DirectX® 3D Graphics
Programming Bible

DirectX® 3D Graphics Programming Bible

Julio Sanchez

Maria P. Canton

IDG Books Worldwide, Inc.
An International Data Group Company

Foster City, CA ✦ Chicago, IL ✦ Indianapolis, IN ✦ New York, NY

DirectX® 3D Graphics Programming Bible

Published by

IDG Books Worldwide, Inc.

An International Data Group Company

919 E. Hillsdale Blvd., Suite 400

Foster City, CA 94404

www.idgbooks.com (IDG Books Worldwide Web site)

Library of Congress Card Number: 00-101538

ISBN: 0-7645-4633-3

Printed in the United States of America

10 9 8 7 6 5 4 3 2 1

1B/SS/QV/QQ/FC

Distributed in the United States by IDG Books Worldwide, Inc.

Distributed by CDG Books Canada Inc. for Canada; by Transworld Publishers Limited in the United Kingdom; by IDG Norge Books for Norway; by IDG Sweden Books for Sweden; by IDG Books Australia Publishing Corporation Pty. Ltd. for Australia and New Zealand; by TransQuest Publishers Pte Ltd. for Singapore, Malaysia, Thailand, Indonesia, and Hong Kong; by Gotop Information Inc. for Taiwan; by ICG Muse, Inc. for Japan; by Intersoft for South Africa; by Eyrolles for France; by International Thomson Publishing for Germany, Austria, and Switzerland; by Distribuidora Cuspide for Argentina; by LR International for Brazil; by Galileo Libros for Chile; by Ediciones ZETA S.C.R. Ltda. for Peru; by WS Computer Publishing Corporation, Inc., for the Philippines; by Contemporanea de Ediciones for Venezuela; by Express Computer Distributors for the Caribbean and West Indies; by Micronesia Media Distributor, Inc. for Micronesia; by Chips Computadoras S.A. de C.V. for Mexico; by Editorial Norma de Panama S.A. for Panama; by American Bookshops for Finland.

For general information on IDG Books Worldwide's books in the U.S., please call our Consumer Customer Service department at 800-762-2974. For reseller information, including discounts and premium sales, please call our Reseller Customer Service department at 800-434-3422.

For information on where to purchase IDG Books Worldwide's books outside the U.S., please contact our International Sales department at 317-596-5530 or fax 317-572-4002.

For consumer information on foreign language translations, please contact our Customer Service department at 800-434-3422, fax 317-572-4002, or e-mail rights@idgbooks.com.

For information on licensing foreign or domestic rights, please phone +1-650-653-7098.

For sales inquiries and special prices for bulk quantities, please contact our Order Services department at 800-434-3422 or write to the address above.

For information on using IDG Books Worldwide's books in the classroom or for ordering examination copies, please contact our Educational Sales department at 800-434-2086 or fax 317-572-4005.

For press review copies, author interviews, or other publicity information, please contact our Public Relations department at 650-653-7000 or fax 650-653-7500.

For authorization to photocopy items for corporate, personal, or educational use, please contact Copyright Clearance Center, 222 Rosewood Drive, Danvers, MA 01923, or fax 978-750-4470.

ABOUT IDG BOOKS WORLDWIDE

Welcome to the world of IDG Books Worldwide.

IDG Books Worldwide, Inc., is a subsidiary of International Data Group, the world's largest publisher of computer-related information and the leading global provider of information services on information technology. IDG was founded more than 30 years ago by Patrick J. McGovern and now employs more than 9,000 people worldwide. IDG publishes more than 290 computer publications in over 75 countries. More than 90 million people read one or more IDG publications each month.

Launched in 1990, IDG Books Worldwide is today the #1 publisher of best-selling computer books in the United States. We are proud to have received eight awards from the Computer Press Association in recognition of editorial excellence and three from Computer Currents' First Annual Readers' Choice Awards. Our best-selling *...For Dummies®* series has more than 50 million copies in print with translations in 31 languages. IDG Books Worldwide, through a joint venture with IDG's Hi-Tech Beijing, became the first U.S. publisher to publish a computer book in the People's Republic of China. In record time, IDG Books Worldwide has become the first choice for millions of readers around the world who want to learn how to better manage their businesses.

Our mission is simple: Every one of our books is designed to bring extra value and skill-building instructions to the reader. Our books are written by experts who understand and care about our readers. The knowledge base of our editorial staff comes from years of experience in publishing, education, and journalism — experience we use to produce books to carry us into the new millennium. In short, we care about books, so we attract the best people. We devote special attention to details such as audience, interior design, use of icons, and illustrations. And because we use an efficient process of authoring, editing, and desktop publishing our books electronically, we can spend more time ensuring superior content and less time on the technicalities of making books.

You can count on our commitment to deliver high-quality books at competitive prices on topics you want to read about. At IDG Books Worldwide, we continue in the IDG tradition of delivering quality for more than 30 years. You'll find no better book on a subject than one from IDG Books Worldwide.

John Kilcullen
Chairman and CEO
IDG Books Worldwide, Inc.

Eighth Annual
Computer Press
Awards ≥1992

Ninth Annual
Computer Press
Awards ≥1993

Tenth Annual
Computer Press
Awards ≥1994

Eleventh Annual
Computer Press
Awards ≥1995

IDG is the world's leading IT media, research and exposition company. Founded in 1964, IDG had 1997 revenues of $2.05 billion and has more than 9,000 employees worldwide. IDG offers the widest range of media options that reach IT buyers in 75 countries representing 95% of worldwide IT spending. IDG's diverse product and services portfolio spans six key areas including print publishing, online publishing, expositions and conferences, market research, education and training, and global marketing services. More than 90 million people read one or more of IDG's 290 magazines and newspapers, including IDG's leading global brands — Computerworld, PC World, Network World, Macworld and the Channel World family of publications. IDG Books Worldwide is one of the fastest-growing computer book publishers in the world, with more than 700 titles in 36 languages. The "...For Dummies®" series alone has more than 50 million copies in print. IDG offers online users the largest network of technology-specific Web sites around the world through IDG.net (http://www.idg.net), which comprises more than 225 targeted Web sites in 55 countries worldwide. International Data Corporation (IDC) is the world's largest provider of information technology data, analysis and consulting, with research centers in over 41 countries and more than 400 research analysts worldwide. IDG World Expo is a leading producer of more than 168 globally branded conferences and expositions in 35 countries including E3 (Electronic Entertainment Expo), Macworld Expo, ComNet, Windows World Expo, ICE (Internet Commerce Expo), Agenda, DEMO, and Spotlight. IDG's training subsidiary, ExecuTrain, is the world's largest computer training company, with more than 230 locations worldwide and 785 training courses. IDG Marketing Services helps industry-leading IT companies build international brand recognition by developing global integrated marketing programs via IDG's print, online and exposition products worldwide. Further information about the company can be found at www.idg.com.

1/26/00

Credits

Acquisitions Editors
Greg Croy
John Osborn

Project Editor
Matthew E. Lusher

Technical Editor
Susan Schilling

Copy Editor
Mildred Sanchez

Media Development Specialist
Jason Luster

Permissions Editor
Lenora Chin Sell

Media Development Manager
Stephen Noetzel

Project Coordinators
Linda Marousek
Danette Nurse
Joe Shines

Graphics and Production Specialists
Robert Bilhmayer
Jude Levinson
Michael Lewis
Victor Pérez-Varela
Dina F Quan

Book Designer
Drew R. Moore

Illustrators
Brian Drumm
Mary Jo Richards

Proofreading and Indexing
York Production Services

Cover Illustration Contributor
David B. Mattingly

Cover Illustration
Peter Kowaleszyn, MBD Design, SF

About the Authors

Julio Sanchez is an associate professor of Computer Science at Minnesota State University, Mankato. Julio is the author of 17 books in the field of computer programming, five of which have been translated into foreign languages. He also teaches courses and seminars in C++, Windows, and Java programming at Minnesota State University.

Maria P. Canton is the president of Skipanon Software, a programming and consulting company that has been in business since 1983. She is also a faculty member at Minnesota State University, Mankato. Maria is the principal author of one book and the coauthor of 13 other titles in the field of computer programming.

Preface

This book covers 3D graphics programming in Windows, using DirectX, and coding in C++. It assumes that you have a basic understanding of C++. Although many applications could profit from object-oriented constructs, we do not use them in this book in order to avoid the additional complications. The book includes one chapter (Chapter 6) on the fundamentals of Windows API programming, but it alone may be insufficient for someone who is totally unfamiliar with this topic. Readers with no previous Windows programming experience may need to devote some time to acquiring these skills before plunging into the details of 3D graphics. We recommend our own book titled *Windows Graphics Programming*, published by M & T Books. This title was designed to provide the necessary skills in Windows graphics without overwhelming the reader with too many complications and details. Nevertheless, any good book on Windows API programming would serve this purpose, such as the ones by Petzold, Rector and Newcomer, and Schildt. Their titles can be found in the Bibliography.

This book is for you if you wish to learn Windows 3D graphics and to apply it to the development of computer games, simulations, or any form of 3D, high-performance, multimedia programming. The road is not an easy one; there is much to learn. 3D is rightly called the "rocket science" of programming. However, the rewards of working on the cutting edge of this technology are enormous.

What Is in the Book

In this book we approach Windows programming at its most basic level, that is, using the Windows Application Programming Interface (API). We do not use the Microsoft Foundation Class Library (MFC) or other wrapper functions that are furnished as part of commercial development environments. Microsoft's MFC is an object-oriented framework that encapsulates many of the functions in the API. It is intended for use with Developer's Studio App Wizard, which facilitates creating a program skeleton for a Windows application. But the MFC interface introduces a processing overhead that slows down execution and limits program functionality. Graphics programs in general, and 3D applications in particular, cannot afford this overhead. Furthermore, DirectX provides no special support for MFC; therefore, its use offers no advantages to the graphics programmer.

Please note that although we do not use the wrapper functions of the MFC, we do rely heavily on the other tools that are part of the Visual C++ development package. These include resource editors for creating menus, dialog boxes, icons, bitmaps, and other standard program components. There are no advantages to hand-coding these program elements.

Part I of this book is devoted to the fundamentals of 3D graphics. Here we present the tools and resources of PC graphics programming and introduce the reader to various graphics representations, image modeling techniques, mathematical transformations, data rendering operations, and animation. The material for this part was selected based on the minimal knowledge required for understanding and using DirectX 3D graphics. The theoretical topics and the mathematics have been reduced to the bare essentials. By presenting this material first, we avoid the distraction of having to explain theoretical concepts when discussing programming topics. This first part also contains a chapter on the fundamentals of Windows API programming.

Part II covers DirectDraw. DirectDraw is the 2D graphics environment in DirectX. We devote considerable space to DirectDraw programming for two reasons. The first one is that 3D graphics in DirectX are based on DirectDraw; a 3D application executes in the DirectDraw environment. The second reason is that few commercial applications are exclusively 3D. Most programs use 3D functions to model some of the objects, whereas others, such as backgrounds and sprites, are rendered in 2D graphics. Mastering 2D in DirectDraw is an essential skill for the DirectX 3D programmer.

Parts III and IV are devoted to 3D graphics programming in DirectX retained mode. Part III introduces 3D graphics and discusses retained mode programming at the system, device, and viewport levels. Part IV discusses programming techniques at the lower levels of the retained mode interface. We do not discuss immediate mode programming, but not because we consider it unimportant. Our reason for not including immediate mode was a simple matter of space. To present a bare-bones discussion of DirectX immediate mode would have required substantially reducing and diluting the rest of the material. The result would have been a book that visited many topics superficially, but no one subject in depth. Because we believe that retained mode is the most reasonable development environment at the application level, as well as the easiest way to learn 3D graphics programming, we concentrated on it. Other factors that influenced our choice are mentioned in the following section.

Direct3D: Past and Future

In more than one sense 3D graphics programming is not for the faint-hearted. We believe that at present, any Windows 3D programming tool, facility, or development environment, should have a warning label stating that it is work in progress. If, as a programmer, you need to operate in a stable, well-defined, consistently evolving platform, then 3D graphics should not be your chosen field.

Although 2D graphics in DirectX always take place in DirectDraw, the 3D DirectX interface changes so much and so frequently that, for many programmers, it is a challenge just to keep up with the updates. When we began writing this book Microsoft's DirectX 5 was recently released. We finished it under DirectX 7. Each of these DirectX versions (5, 6, and 7) contained major expansions, additions, and corrections to the previous ones. Furthermore, each consecutive version of the DirectX SDK seemed to reflect a new vision of the 3D graphics paradigm.

At this time the future of 3D graphics in DirectX remains undefined. For DirectX 8, originally planned for release in the first half of the year 2000, Microsoft announced a completely new development environment, which was code-named *Fahrenheit*. The Fahrenheit product was being developed as a joint venture with Silicon Graphics Corporation. Silicon Graphics is the creator of OpenGL, a 3D environment that has gained considerable prevalence in graphics workstations. Early this year, Silicon Graphics pulled out of the Fahrenheit project. Microsoft has not yet said if it will continue to develop Fahrenheit on its own, or if the project will be scrapped. What will be in DirectX 8 is now a mystery.

All of this generated considerable uncertainty regarding the future of the retained mode and immediate mode interfaces of DirectX. Will Fahrenheit replace retained mode, immediate mode, neither, or both? Because we are not even sure that there will be a Fahrenheit product, or what else DirectX 8 may contain, any answer is pure guesswork. This state-of-affairs in 3D development environments and tools will continue to affect DirectX for many years to come. The fact that Windows is a Microsoft product further complicates matters. Currently DirectX contains three 3D development environments: retained mode, immediate mode, and the DirectX foundation. In the near future the product now called Fahrenheit may be added to the list. Not long after the release of a 3D toolkit or environment, programmers start creating software based on the new interface. These new products are marketed with the expectation that they will continue to execute in future versions of the operating system. As a consequence Microsoft is compelled to provide support for all interfaces or development environments, even after they become outdated, or even obsolete. This all means that a new 3D graphics paradigm does not replace the existing ones because the old interfaces have to be kept operational so as not to break commercial code. In the near future a DirectX 3D programmer may be able to work under retained mode, immediate mode, DirectX foundation, or Fahrenheit — all of this not mentioning other 3D development tools that exist outside of DirectX, such as OpenGL or the proprietary APIs of the various chip manufacturers.

Out of this quagmire of options and development tools we selected DirectX retained mode. Some may question the validity of this choice. In DirectX 7, Microsoft announced that retained mode is now in a maintenance phase. This statement is interpreted to mean that Microsoft lost interest in the future development in retained mode. Another fact is that many professional DirectX 3D programmers work in immediate mode, and recommend it as a more powerful alternative. Although this is true, it is also undeniable that immediate mode complicates 3D programming by several orders of magnitude. Furthermore, there is no assurance that the next release of DirectX will not place immediate mode in a maintenance phase. Retained mode, on the other hand, is easier to learn and use. The fact that it is not being constantly tinkered with at this stage could be seen as an asset, rather than a drawback. We have no doubts that Windows and DirectX must continue to support retained mode for years to come. Not being able to cover both retained mode and immediate mode in a single volume we preferred the one that is easier to learn and, perhaps, a more stable alternative.

About the Sample Programs

How to use code listing in programming books is a controversial topic. On the one hand you see books with little or no code listings, or with short code snippets that miss so many details that they turn out to be virtually useless as programming samples. On the other hand there are books that list entire programs, often so complicated that the reader gets lost in innumerable details unrelated to the point at hand. Most programmers appreciate the value of a code sample that compiles and runs as described. In many cases this is all you need to understand a programming technique or to apply it in your own code. Our approach in this book consists of listing in the text the processing routines and code fragments that are necessary for illustrating the point being discussed. The CD-ROM furnished with the book contains entire programs, which can be re-compiled by the reader in order to assert their validity.

The book's CD-ROM contains all the programs, projects, and templates discussed in the book. Each project is located in its own directory and contains all the files necessary for recreating the samples using Visual C++ versions 5 or 6. The executables were created using the Debug configuration of Microsoft Developer Studio. The authors or the publisher make no copyright claims regarding the code listings, which you are free to copy, edit, or reuse in any way you see fit.

Portability Issues

It must be clearly understood that DirectX is an interface, for which the graphics hardware must provide implementation. Microsoft furnishes some services and facilities that graphics hardware vendors can use to test their product's compliance with the standard, but there is no compulsory protocol. Neither is there a formal certificate that assures a programmer or a user that a hardware device is totally compatible with DirectX. Furthermore, a particular hardware product may support certain DirectX functions and not others. The result is revival of the device-dependency ghosts that Windows was designed to eliminate in the first place.

The DirectX 3D programmer should be ready to tackle many hardware-related problems. Hardware compatibility issues have determined that most high-end 3D applications are developed for a specific subset of graphics cards. It is virtually impossible to create a full-featured 3D program that executes flawlessly in every video card on the market. Even the simple demonstration programs developed for this book have shown compatibility problems when tested in five popular video cards. Ensuring that the 3D application executes correctly in the targeted hardware is one of the programmer's most difficult, and often exasperating, tasks.

Contacting the Authors

Although we can't promise to solve every software- or hardware-related problem that arises from this book, we will take a look at them. You can contact the authors at the following email addresses:

julio.sanchez@mankato.msus.edu

cantom@mail.mankato.msus.edu

Acknowledgments

It has been said that it takes a village to raise a child; to produce a technical book takes a good-sized town. The process is long, arduous, and requires many talents, in addition to the technical knowledge of the authors and editors. A book begins with a sketchy idea, which is then refined, adapted, and polished. The process goes through many phases and stages before it becomes a bound title on the bookstore shelf. In this project we are very fortunate to have the collaboration of many talented professionals. John Osborn and Greg Croy, the acquisitions editors, were invaluable resources by serving as a sounding board for our ideas and providing many of their own. Matt Lusher, the project editor, directed and supervised the production process and furnished many useful comments and suggestions. Susan Schilling was our technical editor. She detected technical inconsistencies and pointed out better ways in which to approach some of the most difficult topics. The book owes much to her talents. Mildred Sanchez (no relation to the author) did the copyediting. Her corrections and suggestions made the book more consistent and readable. We also thank Linda Marousek, production coordinator, and Brian Drumm, graphics processor for the project.

Contents at a Glance

Contents

Part II: DirectDraw   179

Chapter 7: DirectDraw Fundamentals 181

Chapter 8: DirectDraw Configuration and Setup 201

The
Fundamentals

The PC as a Graphics Machine

This chapter contains a smorgasbord of introductory topics that relate to graphics on the PC. The idea is to provide a historical summary of the evolution of PC graphics, an overview of the state-of-the-art, and a short list of related technologies and fields of application. Our rationale for including this material is the difficulty in understanding the characteristics of current PC graphics systems without knowing how and why they came into existence. Many of the PC graphics hardware components in use today evolved through a series of changes, some of which were influenced by concerns of backward compatibility.

History and Evolution

Today, a typical computer is equipped with a high-resolution display, a graphics card or integral video system, and an operating system that supports a graphical user interface (GUI). Graphics are now the norm, but this was not always the case; for several decades computer input and output was text-based and machines were equipped with teletype terminals and line printers. It was in the 1960s that television technology was adapted to producing computer output on a cathode ray tube (CRT).

Sometimes, the transition from text-based systems into inter-active graphics was slow. Today we watch in amazement a video clip taken in the early 1960s of Doug Englebart demon-strating a graphical user interface based on mouse input and CRT graphics. It took fifteen years for this system to become commercially available in the Apple Lisa, predecessor to the Macintosh.

Cathode ray tube technology

Computers were not the first machines to use the *cathode ray tube* (CRT) for graphic display. The oscilloscope, a common laboratory apparatus, performs operations on an input signal to display the graph of the electric or electronic wave on a fluorescent screen. In computer applications the technologies most used for CRT displays can be classified into three groups: *storage tube, vector refresh,* and *raster-scan.*

In its simplest form, the CRT display consists of a glass tube whose interior is coated with a specially formulated phosphor; when struck by an electron beam, it remains fluorescent for up to one hour. This technology, usually called a *storage tube display,* is used as a display and as a storage device. Flooding the tube with a voltage turns the phosphor to its dark state, which erases the image. One limitation is that specific screen areas cannot be erased individually. Because of this, the entire CRT surface must be redrawn to make a small change in a displayed image. Furthermore, the storage tube display has no color capabilities and contrast is low. For these reasons, in spite of its inherent simplicity, storage tube displays are seldom used in computers and never in microcomputers.

In contrast with the storage tube display, the vector-refresh display uses a short-persistence phosphor whose coating must be reactivated by an electron beam at the rate of 30 to 50 times per second. In addition to the cathode ray tube, a vector-refresh system requires a display file and a display controller. The display file is a memory area that holds the instructions for drawing the objects to be displayed. The display controller reads this information from the display file and transforms it into digital commands and data, which are sent to the CRT. Figure 1-1 shows the fundamental elements of a vector-refresh display system.

The main disadvantages of the vector-refresh CRT are its high cost and limited color capabilities. For these reasons vector-refresh displays have not been used in the PC, although they have been used in radar applications and in some of the early video games.

During the 1960s, several important advances took place in television technology that made possible the use of mass-produced components in display devices for computer systems. At that time Conrac Corporation developed a computer image processing technology, known as *raster-scan graphics*, which took advantage of the methods of image refreshing used in television receivers, as well as other television standards and components. In a raster-scan display the electron beam follows a horizontal line-by-line path, usually starting at the top-left corner of the CRT surface. The scanning cycle takes place 50 to 70 times per second. At the start of each horizontal line the controller turns on the electron beam. The beam is turned off during the horizontal and vertical retrace cycles. The scanning path is shown in Figure 1-2.

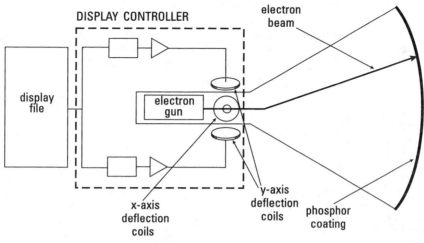

Figure 1-1: Vector-refresh display

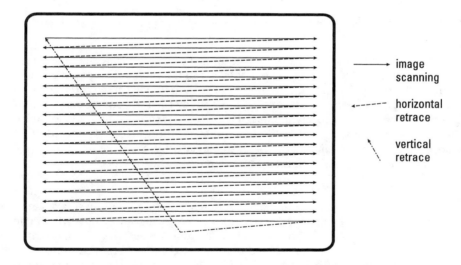

Figure 1-2: Path of the electron beam in a raster-scan system

A raster-scan display surface is divided into a pattern of individual dots, usually called pixels. The term *pixel* was derived from the words ***picture*** and ***elements***. An area of RAM is reserved in the computer's memory space to record the state of each individual screen pixel. The simplest possible storage scheme corresponds to a black and white display system where each pixel requires a single bit. In this scheme, if the memory bit is set, the display scanner renders the corresponding pixel as white. If the memory bit is cleared, the pixel is left dark. The area of memory reserved for the screen display is frequently called the *frame buffer* or the *video buffer*, and the entire video system is said to be memory-mapped. Figure 1-3 shows the elements of a memory-mapped video system.

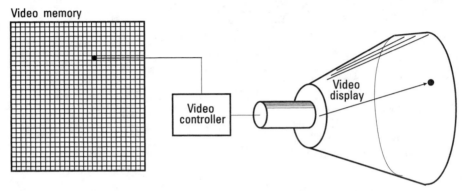

Figure 1-3: Memory-mapped video system

A memory-mapped color video system requires a more elaborate scheme. In color systems the CRT is equipped with an electron gun for each color that is used in activating the pixels. The most common approach is to use three color-sensitive guns: one for the red, one for the green, and one for the blue components. Color data must be stored separately in memory for each of the three colors, either in individual memory maps, or in predefined units of storage. For example, if one memory byte is used to encode the pixel's color attributes, three bits could be assigned to encode the red color, two bits to encode the green color, and three bits for the blue color.

One possible mapping of colors to pixels is shown in color plate 1. In this example we have arbitrarily divided one memory byte into three separate bit fields which encode the three-color values that determine each individual screen pixel. The individual bits are designated with the letters R, G, and B, respectively. Since eight combinations can be encoded in a three-bit field, the blue and red color components could each have eight levels of intensity. Because we have used a two-bit field to encode the green color, it can only be represented in four levels of intensity. The total number of combinations that can be encoded in eight bits is 256, which, in this case, is also the number of different color values that can be represented in one memory byte. The color code is transmitted by the display controller hardware to a *digital-to-analog converter* (DAC), which, in turn, transmits the color video signals to the CRT.

All video systems used in the PC are of the memory-mapped, raster-scan type. The advantages of a raster-scan display are low cost, color capability, and easy interaction with the operator. One major disadvantage is the grainy physical structure of the display surface. Among other aberrations, this causes lines that are not vertical, horizontal, or at exactly 45 degrees, to exhibit a staircase effect, shown in Figure 1-4.

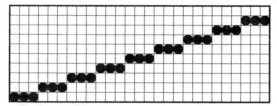

Figure 1-4: Staircase effect in a raster-scan system

Raster-scan systems also have limitations in implementing animation. Two factors contribute to this problem: first, all the screen pixels within a rectangular area must be updated with each image change. Second, the successive images that create the illusion of motion must be flashed on the screen at a fast rate to ensure smoothness. These constraints place a large processing load on the microprocessor and the display system hardware, in any display system.

PC video technologies

In 1981 IBM introduced the first model of its microcomputer line. The original machines were offered with either a *monochrome display adapter* (MDA), or a graphics system named the *color/graphics monitor adapter* (CGA). IBM's notion was that users who intended to use the PC for text operations exclusively would purchase a machine equipped with the MDA video system, while those requiring graphics would buy one equipped with the CGA card. In reality, the CGA video system provided only the most simple and unsophisticated graphics functions. The color card was also plagued with interference problems that created a screen disturbance called "snow." However, the fact that the original IBM Personal Computer was furnished with the optional CGA card signaled that IBM considered video graphics an important part of microcomputing.

At present, PC video hardware includes an assortment of systems, cards, monitors, and options manufactured and marketed by many companies. In the following pages we briefly discuss the history and evolution of the better-known PC video systems. Systems that were short-lived or that gained little popularity, such as the *PCJr,* the *IBM Professional Graphics Controller*, the *Multicolor Graphics Array*, and the *IBM Image Adapter A*, are not discussed.

Monochrome Display Adapter

The MDA is the original alphanumeric display card designed and distributed by IBM for the Personal Computer. Originally, it was sold as the *Monochrome Display and Printer Adapter* because it included a parallel printer port. It could display the entire range of alphanumeric and graphic characters in the IBM character set, but did not provide graphics functions. The MDA was compatible with the IBM PC, PC XT, and PC AT, and some of the earlier models of the PS/2 line. It could not be used in the PCJr, the PC Convertible, or MicroChannel PS/2 machines. The MDA required a monochrome monitor of long-persistence (P39) phosphor. The video hardware was based on the Motorola 6845 CRT controller. The system contained 4K of on-board video memory, mapped to physical address B0000H.

The MDA is a pure alphanumeric display; the programmer cannot access the individual screen pixels, but sees the video screen as a collection of character and attribute cells. The character codes occupy the even-numbered bytes of adapter memory and the display attributes the odd-numbered bytes. This special storage and display scheme was conceived to save memory space and to simplify programming. Figure 1-5 shows the cell structure of the MDA video memory space and the bitmap for the attribute cells.

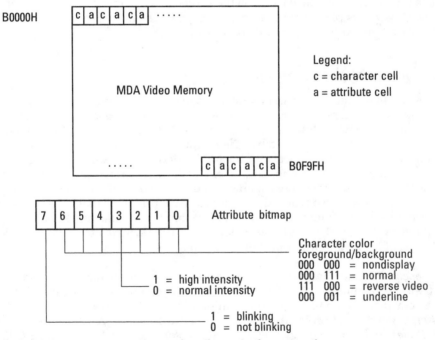

Figure 1-5: Memory mapping and attributes in the MDA adapter

Hercules Graphics Card

The original *Hercules Graphics Card* (HGC), released in 1982, emulates the monochrome functions of the MDA, but also can operate in a graphics mode. Like the MDA, the HGC includes a parallel printer port. Because of its graphics capabilities, the HGC became somewhat of a standard for monochrome systems. The display buffer consists of 64K of video memory. In alphanumeric mode the system sees only the 4K required for the text mode. However, when the HGC is in the graphics mode, the 64K are partitioned as two 32K graphics pages located at physical addresses B0000H to B7FFFH and B8000H to BFFFFH. Graphic applications can select which page is displayed.

Color Graphics Adapter

The *Color Graphics Adapter* (CGA), released early in 1982, was the first color and graphics card for the PC. The CGA could operate in seven modes, which included monochrome and color graphics. The text characters are displayed in 16 shades of gray. Characters are double width and 40 can be fit on a screen line. Graphics mode number 6 provided the highest resolution, which was 640 horizontal by 200 vertical pixels.

One notable difference between the CGA and the MDA was the lower-quality text characters of the color card. The reason for this is related to the size of the respective character cells, which is a box of 9×14 screen pixels in the MDA, and a box of 8×8 pixels in the CGA. The resulting graininess of the CGA text characters is so obvious that many users judged the card as unsuitable for text operations.

The CGA was designed so that it could be used with a standard television set, although it performed best when connected to an RGB color monitor. Timing and control signals were furnished by a Motorola 6845 CRT controller, identical to the one used in the MDA. The CGA contains 16K of memory, which is four times the memory in the MDA. This makes it possible for the CGA to simultaneously hold data for four full screens of alphanumeric text. The video buffer is located at physical address B8000H. The 16K memory space in the adapter is logically divided into four 4K areas, each of which holds up to 2000 characters with their respective attributes. The CGA video memory pages are shown in Figure 1-6.

As in the MDA, video memory in the CGA text modes consists of consecutive character and attribute bytes. (See Figure 1-6.) The mapping of the attribute bits in the black and white alphanumeric modes is identical to the one used in the MDA. (See Figure 1-6.) However, in the color alphanumeric modes the attribute bits are mapped differently. Figure 1-6 shows the bitmap for the attribute cells in the color alpha modes.

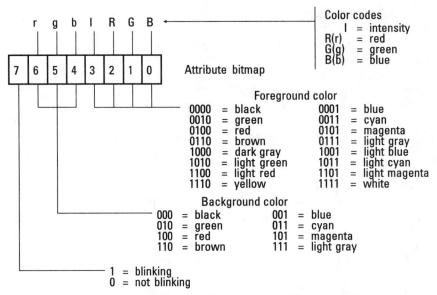

Figure 1-6: Memory mapping and attributes in the CGA color alpha modes

The CGA is plagued with a disturbing screen interference, called snow. This irritating effect is related to CGA's use of RAM chips (called dynamic RAMs) which are considerably slower than the static RAMs used in the MDA card. In a CGA system, if the CPU reads or writes to the video buffer while it is being refreshed by the CRT Controller, a visible screen disturbance takes place. The only remedy is to synchronize screen updates with the vertical retrace signal generated by the 6845. This is only possible during a short time interval, barely sufficient to set a few pixels. Therefore, graphics rendering is considerably slowed down by this synchronization requirement. Furthermore, during screen scroll operations the display functions must be turned off while the buffer is updated. This causes an additionally disturbing screen flicker.

Enhanced Graphics Adapter

The *Enhanced Graphics Adapter* (EGA) was introduced by IBM in 1984 as an alternative to the much maligned CGA card. The EGA could emulate most of the functions and all the display modes of both the CGA and the MDA. On the other hand, the EGA had a greater character definition in the alphanumeric modes than the CGA, higher resolution in the graphics modes, and was not plagued with the snow and flicker problems of the CGA. In addition, EGA could drive an Enhanced Color Display with a graphics resolution of 640 × 350 pixels.

EGA introduced four new graphics resolutions, named the enhanced graphics modes. The new modes were numbered 13 through 16. The highest graphics resolution was obtained in the modes numbered 15 and 16, which displayed

640×350 pixels. The EGA used a custom video controller chip with different port and register assignments than those of the Motorola 6845 controller used in the MDA and CGA cards. For this reason, programs coded for the MDA and CGA that access the 6845 video controller directly did not work on the EGA. EGA was furnished with optional on-board RAM in blocks of 64K. In the minimum configuration the card had 64K of video memory, and 256K in the maximum one.

The EGA system had several serious limitations. In the first place, it supported write operations to most of its internal registers, but not read operations. This made it virtually impossible for software to detect and preserve the state of the adapter, which determined that EGA was unsuitable for memory resident applications or for multitasking or multiprogramming environments, such as Windows. Another limitation of the EGA card was related to its unequal definitions in the vertical and horizontal planes. This problem was also present in the HGC and the CGA cards. In the case of the EGA, with a typical monitor, the vertical resolution in graphic modes 15 and 16 is approximately 54 pixels per inch and the horizontal resolution approximately 75 pixels per inch. This gives a ratio of vertical to horizontal definition of approximately 3:4. Although not as bad as the 2:3 ratio of the HGC, this disproportion still determines that a pixel pattern geometrically representing a square is displayed on the screen as a rectangle and the pattern of a circle is displayed as an ellipse. This geometrical aberration complicates pixel path calculations, which must take this disproportion into account and make the necessary adjustments. The effect of an asymmetrical pixel density is shown in Figure 1-7.

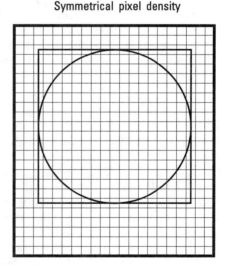

Figure 1-7: Asymmetrical and symmetrical video resolutions

PS/2 video systems

The PS/2 line of microcomputers was released by IBM in 1987. It introduced several new features, including a new system bus and board connectors, named the MicroChannel architecture, a 3.5-inch diskette drive with 1.44MB of storage, and an optional multitasking operating system named OS/2. Machines of the PS/2 line came equipped with one of two new video graphics systems, with a third one available as an option.

The new video standards for the PS/2 line were the *Multicolor Graphics Array* (MCGA), the *Video Graphics Array* (VGA), and the 8514/A Display Adapter. The most notable difference between the PC and the PS/2 video systems is that with the PS/2 line IBM changed the display driver technology from digital to analog, which made the monitors of the PC line incompatible with the PS/2 computers, and vice versa. The main advantage of analog display technology is a much larger color selection. Another important improvement is their symmetrical resolution. The aspect ratio of the new monitors is 4:3, and the best resolution is 640×480 pixels, which results in the same pixel density horizontally and vertically. Symmetrical resolution simplifies programming by eliminating geometrical aberrations during pixel plotting operations.

Video Graphics Array

Video Graphics Array (VGA) is the standard video display system for PS/2 computer models 50, 50z, 60, 70, and 80. IBM furnished VGA on the system board. VGA comes with 256K of video memory, which can be divided into four 64K areas called the *video maps* or *bit planes*. The system supports all the display modes of the MDA, CGA, and EGA cards of the PC family. In addition, VGA introduced graphics mode number 18, with 640×480 pixel resolution in 16 colors. The effective resolution of the text modes is 720×400. To display text in a graphics mode, three text fonts with different box sizes could be loaded from BIOS into the adapter. VGA soon became available as an adapter card for non-IBM machines and remains a PC video standard to this day.

8514/A Display Adapter

The 8514/A Display Adapter is a high-resolution graphics system designed for PS/2 computers and was developed in the United Kingdom at the IBM Hursley Laboratories. The 8514/A system comprises not only the display adapter, but also the 8514 Color Display and an optional Memory Expansion Kit. The original 8514/A is compatible only with PS/2 computers that use the MicroChannel bus; it is not compatible with the PC line, PS/2 models 25 and 30, or non-IBM computers that do not use the MicroChannel architecture. Other companies developed versions of 8514/A that are compatible with the Industry Standard Architecture (ISA) or Expanded Industry Standard Architecture (EISA) bus.

The 8514/A Display Adapter consists of two sandwiched boards inserted into the special MicroChannel slot with the auxiliary video extension. The standard version comes equipped with 512K of video memory. The memory space is divided into four maps of 128K each. In the standard configuration, the 8514/A displays 16 colors. However, if you install the optional Memory Expansion Kit, video memory lis increased to 1MB of space, which is divided into eight maps, extending the number of available colors to 256. The system is capable of four new graphics modes not available in VGA. IBM named them the *advanced function modes*. One of the new modes has 640 × pixels, and the remaining three modes have 1024 × 768 pixels. The 8514/A does not directly support any of the conventional alphanumeric or graphics modes of the other video standards because it executes only in the advanced function modes. In a typical system, VGA automatically takes over when a standard mode is set. The image is routed to the 8514/A monitor when an advanced function mode is enabled. An interesting feature of the 8514/A adapter is that a system containing it can operate with two monitors. In this case the usual setup is to connect the 8514 color display to the 8514/A adapter and a standard monitor to the VGA. Figure 1-8 shows the architecture of a VGA/8514A system.

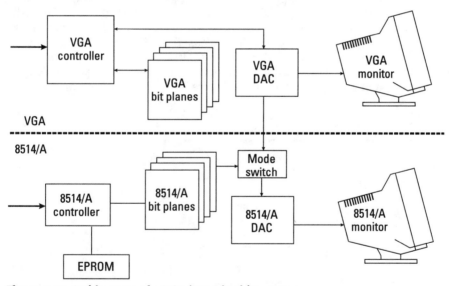

Figure 1-8: Architecture of a VGA/8514/A video system.

An interesting feature of the 8514/A, which presaged things to come, is that it contains a dedicated graphics chip that performs as a graphics coprocessor. Unlike previous systems, the system microprocessor cannot access video memory in 8514/A; instead this function is left to the graphics coprocessor. The greatest advantage of this setup is the improved performance of the graphics subsystem when compared to one in which the CPU is burdened with writing text and graphics to the video display. The 8514/A performs graphics functions through a high-level interface. The furnished software package is called the *Adapter Interface*, or AI. There are a total of 59 drawing functions in the AI, accessible through a software interrupt.

Approximately two years after the introduction of the 8514/A, IBM unveiled another high-performance, high-priced graphics board, designated the *Image Adapter/A*. The Image Adapter/A is compatible with the 8514/A at the Adapter Interface (AI) level but not at the register level. Because of its high price tag and IBM's unveiling of the XGA shortly after its introduction, the Image Adapter/A was short -lived.

Extended Graphics Array

In September 1990, IBM disclosed preliminary information on a new graphics standard designated as the *Extended Graphics Array*, or XGA. The hardware was developed in the UK by the same team that created the 8514/A. An adapter card and a motherboard version of the XGA standard were later implemented. In 1992, IBM released a noninterlaced version of the XGA designated as XGA-2 or XGA-NI (noninterlaced). The XGA adapter is compatible with PS/2 MicroChannel machines equipped with the 80386 or 486 CPU. The system is integrated in the motherboard of IBM Models 90 XP 486 and Model 57 SLC, and is furnished as an adapter board in the Model 95 XP 486. In 1992, Radius Inc. released the Radius XGA-2 Color Graphics Card for computers using the ISA or EISA bus. Other companies developed versions of the XGA system for MicroChannel and nonMicroChannel computers. XGA is found today in many laptop computers. Figure 1-9 is a component diagram of the XGA system.

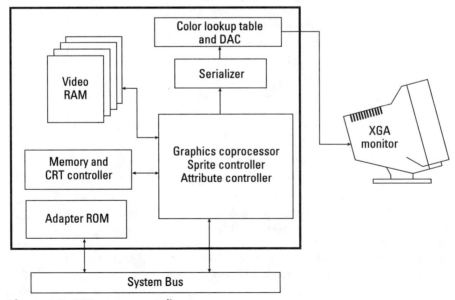

Figure 1-9: XGA component diagram

SuperVGA

SuperVGA refers to enhancements to the VGA standard developed by independent manufacturers and vendors. The general characteristic of SuperVGA boards, as the name implies, is that they exceed the VGA standard in definition, color range, or both. A typical SuperVGA graphics board is capable of executing not only the standard VGA modes, but also other modes that provide higher definition or greater color range than VGA. These are usually called the *SuperVGA Enhanced Modes*.

Originally, the uncontrolled proliferation of SuperVGA hardware caused many compatibility problems. Because of the lack of standardization, the VGA enhancements in the card produced by one manufacturer were often incompatible with the enhancements in a card made by another vendor. Many times this situation presented insurmountable problems to the graphics programmer who would find that an application designed to take advantage of the enhancements in a particular SuperVGA system would not execute correctly in another one. In an attempt to solve this lack of standardization, several manufacturers of SuperVGA boards formed the *Video Electronics Standards Association* (VESA). In October 1989, VESA released its first SuperVGA standard. This standard defined several enhanced video modes and implemented a BIOS extension designed to provide a few fundamental video services in a compatible fashion.

SuperVGA Architecture

All IBM microcomputer video systems are memory-mapped. The video memory space in VGA extends from A0000H to BFFFFH, with 64K, starting at segment base A000H, which is devoted to graphics and 64K, at segment base B000H, which is devoted to alphanumeric modes. This means that the total space reserved for video operations is 128K. But the fact that systems could be set up with two monitors, one in an alphanumeric mode and the other one in a color mode, actually limited the graphics video space to 64K.

Not much video data can be stored in 64K. For example, if each screen pixel is encoded in one memory byte, then the maximum screen data that can be stored in 65,536 bytes corresponds to a square with 256 pixels on each side. But a VGA system set in 640 × 480 pixels resolution, using 1 data byte per pixel, requires 307,200 bytes for storing a single screen. VGA designers were able to compress video data by implementing a latching scheme and a planar architecture. In VGA mode number 18, this enables a pixel to be encoded into a single memory bit, although it can be displayed in 16 different colors. The magic consists of having four physical memory planes mapped to the same address. This explains why VGA systems contain 256K of video memory, all mapped to a 64K address space.

When the VGA was first released, engineers noticed that some VGA modes contained surplus memory. For example, in modes with 640 × 480 pixels resolution the video data stored in each map takes up 38,400 bytes of the available 64K. Notice that, in this case, the previously mentioned VGA latching scheme allows the mapping of each pixel to an individual memory bit. This leaves 27,136 unused bytes. The original idea of enhancing the VGA system was based on using this surplus memory to store video data. It is possible to have an 800×600 pixel display divided into four maps of 60,000 bytes each, and yet not exceed the 64K allowed for each color map. To graphics systems designers, a resolution of 800×600 pixels, in 16 colors, appeared as a natural extension to VGA mode number 18. This new mode, later designated as mode 6AH by the VESA SuperVGA standard, could be programmed in a similar manner as VGA mode number 18. The enhancement, which could be achieved with minor changes in the VGA hardware, provided a 36 percent increase in the display area.

Memory banks

The memory structure for VGA 256-color mode number 19 is not based on a multiplane scheme, but in a much simpler format that maps a single memory byte to each screen pixel. This scheme is shown in Figure 1-10.

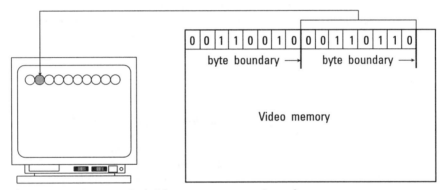

Figure 1-10: Byte-to-pixel video memory-mapping scheme

In byte-to-pixel mapping 256 color combinations can be encoded directly into a data byte, which correspond to the 256 DAC registers of the VGA hardware. The method is straightforward and uncomplicated; however, if the entire video space is contained in 64K, the maximum resolution is limited to the 256×256 pixels previously mentioned. In other words, a rectangular screen of 320×200 pixels nearly fills the allotted 64K.

This determines that if the resolution for a 256-color mode exceeds 256 square pixels, it is necessary to find other ways of mapping video memory into 64K of system RAM. The mechanism adopted by the SuperVGA designers is based on a technique known as *bank switching*. In bank-switched systems the video display hardware maps several 64K blocks of RAM to different locations in video memory. In the PC, addressing the multisegment space is done by means of a hardware mechanism that selects which video memory area is currently located at the system's aperture. In the SuperVGA implementation, the system aperture is usually placed at segment base A000H. The entire process is reminiscent of memory page switching in the LIM (Lotus/Intel/Microsoft) Extended Memory environment. Figure 1-11 schematically shows mapping of several memory banks to the video space and the map selection mechanism for CPU addressing.

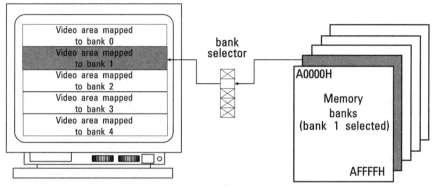

Figure 1-11: SuperVGA banked memory-mapping

In the context of video system architecture, the term *aperture* is often used to denote the processor's window into the system's memory space. For example, if the addressable area of video memory starts at physical address A0000H and extends to B0000H, you can say that the CPU has a 64K aperture into video memory (10000H = 64K). In Figure 1-11 we see that the bank selector determines which area of video memory is mapped to the processor's aperture. This is the video display area that can be updated by the processor. In other words, in the memory-banking scheme the processor cannot access the entire video memory at once. In the case of Figure 1-11 the graphics hardware has to perform five bank switches to update the entire screen.

Implementing 256-color extensions

The SuperVGA alternative for increasing definition beyond the VGA limit is a banking mechanism similar to the one shown in Figure 1-11. This scheme, in which a memory byte encodes the 256 color combinations for each screen pixel, does away with the pixel masking complications of the high-resolution VGA modes. On the other hand, it introduces some new complexities of its own, such as the requirement of a bank selection device. In summary, the SuperVGA approach to extending video memory on the PC has no precedent in CGA, EGA, or VGA systems. It is not interleaved nor does it require memory planes or pixel masking. Although it is similar to VGA mode number 19 regarding color encoding, VGA mode number 19 does not use bank switching.

VESA SuperVGA standard

The Video Electronics Standards Association was created with the purpose of providing a common programming interface for SuperVGA extended modes. In order to achieve this, each manufacturer furnishes a VESA SuperVGA BIOS extension. The BIOS can be in the adapter ROM or furnished as loadable software. The first release of the VESA SuperVGA standard was published in October 1, 1989 (version 1.0). A second release was published in June 2, 1990 (version 1.1). The current one is dated October 22, 1991 (version 1.2).

Graphics coprocessors and accelerators

A group of video systems based on dedicated graphics chips is perhaps the one most difficult to characterize and delimit. These systems are usually defined as those in which graphics performance is enhanced by means of a specialized graphics engine that operates independently from the CPU. The enormous variations in the functionalities and design of graphics accelerators and coprocessors make it impossible to list the specific features of these systems.

Historically speaking, one of the first full-featured dedicated graphics coprocessors used in the PC was the TMS340 chip developed by Texas Instruments. The chip was introduced in 1986, and an upgrade, labeled TMS34020, was introduced in 1990. The project was not a commercial success and in 1993, Texas Instruments started discouraging the development of new products based on the TMS340 chips. However, from 1988 to 1993 these coprocessors were incorporated into many video products, including several high-end video adapters, some of which were capable of a resolution of 1280×1024 pixels in more than 16 million colors. These products, called *True color* or 24-bit color cards, furnished photographic-quality color for the first time on the PC. The quality of the resulting systems was sufficient for image editing, prepress operations, desktop publishing, and CAD applications.

Not all coprocessor-based graphics systems marketed at the time used the TMS 340. For example, the Radius Multiview 24 card contained three 8514/A-compatible chips, while the RasterOps Paintboard PC card was based on the S3. But, undoubtedly, TMS 340 dominated the field of 24-bit color cards at the time. Of ten True-color cards reviewed on the January 1993 edition of *Windows Magazine*, seven were based on the TMS 340.

The TMS 340 was optimized for graphics processing in a 32-bit environment. The technology had its predecessors in TI's TMS320 lines of digital signal processing chips. The following are the distinguishing features of the TMS340 architecture:

1. The instruction set includes both graphics and general-purpose instructions. This made the TMS340 a credible stand-alone processor.

2. The internal data path is 32-bits wide and so are the arithmetic registers. The physical address range is 128MB.

3. The pixel size is programmable at 1, 2, 4, 8, 16, or 32 bits.

4. Raster operations include 16 Boolean and 6 arithmetic modes.

5. The chip contains thirty general-purpose 32-bit registers. This is approximately four times as many registers as in an Intel 80386.

6. A 512-byte instruction cache allows the CPU to place several instructions in the TMS340 queue while continuing to execute in parallel.

7. The coprocessor contains dedicated graphics instructions to draw single pixels and lines, and to perform two-dimensional pixels array operations, such as pixBlts, area fills, and block transfers, as well as several auxiliary graphics functions.

The commercial failure of the TMS 340-based systems was probably caused by the slow development of commercial graphics applications that used the chip's capabilities. Systems based on the TMS 340 sold from $500 to well over $1000 and they had little commercial software support. However, their principal importance was that they demonstrated the PC's capability of high-quality, high-performance graphics.

State-of-the-Art in PC Graphics

During the first half of the 1990s, PC graphics were mostly DOS-based. The versions of Windows and OS/2 operating systems available lacked performance and gave programmers few options and little control outside of the few and limited graphics services offered at the system level. Several major graphics applications were developed and successfully marketed during this period, including professional quality CAD, draw and paint, and digital typesetting programs for the PC. But it was not until the introduction of 32-bit Windows, and especially after the release of Windows 95 that PC graphics took off as a mainstream force.

The hegemony of Windows 95 and its successors greatly contributed to the current graphics prosperity. At the end of the decade DOS has all but disappeared from the PC scene and graphics applications for the DOS environment are no longer commercially viable. By providing graphics hardware transparency, Windows has made possible the proliferation of graphics coprocessors, adapters, and systems with many dissimilar functions and fields of application. At the same time, the cost of high-end graphics systems has diminished considerably. So much so that in late 1999 a top-line PC graphics card equipped with the 3Dfx Voodoo Banshee, the NVidia RIVA TNT, the MGA G200, or other cutting edge graphics coprocessors, along with 16MB of graphics memory, costs from $100 to $150.

From the software side three major forces struggle for domination of PC graphics: DirectX, OpenGL, and several game development packages of which Glide is the best known.

Graphics boards

PC graphics boards available at this time can be roughly classified by their functionality into 2D and 3D accelerators, and by their interface into *Peripheral Component Interconnect* (PCI) and *Accelerated Graphics Port* (AGP) systems. The 16-bit *Industry Standard Architecture* (ISA) expansion bus is in the process of being phased out and few new graphics cards are being made for it.

System bus

Table 1-1 compares the currently available PC system buses.

Table 1-1			
Specifications of PC System Buses			
Bus	**Width**	**Clock Speed**	**Data Rate**
ISA	16 bits	8MHz	(varies)
PCI	32 bits	33MHz	132MBps
AGP 1X	32 bits	66MHz	264MBps
AGP 2X	32 bits	133MHz	528MBps
AGP 4X	32 bits	266MHz	1024MBps

The PCI bus is present in many old-style Pentium motherboards, and graphics cards continue to be made for this interface. It allows full bus mastering and supports data transfer rates in bursts of up to 132MBps. Some PCI buses that use older Pentium 75 to 150 run at 25 or 30MHz, but the vast majority operates at 33MHz. The 66MHz PCI is seen in specialized systems.

The AGP port is dedicated to graphics applications, quadruples PCI performance, and is state-of-the-art. AGP technology is based on Intel's 440LX and 440BX chipsets used in Pentium II and Pentium III motherboards and on the 440 EX chipset designed for the Intel Celeron processors.

The great advantage of AGP over its predecessors is that it provides the graphics coprocessors with a high bandwidth access system memory. This allows applications to store graphics data in system RAM. The 3D graphics applications use this additional memory by means of a process called *direct memory execute* (DIME) or *AGP texturing* to store additional image data and to enhance rendering realism. However, because AGP systems do not require that graphics cards support texturing, this feature cannot be taken for granted in all AGP boards. In fact, few graphics programs to date actually take advantage of this feature.

Graphics coprocessors

Although it is easy to pick AGP as the best available graphics bus for the PC, selecting a graphics coprocessor is much more complicated. Several among half a dozen graphics chips share the foreground at this time. Among them are the Voodoo line from 3Dfx (Voodoo2 and Voodoo Banshee), NVidia's RIVA processors, MGA-G200, and S3 Savage 3D chips. All of these chips are used in top-line boards in PCI and AGP forms. Other well-known graphics chips are 3D Labs Permedia, S3's Virge, Matrox's MGA-64, and Intel's i740.

CPU On-board facilities

Graphics, especially 3D graphics, is a calculation-intensive environment. The calculations are usually simple and can be performed in integer math, but many operations are required to perform even a simple transformation. Graphics coprocessors often rely on the main CPU for performing this basic arithmetic. For this reason, graphics rendering performance is, in part, determined by the CPU's mathematical throughput. Currently the mathematical calculating engines are the math unit and the *multimedia extension* (MMX).

In the older Intel processors the math unit (originally called the 8087 mathematical coprocessor) was either an optional attachment or an optional feature. For example, you could purchase a 486 CPU with or without a built-in math unit. The versions with the math unit were designated with the letters DX and those without it as SX. With the Pentium, the math unit hardware became part of every CPU and the programmer need not be concerned about its presence. The math unit is a fast and efficient numerical calculator that finds many uses in graphics programming. Because 486-based machines can be considered obsolete at this time, our code can safely assume the presence of the Intel math unit and take advantage of its potential.

In 1997, Intel introduced a version of their Pentium processor that contained 57 new instructions and 8 additional registers designed to support the mathematical calculations required in 3D graphics and multimedia applications. This additional unit was named the Multimedia Extension (MMX). The Pentium II and later processors all include MMX. MMX is based on the *Single Instruction Multiple Data* (SIMD) technology, an implementation of parallel processing; it has a single instruction operating on multiple data elements. In the MMX the multiple data is stored in integer arrays of 64 bits. The 64 bits can divided into 8 bytes, four packed words, two doublewords, or a single quadword. The instruction set includes arithmetic operations (add, subtract, and multiply), comparisons, conversions, logical operations (AND, NOT, OR, and XOR), shifts, and data transfers. The result is a parallel, simple, and fast-calculating engine quite suitable for graphics processing, especially in 3D.

3D application programming interfaces

The selection of a PC graphics environment for our application is further complicated by the presence of specialized *application programming interfaces* (APIs) furnished by the various chip manufacturers. For example, 3Dfx furnishes the *Glide* API for their line of graphics coprocessors. Glide-based games and simulations are popular within the 3D gaming community. An application designed to take full advantage of the capabilities of the 3Dfx accelerators is often coded using Glide. However, other graphics coprocessors cannot run the resulting code, which makes the boards incompatible with the software developed using Glide. Furthermore, Glide and Direct3D are mutually exclusive. When a Glide application is running, Direct3D programs cannot start and vice versa.

OpenGL and DirectX

One 3D graphics programming interface that attained considerable support is *OpenGL*. OpenGL, which stands for Open Graphics Language, originated in graphics workstations and is now part of many system platforms, including Windows 95, 98, and NT, DEC's AXP, OpenVMS, and X Window. This led some to believe that it will be the 3D graphics standard of the future.

At this time the mainstream of 3D graphics programming continues to use Microsoft's DirectX. The main advantage offered by this package is portability and universal availability on the PC. DirectX functionality is part of Windows 95, 98, 2000, and NT, and Microsoft provides a complete development package that includes a tutorial, support code, and sample programs — free of charge. Furthermore, developers are given license to provide DirectX runtime code with their products with automatic installation that can be made transparent to the user.

Image Properties

A computer graphics image is a surrogate of reality used to convey visual information. The surrogate is usually a light pattern displayed on a CRT monitor. Some of the characteristics of this image can be scientifically measured, or at least, evaluated objectively. But the human element in the perception of the graphic image introduces factors that are not easily measured. For example, aesthetic considerations can help us decide whether a certain graphic image "looks better" than another one, while another image can give us an eyestrain headache that cancels its technological virtues.

Brightness and contrast

Luminance is defined as the light intensity per unit area reflected or emitted by a surface. The human eye perceives objects by detecting differences in levels of luminance and color. Increasing the brightness of an object also increases the acuity with which it is perceived. However, it has been found that the visibility or legibility of an image is more dependent on contrast than on its absolute color or brightness value.

The visual acuity of an average observer sustains an arc of approximately one minute (1/60 a degree of angle). For this reason, the average observer can resolve an object that measures 5 one-thousands of an inch across on a CRT display viewed at a distance of 18 inches. However, visual acuity falls rapidly with decreased luminance levels and with reduced contrast. This explains why ambient light, reflected off the surface of a CRT, decreases legibility. Another peculiarity of human vision is the decreasing ability of the eye to perceive luminance differences or contrasts as the absolute brightness increases. This explains why the absolute luminance values between object and background are less important to visual perception than their relative luminance, or contrast.

Color

Approximately three-fourths of the light-perceiving cells in the human eye are color-blind, which explains why luminance and contrast are more important to visual perception than color. Nevertheless, it is generally accepted that color is a valuable enhancement to computer graphics. This opinion is probably based on the popular judgment that color photography, cinematography, and television are preferred over the black-and-white versions.

Resolution

The quality of a raster-scan CRT is determined by the total number of separately addressable pixels contained per unit area. This ratio, called the resolution, is usually expressed in pixels-per-inch. For example, a CRT with 8-inch rows containing a total of 640 pixels per row has a horizontal resolution of 80 pixels per inch. By the same token, a CRT measuring 6 inches vertically and containing a total of 480 pixels per column has a vertical resolution of 80 pixels per inch. Previously in this chapter we discussed symmetrical and asymmetrical resolutions (see Figure 1-7).

Aspect ratio

The aspect ratio of a CRT display is the relation between the horizontal and vertical dimensions. For example, the CRT previously mentioned, measuring 8 inches horizontally and 6 inches vertically, is said to have a 4:3 aspect ratio. An 8- by-8-inch display has a 1:1 aspect ratio. Figure 1-12 shows a CRT with a 4:3 aspect ratio.

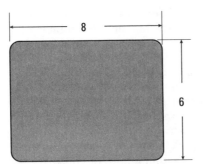

Figure 1-12: CRT with a 4:3 aspect ratio

Graphics Applications

Applications of computer graphics in general and of 3D graphics in particular appear to be limitless. The limitations seem to relate more to economics and to technology than to intrinsic factors. It is difficult to find a sphere of computing that does not profit from graphics in one way or another. This is true not only about applications but also about operating systems. In today's technology, graphics is the reality of computing. The PC has evolved into a powerful graphics machine, and graphics are no longer an option, but a standard feature that cannot be ignored.

Computer games

Since the introduction of Pac Man in the early 1980s, computer games have played an important role in personal entertainment. More recently we have seen an increase in popularity of dedicated computer-controlled systems and user-interaction devices, such as those developed by Nintendo, Sony, and Sega. In the past three or four years, computer games have gone through a remarkable revival. The availability of more powerful graphics systems and of faster processors, as well as the ingenuity and talent of the developers, has brought about the increase in the popularity of this field. Computer games are one of the leading sellers in today's software marketplace, with sales supported by an extensive subculture of passionate followers. Electronic games are always at the cutting edge of computer graphics and animation. A game succeeds or fails according to its performance. It is in this field where the graphics envelope is pushed to the extreme. 3D graphics technologies relate very closely to computer games. In fact, it can be said that computer games have driven graphics technology.

Science, engineering, and technology

Engineering encompasses many disciplines, including architecture, and mechanical, civil, and electrical, and many others. Virtually every field of engineering finds application for computer graphics and most can use 3D representations. The most generally applicable technology is *computer-aided design* (CAD), also called *computer-aided drafting*. CAD systems have replaced the drafting board and the T-square in the design of components for civil, electrical, mechanical, and electronic systems. A few years ago, a CAD system required a mainframe or minicomputer with high-resolution displays and other dedicated hardware. Similar capabilities can be had today with off-the-shelf PC hardware and software. Most CAD packages now include 3D rendering capabilities.

These systems do much more than generate conventional engineering drawings. Libraries of standard objects and shapes can be stored and reused. A CAD program used in mechanical engineering stores nut and bolt designs, which can be resized and used as needed. The same applies to other frequently used components and standard shapes. The use of color adds a visual dimension to computer-generated engineering drawings, a feature that is usually considered too costly and difficult to do manually. Plotters and printers rapidly and efficiently generate high-quality hardcopies of drawings. 3D CAD systems store and manipulate solid views of graphics objects and automatically generate perspective views and projections. Wire-frame and solid modeling techniques allow the visualization of real-world objects and contours. CAD systems can also have *expertise* in a particular field. This *knowledge* can be used to check the correctness and integrity of a design.

In architecture and civil engineering, graphics systems find many applications. Architects used 3D modeling for the display of the interior and exterior of buildings. A graphics technique known as *ray tracing* allows the creation of solid models that show lighting, shading, and mirroring effects.

Computer graphics are used to predict and model system behavior. Simulation techniques allow you to create virtual representations of practically any engineered system, be it mechanical, electrical, or chemical. Mathematical equations are used to manipulate 3D representations and to predict behavior over a period of *simulated* time. Graphics images, usually color-coded and often in 3D, are used to display movement, and to show stress points or other dynamic features which, without this technique, would have been left to the imagination.

Geographic Information Systems (GIS) use computers to manipulate and store geographic, cartographic, and other social data used in the analysis of phenomena where geographical location is an important factor. Usually, the amount of data manipulated in a GIS is much larger than can be handled manually. Much of this data is graphics imagery in the form of maps and charts. GIS systems display their results graphically. They find application in land use and land management, agriculture, forestry, wildlife management, archeology, and geology. Programmable satellites and instruments allow you to obtain multiple images that can be used later in producing 3D images.

Remote sensing refers to collecting data at a distance, usually through satellites and other spacecraft. Today, most natural resource mapping is done using this technology. As the resolution of remotely sensed imagery increases, and its cost decreases, many more practical uses will be found for this technology.

Automation and robotics also find extensive use for computer graphics. Computer numerical control (CNC) and Computer-assisted manufacturing (CAM) systems are usually implemented in a computer graphics environment. State-of-the-art programs in this field display images in 3D.

Art and design

Many artists use computer graphics as a development and experimental platform, and some as a final medium. It is hotly debated whether computer-generated images can be considered fine art, but there is no doubt that graphics technology is one of the most powerful tools for commercial graphics and for product design. As CAD systems have replaced the drafting board, draw and paint programs have replaced the artist's sketchpad. The commercial artist uses a drawing program to produce any desired effect with great ease and speed, and to experiment and fine-tune the design. Computer-generated images can be stretched, scaled, rotated, filled with colors, skewed, mirrored, resized, extruded, contoured, and manipulated in many other ways. Photo editing applications allow scanning and transforming bitmapped images, which later can be vectorized and loaded into the drawing program or incorporated into the design as bitmaps.

Digital composition and typesetting is another specialty field in which computer graphics has achieved great commercial success. Dedicated typesetting systems and desktop publishing programs allow the creation of originals for publication, from a brochure or a newsletter to a complete book. The traditional methods were based on "mechanicals" on which the compositor glued strips of text and images to form pages. The pages were later photographed and the printing plates manufactured from the resulting negatives. Today, composition is done electronically. Text and images are merged in digital form. The resulting page can be transferred into a digital typesetter or used to produce the printing plates directly. The entire process is based on computer graphics.

Business

In recent years a data explosion has taken place. In most fields, more data is being generated than there are people to process it. Imagine a day in the near future in which fifteen remote sensing satellites orbit the earth, each of them transmitting every fifteen minutes an image of an area that covers 150 square miles. The resulting acquisition rate of an image per minute is likely to create processing and storage problems, but perhaps the greatest challenge will be to find ways to use this information. How many experts will be required simply to look at these images? Recently there were only two or three remote sensing satellites acquiring earth images and it is estimated that no more than 10 percent of these images ever were analyzed. Along this same line, businesses are discovering that they accumulate and store more data than can be used. *Data mining* and *data warehousing* are techniques developed to find some useful nugget of information in these enormous repositories of raw data.

Digital methods of data and image processing, together with computer graphics, provide our only hope of ever catching up with this mountain of unprocessed data. A business graph is used to compress and make available a large amount of information, in a form that can be used in the decision-making process. Computers are required to sort and manipulate the data and to generate these graphs. The field of image processing is providing methods for operating on image data. Technologies are being developed to allow computers to "look at" imagery and obtain useful information. If we cannot dedicate a sufficient number of human experts to look at a daily heap of satellite imagery, perhaps we will be able to train computers for this task.

Computer-based command and control systems are used in the distribution and management of electricity, water, and gas, in the scheduling of railways and aircraft, and in military applications. These systems are based on automated data processing and on graphics representations. At the factory level they are sometimes called *process controls*. In small and large systems, graphics displays are required to help operators and experts visualize the enormous amount of information that must be considered in the decision-making process. For example, the pilot of a modern-day commercial aircraft can obtain, at a glance, considerable information about the airplane and its components as they are depicted graphically on a video display. This same information was much more difficult to grasp and mentally process when it originated in a dozen or more analog instruments.

Computer graphics also serve to enhance the presentation of statistical data for business. Graphics data rendering and computer animation serve to make the presentation more interesting; for example, the evolution of a product from raw materials to finished form, the growth of a real estate development from a few houses to a small city, or the graphic depiction of a statistical trend. Business graphics serve to make more convincing presentations of products or services offered to a client, as a training tool for company personnel, or as an alternative representation of statistical data. In sales, computer graphics techniques can make a company's product or service more interesting, adding much to an otherwise dull and boring description of properties and features.

Simulations

Both natural and man-made objects can be represented in computer graphics. The optical planetarium is used to teach astronomy in an environment that does not require costly instruments and that is independent of the weather and other conditions. One such type of computer-assisted device, sometimes called a *simulator*, finds practical and economic use in experimentation and instruction. Simulators are further discussed in Chapter 5 in relation to animation programming.

Virtual reality

Technological developments have made possible a new level of user interaction with a computing machine, called *virtual reality*. Virtual reality creates a digital universe in which the user is immersed. This topic is discussed in Chapter 5 in relation to animation programming.

Artificial life

Artificial life, or *ALife*, has evolved around the computer modeling of biosystems. It is based on biology, robotics, and artificial intelligence. The results are digital entities that resemble self-reproducing and self-organizing biological life forms. Artificial life is discussed in Chapter 5.

Fractal graphics

Natural surfaces are highly irregular. For this reason, many natural objects cannot be represented by means of polygons or smooth curves. However, it is possible to represent some types of natural objects by means of a mathematical entity called a *fractal*. The word *fractal* was derived from *fractional dimensions*. Fractals are discussed in Chapter 5.

Summary

In this first chapter we discussed a host of topics that are at the core of computer graphics and that should be familiar to every PC graphics programmer. We discussed the history and evolution of graphics on the PC, the best-known and most widely used PC video technologies, the state-of-the-art in PC graphics, the various Application Programming Interfaces, image properties, and applications of computer graphics. In Chapter 2 we consider how images and graphics image data are represented and stored in a computer system, introducing the core notions of segments and of polygonal modeling.

✦　　　✦　　　✦

Graphics Representation and Modeling

This chapter is an overview of the database and geometrical concepts that underlie computer graphics. The material has been chosen so that it applies to the 3D rendering engines discussed in the book. The specifics that refer to each of the major 3D rendering systems used on the PC, Direct3D and OpenGL, are discussed in the corresponding chapters.

Types of Graphics Data

Computer images are classified into two general types: those defined as a pixel map and those defined as one or more vector commands. In the first case we refer to raster graphics and in the second case to vector graphics. Figure 2-1 shows two images of a cross, first defined as a bitmap, and then as a set of vector commands.

On the left side image of Figure 2-1, the attribute of each pixel is encoded in the bitmap. The simplest scheme consists of using a 0-bit in the bitmap to represent a white pixel and a 1-bit to represent a black or colored pixel. Vector commands, on the other hand, refer to the geometrical elements in the image. The vector commands in Figure 2-1 define the image in terms of two intersecting straight lines. Each command contains the start and end points of the corresponding line in a Cartesian coordinate plane that represents the system's video display.

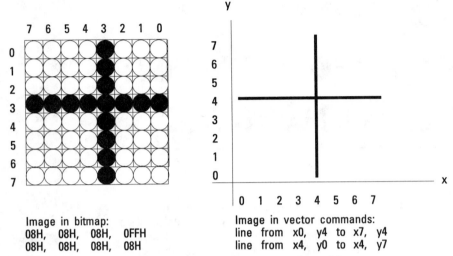

Image in bitmap:
08H, 08H, 08H, 0FFH
08H, 08H, 08H, 08H

Image in vector commands:
line from x0, y4 to x7, y4
line from x4, y0 to x4, y7

Figure 2-1: Raster and vector representation of a graphics object

An image composed exclusively of geometrical elements, such as a line drawing of a building, or a machine part, can usually be defined by vector commands. On the other hand, a naturalistic representation of a landscape may best be done with a bitmap. Each method of image encoding, raster- or vector-based, has its advantages and drawbacks. One fact often claimed in favor of vector representation is the resulting memory savings. For example, in a video surface of 600-by-400 screen dots, the bitmap for representing two intersecting straight lines encodes the individual states of 240,000 pixels. If the encoding is in a two-color form, as in Figure 2-1, then one memory byte is required for each eight screen pixels, requiring a 30,000-byte memory area for the entire image. This same image can be encoded in two vector commands that define the start and end points of each line. By the same token, to describe in vector commands a screen image of Leonardo's Mona Lisa would be more complicated and memory-consuming than a bitmap.

In the context of 3D graphics programming rasterized images are mostly used as textures and backgrounds. 3D rendering is based on transformations that require graphics objects defined by their coordinate points. Software operates mathematically on these points to transform the encoded images. For example, a geometrically defined object can be moved to another screen location by adding a constant to each of its coordinate points. In Figure 2-2 the rectangle with its lower left-most vertex at coordinates $x = 1$, $y = 2$, is translated to the position $x = 12$, $y = 8$, by adding 11 units to its x coordinate and 6 units to its y coordinate.

In Chapter 3 we explore geometrical image transformations in greater detail.

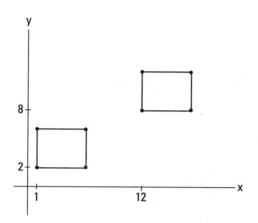

Figure 2-2: Translating an object by coordinate arithmetic

Coordinate systems

The French mathematician Rene Descartes (1596-1650) developed a method for representing geometrical objects. Descartes's system divides the plane with two intersecting lines, known as the *abscissa* and the *ordinate* axis. Conventionally, the abscissa axis is labeled with the letter x and the ordinate axis with the letter y. When the axes are perpendicular, we refer to the coordinate system as *rectangular;* otherwise, it is said to be oblique. The *origin* is the point of intersection of the abscissa and the ordinate axes. A point at the origin has coordinates (0, 0). When coordinates are expressed in this manner, the first element inside the parentheses corresponds to the x-axis and the second one to the y-axis. Therefore a point at (2, 7) is located at coordinates $x = 2$, $y = 7$. Figure 2-3 shows the rectangular Cartesian plane.

In Figure 2-3 we observe that a point on the x-axis has coordinates $(x, 0)$ and a point on the y-axis has coordinates $(0, y)$. The origin is defined as the point with coordinates (0, 0). The axes divide the plane into four quadrants, usually labeled counterclockwise with Roman numerals I to IV. In the first quadrant x and y have positive values. In the second quadrant x is negative and y is positive. In the third quadrant both x and y are negative. In the fourth quadrant x is positive and y is negative.

The Cartesian coordinates plane can be extended to three-dimensional space by adding another axis, usually labeled z. A point in space is defined by a triplet that expresses its x, y, and z coordinates. Here again, a point at the origin has coordinates (0, 0, 0), and a point on any of the three axes has zero coordinates on the other two. In a rectangular coordinate system the axes are perpendicular. Each pair of axis determines a coordinate plane: the xy-plane, the xz-plane, and the yz-plane. The three planes are mutually perpendicular. A point in the xy-plane has coordinates $(x, y, 0)$, a point in the xz-plane has coordinates $(x, 0, z)$, and so on. By the same token, a point not located on any particular plane has non-zero coordinates for all three axes. Figure 2-4 shows the Cartesian 3D coordinate plane.

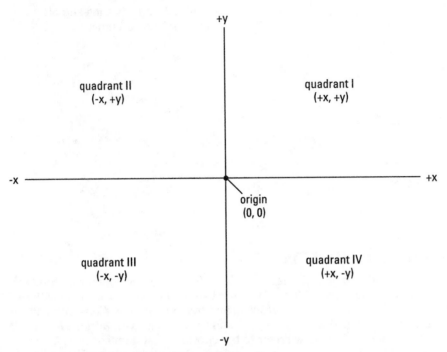

Figure 2-3: Cartesian rectangular coordinate plane

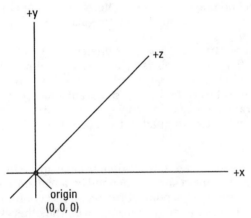

Figure 2-4: 3D Cartesian rectangular coordinates plane

The labeling of the axes in 3D space is conventional. In Figure 2-4 we could have labeled the *x*-axis as *z*, and the *z*-axis as *x* without affecting the validity of the representation. In computer graphics the most common labeling preserves the conventional labeling of the x- and y-axis in two-dimensional space and adds the z-axis in the viewer's direction, as in Figure 2-4. This labeling style is consistent with the notion of a video system in which image depth is thought to be inside the CRT. However, adopting the axis labeling style in which positive x points to the right, and positive y points upward, still leaves undefined the positive direction of the z axis. For example, we could represent positive z-axis values in the direction of the viewer or in the opposite one. The case in which the positive values of the z-axis are in the direction of the viewer is called a right-handed coordinate system. The one in which the positive values of the z-axis are away from the viewer is called a left-handed system. Left- and right-handed systems are shown in Figure 2-5.

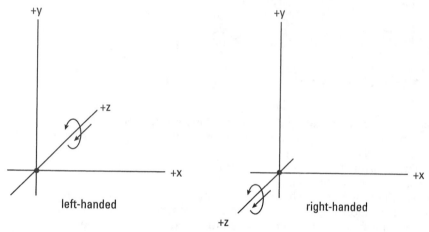

Figure 2-5: Left- and right-handed 3D coordinate systems

To remember if a system is left- or right-handed we can visualize which hand needs to be curled over the z-axis so that the thumb points in the positive direction, as shown in Figure 2-5. In a left-handed system the left hand with the fingers curled on the z-axis has the thumb pointing away from the viewer. In a right-handed system the thumb points toward the viewer.

There is considerable variation in the axes labeling among 3D modeling systems. In some systems the z-axis is represented horizontally, the y-axis in the direction of the viewer, and the x-axis is represented vertically. In any case, the right- and left-handedness of a system is determined by observing the axis that lays in the viewer's direction, independently of its labeling. Image data can be easily ported between different axes labeling styles by applying a rotation transformation, described in Chapter 3.

The 3D Cartesian coordinates planes are a 2D representation of a solid modeling system. In Figure 2-6 we have modeled a rectangular solid with dimensions $x = 5$, $y = 4$, $z = 3$.

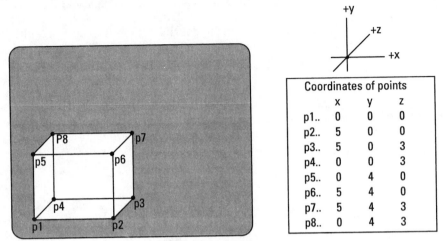

Figure 2-6: Vertex representation of a rectangular solid

The table of points, on the right side of the illustration, shows the coordinates for each of the vertices of the solid figure. However, because the illustration is a 2D rendering of a 3D object, it is not possible to use a physical scale in order to determine coordinate values from the drawing. For example, vertices $p1$ and $p4$ have identical x and y coordinates; however, they appear at different locations on the flat surface of the drawing. In other words, the image data stores the coordinates points of each vertex in 3D space. How these points are rendered on a 2D surface depends on the viewing system, sometimes called the projection. Projections and viewing systems are discussed in Chapter 4.

An alternative visualization of the 3D rectangular Cartesian coordinate system is based on planes. In this case each axes pair determines a *coordinate plane*, named the *xy*-plane, the *xz*-plane, and the *yz*-plane. Like the axes, the coordinate planes are mutually perpendicular. In this manner, the z coordinate of a point p is the value of the intersection of the z-axis with a plane through p that is parallel to the *yx*-plane. If the planes intersect the origin, then a point in the *xy*-plane has zero value for the z coordinate, a point in the *yz*-plane has zero value for the x coordinate, and a point in the *xz*-plane has zero for the y coordinate. Figure 2-7 shows the three planes of the 3D Cartesian coordinate system.

We have transferred to Figure 2-7 points $p6$ and $p7$ of Figure 2-6. Point $p6$ is located on *xy*-plane 1, and point $p7$ in *xy*-plane 2. The plane labeled *xy*-plane 2 can be visualized as *xy*-plane 1 which has been slid along the z-axis to the position $z = 3$. This explains why the x and y coordinates of points $p6$ and $p7$ are identical, as in the table of Figure 2-6.

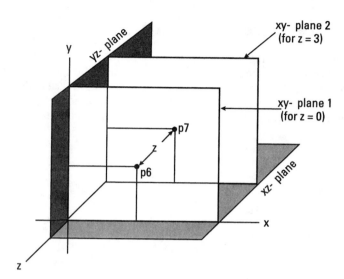

Figure 2-7: Coordinate planes in the rectangular Cartesian system

Representing geometrical objects

Much of 3D graphics programming relates to representing, storing, manipulating, and rendering vector-coded geometrical objects. In this sense, the problem of representation precedes all others. Many representational forms are used in 3D graphics; most are related to the rendering algorithms used in a particular package. In addition, representational forms determine data structures, processing cost, final appearance, and editing ease. The following are the most frequently used:

1. *Polygonal representations* are based on reducing the object to a set of polygonal surfaces. This approach is the most popular one due to its simplicity and ease of rendering.

2. Objects can also be represented as *bicubic parameteric patch nets*. A patch net is a set of curvilinear polygons that approximate the object being modeled. Although more difficult to implement than polygonal representations, objects represented by parametric patches are more fluid; this explains their popularity for developing CAD applications.

3. *Constructive solid geometry* (CSG) modeling is based on representing complex objects by means of simpler, more elementary ones, such as cylinders, boxes, and spheres. This representation finds use in manufacturing-related applications.

4. *Space subdivision techniques* consider the whole object space and define each point accordingly. The best-known application of space subdivision technique is *ray tracing*. With ray tracing processing is considerably simplified by avoiding brute force operations on the entire object space.

Out of this list, we concentrate our attention on polygonal modeling, with occasional reference to parametric patches.

Polygons and Polygonal Modeling

A simple polygon is a two-dimensional geometrical figure formed by more than two connected and non-intersecting line segments. The connection points for the line segments are called the *vertices* of the polygon and the line segments are called the *sides*. The fundamental requirements that the line segments be connected and non-intersecting eliminates from the polygon category certain geometrical figures, as shown in Figure 2-8.

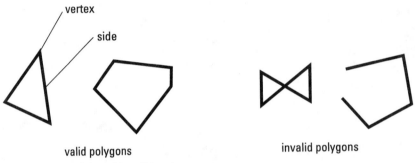

Figure 2-8: Valid and invalid polygons

Polygons are named according to their number of sides or vertices. A triangle, which is the simplest possible polygon, has three vertices. A quadrilateral has four, a pentagon has five, and so on. A polygon is said to be *equilateral* if all its sides are equal, and *equiangular* if all its angles are equal. A *regular* polygon is both equilateral and equiangular. Figure 2-9 shows several regular polygons.

Figure 2-9: Regular polygons

Polygons can be *convex* or *concave*. In a convex polygon the extension of any of its sides does not cut across the interior of the figure. Optionally, we can say that in a convex polygon the extensions of the lines that form the sides never meet another side. Figure 2-10 shows a convex and a concave polygon.

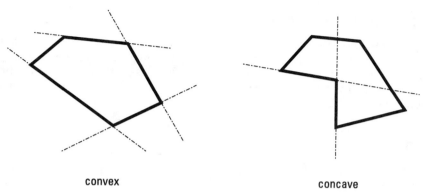

convex   concave

Figure 2-10: Concave and convex polygons

Specific software packages often impose additional restrictions on polygon validity in order to simplify the rendering and processing algorithms. For example, OpenGL requires that polygons be concave and that they be drawn without lifting the pen. In OpenGL, a polygon that contains a non-contiguous boundary is considered invalid.

Triangular representations

Of all the polygons, the one most used in 3D graphics is the triangle. Not only is it the simplest of the polygons, but all the points in the surface of a triangular polygon must lie on the same plane. In other polygons this may or may not be the case. In other words, the figure defined by three vertices must always be a plane, but four or more vertices can describe a figure with more than one plane. When all the points on the figure are located on the same surface, the figure is said to be *coplanar*. This is not the case in non-coplanar objects. Figure 2-11 shows coplanar and non-coplanar polygons.

coplanar
polygon

non-coplanar
polygon

Figure 2-11: Coplanar and non-coplanar polygons

The coplanar property of triangular polygons simplifies rendering. In addition, triangles are always convex figures. For this reason 3D software such as Microsoft's Direct3D rely heavily on triangular polygons.

Polygonal approximations

Solid objects with curved surfaces can be approximately represented by means of polygonal facets. For example, a circle can be approximated by means of a polygon. The more vertices in the polygon, the better the approximation. Figure 2-12 shows the polygonal approximation of a circle. The first polygon has eight vertices, while the second one has sixteen.

Figure 2-12: Polygonal approximation of a circle

A solid object, such as a cylinder, can be approximately represented by means of several polygonal surfaces. Here again, the greater the number of polygons, the more accurate the approximation, as shown in Figure 2-13.

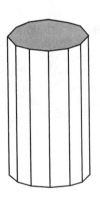

Figure 2-13: Polygonal approximation of a cylinder

Edges

When objects are represented by polygonal approximations, often two polygons share a common side. This connection between vertex locations that define a boundary is called an *edge*. Edge representations of polygons simplify the database by avoiding redundancy. This is particularly useful in models that share a large number of edges. Figure 2-14 shows a figure represented by two adjacent triangular polygons that share a common edge.

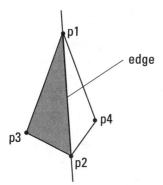

Figure 2-14: Polygon edge

In an edge representation the gray triangle in Figure 2-14 is defined in terms of its three vertices, labeled $p1$, $p2$, and $p3$. The white triangle is defined in terms of its edge and point $p4$. Thus, points $p2$ and $p3$ appear but once in the database. Edge-based image databases provide a list of edges rather than of vertex locations. Figure 2-15 shows an object consisting of rectangular polygons.

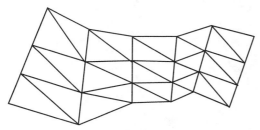

Figure 2-15: Edge representation of polygons

In Figure 2-15 each vertical panel consists of six triangles, for a total of 30 triangles. If each triangle were defined by its three vertices, the image database would require 90 vertices. Alternatively, the image could be defined in terms of sides and edges. There are 16 external sides which are not shared, and 32 internal sides, which are edges. Therefore, the edge-based representation could be done by defining 48 edges. The rendering system keeps track of which edges have already been drawn, avoiding duplication and the consequential processing overheads, and facilitating transparency.

Polygonal mesh

In 3D graphics an object can be represented as a polygon mesh. Facets are used to approximate curved surfaces; the more facets the better the approximation. Polygon-based modeling is straightforward, and polygon meshes are quite suitable for using shading algorithms that diminish the linearity that results from the straight-line representation. In the simplest form a polygon mesh is encoded by means of the x, y, and z coordinates of each polygon vertex. Alternatively, polygons can be represented by their shared sides, or edges. In either case, each polygon is an independent entity that can be rendered as a unit. 3D renderers are often based on this strategy as a means of shading and removing hidden surfaces. Figure 2-16 shows the polygon mesh representation of a teacup and the resulting rendered image.

Figure 2-16: Rendering a polygon mesh representation of a teacup

The Graphics Primitives

Many graphics systems are imaging tools, therefore, they must be capable of performing elementary graphics functions, such as drawing lines and geometric figures, displaying text characters, and shading or coloring screen areas. The set of available image-creating operations are called the *output functions* or *graphics primitives* of the system. A general- purpose graphics library generally includes a collection of graphics primitives. A graphics application often includes only those functions required for its specific purpose. A minimal, general-purpose 2D graphics library may contains the following primitives:

1. *Viewport primitives:* clear the viewport, set the entire viewport to a color or attribute, save the displayed image in memory, and restore a saved image.

2. *Window primitives:* set a rectangular screen area to a given color or attribute, save a rectangular screen area in memory, and restore a saved rectangular screen area.

3. *Attribute selection primitives:* set the current drawing color, set the current fill color, set the current shading attribute, set the current text color, set the current text font, set the current line type (continuous, dotted, dashed, etc.), and set the current drawing thickness.

4. *Geometrical primitives:* draw a straight line, draw a circular arc, draw an elliptical arc, draw a parabolic arc, draw a hyperbolic arc, and draw Bezier curves.

5. *Image transformation primitives:* scale, rotate, translate, and clip image.

6. *Painting primitives:* fill a closed figure with current fill color or shading attribute.

7. *Bit block primitives:* XOR text or bit block, AND text or bit block, and OR text or bit block.

The Windows API provide some of the listed functionality, except for the image transformation functions mentioned in item Number 5.

Input functions

In addition to generating geometrical objects, a computer graphics system must usually be capable of interacting with a human operator. The interaction typically takes place through an input device such as a keyboard, a mouse, a graphical input tablet, or any other similar gadgetry. Input can be roughly classified into two types: *valuator* and *locator*. Valuator input takes place when the data entered is in alphanumerical form. For example, the coordinates of the end points of a line constitute valuator input. Locator input takes place when the user interaction serves to establish the position of a graphics object called the locator. A mouse-controlled icon produces locator input.

Valuator and locator input normally follow this sequence of input phases:

1. Input request phase: The graphics system goes into the input mode and prompts the user to produce an input action.

2. Echo phase: As the user interacts with the input device, its actions are echoed by the graphics system. For instance, the characters are displayed as they are typed, or an icon moves on the screen as the mouse is dragged. Phases 1 and 2 are sometimes called the prompt-and-echo phase.

3. Trigger phase: The user signals the completion of input by pressing a specially designated key or a button on the input device. One way to conclude the input phase is to abort the operation, usually by pressing the escape or break key or clicking a specific button.

4. Acknowledge phase: The graphics system acknowledges that the interaction has concluded by disabling the input prompt and by notifying the user of the result of the input. In the case of locator input the acknowledge phase often consists of displaying a specific symbol that fixes the locator position. In the case of valuator input the acknowledge phase can make the cursor disappear. Another action of the acknowledge phase is that the characters entered are reformatted and redisplayed, or they are stored internally and erased from the CRT.

A general-purpose graphics library includes the following interaction primitives:

1. *Valuator input primitives*: input coordinate, input integer, input string, and input real number

2. *Locator selection primitives*: select cursor type, such as crosshair, vertical bar, flashing rectangle, or rubber band

3. *Locator input primitives*: enable and disable screen icon, move screen icon, select graphics item on screen and menu item

Display file structure

A graphics application must be capable of storing and transforming graphics data. The logical structure that contains this data is sometimes called the display file. One of the advantages of a display file is that it allows the compact storage of graphics data and its transformation through logical and mathematical operations. For example, an image may be enlarged by means of a mathematical transformation of its coordinate points, called a scaling transformation. Or the graphics object can be viewed from a different angle by means of a rotation transformation. Another transformation, called translation, allows changing the position of a specific object. Geometrical transformations are the subject of Chapter 3.

Before these manipulations can take place, the program designers must devise the logical structure that encodes image data in a form that is convenient for the mathematical operations to be performed. High-level graphics environments, graphical languages, and operating systems with graphics functions provide pre-canned display file structures that are available to applications. The programmer working in a customized environment, on the other hand, usually designs the display file to best accommodate and manipulate the data at hand. The first step in defining this structure usually consists of standardizing the screen coordinates.

A screen normalization schemes usually aims at maximum simplification. A common approach is to select the top-left corner of the screen as the origin of the coordinate system and make all locations positive, as shown in Figure 2-17.

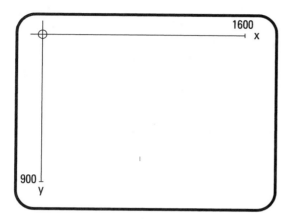

Figure 2-17: Cartesian plane representation of the display surface

The range of values that can be represented in either axis is determined by the system's resolution. If an application is to support a single display definition, it may be convenient to normalize the screen coordinates to this range. However, this decision should be taken cautiously, since equating the virtual to the physical device means that any future support for a system with a different definition probably implies modifying the entire software package.

Screen normalization is necessary so that image data in the display file can be shown on a physical device, but stored image data does not have to conform to the adopted screen normalization. At display time the processing routines perform the image-to-pixel conversions. This *pixelation*, sometimes called the window-to-viewport transformation, is described later in this chapter and in Chapter 4.

Image data in the display file

How the image is stored in the display file depends on the image itself and on the operations to be performed on its elements. Graphical images can be vectorized or bit-mapped. This requires a decision on whether a particular image is to be stored as a set of vector commands, as a bitmap, or as a combination of both. In many cases the nature of the image itself determines the most suitable approach. For example, an application that manipulates geometrical figures, such as a drawing program, probably stores image data in vector form. Some images, as is the case with alphanumeric characters, can be represented either in vector form or as bitmaps. Postscript and other conventions use vector representation of text characters in order to facilitate scaling.

There can be considerable variation in the encoding of a graphics object, whether it is represented as a bitmap, as a set of vector commands, or as both. A straight line is defined by its two end-points coordinates, or by its start point, angle, and length.

A rectangle is defined by the coordinates of its four vertices, or by the coordinates of two diagonally opposite vertices. In the case of a rectangle, the first option allows the representation of parallelograms, but the second one is more compact. There are also variations in the encoding of bit-mapped objects. If the object is unique, its bitmap can be included in the display file. However, if the application is to manipulate several objects with the same bitmap, then it may be preferable to encode a reference to the bitmap image in the display file.

The design of the image data formats for a customized display file requires careful planning and detailed design. Even then, changes usually become necessary in the program development stage. Anticipation of change is one of the basic principles of good database design.

Display file commands

A graphics system must not only store image data, it must also be capable of manipulating this data in order to generate and transform images. The set of orders that operate on image data is called *display file commands*. The notion of a display file containing both data and processing methods is consistent with the principles of object-oriented programming. As an illustration consider a screen triangle represented by three straight lines. The display file contains the coordinate points of the three lines as well as the commands to draw these lines, as shown in Figure 2-18.

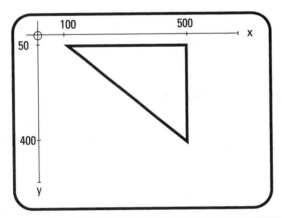

Display File				
commands:	image data:			
	x	y	x'	y'
draw line	100	50	500	50
draw line	500	50	500	400
draw line	500	100	100	50

Figure 2-18: Display file for a triangle

In Figure 2-18 the screen coordinates coincide with the display file coordinates, which is not usually the case. More often graphics software must perform mapping operations and convert image data to viewport coordinates at display time, as described in the following sections.

Image Mapping

The graphical image exists in a physical universe. The storage media is typically a memory or a permanent digital recording, and the display media is a pixel-mapped video surface. In either case there are certain concepts, terminology, and logical structures that find frequent use in image mapping, storage, and retrieval.

Video buffer

The video buffer is the portion of system memory reserved for video display use. It is a system-specific concept: the location and structure of the video buffer depends on the architecture of the specific graphics hardware and on the operating system. In MS-DOS graphics programming the video buffer architecture changes in the different display modes. For example, in VGA mode 18 the video buffer consists of four color planes, each plane storing a 640-by-480 pixel image, while in mode 19 the video buffer consists of 320-by-200 pixels, each of which is mapped to a memory byte that encodes the pixel's attribute. SuperVGA memory structures were mentioned in Chapter 1. In any case, the physical address of the MS-DOS video buffer in the graphics modes is A0000H. Microsoft DirectX allows Windows graphics applications to obtain access to the video buffer. Direct access to video memory in Windows programming is discussed in detail in Part II.

The video buffer is also called the *display buffer*, the *regen buffer* (short for image regeneration buffer), video memory, and the *video display buffer*. The term *frame buffer* is used occasionally, and somewhat imprecisely. Most PC display systems allow access to the video buffer by the CPU (programmer's port) and by the display hardware (video controller's port). For this reason it is described as a dual-ported system.

Image buffer

While the video buffer is a physical entity, the notion of an *image buffer* is a logical one. It is usually associated with the virtual graphics device. Since the attributes of the virtual machine can exceed those of the physical one, the dimensions and attribute range of the image buffer can exceed those of the video buffer. In fact, an application can manage and manipulate more than one image buffer. In DirectX image buffers are called *surfaces*. Image data in the image buffer is usually represented in *world coordinates* using whatever units are meaningful in the program's context. For example, an engineering application may store image data in meters, while an astronomical program uses light years.

Window and viewport

The terms *window* and *viewport* are used often, and sometimes imprecisely, in computer graphics. The fact that Microsoft's multitasking operating system for the PC is called Windows adds to the confusion. Strictly speaking, a window is a rectangular area in the image buffer, also called a *world-coordinate window*. A screen region is called a viewport. In this sense, an application displays a portion of the image data by performing a *window-to-viewport* transformation. But recently, the word *window* has been used as a loose synonym for viewport. This type of window is sometimes qualified as *window-manager window*, to distinguish it from world-coordinate window.

In the PC world the word "window" is used, in the sense of a window-manager window, to denote a screen area. This connotation is at least as common as the more correct term "viewport." In this book we use either term, according to the topic's context. We refer specifically to "world-coordinate window" and "window-manager window" when the clarification is necessary. Figure 2-19 shows these terms and concepts.

world-coordinate window

viewport
(window-manager window)

image buffer (world coordinates)

Figure 2-19: Window and viewport

Graphics Modeling Elements

Graphic modeling assumes that any picture, no matter how elaborate or ornate, can be constructed out of relatively few, simple components. The term *descriptor* is often used to represent an element in a drawing, which cannot be subdivided into simpler parts.

Descriptor

The descriptor concept is an abstraction adopted by the graphics system. Theoretically, any geometrical figure except a point can be represented in a simplified form. A *description* is defined as a collection of at least one descriptor. In general, a graphics model is the representation of objects using literal or mathematical descriptions. In functional programming, the model is a representation of the object, but does not include instructions on how to display it. In object-oriented terms the model includes the data that defines the image and the methods that are used in manipulating and rendering it. Whether object-oriented or not most graphics systems adopt this last approach.

The specific format and syntax of the model and the available descriptors vary with each development system or graphics language, and even in the specific implementations of these packages. For example, a simple graphic modeling system could be based on the following descriptors:

1. *move (x,y)* is a command to set the current location of the drawing pen at coordinates *x,y*.

2. *line (x,y)* is a command to draw a line from the current location to a location with coordinates *x,y*.

3. *circle (r)* is a command to draw a circle of radius *r* with its center positioned at the current location of the drawing pen.

Description

A description can include as many descriptors as necessary to represent the figure. In some graphics languages, descriptions are assigned a variable name. The following description encodes the operations necessary to draw a circle enclosed by a square:

```
Dname (A)
   move (0,0)
   line (8,0) > line (8,8) > line (0,8) >line (0,0)
   move (4,4)
   circle (3)
A ends
```

In this case the operator Dname marks the start of a description and the operator ends signals its end. Also note that the greater-than symbol (>) is used to separate descriptors in the same line, as well as to indicate program flow. Notice that these symbols and structures are used by the authors for the purpose of the current illustration, and that they do not correspond to the actual operators of any graphics language or system.

The model of a graphics object may also specify transformations to be performed on its description. These transformations are the usual operations of translation, rotation, scaling, or others specific to the language or environment. Sometimes the transformed description is called a *graphical object*. A possible scheme for representing transformations in a graphical language can use parentheses, brackets, and capital letters, as in the following example of a translation of the graphical description, labeled A, previously listed:

```
SHIFT (14,2) [A]
```

Figure 2-20 represents the description for the object (A) and the translation that results from the SHIFT *(x,y)* [A] operator.

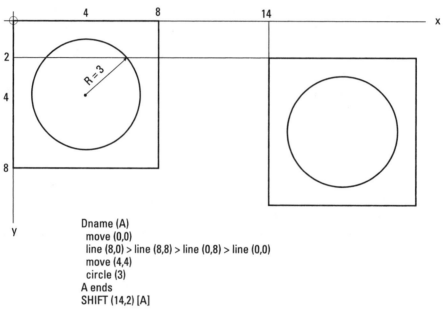

```
Dname (A)
  move (0,0)
  line (8,0) > line (8,8) > line (0,8) > line (0,0)
  move (4,4)
  circle (3)
A ends
SHIFT (14,2) [A]
```

Figure 2-20: Descriptors and descriptions in a graphical language

The Display File

The data structure that serves to encode graphical images is called the *display file*. Because descriptors and descriptions are the rational foundation for any modeling scheme, display file design is based on the principles of graphics modeling. The first step in display file design is usually determining the general structure of the filing system. The level of complexity of the display file structure should be consistent with the requirements of the system or application. The implementation of a full-featured graphical language requires several logical levels and sublevels of image encoding. A specific application, on the other hand, can sometimes do without some of these complications.

The most common elements of the display file are the image file, the image segment, and the image descriptors.

Image file

Image files are subdivisions of a display file. Each image file encodes a single screen image. Image file data, or data references, can be in the form of bitmaps, vector graphics, and text elements. In some cases the image file also includes manipulating and rendering logic. Figure 2-21 shows the results of displaying an image file that contains a bitmap, a vector-based rectangle, and several text elements.

Figure 2-21: Rendered image file

Storing bitmaps, vector-based graphics, and text data separately makes available the individual components to other images. In Figure 2-21 the partial view of the planet Saturn is a portion of a much larger image stored in the image buffer, represented in Figure 2-19. In this case the display file need contain only a reference that allows identifying the rectangular tile of the image buffer that is to be used in this particular screen. In addition, the image file contains information describing the transformations, if any, to be performed on the data.

Text elements can be stored in the image file or elsewhere, according to their purpose, complexity, and extension. For example, if the use of text is limited to short messages that are part of the graphics images, the most reasonable approach may be to store the text strings in the image file itself. On the other hand, if the program uses and reuses extensive text areas it is more efficient to store the text separately and include in the image file a reference to this location.

Image segments

An image segment is a portion of the image that can be considered as a graphic unit. Therefore, the image file can contain more than one image segment. The portion of the image contained in each segment is displayed as a single element. Figure 2-22 shows an image file consisting of two separate segments: the mailbox segment and the flag segment. In the right-hand drawing the flag segment has been rotated to the vertical position.

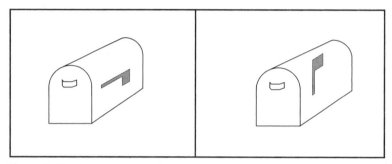

Figure 2-22: Image segments

Most graphics manipulations take place at the level of the image segment.

Image descriptors

The *image descriptors* are the basic elements of the encoding. They are also called *display file commands*, and less appropriately, *graphics primitives*. A descriptor contains the instructions, data, and data references necessary for displaying a graphical element. The descriptors in Figure 2-20 (move, line, and circle) are used to form the segment (or description) labeled (A). A segment can contain one or more descriptors. For example, the segment for the mailbox in Figure 2-22 requires descriptors for the straight-line segments that form the top and bottom of the box and for the arcs that form its ends. The segment for the mailbox flag can contain a single descriptor for a polygon.

The components of a descriptor are the operation code and the operands. The operation code, sometimes called opcode, is a mnemonic description of the operations to be performed. The terms move, line, and circle in Figure 2-20 are opcodes. The operands are the data items required by the opcode. In this example the operands follow the opcodes and are enclosed in parentheses or brackets.

Summary

This chapter is an overview of the basic concepts and constructs that serve as a foundation to computer graphics in general, and to 3D graphics in particular. The chapter's main purpose is to acquaint the reader with types of graphics data and their most common representations, with graphics modeling systems and techniques, and with the basic ideas of image mapping. In Chapter 3 we use this knowledge obtained here to explain the geometrical transformations that are at the core of 3D graphics manipulations.

✦　　✦　　✦

3D Image Transformations

Computer graphics rely heavily on geometrical transformations for the generation and animation of 2D and 3D imagery. In this chapter we introduce the essential transformations of translation, rotation, and scaling. For didactical reasons the geometrical transformations are first presented in the context of 2D imagery, and then expanded to 3D.

Coordinate Systems and Matrix Representations

In computer graphics you often need to manipulate vector images in order to transform them. For example, an arrow indicating a northerly direction can be rotated 45 degrees clockwise to indicate a northeasterly direction. If an image is defined as a series of points in the Cartesian plane, then the rotation can be performed by a mathematical operation on the coordinates that define each point. Similarly, if an image is defined as a series of straight lines connecting points in the plane, as would be the case in the representation of an arrow, then the transformation applied to the image points is also a transformation of the image itself.

The process is simplified further by storing the coordinates of each image point in a rectangular array. The mathematical notion of a matrix as a rectangular array of values turns out to be quite suitable for storing the coordinates of image points. After the coordinate points are stored in a matrix, you can use standard operations of linear algebra to perform geometrical transformations on the images. Figure 3-1 shows the approximate location of seven stars of the constellation Ursa Minor, also known as the Little Dipper. The individual stars are labeled with the letters a through g. The star labeled a corresponds to Polaris (the Pole star).

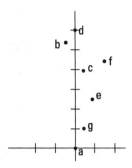

Figure 3-1: Point representation of the stars in the constellation Ursa Minor (Little Dipper)

The coordinates of each star of the Little Dipper, shown in Figure 3-1, can be represented in tabular form, as follows:

Star	X	Y
A	0	0
B	-1	11
C	1	8
D	0	12
E	2	5
F	3	9
G	1	2

In 2D graphics the coordinate matrix is a set of x, y coordinate pairs, as shown in the preceding example. 3D representations require an additional z-coordinate that stores the depth of each point. 3D matrix representations are discussed later in this chapter. In the following sections we explain the matrix operations that are most useful in graphics programming.

Image transformations

An image can be changed into another one by performing mathematical operations on its coordinate points. Figure 3-2 shows the translation of a line from coordinates (2,2) and (10,14) to coordinates (10,2) and (18,14).

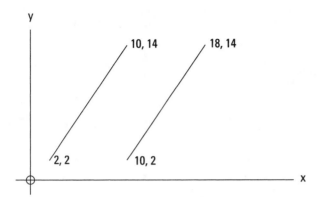

Figure 3-2: Translation of a straight line

Notice that in Figure 3-2 the translation is performed by adding 8 to the start and end *x*-coordinates of the original line. This operation on the *x*-axis performs a horizontal translation. A vertical translation requires manipulating the *y*-coordinate. To translate the line both horizontally and vertically you must operate on both coordinate axes simultaneously.

Matrix Arithmetic

Matrices are used in several fields of mathematics. In linear algebra matrices can hold the coefficients of linear equations. When the equations are represented in this manner, they can be manipulated (and often solved) by performing operations on the rows and columns of the matrix. At this time we are interested only in matrix operations that are used to perform geometrical image transformations. The most primitive of these — translation, rotation, and scaling — are common in graphics and animation programming. Other less common transformations are reflection (mirroring) and shearing.

We start by defining a matrix as a rectangular array usually containing a set of numeric values. It is customary to represent a matrix by means of a capital letter. For example, the following matrix, designated by the letter A, has three rows and two columns.

Example 1

$$A = \begin{array}{cc} 10 & 22 \\ 3 & 4 \\ 7 & 1 \end{array}$$

The size of a matrix is determined by its number of rows and columns. It is common to state matrix size as a product of rows by columns. For example, matrix A, in Example (1), is a 3-by-2 matrix.

Scalar-by-matrix operations

A single numerical quantity is called a *scalar*. Scalar-by-matrix operations are the simplest procedures of matrix arithmetic. Example 2 shows the multiplication of matrix A by the scalar 3.

Example 2

$$3\,A = \begin{array}{cc} 30 & 66 \\ 9 & 12 \\ 21 & 3 \end{array}$$

If a scalar is represented by the variable s, the product matrix sA is the result of multiplying each element in matrix A by the scalar s.

Matrix addition and subtraction

Matrix addition and subtraction are performed by adding or subtracting each element in a matrix to the corresponding element of another matrix of equal size. Example 3 shows matrix addition. Matrix C is the algebraic sum of each element in matrices A and B.

Example 3

$$\begin{array}{ccc} A & + & B & = & C \end{array}$$

$$\begin{array}{cc} 2 & 4 \\ 3 & 11 \\ 1 & 4 \\ 1 & -1 \end{array} + \begin{array}{cc} 1 & 2 \\ 2 & 2 \\ -1 & -3 \\ 0 & 0 \end{array} = \begin{array}{cc} 3 & 6 \\ 5 & 13 \\ 0 & 2 \\ 1 & -1 \end{array}$$

The fundamental restriction of matrix addition and subtraction is that both matrices must be of equal size, that is, they must have the same number of rows and columns. Matrices of different sizes cannot be added or subtracted.

Matrix multiplication

Matrix addition and subtraction intuitively correspond to conventional addition and subtraction. The elements of the two matrices are added or subtracted, one-to-one, to obtain the result. The fact that both matrices must be of the same size makes the operations easy to visualize. Matrix multiplication, on the other hand, is not the multiplication of the corresponding elements of two matrices, but a unique sum-of-products operation. In this case, the elements of a row in the multiplicand (first) matrix are multiplied by the elements in a column of the multiplier (second) matrix. These resulting products are then added to obtain the final result. The process is best explained by describing the individual steps. Consider the matrices in Example 4.

Example 4

$$A = \begin{matrix} 1 & 3 & 5 \\ 2 & 1 & 0 \end{matrix} \qquad B = \begin{matrix} 5 & 10 & 2 \\ 1 & 2 & 3 \\ 11 & 5 & 4 \end{matrix}$$

From the definition of matrix multiplication we deduce that if the columns of the first matrix are multiplied by the rows of the second matrix, then each row of the multiplier must have the same number of elements as each column of the multiplicand. Notice that matrices A and B in Example 4 meet this requirement. However, observe that product B × A is not possible, since matrix B has three elements per row and matrix A has only two elements in each column. For this reason, in Example 4, the matrix operation A × B is possible but B × A is undefined. The row by column operation in A × B is performed as follows:

Example 5

First row of A				Columns of B				Products				Sum
[1	3	5]	×	[5	1	11]	=	[5	3	55]	=	63
[1	3	5]	×	[10	2	5]	=	[10	6	25]	=	41
[1	3	5]	×	[2	3	4]	=	[2	9	20]	=	31

Second row of A				Columns of B				Products				Sum
[2	1	0]	×	[5	1	11]	=	[10	1	0]	=	11
[2	1	0]	×	[10	2	5]	=	[20	2	0]	=	22
[2	1	0]	×	[2	3	4]	=	[4	3	0]	=	7

The products matrix has the same number of columns as the multiplicand matrix and the same number of rows as the multiplier matrix. In Example 6, the products matrix C has the same number of rows as A and the same number of columns as B. In other words, C is a 2 × 3 matrix. The elements obtained by the preceding operations appear in matrix C in the following manner:

Example 6

$$C = \begin{matrix} 63 & 41 & 31 \\ 11 & 22 & 7 \end{matrix}$$

You have seen that in relation to matrices A and B in the previous example, the operation A × B is possible but B × A is undefined. This fact is often described by saying that matrix multiplication is not commutative. For this reason, the product of two matrices can be different if the matrices are taken in different order. In fact, in regards to nonsquare matrices, if the matrix product A × B is defined, then the product B × A is undefined.

On the other hand, matrix multiplication is associative. This means that the product of three or more matrices is equal independently of the order in which they are multiplied. For example, in relation to three matrices, A, B, and C, youi can state that (A × B) × C equals A × (B × C). In the coming sections you often find use for the associative and noncommutative properties of matrix multiplication.

2D Geometrical Transformations

A geometrical transformation can be described as the conversion of one image onto another one by performing mathematical operations on its coordinate points. Geometrical transformations are simplified by storing the image coordinates in a rectangular array, called a matrix. In the following sections, we describe the most common transformations: translation, scaling, and rotation. The transformations are first described in terms of matrix addition and multiplication, and later standardized so that they can be expressed in terms only of matrix multiplications.

Translation

A *translation transformation* is the movement of a graphical object to a new location by adding a constant value to each coordinate point that defines the object. The operation requires that a constant is added to all the coordinates in each plane, but the constants can be different for each plane. For example, a translation takes place if the constant 5 is added to all *x*-coordinates and the constant 2 to all *y*-coordinates of an object represented in a two-dimensional plane.

At the top of Figure 3-3 you see the graph and matrix of seven stars in the constellation Ursa Minor. A translation transformation is performed by adding 5 to the *x*-coordinate of each star and 2 to the *y*-coordinate. The bottom part of Figure 3-3 shows the translated image and the new coordinates.

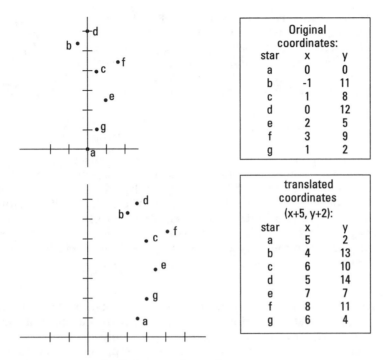

Figure 3-3: A translation transformation

In terms of matrix operations, the translation can also be viewed as follows:

Original coordinates matrix A		Transformation matrix B		Transformed coordinates matrix C	
x	y	x	y	x	y
0	0	5	2	5	2
-1	11	5	2	4	13
1	8	5	2	6	10
0	12	5	2	5	1
2	5	5	2	7	7
3	9	5	2	8	11
1	2	5	2	6	4

The transformation is expressed in the following matrix equation:

$A + B = C$

where A represents the original coordinates matrix, B the transformation matrix, and C the matrix holding the transformed coordinates. Notice that the transformation matrix holds the constants to be added to the x- and y-coordinates. By definition of the translation transformation, because the same value must be added to all the elements of a coordinate plane, it is evident that the columns of the transformation matrix always hold the same numerical value.

Scaling

To scale is to apply a multiplying factor to the linear dimension of an object. A *scaling transformation* is the conversion of a graphical object into another one by multiplying each coordinate point that defines the object by a scalar. The operation requires that all the coordinates in each plane are multiplied by the scaling factor, although the scaling factors can be different for each plane. For example, a scaling transformation takes place when all the x-coordinates of an object represented in a two-dimensional plane are multiplied by 2, and all the y-coordinates of this same object are multiplied by 3. In this case the scaling operation is said to be asymmetrical.

In comparing the definition of the scaling transformation to that of the translation transformation you notice that translation is performed by adding a constant value to the coordinates in each plane, while scaling requires multiplying these coordinates by a factor. The scaling transformation can be represented in matrix form by taking advantage of the properties of matrix multiplication.

Figure 3-4 shows a scaling transformation that converts a square into a rectangle.

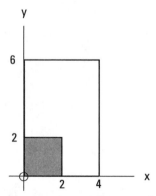

Figure 3-4: A scaling transformation

The coordinates of the square in Figure 3-4 can be stored in a 4-by-2 matrix, as follows:

	Coordinates	
	x	y
Start point	0	0
	2	0
End point	2	2
	0	2

The transformation matrix holds the factors that must be multiplied by the *x*- and *y*-coordinates in order to perform the scaling operation. Using the letters Sx to represent the scaling factor for the *x*-coordinates, and the letters Sy to represent the scaling factor for the *y*-coordinates, the scaling transformation matrix can be expressed as follows:

Sx	0
0	Sy

The transformation of Figure 3-4, which converts the square into a rectangle, is expressed in matrix form as follows:

Original coordinates matrix			Scaling matrix			Transformed coordinates matrix	
x	y		Sx	Sy		x	y
0	0					0	0
2	0	×	2	0	=	4	0
2	2		0	3		4	6
0	2					0	6

The intermediate steps in the matrix multiplication operation can be obtained following the rules of matrix multiplication described previously in this chapter.

Figure 3-5 shows the scaling transformation of the graph of the constellation Ursa Minor. In this case, in order to produce a symmetrical scaling, the multiplying factor is the same for both axes. A symmetrical scaling operation is sometimes referred to as a *zoom*.

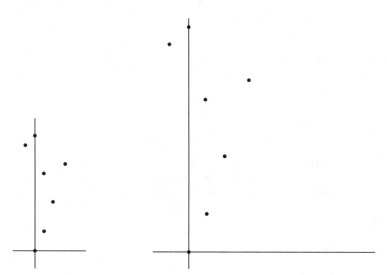

Figure 3-5: Symmetrical scaling (zooming)

Rotation

A *rotation transformation* is the conversion of a graphical object into another one by moving all coordinate points that define the original object, by the same angular value, along circular arcs with a common center. The angular value is called the *angle of rotation,* and the fixed point that is common to all the arcs is called the *center of rotation.* Notice that some geometrical figures are unchanged by specific rotations. For example, a circle is unchanged by a rotation about its center, and a square is unchanged if rotated by an angle that is a multiple of 90 degrees, provided that the center of rotation is the intersection point of both diagonals.

The mathematical interpretation of the rotation is obtained by applying elementary trigonometry. Figure 3-6 shows the counterclockwise rotation, through an angle r, of points located on the coordinate axes at unit distances from the center of rotation.

The left-side drawing in Figure 3-6 shows the counterclockwise rotation of point $p1$, with coordinates (1,0), through angle *r*. The coordinates of the rotated point ($pr1$) can be determined by solving the triangle with vertices at O, $p1$ and $pr1$, as follows:

```
cos r = x/1, therefore x = cos r
sin r = y/1, therefore y = sin r
```

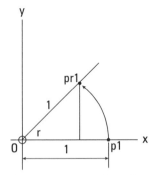 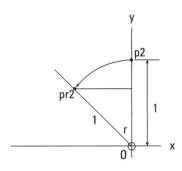

Figure 3-6: Rotation of a point

The coordinates of the rotated point *pr2*, shown on the right-side drawing in Figure 3-6, can be determined by solving the triangle with vertices at O, *p2* and *pr2*.

```
sin r = -x/1, therefore x = - sin r
cos r = y/1, therefore y = cos r
```

Now the coordinates of the rotated points can be expressed as follows.

```
coordinates of pr1 = (cos r, sin r)
coordinates of pr2 = (-sin r, cos r)
```

From these equations you can derive a transformation matrix, which, through matrix multiplication, yields the new coordinates for the counterclockwise rotation about the origin, through angle *r*, as shown in the following example:

cos*r*   -sin*r*

sin*r*   cos*r*

You are now ready to perform a rotation transformation through matrix multiplication. Figure 3-7 shows the clockwise rotation of the stars in the constellation Ursa Minor, through an angle of 60 degrees, with center of rotation at the origin of the coordinate axes.

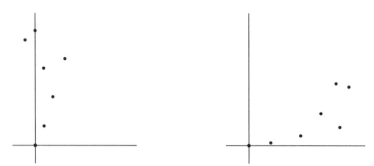

Figure 3-7: Rotation transformation

Suppose that the coordinates of the four vertices of a polygon are stored in a matrix, as follows:

		Coordinates	
		x	y
p1	→	10	2
p2	→	12	0
p3	→	14	2
p4	→	12	4

The transformation matrix for clockwise rotation through angle r is as follows:

cosr	sinr
·sinr	cosr

Evaluating this matrix for a 60-degree rotation gives the following trigonometric functions.

0.5	0.867
0.867	0.5

Now the rotation can be expressed as a product of two matrices as shown in the following example.

The intermediate steps in the matrix multiplication operation are obtained following the rules of matrix multiplication described earlier in this chapter.

		Original polygon coordinates			Rotation matrix 60 degrees clockwise			Rotated polygon coordinates			
		x	y					x	y		
p1	→	10	2					3.87	9.87	←	pr 1
p2	→	12	0	×	0.5	0.867	=	6	10.4	←	pr 2
p3	→	14	2		-0.867	0.5		5.27	13.4	←	pr 3
p4	→	12	4					2.53	12.4	←	pr 4

Homogeneous coordinates

Expressing translation, scaling, and rotation mathematically, in terms of matrix operations, allows a more efficient approach to graphical transformations. However, you notice that in the method previously described rotation and scaling are expressed in terms of matrix multiplication, while translation is expressed as matrix addition. It would be a valuable simplification if you could express all three basic transformations in terms of the same mathematical operation. Fortunately, it is possible to represent the translation transformation as matrix multiplication. The scheme requires adding a dummy parameter to the coordinate matrices and expanding the transformation matrices to 3×3. The following example shows the necessary manipulations where the coordinates of a point can be expressed in a matrix.

		Coordinates	
		x	y
point	→	[5	2]

This matrix can be expanded to three columns by using a dummy matrix parameter, labeled w. If w is not to affect coordinates x and y in two-dimensional transformations, it must meet the following requirement:

$$x = x * w, \quad y = y * w$$

It follows that 1 is the only value that can be assigned to w so that it meets the condition in the preceding example. This results in the matrix:

		Coordinates		
		x	y	w
point	→	[5	2	1]

You can use the terms *Tx* and *Ty* to represent the horizontal and vertical units of a translation. A transformation matrix for the translation operation can be expressed when you use homogenous coordinates as follows:

Translation
transformation
matrix

1	0	0
0	1	0
Tx	Ty	1

You test these results by performing a translation of eight units in the horizontal direction (*Tx* = 8) and zero units in the vertical direction (*Ty* = 0) of the point located at coordinates (5,2). The matrix multiplication is expressed as follows:

$$[5 \quad 2 \quad 1] * \begin{array}{ccc} 1 & 0 & 0 \\ 0 & 1 & 0 \\ 8 & 0 & 1 \end{array} = \begin{array}{l} 5 + 0 + 8 \ = \ 13 \\ 0 + 2 + 0 \ = \ 2 \\ 0 + 0 + 1 \ = \ 1 \end{array} = [13 \quad 2 \quad 1]$$

This operation shows the point at *x* = 5, *y* = 2 translated 8 units to the right, with destination coordinates of *x* = 13, *y* = 2. Observe that the *w* parameter, set to 1 in the original matrix, remains the same in the final matrix. For this reason, in actual processing operations the additional parameter can be ignored.

Concatenation

To take full advantage of the system of homogeneous coordinates you must express all the transformation matrices in terms of 3-by-3 matrices. The translation transformation can be expressed using homogenous coordinates in the following matrix:

Translation
transformation
matrix

1	0	0
0	1	0
Tx	Ty	1

The scaling transformation matrix can also be expanded to a 3-by-3 matrix as follows:

Scaling
transformation
matrix

Sx	0	0
0	Sy	0
0	0	1

At the same time, the translation transformation matrix for a counterclockwise rotation through angle *r* can be converted to homogeneous coordinates as follows:

Rotation
transformation
matrix

cos r	sin r	0
-sin r	cos r	0
0	0	1

Notice that this rotation transformation assumes that the center of rotation is at the origin of the coordinate system.

Matrix multiplication is associative. This means that the product of three or more matrices is equal, no matter which two matrices are multiplied first. By virtue of this property, you are now able to express a complex transformation by combining several basic transformations. This process is generally known as *matrix concatenation*.

For example, in Figure 3-7 the image of the constellation Ursa Minor is rotated clockwise 60 degrees about the origin. But it is possible to perform this transformation using any arbitrary point in the coordinate system as a pivot point. For instance, to rotate a polygon about any arbitrary point *pa*, the following sequence of transformations is executed:

1. Translate the polygon so that point *pa* is at the coordinate origin.

2. Rotate the polygon.

3. Translate the polygon so that point *pa* returns to its original position.

In matrix form the sequence of transformations can be expressed as the following product:

1	0	0		cos r	sin r	0		1	0	0
0	1	0	×	-sin r	cos r	0	×	0	1	0
-Tx	-Ty	1		0	0	1		Tx	Ty	1

Performing the indicated multiplication yields the matrix for a counterclockwise rotation, through angle r, about point pa, with coordinates (Tx, Ty).

cos r	sin r	0
-sin r	cos r	0
-Tx cos$r$ + Ty sin r + Tx	-Tx sin r - Ty cos r + Ty	1

Although matrix multiplication is associative, it is not commutative. Therefore, the order in which the operations are performed can affect the results. A fact that confirms the validity of the matrix representation of graphics transformations is that, graphically, the results of performing transformations in different sequences can also yield different results. For example, the image resulting from a certain rotation, followed by a translation transformation, may not be identical to the one resulting from performing the translation first and then the rotation.

Figure 3-8 shows a case in which the order of the transformations determines a difference in the final object.

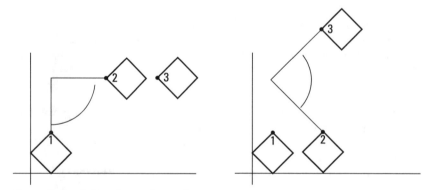

Figure 3-8: Order of transformations

3D Transformations

Two-dimensional objects are defined by their coordinate pairs in 2D space. By extending this model you can represent a three-dimensional object by means of a set of coordinate triples in 3D space. Adding a z-axis that encodes the depth component of each image point produces a three-dimensional coordinate system. The coordinates that define each image point in 3D space are a triplet of x, y, and z values. Because the three-dimensional model is an extension of the two-dimensional one, you can apply geometrical transformations in a similar manner as you did with two-dimensional objects. Figure 3-9 shows a rectangular solid in 3D space.

The solid in Figure 3-9 is defined by means of the coordinate triplets of each of its eight points, which are represented by the labeled black dots. In tabular form the coordinates of each point are defined as follows:

	x	y	z
p1	0	0	2
p2	4	0	2
p3	4	2	2
p4	0	2	2
p5	0	0	0
p6	4	0	0
p7	4	2	0
p8	0	2	0

Point p5, which is at the origin, has values of zero for all three coordinates. Point p1 is located 2 units along the z-axis, therefore its coordinates are $x = 0$, $y = 0$, $z = 2$. Notice that if you disregard the z-axis coordinates, then the two planes formed by points p1, p2, p3, and p4 and points p5, p6, p7, and p8 would have identical values for the x- and y-axis. This is consistent with the notion of a rectangular solid as a solid formed by two rectangles residing in 3D space.

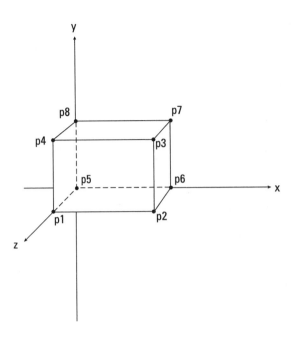

Figure 3-9: 3D representation of a rectangular solid

3D translation

In 2D representations, a translation transformation is performed by adding a constant value to each coordinate point that defines the object. This continues to be true when the point's coordinates are contained in three planes. As in the case of a 2D object, the transformation constant is applied to each plane to determine the new position of each image point. Figure 3-10 shows the translation of a cube defined in 3D space by adding 2 units to the x-axis coordinates, 6 units to the y-axis, and -2 units to the z-axis.

If the coordinate points of the eight vertices of the cube in Figure 3-10 were represented in a 3-by-8 matrix (designated as matrix A) and the transformation constants in a second 8-by-3 matrix (designated as matrix B), then you could perform the translation transformation by means of matrix addition and store the transformed coordinates in a results matrix (designated as matrix C). The matrix operation $A + B = C$ operation would be expressed as follows:

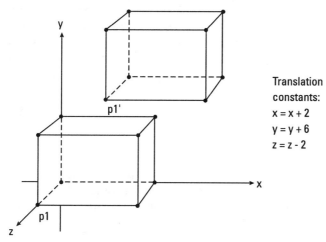

Translation
constants:
x = x + 2
y = y + 6
z = z - 2

Figure 3-10: Translation transformation of a cube

		Original coordinates matrix A				Transformation matrix B				Transformed coordinates matrix C				
		x	y	z		x	y	z		x	y	z		
p2	→	4	0	2		2	6	-2		6	6	0	→	p2 '
p3	→	4	2	2		2	6	-2		6	8	0	→	p3 '
p4	→	0	2	2		2	6	-2		2	8	0	→	p4 '
p5	→	0	0	0	+	2	6	-2	=	2	6	-2	→	p5 '
p6	→	4	0	0		2	6	-2		6	6	-2	→	p6 '
p7	→	4	2	0		2	6	-2		6	8	-2	→	p7 '
p8	→	0	2	0		2	6	-2		2	8	-2	→	p8 '

Here again, you can express the geometric transformation in terms of homogeneous coordinates. The translation transformation matrix for 3D space would be as follows:

3D translation
transformation
matrix

1	0	0	0
0	1	0	0
0	0	1	0
Tx	Ty	Tz	1

The parameters Tx, Ty, and Tz represent the translation constants for each axis. As in the case of a 2D transformation, the new coordinates are determined by adding the corresponding constant to each coordinate point of the figure to be translated. If x', y', and z' are the translated coordinates of the point at x, y, and z, the translation transformation takes place as follows:

$x' = x + Tx$

$y' = y + Ty$

$z' = z + Tz$

As in the case of 2D geometrical transformations, the transformed results are obtained by matrix multiplication using the matrix with the object's coordinate points as the first product matrix, and the homogenous translation transformation matrix as the second one.

3D scaling

A scaling transformation consists of applying a multiplying factor to each coordinate point that defines the object. A scaling transformation in 3D space is consistent with the scaling in 2D space. The only difference is that in 3D space the scaling factor is applied to each of three planes, instead of the two planes of 2D space. Here again the scaling factors can be different for each plane. If this is the case, the resulting transformation is described as an asymmetrical scaling. When the scaling factor is the same for all three axes, the scaling is described as symmetrical or uniform. Figure 3-11 shows the uniform scaling of a cube by applying a scaling factor of 2 to the coordinates of each figure vertex.

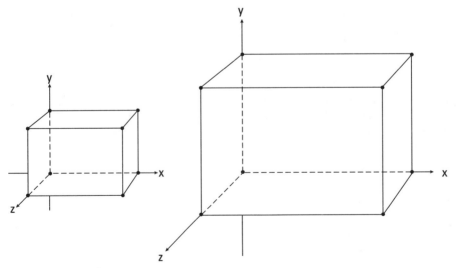

Figure 3-11: Scaling transformation of a cube

The homogeneous matrix for a 3D scaling transformation is as follows:

3D scaling
transformation
matrix

$$\begin{bmatrix} Sx & 0 & 0 & 0 \\ 0 & Sy & 0 & 0 \\ 0 & 0 & Sz & 0 \\ 0 & 0 & 0 & 1 \end{bmatrix}$$

The parameters Sx, Sy, and Sz represent the scaling factors for each axis. As in the case of a 2D transformation, the new coordinates are determined by multiplying the corresponding scaling factor with each coordinate point of the figure to be scaled. If x', y', and z' are the scaled coordinates of the point at x, y, and z, the scaling transformation takes place as follows:

$x' = x * Sx$

$y' = y * Sy$

$z' = z * Sz$

In homogeneous terms, the transformed results are obtained by matrix multiplication using the matrix with the object's coordinate points as the first product matrix, and the homogeneous scaling transformation matrix as the second one. When the object to be scaled is not located at the origin of the coordinates axes, a scaling transformation will also result in a translation of the object to another location. This effect is shown in Figure 3-12.

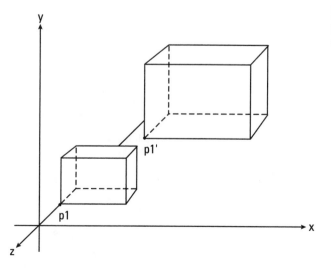

Figure 3-12: Scaling transformation of an object not at the origin

Assuming that point p1 in Figure 3-12 is located at coordinates $x = 2, y = 2, z = -2$, and that a uniform scaling of 3 units is applied, then the coordinates of translated point p1' are as follows:

		x	y	z
p1'	$\rightarrow$	[2	2	-2]
p1'	$\rightarrow$	[6	6	-12]

The result is that not only is the cube tripled in size, it is moved to a new position in the coordinates plane as well. To scale an image with respect to a fixed position, it is necessary to first translate it to the origin, apply the scaling factor next, and finally translate it back to its original location. The necessary manipulations are shown in Figure 3-13.

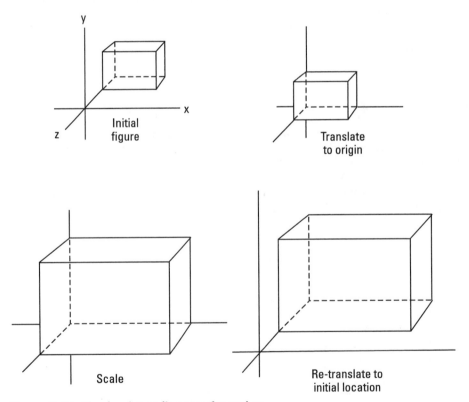

Figure 3-13: Fixed-point scaling transformation

In terms of matrix operations a fixed-point scaling transformation consists of applying a translation transformation to move the point to the origin, and then the scaling transformation, followed by another translation to return the point to its original location. If you represent the fixed position of the point as *xf, yf, zf*, then the translation to the origin is represented by the transformation:

$$T \left(-x^f, \ -y^f, \ -z^f \right)$$

Where T is any transformation applied to the points inside the parentheses. The transformation to return the point to its original location is as follows:

$$T \left(x^f, \ y^f, \ z^f \right)$$

Therefore, the fixed-point scaling consists of

$$T \left(-x^f, \ -y^f, \ -z^f \right) \leftrightarrow S \left(Sx, Sy, Sz \right) \leftrightarrow T \left(x^f, y^f, z^f \right)$$

and the homogeneous matrix is

Sx	0	0	0
0	Sy	0	0
0	0	Sz	0
$(1 - Sx) x^f$	$(1 - Sy) y^f$	$(1 - Sz) z^f$	0

where *S* is the scaling matrix and *T* the transformation matrix, as previously described.

3D rotation

Although 3D translation and scaling transformations are described as simple extensions of the corresponding 2D operations, the 3D rotation transformation is more complex than its 2D counterpart. The additional complications arise from the fact that in 3D space, rotation can take place in reference to any one of the three axes. Therefore an object can be rotated about the *x-*, *y-*, or *z*-axes, as shown in Figure 3-14.

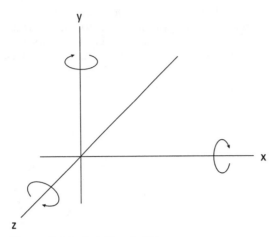

Figure 3-14: Rotation in 3D space

In defining 2D rotation, we adopted the convention that positive rotations produce a clockwise movement about the coordinate axes as shown by the elliptical arrows in Figure 3-14. Figure 3-15 shows the positive, *x*-axis rotation of a cube.

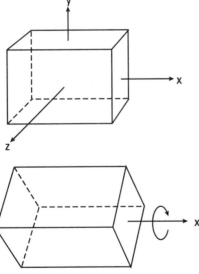

Figure 3-15: Positive, x-axis rotation of a cube

A rotation transformation leaves unchanged the coordinate values along the axis of rotation. For example, the x-coordinates of the rotated cube in Figure 3-15 are the same as those of the figure at the top of the illustration. By the same token, rotating an object along the z-axis changes its y- and x-coordinates while the z-coordinates remain the same. Therefore, the 2D rotation transformation equations can be extended to a 3D rotation along the z-axis, as follows:

z-axis, 3D rotation
transformation matrix

cos r	sin r	0	0
-sin r	cos r	0	0
0	0	1	0
0	0	0	1

Here again, r is the negative angle of rotation.

By performing a cyclic permutation of the coordinate parameters you can obtain the transformation matrices for rotations along the x- and y-axis. In homogeneous coordinates they are as follows:

x-axis, 3D rotation
transformation matrix

1	0	0	0
0	cos r	sin r	0
0	-sin r	cos r	0
0	0	0	1

y-axis, 3D rotation
transformation matrix

cos r	0	-sin r	0
0	1	0	0
sin r	0	cos r	0
0	0	0	1

Rotation about an arbitrary axis

You often need to rotate an object about an axis parallel to the coordinate axis but different from the one in which the object is placed. In the case of the 3D fixed-point scaling transformation shown in Figure 3-13, we performed a translation transformation to reposition the object in the coordinates planes, performed the scaling transformation, and concluded by retranslating the object to its initial location. Similarly, you can rotate a 3D object about an arbitrary axis by first translating it to the required position on the coordinate plane, performing the rotation, and finally relocating the object at its original position. For example, suppose you want to rotate a cube, with one of its faces parallel to one of the principal planes, along its own x-axis. In this case you may need to relocate the object so that the desired axis of rotation lies along the x-axis of the coordinate system. When in this position, you can perform the rotation applying the rotation transformation matrix for the x-axis. After the rotation, the object is repositioned to its original location. The sequence of operations is shown in Figure 3-16.

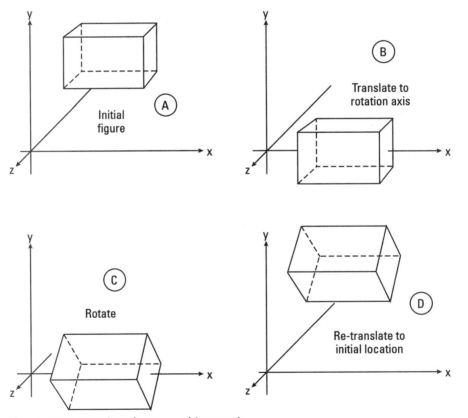

Figure 3-16: Rotation about an arbitrary axis

In this case it is possible to see one of the advantages of homogeneous coordinates. Instead of performing three different transformations, you can combine the three matrices necessary for the entire transformation into a single one that performs the two translations and the rotation through concatenation. Matrix concatenation was covered earlier in this chapter.

Coding Geometrical Transformations

Most graphics packages, including Microsoft DirectX 6, contain utilities for performing geometrical transformations and matrix concatenation. The file named D3dutil.cpp in the DirectX package includes primitives to perform 3D rotations, translations, and scaling operations. Three utilities are provided in D3dutil.cpp for performing rotation transformations, one for each coordinate axis.

After the transformation matrices have been obtained, you can develop your own routines for performing translation, rotation, scaling, and matrix concatenation transformations. The following code sample contains code for the following functions:

1. The `MatrixMult()` function performs matrix multiplication. The first parameter is an array of points holding *x*- and *y*-coordinates of a figure in 2D space. The second parameter is a 3-by-3 matrix used as the multiplier. The third parameter is an array that holds the new point in homogeneous coordinates.

2. The `Transform()` function applies a transformation to an array of *x*- and *y*-coordinate pairs in homogeneous coordinates. The first parameter is a matrix containing the coordinates of the points to be transformed. The second parameter is the matrix that is applied in performing the transformation.

3. The `TranslateFig()` function demonstrates the use of the `Transform()` function by calling it with a translation matrix as an argument.

```
//*********************************************************
//       code sample for 2D geometrical transformations
//*********************************************************

// Matrix multiplication
void MatrixMult(double s[], double matrix[3][3],
                double r[])
// First parameter holds the coordinates of a point.

// The second parameter is a 3 x 3 transformation matrix.
// The third parameter is an array of vertices
// that result from the matrix multiplication,
// as follows:
//      SOURCE          MATRIX          RESULT
//                    | 1  0  0 |
//    [sx  sy  1] *   | 0  1  0 |  = [rx  ry  1]
//                    | 2  4  1 |
//
// Matrix multiplication operation:
//    rx = sx*1 + sx*0 + sx*2
```

```
//    ry = sy*0 + sy*1 + sy*4
//
// if sx = 10 and sy = 40
// to perform a translation of x = 200 and y = 50
//      SOURCE          MATRIX
//                    | 1    0    0 |
//    [10   40   1] * | 0    1    0 |
//                    | 200  50   1 |

// rx = 10*1 + 40*0 + 1*200 = 210
// ry = 10*0 + 40*1 + 1*50  = 90

    {
      for(int col = 0; col < 3; col++)
      {
        r[col] = 0.0;
          for(int row = 0; row < 3; row++)
          {
            r[col] = r[col] + s[row] * matrix[row][col];
          }
      }
    }

// Apply a transformation to a shape stored in an
// array of x and y coordinate pairs. tMatrix holds
// a 3 x 3 transformation matrix
void Transform(int shape[][3], double tMatrix[3][3])
    {
      double oldPos[] = {0, 0, 1 };
      double newPos[] = {0, 0, 1 };

// Set up loop. A value of -1 forces loop termination
      for(int i = 0; shape[i][0] != -1; i++)
      {
        oldPos[0] = shape[i][0];
        oldPos[1] = shape[i][1];
        MatrixMult(oldPos, tMatrix, newPos);
        shape[i][0] = (int) newPos[0];
        shape[i][1] = (int) newPos[1];
      }
    }

// Translate shape
void TranslateFig(int shape[3][3], int xVal, int yVal)
    {
      double translateMat[][3] = {
                                   { 1,     0,      0 },
                                   { 0,     1,      0 },
                                   { xVal,  yVal,   1 },
                                 };

      Transform(shape, translateMat);
    }
```

Applications of Geometrical Transformations

Geometrical transformations provide a convenient technique for creating consecutive images of a graphical object. If the consecutive images are projected and erased at sufficient speed, they can be used to create an illusion of movement or change, called *animation*.

Because of image retention, the animated images must be flashed at a rate of approximately 70 images per second to produce a smooth and realistic effect. Even when dealing with images of moderate complexity, the task of creating and displaying them at this rate can impose an extremely large processing load on the graphics system. Therefore, in animation programming every device or stratagem that improves graphics performance is critically important. Performing the image transformation by mathematically operating on matrices of coordinate points saves considerable processing time and effort.

It is possible to combine more than one transformation in the creation of more refined animation effects. For example, by combining translation and rotation transformations, a wheel can be made to appear to roll on the screen. Or, by combining translation and scaling transformations, an object can be made to disappear into the background. Figure 3-17 shows the application of scaling and rotation to the image of an airplane in order to simulate it being approached in combat. The effect could be enhanced by applying additional transformations to the background image.

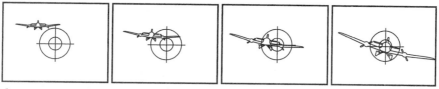

Figure 3-17: Animation by rotation and scaling transformations

Summary

In Chapter 3, you see how geometrical transformations facilitate graphics representations 2D and 3D space. The transformation matrices developed in this chapter, coupled with matrix concatenation operations, constitute the basic transformation tool of 3D graphics. These techniques find frequent use in the remainder of the book. We covered the following fundamental topics:

   ✦ Matrix arithmetic

   ✦ 2D transformations

✦ Homogenous coordinates

✦ 3D transformations

✦ Applications and code sample

In Chapter 4, we continue our overview of 3D graphics techniques with modeling and rendering, introducing the plane as a polygonal modeling tool, and discussing splines, cameras, lights, rendering algorithms, and texture mapping.

✦   ✦   ✦

3D Rendering

Before you can view a graphics object, you must find a way of storing it in a computer-compatible way, and before you can store an image, you must find a way of defining it. In other words, you must be able to digitize it. Because the current state-of-the-art in computer displays is two-dimensional, the solid image must be transformed so that it is displayed on a flat surface. The task can be broken down into three separate chores: representing, encoding, and rendering. Representing and encoding graphics images were discussed in previous chapters. Here we are concerned with rendering.

Rendering a real-world solid, encoded in digital form, onto a flat display surface is indeed complicated. Many books and hundreds of articles and research papers have been written on this topic and as many algorithms have been developed, each with its own advantages and drawbacks.

Projections and Perspective

We start from the assumption that the computer screen is a planar surface. In Chapters 2 and 3 you learned how to represent and transform image data stored in the computer in numerical form. The result is a data structure of coordinate points that defines the image, which can be translated, scaled, and rotated by means of geometrical transformations. But this data structure cannot be directly displayed on a flat screen. A similar problem is encountered by an engineer who needs to represent a solid object on the flat surface of the drawing paper. In either case you must find ways of rendering a solid onto a plane. Various approaches to this problem produce several types of projections. Figure 4-1 shows the more common classification of projections.

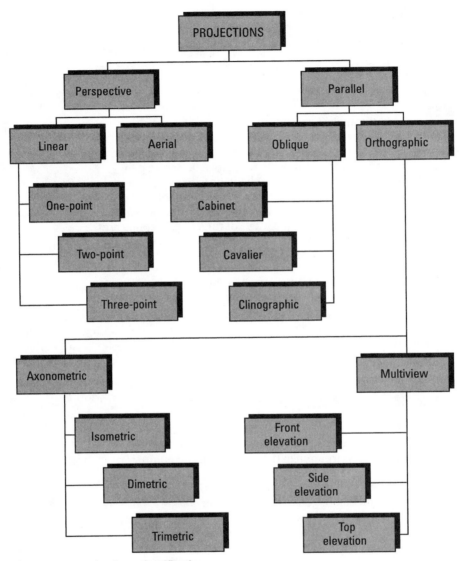

Figure 4-1: Projections classification

Projective geometry

Projective geometry is the field of mathematics that studies the transformations of objects during projections. The following imaginary elements participate in every projection:

1. The observer's eye, also called the *center of projection*, or viewpoint

2. The object being projected

3. The plane or *planes of projection*

4. The visual rays that determine the line of sight, called the *projectors*

Figure 4-2 shows these elements.

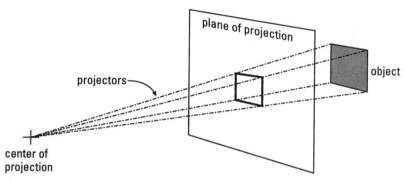

Figure 4-2: Projection elements

From a geometrical point of view, the projection of a point on a plane is the point of intersection on the plane of projection of a line that extends from the object's point to the center of projection. Because this line is called the projector, you can also say that the projection of a point is the intersection between the point's projector and the plane of projection. This definition can be refined further by requiring that the center of projection not be located in the object nor in the plane of projection. This constraint makes this type of projection a *central projection*.

The location of the center of projection in relation to the plane of projection and the object determines the two main types of projections. When the center of projection is at a discrete distance from the plane of projection the result is called a *perspective projection*. When the center of projection is located at infinity, the projection is called a *parallel projection*. Figure 4-3 shows perspective and parallel projections.

In a central projection the geometrical elements in the object plane are transformed into similar ones in the plane of projection. In this case a line is projected as a line, a triangle as a triangle, and a polygon as a polygon. Other properties are not preserved. For example, the length of line segments, the angular values, and the congruence of polygons can be different in the projected image. Furthermore, geometrical elements that are conic sections (circle, ellipse, parabola, and hyperbola) retain the conic section property, but not necessarily the type. A circle can be projected as an ellipse, an ellipse as a parabola, and so on. Figure 4-4 shows the perspective projection of a circle as an ellipse.

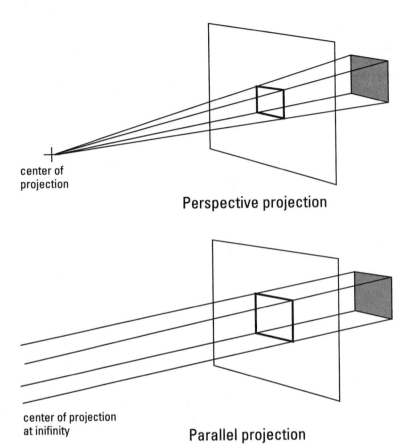

Perspective projection

Parallel projection

center of projection
at inifinity

Figure 4-3: Perspective and parallel projections

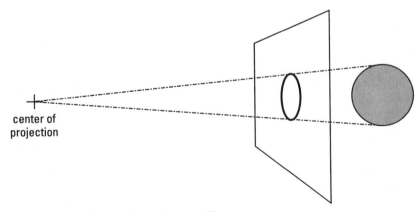

Figure 4-4: A circle projected as an ellipse

Parallel projections

Parallel projections have found extensive use in technical drafting, engineering drawings, and architecture. They are divided into two types: oblique and orthographic. The orthographic or right-angle projection, which is the simplest of all, assumes that the direction of projection is perpendicular to the projection plane. In this case the projectors are normal (perpendicular) to the plane of projection. In the oblique projection the projectors are not normal to the plane of projection.

A type of orthographic projection, called a *multiview projection*, is used often in technical drawings. The images that result from a multiview projection are planar and true-to-scale. Therefore, the engineer or draftperson can take measurements directly from a multiview projection. Figure 4-5 shows a multiview projection of an engineered object.

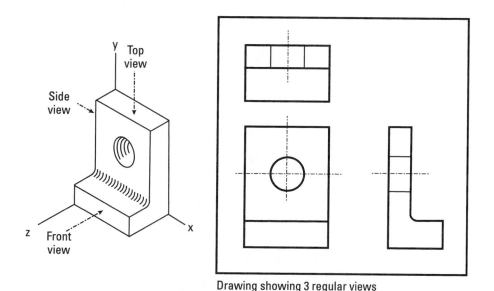

Drawing showing 3 regular views

Figure 4-5: Parallel, orthographic, multiview projection

The front, side, and top views shown in the drawing in Figure 4-5 are called the *regular views*. There are three additional views not shown in the illustration, called the bottom, right-side, and rear views. These are drawn whenever it is necessary to show details not visible in the regular views. The Cartesian interpretation of the front view is the orthographic projection of the object onto the *xy*-plane, the side view is the projection onto the *yz*-plane, and the top view is the projection onto the *xz*-plane. Sometimes, these views are called the front-elevation, side-elevation, and top- or plan-elevation.

Although each multiview projection shows a single side of the object, it is often convenient to show the object pictorially. The left-side drawing in Figure 4-5 shows several sides of the object in a single view, thus rendering a pictorial view of the object. The orthographic-axonometric projections are pictorial projections often used in technical applications.

The term *axonometric* originates in the Greek words "axon" (axis) and "metrik" (measurement). It relates to the measurements of the axes used in the projection. In Figure 4-1 the axonometric projections are further classified into *isometric, dimetric,* and *trimetric*. Isometric means "equal measure," which determines that the object axes make equal angles with the plane of projection. In the dimetric projection two of the three object axes make equal angles with the plane of projection. In the trimetric, all three axes angles are different. Figure 4-6 shows the isometric, dimetric, and trimetric projections of a cube.

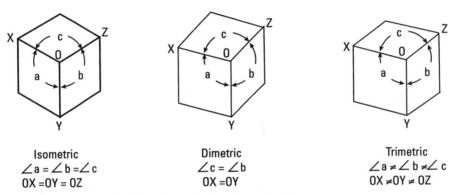

Figure 4-6: Isometric, dimetric, and trimetric projections

Perspective projections

The orthographic projections have features that make them useful in technical applications. The multiview projections provide information to the technician, engineer, and the architect. The axonometric projections shown in Figure 4-6 can be mechanically generated from multiview drawings. In general, the main feature of the parallel projections is their information value. In the world of 3D rendering the objection to the parallel projections is their lack of realism. For example, Figure 4-7 shows two isometric cubes, labeled A and B, at different distances from the observer. However, both objects have projected images of the same size. This is not a realistic representation because cube B, farther away from the observer, should appear smaller than cube A.

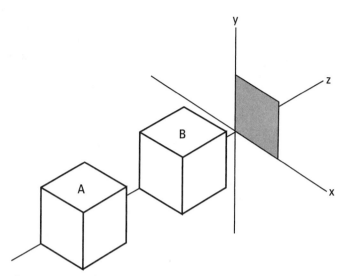

Figure 4-7: Lack of realism in an isometric projection

A perspective projection attempts to improve the realism of the image by providing *depth cues* that enhance relative positions, distances, and diminishing size. One of the most important depth cues is the relative size of the object at different distances from the viewpoint. This effect can be achieved by means of perspective projections. The perspective projections depend on a *vanishing point* that is used to determine the object's relative size. Three types of perspective projections are in use, according to the number of vanishing points. They are named *one-point, two-point, and three-point perspectives.*

The number of vanishing points is determined by the positioning of the object in relation to the plane of projection. If a cube is placed so its front face is parallel to the plane of projection, then one set of edges converges to a single vanishing point. If the same cube is positioned so that one set of parallel edges (usually, the vertical) is parallel to the picture plane and the other two sets are not, then each of those two sets of parallel edges not parallel to the picture plane has a vanishing point. Finally, if the cube is placed so that none of its principal edges are parallel to the plane of projection, then there are three vanishing points.

In contrast to the parallel projections previously described, perspective projections have unique characteristics. In a parallel projection you take a three-dimensional object and produce a two-dimensional image. In a perspective projection you start with a three-dimensional object and produce another three-dimensional object, which is modified to enhance its depth cues. This means that a projection is a transformation, much like the rotation, translation, and scaling transformations discussed in Chapter 3. Unlike rotation, translation, and scaling, a perspective transformation distorts the shape of the object transformed. After a perspective transformation, forms that were originally circles may turn into ellipses, parallelograms into trapezoids, and so forth. It is this distortion that reinforces our depth perception.

One-point perspective

The simplest perspective projection is based on a single vanishing point. This projection is also called *single-point perspective*. In the one-point perspective the object is placed so that one of its surfaces is parallel to the plane of projection. Figure 4-8 shows a one-point perspective of a cube.

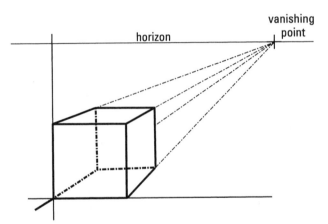

Figure 4-8: One-point perspective projection

One-point perspective projections are simple to produce and find many practical uses in engineering, architecture, and computer graphics. One of the features of the one-point perspective is that if an object has cylindrical or circular forms, and these are placed parallel to the plane of projection, then the forms are represented as circles or circular arcs in the perspective. This can be an advantage, considering that circles and circular arcs are easier to produce than ellipses or other conics. Figure 4-9 is a one-point projection of a mechanical part that contains cylindrical and circular forms.

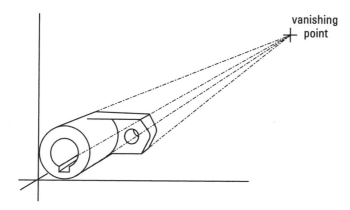

Figure 4-9: One-point projection of a part with cylindrical and circular forms

A special form of the one-point perspective projection takes place when the vanishing point is placed centrally within the figure. This type of projection, which has limited use, is sometimes called a *tunnel perspective* or *tunnel projection*. Because of the particular positioning of the object in the coordinate axes, the depth cues in a tunnel projection are not very obvious. Figure 4-10 shows the tunnel projection of a cube.

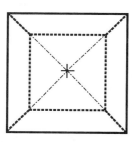

Figure 4-10: Tunnel projection of a cube

Two-point perspective

The depth cues in a linear perspective of a multifaced object can be improved by rotating the object so that two of its surfaces have vanishing points. In the case of a cube this is achieved if it is rotated along its *y*-axis, so that lines along that axis remain parallel to the viewing plane, but those along the two other axes have vanishing points. Figure 4-11 shows a two-point perspective of a cube.

Two-point perspective projections are the most commonly used in 3D graphics.

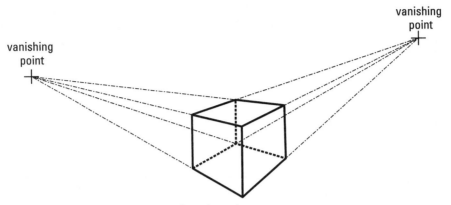

Figure 4-11: Two-point perspective of a cube

Three-point perspective

You create a three-point perspective by positioning the object so that none of its axes are parallel to the plane of projection. Although, in this case, the visual depth cues are stronger than in the two-point perspective, the resulting geometrical deformations are sometimes disturbing to the viewer. Figure 4-12 is a three-point perspective projection of a cube.

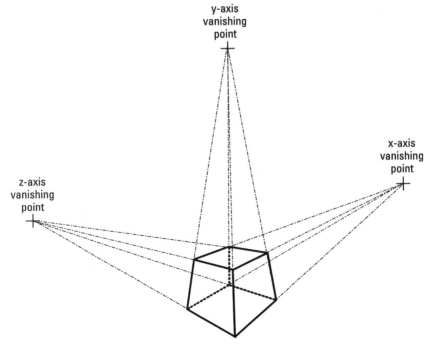

Figure 4-12: Three-point perspective of a cube

Perspective as a transformation

The data that defines a three-dimensional object can be changed into another one that contains enhanced depth cues by performing a mathematical transformation. In other words, a perspective projection can be accomplished by means of a transformation. In calculating the projection transformation it is convenient to define a 4 × 4 matrix so the transformation is compatible with the ones used for rotation, translation, and scaling described in Chapter 3. In this manner you can use matrix concatenation to create matrices that simultaneously perform one or more geometrical transformations, as well as a perspective projection.

The simplest approach for deriving the matrix for a perspective projection is to assume that the projection plane is normal to the z-axis and located at $z = d$. Figure 4-13 shows the variables for this case.

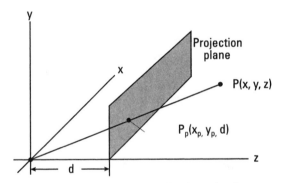

Figure 4-13: Perspective projection of point P

Point P_p, in Figure 4-13, is the perspective projection of point P. According to the predefined constraints for this projection, you already know that the z-coordinate of point P_p is d. To determine the formulas for calculating the x- and y-coordinates you can take views along either axis, and solve the resulting triangles, as shown in Figure 4-14.

Because the gray triangles in Figure 4-14 are similar, you can establish the following ratios:

$$\frac{x_p}{d} = \frac{x}{z}$$

and

$$\frac{y_p}{d} = \frac{y}{z}$$

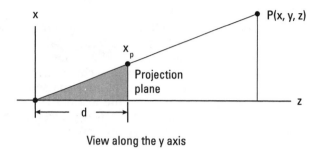

View along the y axis

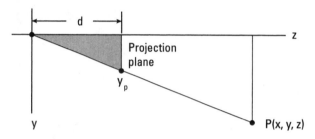

View along the x axis

Figure 4-14: Calculating x- and y-coordinates of P_p

Solving for xp and yp produces the equations:

$$x_p = \frac{x}{z/d}, \; y_p = \frac{y}{z/d}$$

Because the distance d is a scaling factor in both equations, the division by z has the effect of reducing the size of more distant objects. In this case the value of z can be positive or negative, but not zero, because $z = 0$ defines a parallel projection. These equations can be expressed in matrix form, as follows:

3D perspective
transformation
matrix

$$\begin{matrix} 1 & 0 & 0 & 0 \\ 0 & 1 & 0 & 0 \\ 0 & 0 & 1 & 0 \\ 0 & 0 & 1/d & 0 \end{matrix}$$

The Rendering Pipeline

One possible interpretation considers the rendering process as a series of transformations that take the object from the coordinate system in which it is encoded, into the coordinate system of the display surface. This process, sometimes referred to as the *rendering pipeline*, is described as a series of *spaces* through which the object migrates in its route from database to screen. One model of the rendering pipeline is shown in Figure 4-15.

Local space

Objects are usually easier to model if they are positioned conveniently in the coordinate plane. For example, when you place the bottom-left vertex of a cube at the origin of the coordinate system, the coordinates are all positive values, as in Figure 4-16.

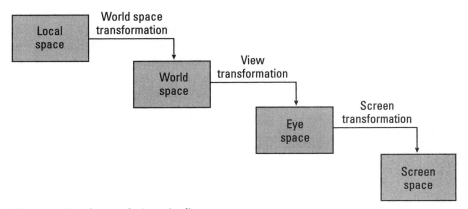

Figure 4-15: The rendering pipeline

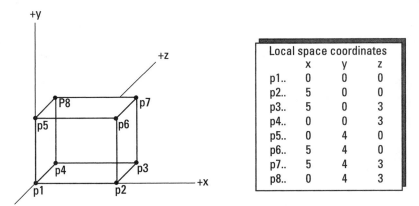

Figure 4-16: Local space coordinates of a cube with vertex at the origin

This scheme, called the *local space* or *modeling coordinates system*, facilitates numerical representation and transformations. When objects are represented by polygons, the modeling database usually includes not only the object coordinates points but the normals to the polygon vertices and the normal to the polygon itself. This information is necessary to perform many of the rendering transformations discussed in this chapter.

World space

The coordinate system of the scene is called the *world space*, or *world coordinate system*. Objects modeled in local space usually have to be transformed into world space at the time they are placed in a scene. For example, a particular scene may require a cube placed so that its left-bottom vertex is at coordinates $x = 2$, $y = 3$, $z = 0$. The process requires applying a translation transformation to the cube defined in local space. In addition, lighting conditions are usually defined in world space. After the light sources are specified and located, shading and other rendering transformations can be applied to the polygons so as to determine how the object appears under the current illumination. Surface attributes of the object, such as texture and color, may affect the shading process. Figure 4-17 shows the world space transformation of a cube under unspecified illumination conditions and with undefined texture and color attributes.

Eye space

Note in Figure 4-17 that the image is now in world space, and that some shading of the polygonal surfaces has taken place; however, the rendering is still far from complete. The first defect that is immediately evident is the lack of perspective. The second one is that all of the cube's surfaces are still visible. The *eye space*, or *camera coordinate system*, introduces the necessary transformations to improve rendering to a desired degree. Perspective transformations require knowledge of the camera position and the projection plane. The second of these is not known until you reach the screen space phase in the rendering pipeline. Therefore, determining the projection plane must be postponed until you reach this stage.

The notions of eye and camera positions can be taken as equivalent, although the word "camera" is used more often in 3D graphics. The camera can be positioned anywhere in the world space and pointed in any direction. Once the camera position is determined, it is possible to eliminate those elements of the scene that are not visible. In the context of polygonal modeling, this process is generically called *backface elimination*.

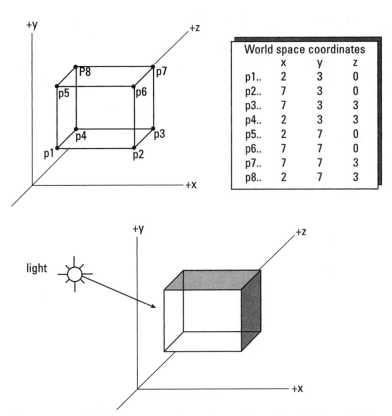

Figure 4-17: World space transformation of the cube in Figure 4-16

World space coordinates		
	x	y	z
p1..	2	3	0
p2..	7	3	0
p3..	7	3	3
p4..	2	3	3
p5..	2	7	0
p6..	7	7	0
p7..	7	7	3
p8..	2	7	3

Backface elimination

One of the most important rendering problems that must be solved at this stage of the pipeline is the elimination of the polygonal faces that are not visible from the eye position. In the simplest case, entire polygons that are not visible are removed at this time. This operation is known as *culling*. When dealing with a single convex object, as is a cube, culling alone solves the backface elimination problem. However, if there are multiple objects in a scene, where one object may partially obscure another one, or in the case of concave objects, then a more general backface elimination algorithm must be used.

A solid object composed of polygonal surfaces that completely enclose its volume is called a polyhedron. In 3D graphics a polyhedron is usually defined so that the normals to its polygonal surfaces point away from its center. In this case, you can assume that the polygons whose normals point away from the eye or camera are blocked by other, closer polygons, and are thus invisible. Figure 4-18 shows a cube with rods normal to each of its six polygonal surfaces. Solid arrows indicate surfaces whose normals point in the direction of the viewer. Dotted arrows indicate surfaces whose normals point away from the viewer and can, therefore, be eliminated.

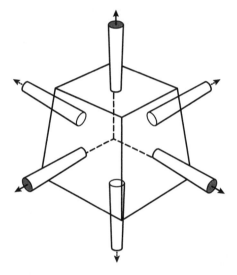

Figure 4-18: Backspace culling of a polyhedron

A single mathematical test can be used to determine if a polygonal face is visible. The geometric normal to the polygonal face is compared with a vector from the polygon center to the camera or eye position. This is called the line-of-sight vector. If the resulting angle is greater than 90 degrees, then the polygonal surface faces away from the camera and can be culled. Figure 4-19 shows the use of polygonal surface and line-of-sight vectors in culling.

When the position of the camera is determined in the scene, it is possible to perform the backface elimination. Figure 4-20 shows the cube of Figure 4-17 after this operation.

Screen space

The image, as it exists at this point of the rendering pipeline, is a numerical representation of the object. The previous illustrations, such as Figure 4-20, should not be taken literally because the image has not been displayed yet. The last step of the rendering pipeline is the transformation onto screen space.

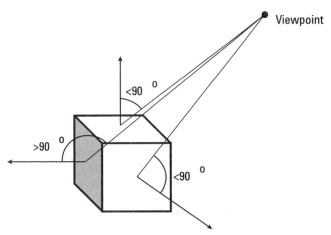

Figure 4-19: Line-of-sight and surface vectors in culling

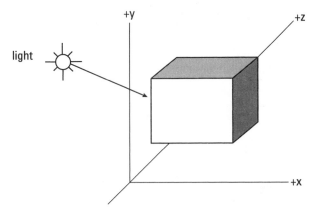

Figure 4-20: Eye space transformation of the cube in Figure 4-17

Changing the positioning of the camera is equivalent to rotating the object in the coordinate space. Either operation determines the type of perspective transformation: one-point, two-point, or three-point. In relation to Figure 4-17, if you position the camera so that it is normal to the face of the cube defined by points $p1$, $p2$, $p6$, and $p5$, the result will be a one-point perspective. If you position the camera so that only the vertical edges of the cube remain parallel to the viewer, the result will be a two-point perspective. Similarly, you can reposition the object for a three-point perspective. In addition, the perspective transformation requires determining the distance to the plane of projection, which is known at the screen space stage of the rendering pipeline.

Screen space is defined in terms of the viewport. The final transformation in the rendering pipeline consists of eliminating those elements of the eye space that fall outside the boundaries of the screen space. This transformation is known as *clipping*. The perspective and clipping transformations are applied as the image reaches the last stage of the rendering pipeline. Figure 4-21 shows the results of this stage.

Eye-space

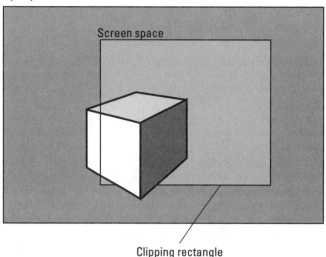

Screen space

Clipping rectangle

Figure 4-21: Screen space transformation of the cube in Figure 4-20

Other pipeline models

The model of the rendering pipeline described here is not the only one in use. In fact, practically every 3D graphics package or development environment describes its own version of the rendering pipeline. For example, the model used in Microsoft's Direct 3D is based on a transformation sequence that starts with polygon vertices being fed into a transformation pipeline. The pipeline performs world, view, projection, and clipping transformations before data is sent to the rasterizer for display. These other versions of the rendering pipeline are discussed in the context of the particular systems to which they refer.

Lighting

Lighting of a three-dimensional object determines its rendered realism to a great degree. In fact, some solid objects are virtually impossible to represent without lighting effects. For example, a billiard ball could not be convincingly rendered as a flat disk. Figure 4-22 shows the enhanced realism that results from lighting effects on a solid object.

Figure 4-22: Lighting enhances realism

Rendering lighting is one of the most computationally expensive operations of 3D graphics. You often have to consider not the ideal lighting effects on a scene, but the minimum acceptable levels of lighting that will produce a satisfactory rendering. The value of this "acceptable level" depends on the application. An interactive program that executes in real-time, such as a flight simulator or a computer game, usually places stringent limitations on lighting effects. For the PC animation programmer it often comes down to a tradeoff between the smoothness of the animation and the quality of the scene lighting. On the other hand, when developing applications that are not so sensitive to execution speed, such as a paint program, you are able to grant a greater time slice to lighting operations, even at some sacrifice of speed of execution.

Two related models are usually mentioned in the context of lighting: the *reflection model* and the *illumination model*. The reflection model describes the interaction of light within a surface. The illumination model refers to the nature of light and its intensity distribution. Both are important in developing rendering algorithms that take lighting into account.

Illumination models

The intensity and distribution of light on the surface of an object are determined both by the characteristics of the light itself and by the texture of the object. A polished glass ball and a velvet-covered one show different lighting under the same illumination. The subject of textures is covered later in this chapter. At this point you are concerned with the light source and its characteristics.

The simplest illumination model, and one that you must sometimes accept for the sake of performance, is one with no external light source. In this case each polygon that forms the object is displayed in a single shade of its own color. The result is a flat, monochromatic rendering in which self-luminous objects are visible by their silhouette only. One exception is if the individual polygons that form the object are assigned different colors or shades. The circular disk on the left side of Figure 4-22 is an example of rendering without lighting effects.

An object can receive two types of illumination: direct and indirect. This, in turn, relates to two basic types of light sources: light-emitting and light reflecting. The illumination that an object receives from a light-emitting source is direct. The illumination received from a light-reflecting source is indirect. Consider a polished sphere in a room illuminated by a single light bulb. If no other opaque object is placed between the light bulb and the sphere, then most of the light that falls on the sphere is direct. Indirect light, proceeding from reflection of other objects, may also take part in illuminating the sphere. If an opaque object is placed between the light bulb and the sphere, then the sphere is illuminated indirectly, which means, by reflected light only. Figure 4-23 shows a polished sphere illuminated by direct and indirect lighting, and by a combination of both.

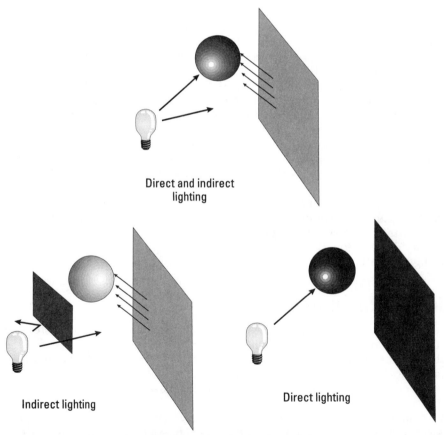

Direct and indirect
lighting

Indirect lighting

Direct lighting

Figure 4-23: Sphere illuminated by direct and indirect lighting

Light sources can also differ by their comparative size. A small light source, such as the sun, is considered a *point source*. A rather extensive light source, such as a battery of fluorescent light, is considered an *extended source*. Reflected light is usually an extended source. Here again, the lighting effect of a point or extended source is modified by the object's texture. Figure 4-24 shows a polished sphere illuminated by a point and an extended source.

Point source   Extended source

Figure 4-24: Sphere illuminated by a point and an extended light source

Reflection

Excluding luminescent objects, most of the lighting effects result from reflection. In this context *ambient illumination* is defined as light that has been scattered to such a degree that it is no longer possible to determine its direction. Backlighting produces ambient illumination, as is the case in the second sphere in Figure 4-23. Ambient light and matte surfaces produce *diffuse reflection*. Point sources and polished surfaces produce *specular reflection*. Variations in the light source, and surface textures, produce unlimited variations between pure diffuse and pure specular reflection.

where *I* is the intensity of illumination and *k* is the *ambient reflection coefficient*, or *reflectivity*, of the surface. Notice that this coefficient is a property of the material from which the surface is made. In calculations, *k* is assigned a constant value in the range 0 to 1. Highly reflective surfaces have values near 1. When this is the case, reflected light has nearly the same effects as incident light. Surfaces that absorb most of the light have reflectivities near 0.

The second element in determining diffuse reflection is the *angle of illumination*, or *angle of incidence*. A surface perpendicular to the direction of incident light reflects more light than a surface at an angle to the incident light. For a point source, the calculation of diffuse reflection can be made according to Lambert's cosine law, which states that the intensity of reflected light is proportional to the cosine of the angle of incidence. Figure 4-25 shows this effect.

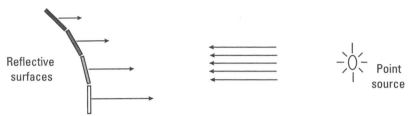

Figure 4-25: Reflected light depends on the angle of incidence

Diffuse reflection is also called *Lambertian reflection* because it obeys Lambert's cosine law. It is associated with matte, dull surfaces such as rubber, chalk, and cloth. The degree of diffusion depends on the material and the illumination. Given the same texture and lighting conditions, the diffuse reflection is determined solely by the angle of incidence. In addition, the type of the light source and atmospheric attenuation can influence the degree of diffusion. The spheres in Figure 4-26 show various degrees of diffuse reflection.

Specular reflection

Specular reflection is observed in naturally shiny or polished surfaces. Illuminating a polished sphere, such as a billiard ball, with a bright white light, produces a highlight of the same color as the incident light. Color plate 2 shows specular reflection on the surface of a teapot. Notice that the reflected highlights are the color or the incident light, not that of the surface material.

Specular reflection is also influenced by the angle of incidence. In a perfect reflector the angle of incidence, which is the inclination of the light source to the surface normal, is the same as the angle of reflection. Figure 4-27 shows the angles in specular reflection.

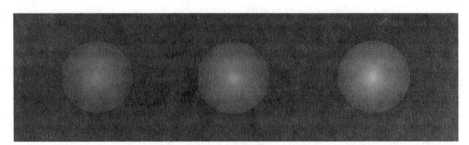

Figure 4-26: Spheres showing diffuse reflection

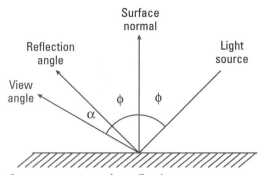

Figure 4-27: Specular reflection

In Figure 4-27 you see that in specular reflection, the angle of incidence (is the same as the angle of reflection. In the case of a perfect reflector, specular reflection is visible only when the viewer is located at the angle of reflection, in other words, when (= 0. Objects that are not perfect reflectors exhibit specular reflection over a range of viewing positions about the angle of reflection. Polished surfaces have a narrow reflection angle while dull surfaces have a wider one.

Phong illumination model

In 1975, Phong Bui-Toung described a model for nonperfect reflectors, such as the teapot in color plate 2. The Phong model, which is widely used in 3D graphics, assumes that specular reflectance is great in the direction of the reflection angle, and decreases as the viewing angle increases. The Phong model sets the intensity of reflection according to the function

$I = \cos^n \alpha$

where n is called the *material's specular reflection exponent*. For a perfect reflector n would be infinite and the falloff would be instant. Normal values of n range from 1 to several hundreds, depending on the reflectivity of the surface material. The shaded areas in Figure 4-28 show Phong reflection for a shiny and a dull surface. The larger the value of n, the faster the falloff and the smaller the angle at which specular reflection is visible. A polished surface is associated with a large value of n, while a dull surface has a small value of n.

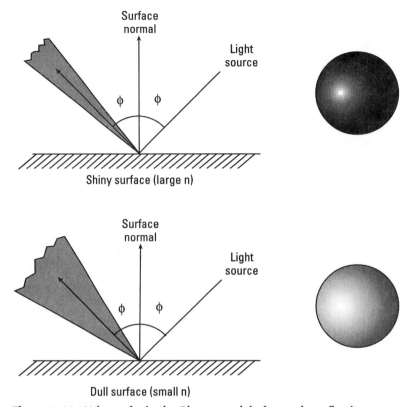

Figure 4-28: Values of *n* in the Phong model of specular reflection

The Phong model enjoys considerable popularity because of its simplicity and because it provides sufficient realism for many applications. However, it also has some important drawbacks:

1. All light sources are assumed to be points.
2. Light sources and viewers are assumed to be at infinity.
3. Diffuse and specular reflections are modeled as local components.
4. The decrease of reflection around the reflection vector is empirically determined.
5. Highlights are rendered white, regardless of the color of the surface.

The following limitations have been pointed out for the Phong model:

1. Because highlights are rendered white, no matter the color of the material, the Phong model does not render plastics and other colored solids very well.

2. The Phong model does not generate shadows. Therefore, objects in a scene do not interact with each other and appear floating and lifeless.

3. Object concavities are often rendered incorrectly. This means that the model often produces specular highlights in concave areas that should not have them.

Shading

In computer graphics the word *shading* refers to the application of a reflection model over the surface of an object. Because graphics objects are often represented by polygons, a brute force shading method can be based on calculating the normal to each polygon surface, and then applying an illumination model, such as Phong's, to that point.

Flat shading

The simplest shading algorithm for a polygonal object is to use an illumination model to determine the corresponding intensity value for the incident light, and then shade the entire polygon according to this value. This type of shading, also known as *constant shading* or *constant intensity shading*, is easy to implement. Flat shading produces satisfactory results when the following conditions apply:

1. The subject is illuminated by ambient light and there are no surface textures or shadows

2. In the case of curved objects when the surface changes gradually and the light source and viewer are far from the surface

3. In general, when there are large numbers of plane surfaces

Figure 4-29 shows three cases of flat shading of a conical surface. The more polygons there are, the better the rendering.

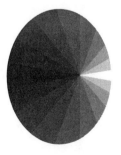

18 Polygons   36 Polygons   72 Polygons

Figure 4-29: Flat shading

Interpolative shading

The fundamental limitation of flat shading is that each polygon is rendered in a single color. Very often the only way to improve the rendering is to increase the number of polygons, as shown in Figure 4-29. An alternative shading scheme is based on using more than one shade in each polygon by interpolating the values calculated for the vertices to the polygon's interior points. This type of manipulation, called *interpolative* or *incremental shading*, is capable of producing, under some circumstances, a more satisfactory shade rendering with a smaller number of polygons in the model. Two incremental shading methods, called *Gouraud* and *Phong shading* are almost ubiquitous in 3D rendering software.

Gouraud shading

This shading algorithm was described by H. Gouraud in 1971. It is also called *bilinear intensity interpolation*. Gouraud shading is best explained in the context of the scan-line algorithm used in hidden surface removal. Scan-line processing is discussed in greater detail later in this chapter; for now, assume that each pixel is examined according to its horizontal (scan-line) placement, usually left-to-right. Figure 4-30 shows a triangular polygon with vertices at *A*, *B*, and *C*.

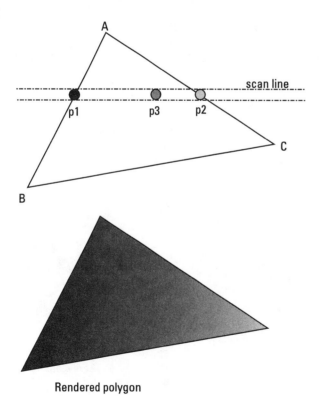

Rendered polygon

Figure 4-30: Intensity interpolation in Gouraud shading

The intensity value at each of these vertices is determined from the reflection model. As scan-line processing proceeds, the intensity of pixel *p1* is determined by interpolating the intensities at vertices *A* and *B*, according to the formula

$$I_{p1} = \frac{y_{p1} - y_B}{y_A - y_B} + \frac{y_A - y_{p1}}{y_A - y_B}$$

In Figure 4-30, the intensity of *p1* is closer to the intensity of vertex *A* than that of vertex *B*. The intensity of *p2* is determined similarly by interpolating the intensities of vertices *A* and *C*. After the boundary intensities for the scan line are determined, any pixel along the scan line is calculated by interpolating, according to the following formula:

$$I_{p3} = I_{p1} \frac{x_{p2} - x_{p3}}{x_{p2} - x_{p1}} + I_{p2} \frac{x_{p3} - x_{p1}}{x_{p2} - x_{p1}}$$

The process is continued for each pixel in the polygon, and for each polygon in the scene. Gouraud shading calculations are usually combined with a scan-line hidden surface removal algorithm and performed at the same time.

Gouraud shading also has limitations. One of the most important ones is the loss of highlights on surfaces and highlights that are displayed with unusual shapes. Figure 4-31 shows a polygon with an interior highlight. However, because Gouraud shading is based on the intensity of the pixels located at the polygon edges, this highlight is missed. In this case pixel *p3* is rendered by interpolating the values of *p1* and *p2*, which produces a darker color than the one required.

Another error associated with Gouraud shading is the appearance of bright or dark streaks, called *Mach bands*.

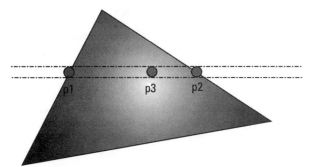

Figure 4-31: Highlight rendering error in Gouraud shading

Phong shading

Phong shading is the most popular shading algorithm in use today. This method was developed by Phong Bui-Toung, the author of the illumination model described previously. Pong shading, also called *normal-vector interpolation*, is based on calculating pixel intensities by means of the approximated normal vector at the point in the polygon. Although more calculation-expensive, Phong shading improves the rendering of bright points and highlights that are miss-rendered in Gouraud shading.

Ray tracing

Other shading models have been developed and find occasional use in 3D graphics. The ones discussed to this point, Phong and Gouraud shading, as well as others of intermediate complexity, are not based on the physics of light, but on the way that light interacts with objects. Although the notion of light *intensity* is used in these models, it is not formally defined. Physically based methods, although much more expensive computationally, can produce more accurate rendering. One such method, called *ray tracing*, is based on backtracking the light rays from the center of projection (viewing position) to the light source.

Ray tracing originated not in computer graphics, but in geometric optics. In 1637, Rene Descartes used ray tracing on a glass ball filled with water to explain rainbow formation. Around 1980, computer graphics researchers began applying ray-tracing techniques in the production of very high quality images, at a very high processing expense. Ray tracing is a versatile and powerful rendering tool. It incorporates the processing done in reflection, hidden surface removal, and shading operations. Its only objection is its processing cost. When execution time is not a factor, ray tracing produces superior results, better than any other rendering scheme. This fact has led to the general judgment that ray tracing is currently the best implementation of an illumination model.

Color plate 3 shows two renderings of a coffee cup. The one on the left is obtained through incremental shading, and the one on the right, through ray tracing. Note the reflection of the cup's handle that is visible on the ray-traced image. In a simple reflection model, only the interaction of a surface with the light source is considered. For this reason, when a light ray reaches a surface through interaction with another surface, or when it is transmitted through a partially transparent object, or by a combination of these factors, the rendering fails. This is the case with the reflection of the cup handle in color plate 3. Color plate 4 shows how ray tracing captures the reflected image of a blue cube on the surface of a polished red sphere.

Other rendering algorithms

So far we have discussed rendering algorithms that relate to projection, culling and hidden surface removal, illumination, and shading. In this section we look at other rendering methods that complement or support the ones already mentioned. Note that we have selected a few of the better-known schemes. In making this selection we emphasize the algorithms used in the graphics programming packages discussed in the text.

Scan-line operations

In computer graphics the term *scan-line processing* or *scan-line algorithms* refers to a general-processing method whereby each successive pixel is examined in row-by-row (scan-line) order. You already have seen scan-line processing in Gouraud shading. Scan-line methods are used in filling the interior of polygons also. Most rendering engines use some form of scan-line processing. Usually, several algorithms are incorporated into a scan-line routine. For example, as each pixel is examined in the scan-line routine, hidden-surface removal, shading, and shadow generation logic are applied to determine how it should be rendered. The result is a considerable saving compared to the time it would take to apply each rendering operation independently.

Scan-line hidden surface removal

A scan-line algorithm called the *image space method* is often used for removing hidden surfaces in a scene. This method is actually a variation of the scan-line polygon-filling algorithm. The processing requires that the image database contain the coordinate points for each polygon vertex. This is usually called the *edge table*. Figure 4-32 shows two overlapping triangles whose vertices (*A*, *B*, *C*, *D*, *E*, and *F*) are stored in the edge table.

The scan-line algorithm uses a binary flag to indicate whether a pixel in the scan line is inside or outside a surface. Each surface on the scene is given one such flag. As the left-most boundary of a surface is reached, the flag is turned *on*. At the surface's right-most boundary, the flag is turned *off*. When a single surface flag is *on*, the surface is rendered at that pixel. Scan line 1 in Figure 4-32 has some pixels in which the flag is on for triangle *ABC*. Scan line 2 in Figure 4-32 also poses no problem because a single surface has its flag *on* at one time. In scan line 3 the flag for triangle *ABC* is turned on at its left-most boundary. Before the surface's right-most boundary is reached, the flag for triangle *DEF* is turned *on*. When two flags are on for a given pixel, the processing algorithm examines the database to determine the depth of each surface. The surface with less depth is rendered, and all the other ones are removed. As the scan-line processing crosses the boundary defined by edge *BC*, the flag for triangle *ABC* is turned *off*. From that point on, the flag for triangle *DEF* is the only one turned on; therefore, its surface is rendered.

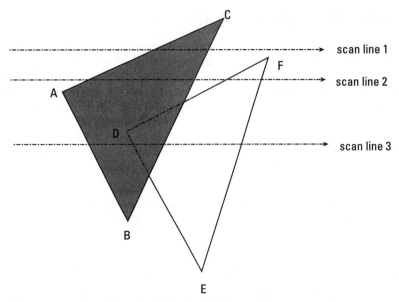

Figure 4-32: Scan-line algorithm for hidden surface removal

Scan-line shadow projections

Ray-tracing algorithms can be implemented so as to generate shadows; however, other rendering methods require a separate handling of shadows. Sometimes, it is convenient to add shadow processing to a scan-line routine. To do this, the image database must contain a list of polygons that may mutually shadow each other. This list, called the *shadow pairs*, is constructed by projecting all polygons onto a sphere located at the light source. Only polygon pairs that can interact are included in the shadow pairs list. The list saves considerable processing effort by eliminating those polygons that cannot possibly cast a shadow on each other.

The actual processing is similar to the scan-line algorithm for hidden surface removal. Figure 4-33 shows two polygons, labeled *A* and *B*. In this case you assume a single light source placed so that polygon *A* casts a shadow on polygon *B*. The shadow pairs in the database tell us that polygon *B* cannot shadow polygon *A*, but polygon *A* can shadow polygon *B*. For this reason, polygon *A* is rendered without further query in scan line 1. In scan line 2, polygon *B* is shadowed by polygon *A*. Therefore, the pixels are modified appropriately. In scan line 3, polygon *B* is rendered.

Figure 4-34 shows two renderings of the same scene. The one on the left side is done without shadow projection. The one on the right side is rendered using a shadow projection algorithm.

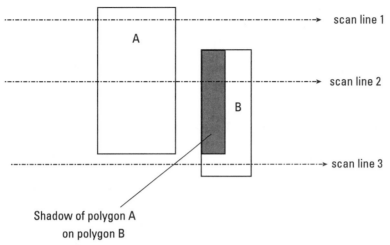

scan line 1

A

scan line 2

B

scan line 3

Shadow of polygon A
on polygon B

Figure 4-33: Scan-line algorithm for shadow projection

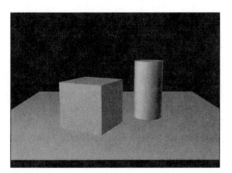
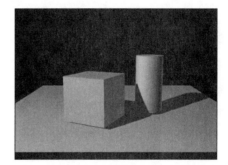

Figure 4-34: Shadow rendering of multiple objects in a scene

Z-buffer algorithm

Developed by Catmull in 1975, the *z-buffer* or *depth buffer* algorithm for eliminating hidden surfaces has become a staple in 3D computer graphics. The reason for its popularity is its simplicity of implementation.

The algorithm's name relates to the fact that the processing routine stores in a buffer the z-coordinates for the (x, y) points of all objects in the scene. This is the z-buffer. A second buffer, sometimes called the *refresh buffer*, is used to hold the intensities for each pixel. In processing, all positions in the z-buffer are first initialized to the maximum depth value, and all positions in the refresh buffer to the background attribute. At each pixel position, each polygon surface in the scene is examined for its z-coordinate value. If the z-coordinate for the surface is less than the value stored in the z-buffer, then the value in the z-buffer is replaced with the one corresponding to the surface being examined. At this point the refresh buffer is also updated with the intensity value for that pixel. If the z value for the surface is greater than the value in the z-buffer, then the point is not visible and can be ignored.

Figure 4-35 shows the z-buffer algorithm operation. Three surfaces, a square, a circle, and a triangle, are located at various depths. When the z-buffer is initialized the pixel shown in the illustration is assigned the depth of the background surface, S0. The surface for the circle is examined next. Because S2 is at less depth than S0, the value S2 replaces the value S0 in the z-buffer. Now S2 is the current value in the z-buffer. Next, the value for the triangular surface S1 is examined. Because S1 has greater depth than S2, it is ignored. However, when S3 is examined it replaces S2 in the buffer, because it is at less depth.

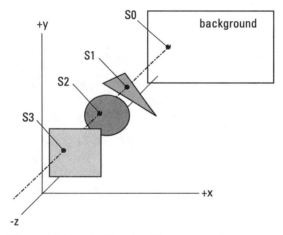

Figure 4-35: Z-buffer algorithm processing

Textures

The surface composition of an object influences how the surface reflects light. The reflectivity of a surface is taken into account when calculating illumination effects. Textures were completely ignored in early 3D packages. At that time all surfaces were assumed to have identical refection properties. The results were scenes that appeared unnatural because of their uniformity. Since then, textures have been steadily gaining popularity. All of the 3D development systems discussed in this book support textures, in one form or another.

In the PC, the simplest and most common implementation of textures is with bitmaps. Because of this, the notion of texture refers only to the color pattern of the surface, and not to its degree of smoothness. Texture bitmaps are easy to apply to objects and are rendered as a surface attribute. In addition, texture blending and light mapping with textures provide additional enhancements to the rendering. The specifics of texture rendering are discussed in the context of the individual 3D packages.

Summary

In this chapter we examined the problems associated with rendering a graphics object. In doing this, we looked at projections and perspective, followed the rendering pipeline, and studied the fundamentals of lighting and illumination and shading. In the process we discussed some of the fundamental algorithms of 3D graphics: Gouraud and Phong shading, scan-line processing, and the z-buffer method for hidden surface removal, among others. We also mentioned textures and shadow processing. In Chapter 5, we discuss animation techniques, one of the most difficult, intriguing, and rewarding topics of 3D graphics programming.

✦   ✦   ✦

Computer Animation

This chapter is about computer animation. A few years
ago, real-time, convincing animation was not possible on
a PC machine. Over the past five or six years, improvements
in processing speed and rendering capabilities have made PC
animation a reality. Today, a PC programmer can simulate
movement on the computer screen in a realistic, effective,
and pleasant way. Several screen objects can be manipulated
simultaneously over a panoramic background, producing
lifelike actions that are comparable to cinematography and
cartoon animation. The spectacular growth of PC computer
games and simulations that has taken place in the past few
years is a direct result of this technological watershed.

The details of PC animation programming are left for Part II
of the book. At this time we discuss mostly the fundamental
principles.

Cartoon Animation

Computer animation originated in cartoons and is closely
related to them. Many of the technologies used in the
production of cartoons are directly applicable to computer
animation. The original cartoon techniques are based on the
work of Walt Disney, Hanna-Barbera, and others. The standard
method consists of photographing a series of progressive
drawings. The photographs are then developed as color
transparencies and animation achieved by successively
projecting the transparencies on the screen.

Historical note

In 1831, a Frenchman named Joseph Antoine Plateau was able to create the illusion of movement by means of a machine, which he called a *phenakistoscope*. The device consisted of a disk with a series of progressive drawings and a viewing window. When the disk was rotated, the viewer would see the drawings in rapid sequence, which created an illusion of movement. Three years later, an Englishman named Horner modified the phenakistoscope into a device, which he called the *zoetrope*. The zoetrope consisted of a drum with drawings on its inner walls. A series of slits allowed the viewer to see the different drawings as the drum rotated. Emile Reynaud, another Frenchman, further refined the zoetrope by replacing the viewing slits with mirrors. This device was named the *praxisnoscope*.

The first movie theater was founded by Emile Reynaud in 1892. It was called the *Theater Optique*. The first animated film was produced in 1906. By 1913, several American companies were regularly producing cartoons for the thriving motion picture theaters. *Felix the Cat*, by Pat Sullivan, is possibly the best-known cartoon character of this era. Walt Disney, who is usually considered the father of animated cartoons, produced a *Mickey Mouse* film in 1928. This was the first cartoon to incorporate sound. *Donald Duck* and other characters followed shortly thereafter. *Snow White and the Seven Dwarfs* was the first feature film–length cartoon.

Drawing techniques

Computers play an important role in the commercial production of cartoons. They are used in the coloring of drawings and in the generation of intermediate images, an operation called *in-betweening* or *tweening*. Drawing, coloring, and in-betweening are tedious and time-consuming operations when performed by hand. The organizational elements in the production of an animated cartoon can be seen in Figure 5-1.

In a cartoon the story is developed in three progressively refined steps, shown in Figure 5-1. The *synopsis* is a short summary of the story, usually in less than one page. The *scenario* describes the story more completely and it includes details of characters and scenery. The *storyboard* is a series of drawings and captions that capture the most important moments depicted in the film. From the storyboard it is possible to derive the film *sequences*. Each sequence refers to a film action and consists of one or more *scenes*. Typically, scenes are associated with a particular location, or with one or more characters. The units of cartoon execution are the individual *shots* that compose each scene. The production of each animated scene is performed by artists called *animators* who layout, design, and draw the key images in each scene. At this time the sound track for the cartoon must have already been defined because the motion of the animated figures takes place in relation to dialog and music. Note that computer games are often developed following the synopsis-scenario-storyboard sequence that is used in cartoons.

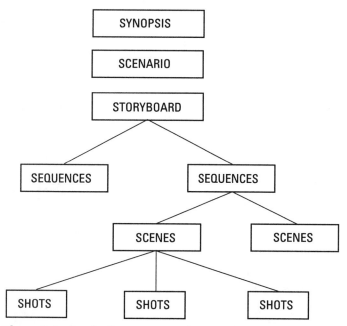

Figure 5-1: Production sequence for a cartoon

In the production of the actual cartoon drawings the artists use two key positions, called frames, as reference. Figure 5-2 shows the drawings used in a cartoon scene in which a dagger appears to travel from the hand of an imaginary thrower to a target. The key frames are the start frame and the end frame. The drawings that are necessary to animate the movement between both key frames are the in-between frames. In cartoon animation *in-betweening* is a routine task usually performed by assistants to the animators.

The number of progressions between the start frame and the end frame of a sequence depends on the time assigned to the frame and the display rate. For example, if the animation is to take 1.5 seconds, and the display rate is 24 frames per second, then 36 frames are required for the animation, of which 34 are in-between frames.

Photographic techniques

The progressive drawings simulate movement, and photographic manipulations are used to enhance the effects. Because the drawings for cartoons are made on a transparent plastic film, the clear portions of the drawing are invisible to the camera. The equipment used in the production of cartoons is a specialized motion picture camera called a *multiplane*. The animation surface consists of several glass layers at varying distances from the camera lens. Figure 5-3 is a diagram of a multiplane camera.

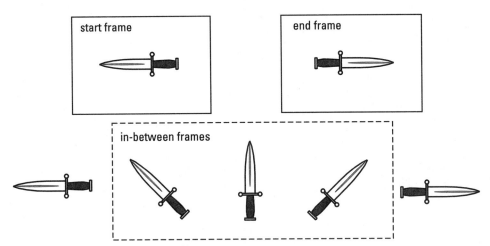

Figure 5-2: In-betweening in cartoon animation

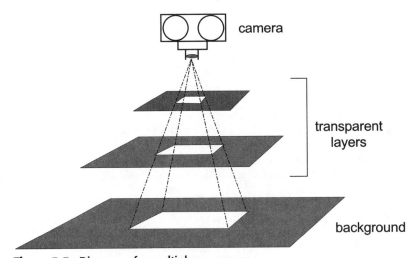

Figure 5-3: Diagram of a multiplane camera

The multiplane camera is used in creating special effects. The camera can be moved horizontally to *pan* an image, or moved along the optic axis to enlarge or reduce the apparent size of an object (*zooming*). Rotating the camera creates an effect called *spin*. Several *fade* and *dissolve* effects are used to provide a soft transit between scenes. The *fade-in* is a progressive transition of the image from black, and the *fade-out* is a transition to black. The fade-in is typically used at the start of a scene and the fade-out at the conclusion.

In multiplane animation the image is separated into several elements according to their distance from the viewer. For example, in animating the scenery visible from a moving train it is possible to divide the image into several strips, as shown in Figure 5-4.

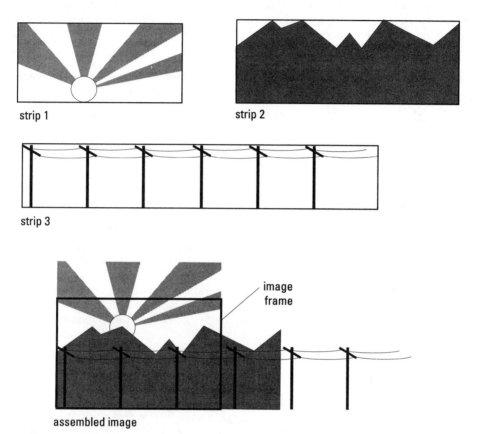

strip 1

strip 2

strip 3

image frame

assembled image

Figure 5-4: A multiplane image

The landscape in Figure 5-4 is animated by moving the three image strips at different rates under the multiplane camera. In this case the image strip that depicts the setting sun is scrolled downward. At the same time, the strip depicting the mountain range is moved horizontally, at a slow rate, while the strip with the telephone poles is moved at a faster rate. The resulting animation simulates what a person traveling in a train or automobile would see as the sun slowly sets behind a mountain range. Notice that the length of the images is proportional to their rate of movement during animation. The multiple plane animation technique is quite suited to computer animation.

Computer Animation

A computer can assume one of two roles in implementing animation: it can assist in the creation of animated imagery (computer-assisted animation) or it can generate and portray the animated action (real-time animation). The most time-consuming and tedious task of computer-assisted cartoon animation is the generation of the many intermediate images required by the process (tweening). During this phase a computer plays the following roles:

1. During the drawing stage the computer is used to scan and digitize image elements and to create drawings or parts of drawings.

2. In the animation process the computer is used to generate in-betweens and to color the drawings.

3. During the photography stage the computer controls the multiplane camera and assists in the creation of special effects.

4. In the production stage the computer is used in editing and in adding sound to the animated film.

Every day animators find new uses for computers; new technologies are developed which create novel possibilities and applications in animated graphics. Computer technology is used in the creation of spectacular special effects based on the digitization of screen objects, which are later manipulated by the software. Original efforts in this type of computer-assisted animation first appeared in the films TRON, produced by Walt Disney Studios, in *Return of the Jedi*, by Lucasfilm, and *The Last Starfighter*. In recent years animation by image digitization has become a standard manipulation.

Real-time animation

Real-time animation is found in arcade machines, simulators and trainers, electronic games, including Nintendo and Sega, and in interactive simulations and computer games. In real-time animation the computer is both an image generator and a display media.

Animation is based on the physiology of the human eye–brain complex. The basic fact is that the image of an object persists in the brain for a brief period of time after it no longer exists in the real world. This phenomenon, called *visual retention*, is related to the chemistry of the retina and to the structure of cells and neurons in the eye. Smooth animation is achieved in cinematography and television by consecutively displaying images at a faster rate than the period of visual retention. This operation, by which a new image replaces the old one before the period of retention has expired, creates in our minds the illusion of movement.

Visual retention lasts a few hundredths of a second. Experiments set the critical image update rate for smooth animation between 22 and 30 images per second, depending on the individual. Modern day moving picture films are recorded and displayed at a rate of 24 images per second. Commercial television takes place at a slightly faster rate, that is, at 30 images per second. In general, the threshold rate, subject to individual variations, is usually estimated at 18 images per second. This means that if the consecutive images are projected at a rate slower than this threshold, the average individual perceives jerkiness. When the image rate equals or exceeds this threshold, our brains merge the images together and we sense a smoothly animated action.

Assuming that animation must take place at an image rate of 20 per second, then each image must be updated and rendered in 1/20th of a second. Some rendering routines require that the old image is erased from the display before a new one is drawn, otherwise the animation leaves a visible track of objects on the video display. For this reason the image update sequence is a series of redraw, erase, redraw operations, which means that the critical display rate must be calculated from one redraw cycle to the next one. The allotted time for the redraw phase is one-half the image rate, in this case, 1/40th of a second.

All of this explains why computer animation is often a battle against time. The animation programmer resorts to every known trick and stratagem in order to squeeze the maximum performance out of the image update and rendering routines. Occasionally the programmer cannot overcome the system's limitations, and the result is a bumpy and coarse animation that is but a remote likeness of cinematography and television.

Frame-by-frame animation

In frame-by-frame animation the computer generates the required images, which are recorded or stored for playback at a later time. This playback can take place in the same machine that generated the image set or in another machine or media. For example, a computer can be used to manipulate the image strips in Figure 5-4 so as to generate a set of 100 progressive pictures. As the images are generated, they are recorded on videotape, or any other compatible media. When the image set is complete, the animation can be viewed by playing back the tape. Alternatively, the images can be stored in computer memory played back from this storage. In frame-by-frame animation the rendering is not time-critical because the image creation step does not have to take place in real-time.

Interactive animation

Interactive animation refers to computer objects that are moved at the user's will. At present, the most common interactive devices in the PC are the mouse, the joystick, and the command center. In general, the notion of interactive animation includes any technology in which the user exercises some level of control over computer-animated action. By today's standards the ultimate level of interactive animation is called *virtual reality*, discussed later in this chapter.

Unpredictability

Conventionally, the computer simulation of movement is based on programmable or predictable stages. In this manner, the cartoon animator knows beforehand (from the storyboard) all the actions and interactions that will be portrayed in the final rendition. In most implementations of virtual reality, every possible result can be predicted from the user's interaction with the device. Therefore, we can say that the system is deterministic.

However, many natural systems are not deterministic. Biology students often observe that colonies of bacteria developing in an identical media show different patterns of growth. This is because many factors cannot be determined beforehand in a complex biological system. Random or unpredictable elements influence the evolution of a biosystem. One modern theory states that the disappearance of the dinosaurs was caused by the collision of an asteroid with the earth. If this hypothesis is true, then a small change in the trajectory of the asteroid would have made it miss our planet, and the evolution of life on earth would have followed an entirely different path.

Statistics can be used to describe the unpredictable behavior of a biosystem. In the gene exchange process it is often possible to determine, according to their location in the chromosome, that certain genes are more or less likely to be transmitted. However, anything less than absolute certainty implies some degree of randomness or unpredictability. If a computer were to simulate the reproduction of a biosystem it would have to take into consideration these random or unpredictable factors.

Animation Techniques

If computer animation is roughly equated with the screen simulation of movement, the methodology for producing the animated effect can be described as a set of motion control techniques. Allan and Mark Watt, in their book *Advanced Animation and Rendering Techniques,* refer to procedural, representational, stochastic, and behavioral as the main categories of the animation hierarchy.

From a programmer's viewpoint, animation is implemented by applying one of many low-level methods of motion simulation and control. Some of these methods have been passed on to us by cartoon animators, while others are digital in nature; therefore, unique products of the computer environment.

The computer animator is confronted by many limitations and constraints. Often the animation is produced by means of mathematical transformations on the parameters that define one or more screen images. It is possible to perform image rotation, translation, scaling, and other transformations, by geometrical means. Because movement is a function of time, the laws of physics are often taken into account. For example, in representing a falling object the animator may use the formula that expresses acceleration in a gravitational field to determine the rate of in-betweening that most naturally represents the action. On the other hand, artistic considerations can determine an intentional variation from the physical laws of motion.

Tweening and morphing

The cartoon animator proceeds from two key positions, known as frames, and creates a set of in-between drawings, as in Figure 5-2. The entire sequence is photographed and projected to create an illusion of movement. The depiction of animated action by creating and projecting a set of in-between drawings is often called *tweening*; the intermediate drawings are the *tweens*. Computer animators have successfully borrowed the tweening technique from cartoon animators. Furthermore, in a computer environment the machine can often aid in the creation of the in-between frames by performing geometrical transformations on the key frames.

The tweening required for representing the flight of the dagger shown in Figure 5-2 is obtained by rotating and translating the initial frame. In this case, the animation image set can be produced by mathematical manipulations of a single file.

Another animation technique that originated in cartoons is *morphing*. The term relates to the notion of a metamorphosis: a transformation in shape, form, or substance that takes place by biological change or by magic and sorcery. Morphing techniques are now extensively used in motion pictures. We are all familiar with the image of an actor transforming into a wolf or a cat. Figure 5-5 shows the morphing of a circle into a square.

Path-of-motion calculations

The rules for path-of-motion calculations in animation depend on the image file encoding and on the transformation to be performed. In morphing, the intermediate frames are determined according to different rules than in tweening. The morphing transformation of a circle into a square shown in Figure 5-5 cannot be made by rotation and translation alone, as is the case in the tweening shown in Figure 5-2. Figure 5-6 shows the path, along a vector that is at a 45-degree angle with the horizontal, that a point on the circle would follow in the process of morphing into a square.

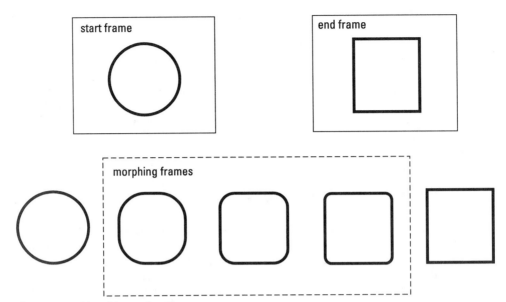

Figure 5-5: Morphing animation

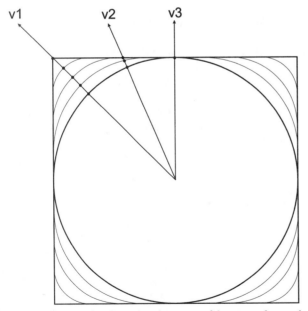

Figure 5-6: Path-of-motion in a morphing transformation

In Figure 5-6 you see that points along different vectors follow a different motion path. For this reason, morphing usually requires more complicated processing than other geometrical transformations. Notice that the path-of-motion along vector *v1* requires three intermediate steps in the transformation of a circle into a square. Along vector *v2* only one intermediate step is necessary, while there is no motion along vector *v3*. Path-of-motion calculations in tweening and morphing are often based on polygonal rendering, discussed in previous chapters. This approximation is shown in Figure 5-7.

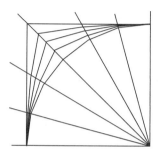

Figure 5-7: Polygonal approximation in morphing

Color-shift animation

The animator manipulates the color attribute of screen objects to create the illusion of movement or change. One common application of this technique is *fading*. An object or scene is faded-in when its color is progressively changed so as to make it slowly appear on the screen. A cross-dissolve operation takes place when one scene or object is faded-out while another one is faded-in. Figure 5-8 shows fade-in of a rectangle and fade-out of a circle.

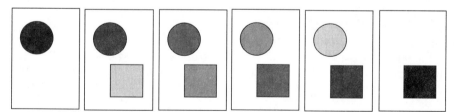

Figure 5-8: Fade-in and fade-out

Sometimes fade operations can be implemented by progressively changing the hue or saturation of one or more objects, or of the entire scene. A screen fade-out can be accomplished by progressively increasing the white saturation of all the objects until the entire screen is white. In some PC display modes, modifying the color palette itself, instead of the color attributes of individual objects, can perform the fade operations. *Palette animation*, as these methods are sometimes called, is relatively easy to implement and often generates satisfactory results at a low processing cost.

Color animation is also used in other creative manipulations. For example, increasing the black, red, and orange color saturation of selected screen objects can mimic a sunset scene. Or the illusion of movement can be enhanced by having the object leave tracks of its image with a decreasing color saturation. This effect, sometimes called a *motion blur*, is depicted by the bouncing ball shown in Figure 5-9.

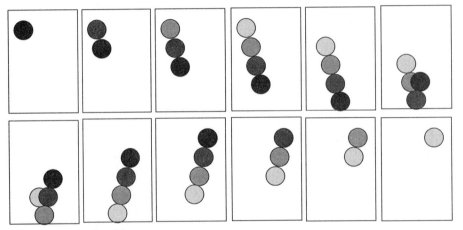

Figure 5-9: Motion blur

Background animation

A computer game or real-time simulation contains two different types of graphics objects: backgrounds and sprites. The backgrounds consist of larger bitmaps over which the action takes place. For example, in a flight simulator program there can be several background images representing views from the cockpit. These may include landscapes, seascapes, and views of airports and runways used during takeoff and landing. A computer game that takes place in a medieval castle may have backgrounds consisting of the various castle rooms and corridors on which the action takes place. Sprites are small objects represented in two or three dimensions. In the flight simulator program, the sprites are other aircraft visible from the cockpit and the cabin instruments and controls that are animated during the simulation. In the computer game the sprites are medieval knights that do battle in the castle, as well as the objects animated during the battle. The methods discussed so far refer mostly to sprite animation. But backgrounds can also be animated, usually with very effective results. Panning and zooming are two popular techniques for background animation.

Panning

The design, display, and manipulation of background images in a graphics application are relatively straightforward. One of the most common methods consists of creating backgrounds that are larger than the viewport and using clipping and blit-time transformations to generate panning and zoom effects. Figure 5-10 shows a bitmapped scene, a portion of which is selected by a rectangular viewport.

Figure 5-10: Source rectangles in panning animation

In panning, the portion of the image mapped to the viewport is changed a few pixels at a time. In Figure 5-10, the progression from the portion of the image enclosed by the solid rectangle to the one enclosed by the dashed rectangle could take over one hundred steps. The result appears as if the camera were slowly moved from the start position to the final one. In actual programming, panning effects are easy to produce and are effective and natural.

Zoom

Zooming is another background animation that is implemented at display time. In zooming, the image size is progressively reduced or enlarged, while the corresponding portion of the image bitmap is stretched or compressed to fill the viewport. The effect simulates progressively changing the magnification of a viewing instrument, such as binoculars or a telescope. Figure 5-11 shows the source rectangles in the original bitmap, which, in this case, are expanded to fit the viewport. Like panning, zoom animation can be programmed simply and effectively.

Figure 5-11: Source rectangles in zoom animation

Notice that the dimension of the rectangles in zoom animation must take into account the aspect ratio of the viewport. This is necessary so that the image is not deformed by the required compression and stretching operations.

XOR animation

To animate a screen object, its image must be erased from the current screen position before being redrawn at the new position. In this respect animation programmers sometimes speak of a *draw-erase-redraw* cycle. If the object is not erased, the consecutive images leave a visible track on the display surface. In lateral translation an object appears to move across the screen, from left to right, by progressively redrawing and erasing its screen image at consecutively larger x coordinates. In this case erasing the old screen object is at least as time-consuming as drawing the new one. In either case, each pixel in the object must be changed.

Several techniques have been devised for performing the draw-erase-redraw cycle required in animation. The most obvious method is to save that portion of the screen image that is to be occupied by the object. Redisplaying the saved image can then erase the object. The problem with this double blit manipulation is that it requires a preliminary, and time-consuming, read operation to store the screen area that is to be occupied by the animated object. Therefore, the draw-erase-redraw cycle is performed by a video-to-RAM blit (save screen), RAM-to-video blit (display object), and a RAM-to-video blit (restore screen).

An interesting method of erasing and redrawing the screen is based on the properties of the logical exclusive (XOR) operation. The action of the logical XOR is that a bit in the result is set if both operands contain opposite values. Consequently, XORing the same value twice restores the original contents, as in the following case:

```
                 10000001B
     XOR mask    10110011B
                 ----------
                 00110010B
     XOR mask    10110011B
                 ----------
                 10000001B
```

In this example the final bitmap (10000001B) is the same as the original one. This property of the logical XOR makes it a convenient and fast way for consecutively drawing and erasing a screen object. Its main advantage is that it does not require a previous read operation to store the original screen contents. This results in a faster and simpler read-erase cycle. The XOR method is particularly useful when more than one animated object can coincide on the same screen position because it ensures that the original screen image is always restored.

The biggest disadvantage of the XOR method is that the resulting image depends on the background. In other words, each individual pixel in the object displayed by means of a logical XOR operation is determined both by the XORed value and by the present pixel contents. For example, the following XOR operation produces a red object (in RGB format) on a bright white screen background:

```
                  R G B
background    =   1 1 1   (white)
XOR mask      =   0 1 1
                  -------
image         =   1 0 0   (red)
```

However, if the same XOR mask is used over a green background the resulting pixel is blue, as in the following example:

```
                  R G B
background    =   0 1 0   (bright green)
XOR mask      =   0 1 1
                  -------
image         =   0 0 1   (blue)
```

The effect whereby an object's color changes as it moves over different backgrounds can be an advantage or a disadvantage in graphics applications. For example, a marker symbol conventionally displayed may disappear as it moves over a background of its same color, whereas a marker displayed by means of a logical XOR is likely to be visible over many different backgrounds. On the other hand, the color of a graphics object could be an important characteristic. In this case any changes during display operations would be objectionable.

Figure 5-12 graphically shows how the XOR operation changes the attributes of a sprite as it is displayed over different backgrounds.

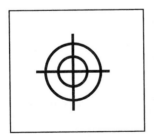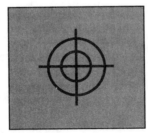

Figure 5-12: XOR rendering

Most video graphics systems and processors directly support the XOR operation. By using the XOR function the graphics programmer can move the sprite symbol simply by defining its new coordinates. In this case the hardware takes care of erasing the old marker and restoring the underlying image.

Rendering in animation

In creating the image set the animator is often confronted with modeling problems. As the number of dimensions of the representation and the complexity of the objects increase, so do the difficulties in obtaining the in-between images and the complications in performing the mathematical transformations required for the animation. In general, two-dimensional objects are easier to model than three-dimensional ones, symmetrical objects are easier than asymmetrical ones, and geometrical entities are easier than living organisms, although there are exceptions to these general rules.

The modeling of realistic living organisms introduces additional difficulties. Higher animals and human forms, in particular, present challenging rendering problems. In this case the models are complex and muscle action is difficult to predict and imitate. Several techniques have been developed to model the human body in three dimensions. Stick figures, surfaces, and volume models have all been used with moderate success. Stick figures, in particular, provide a simplification during the early development stages by reducing the complexity of animating a human body. Figure 5-13 is a stick figure of a man.

Figure 5-13: Stick figure of a man

But even in the most schematic representations of the human body, developing the image set involves the interaction of several limbs and joints. Figure 5-14 shows the animation of a stick figure to simulate a walking man.

Several techniques and algorithms have been developed for the computer modeling of human motion. In one methodology (Labanotation) the body is described as sets of limbs and joints. Each joint is specified in terms of axes that can be oriented in various ways. Joint movements are described by operations that fall into several categories. A special symbol represents each class of operation. This approach makes possible the study and representation of human motion in an abstract way.

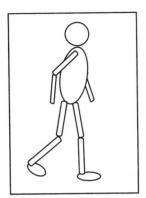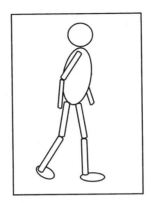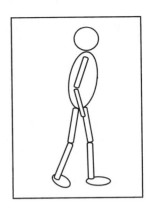

Figure 5-14: Stick figure animation

Applications of Computer Animation

The applications of computer animation practically coincide with the applications of computer graphics. For instance, computer graphics are often used in business to draw charts of economic and financial functions. The usual purpose of these charts and graphs is to facilitate the understanding of complex phenomena and to aid in decision making. These purposes are enhanced when the graphs and charts are animated so as to represent historical changes or future trends of the depicted data. The use of animation in business computing is made evident by the fact that standard business software tools, such as Microsoft's PowerPoint, now support animation.

Simulators and trainers

Many natural or man-made objects and environments can be represented artificially in a satisfactory manner. For many years we have used optical planetariums to illustrate and teach astronomy in an environment that does not require costly optical instruments and that is independent of the weather and other meteorological conditions. In the planetarium, the viewer sits in a comfortable chair located in an air-conditioned amphitheater and watches the procession of constellations and deep-sky objects, as well as the trajectory of the moon and the planets, over a realistically depicted sky. The operator of the planetarium controls the rate of movement so that the celestial transformations that take place over years or centuries can appear to occur in a few seconds or in minutes. The operator can enlarge the magnification of a particular object so that the viewer can appreciate in detail the rings of Saturn or the satellites of Jupiter. Furthermore, it is possible in an artificial environment to reproduce the stellar objects and viewing conditions of any particular date in history. In this manner a viewer is able to relive the astronomical observations and experiences of Galileo or Newton. Most modern planetariums use computers to aid the control and rendering processes.

Other natural phenomena cannot be conveniently reproduced in a physical or optical laboratory. For example, the transformation of mass according to the theory of relativity would be practically impossible to reproduce physically. We can use animated graphics to simulate physical entities or to represent complex scientific phenomena such as nuclear and chemical reactions, hydraulic flow, physiological systems and organs, or structures under load. We can also use animated graphics in reproducing physical simulators, such as the planetarium, in depicting systems that cannot be conveniently imitated in other ways, or in creating a more feasible or economical emulation of physical phenomena.

One such type of computer-assisted device, sometimes called a *simulator*, finds practical and economical use in experimentation and instruction. Astronauts training for a lunar landing practiced in simulators of the landing module and the mother ship. Airplane pilots often train in computer-assisted simulators that can safely reproduce unusual or dangerous flying conditions.

Computer games

Since the release of Pac Man in the early 1980s computer animation has played an increasingly important role in the personal entertainment field. More recently we have seen a remarkable increase in popularity of dedicated computer-controlled systems and user-interaction devices, such as those developed by Nintendo and Sega. During this time the arcade-type electronic game continued to prosper.

Even more recently, PC games and simulations have gained their own status. High-performance video systems, CD-ROM, digital audio, and specialized user-interaction devices have been combined in an environment called *multimedia*. The quality of the animated imagery and sound effects that can be obtained in multimedia computer systems often competes with those in dedicated systems. Some applications for personal computers have achieved such a degree of realism that moral and ethical issues are being raised regarding the use of sexually explicit or violent representations.

Artificial life

A new discipline of computer science, named *artificial life*, or *ALife*, has evolved around the computer modeling of biosystems. Practitioners of this new field state that it is based on biology, robotics, and artificial intelligence. The results are digital entities that resemble self-reproducing and self-organizing biological life forms. Computer viruses of the harmful and benign forms are examples of artificial life.

The notion of a cellular automaton is at the core of artificial life. The idea was first described by John von Neumann as a theoretical model of a parallel computing device. The model is made subject to various restrictions to facilitate the formal investigation of its computing powers. The cellular automaton is reminiscent of a living organism because it is based on an interconnection of identical cells. Each cell behaves as a finite-state machine: it computes an output based on input received from a finite set of other similar cells, which are said to form its *neighborhood*. A cell can also receive input from an external source. A timer determines that all cells produce a simultaneous output. The output is directed to all cells in the neighborhood, and possibly to an external destination or receiver.

The first formal discussion of cellular automata was by E. F. Codd in 1968. The subject of cellular automata is also discussed in a book edited by A.W. Burks titled *Theory of Self-Reproducing Automata* (1970). A more recent title by Edward Rietman, *Creating Artificial Life Self Organization,* provides a rigorous, and at the same time, entertaining presentation of this subject. The implementation of cellular automata is often represented as a sequence of images. Each clock cycle is an iteration update of the automata system, which can be viewed graphically on the computer screen. The resulting changes in the system give rise to an image set that simulates an animated entity. In general, the notion of artificial life is naturally associated with biological forms capable of self-reproduction and self-organization. These actions imply changes that can be represented graphically.

Virtual reality

Recent breakthroughs in input/output technology have made possible a new level of user interaction with a computing machine. In *virtual reality* (VR) a computer system is equipped with one or more interaction devices (typically in the form of *virtual reality goggles* or *head-mounted display*), and one or more input devices, which enable the user to interact with the animation system. The result of virtual reality is a digital universe created by the computer system in which the user is submerged, according to its level of isolation from the surrounding environment. This digital universe has been named *cyberspace*, using a term coined by science fiction writer William Gibson in his 1984 book *Neuromancer*. The possible applications of VR technology range from pure entertainment to practical industrial controls. For example, we can use VR to travel to planet Mars and walk on its surface, to control a complex robot used in industry or manufacturing, or to dance to the tango with a virtual partner. Other applications of virtual reality technology include scientific and medical research, art, music, CAD, electronic games, information management, engineering, education, and surgery.

Animation techniques are usually required in virtual reality as part of the computer feedback mechanism. In a typical VR system the goggles take the place of the video display. Animators use their art to present to the user a convincing image of the virtual environment created by the system. For example, when the system detects a rotation of the user's head toward the left, the video image displayed on the VR goggles is smoothly panned in that direction. This action makes visible the objects that were previously outside of the user's field of view, as would naturally result from the new position of the eyes. If the virtual universe includes entities that move, the system must use sprite animation to reflect this action in the virtual environment. For example, a virtual reality representation of the Jurassic period could be based on images of dinosaurs that move in predetermined or random fashion, perhaps interacting with the user.

On the PC we have not yet achieved the level of technical refinement and the image processing power necessary for creating a completely realistic virtual environment. In an ideal system many virtual entities would be animated simultaneously, according to the user's interaction with the system, or to predetermined or random factors. In the years to come we are likely to create virtual realities in which a user is able to experience being a brain surgeon, a time traveler, or a rather skimpy meal for a large, flesh-eating animal from the Jurassic period.

Fractal graphics

When examined closely, natural surfaces are highly irregular and do not follow predictable geometrical patterns. Such is the case with coastlines, islands, rivers, snowflakes, and galaxies. For this reason, many natural objects cannot be satisfactorily represented using polygons or even smooth curves because the resulting image is too regular and contrived. However, it is possible to represent some types of natural objects realistically with a mathematical entity called a *fractal*. The term was derived from the words *fractional dimensions* and first used by Benoit Mandelbrot in his book *The Fractal Geometry of Nature*.

A fractal is often explained by a structure called a *triadic Koch curve*. The evolution of the Koch curve starts with a straight line of length one. The middle third of this line (one-third fraction) is replaced by two lines of the same length that form a 60-degree angle. The result is a curve that is more rugged than the original one. This second-order curve can be transformed into a curve of the third order by repeating the same process with each of its four segments. The evolution of a Koch curve to the third order is shown in Figure 5-15.

first order   second order   third order

Figure 5-15: Triadic Koch fractal

We observe that the length of the Koch curve in Figure 5-15 increases in proportion to the number of straight line segments that it contains. This means that the second-order Koch curve has a greater length than the first-order curve, and the third order is longer than the second order. By continuing the process to infinity, the length of the curve also increases to infinity. Therefore, the curve cannot be measured in one dimension. On the other hand, the Koch curve cannot be measured in two dimensions because, by definition, its area is always zero. This leads to the conclusion that the curve must have a dimension that is greater than one and less than two, that is, a fractional dimension, or fractal. Following the Hausdorff-Besicovich method, the dimension of the Koch curve is determined to be approximately 1.2857.

One interesting feature of fractals is that they can be generated by computers following what is called a *production rule*. The method of subdividing each intermediate line segment into two others is the production rule for the Koch fractal. The Koch curve exhibits a feature known as *self-similarity*. Parts of the curves are similar to the whole curve. Natural objects, on the other hand, rarely exhibit self-similarity, although they do show what is called *statistical self-similarity*. In using fractal curves to simulate natural objects it is necessary to introduce a random factor that diminishes the curve's self-similarity property. The result is comparable to the image formed in a kaleidoscope in which the random placement of the colored glass fragments ensures a unique image with every change.

Computer animation can be used to show the progression in the approximation of random fractals. Notice that a truly random fractal has an infinitely complex shape; therefore, it cannot actually exist as a visible object. The introduction of a random element in the creation of the fractal curve ensures that the result will be unpredictably different every time the fractal is approximated. The animated imagery that results from the generation of a random fractal graphic approximation is quite interesting from both an artistic and a mathematical viewpoint.

The Animator's Predicament

At the current levels of technology, a 3D programmer on the PC rarely has available all the resources ideally necessary for the project at hand. The most common dilemma requires a sacrifice of image quality for the sake of performance, or vice-versa. Real-time animation in the PC environment, such as is required in games and simulations, may result in a bumpy, coarse, and unrealistic rendering that is aesthetically unpleasant, and even physiologically disturbing. The 3D programmer's art consists of making the best possible use of limited resources in solving the processing and image representation problems to produce results that are as smooth and pleasant as the media allows. This often requires stretching the system's capabilities to its extremes as well as resorting to every scheme and stratagem in the programmer's bag of tricks.

The least rewarding part of the programmer-animator's work is making the compromises that ensure acceptable levels of undesirable effects. In this sense, the animator often has to decide how small an image satisfactorily depicts the object, how much bumpiness is acceptable in representing a movement, how little definition is sufficient for a certain scenery, or with how few attributes can an object be realistically depicted. In the hands of the expert, these compromises and concessions result in the best possible representation in a particular system.

Summary

Here we reviewed the fundamental concepts in computer animation. We started with cartoon technology because computer animation originated in cartoons and continues to follow similar methods. We also looked at frame-by-frame and real-time animation, at programming methods, and rendering problems. The chapter also covered applications of animation and concluded with a discussion of the compromises and concessions that the animation programmer often must make.

At this point in the book we are almost finished with the fundamentals. One topic that is pending is covered in the next chapter: the fundamentals of Windows programming.

✦   ✦   ✦

Windows API Programming

Although this book assumes that you have some Windows programming experience, in this Chapter we review API programming in Windows. The idea is to establish a programming environment for the chapters that follow and to agree upon a program development methodology. Our approach to Windows programming is at the API level. Although we don't use class libraries or other wrappers, we take advantage of the editing and code generating facilities provided by Developer Studio. The process of fabricating a program requires not only knowledge of the language constructs that go into it, but also skills in using the environment. For example, to create a program icon for an application you need to know about the API services that are used in defining and loading the icon, but you also need to have skills in activating and using the icon editor that is part of Developer Studio. Furthermore, when the icon graphics are stored in a file, you need to follow a series of steps that make this resource available to the program.

Preparatory Steps

We assume that you already installed one of the supported software development products. The text is compatible with Microsoft Visual C++ versions 5 and 6. The following section describes the steps in creating a new project in Microsoft Developer Studio, inserting a source code template into the project, modifying and saving the template with a new name, and compiling the resulting file into a Windows executable.

Creating a project

After Visual C++ is installed, start Developer Studio by double-clicking on the program icon on the desktop, or by selecting it from the Microsoft Visual C++ **program group**. The initial

Developer Studio screen varies with the program version, the Windows configuration, the options selected when Developer Studio was last executed, and the project under development. Visual C++ version 5.0 introduced the notion of a *project workspace*, or simply a workspace, as a container for several related projects. In version 5 the extension .mdp, used previously for project files, was changed to .dsw, which now refers to a workspace. The dialog boxes for creating workspaces, projects, and files were also changed. The workspace/project structure and the basic interface are also used in Visual C++ version 6.0.

We start with a walk through the process of creating a project from a template file. The walkthrough is intended to familiarize you with the Developer Studio environment. Later in this chapter you will learn about the different parts of a Windows program and develop a sample application. We call this first project *Program Zero Demo*, for the lack of a better name. The project files are found in the Program Zero project folder in the book's CD-ROM.

A project is located in a workspace, which can include several projects. Project and workspace can be located in the same folder or subfolder or in different ones, and can have the same or different names. In the examples and demonstration programs used in this book we use the same folder for the project and the workspace. The result of this approach is that the workspace disappears as a separate entity, simplifying the creation process.

A new project is started by selecting the New command from the Developer Studio File menu. When the New dialog box is displayed, click on the Project tab option and select a project type from the displayed list. In this case our project is Win32 Application. Make sure that the project location entry corresponds to the desired drive and folder. If not, click the button to the right of the location text box and select another one. Next, enter a project name in the corresponding text box at the upper right of the form. The name of the project is the same one used by Development Studio to create a project folder. In this example we create a project named Do Nothing Demo, which is located in a folder named 3DB_PROJECTS. You can use these same names or create your own. Note that as you type the project name it is added to the path shown in the location text box. At this point the New dialog box appears as in Figure 6-1.

Make sure that the radio button labeled Create new workspace is selected so that clicking OK on the dialog box creates both the project and the workspace. At this point, you have created a project, as well as a workspace of the same name, but there are no program files in it yet. How you proceed from here depends on whether you are using another source file as a base or template or starting from scratch.

If you wish to start a source file from scratch, click the Developer Studio Project menu, select Add To Project, and then New commands. This action displays the same dialog box as when creating a project, but now the Files tab is open. In the case of a source file, select the C++ Source File option from the displayed list and type a filename in the corresponding text box. The dialog appears as shown in Figure 6-2.

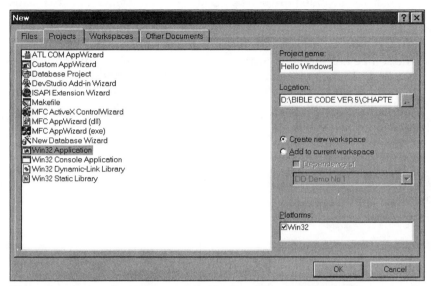

Figure 6-1: Using the New command in Developer Studio FileMenu

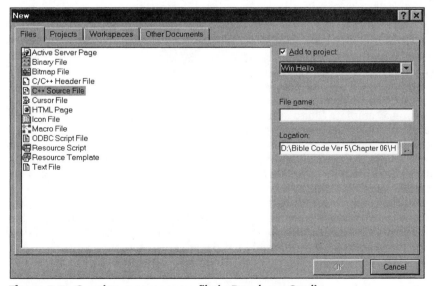

Figure 6-2: Creating a new source file in Developer Studio

The development method we use in this book is based on using source code templates. To use a template as a base, or another source file, you must follow a different series of steps. Assuming that you have created a project, the next step is to select and load the program template or source file. We use the template named Templ01.cpp. If you installed the book's CD-ROM in your system, the template file is in the path 3DB/Templates. If you did not install the CD-ROM, then you can copy the program file Templ01.cpp from the CD-ROM into your project folder.

To load the source file into your current project, open the Developer Studio Project menu, select Add To Project item, and then the Files commands. This action displays an Insert Files into Project dialog box. Use the buttons to the right of the Look in text box to navigate into the desired drive and folder until the desired file is selected. Figure 6-3 shows the file WinHello.cpp highlighted and ready for inserting into the project.

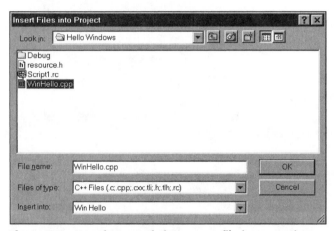

Figure 6-3: Inserting an existing source file into a project

When using a template file to start a new project you must be careful not to destroy or change the original source. The template file is usually renamed when it is inserted into the project. It is possible to insert a template file in a project, rename it, delete it from the project, and then reinsert the renamed file. However, it is easier to rename a copy of the template file before it is inserted into the project. The following sequence of operations is used:

1. Click the File menu and select the Open command. Navigate through the directory structure to locate the file to be used as a template. In this case the file Templ01.cpp is located in 3DB/Templates folder.

2. With the cursor still in Developer Studio editor pane, open the File menu and click Save As. Navigate through the directory structure again until you reach the 3DB_PROJECTS\Program Zero Demo folder. Save the file using the name Prog_zero.cpp.

3. Click on the Project menu and select the commands Add to Project and Files. Locate the file named Prog_zero.cpp in the Insert Files into Project dialog box, select it, and click **OK**.

The file Prog_zero.cpp now appears in the Program Zero Demo file list in Developer Studio workspace pane. It is also displayed in the Editor window.

The Developer Studio main screen is configurable by the user. Furthermore, the size of its display areas is determined by the system resolution. For this reason, it is impossible to depict a Developer Studio screen display that matches the one that every user will see. In the illustrations and screen dumps throughout this book we have used a resolution of 1152 × 854 pixels in 16-bit color with large fonts. However, our screen format may not match yours exactly. Figure 6-4 shows a full screen display of Developer Studio with the file Prog_zero.cpp loaded in the Editor area.

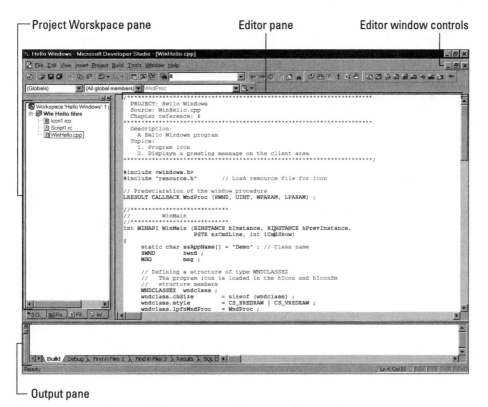

Figure 6-4: Developer Studio Project Workspace, Editor, and Output pane

The Project Workspace pane of Developer Studio was introduced in version 4.0. It has four possible views: Class View, File View, Info View, and Resource View. The Resource View is not visible in Figure 6-4. To display the source file in the editor pane, you must first select File View tab and double-click on the Prog_zero.cpp filename.

At this point, you can proceed to develop the new project using the renamed template file as the main source. The first step is to make sure that the development software is working correctly. To do this, open the Developer Studio Build menu and click Rebuild All. Developer Studio compiles and builds your program, which is at this stage nothing more than the renamed template file. The results are shown in the Output area. If compilation and linking took place without error, reopen the Build menu and select the Execute Prog_zero.exe command button. If everything is in order, a do-nothing program executes in your system.

Now click Save on the File menu to make sure that all project files are saved on your hard drive.

Elements of a Windows program

The template file Templ01.cpp, which we used and renamed in the previous example, is a bare bones Windows program with no functionality except to display a window on the screen. Before proceeding to edit this template into a useful program, you should become acquainted with its fundamental elements. In this section, we take apart the template file Templ01.cpp for a detailed look into each of its components. The program contains two fundamental components: WinMain() and the window procedure.

WinMain()

All Windows GUI applications must have a WinMain() function. WinMain() is to a Windows GUI program what main() is to a DOS application. It is usually said that WinMain() is the program's entry point, but this is not exactly true. C/C++ compilers generate a startup code that calls WinMain(), so it is the startup code and not WinMain() that is actually called by Windows. The WinMain() header line is as follows:

```
           |------------------- Return type
           |   |--------------- One of the standard calling conventions
           |   |                 defined in windows.h
           |   |   |------- Function name
           |   |   |
           |   |   |    [          parameter list ....
--- ------ ------- -------------------------------------------------
int WINAPI WinMain (HINSTANCE hInstance, HINSTANCE
                    hPrevInstance,
                    PSTR szCmdLine, int iCmdShow) {
```

WINAPI is a macro defined in the windows.h header file, which translates the function call to the appropriate calling convention. Recall that calling conventions refer to how the function arguments are placed in the stack at call time, and if the caller or the called routine is responsible for restoring stack integrity after the call. Microsoft versions of Basic, FORTRAN, and Pascal push the parameters onto the stack in the same order in which they are declared. In these languages the stack must be restored by the caller. In C and C++, the parameters are pushed in reverse order, and the stack is restored automatically after the call returns. For historical reasons (and to take advantage of hardware features of the Intel processors) Windows requires the Pascal calling convention. In previous versions of Windows the calling convention for WinMain() was PASCAL or FAR PASCAL. You can still replace WINAPI with FAR PASCAL and the program will compile and link correctly, but using the WINAPI macro makes your program more portable.

Parameters

Most often parameters are passed to WinMain() by Windows but some can be passed by whatever program executes your application. Your code can inspect these parameters to obtain information about the conditions in which the program executes. Four parameters are passed to WinMain():

✦ HINSTANCE. HINSTANCE is a handle-type identifier. The variable hInstance is an integer that identifies the instance of the program. Consider a multitasking environment where several copies (instances) of the same program are running simultaneously. In this case Windows sets the value of the instance and passes it to your code. Your program needs to access this parameter to enter it in the WNDCLASSEX structure, and to call the CreateWindow() function. Because the handle to the instance is required outside of WinMain() by many functions of the Windows API, the template file stores it in a public variable, named pInstance. In general, the use of public variables is undesirable in Windows programming, but this case is one of the valid exceptions to the rule.

✦ hPrevInstance. The variable hPrevInstance is also of type HINSTANCE. This parameter is included in the call for compatibility with previous versions of Windows, which used a single copy of the code to run more than one program instance. In 16-bit Windows the first instance had a special role in the management of resources. Therefore, an application needed to know if it was the first instance. hPrevInstance held the handle of the previous instance. In Windows 95/98/NT this parameter is unused and its value is set to NULL.

✦ PSTR szCmdLine. This is a pointer to a string that contains the command tail entered by the user when the program is executed. It works only when the program name is entered from the DOS command line or from the Run dialog box. For this reason, it is rarely used by code.

✦ int iCmdShow. This parameter determines how the window is to be initially displayed. The program that executes your application (normally Windows) assigns a value to this parameter, as shown in Table 6-1.

Table 6-1
WinMain() Display Mode Parameter

Value	Meaning
SW_HIDE	Hides the window and activates another window.
SW_MINIMIZE	Minimizes the specified window and activates the top-level window in the system's list.
SW_RESTORE	Activates and displays a window. If the window is minimized or maximized, Windows restores it to its original size and position (same as SW_SHOWNORMAL).
SW_SHOW	Activates a window and displays it in its current size and position.
SW_SHOWMAXIMIZED	Activates a window and displays it as a maximized window.
SW_SHOWMINIMIZED	Activates a window and displays it as an icon.
SW_SHOWMINNOACTIVE	Displays a window as an icon. The active window remains active.
SW_SHOWNA	Displays a window in its current state. The active window remains active.
SW_SHOWNOACTIVATE	Displays a window in its most recent size and position. The active window remains active.
SW_SHOWNORMAL	Activates and displays a window. If the window is minimized or maximized, Windows restores it to its original size and position (same as SW_RESTORE).

Data variables

The program file Templ01.cpp defines several variables. One of them, the handle to the program's main window, is defined globally. The other variables are local to WinMain() or the window procedure. The variable defined globally is

```
HWND        hwnd ;
```

HWND is a 16-bit unsigned integer that serves as a handle to a window. The variable HWND refers to the actual program window. The variable is initialized when we make the call to CreateWindow() service, described later in this section.

The variables defined in WinMain() are as follows:

```
static char szClassName[] = "MainClass" ; // Class name
MSG         msg ;
```

The first one is an array of char that shows the application's class name. In the template it is given the name MainClass, which you can replace for a more meaningful one. The application class name must be the same one used in the WNDCLASSEX structure.

MSG is a message-type structure of which msg is a variable. The MSG structure is defined in the Windows header files as follows:

```
typedef struct tagMSG {      // msg
    HWND    hwnd;       // Handle to window receiving message
    UINT    message;   // message number
    WPARAM wParam;     // Context-dependent additional
information
    LPARAM lParam;     // about the message
    DWORD  time;       // Time at which message was posted
    POINT  pt;         // Cursor position when message was posted
} MSG;
```

The comments to the structure members show that the variable holds information that is important to the executing code. The values of the message variable are reloaded every time a new message is received.

WNDCLASSEX structure

This structure is defined in the Windows header files, as follows:

```
typedef struct tagWNDCLASSEX {
UINT       cbSize ;
UINT       style ;
WNDPROC    lpfnWndProc ;
int        cbClsExtra ;
int        cbWndExtra ;
HINSTANCE  hInstance ;
HICON      hIcon ;
HCURSOR    hCursor ;
HBRUSH     hbrBackground ;
LPCSTR     lpszMenuName ;
LPCSTR     lpszClassName ;
HICON      hIconSm ;
} WNDCLASSEX;
```

The WNDCLASSEX structure contains window class information. It is used with the RegisterClassEx() and GetClassInfoEx() functions. The structure is similar to the WNDCLASS structure used in 16-bit Windows. The differences between the two structures is that WNDCLASSEX has a cbSize member, which specifies the size of the structure, and the hIconSm member, which contains a handle to a small icon associated with the window class. In the template file Templ01.cpp the structure is declared and the variable initialized as follows:

```
// Defining a structure of type WNDCLASSEX
WNDCLASSEX  wndclass ;
wndclass.cbSize        = sizeof (WNDCLASSEX) ;
wndclass.style         = CS_HREDRAW | CS_VREDRAW ;
wndclass.lpfnWndProc   = WndProc ;
wndclass.cbClsExtra    = 0 ;
wndclass.cbWndExtra    = 0 ;
wndclass.hInstance     = hInstance ;
wndclass.hIcon         = LoadIcon (NULL, IDI_APPLICATION) ;
wndclass.hCursor       = LoadCursor (NULL, IDC_ARROW) ;
wndclass.hbrBackground = (HBRUSH) GetStockObject
                         (WHITE_BRUSH) ;
wndclass.lpszMenuName  = NULL ;
wndclass.lpszClassName = szClassName ;
wndclass.hIconSm       = LoadIcon (NULL, IDI_APPLICATION) ;
```

The window class is a template that defines the characteristics of a particular window, such as the type of cursor and the background color. The class also specifies the address of the window procedure that carries out the work for the window. The structure variables define the window class, as follows:

1. The cbSize variable specifies the size, in bytes, of the structure. The member is set using the sizeof operator in the statement:

   ```
   sizeof(WNDCLASSEX);
   ```

2. The style variable specifies the class style or styles. Two or more styles can be combined by means of the C bitwise OR (|) operator. This member can be any combination of the values in Table 6-2.

Table 6-2 Summary of Window Class Styles	
Symbolic Constant	**Action**
CS_BYTEALIGNCLIENT	Aligns the window's client area on the byte boundary (in the *x* direction) to enhance performance during drawing operations. This style affects the width of the window and its horizontal position on the display.
CS_BYTEALIGNWINDOW	Aligns a window on a byte boundary (in the *x* direction) to enhance performance during operations that involve moving or sizing the window. This style affects the width of the window and its horizontal position on the display.

Symbolic Constant	Action
CS_CLASSDC	Allocates one device context to be shared by all windows in the class. Window classes are process specific; therefore, different threads can create windows of the same class.
CS_DBLCLKS	Sends double-click messages to the window procedure when the user double-clicks the mouse while the cursor is within a window belonging to the class.
CS_GLOBALCLASS	Allows an application to create a window of the class regardless of the value of the hInstance parameter passed to the CreateWindowEx() function. If you do not specify this style, the hInstance parameter passed to CreateWindowEx() function must be the same as the one passed to the RegisterClass() function.
CS_HREDRAW	Redraws the entire window if a movement or size adjustment changes the width of the client area.
CS_NOCLOSE	Disables the Close command on the System menu.
CS_OWNDC	Allocates a unique device context for each window in the class.
CS_PARENTDC	Specifies that child windows inherit their parent window's device context. Specifying CS_PARENTDC enhances an application's performance.
CS_SAVEBITS	Saves, as a bitmap, the portion of the screen image obscured by a window. Windows uses the saved bitmap to recreate the screen image when the window is removed. This style is useful for small windows (such as menus or dialog boxes) that are displayed briefly and then removed before other screen activity takes place.
CS_VREDRAW	Redraws the entire window if a movement or size adjustment changes the height of the client area.

Of these, the styles CS_HREDRAW and CS_VREDRAW are most commonly used. They can be combined by means of the OR operator to produce a window that is automatically redrawn if it is resized vertically or horizontally, as implemented in the Templ01.cpp code.

lpfnWndProc is a pointer to the window procedure, described later in this chapter. In the template Templ01.cpp it is initialized to the name of the window procedure as follows:

```
wndclass.lpfnWndProc = WndProc;
```

cbClsExtra is a count of the number of extra bytes to be allocated following the window class structure. The operating system initializes the bytes to zero. In the template this member is set to zero.

cbWndExtra is a count of the number of extra bytes to allocate following the window instance. The operating system initializes the bytes to zero. In the template this member is set to zero.

hInstance is a handle to the instance of the window procedure.

hIcon is a handle to the class icon. If this member is NULL, an application must draw an icon whenever the user minimizes the application's window. In the template this member is initialized by calling the LoadIcon() function.

hCursor is a handle to the class cursor. If this member is NULL, an application must explicitly set the cursor shape whenever the mouse moves into the application's window. In the template this member is initialized by calling the LoadCursor() function.

hbrBackground is a background brush. This member can be a handle to the physical brush to be used for painting the background, or it can be a color value. If it is a color value, then it must be one of the standard system colors listed in Table 6-3.

Table 6-3
Common Windows Standard System Colors

Symbolic Constant	Meaning
COLOR_ACTIVEBORDER	Border color of the active window
COLOR_ACTIVECAPTION	Caption color of the active window
COLOR_APPWORKSPACE	Window background of MDI clients
COLOR_BACKGROUND	Desktop color
COLOR_BTNFACE	Face color for buttons
COLOR_BTNSHADOW	Shadow color for buttons
COLOR_BTNTEXT	Text color on buttons
COLOR_CAPTIONTEXT	Text color for captions, size boxes, and scroll bar arrow boxes
COLOR_GRAYTEXT	Color for disabled text

Symbolic Constant	Meaning
COLOR_HIGHLIGHT	Color of a selected item
COLOR_HIGHLIGHTTEXT	Text color of a selected item
COLOR_INACTIVEBORDER	Border color of inactive window
COLOR_INACTIVECAPTION	Caption color of an inactive window
COLOR_MENU	Background color of a menu
COLOR_MENUTEXT	Text color of a menu
COLOR_Scroll bar	Color of a scroll bar's gray area
COLOR_WINDOW	Background color of a window
COLOR_WINDOWFRAME	Frame color of a window
COLOR_WINDOWTEXT	Text color of a window

When this member is NULL, an application must paint its own background whenever it is required to paint its client area. In the template this member is initialized by calling the GetStockObject() function.

lpszMenuName is a pointer to a null-terminated character string that specifies the resource name of the class menu, as it appears in the resource file. If you use an integer to identify the menu, then you must use the MAKEINTRESOURCE macro. If this member is NULL, the windows belonging to this class have no default menu, as is the case in the template file.

lpszClassName is a pointer to a null-terminated string or it is an atom. If this parameter is an atom, it must be a global atom created by a previous call to the GlobalAddAtom() function. The atom, a 16-bit value, must be in the low-order word of lpszClassName; the high-order word must be zero. If lpszClassName is a string, it specifies the window class name. In Templ01.cpp this member is set to the szClassName[] array.

In Windows 95/98, hIconSm is a handle to a small icon that is associated with the window class. This is the icon shown in Windows Explorer and in dialog boxes that list filenames. A Windows 95/98 application can use a predefined icon in this case, using the LoadIcon function with the same parameters as for the hIcon member. In Windows NT this member is not used and should be set to NULL. Windows 95/98 applications that set the small icon to NULL still have the default small icon displayed on the task bar.

In most cases it is better to create both the large and the small icon than to let Windows create the small one from the large bitmap. Later in this chapter we describe how to create both icons as a program resource and how to make these resources available to the application.

Contrary to what is sometimes stated, the LoadIcon() function cannot be used to load both large and small icons from the same resource. For example, if the icon resource is named IDI_ICON1, and we proceed as follows:

```
wndclass.hicon       = LoadIcon (hInstance,
                            MAKEINTRESOURCE(IDI_ICON1);
      .
      .
      .
wndclass.hiconSm     = LoadIcon (hInstance,
                            MAKEINTRESOURCE(IDI_ICON1);
```

the result is that the large icon is loaded from the resource file, but not the small one. This happens even if the resource file contains both images. Instead, you must use the LoadImage() function, as follows:

```
wndclass.hIcon           = LoadImage(hInstance,
                            MAKEINTRESOURCE(IDI_ICON1),
                            IMAGE_ICON,       // Type
                            32, 32,           // Pixel size
                            LR_DEFAULTCOLOR) ;
      .
      .
      .
wndclass.hIconSm         = LoadImage(hInstance,
                            MAKEINTRESOURCE(IDI_ICON1),
                            IMAGE_ICON,       // Type
                            16, 16,           // Pixel size
                            LR_DEFAULTCOLOR) ;
```

Now both the large and the small icon resources are loaded correctly and are used as required.

Registering the window class

After your code has declared the WNDCLASSEX structure and initialized its member variables, it has defined a window class that encompasses all the structure attributes. The most important ones are the window style (wndclass.style), the pointer to the window procedure (wndclass.lpfnWndProc), and the window class name (wndclass.lpszClassName). The RegisterClassEx() function is used to notify Windows of the existence of a particular window class, as defined in the WNDCLASSEX structure variable. The address-of (&) operator is used to reference the location of the specific structure variable, as in the following statement:

```
RegisterClassEx (&wndclass) ;
```

The `RegisterClassEx()` function returns an atom (16-bit value). This value is nonzero if the class is successfully registered. Code should check for a successful registration because you cannot create a window otherwise. The following construct ensures that execution does not proceed if the function fails.

```
if(!RegisterClassEx (&wndclass))
    return(0);
```

This coding style is the one used in the template Templ01.cpp.

Creating the window

A window class is a general classification. Other data must be provided at the time the actual window is created. The `CreateWindowEx()` function receives the additional information as parameters. `CreateWindowEx()` is a Windows 95 version of the `CreateWindow()` function. The only difference between them is that the new version supports an extended window style passed as its first parameter.

The `CreateWindowEx()` function is very rich in arguments, many of which apply only to special window styles. For example, buttons, combo boxes, list boxes, edit boxes, and static controls can be created with a `CreateWindowEx()` call. At this time, we refer only to the most important function parameters that relate to a program's main window.

In the file Templ01.cpp the call to `CreateWindowEx()` is coded as follows:

```
hwnd = CreateWindowEx (
        WS_EX_LEFT,             // left aligned (default)
        szClassName,            // pointer to class name
        "Window Caption",       // window caption (title bar)
        WS_OVERLAPPEDWINDOW,    // window style
        CW_USEDEFAULT,          // initial x position
        CW_USEDEFAULT,          // initial y position
        CW_USEDEFAULT,          // initial x size
        CW_USEDEFAULT,          // initial y size
        NULL,                   // parent window handle
        NULL,                   // window menu handle
        hInstance,              // program instance handle
        NULL) ;                 // creation parameters
```

The first parameter passed to the `CreateWindowEx()` function is the extended window style introduced in the Win32 API. The one used in the file Templ01.cpp, `WS_EX_LEFT`, acts as a placeholder for others that you may want to select because it is actually the default value. Table 6-4 lists some of the most common extended styles.

Table 6-4
Most Commonly Used Windows Extended Styles

Symbolic Constant	Meaning
WS_EX_ACCEPTFILES	The window created with this style accepts drag-and-drop files.
WS_EX_APPWINDOW	A top-level window is forced onto the application taskbar when the window is minimized.
WS_EX_CLIENTEDGE	The window has a border with a sunken edge.
WS_EX_CONTEXTHELP	The title bar includes a question mark. When the user clicks the question mark, the cursor changes to a question mark with a pointer. If the user then clicks a child window, it receives a WM_HELP message.
WS_EX_CONTROLPARENT	Enables the user to navigate among the child windows of the window by using the Tab key.
WS_EX_DLGMODALFRAME	The window has a double border. Optionally, the window can be created with a title bar by specifying the WS_CAPTION style in the dwStyle parameter.
WS_EX_LEFT	The window has generic "left-aligned" properties. This is the default.
WS_EX_MDICHILD	This style creates an MDI child window.
WS_EX_NOPARENTNOTIFY	This style creates a child window that does not send the WM_PARENTNOTIFY message to its parent window when it is created or destroyed.
WS_EX_OVERLAPPEDWINDOW	This style combines the WS_EX_CLIENTEDGE and WS_EX_WINDOWEDGE styles.
WS_EX_PALETTEWINDOW	This style combines the WS_EX_WINDOWEDGE, WS_EX_TOOLWINDOW, and WS_EX_TOPMOST styles.
WS_EX_RIGHTScroll bar	The vertical scroll bar (if present) is to the right of the client area. This is the default placement for the vertical scrollbar.
WS_EX_STATICEDGE	This style creates a window with a three-dimensional border style intended for use with items that do not accept user input.
WS_EX_TOOLWINDOW	This style creates a tool window. This type of window's intended use is as a floating toolbar.
WS_EX_TOPMOST	A window created with this style should be placed above all non-topmost windows and should stay above them, even when the window is deactivated.

Symbolic Constant	Meaning
WS_EX_TRANSPARENT	A window created with this style is transparent. That is, any windows that are beneath it are not obscured by it.
WS_EX_WINDOWEDGE	The window has a border with a raised edge.

The second parameter passed to the CreateWindowEx() function call is either a pointer to a string with the name of the window type, a string enclosed in double quotation marks, or a predefined name for a control class.

In the template file, szClassName is a pointer to the string defined at the start of WinMain(), with the text "MainClass." You can edit this string in your own applications so that the class name is more meaningful. For example, if you were coding an editor program you may rename the application class as TextEdClass. However, this is merely a name used by Windows to associate a window with its class; it is not displayed as a caption or used otherwise.

Control classes can also be used as a window class name. These classes are the symbolic constants BUTTON, Combo box, EDIT, List box, MDICLIENT, Scroll bar, and STATIC.

The third parameter can be a pointer to a string or a string enclosed in double quotation marks entered directly as a parameter. In either case, this string is used as the caption to the program window and is displayed in the program's title bar. Often this caption coincides with the name of the program. You should edit this string to suit your own program.

The fourth parameter is the window style. Over 25 styles are defined as symbolic constants. The most used styles are listed in Table 6-5.

Table 6-5 **Window Styles**	
Symbolic Constant	Meaning
WS_BORDER	Creates a window that has a thin-line border.
WS_CAPTION	Creates a window that has a title bar (includes the WS_BORDER style).
WS_CHILD	Creates a child window. This style cannot be used with the WS_POPUP style.

Continued

Table 6-5 *(continued)*	
Symbolic Constant	*Meaning*
WS_CLIPCHILDREN	Excludes the area occupied by child windows when drawing occurs within the parent window.
WS_CLIPSIBLINGS	Clips child windows relative to each other. When a particular child window receives a WM_PAINT message, this style clips all other overlapping child windows out of the region of the child window to be updated. If WS_CLIPSIBLINGS is not specified and child windows overlap, it is possible to draw within the client area of a neighboring child window.
WS_DISABLED	Disables the window. A disabled window cannot receive input from the user.
WS_DLGFRAME	Creates a window that has a border of a style typically used with dialog boxes. The window does not have a title bar.
WS_HSCROLL	Creates a window that has a horizontal scroll bar.
WS_ICONIC	Minimizes the Window; same as the WS_MINIMIZE style.
WS_MAXIMIZE	Maximizes the window.
WS_MAXIMIZEBOX	Creates a window that has a Maximize button. Cannot be combined with the WS_EX_CONTEXTHELP style.
WS_MINIMIZE	Minimizes the window; same as the WS_ICONIC style.
WS_MINIMIZEBOX	Creates a window that has a Minimize button. Cannot be combined with the WS_EX_CONTEXTHELP style.
WS_OVERLAPPED	Overlapped window. Has a title bar and a border.
WS_OVERLAPPEDWINDOW	Overlapped window with the WS_OVERLAPPED, WS_CAPTION, WS_SYSMENU, WS_THICKFRAME, WS_MINIMIZEBOX, and WS_MAXIMIZEBOX styles. Same as the WS_TILEDWINDOW style.
WS_POPUP	Creates a pop-up window. Cannot be used with the WS_CHILD style.
WS_POPUPWINDOW	Creates a pop-up window with WS_BORDER, WS_POPUP, and WS_SYSMENU styles. The WS_CAPTION and WS_POPUPWINDOW styles must be combined to make the System menu visible.
WS_SIZEBOX	Creates a window that has a sizing border. Same as the WS_THICKFRAME style.

Symbolic Constant	Meaning
WS_SYSMENU	Creates a window that has a System–menu box in its title bar. The WS_CAPTION style must also be specified.
WS_TILED	Overlapped window. Has a title bar and a border. Same as the WS_OVERLAPPED style.
WS_TILEDWINDOW	Overlapped window with the WS_OVERLAPPED, WS_CAPTION, WS_SYSMENU, WS_THICKFRAME, WS_MINIMIZEBOX, and WS_MAXIMIZEBOX styles. Same as the WS_OVERLAPPEDWINDOW style.
WS_VISIBLE	Window is initially visible.
WS_VSCROLL	Creates a window that has a vertical scroll bar.

The style defined in the template file Templ01.ccp is WS_OVERLAPPEDWINDOW. This style creates a window that has the styles WS_OVERLAPPED, WS_CAPTION, WS_SYSMENU, WS_THICKFRAME, WS_MINIMIZEBOX, and WS_MAXIMIZEBOX. It is the most common style of windows.

The fifth parameter to the CreateWindowEx() service defines the initial horizontal position of the window. The value CS_USERDEFAULT (0x80000000) determines the use of the default position. The template file uses the same CS_USERDEFAULT symbolic constant for the *y* position, and the windows *x* and *y* size.

The ninth and tenth parameters are set to NULL because this window has no parent and no default menu.

The eleventh parameter, hInstance, is the handle to the instance that was passed to WinMain() by Windows.

The last entry, called the creation parameters, can be used to pass data to a program. A CREATESTRUCT-type structure is used to store the initialization parameters passed to the window procedure of an application. The data can include an instance handle, a new menu, the window's size and location, the style, the window's name and class name, and the extended style. Because no creation parameters are passed, the field is set to NULL.

The CreateWindowEx() function returns a handle to the window of type HWND. The template file Templ01.cpp stores this handle in a global variable named hwnd. The reason for this is that many functions in the Windows API require this handle. By storing it in a global variable, we make it visible throughout the code.

If `CreateWindowsEx()` fails, it returns NULL. Code in `WinMain()` can test for this error condition with the statement

```
if(!hwnd)
    return(0);
```

We do not use this test in the template file Templ01.cpp because it is usually not necessary. If `WinMain()` fails, you may use the debugger to inspect the value of hwnd after `CreateWindowEx()` to make sure that a valid handle was returned.

Displaying the window

`CreateWindowEx()` creates the window internally but does not display it. To display the window your code must call two other functions: `ShowWindow()` and `UpdateWindow()`. `ShowWindow()` sets the window's show state and `UpdateWindow()` updates the window's client area. In the case of the program's main window, `ShowWindow()` must be called once, using as a parameter the `iCmdShow` value passed by Windows to `WinMain()`. In the template file the call is coded as follows:

```
ShowWindow (hwnd, iCmdShow) ;
```

The first parameter to `ShowWindow()` is the handle to the window returned by `CreateWindowEx()`. The second parameter is the window's display mode parameter, which determines how the window must be initially displayed. The display mode parameters are listed in Table 6-1, but in this first call to `ShowWindow()` you must use the value received by `WinMain()`.

`UpdateWindow()` actually instructs the window to paint itself by sending a WM_PAINT message to the window procedure. The processing of the WM_PAINT message is described later in this chapter. The actual code in the template file is as follows:

```
UpdateWindow (hwnd) ;
```

If all has gone well, at this point your program is displayed on the screen. It is now time to implement the message passing mechanisms that are at the heart of event-driven programming.

The message loop

In an event-driven environment there can be no guarantee that messages are processed faster than they originate. For this reason Windows maintains two message queues. The first type of queue, called the *system queue*, is used to store messages that originate in hardware devices, such as the keyboard and the mouse.

In addition, every thread of execution has its own *message queue*. The message handling mechanism can be described with a simplified example: when a keyboard event occurs, the device driver software places a message in the system queue. Windows uses information about the input focus to decide which thread should handle the message. It then moves the message from the system queue into the corresponding thread queue.

A simple block of code, called the *message loop*, removes a message from the thread queue and dispatches it to the function or routine that must handle it. When a special message is received, the message loop terminates, and so does the thread. The message loop in Templ01.cpp is coded as follows:

```
while (GetMessage (&msg, NULL, 0, 0))
    {
    TranslateMessage (&msg) ;
    DispatchMessage (&msg) ;
    }
  return msg.wParam ;
```

The while statement calls the function GetMessage(). The first parameter to GetMessage() is a variable of the structure type MSG, described earlier in this chapter and reproduced in Appendix A. The structure variable is filled with information about the message in the queue, if there is one. If no message is waiting in the queue, Windows suspends the application and assigns its time slice to other threads of execution. In an event-driven environment, programs act only in response to events. If no event occurs no message is sent and no action takes place.

The second parameter to GetMessage() is the handle to a window for which to retrieve a message. Most applications set this parameter to NULL, which signals that all messages for windows that belong to the application making the call should be retrieved. The third and the fourth parameters to GetMessage() are the lowest and the highest message numbers to be retrieved. Threads that only retrieve messages within a particular range can use these parameters as a filter. When the special value 0 is assigned to both of these parameters (as is the case in our message loop) then no filtering is performed and all messages are passed to the application.

There are two functions inside the message loop. TranslateMessage() is a keyboard processing function that converts keystrokes into characters. The characters are then posted to the message queue. If the message is not a keystroke that needs translation, then no special action is taken. The DispatchMessage() function sends the message to the window procedure, where it is further processed and either acted upon or ignored. The window procedure is discussed in the following section. GetMessage() returns 0 when a message labeled WM_QUIT is received. This signals the end of the message loop; at this point execution returns from WinMain(), and the application terminates.

The Window Procedure

At this moment in a program's execution the window class has been registered, the window has been created and displayed, and all messages are being routed to your code. The *window procedure*, sometimes called the *window function*, is where you write code to handle the messages received from the message loop. It is in the window procedure that you respond to the events that pertain to your program.

Every window must have a window procedure. Although the name WinProc() is commonly used, you can use any other name for the window procedure provided that it appears in the procedure header, the prototype, in the corresponding entry of the WNDCLASSEX structure, and that it does not conflict with another name in your application. Also, a Windows program can have more than one window procedure. The program's main window is usually registered in WinMain() but others can be registered elsewhere in an application. Here again, each window procedure corresponds to a window class, has its own WNDCLASSEX structure, as well as a unique name.

In the template, the window procedure is coded as follows:

```
        |----------------------- Return type, equivalent to a long
        |                         type
        |       |--------------- Same as FAR PASCAL calling
        |       |                 convention.
        |       |                 Used in windows and dialog
        |       |                 procedures.
        |       |       |------- Procedure name
        |       |       |        [ parameter list ...              ]
------- -------- ------- ------------------------------------------
----
LRESULT CALLBACK WndProc (HWND hwnd, UINT iMsg, WPARAM wParam,
                         LPARAM lParam) {
```

The window procedure is of callback type. The CALLBACK symbol was first introduced in Windows 3.1 and is equivalent to FAR PASCAL, and also to WINAPI because all of them currently correspond to the __stdcall calling convention. Although it is possible to substitute __stdcall for CALLBACK in the function header, it is not advisable because this could compromise the application's portability to other platforms or to future versions of the operating system.

The return value of a window procedure is of type LRESULT, which is a 32-bit integer. The actual value depends on the message, but it is rarely used by application code. However, there are a few messages for which the window procedure is expected to return a specific value. It is a good idea to check the Windows documentation when in doubt.

Window procedure parameters

The four parameters to the window procedure are the first four fields in the MSG structure. Because the window procedure is called by Windows, the parameters are provided by the operating system at call time, as follows:

✦ hwnd is the handle to the window receiving the message. This is the same handle returned by CreateWindow().

✦ iMsg is a 32-bit unsigned integer (UINT) that identifies each particular message. The constants for the various messages are defined in the Windows header files. They all start with the letters WM_, which stand for *window message*.

✦ wParam and lParam are called the message parameters. They provide additional information about the message. Both values are specific to each message.

The last two members of the message structure, which correspond to the message's time of posting and cursor position, are not passed to the window procedure. However, application code can use the functions GetMessageTime() and GetMessagePos() to retrieve these values.

Window procedure variables

The implementation of the window procedure in Templ01.cpp starts by declaring a scalar of type HDC and two structure variables of type HWND and MSG, respectively. The variables are as follows:

✦ hdc is a handle to the device context. A device context is a data structure maintained by Windows, which is used in defining the graphics objects and their attributes, as well as their associated graphics modes. Devices such as the video display, printers, and plotters must be accessed through a handle to their device contexts, which is obtained from Windows.

✦ ps is a PAINTSTRUCT variable. The structure is defined by Windows as follows:

```
typedef struct tagPAINTSTRUCT
{
  HDC    hdc;              // identifies display device
  BOOL   fErase;          // not-zero if background must be
                          // erased
  RECT   rcPaint;         // Rectangle structure in which
                          // painting is requested
  BOOL   fRestore;        // RESERVED
  BOOL   fIncUpdate;      // RESERVED
  BYTE   rgbReserved[32]; // RESERVED
} PAINTSTRUCT;
```

The structure contains information that is used by the application to paint its own client area.

✦ rect is a RECT structure variable. The RECT structure is also defined by Windows:

```
typdef struct _RECT {
   LONG    left;      // x coordinate of upper-left corner
   LONG    top;       // y of upper-left corner
   LONG    right;     // x coordinate of bottom-right corner
   LONG    bottom;    // y of bottom-right
} RECT;
```

The RECT structure is used to define the corners of a rectangle, in this case of the application's display area, which is also called the *client area*.

Message processing

The window procedure receives and processes messages. The message can originate as follows:

✦ Some messages are dispatched by WinMain(). In this group are the messages placed in the thread's message queue by the DispatchMessage() function in the message loop. Messages handled in this manner are referred to as *queued messages*. Queued messages originate in keystrokes, mouse movements, mouse button clicks, the system timer, and in orders to redraw the window.

✦ All other messages come directly from Windows. These are called *nonqueued messages*.

The window procedure examines each message, queue or nonqueued, and either takes action or passes the message back for default processing. In the template file Templ01.cpp the message processing skeleton is coded as follows:

```
switch (iMsg)
      {
// Windows message processing
      // Preliminary operations
      case WM_CREATE:
            return (0);

      // Redraw window
      case WM_PAINT :
            hdc = BeginPaint (hwnd, &ps) ;
            GetClientRect (hwnd, &rect) ;
// Initial display operations here
            EndPaint (hwnd, &ps) ;
            return 0 ;
```

```
                    // End of program execution
                    case WM_DESTROY :
                         PostQuitMessage (0) ;
                         return 0 ;
                    }
               return DefWindowProc (hwnd, iMsg, wParam, lParam) ;
```

Messages are identified by uppercase symbolic constants that start with the characters WM_ (window message). Over two hundred message constants are defined in Windows. Three messages are processed in the template file: WM_CREATE, WM_PAINT, and WM_DESTROY.

When the window procedure processes a message it must return 0. If it does not process a particular message, then the function DefWindowsProc() is called to provide a default action.

WM_CREATE message processing

The WM_CREATE message is sent to an application as a result of the Create WindowEx() function in WinMain(). This message gives the application a chance to perform preliminary initialization, such as displaying a greeting screen, or playing a sound file. In the template, the WM_CREATE processing routine does nothing. It serves as a placeholder where the programmer can insert the appropriate code.

WM_PAINT message processing

The WM_PAINT message informs the program that all or part of the client window must be repainted. This happens when the user minimizes, overlaps, or resizes the client window area. Recall that the style of the program's main window is defined in the template with the statement:

```
        wndclass.style     = CS_HREDRAW | CS_VREDRAW ;
```

This style determines that the screen is redrawn if it is resized vertically or horizontally.

In WM_PAINT, processing begins with the BeginPaint() function. BeginPaint() serves to prepare the window for a paint operation by filling a variable of type PAINTSTRUCT, previously discussed. The call to BeginPaint() requires the hwnd variable, which is the handle to the window that will be painted. ps, a PAINTSTRUCT variable, is also filled by the call. During BeginPaint() Windows erases the background using the currently defined brush.

The call to GetClientRect() requires two parameters. The first one is the handle to the window (hwnd), which is passed to the window procedure as a parameter. In the template file this value is also stored in a public variable. The second parameter is the address of a structure variable of type RECT, where Windows places the coordinates of the rectangle that defines the client area. The left and top values are always set to zero.

Processing ends with EndPaint(). EndPaint() notifies Windows that the paint operation has concluded. The parameters passed to EndPaint() are the same ones passed to BeginPaint(): the handle to the window and the address of the structure variable of type PAINTSTRUCT.

WM_DESTROY message processing

The WM_DESTROY message is received by the window procedure when the user takes an action to destroy the window, usually by clicking the Close button or selecting the Close or Exit commands from the File or the System menus. The standard processing performed in WM_DESTROY is

```
PostQuitMessage (0) ;
```

The PostQuitMessage() function inserts a WM_QUIT message in the message queue, thus terminating the GetMessage loop and ending the program.

The default windows procedure

The code in the template file contains a return statement for each of the messages that it handles. For example

```
case WM_PAINT :
        hdc = BeginPaint (hwnd, &ps) ;
        GetClientRect (hwnd, &rect) ;
// Initial display operations here
        EndPaint (hwnd, &ps) ;
        return 0 ;
```

The last statement in this routine returns a value of zero to Windows. The Windows documentation states that zero must be returned when an application processes the WM_PAINT message. Some Windows messages, not many, require a return value other than zero.

Many of the messages received from Windows, or retrieved from the message queue, are of no interest to your application. In this case, code must provide a default action for those messages that it does not handle. Windows contains a function, named DefWindowsProc(), that ensures this default action. DefWindowsProc() provides specific processing for those messages that require it, thus implementing a default behavior. For those messages that can be ignored, DefWindowsProc() returns zero. Your application uses the return value of DefWindowsProc() as its own return value from the window procedure. This action is coded as follows in the template file:

```
return DefWindowProc (hwnd, iMsg, wParam, lParam) ;
```

The parameters passed to DefWindowsProc() are the same message parameters received by your window procedure from the operating system.

The WinHello Program

In the first walkthrough, at the beginning of this chapter, we used the template file Templ01.cpp to create a new project, which we named *Program Zero Demo*. Program Zero Demo resulted in a do-nothing program because no modifications were made to the template file at that time. In the present walkthrough we proceed to make modifications to the template file to create a Windows program different from the template. This project, which we named *Hello Windows*, is a Windows version of the classic "Hello World" program.

We first create a new project and use the template file Templ01.cpp as the source code base for it. To do this we must follow all the steps in the first walkthrough, except that the project name is now *Hello Windows* and the name template file Templ01.cpp is copied and renamed WinHello.cpp. After you have finished all the steps in the walkthrough you will have a project named Hello Windows and the source file named WinHello.cpp listed in the Project Workspace and displayed in the Editor window. After the source file is renamed, you should edit the header block to reflect the file's new name and the program's purpose. Figure 6-5 shows the Developer Studio screen at this point.

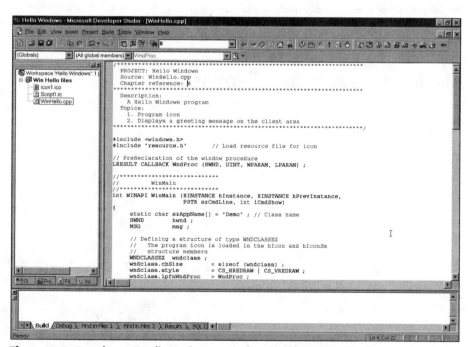

Figure 6-5: Developer Studio main screen showing the Hello Windows Project and source file

The project Hello Windows, which we are about to code, has the following features:

✦ The caption displayed on the program title bar is changed to "Hello Windows."

✦ When the program executes, it displays a greeting message on the center of its client area.

✦ The program now contains a customized icon. A small version of the icon is displayed in the title bar and a larger one is used when the program's executable is represented by a shortcut on the Windows desktop.

After you create the project named Hello Windows and include in it the source file WinHello.cpp, you are ready to start making modifications to the source and inserting new elements into the project.

Modifying the program caption

The first modification that we make to the source is to change the caption that is displayed on the title bar when the program executes. This requires editing the third parameter passed to the CreateWindowsEx() function in WinMain(). The parameter now reads "Hello Windows." Throughout this book we use the project's name, or a variation of it, as the title bar caption. Our reason for this is to make it easy to find the project files from a screen dump of the executable.

Displaying text in the client area

The second modification requires entering a call to the DrawText() API function, in the case WM_PAINT processing routine. The routine now is

```
case WM_PAINT :
    hdc = BeginPaint (hwnd, &ps) ;
    GetClientRect (hwnd, &rect) ;

    // Display message in the client area
        DrawText (hdc,
                  "Hello World from Windows",
                  -1,
                  &rect,
                  DT_SINGLELINE | DT_CENTER | DT_VCENTER);

    EndPaint (hwnd, &ps) ;
    return 0 ;
```

The call to DrawText() requires five parameters. When calls require several parameters, we can improve the readability of the source by devoting a separate text line to each parameter, or to several associated parameters, as in the previous listing.

The first parameter to DrawText() is the handle to the device context. This value was returned by the call to BeginPaint(), described previously in this chapter.

The second parameter to DrawText() points to the string to be displayed. The string can also be enclosed in double quotation marks, as in the previous listing.

The third parameter is -1 if the string defined in the second parameter terminates in NULL. If not, then the third parameter is the count of the number of characters in the string.

The fourth parameter is the address of a structure of type RECT, which contains the logical coordinates of the area in which the string is to be displayed. The call to GetClientRect(), made in the WM_PAINT message intercept, filled the members of the rect structure variable.

In the fifth parameter are the text formatting options. Table 6-6 lists the most used of these controls.

Table 6-6
Symbolic Constants Used in DrawText() Function

Value	Meaning
DT_BOTTOM	Bottom-justifies text. Must be combined with DT_SINGLELINE.
DT_CALCRECT	This constant is used to determine the width and height of the rectangle. If there are multiple lines of text, DrawText uses the width of the rectangle in the RECT structure variable supplied in the call and extends the base of the rectangle to bound the last line of text. If there is only one line of text, DrawText modifies the right side of the rectangle so that no text is displayed.
DT_CENTER	Centers text horizontally.
DT_EXPANDTABS	Expands tab characters. The default number of characters per tab is eight.
DT_EXTERNALLEADING	Includes the font external leading in line height. Normally, it is not included.
DT_LEFT	Aligns text to the left.
DT_NOCLIP	Draws without clipping. The function executes somewhat faster when DT_NOCLIP is used.

Continued

	Table 6-6 *(continued)*
Value	**Meaning**
DT_NOPREFIX	DrawText() interprets the control character & as a command to underscore the character that follows. The control characters && print a single &. This processing is turned off by specifying DT_NOPREFIX.
DT_RIGHT	Aligns text to the right.
DT_SINGLELINE	Displays text on a single line only. Carriage returns and linefeeds are ignored.
DT_TOP	Top-justifies text (single line only).
DT_VCENTER	Centers text vertically (single line only).
DT_WORDBREAK	Breaks words. Lines are automatically broken between words if a word extends past the edge of the rectangle specified by the lpRect parameter. A carriage-return–linefeed sequence also breaks the line.

Creating a program resource

The last customization that you have to perform on the template file is to create two customized icons, which are associated with the program window. The icons correspond to the hIcon and hIconSm members of the WNDCLASSEX structure described previously and listed in Appendix A. hIcon is the window's standard icon. Its default size is 32-by-32 pixels, although Windows automatically resizes this icon as required. The standard icon is used on the Windows desktop when a shortcut is created and in some file listing modes of utilities like Windows Explorer. The small icon is 16-by-16 pixels, which makes it one-fourth the size of the large one. This is the icon shown in dialog boxes that list filenames, by Windows Explorer, and in the program's title bar. Windows NT uses a scaled version of the standard icon when a smaller one is required.

An icon is a resource. Resources are stored in read-only, binary data files, which the application can access by means of a handle. We introduce icons at this time because other program resources such as cursors, menus, dialog boxes, bitmaps, and fonts are handled similarly. The icons that we create in this walkthrough are considered an application-defined resource.

The most convenient way of creating and using resources is to take advantage of the facilities in the development environment. Visual C++ provides several resource editors, and Developer Studio facilitates the creation and manipulation of the support files required for using resources. Graphics programmers often want to retain the highest possible control over their code; however, the use of these facilities in creating and managing resources does not compromise this principle. The files created by the development environment are both visible and editable. As you gain confidence and knowledge about them, you can progressively take over some or all of the operations performed by the development software. In this book, we sometimes let the development environment generate one or more of the program files and then proceed to edit them so that it better suits our purpose.

The convenience of using the automated functions of the development environment is made evident by the fact that a simple resource often requires several software elements. For example, a program icon requires the following components:

✦ A bitmap that graphically encodes the icon. If the operating system and the application support the small icon, then two bitmaps are required.

✦ A script file (also called a resource definition file), which lists all the resources in the application and may describe some of them in detail. The resource script can also reference other files and may include comments and pre-processor directives. The resource compiler (RC.EXE) compiles the script file into a binary file with the extension .RES. This binary file is referenced at link time. The resource file has the extension .RC.

✦ The script file uses a resource header file, with the default filename resource.h, which contains preprocessor directives related to the resources used by the application. The application must reference this file with an #include statement.

Creating the icon bitmap

Developer Studio provides support for the following resources: dialog boxes, menus, cursors, icons, bitmaps, toolbars, accelerators, string tables, and version controls. Each resource has either a graphics editor or a wizard that helps create the resource. In this discussion we refer to either one of them as a resource editor.

Resource editors can be activated by clicking Resource in the Insert menu. At this time Developer Studio displays a dialog box with an entry for each type of resource. Alternatively, you can access the resource editors faster by displaying the Resource toolbar. In Visual C++ 4 and later this is accomplished by clicking Toolbars in the View menu, and then selecting the check box for the Resource option. In versions 5 and 6 select Customize in the Tools menu, open the Toolbars tab in the Customize dialog box, and select the check box for the Resource option. The Graphics and Colors boxes should also be checked to display the normal controls in the resource editors. The resulting toolbar is identical in both cases. When the Resource toolbar is displayed, you can drag it into the toolbar area or to any other convenient screen location. The Insert Resource dialog screen and the resource toolbar are shown in Figure 6-6.

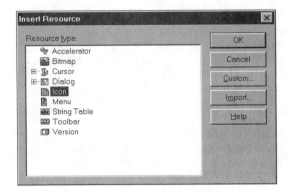

Figure 6-6: Developer Studio Insert Resource dialog screen and toolbar

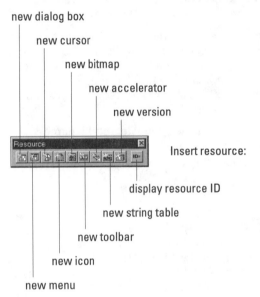

new dialog box

new cursor

new bitmap

new accelerator

new version

Insert resource:

display resource ID

new string table

new toolbar

new icon

new menu

You can activate the icon editor either by selecting the icon option in the Resource dialog box or by clicking the appropriate button on the toolbar. The icon editor is simple to use and serves well in most cases. It enables you to create the bitmap for several sizes of icons. Although the interface to the icon editor is simple, it is also powerful and flexible. You should experiment with the icon editor, as well as with the other resource editors, until you have mastered all their options and modes. Figure 6-7 shows the icon editor in Developer Studio.

The toolbar on the right of the icon editor is similar to the one used in the Windows Paint utility and in other popular graphics programs. There are several tools that enable you to draw lines, curves, and geometrical figures in outline or filled form. Also, there is a palette box from which colors for foreground and background can be selected.

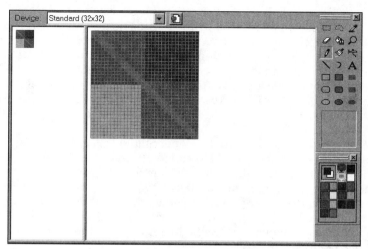

Figure 6-7: Creating an icon resource with Developer Studio icon editor

Developer Studio makes possible the creation of a large and a small icon from the same resource. To request the small icon, click on the New Device Image button and then select the 16-by-16 icon. The two icons, 32-by-32 pixels and 16-by-16 pixels, can be developed alternatively by selecting one of them in the Open Device Image scroll box in the icon editor. Windows automatically uses the large and the small icons as required.

In the WinHello program the WNDCLASSEX structure is edited to support user-created large and small icons, as follows:

```
//   The program icon is loaded in the hIcon and hIconSm
//     structure members
WNDCLASSEX  wndclass ;
wndclass.hIcon          = LoadImage(hInstance,
                          MAKEINTRESOURCE(IDI_ICON1),
                          IMAGE_ICON,      // Type
                          32, 32,          // Pixel size
                          LR_DEFAULTCOLOR) ;
    .
    .
    .
wndclass.hIconSm        = LoadImage(hInstance,
                          MAKEINTRESOURCE(IDI_ICON1),
                          IMAGE_ICON,      // Type
                          16, 16,          // Pixel size
                          LR_DEFAULTCOLOR) ;
```

The MAKEINTRESOURCE macro is used to convert an integer value into a resource. Although resources can also be referenced by their string names, Microsoft recommends the use of the integer value. The name of the icon resource, IDI_ICON1, can be obtained from the resource script file. However, an easier way of finding the resource name is to click the Resource Symbols button on the Resource toolbar (labeled ID=) or select Resource Symbols in the View menu. Either the symbolic name or the numerical value for the icon resource that is shown on the Resource Symbols screen can also be used in the MAKEINTRESOURCE macro.

In the process of creating an icon bitmap, Developer Studio also creates a new script file, or adds the information to an existing one. However, when working outside of the Microsoft Foundation Class library, you must manually insert the script file into the project. You can do this by selecting Add to Project in the Project menu and then clicking on the Files option. In the Insert Files into Project dialog box, select the script file, which in this case is the one named Script1.rc, and then press OK. The script file now appears on the Source Files list in the Files View window of the Project Workspace.

In addition to the script file, Developer Studio also creates a header file for resources. The default name of this file is *resource.h*. In order for resources to be available to the code you must enter an #include statement in the main source file, as follows:

```
#include "resource.h"
```

Notice that the double quotation marks surrounding the filename indicate that it is in the current folder.

At this point, all that is left to do is to compile the resources, the source files, and link the program into an executable. You can do this by selecting Rebuild All in the Build menu. Figure 6-8 shows the screen display of the WinHello program.

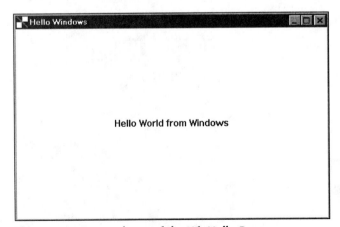

Figure 6-8: Screen dump of the WinHello Program

WinHello Program Listing

The following is a listing of the WinHello program. We excluded the header block to economize space.

```cpp
//   WinHello.cpp

#include <windows.h>
#include "resource.h"            // Load resource file

// Storage for program instance
HINSTANCE     pInstance;

// Predeclaration of the Window Procedure
LRESULT CALLBACK WndProc (HWND, UINT, WPARAM, LPARAM) ;

//****************************
//          WinMain
//****************************
int WINAPI WinMain (HINSTANCE hInstance, HINSTANCE
hPrevInstance,
                    PSTR szCmdLine, int iCmdShow)
{
    static char szClassName[] = "MainClass" ; // Class name
    HWND          hwnd ;
    MSG           msg ;

    // Defining a structure of type WNDCLASSEX
    //   The program icon is loaded in the hIcon and hIconSm
    //     structure members
    WNDCLASSEX  wndclass ;
    wndclass.cbSize         = sizeof (wndclass) ;
    wndclass.style          = CS_HREDRAW | CS_VREDRAW ;
    wndclass.lpfnWndProc    = WndProc ;
    wndclass.cbClsExtra     = 0 ;
    wndclass.cbWndExtra     = 0 ;
    wndclass.hInstance      = hInstance ;
    wndclass.hIcon          = LoadImage(hInstance,
                              MAKEINTRESOURCE(IDI_ICON1),
                              IMAGE_ICON,        // Type
                              32, 32,            // Pixel size
                              LR_DEFAULTCOLOR) ;
    wndclass.hCursor        = LoadCursor (NULL, IDC_ARROW) ;
    wndclass.hbrBackground  = (HBRUSH) GetStockObject
                              (WHITE_BRUSH) ;
    wndclass.lpszMenuName   = NULL ;
    wndclass.lpszClassName  = szClassName ;
    wndclass.hIconSm        = LoadImage(hInstance,
                              MAKEINTRESOURCE(IDI_ICON1),
                              IMAGE_ICON,        // Type
                              16, 16,            // Pixel size
                              LR_DEFAULTCOLOR) ;
```

```
        // Store program instance
        pInstance = hInstance;

        // Registering the structure wmdclass
        RegisterClassEx (&wndclass) ;

        // CreateWindow()
        hwnd = CreateWindowEx (
            WS_EX_LEFT,                 // Left aligned (default)
            szClassName,                // pointer to class name
              "WinHello Program",        // window caption
              WS_OVERLAPPEDWINDOW,       // window style
              CW_USEDEFAULT,             // initial x position
              CW_USEDEFAULT,             // initial y position
              CW_USEDEFAULT,             // initial x size
              CW_USEDEFAULT,             // initial y size
              NULL,                      // parent window handle
              NULL,                      // window menu handle
              hInstance,                 // program instance handle
              NULL) ;                    // creation parameters

        ShowWindow (hwnd, iCmdShow) ;
        UpdateWindow (hwnd) ;

        // Message loop
        while (GetMessage (&msg, NULL, 0, 0))
            {
            TranslateMessage (&msg) ;
            DispatchMessage (&msg) ;
            }
        return msg.wParam ;
}
//****************************
//    Window Procedure
//****************************
LRESULT CALLBACK WndProc (HWND hwnd, UINT iMsg, WPARAM wParam,
LPARAM lParam)
{
    HDC        hdc ;
    PAINTSTRUCT ps ;
    RECT        rect ;

    switch (iMsg)
        {
    // Windows message processing
     case WM_CREATE:
             return 0;

        case WM_PAINT :
             hdc = BeginPaint (hwnd, &ps) ;
             GetClientRect (hwnd, &rect) ;
```

```
// Display message in the client area
DrawText (hdc,
    "Hello World from Windows",
    -1,
    &rect,
    T_SINGLELINE | DT_CENTER | DT_VCENTER);

EndPaint (hwnd, &ps) ;
return 0 ;

// End of program execution
case WM_DESTROY :
    PostQuitMessage (0) ;
    return 0 ;
    }
return DefWindowProc (hwnd, iMsg, wParam, lParam) ;
}
```

Summary

In this chapter we concluded our review of API programming in Windows. At this point we established the programming environment for the chapters that follow and showed you our program development methodology. In addition, you gained some familiarity with the Developer Studio environment so that you are able to create a simple project using the program templates furnished in the book's CD-ROM. The chapter includes two walkthroughs: in the first one you created a do-nothing program by simply inserting the template file into a project. In the second walkthrough you edited the template file to create an actual Windows program, with its own icons, and which displays a message on its client area.

Here we conclude Part I of the book, devoted to the fundamentals, and now proceed with DirectDraw programming. DirectDraw is the rendering engine of Direct3D; therefore it is a core subject in our context.

✦　　✦　　✦

DirectDraw

◆ ◆ ◆ ◆

◆ ◆ ◆ ◆

DirectDraw Fundamentals

With this chapter we begin our discussion on DirectDraw. DirectDraw is one of the components of Microsoft's DirectX Software Development Kit, version 7, usually called the DirectX 7 SDK. It provides graphics programmers with direct access to video memory and to special hardware features in the video card. This results in better performance and a higher level of control. The disadvantage is that direct access to the video memory and hardware complicates programming and creates portability and device dependency problems.

Game Development on the PC

Computer games, and other high-performance graphics programs, require interactive graphics, animation, and realistic object rendering: all of these features rapidly consume CPU cycles and video resources. In their effort to achieve maximum quality for their products, game programmers are constantly pressing the boundaries of machine performance.

PC game development started in DOS. In this environment, applications can use any operation code or operand in the instruction set. In this case the running application is the "god of the machine." But this power can be dangerous. A DOS program can accidentally (or intentionally) destroy files and resources that are not its own, including the operating system itself. As the PC gradually evolved into a serious business machine, the possibility that an application could destroy code, erase data belonging to other programs, and even create havoc with the operating system became intolerable. How would anyone trust its valuable business information and processing to such an unsafe environment?

The problem had to be addressed both in hardware and software. An operating system capable of providing a safe and reliable environment requires hardware that supports this protection. Intel started on this route with the 286 microprocessor, which came equipped with hardware features that allow the operating system to detect and prevent access to restricted memory areas and to disallow instructions that are considered dangerous to the integrity of other programs or to the environment's stability. The features were enhanced in the 386 and the various versions of the Pentium. In the mid 1980s Microsoft and others started developing operating systems that would take advantage of the CPU features recently introduced. The results were several protected-mode operating systems, of which Windows has been the only survivor.

Although safer and more reliable, Microsoft Windows imposed many restrictions on applications. One result of this situation was that games, and other high-performance graphics applications, could no longer access the hardware resources directly in order to maximize performance and expand functionalities. For several years game programmers continued to exercise the craft in DOS, and Windows users had to switch to the DOS mode to run games, simulations, and other graphics programs. The resulting situation implied a major contradiction: a graphical operating system in which graphics applications would execute with marginal performance.

Microsoft decided to remedy the situation by providing programmers with limited access to hardware and system resources. The goal was to allow applications sufficient control of video hardware and other resources so as to improve performance and control, and to do it in a way that would not compromise system stability. The first effort in this direction was a product named WinG, in reference to *Windows for Games*. WinG was first made available in 1994 and it required Win32 in Windows 3.1. Its main feature is that WinG enabled the game programmer to rapidly transfer bitmaps from system memory into video memory. This made possible the creation of Windows games that executed with much better performance. Because of the success of WinG, Microsoft developed a more elaborate product called the *Game Software Development Kit*, or Game SDK.

DirectX

The Microsoft Game SDK made evident that the usefulness of direct access to video memory and hardware was not limited to games. Many multimedia applications, and other graphics programs that required high performance, could benefit from these enhanced facilities. In response, Microsoft renamed the new version of the Game SDK, calling it DirectX 2. Other versions later released were named DirectX 3, DirectX 5, DirectX 6, and currently, DirectX 7. Note that no DirectX 4 version exists. DirectX version 7 SDK, released in 1999, is discussed in this book.

The functionality of the DirectX SDKs is available to applications running in Windows 95/98 and Windows NT 3.1 and later. In fact, the full functionality of DirectX 7 SDK is incorporated into Windows 98 and will also be found in Windows NT 5.0 and Windows 2000. This means that applications running under Windows 98 and later will be able to execute programs that use DirectX without loading additional drivers or other support software. In addition, Microsoft provides a setup utility that enables you to upgrade a compatible machine to a new version of DirectX.

Installing the SDK

Several versions of the DirectX SDK are available for download, at no cost, on the Microsoft Web sites. DirectX has grown in size during its evolution. The current version takes up approximately 360MB, which requires several hours online, even with the fastest commercial modems. For this reason we have included the DirectX 7 SDK in the book's CD-ROM. DirectX SDK CD-ROMs can also be ordered from Microsoft.

DirectX 7 contains an installation utility that loads and sets up the software on the target system. Microsoft recommends that you uninstall any previous versions of the SDK before the setup program is executed; however, only the most recent versions of the SDK are equipped with uninstall utilities. The SDK installs to a default folder c:\mssdk. Certain uncommon features of the SDK directory structure are designed for compatibility with Microsoft Developers Network (MSDN) Platform SDK, which duplicates most of DirectX 7.

Compiler support

DirectX 7 is compatible with Microsoft Visual C++ version 4.2 and later as well as with Watcom 11.0 and Borland C Builder 3 and 4. Visual C++ project files (.mdp) are included in the demonstration programs contained in the package. Microsoft states in the SDK documentation that some of the sample programs are not compatible with Borland or Watcom.

Testing the installation

The folder mssdk\bin\DXUtils of the installed DirectX 7 SDK contains several programs that can be used for testing DirectX in the host system. The most useful one, named dxdiag, allows testing the DirectDraw, Direct3D, and DirectSound components of the SDK. The tests also provide a brief demonstration of the capabilities of each of these components. Figure 7-1 shows the Display test tab of the DirectX diagnostics program.

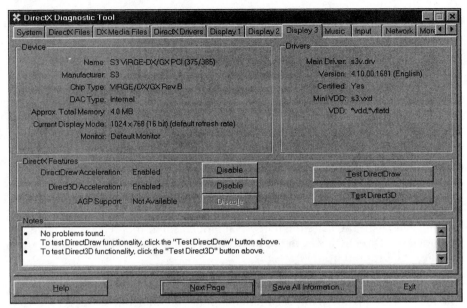

Figure 7-1: Display test function of the DirectX diagnostics program

When the Test button associated with the DirectDraw function is clicked, the program executes several tests to determine compatibility. A series of tests related to the Direct3D function activate when the corresponding test button is selected. In the Still Stuck? tab the program provides several troubleshooting options. Figure 7-2 shows the initial display of the troubleshooting screen.

DirectX components

The DirectX SDK includes the following components:

✦ *DirectDraw* provides hardware acceleration and direct access to video memory. This component accelerates the performance of bit block transfers (bitblts) and buffer flipping. The features are particularly useful in animation techniques because they considerably improve the graphics performance.

✦ *DirectSound* provides hardware and software sound mixing and playback.

✦ *DirectMusic* works with message-based musical data. It supports the Musical Instrument Digital Interface (MIDI) and provides authoring tools for creating interactive music.

✦ *DirectPlay* makes possible the connecting of applications over a modem link or a network.

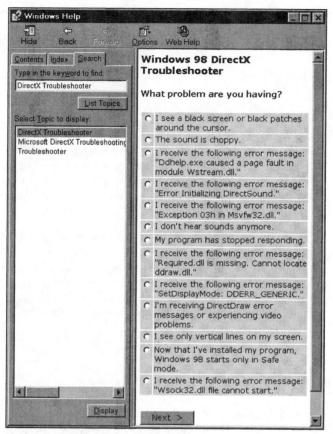

Figure 7-2: Troubleshooting screen of the DirectX diagnostics program

✦ *Direct3D* is a 3D graphics package that provides a high-level interface that enables you to implement a 3D graphical system. It also contains a low-level interface that lets applications take complete control of the rendering pipeline.

✦ *DirectInput* provides support for input devices including joystick, mouse, keyboard, and game controllers. It also provides support for feedback game devices.

✦ *DirectSetup* provides a simple installation procedure for DirectX. It simplifies the updating of display and audio drivers and makes sure that there are no software or hardware conflicts.

✦ *AutoPlay* enables you to create a CD-ROM disc that installs automatically after it is inserted in the drive. AutoPlay is not unique to DirectX since it is part of the Microsoft Win32 API.

The SDK also includes several sample programs with the corresponding source code.

In this section we mainly discuss the DirectDraw component of the DirectX SDK.

DirectX and COM

Microsoft's *Component Object Model* (COM) is a foundation for an object-oriented system that attempts to improve on the C++ model. COM is also an object model at the operating system level, which supports and promotes the reuse of interfaces. DirectDraw is presented to the programmer using the Component Object Model. The COM object is defined as a data structure that contains a pointer to the associated functions. One of the advantages of the COM is that it does not require C++. Programs written in C, or even in a non-C development system, can use APIs based on the COM protocol.

The DirectX Programmer has several ways of accessing the COM interface. From C++, the COM object appears like an abstract class. In this case access is by means of the pointer to the DirectDraw COM object. However, when using straight C, the function must pass the pointer to the COM object as an additional parameter. In addition, the call must include a pointer to a property of the COM object called the `vtable`. Because this book assumes C++ programming, we use the simpler interface to the COM.

Introduction to DirectDraw

DirectDraw is usually considered the most basic and useful component of DirectX. It enables an application to access display memory as well as some of the hardware functions in the video card. The result is that a Windows program can obtain a high level of graphics performance without sacrificing device independence and while maintaining compatibility with the Graphics Device Interface (GDI). DirectDraw is implemented as a software interface to the card's video memory and graphics functions. Although its original intention was merely to facilitate game development under Windows, many other types of graphics applications can benefit from the higher degree of control and the performance gains that it provides.

In this sense DirectDraw can be described as a display memory manager, which also furnishes access to some hardware acceleration features and other graphics facilities that may be available on the video card. Most current video cards used in the PC support DirectDraw, but some do so to a limited extent. Furthermore, there is no uniform set of acceleration features and graphics functions that all DirectDraw devices must provide. For these reasons, the decision to use DirectDraw also entails the burden of accommodating varying degrees of DirectDraw functionalities. DirectDraw provides services that enable applications to query the capabilities of a particular video card as well as the level of hardware support. Most features not supported by the hardware are emulated in software by DirectX, but at a substantial performance penalty.

A DirectDraw system implements its functionality both in hardware and in software emulation, each one with its own capabilities. Applications can query DirectDraw to retrieve the hardware and software capabilities of the specific implementation in the installed video card. DirectDraw is furnished as a 32-bit dynamic link library named DDRAW.DLL.

DirectDraw features

The following are the most important features of DirectDraw:

✦ Direct access to video memory

✦ Manipulation of multiple display surfaces

✦ Page flipping

✦ Back buffering

✦ Clipping

✦ Palette management

✦ Video system support level information

Advantages and drawbacks

The possible advantages of using DirectDraw are:

1. It provides direct access to video memory, thus increasing performance and allowing the graphics programmer a higher degree of control. This feature also makes it easier to port some DOS graphics programs and routines into the Windows environment.

2. It improves application performance by making use of video hardware capabilities. For example, if the video card supports hardware blits, DirectDraw uses this feature. DirectDraw also provides a hardware emulation layer (HEL) to simulate features that are not supported by the hardware.

3. DirectDraw uses 32-bit flat memory addressing of video memory. This model is much easier to handle by code than one that is based on the Intel segmented architecture.

4. In full screen, exclusive mode applications, DirectDraw supports page flipping with multiple back buffers. This technique enables you to implement animation effects that were previously unsatisfactory. In windowed programs DirectDraw supports clipping, hardware-assisted overlays, image stretching, and other graphics manipulations.

The major disadvantages are:

1. Programming in DirectDraw is more complicated and difficult than using the Windows GDI. Programs that do not need the additional performance or control provided by DirectDraw might find little additional justification for using it.

2. The graphics functions emulated by DirectDraw are often slower than those in the GDI.

3. Applications that rely on DirectDraw are less portable than those that do not.

Architecture

The architecture of DirectDraw is defined by its interface, its object composition, the hardware abstraction layer (HAL), and the hardware emulation layer (HEL).

Interface

DirectDraw provides services through COM-based interfaces. The various versions of this interface are named IDirectDraw, IDirectDraw2, and IDirectDraw4. Note that IDirectDraw3 does not exist, although it is erroneously mentioned in some Microsoft documents. These interfaces to DirectDraw correspond to different releases of the Game SDK and of DirectX.

Programs can gain access to DirectDraw by means of the DirectDrawCreate() function or by the CoCreateInstance() COM function. In this book we use DirectDrawCreate(), which is the easier and more common one. Later in this chapter we discuss how a program can query which of the three DirectDraw interfaces is available at run time.

Object composition

DirectX APIs are sometimes implemented as instances of COM objects. Communication with these objects is by means of methods; for example, if IDirectDraw4 is the interface, the method SetDisplayMode is accessed through the interface as follows:

```
IDirectDraw4::SetDisplayMode
```

COM interfaces are derived from a base class called IUnknown. The following DirectDraw object types are currently defined: DirectDraw, DirectDrawSurface, DirectDrawPalette, DirectDrawClipper, and DirectDrawVideoPort. Figure 7-3 shows the object composition of the IDirectDraw interface.

The DirectDraw objects are described as follows:

✦ DirectDraw is the basic object of all applications. It is considered to represent the display adapter card. The corresponding COM object is named IDirectDraw. This is the first object created by a program, and it relates to all other DirectDraw objects. A call to DirectDrawCreate() creates a DirectDraw object. If the call is successful, it returns a pointer to either IDirectDraw, IDirectDraw2, or IDirectDraw4 interfaces.

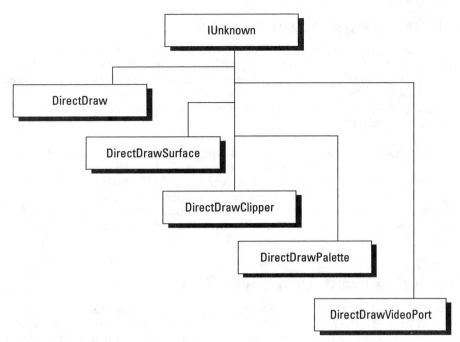

Figure 7-3: IDirectDraw object types

✦ `DirectDrawSurface` object, sometimes called a surface, represents an area in memory. The COM object name is `IDirectDrawSurface`. This object holds the image data to be displayed, or images to be moved to other surfaces. Applications usually create a surface by calling the `IDirectDraw::CreateSurface` method of the DirectDraw object.

✦ `DirectDrawPalette` object, sometimes referred to as a palette, represents a 16- or 256-color indexed palette. The palette object simplifies palette manipulations. It contains a series of indexed RGB triplets that describe colors associated with values within a surface. Palettes are limited to surfaces that use a pixel format of 8 bits or less. Palette objects are usually associated with corresponding surface objects, whose color attributes the palette object defines.

✦ `DirectDrawClipper` object, sometimes referred to as a clipper, serves to prevent applications from drawing outside a predefined area. Clipper objects are usually convenient when a DirectDraw application is displayed in a window. In this case the clipper object prevents the application from drawing outside of its client area.

✦ `DirectDrawVideoPort` object, which was introduced in DirectX 5, represents the video-port hardware present in some systems. It allows direct access to the frame buffer without intervention of the CPU or the PCI bus.

Hardware Abstraction Layer (HAL)

DirectDraw ensures device independence by implementing a *Hardware Abstraction Layer*, or HAL. The HAL is provided by the video card manufacturer, board manufacturer, or OEM, according to Microsoft's DirectDraw specifications. However, applications have no direct access to the HAL, but to the interfaces exposed by DirectDraw. It is this indirect access mechanism that ensures HAL consistency and reliability.

In Windows 95/98, device manufacturers implement the HAL in both 16-bit and 32-bit code. In Windows NT the HAL is always in 32-bit code. It can be furnished as part of the card's display driver or as a separate DLL. The HAL contains device-dependent code. It performs no emulation and provides no programmer-accessible services. The only point of contact between an application and the HAL is when the application needs to query DirectDraw to find out what capabilities are directly supported.

Hardware Emulation Layer (HEL)

DirectDraw emulates in software those basic features that are not supported through the HAL. The *Hardware Emulation Layer* (HEL) is the part of DirectDraw that provides this functionality. Applications do not access the HEL directly. Whether a given functionality is provided through hardware features, or through emulation, is transparent to an application using DirectDraw. Code must specifically query DirectDraw to determine the origin of a given functionality. The GetCaps() function, discussed later in this chapter, furnishes this information.

Unfortunately, some combinations of hardware-supported and emulated functions may lead to slower performance than pure emulation. DirectDraw documentation cites an example in which a display device driver supports DirectDraw but not stretch blitting. When the stretch blit function is emulated in video memory, a noticeable performance loss occurs. The reason is that video memory is often slower than system memory; therefore, the CPU is forced to wait when accessing video memory surfaces. Such cases make evident one of the greatest drawbacks of DirectDraw, which is that applications must provide alternate processing for hardware dependencies.

Relations with Windows

Several Windows graphics components lie between the application code and the video card hardware. Figure 7-4 shows the relations between the various Windows graphics components.

The right-hand side of Figure 7-4 shows that an application can access the Windows video functions through the GDI, which, in turn, uses the Display Device Interface (DDI). On the left-hand side you can see that, alternatively, an application can access the video functions through DirectDraw. DirectDraw, in turn, uses the Hardware Abstraction Layer and the Hardware Emulation Layer to provide the necessary functionality. The horizontal arrow connecting the HAL and the DDI indicates that applications that use DirectDraw can also use the GDI functions because both channels of video card access are open simultaneously.

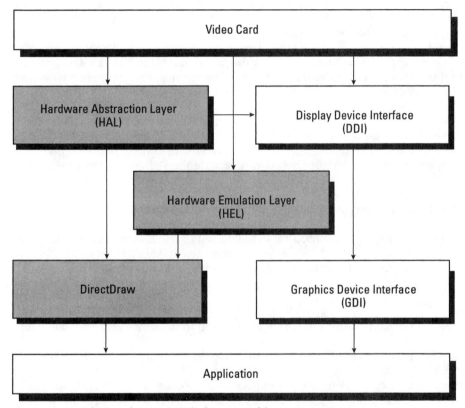

Figure 7-4: Relations between Windows graphics components

DirectDraw Fundamentals

There are several core topics that relate specifically to DirectDraw. Understanding these fundamental concepts is a prerequisite to successful DirectDraw programming. Following are the core topics of DirectDraw:

✦ Cooperative levels

✦ Display modes

✦ Surfaces

✦ Palettes

✦ Clippers

Cooperative levels

The notion of cooperative levels refers to the relation between DirectDraw and other Windows applications. A DirectDraw program can execute full-screen, with exclusive access to the display resources, or it can execute in a window and share the video resources with other running programs. In this last case the DirectDraw application and the other Windows programs executing concurrently must cooperate in their use of the video resources. When a DirectDraw application requests and obtains total control of the video functions it is said to execute in exclusive mode. DirectDraw applications that do not execute in exclusive mode are usually referred to as windowed DirectDraw programs.

The SetCooperativeLevel() function is used by an application to set cooperative levels. The predefined constants DDSCL_FULLSCREEN and DDSCL_EXCLUSIVE enable the application to execute full-screen and to ensure control of the display mode and the palette. In this case the DirectDraw program has almost exclusive control of the video resources. The use of this function is described later in this chapter.

DirectDraw cooperative levels have the following additional features:

✦ You can enable a DirectDraw application to use a nonstandard VGA resolution known as Mode X. Mode X, which executes in 320 × 240 pixels in 256 colors, was a very popular mode with DOS game programmers.

✦ You can prevent DirectDraw applications that execute in exclusive mode from responding to CTRL + ALT + DEL keystrokes.

✦ You can enable a DirectDraw application to minimize or maximize itself.

Microsoft considers the normal cooperative level the one in which the DirectDraw application cooperates as a windowed program. However, the DirectDraw applications that execute in windowed mode are not capable of changing the display mode or of performing page flipping. Display mode control and page flipping are essential to many high-performance graphics programs, especially those that use animation. Therefore, many high-performance DirectDraw programs execute in exclusive mode.

Display modes

Display modes were introduced with the first video system used in the PC. The Video Graphics Array (VGA) video system, released in 1987, supports 18 display modes. A display mode, which enables a particular resolution and color depth, is a hardware configuration of the video system internal registers. For this reason, display modes are described by their pixel width, height, and bit-depth. For example, VGA mode 18H has a resolution of 640 by 480 by 4. This means that it displays 640 pixel columns and 480 pixel rows in 16 colors. The last digit of the mode specification is the number of bits used in the pixel color encoding. In VGA mode 18H the color range is 16, which is the maximum number of combinations of the 4 binary digits devoted to the color encoding.

PC display modes are often classified as palettized and nonpalettized. In palettized display modes each color value is an index into an associated color table, called the *palette*. The bit depth of the display mode determines the number of colors in the palette. For example, in a 4-bit palettized display mode, such as VGA mode 18H, each pixel attribute is a value from 0 to 15, which makes possible a palette with 16 entries. The actual colors displayed depend on the palette settings. The programmer can select and change the palette colors at any time, thus selecting a subrange of displayed colors. However, when the palette is changed, all displayed objects are shown with the new settings.

Nonpalettized display modes, on the other hand, encode pixel colors directly. In this case the bit depth represents the total number of color attributes that can be assigned to each pixel. In nonpalettized modes there is no look-up table to define the color attributes.

The higher the resolution and the color depth of a display mode, the more video memory is required in the adapter. Because not all video adapters contain the same amount of memory, not all of them support the same video modes. The DirectDraw `EnumDisplayModes()` function is used to list all the display modes supported by a device, or to confirm if a particular display mode is available in the video card.

Applications using DirectDraw can call the `SetDisplayMode()` function. The parameters passed to the call describe the dimensions, bit depth, and refresh rate of the mode to be set. A fifth parameter indicates special options for the given mode. Currently, this parameter is used only to differentiate between Mode 13H, with 320 by 200 resolution and 16 colors, and VGA Mode X, also with 320 by 200 resolution but in 256 colors. Although an application can request a specific display mode resolution and bit depth, it cannot specify how the pixel depth is achieved by the hardware. After a mode is set, the application can call the `GetDisplayMode()` function to determine if the mode is palettized and to examine the pixel format. In other words, DirectDraw reserves the right to implement a particular color depth in a palettized or nonpalettized mode.

DirectDraw programs that do not execute in exclusive mode allow other applications to change the video mode. However, an application can change the bit depth of the display mode only if it has exclusive access to the DirectDraw object. DirectDraw applications that execute in exclusive mode allow other applications to allocate `DirectDrawSurface` objects, and to use DirectDraw and GDI services. However, only applications that execute at the exclusive cooperative level can change the display mode or manipulate the palette.

A DirectDraw application can explicitly restore the display hardware to its original mode by calling the `RestoreDisplayMode()`. Since the DirectDraw2 interface, a DirectDraw exclusive mode application that sets the display mode by calling `SetDisplayMode()` can restore the original display mode automatically by calling `RestoreDisplayMode()`.

DirectDraw supports all screen resolutions and pixel depths that are available in the card's device driver. Thus, a DirectDraw application can change to any mode supported by the display driver, including all 24- and 32-bit True-color modes.

Surfaces

A DirectDraw surface is a linear memory area used to hold image data. A DirectDrawSurface object is a COM object derived from IUnknown, as shown in Figure 7-3. Surfaces can reside in display memory, which is located in the video card, or in system memory. Applications create a DirectDraw surface by calling the CreateSurface() function. The call can create a single surface object, a complex surface-flipping chain, or a three-dimensional surface. The IDirectDrawSurface interface allows an application to indirectly access memory through blit functions, such as Blt() and BltFast(). In addition, a surface provides a device context to the display, which can be used with GDI functions.

IDirectDrawSurface surface functions can be used to access display memory directly. The Lock() function retrieves the address of an area of display memory and ensures exclusive access to this area. This operation is said to lock the surface. A primary surface is one in which the display memory area is mapped to the video display. Alternatively, a surface can refer to a nondisplayed area. In this case the surface is called an off-screen or overlay surface. Nonvisible buffers usually reside in display memory, but they can be created in system memory if DirectDraw is performing a hardware emulation, or if it is otherwise necessary because of hardware limitations. Surface objects that use a pixel depth of 8 bits or less are assigned a palette that defines the color attributes in the encoding. Figure 7-5 shows the surface-based layout of video memory.

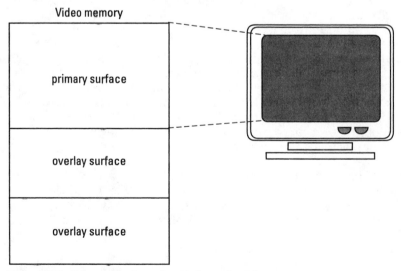

Figure 7-5: Primary and overlay surfaces in video memory

When a DirectDraw application receives a pointer to video memory it can use this pointer to draw on the screen, with considerable gain in control and performance. However, a program that accesses video memory directly must concern itself with many video system layout details that are transparent at a higher programming level. The first complicating factor is that video buffer mapping may be different in two modes with the same resolution but different color depths. The reason for this variation is related to the fact that the video buffer is actually storage for pixel attributes. If an attribute is encoded in 8 bits, then the buffer requires one byte per pixel. However, if a pixel attribute is stored in 24 bits, then the buffer requires 3 bytes per pixel.

Figure 7-6 shows two video modes with different pixel depths. In the 8 bits per pixel mode the fourth memory byte is mapped to the fourth screen pixel. However, in the 24 bits per pixel mode, the thirteenth to the fifteenth video memory bytes are mapped to the fourth pixel. The calculations required to obtain the offset in video memory for a particular screen pixel will be different in each case.

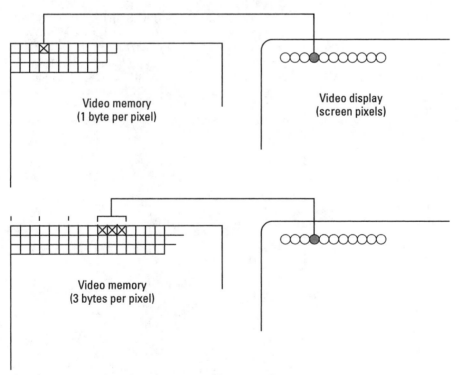

Figure 7-6: Variations in memory-to-video mapping

There is another complication in direct access programming: in some display modes the number of bytes in each video buffer row is not the product of the number of pixels on each video display row by the number of bytes per pixel.

The reason is related usually to video system design and performance considerations, which make it necessary to allocate a number of bytes in each buffer row that is a multiple of some specific number. This determines that some display modes have data areas in each row that are not mapped to screen pixels. For example, a display mode with a resolution of 640 pixels per row and a color depth of 24 bits per pixel requires 1920 bytes to store the data corresponding to a single row of screen pixels. However, the video card designers may have assigned 2560 bytes of video buffer space for each screen row, so that the same buffer size can be used in a 32-bits-per-pixel mapping. The result is that in the 24-bit mode there is an area of 640 unmapped bytes at the end of each row. The term *pitch* is used to describe the actual byte length of each row in the video buffer, while the term *width* refers to the number of pixels in each screen row.

Palettes

A palette is a color look-up table. It provides a convenient way of indirectly mapping pixel attributes, which results in extending the number of displayable colors in modes with limited color depths. For example, a display mode with a 4-bits-per-pixel color depth represents 16 different color attributes. When a palette is associated with the display surface, each video buffer value serves as an index into the palette, which in turn defines the pixel color. By changing the palette, the application can map many 16-color sets to the display attributes. By means of the palette scheme the number of simultaneously displayable colors remains the same, but the actual colors mapped to the video buffer values can be changed by the application. Figure 7-7 shows how a palette provides an indirect mapping for the color attributes stored in the video buffer.

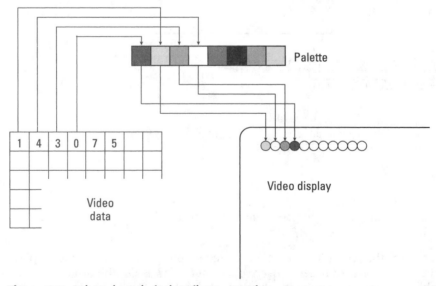

Figure 7-7: Palette-based pixel attribute mapping

In DirectDraw palettes are linked to surfaces. Surfaces that use a 16-bit or greater pixel format do not use palettes. Therefore, the so-called real color modes (16 bits per pixel) and True-color modes (24 and 32 bits per pixel) are nonpalettized. A DirectDraw palette can have 2, 4, 16, or 256 entries. A palette can only be attached to a surface with the same color depth. In addition, it is possible to create palettes that do not contain a color table. In these so-called index palettes, the palette values serve as an index into another palette's color table.

Each palette entry is in the form of an RGB triplet that describes the color to be used when displaying pixel values at the corresponding entry. The RGB values in the color table can be in 16- or 24-bit format. In 16-bit RGB format each palette entry is encoded in 5-6-5 form. The first 5 pixels are mapped to the red attribute, the second 6 pixels to the green attribute, and the last 5 pixels to the blue attribute. This is the same mapping scheme used in the real color modes. In the 24-bit RGB palette format each of the primary colors (red, green, and blue) is mapped to 8 pixels, as is the case in the True-color modes.

An application creates a palette by calling the DirectDraw `CreatePalette()` function. At call time the application defines if the palette contains 2, 4, 16, or 256 entries and provides a pointer to a color table used in initializing the palette. If the call is successful, DirectDraw returns the address of the newly created `DirectDrawPalette` object. This palette object can then be used to attach the palette to a DirectDraw surface. The same palette can be attached to multiple surfaces. After a palette is attached to a surface, an application can call the `GetPalette()` and `SetPalette()` functions to query or change the palette entries.

A type of animation is based on changing the appearance of a surface object by modifying the palette attached to the surface that contains it. By repeatedly changing the palette, the surface object can be made to appear differently without actually modifying the contents of video memory. Two different types of palette manipulations can be used for this. The first method is based on modifying the values in a single palette. The second method is based on switching between several palettes. Because palette modifications are not hardware intensive, either method often produces satisfactory results.

The development and use of palettes were a direct consequence of the memory limitations of the original video systems used in the PC. In VGA the video space was limited to a few hundred kilobytes, whereas the low-end PCs of today are furnished with video cards that have 2 or 4 MB of space on board video memory. This abundance of video memory makes palette modes almost obsolete. Perhaps the one remaining justification for palettized modes relates to some interesting animation effects that can be achieved by performing palette manipulations. For example, you can make an object disappear from the screen by changing to a palette in which the object attributes are the same as the background. Then you can make the object reappear by restoring the original palette.

Clipping

DirectDraw *clipping* is a manipulation by which video output is limited to one or more rectangular-shaped regions. DirectDraw supports clipping in applications that execute in exclusive mode and windowed. The term, clippers, is often used to refer to `DirectDrawClipper` objects. A single bounding rectangle is sometimes used to limit the display to the application's client area. Several associated bounding rectangles are called a *clip list*.

The most common use for a clipper is to define the boundaries of the screen or of a rectangular window. A DirectDraw clipper can be used to define the screen area of an application so as to ensure that a bitmap is progressively displayed as it moves into this area. If a clipping area is not defined, then the blit fails because the destination drawing surface is outside the display limits. However, when the boundaries of the video display area are defined by means of a clipper, DirectDraw knows not to display outside this area and the blit succeeds. Blitting a bitmap to unclipped and clipped display areas is shown in Figure 7-8.

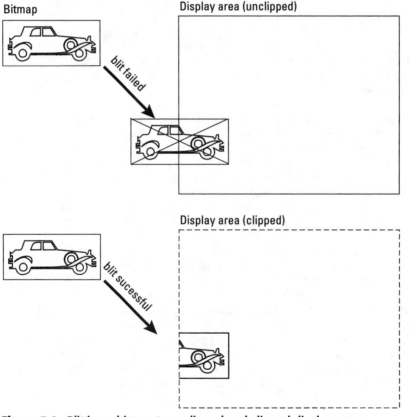

Figure 7-8: Blitting a bitmap to unclipped and clipped display areas

In Figure 7-8 we see that clipping makes it possible to display a bitmap that does not entirely fit in the display area. Without clipping, the blit operation fails if the source bitmap doesn't fit in the destination area, as shown in the top part of the illustration. With clipping it is possible to display the bitmap of the automobile as it progressively enters the screen area, instead of making it pop onto the screen all at once. All that is required to implement clipping in DirectDraw is to create a clipper with the screen rectangle as its clip list. Trimming of the bitmap is performed automatically. Clipper objects are also used to designate areas within a destination surface. The designated areas are tagged as writable, while DirectDraw automatically crops images that fall outside this area. Figure 7-9 shows a display area with a clipper defined by two rectangles. When the text bitmap is blitted onto the screen, only those parts that fall inside the clipper are displayed. The pixel data is preserved in the screen areas not included in the clipper. In this case the clip list consists of the two rectangles for which output is validated.

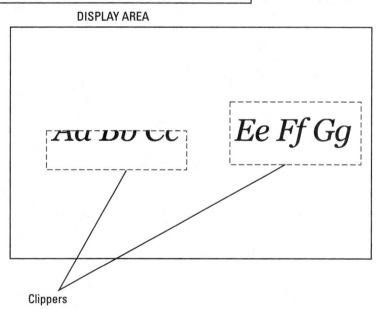

Figure 7-9: A clipper consisting of two rectangular areas

Summary

In this chapter you learned the essential elements of DirectDraw. The discussion included topics related to computer games, Windows programming using the DirectX 7 SDK, as well as an overview of DirectDraw features, architecture, and basic concepts. Now that you are acquainted with DirectDraw, we can proceed with DirectDraw installation and setup operations, which are the topics discussed in Chapter 8.

✦   ✦   ✦

DirectDraw Configuration and Setup

◆ ◆ ◆ ◆

In This Chapter

Setting up Developer Studio to access DirectDraw

Creating the DirectDraw object

Determining the interface version

Setting the level of interaction with concurrent applications

Obtaining the hardware capabilities

Setting the DirectDraw display mode

◆ ◆ ◆ ◆

Before an application can use DirectDraw it must initialize the software and perform a series of configuration tests to determine how the program cooperates with concurrent Windows programs. In this chapter we describe the initialization and setup operations and develop the code that serves as a backbone for a DirectDraw program.

DirectDraw Setup

Before you can develop a DirectDraw program you must first set up your development system so that it can access the DirectDraw software. The first step is to include the DirectDraw header file, named ddraw.h. The file is furnished with the DirectX package and also with the newer versions of the Windows operating system.

DirectDraw header file

As a system is updated with newer versions of the DirectX SDK, and perhaps with operating system patches and new releases, it is possible to find several versions of the ddraw.h file on the same machine. The developer needs to make sure that the software is using the most recent release of the header file. One way to accomplish this is to search for all files named ddraw.h by means of the file-finding feature of Windows Explorer, or of a similar utility. After the files are located, you can rename or delete the older versions of ddraw.h. In most cases the directory path, the date stamp, and the file size can serve to identify the most recent one. It is unwise to assume that the installation program for the operating system, the SDK, or the development environment, performs the necessary setup operations.

In addition, the newest version of the ddraw.h file must be located so that it is accessible to the development software. This may require moving or copying the newest version of ddraw.h to the corresponding include directory, as well as making certain that the path in the development environment corresponds with this directory. In Visual C++ the directories searched by the development system can be viewed by clicking Options in the Tools menu. In this case the Show directories for: scroll box should be set for include files. You may now enter the path to the DirectDraw include and library files in the edit box at the bottom of the Directories: window. Once entered, the boxes can be dragged to the top of the list so that these directories are searched first. If DirectX is installed in the default drive and path, then the results are as shown in Figure 8-1.

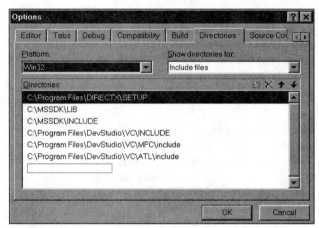

Figure 8-1: Directories tab in Developer Studio Options dialog box

DirectDraw libraries

The second software element necessary for DirectDraw programming is the ddraw.lib library file. What was said in relation to ddraw.h also applies to ddraw.lib: possible duplicated versions of the software must be identified and all but the most recent one eliminated. Here again, a search function can be used to find the duplicate files. After the most recent library file is identified, the older ones can be deleted or renamed. If after performing this step, the development system is still unable to locate the library files, then you must copy ddraw.lib to the corresponding include directory or modify the path, as previously explained for the ddraw.h file.

In addition to finding the newest version of the library, and installing it in the system's library path, Visual C++ users must also make sure that the development environment is set up to look for the DirectDraw libraries. To make sure of this you can inspect the dialog box that is displayed when Settings is selected in the Developer Studio Project menu. The ddraw.lib and dxguid.lib files must be listed in both the Object/library modules and the Project Options windows of the Link tab in the Project Settings dialog box, as shown in Figure 8-2. If not, you can manually insert the library names in the Object/library modules edit box. The library names are copied automatically to the Project Options box.

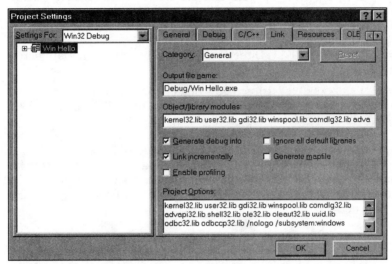

Figure 8-2: Link tab in Developer Studio Project Settings dialog box

The ddraw.lib file contains the DirectDraw functions, and the dxguid.lib file has the GUID identifiers required for accessing the various interface versions. When access to the DirectDraw header file and the libraries are in place, the development system is ready to use.

Creating the DirectDraw Object

In order to use DirectDraw, an application must first create a DirectDraw object. This object is actually a pointer to the DirectDraw interface as implemented in the video card. The pointer is required for accessing all other DirectDraw functions, which means that a DirectDraw application can do little else without this object.

The `DirectDrawCreate()` function creates an instance of the DirectDraw object. The function's general form is as follows:

```
HRESULT DirectDrawCreate (
            GUID FAR lpGUID,              // 1
            LPDIRECTDRAW FAR *lplpDD,     // 2
            IUnknown FAR *pUnkOutter,     // 3
            );
```

The first parameter is a globally unique identifier (GUID) that represents the driver to be created. If this parameter is NULL, then the call refers to the active display driver. The newer versions of DirectDraw allow passing one of two flags in this parameter. The flags control the behavior of the active display, as follows:

✦ `DDCREATE_EMULATIONONLY`: DirectDraw uses only emulation. Hardware support features cannot be used.

✦ `DDCREATE_HARDWAREONLY`: DirectDraw object does not use emulated features. If a hardware supported features is not available the call returns `DDERR_UNSUPPORTED`.

The second parameter is a pointer that the call initializes if it succeeds. This is the object returned by `DirectDrawCreate()`. The third parameter is provided for future compatibility with the COM interface. At present it should be set to NULL. The call returns `DD_OK` if it succeeds. If it fails, one of the following predefined constants is returned:

```
DDERR_DIRECTDRAWALREADYCREATED
```

```
DDERR_GENERIC
```

```
DDERR_INVALIDDIRECTDRAWGUID
```

```
DDERR_INVALIDPARAMS
```

```
DDERR_NODIRECTDRAWHW
```

```
DDERR_OUTOFMEMORY
```

On systems with multiple monitors, specifying NULL for the first parameter causes the DirectDraw object to run in emulation mode. In these systems the call must specify the device's GUID to use hardware acceleration.

Obtaining the interface version

The component object model (COM) requires that objects update their functionality by means of new interfaces that provide the new features, rather than by changing methods within existing interfaces. The objective is to keep existing interfaces static so that older applications continue to be compatible with the newer interfaces. DirectX, and therefore, DirectDraw, follow the COM object model.

Although the availability of various interfaces facilitates component updating, it also creates some coding complications. For example, currently the DirectDraw surface object supports three different interfaces, named IDirectDrawSurface, IDirectDrawSurface2, and IDirectDrawSurface4. Each version supports all the methods of its predecessor and adds new ones for the new features. For an application to use these new features it must query DirectDraw to determine which interface or interfaces are available in the host, then provide alternative processing routes for each case. The situation is further complicated by the fact that, at least in some instances, a new interface may not support methods provided in a previous one. The result is a return to device-dependent programming that Windows was designed to avoid in the first place. This is the price that must be paid for the power and functionality of direct hardware access.

Once the DirectDraw application has used the DirectDrawCreate() function to obtain a pointer to the DirectDraw object, COM provides a mechanism that enables you to find out whether the object supports other interfaces. The QueryInterface() method of IUnknown can be used for this purpose. If a particular interface is supported, the call returns a pointer to this interface. It is through this pointer that code gains access to the methods of the new interface. If the QueryInterface() function returns NULL, or an error, then the calling code must decide if it can use the previous interface, if it can provide some sort of work-around the missing functionalities, or if it must abort execution for lack of processing capabilities in the host machine. The processing usually consists of one or more tests and the contingency code required in each case.

The QueryInterface() has the following general form:

```
HRESULT QueryInterface(
                    REFIID riid,            // 1
                    LPVOID* obj,            // 2
                    );
```

The first parameter is a reference identifier for the object being queried. The calling code must know this unique identifier before the call is made. The second parameter is the address of a variable that will contain a pointer to the new interface if the call is successful. The return value is S_OK if the call succeeds, or one of the following error messages if it fails:

DDERR_INVALIDOBJECT

DDERR_INVALIDPARAMS

DDERR_OUTOFMEMORY

The DDERRR_OUTOFMEMORY error message is returned by IDirectDrawSurface2 and IDirectDrawSurface4 objects only. If after making the call, the application determines that it does not need to use the interface, it must call the Release() function to free it.

At this time there are three IDirectDraw interfaces implemented. The corresponding reference identifiers are IID_DirectDraw, IID_DirectDraw2, and IID_DirectDraw4. It is not recommended that an application mix methods from two or more interfaces because the results are sometimes unpredictable. Furthermore, it is virtually impossible to code a DirectDraw application of any substance that executes in more than one implementation. In the first place, the pointers returned by the various versions are often of formally different types. For example, IID_DirectDraw returns a pointer of type LPDIRECTDRAW, IID_DirectDraw2 returns a pointer of type LPDIRECTDRAW2, and IID_DirectDraw4 returns a pointer of type LPDIRECTDRAW4. The same is true of other objects and data structures, as well as the parameters to some calls. For instance, the SetDisplayMode() function takes three parameters in IID_DirectDraw and five parameters in IID_DirectDraw2 and IID_DirectDraw4.

Microsoft attempts to ensure the portability of applications that commit to a specific DirectX implementation by furnishing an installation utility that upgrades the host system to the newest components. In the DirectSetup element of DirectX there are the diagnostics and installation programs, as well as the drivers and library files, that serve to update a system to the corresponding version of the SDK. DirectSetup also includes a ready-to-use installation utility, which copies all the system components to the corresponding directories of the client's hard drive and performs the necessary modifications in the Windows registry. In the DirectX SDK Microsoft also provides all the required project files for a sample installation application named *dinstall*. The DirectX programmer can use the source code of the dinstall program as a base on which to create a customized installation utility for DirectX.

The following code fragment shows the necessary processing for obtaining the version of DirectX installed in the host system:

```
// Global variables for DirectDraw operations
HRESULT          DDConnect;
// Interfaces pointers
LPDIRECTDRAW     lpDD;
LPDIRECTDRAW2    lpDD2;
LPDIRECTDRAW4    lpDD4;
int dDLevel      = 0;        // Implementation level
//*************************
//    DirectDraw Init
//*************************
// Create a DirectDraw object
  DDConnect = DirectDrawCreate ( NULL,
              &lpDD,            // Pointer to object
              NULL);
// Querying the interface to determine most recent
// version
```

```
       if(DDConnect == DD_OK) {
          dDLevel = 1;                // Store level
       // Query the next interface level
          DDConnect = lpDD->QueryInterface(
                       IID_IDirectDraw2,
                       (LPVOID *) &lpDD2);
       }
       if(DDConnect == S_OK){
          dDLevel = 2;                // Update level
          lpDD->Release();            // Release old pointer
       // Query the next interface level
          DDConnect = lpDD2->QueryInterface(
                       IID_IDirectDraw4,
                       (LPVOID *) &lpDD4);
       }
       if(DDConnect == S_OK){
          dDLevel = 4;                // Update level
          lpDD2->Release();           // Release old pointer
          lpDD4->Release();           // and current one
       }
   // ASSERT:
   //   dDlevel holds the current interface levels (values are
   //   1, 2 or 4). If dDLevel == 0, then no DirectDraw interface
   //   was found.
   //   All pointers to interfaces have been released
```

Some of the examples in the DirectDraw literature use the return value from the DirectDrawCreate() or QueryInterface() calls to determine if a DirectDraw object is available. In the previous code fragment we use the dDlevel variable for this same purpose. If this variable is zero, then no DirectDraw object has been created and DirectDraw functions are unavailable. Notice in the code that as each new valid object is found, the preceding one is released by means of the Release() function. The reason is that the COM interface maintains a count of the number of objects created. IUnknown contains a function named AddRef() which increments the object's reference count by 1 when an interface or an application binds itself to an object. The Release() function then decrements the object's reference count by 1 when it is no longer needed. When the count reaches 0, the object is deallocated.

Normally, every function that returns a pointer to an interface calls AddRef() to increment the object reference count. By the same token, the application calls Release() to decrement the object reference count. When an object's reference count reaches 0, it is destroyed and all interfaces to it become invalid. In the previous sample code we need not call the AddRef() method because QueryInterface() implicitly calls AddRef() when a valid object is found. However, the code must still call Release() to decrement the reference object count and destroy the pointer to the interface.

Setting the cooperative level

A DirectDraw application can obtain almost exclusive control over the hardware resources that a normal Windows application must share. Control over the video system is necessary for implementing some types of interactive, animated games and other high-performance graphics programs. On the other hand, some DirectDraw programs may not need this special functionality and behave more like a normal Windows application. The SetCooperativeLevel() function is used to request a specific level of resource control which establishes the level of cooperation with other Windows programs.

The function SetCooperativeLevel() has slightly different implementations in the IDirectDraw, IDirectDraw2, and IDirectDraw4 interfaces. The basic decision that must be made at the time of calling SetCooperativeLevel() is whether the application is to run full-screen, with exclusive access to the display resources, or as a normal windowed program. In addition, DirectDraw cooperative levels enable the use of Mode X resolutions, prevent DirectDraw from releasing exclusive control of the display and from rebooting if the user presses Ctrl+Alt+Del, and enable DirectDraw to minimize or maximize the application in response to user events. Table 8-1 lists the predefined constants that are recognized by the SetCooperativeLevel() function.

Table 8-1
Cooperative Level Symbolic Constants

Flag	Description
DDSCL_ALLOWMODEX	Enables the use of Mode X display modes. This flag can only be used with the DDSCL_EXCLUSIVE and DDSCL_FULLSCREEN modes.
DDSCL_ALLOWREBOOT	Enables the Ctrl+Alt+Del keystroke to function while in exclusive mode.
DDSCL_CREATEDEVICEWINDOW	DirectDraw creates and manages a default device window for this DirectDraw object; supported by Windows 98 and NT 5.0 only.
DDSCL_EXCLUSIVE	Requests the exclusive level. This flag must be used with DDSCL_FULLSCREEN.
DDSCL_FPUSETUP	Indicates that the DirectDraw application will keep the math unit set up for single precision and exceptions disabled, which is the best setting for optimal Direct3D performance.

Flag	Description
DDSCL_FULLSCREEN	The exclusive-mode owner is responsible for the entire primary surface. GDI is ignored. This flag must be used with DDSCL_EXCLUSIVE.
DDSCL_MULTITHREADED	Requests multithread-safe DirectDraw behavior. This causes Direct3D to execute the global critical section more frequently.
DDSCL_NORMAL	Indicates a regular Windows application. Cannot be used with the DDSCL_ALLOWMODEX, DDSCL_EXCLUSIVE, or DDSCL_FULLSCREEN flags. Applications executing in this mode cannot perform page flipping or change the primary palette.
DDSCL_NOWINDOWCHANGES	DirectDraw is not allowed to minimize or restore the application window.
DDSCL_SETDEVICEWINDOW	The hWnd parameter is the window handle of the device window for this DirectDraw object. This flag cannot be used with the DDSCL_SETFOCUSWINDOW flag. Supported by Windows 98 and NT 5.0 only.
DDSCL_SETFOCUSWINDOW	The hWnd parameter is the window handle of the focus window for the DirectDraw object. Cannot be used with the DDSCL_SETDEVICEWINDOW flag. Supported by Windows 98 and NT 5.0 only.

The SetCooperativeLevel() function's general form is as follows:

```
HRESULT SetCooperativeLevel(
                    HWND hwnd,      // 1
                    DWORD  dword    // 2
                    );
```

The first parameter is the handle to the application window; however, if an application requests DDSCL_NORMAL in the second parameter, it can use NULL for the window handle. The second parameter is one or more of the flags defined by the symbolic constants listed in Table 8-1. The function returns DD_OK if the call succeeds, or one of the following error messages:

DDERR_EXCLUSIVEMODEALREADYSET   DDERR_INVALIDOBJECT

DDERR_HWNDALREADYSET   DDERR_INVALIDPARAMS

DDERR_HWNDSUBCLASSED   DDERR_OUTOFMEMORY

The DDERR_EXCLUSIVEMODEALREADYSET message refers to the fact that only one application can request the exclusive mode. If this message is received, then there is another application that has been granted the exclusive mode and code should provide alternative processing or an exit.

Full-screen applications receive the DDERR_NOEXCLUSIVEMODE return value if they lose exclusive device access, as is the case when the user presses Alt+Tab to switch to another program. In this event one possible coding alternative is to call the TestCooperativeLevel() function in a loop, exiting only when it returns DD_OK, which indicates that exclusive mode is now available.

Applications that use the normal cooperative level (DDSCL_NORMAL flag) receive DDERR_EXCLUSIVEMODEALREADYSET if another application has taken exclusive device access. In this case a windowed application can be coded to loop until TestCooperativeLevel() returns DD_OK.

The two most common flag combinations used in the SetCooperativeLevel() call are the ones used for programs that execute in exclusive mode and those that are windowed. The following code fragment shows the call to SetCooperativeLevel() for a DirectDraw application that requests exclusive mode:

```
LPDIRECTDRAW      lpDD4;     // DirectDraw object
HWND              hwnd;      // Handle to the window
...
lpDD4->SetCooperativeLevel(hwnd, DDSCL_EXCLUSIVE |
DDSCL_FULLSCREEN);
```

Two flags are required to set DirectDraw exclusive mode: DDSCL_EXCLUSIVE and DDSCL_FULLSCREEN. In reality all exclusive mode applications execute full-screen so the second flag is actually redundant.

To set the cooperative level to the normal mode the code can be as follows:

```
LPDIRECTDRAW      lpDD4;     // DirectDraw object
...
lpDD4->SetCooperativeLevel(NULL, DDSCL_NORMAL);
```

Note that exclusive mode applications pass the handle to the window (hWnd) parameter so that Windows has a way of recovering from conditions that freeze the otherwise disabled video system. This is not required for normal Windows programs that use conventional recovery procedures.

Hardware capabilities

Whereas in conventional Windows programming application code often ignores the specific configuration of the system hardware, this is not the case in programs that use DirectDraw. Video cards that support DirectDraw do so at varying degrees of hardware compatibility and of DirectDraw functionality. In most cases an application needs to know what level of DirectDraw hardware support is available in a particular machine, as well as the amount of available video memory, before deciding if the code is compatible with the host, or how to proceed if a given functionality is not present.

Applications can enumerate the capabilities of the hardware to determine the supported hardware-accelerated features. DirectX emulates most features that are not implemented in hardware; however, there are a few in which this is not the case. It is this emulation that makes possible some degree of device independence. The DirectDraw GetCaps() function returns run-time information about video resources and hardware capabilities. By examining these capabilities during the initialization stage, an application can decide whether the available functionality is insufficient and abort execution, or make other adjustments to provide the best possible performance over varying levels of support.

For this reason, applications that use features not supported by the hardware are usually better off creating surfaces in system memory, rather than in video memory.

The GetCaps() function returns the capabilities of the device driver for the hardware abstraction layer (HAL) and for the hardware emulation layer (HEL). The general form of the GetCaps() function is as follows:

```
HRESULT GetCaps(
                LPDDCAPS lpDDDriverCaps,    // 1
                LPDDCAPS lpDDHelCaps        // 2
                );
```

The first parameter is the address of a structure of type DDCAPS that is filled with the capabilities of the HAL, as reported by the device driver. Code can set this parameter to NULL if the hardware capabilities are not necessary. The second parameter is the address of a structure, also of type DDCAPS, which is filled with the capabilities of the HEL. This parameter can also be set to NULL if these capabilities should not be retrieved. Code can set only one of the two parameters to NULL. If the method succeeds, the return value is DD_OK. If the method fails, the return value is one of the following error constants:

DDERR_INVALIDOBJECT

DDERR_INVALIDPARAMS

The DDCAPS structure is a large one indeed; it contains 58 members in the DirectDraw4 version. The structure is defined as follows:

```
typedef struct _DDCAPS {
    DWORD     dwSize;                            // size of structure DDCAPS
    DWORD     dwCaps;                            // driver-specific caps
    DWORD     dwCaps2;                           // more driver-specific
                                                // caps
    DWORD     dwCKeyCaps;                        // color key caps
    DWORD     dwFXCaps;                          // stretching and effects
                                                // caps
    DWORD     dwFXAlphaCaps;                     // alpha caps
    DWORD     dwPalCaps;                         // palette caps
    DWORD     dwSVCaps;                          // stereo vision caps
    DWORD     dwAlphaBltConstBitDepths;
                                                // alpha bit-depth members
    DWORD     dwAlphaBltPixelBitDepths;        //  .
    DWORD     dwAlphaBltSurfaceBitDepths;      //  .
    DWORD     dwAlphaOverlayConstBitDepths;    //  .
    DWORD     dwAlphaOverlayPixelBitDepths;    //  .
    DWORD     dwAlphaOverlaySurfaceBitDepths; //  .
    DWORD     dwZBufferBitDepths;               // Z-buffer bit depth
    DWORD     dwVidMemTotal;                     // total video memory
    DWORD     dwVidMemFree;                      // total free video memory
    DWORD     dwMaxVisibleOverlays;             // maximum visible overlays
    DWORD     dwCurrVisibleOverlays;            // overlays currently
                                                // visible
    DWORD     dwNumFourCCCodes;                 // number of supported
                                                // FOURCC
                                                // codes
    DWORD     dwAlignBoundarySrc;               // overlay alignment
                                                // restrictions
    DWORD     dwAlignSizeSrc;                    //  .
    DWORD     dwAlignBoundaryDest;              //  .
    DWORD     dwAlignSizeDest;                   //  .
    DWORD     dwAlignStrideAlign;               // stride alignment
    DWORD     dwRops[DD_ROP_SPACE];             // supported raster ops
    DWORD     dwReservedCaps;                    // reserved
    DWORD     dwMinOverlayStretch;              // overlay stretch factors
    DWORD     dwMaxOverlayStretch;              //  .
    DWORD     dwMinLiveVideoStretch;            // obsolete
    DWORD     dwMaxLiveVideoStretch;            //  .
    DWORD     dwMinHwCodecStretch;              //  .
    DWORD     dwMaxHwCodecStretch;              //  .
    DWORD     dwReserved1;                       // reserved
    DWORD     dwReserved2;                       //  .
    DWORD     dwReserved3;                       //  .
    DWORD     dwSVBCaps;                         // system-to-video blit
                                                // related
                                                // caps
    DWORD     dwSVBCKeyCaps;                     //  .
    DWORD     dwSVBFXCaps;                       //  .
```

```
DWORD      dwSVBRops[DD_ROP_SPACE]; //  .
DWORD      dwVSBCaps;               // video-to-system blit
                                    // related
                                    // caps
DWORD      dwVSBCKeyCaps;           //  .
DWORD      dwVSBFXCaps;             //  .
DWORD      dwVSBRops[DD_ROP_SPACE]; //  .
DWORD      dwSSBCaps;               // system—to-system blit
                                    // related
                                    // caps
DWORD      dwSSBCKeyCaps;           //  .
DWORD      dwSSBCFXCaps;            //  .
DWORD      dwSSBRops[DD_ROP_SPACE]; //  .
DWORD      dwMaxVideoPorts;         // maximum number of live
                                    // video
                                    // ports
DWORD      dwCurrVideoPorts;        // current number of live
                                    // video
                                    // ports
DWORD      dwSVBCaps2;              // additional system-to-
                                    // video
                                    // blit
                                    // caps
DWORD      dwNLVBCaps;              // nonlocal-to-local video
                                    // memory
                                    //  blit caps
DWORD      dwNLVBCaps2;             //  .
DWORD      dwNLVBCKeyCaps;          //  .
DWORD      dwNLVBFXCaps;            //  .
DWORD      dwNLVBRops[DD_ROP_SPACE];//  .
DDSCAPS2 ddsCaps;                   // general surface caps
DDCAPS,FAR* LPDDCAPS;
```

Most applications are concerned with only a few of the capabilities of a DirectDraw device. Table 8-2 lists some of the most often needed capabilities.

Table 8-2
Selected Device Capabilities Reported by the GetCaps() Function

Capability	Description
dwCaps member constants:	
DDCAPS_3D	Display hardware has 3D acceleration.
DDCAPS_ALPHA	Display hardware supports alpha-only surfaces.
DDCAPS_BANKSWITCHED	Display hardware is bank-switched. Therefore it is very slow at random access operations to display memory.

Continued

Table 8-2 *(continued)*

Capability	Description
DDCAPS_BLT	Display hardware is capable of blit operations.
DDCAPS_BLTCOLORFILL	Display hardware is capable of color filling with a blitter.
DDCAPS_BLTSTRETCH	Display hardware is capable of stretching during blit operations.
DDCAPS_CANBLTSYSMEM	Display hardware is capable of blitting to or from system memory.
DDCAPS_CANCLIP	Display hardware is capable of clipping with blitting.
DDCAPS_CANCLIPSTRETCHED	Display hardware is capable of clipping while stretch blitting.
DDCAPS_COLORKEY	System supports some form of color key in either overlay or blit operations.
DDCAPS_GDI	Display hardware is shared with GDI.
DDCAPS_NOHARDWARE	No hardware support.
DDCAPS_OVERLAY	Display hardware supports overlays.
DDCAPS_OVERLAYCANTCLIP	Display hardware supports overlays but cannot clip.
DDCAPS_PALETTE	DirectDraw is capable of creating and supporting DirectDrawPalette objects for more surfaces than the primary one.
DDCAPS_READSCANLINE	Display hardware is capable of returning the current scan line.
DDCAPS_ZBLTS	Supports the use of z-buffers with blit Operations.

dwCaps2 member constants:

DDCAPS2_VIDEOPORT	Display hardware supports live video.
DDCAPS2_WIDESURFACES	Display surfaces supports surfaces wider than the primary surface.

dwPalCaps member constants:

DDPCAPS_1BIT	Supports 2-color palettes.
DDPCAPS_2BIT	Supports 4-color palettes.
DDPCAPS_4BIT	Supports 16-color palettes.
DDPCAPS_8BIT	Supports 256-color palettes.
DDPCAPS_8BITENTRIES	Specifies an index to an 8-bit color index. This field is valid only when used with the DDPCAPS_1BIT, DDPCAPS_2BIT, or DDPCAPS_4BIT capability.

Capability	Description
DDPCAPS_ALPHA	Supports palettes that include an alpha component.
DDPCAPS_ALLOW256	Supports palettes that can have all 256 entries defined.
DDPCAPS_PRIMARYSURFACE	The palette is attached to the primary surface. Changing the palette has an immediate effect on the display unless the DDPCAPS_VSYNC capability is specified and supported.
Other structure members:	
dwVidMemTotal	Total amount of display memory.
dwVidMemFree	Amount of free display memory.
dwMaxVisibleOverlays	Maximum number of visible overlays or overlay sprites.
dwCurrVisibleOverlays	Current number of visible overlays or overlay sprites.
dwReservedCaps	Reserved. Prior to DirectX 6.0, this member contained general surface capabilities.
DwMinOverlayStretch	
DwMaxOverlayStretch	Minimum and maximum overlay stretch factors multiplied by 1000. For example, 1.3 = 1300.
dwSVBCaps	Driver-specific capabilities for system-memory-to-display-memory blits.
dwVSBRops	Raster operations supported for display-memory-to-system-memory blits.
dwSSBCaps	Driver-specific capabilities for system-memory-to-system-memory blits.

The following code fragment shows the processing required to read the hardware capabilities using the DirectDraw GetCaps() function. The code reads various capabilities and displays the corresponding screen messages. After each message is displayed, the screen position is indexed by one or more lines. The project named DDInfo Demo, in the book's CD-ROM, uses similar processing.

```
DDCAPS          DrawCaps;     // DDCAPS structure
LPDIRECTDRAW4   lpDD4;          // DirectDraw object
...
//**********************************
// DirectDraw hardware capabilities
//**********************************
DrawCaps.dwSize = sizeof ( DrawCaps );
// Call to capabilities function
```

```
        lpDD4->GetCaps (&DrawCaps, NULL );
// Video memory
    strcpy ( message, " Total Video Memory: ");
    sprintf ( message+strlen(" Total Video Memory: "),
              "%i",DrawCaps.dwVidMemTotal );
    TextOut ( hdc, text_x, text_y, message, strlen (message) );
    text_y += tm.tmHeight+tm.tmExternalLeading;
// Free video memory
    strcpy ( message, " Free Video Memory: ");
    sprintf ( message+strlen(" Free Video Memory: "),
              "%i",DrawCaps.dwVidMemFree );
    TextOut ( hdc, text_x, text_y, message, strlen (message) );
    text_y += tm.tmHeight+tm.tmExternalLeading;
    text_y += tm.tmHeight+tm.tmExternalLeading;

    // Video card hardware
    strcpy ( message,
            " Video card hardware support as follows:");
    TextOut ( hdc, text_x, text_y, message, strlen (message) );
    text_y += tm.tmHeight+tm.tmExternalLeading;
    text_x = 16;
    if (DrawCaps.dwCaps & DDCAPS_NOHARDWARE)
    {
    strcpy ( message, "  No DirectDraw hardware support
available" );
        TextOut ( hdc, text_x, text_y, message, strlen
(message) );
        text_y += tm.tmHeight+tm.tmExternalLeading;
        return;
    }
    if (DrawCaps.dwCaps & DDCAPS_3D)
    {
        strcpy ( message, "  3D support" );
        TextOut ( hdc, text_x, text_y, message, strlen
(message) );
        text_y += tm.tmHeight+tm.tmExternalLeading;
    }
    else
    {
        strcpy ( message, "  No 3D support" );
        TextOut ( hdc, text_x, text_y, message, strlen
(message) );
        text_y += tm.tmHeight+tm.tmExternalLeading;
    }
    if (DrawCaps.dwCaps & DDCAPS_BLT)
    {
        strcpy ( message, "  Hardware Bitblt support" );
        TextOut ( hdc, text_x, text_y, message, strlen
(message) );
        text_y += tm.tmHeight+tm.tmExternalLeading;
    }
    else
    {
```

```
          strcpy ( message, " No hardware Bitblt support" );
          TextOut ( hdc, text_x, text_y, message, strlen
                  (message) );
          text_y += tm.tmHeight+tm.tmExternalLeading;
    }
    if (DrawCaps.dwCaps & DDCAPS_OVERLAY)
    {
          strcpy ( message, " Hardware overlays supported");
          TextOut ( hdc, text_x, text_y, message, strlen
                  (message) );
          text_y += tm.tmHeight+tm.tmExternalLeading;
    }
    else
    {
          strcpy ( message, " No hardware overlays ");
          TextOut ( hdc, text_x, text_y, message, strlen
                  (message) );
          text_y += tm.tmHeight+tm.tmExternalLeading;
    }

    if (DrawCaps.dwCaps & DDCAPS_CANCLIP)
    {
          strcpy ( message, " Clipping supported in hardware");
          TextOut ( hdc, text_x, text_y, message, strlen
                  (message) );
          text_y += tm.tmHeight+tm.tmExternalLeading;
    }
    else
    {
          strcpy ( message, " No hardware clipping support ");
          TextOut ( hdc, text_x, text_y, message, strlen
                  (message) );
          text_y += tm.tmHeight+tm.tmExternalLeading;
    }
    if (DrawCaps.dwCaps & DDCAPS_BANKSWITCHED)
    {
          strcpy ( message, " Memory is bank switched");
          TextOut ( hdc, text_x, text_y, message, strlen
                  (message) );
          text_y += tm.tmHeight+tm.tmExternalLeading;
    }
    else
    {
          strcpy ( message, " Memory not bank switched");
          TextOut ( hdc, text_x, text_y, message, strlen
                  (message) );
          text_y += tm.tmHeight+tm.tmExternalLeading;
    }
      if (DrawCaps.dwCaps & DDCAPS_BLTCOLORFILL)
    {
          strcpy ( message, " Color fill Blt support");
```

```
            TextOut ( hdc, text_x, text_y, message, strlen
                    (message) );
            text_y += tm.tmHeight+tm.tmExternalLeading;
    }
  else
  {
        strcpy ( message, "  No Blt color fill support");
        TextOut ( hdc, text_x, text_y, message, strlen
                (message) );
        text_y += tm.tmHeight+tm.tmExternalLeading;
  }
  if (DrawCaps.dwCaps & DDCAPS_COLORKEY)
  {
        strcpy ( message, "  Color key hardware support ");
        TextOut ( hdc, text_x, text_y, message, strlen
                (message) );
        text_y += tm.tmHeight+tm.tmExternalLeading;
  }
  else
  {
        strcpy ( message, "  No color key support");
        TextOut ( hdc, text_x, text_y, message, strlen
                (message) );
        text_y += tm.tmHeight+tm.tmExternalLeading;
  }
  if (DrawCaps.dwCaps & DDCAPS_ALPHA)
  {
        strcpy ( message, "  Alpha channels supported");
        TextOut ( hdc, text_x, text_y, message, strlen
                (message) );
        text_y += tm.tmHeight+tm.tmExternalLeading;
  }
  else
  {
        strcpy ( message, "  No Alpha channels support");
        TextOut ( hdc, text_x, text_y, message, strlen
                (message) );
        text_y += tm.tmHeight+tm.tmExternalLeading;
  }
```

Display modes

Earlier we discussed the concept of display modes in DirectDraw programming. In DirectDraw a display mode is defined by its resolution and color depth. Therefore, a display mode of 640 by 480 by 8 executes with a resolution of 640 pixel columns, 480 pixel rows, and encodes the pixel attribute in 8 bits. Because 8 bits support 256 combinations, this mode supports a range of 256 colors. DirectDraw applications can obtain the available display modes. An application that executes in exclusive mode can also set a display mode and restore the previous one when it concludes.

Not all devices support all display modes. To determine the display modes supported on a given system, an application can call the EnumDisplayModes() functions. EnumDisplayModes() can be used to list all supported display modes or to confirm that a single display mode is available in the hardware. The function's general form is as follows:

```
HRESULT EnumDisplayModes(
        DWORD dwFlags,                              // 1
        LPDDSURFACEDESC2 lpDDSurfaceDesc,           // 2
        LPVOID lpContext,                           // 3
        LPDDENUMMODESCALLBACK2 lpCallBack           // 4
        );
```

The first parameter determines the function's options by means of two flags. DDEDM_REFRESHRATES enumerates the modes that have different refresh rates separately, even if they have the same resolution and color depth. The second flag DDEDM_STANDARDVGAMODES enumerates Mode X and VGA Mode 13H as different modes. This parameter can be set to zero to ignore both of these options. The second parameter is the address of a DDSURFACEDESC2 structure. The structure is used to store the parameters of a particular display mode, which is confirmed or not by the call. Applications that request a listing of all available modes set this parameter to NULL. The third parameter is a pointer to an application-defined structure that is passed to the callback function associated with EnumDisplayModes(). This provides a mechanism whereby the application code can make local data visible to the callback function. If not used, as is most often the case, then the third parameter is set to NULL. The fourth parameter is the address of a special callback function, of prototype EnumModesCallback2(). This function is called every time a supported mode is found. Applications use this callback function to provide the necessary processing for each display mode found by the call.

The callback function, for which your code supplies an address when it calls EnumDisplayModes(), must match the prototype for EnumModesCallback2(). Each time that a supported mode is found, the callback function receives control. The function's general form is:

```
HRESULT WINAPI EnumModesCallback(
        LPDDSURFACEDESC2 lpDDSurfaceDesc2,          // 1
        LPVOID lpContext                            // 2
        );
```

The first parameter is the address of a DDSURFACEDESC2 structure that describes the display mode. The second one is the address of the application-defined data structure, which may have been passed in the third parameter of the EnumDisplay Modes() function call. Code can examine the values in the DDSURFACEDESC2 structure to determine the characteristics of each available display mode. The most important members of the DDSURFACEDESC2 structure are dwWidth, dwHeight, and ddpfPixelFormat. The dwWidth and dwHeight hold the display mode's dimensions.

The ddpfPixelFormat member is a DDPIXELFORMAT structure that contains
information about the mode's bit depth and describes whether the display mode is
palettized or not. If the dwFlags member contains the DDPF_PALETTEINDEXED1,
DDPF_PALETTEINDEXED2, DDPF_PALETTEINDEXED4, or DDPF_PALETTEINDEXED8 flag,
then the display mode's bit depth is 1, 2, 4, or 8 bits. In this case the pixel value is an
index into the corresponding palette. If dwFlags contains DDPF_RGB, then the display
mode's bit depth in the dwRGBBitCount member of the DDPIXELFORMAT structure
is valid.

Applications that call EnumDisplayModes() usually do most of the processing in the
EnumModesCallback() function. For example, a program can list all the DirectDraw
display modes on the screen by storing the display modes data in one or more arrays
each time the callback function receives control. When execution returns to the
caller, then all modes are stored or a predetermined maximum is reached. The calling
code can now read the mode data from the arrays and display the values on the
screen. In this case the callback function could be coded as follows:

```
// Global variables for DirectDraw operations
HRESULT         DDConnect;
DDCAPS          DrawCaps;
// DirectDraw object
LPDIRECTDRAW2  lpDD4;
int             DDLevel = 0;          // DirectDraw implementation
// DirectDraw modes data
int modesCount = 0;          // Counter for DirectDraw modes
static int MAX_MODES = 30; // Maximum number of modes
DWORD modesArray[90];        // Array for mode parameters
...
//*********************************************************
// Callback function for EnumDisplayModes()
//*********************************************************
static WINAPI ModesProc(LPDDSURFACEDESC aSurface,
                        LPVOID Context)
{
    static int i;          // Index into array
    i = modesCount * 3;    // Set array pointer
    // Store mode parameters in public array
    // Note: code assumes that the dwRGBBitFormat member of
    //       the DDPIXELFORMAT structure contains valid data
    modesArray[i]     = aSurface->dwWidth;
    modesArray[i + 1] = aSurface->dwHeight;
    modesArray[i + 2] = aSurface->ddpfPixelFormat.dwRGBBitCount;
    modesCount++;             // Bump display modes counter
    // Check for maximum number of display modes
    if( modesCount >= MAX_MODES )
      return DDENUMRET_CANCEL;  // Stop mode listing

    else
      return DDENUMRET_OK;  // Continue
}
```

The callback function, named ModesProc(), uses an array of type DWORD to store the height, width, and color depth for each mode reported by DirectDraw. A public variable named modesCount keeps track of the total number of modes. In this case the calling code can be implemented in a function called DDModes, as follows:

```
//**********************************************************
//      DDModes - Obtain and list DD display modes
//**********************************************************
void DDModes ( HDC hdc )
{
    TEXTMETRIC  tm;
    char        message[255];
    int j;                          // Display buffer offset
    static int textLines;           // Display lines counter
    int         text_x = 0;
    int         text_y = 0;
    int         cxChar;
    GetTextMetrics ( hdc, &tm );
    cxChar = tm.tmAveCharWidth ;
 // Test for no DirectDraw interface
    if (DDLevel == 0) {
    strcpy ( message, "No DirectDraw interface" );
        TextOut ( hdc, text_x, text_y, message, strlen
                (message) );
    return;
    }
    //********************************
    //  There is DirectDraw. Obtain
    //    and list display modes
    //********************************
    strcpy ( message, "       DirectDraw Display Modes" );
    TextOut ( hdc, text_x, text_y, message, strlen (message) );
    text_y += tm.tmHeight+tm.tmExternalLeading;
 // Call EnumDisplayModes()
    DDConnect = lpDD4->EnumDisplayModes(0, NULL, NULL,
ModesProc);
    if (DDConnect == DD_OK) {
    strcpy ( message, "       Number of display modes: ");
    sprintf ( message+strlen("       Number of display modes:
                        "),
            "%i", modesCount);
    TextOut ( hdc, text_x, text_y, message, strlen (message) );
    text_y += tm.tmHeight+tm.tmExternalLeading;
    // Format and display mode data
    // First column
    textLines = modesCount;
    if(modesCount > 15){
      textLines = modesCount - 15;
      for(int x = 0; x < 15; x++){
        j = sprintf ( message, "  %d", modesArray[x*3] );
        j += sprintf (message + j, " x %d", modesArray[x*3+1] );
```

```
            j += sprintf (message + j, " x %d", modesArray[x*3+2] );
            TextOut ( hdc, text_x, text_y, message, strlen
(message) );
            text_y += tm.tmHeight+tm.tmExternalLeading;
         }
      }
   if(modesCount < 16)
      return;
   // Display second column if more than 15 modes
   text_x = cxChar * 20;
   text_y = 2 * tm.tmHeight+tm.tmExternalLeading;
      for(int y = 15; y < modesCount; y++){
         j = sprintf ( message, " %d", modesArray[y*3] );
         j += sprintf (message + j, " x %d", modesArray[y*3+1] );
         j += sprintf (message + j, " x %d", modesArray[y*3+2] );
         TextOut ( hdc, text_x, text_y, message, strlen (message) );
            text_y += tm.tmHeight+tm.tmExternalLeading;
         text_x = cxChar * 20;
      }
   return;
   }
}
```

The processing calls EnumDisplayModes() in the statement:

```
    DDConnect = lpDD4->EnumDisplayModes(0, NULL, NULL,
ModesProc);
```

The first parameter is set to zero to indicate that no special control flags are
required. Therefore, the refresh rate is not taken into consideration and Mode X is
not reported separately. The second parameter is NULL to indicate that no structure
data for checking against available modes is used. The NULL value for the third
parameter relates to the fact that no user-defined data structure is being passed to
the callback function. The last parameter is the address of the callback function, in
this case the ModesProc() function previously listed. When the callback function
returns, the code tests for a return value of DD_OK, which indicates that the call was
successful, and then proceeds to display the header messages and to convert the
code data stored in ModesArray[] into ASCII strings for display.

DDInfo Demo Project

The program named DD_info.cpp, located in the DDInfo Demo project folder of the
book's CD-ROM, is a demonstration of the initialization and preparatory operations for
a DirectDraw application. The program starts by initializing DirectDraw. The program's

menu contains commands to read and display system hardware information and to list the available display modes. Figure 8-3 is a screen dump of both menu commands in a machine equipped with a Matrox Millennium video card and 2 MB of video memory.

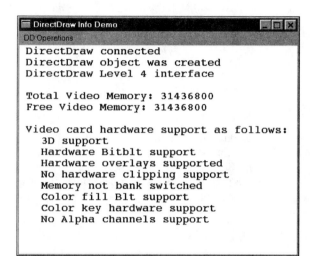

Figure 8-3: Screen dump of the DD Information and Display Modes commands in DDInfo Demo project

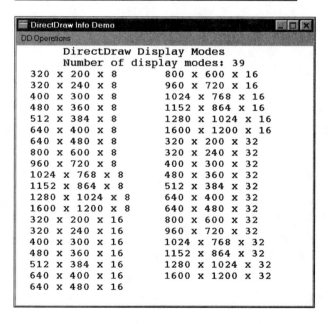

One of the first operations performed by the DD_info.cpp program, which is the source for the DDInfo Demo Project, is to determine which version of the DirectDraw interface is installed in the target system. Then the code continues to obtain and display hardware support and lists the available display modes whatever DirectDraw interface is present. To accomplish this, the program typecasts the interface pointer, which can be of type `LPDIRECTDRAW`, `LPDIRECTDRAW2`, or `LPDIRECTDRAW4`, to a type `LPDIRECTDRAW`. This manipulation is not conventional and works only in very simple processing conditions. Application code should not typecast DirectDraw pointer into those of other interfaces.

Summary

You now have learned the essential elements of DirectDraw, as well as the fundamental steps in creating and initializing an application that uses DirectDraw functions. The programming operations discussed referred mainly to configuration and initialization. We have not yet discussed using DirectDraw to perform graphics display operations. In the following chapter we cover graphics programming with DirectDraw.

✦   ✦   ✦

Direct Access to Video Memory

✦ ✦ ✦ ✦

In This Chapter

Programming
template for
DirectDraw
exclusive mode

Using direct
memory access

Using in-line
assembly

Developing direct
access primitives

Raster operations
in direct access

✦ ✦ ✦ ✦

Y ou have seen how a DirectDraw application is set up
and initialized and learned the basics of DirectDraw
architecture in the context of a conventional, windowed
program. However, the fundamental purpose of DirectDraw
is to make possible high-performance graphics. Two elements
are necessary to achieve this: accessing video memory directly
and taking advantage of the hardware facilities furnished in the
video card. In this chapter we cover the first of these topics.

Before we tackle the complications of DirectDraw programming
in exclusive mode, it is convenient to develop a code backbone
that supports any such program. In this effort two tasks appear
to be critical: creating a WinMain() function suited for Direct-
Draw applications in exclusive mode, and ensuring access to
the latest version of the interface, currently DirectX 7.

WinMain() Function for DirectDraw

The WinMain() function for a DirectDraw program that
operates in exclusive mode has some unique features. This
implies making some variations in the conventional WinMain()
function that is used for a standard Windows application.
Our new WinMain() function needs to perform several
DirectDraw-specific initializations that are not common
in standard Windows programming. The result is a new
template for DirectDraw exclusive mode programming.

If the program's main window is created by DirectDraw, then
a reasonable approach is to perform most of the initialization
and setup operations in WinMain(). In addition to the usual
windows initialization operations, the following DirectDraw-
specific steps are typically required:

✦ Obtain the DirectDraw4 interface and store the pointer
object for future use.

✦ Check that the desired mode is available in the host machine.

✦ Set the cooperative level.

✦ Set the display mode.

✦ Create the drawing surfaces. Most DirectDraw programs require at least a primary surface.

✦ Obtain the DirectDraw device context if the program is to execute GDI functions.

DirectDraw version of WinMain()

Your first task is to code a `WinMain()` function that creates an application window compatible with a DirectDraw exclusive mode program. In addition to creating the program window you can perform DirectDraw-specific initialization and output operations in `WinMain()`. This part of the code is usually placed before the message loop. The fundamental parts of the `WinMain()` backbone are the same as those of any Windows program:

✦ Creating and filling the members of a data structure of type `WNDCLASS`

✦ Registering the window class

✦ Creating the DirectDraw-compatible window

✦ Setting the window's show state

✦ Providing a program message loop

Filling the WNDCLASSEX structure

The `WINDCLASSEX` structure contains window class information. In this case it is used in the `RegisterClassEx()` function call. There are few differences between the `WNDCLASSEX` structure that you use in conventional Windows programming, and the one required for an exclusive mode DirectDraw application. One such difference relates to the fact that a DirectDraw window class does not use a private device context; therefore, the `CS_OWNDC` constant is not present in the style member of the `WNDCLASSEX` structure member. The only other structure member that requires comment is `hbrBackground`. In this case the application can select a standard brush to color the initial program background. In the template file the structure is filled as follows:

```
WNDCLASSEX  wndclass ;
wndclass.cbSize        = sizeof (wndclass) ;
wndclass.style         = CS_HREDRAW | CS_VREDRAW;
wndclass.lpfnWndProc   = WndProc ;
wndclass.cbClsExtra    = 0 ;
wndclass.cbWndExtra    = 0 ;
wndclass.hInstance     = hInstance ;
```

```
wndclass.hIcon           = LoadIcon (NULL, IDI_APPLICATION) ;
wndclass.hCursor         = LoadCursor (NULL, IDC_ARROW) ;
wndclass.hbrBackground   = (HBRUSH) GetStockObject
                                    (GRAY_BRUSH) ;
wndclass.lpszMenuName    = szAppName;
wndclass.lpszClassName   = szAppName;
wndclass.hIconSm         = LoadIcon (NULL, IDI_APPLICATION) ;
```

Registering the window class

The window class is a template that defines the characteristics of a particular window. It also defines the address of the window procedure, as in the preceding code fragment. After filling the structure members, code can now register the class, with the following call:

```
RegisterClass(&wndclass);
```

Creating the window

It is now time to create the window using CreateWindowEx(). You can use many combinations of parameters in the call according to the characteristics desired for the particular application window that you are creating. In a DirectDraw exclusive mode application, many of the predefined values are meaningless.

The extended style WS_EX_TOPMOST defines a window that is placed above all non-topmost windows. For a DirectDraw exclusive mode program, WS_EX_TOPMOST is usually the appropriate style. The window style parameter is WS_POPUP. If the DirectDraw application executes full screen, which is always the case in exclusive mode, then the horizontal and vertical origins are set to zero and the xsize and ysize parameters are filled using GetSystemMetrics(). The GetSystemMetrics() call returns the full pixel size of the screen area. In the template file the structure is filled as follows:

```
hWnd = CreateWindowEx(
        WS_EX_TOPMOST,          // Extended style
        szAppName,              // Application name
        "DirectDraw Demo No. 2",
        WS_POPUP,               // Window style
        0,                      // Horizontal origin
        0,                      // Vertical origin
        GetSystemMetrics(SM_CXSCREEN), // x size
        GetSystemMetrics(SM_CYSCREEN), // y size
        NULL,                   // Handle of parent
        NULL,                   // Handle to menu
        hInstance,              // Application instance
        NULL);                  // Additional data
if (!hWnd)
    return FALSE;
```

Defining the window show state

CreateWindowEx() creates the window internally but does not display it. When ShowWindow() is called, the code specifies how the window is shown. To display the window, a conventional Windows program first calls ShowWindow() to set the show state, and then calls UpdateWindow() to update the client area by sending a WM_PAINT message to the window procedure. It is different in a DirectDraw exclusive mode application. Because the DirectDraw interface has not yet been established, no WM_PAINT message can be sent at this point in the code. Therefore, the template file makes the call to the ShowWindow() function, but not the one to UpdateWindow(). The code is as follows:

```
ShowWindow (hwnd, iCmdShow) ;
```

The first parameter is the handle to the window returned by CreateWindowEx() function. The second parameter is the window's display mode parameter. In this first call to ShowWindow() applications must use the value received by WinMain().

Creating the message loop

The coding is now at a point in which WinMain() can initialize DirectDraw and perhaps perform some preliminary display operations. The processing details in the following sample program are discussed in the next section. The last step in WinMain() is the ever-present message loop. In a standard DirectDraw exclusive mode application, the message loop is no different than the one in a conventional windows program. In Chapter 11 we discuss a different type of message loop, used in DirectDraw animation. The present code is as follows:

```
while (GetMessage(&msg, NULL, 0, 0))
    {
        TranslateMessage(&msg);
        DispatchMessage(&msg);
    }
    return msg.wParam;
}
```

DirectDraw initialization

A DirectDraw exclusive mode application is often initialized in WinMain(). The reason for this is that an exclusive mode application cannot perform display operations until it obtains the interface and sets the cooperative level and display mode. If display operations are performed by means of GDI functions, then the application must also obtain the DirectDraw device context. Note that some DirectDraw applications draw on the screen using both GDI and direct memory access methods.

Typically, the DirectDraw initialization for exclusive mode operation includes the following steps:

✦ Obtain the current interface. In DirectX 6 this is IDirectDraw4.

✦ Check that the desired display mode is available in the host machine.

✦ Set the cooperative level and display mode.

✦ Create the drawing surfaces. This usually means at least a primary surface, but often other surfaces are also necessary.

✦ Display some initial screen text or graphics.

This last operation can be accomplished by means of conventional GDI functions, by direct access to video memory, by DirectDraw-specific functions, or by a combination of these methods. Programs of greater complexity usually perform other initialization, setup, and initial display functions at this time. The sample program DD Access Demo, developed later in this chapter, has minimal DirectDraw functionality. In the chapters that follow we develop DirectDraw programs of a greater level of complexity.

An important issue related to preliminary DirectDraw operations is to provide a mechanism whereby the application can recover if a terminal condition is encountered during the initialization process. In the DirectDraw template program we include a function named DDInitFailed() that creates a message box with the corresponding diagnostic prompt and waits for the user to press OK. When the user acknowledges, the terminal error handler destroys the application window and returns control to the operating system. The function is coded as follows:

```
//*************************************
// Name: DDInitFailed()
// Desc: This function is called if an
//       initialization operation fails
//*************************************
HRESULT DDInitFailed(HWND hWnd, HRESULT hRet, LPCTSTR szError)
{
    char    szBuff[128];

    sprintf(szBuff, szError);
    ReleaseObjects();
    MessageBox(hWnd, szBuff, "DirectDraw Demo No. 2", MB_OK);
    DestroyWindow(hWnd);
    return hRet;
}
```

The parameters for the DDInitFailed() function are the handle to the window, the result code from the call that caused the failure, and a string pointer with the diagnostic text to be displayed in the message box. All DirectDraw initialization calls performed in the template code test for a valid result code; and if no valid code is found, they exit execution through the DDInitFailed() function. The same is true of the DirectDraw examples used in the rest of the book.

Obtaining the current interface

The first processing step is to obtain the DirectDraw object that corresponds to the current version of the interface. It is usually a good idea to store the pointer in a global variable, which can be accessed by other program elements. The function named DD4Interface() attempts to find this object. It is coded as follows:

```
// Global data
LPDIRECTDRAW4    lpDD4;      // Pointer to current interface
. . .
//*********************************************
// Name: DD4Interface()
// Desc: Finds DirectDraw4 object
// PRE CONDITIONS:
//    lpDD4 is a global variable of type
//    LPDIRECTDRAW4
//
// POST CONDITIONS:
//    returns 0 if no DirectDraw4 interface
//    returns 1 if DirectDraw4 found
//*********************************************
int DD4Interface()
{

  HRESULT         DDConnect;
  LPDIRECTDRAW    lpDD;          // Pointer to DirectDraw

 DDConnect = DirectDrawCreate ( NULL, &lpDD, NULL);

 if(DDConnect != DD_OK)
  return 0;
    // Attempt to locate DirectDraw4 interface
    DDConnect = lpDD->QueryInterface( IID_IDirectDraw4,
                                 (LPVOID *) &lpDD4);
    if(DDConnect != S_OK)
    return 0;
    lpDD->Release();        // Release old pointer
      return 1;
  }
```

The preceding code releases the local pointer to DirectDraw if the DirectDraw4 pointer is found. In this manner the application code need only be concerned with releasing the object actually in use. Note that the pointer to the DirectDraw4 interface is defined globally, so that it can be seen throughout the application. In `WinMain()` the call to the `DD4Interface()` function is as follows:

```
// Attempt to fetch the DirectDraw4 interface
   hRet = DD4Interface();
     if (hRet == 0)
     return DDInitFailed(hWnd, hRet,
                         "QueryInterface() call failed");
```

If the DirectDraw4 interface is not found, then the program exits through the `DDInitFailed()` function previously described. In the template file the diagnostic messages simply express the name of the failed function. In your own programs you will probably substitute these text messages for more appropriate ones. For example, the failure of the `QueryInterface()` call can be interpreted to mean that the user needs to upgrade the host system to DirectX 7. A more detailed diagnostic function may be advisable in this case.

Checking mode availability

If the call succeeds, you have obtained a pointer to the DirectDraw4 interface. You can use the pointer in all other DirectDraw function calls. The fact that you have a pointer to the newest version of the DirectDraw interface does not mean that the application will execute correctly. DirectDraw programming sometimes introduces hardware dependencies that are not a found in conventional Windows programming. This fact is evident in operations related to the display mode. For this reason, before you attempt to set a display mode, it is usually a good idea to investigate if the desired mode is available in the host system. This gives our code the opportunity to select an alternative mode if the ideal one is not available, or to exit with a diagnostic message if no satisfactory display mode is found.

In Chapter 8 we explored the use of the `EnumDisplayModes()` function; at that time it was used to list the display modes available in a system. You can use the same function to determine if a particular mode is available. The code used in the template file is as follows:

```
//************************************************
// Name: ModesProc
// Desc: Callback function for EnumDisplayModes()
//************************************************
HRESULT WINAPI ModesProc(LPDDSURFACEDESC2 aSurface,
         LPVOID Context)
{
    static int i;          // Index into array of mode data

    i = modesCount * 3;    // Set array pointer

    if( modesCount >= MAX_MODES )
     return DDENUMRET_CANCEL;  // Stop mode listing
```

```
        // Store mode parameters in public array
        // Note: code assumes that the dwRGBBitFormat member if
        //       the DDPIXELFORMAT structure contains valid data
        modesArray[i]     = aSurface->dwWidth;
        modesArray[i + 1] = aSurface->dwHeight;
        modesArray[i + 2] = aSurface->ddpfPixelFormat.dwRGBBitCount;

        modesCount++;               // Bump display modes counter
        return DDENUMRET_OK;  // Continue
}

//****************************************************************
// Name: hasDDMode
// Desc: Tests for mode availability
//****************************************************************
// PRE CONDITIONS:
// 1. Public variable modesArray[] to store mode data
// 2. Public int variable modesCount to store number of
//    display modes
// 3. ModesProc() is an associated function that stores
//    mode data in array and count modes
//
// POST CONDITIONS:
//  1. Returns 1 if mode is available
//****************************************************************

int HasDDMode(DWORD pixWidth, DWORD pixHeight, DWORD pixBits)
{

  static HRESULT DDConnect;

      // Call EnumDisplayModes()
  if(MODES_ON == 0){
   MODES_ON = 1;            // set switch
   DDConnect = lpDD4->EnumDisplayModes(0, NULL, NULL,
                              ModesProc);
  }
// Modes are now stored in modeArray[] as triplets encoding
// width, height, and pixel bit size
// Variable modesCount holds the total number of display modes
  for(int x = 0; x < (modesCount * 3); x += 3){
   if(modesArray[x]==pixWidth && modesArray[x+1]==pixHeight\
   && modesArray[x+2]==pixBits)
   return 1;
  }
  return 0;
}
```

DirectDraw documentation states the EnumDisplayModes() function can be passed
the address of a DDSURFACEDESC2 structure that is checked for a specific mode.
We found that this mode of operation is not always reliable. To make sure that all

available modes are checked, the HasDDMode() function loads all the available modes into a global array variable and then searches the array for the desired one.

```
In the WinMain() template, the call to the HasDDMode() function
is coded as follows:
// Check for available mode (640 X 480 in 24-bit color)
  if (HasDDMode(640, 480, 24) == 0)
        return DDInitFailed(hWnd, hRet, "Display mode not
available");
```

We provided no alternative processing for the case in which the desired True-color mode is not available in the system. In your own programs you may want to provide alternative modes if the ideal one is not found. Here again, you should note that this programming style creates device-dependent code that may bring about other complications.

Setting the cooperative level and mode

If the desired mode is available, then the code must determine the cooperative level and proceed to set the mode. Exclusive mode DirectDraw programs require the constants DDSLC_EXCLUSIVE and DDSCL_FULLSCREEN, which were discussed in Chapter 8. The processing is as follows:

```
// Set cooperative level to exclusive and full screen
   hRet = lpDD4->SetCooperativeLevel(hWnd, DDSCL_EXCLUSIVE
                                   | DDSCL_FULLSCREEN);
   if (hRet != DD_OK)
       return DDInitFailed(hWnd, hRet,
                    "SetCooperativeLevel() call failed");
   // Set the video mode to 640 x 480 x 24
   hRet = lpDD4->SetDisplayMode(640, 480, 24, 0, 0);
   if (hRet != DD_OK)
       return DDInitFailed(hWnd, hRet,
                    "SetDisplayMode() call failed");
```

Creating the surfaces

In Chapter 7 we first learned about DirectDraw surfaces. At that time we defined a drawing surface as an area of video memory, typically used to hold image data, and DirectDrawSurface as a COM object in itself. Most DirectDraw4 applications require at least two types of COM objects: one, of type LPDIRECTDRAW4, is a pointer to the DirectDraw object. The second one, of type LPDIRECTDRAWSURFACE4, is a pointer to a surface. All surface-related functions use this second pointer type, whereas the core DirectDraw calls require the first one. Applications that manipulate several surfaces often cast a pointer for each surface. A third type of object, called a DirectDraw palette object, is necessary for programs that perform palette manipulations, whereas DirectDraw clipper objects are used in clipping operations.

Before accessing a DirectDraw surface you must create it by means of a call to the `CreateSurface()` function. The call can produce a single surface object, a complex surface-flipping chain, or a three-dimensional surface. The call to `CreateSurface()` specifies the dimensions of the surface, whether it is a single surface or a complex surface, and the pixel format. These characteristics are previously stored in a `DDSURFACEDESC2` structure, for which an address is included in call's parameters. The function's general form is as follows:

```
HRESULT CreateSurface(
        LPDDSURFACEDESC2 lpDDSurfaceDesc,           // 1
        LPDIRECTDRAWSURFACE4 FAR *lplpDDSurface,     // 2
        IUnknown FAR *pkUnkOutter                    // 3
        );
```

The first parameter is the address of a structure variable of type `LPDDSURFACEDESC2`. The `CreateSurface()` API requires that all unused members of the structure are set to zero. In the code sample that follows you will see how this can be accomplished easily. The second parameter is the address of a variable of type `LPDIRECTDRAWSURFACE4`, which is set to the interface address if the call succeeds. This is the pointer used in the calls that relate to this surface. Applications often store this pointer in a global variable so that it is visible throughout the code. The third parameter is provided for future expansion of the COM. Presently, applications must set this parameter to NULL.

If the call succeeds, the return value is `DD_OK`. If it fails the following self-explanatory error values are returned:

    DDERR_INCOMPATIBLEPRIMARY

    DDERR_INVALIDCAPS

    DDERR_INVALIDOBJECT

    DDERR_INVALIDPARAMS

    DDERR_INVALIDPIXELFORMAT

    DDERR_NOALPHAHW

    DDERR_NOCOOPERATIVELEVELSET

    DDERR_NODIRECTDRAWHW

    DDERR_NOEMULATION

    DDERR_NOEXCLUSIVEMODE

    DDERR_NOFLIPHW

    DDERR_NOMIPMAPHW

    DDERR_NOOVERLAYHW

    DDERR_NOZBUFFERHW

```
DDERR_OUTOFMEMORY

DDERR_OUTOFVIDEOMEMORY

DDERR_PRIMARYSURFACEALREADYEXISTS

DDERR_UNSUPPORTEDMODE
```

DirectDraw always attempts to create a surface in local video memory. If there is not enough local video memory available, then DirectDraw tries to use nonlocal video memory. Finally, if no video memory is available at all, then the surface is created in system memory. The call to `CreateSurface()` can explicitly request that a surface is created in a certain type of memory. This is done by means of the appropriate flags in the associated `DDSCAPS2` structure, which is part of `DDSURFACEDESC2`.

The primary surface is the one currently displayed on the monitor and is identified by the `DDSCAPS_PRIMARYSURFACE` flag. There is only one primary surface for each DirectDraw object. The dimensions and pixel format of the primary surface must match the current display mode. It is not necessary to explicitly enter these values when calling `CreateSurface()`; in fact, specifying these parameters generates an error even if they match the ones in the current display mode. In this template program you create the simplest possible surface object, which is the one that corresponds to a primary surface. The code is as follows:

```
// Global data
LPDIRECTDRAWSURFACE4         lpDDSPrimary = NULL; // DirectDraw
primary
DDSURFACEDESC2               ddsd;
. . .
 // Create a primary surface
 // ddsd is a structure of type DDSRUFACEDESC2
 // First, zero all structure variables using the ZeroMemory()
 // function
   ZeroMemory(&ddsd, sizeof(ddsd));
 // Now fill in the required members
   ddsd.dwSize = sizeof(ddsd);       // Structure size
   ddsd.dwFlags = DDSD_CAPS ;
   ddsd.ddsCaps.dwCaps = DDSCAPS_PRIMARYSURFACE;

   hRet = lpDD4->CreateSurface(&ddsd, &lpDDSPrimary, NULL);
   if (hRet != DD_OK)
       return DDInitFailed(hWnd, hRet,
                   "CreateSurface() call failed");
```

If the call succeeds, you obtain a pointer by which to access the functions that relate to DirectDraw surfaces. The pointer, named `lpDDSPrimary`, is stored in a global variable of type `LPDIRECTDRAWSURFACE4`. You can use the surface pointer to obtain a DirectDraw device context, which enables you to use GDI graphics in the application, or to lock the surface for direct access and retrieve its base address and pitch.

Performing display operations

If the application now needs to display some screen text, such as a "Hello World" message, it has to obtain a handle to the device context. The `DirectDrawSurface4` interface contains a function called `GetDC()` that you can use for this purpose. This function is not the same one as `GetDC()` in the general Windows API. Its general form is as follows:

```
HRESULT GetDC( HDC );
```

The function's only parameter is the address of the handle to the device context that is associated with the surface. If the call succeeds it returns `DD_OK`. If it fails it returns one of the following error codes:

```
DDERR_DCALREADYCREATED

DDERR_GENERIC

DDERR_INVALIDOBJECT

DDERR_INVALIDPARAMS

DDERR_INVALIDSURFACETYPE

DDERR_SURFACELOST

DDERR_UNSUPPORTED

DDERR_WASSTILLDRAWING
```

Note that the `GetDC()` function uses an internal version of the `IDirectDraw-Surface4::Lock` function to lock the surface. The surface remains locked until the `IDirectDrawSurface4::ReleaseDC` function is called. In the template program the code proceeds as follows:

```
static char szDDMessage1[] =
 "Hello World -- Press <Esc> to end program";
. . .
// Display some text on the primary surface
if(lpDDSPrimary->GetDC(&hdc) != DD_OK)
 return DDInitFailed(hWnd, hRet, "GetDC() call failed");
// Display screen message
   SetBkColor(hdc, RGB(0, 0, 255));         // Blue background
   SetTextColor(hdc, RGB(255, 255, 0));    // Yellow letters
   TextOut(hdc, 120, 200, szDDMessage1,
         lstrlen(szDDMessage1));
   lpDDSPrimary->ReleaseDC(hdc);
```

The DD Exc Mode project

The project file named DD Exc Mode in the book's CD-ROM contains the program DD Exc Mode.cpp which you can use as a template for developing simple DirectDraw applications in exclusive mode. The template contains all of the support functions previously mentioned, that is, functions to find a DirectDraw4 interface object, to test for availability of a particular display mode, to release objects, and to handle terminal errors during DirectDraw initialization. The processing consists of displaying a screen message using the text output GDI service. The code also includes a skeletal window procedure to handle keyboard input, disable the cursor, and terminate execution.

Direct Access Programming

The program found in the DD Exc Mode Project directory initializes DirectDraw, defines the cooperative level, sets a display mode, and draws text on the screen using a GDI function. These are necessary in many DirectDraw applications, but bring little advantages over conventional Windows programming. Not much is gained in performance and control by a DirectDraw application that is limited to the GDI functions. The purpose of DirectDraw is to obtain a higher level of control and to improve graphics performance. Neither of these is achieved by merely setting a display mode and displaying text or graphics to the screen using the GDI services. Before an application's performance is improved by the advantages that derived from the DirectDraw interface, it must gain access to video memory. The second level of DirectDraw advantages, those that result from using the hardware features in the video card, are discussed in the chapters that follow.

Memory-mapped video

Graphics programming in DOS is based on the fact that PC video functions are mapped to a specific area of system memory. The DOS graphics programmer determines the base address to which the video system is mapped, and the pixel format used in the current display mode. The code then proceeds to store pixel data in this memory area, and the video hardware takes care of automatically updating the display by reflecting the contents of the memory region to which it is mapped. The process is simple, although in some display modes the manipulations can become relatively complicated.

One of the difficulties of direct access to video memory in DOS programming relates to the segmented architecture of the Intel CPUs. The 16-bit internal architecture of the original Intel CPUs consisted of 16 segments, each segment containing 64 KB. A display mode of 640×480 pixels in which each pixel is stored in 1 byte of data, requires 307,200 bytes, which exceeds the span of a single segment. In fact, 307,200 data bytes require five segments for storing the pixel information. This forces the programming into the so-called *banking mechanisms*. By switching a hardware element called the bank, it is possible to map several areas of system memory to the same segment. The programming appears complicated, but after the access routines are developed for a particular display mode, the code can set any screen pixel to any desired color attribute by simply passing the pixel's screen column and row address and the desired color code.

Until the advent of DirectDraw, Windows graphics programmers had no way of accessing video memory directly. Even if a Windows programmer had been capable of finding the address to which the video display was mapped in a particular system, any attempt to access this area of memory generated a general protection fault at the operating system level. DirectDraw solves both problems: it temporarily relaxes the operating system's access restriction, and it provides information about the location and mapping of the video system.

An additional advantage is that in Win32, video display area is defined in a flat, unsegmented memory space. When the application obtains the base address of video memory, and its bit-to-pixel mapping, it can proceed to perform display operations without any banking complications nor attribute mapping schemes that complicate DOS graphics.

Hi-color modes

The development of SuperVGA video cards, which contained more video memory than the standard VGA, made possible display modes with a much richer color range than had been previously available on the PC. The modes that devote 16 or more bits for the color encoding of each screen pixel are called the *hi-color modes*. Although no formal designation for these modes has been established, the 16-bit per pixel modes are usually referred to as *real-color* modes, and those with 24- and 32-bits per pixel are called the *True-color* modes. An adapter with 2MB of video memory, which is common in today's hardware, enables several real-color and True-color modes. Real-color modes are available up to a resolution of 1600×1200 pixels, and True-color modes up to 1280×1024 pixels. The graphics programmer working with current video system technology can safely assume that most PCs support real-color and True-color modes with standard resolutions.

In Windows, all display modes with a resolution of 16-bits per pixel or higher are nonpalettized. Palettes were developed mostly to increase the colors available in modes with limited pixel depth. For general graphics programming the use of palette-independent display modes considerably simplifies the design and coding effort. In today's video cards, with several megabytes of display memory, there is little justification for using palettized modes. All real-color and true-color modes are, by definition, nonpalettized. Figure 9-1 shows the mapping of video memory bits to pixel attributes in a real-color mode.

Real-color modes are often mapped differently in the various SuperVGA cards. One problem results from the fact that 16 bits cannot be divided exactly into the three primary colors. One possible solution is to leave one bit unused and map each primary color to a 5-bit field. A more reasonable alternative is to map green to a 6-bit field because the human eye is more sensitive to this color than to red and blue. This scheme, sometimes called a 5-6-5 mapping, is the one shown in Figure 9-1.

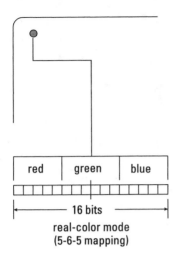

Figure 9-1: Pixel mapping in real-color modes

The fact that the individual colors are not located at a byte boundary introduces some programming in the real-color modes. In this case code must perform bitwise operations to set the corresponding fields to the required values. In the true-color modes, on the other hand, eight bits are mapped to each of the primary colors. This makes the direct access operations much easier to implement.

True-color modes

In the True-color modes each primary color (red, green, and blue) is mapped to an 8-bit field. The name True-color relates to the opinion that these modes are capable of reproducing a color range that is approximately equivalent to the sensitivity of the human eye. It is often said that the True-color modes produce a rendition that I is of photographic quality. Two different mappings are used in the True-color modes. The 24-bit mapping, shown at the top of Figure 9-2, uses three consecutive bytes to represent each of the primary colors. In the 32-bit mapping, shown at the bottom of Figure 9-2, there is an extra byte, which is unused, at the end of each pixel field.

The reason for the unused byte in the 32-bit True-color modes relates to the 32-bit architecture of the Intel CPUs, which is also the bus width of most video cards. By assigning 4 bytes to encoding the color attribute it is possible to fill a pixel with a single 32-bit memory transfer. A low-level program running in an Intel machine can store the pixel attribute in an extended machine register, such as EAX, and then transfer it into video memory with a single move instruction. By the same token, a C or C++ program can place the value into a variable of type LONG and use a pointer to LONG to move the data, also in a single operation. In the 32-bit mapping scheme, memory storage space is sacrificed for the sake of faster access.

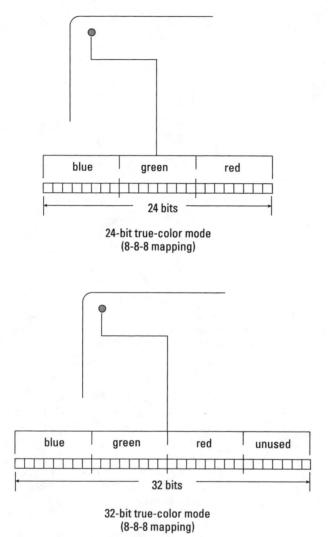

24-bit true-color mode
(8-8-8 mapping)

32-bit true-color mode
(8-8-8 mapping)

Figure 9-2: Pixel mapping in the True-color modes

Locking the surface

Applications directly access the video buffer, or any surface memory area, by first calling the Lock() function. The Lock() function returns a pointer to the top-left corner of the rectangle that defines the surface, as well as the surface pitch and l other relevant information necessary for accessing the surface. When calling the Lock() function the application can define a rectangular area within the surface, or the entire surface. If the surface is a primary surface, and the entire area is requested, then Lock() returns the base address of the video buffer and the number of bytes in each buffer row. This last parameter is called the surface pitch. At this point the DirectDraw application gains total control as well as direct access to the video display.

The Lock() function is related to the surface; therefore, it is accessed by means of the surface object returned by the call to CreateSurface(), not by a DirectDraw object. The function's general form is as follows:

```
HRESULT Lock(
        LPRECT lpDestRect,                  // 1
        LPDDSURFACEDESC2 lpDDSurfaceDesc,   // 2
        DWORD dwFlags,                      // 3
        HANDLE hEvent                       // 4
        );
```

The first parameter is a pointer to a RECT structure that describes a rectangular area on the surface that is to be accessed directly. To lock the entire surface this parameter is set to NULL. If more than one rectangle is locked, they cannot overlap. The second parameter is the address of a structure variable of type DDSURFACEDESC2, which is filled with all the information necessary to access the surface memory directly. The information that is returned in this structure includes the base address of the surface, its pitch, and its pixel format. Applications should never make assumptions about the surface pitch because this value changes according to the location of surface memory and even the version of the DirectDraw driver. The third parameter contains one or more flags that define the function's mode of operation. Table 9-1 lists the constants currently implemented in the IDirectDrawSurface4 interface.

Table 9-1	
Flags Used in the IDirectDrawSurface4::Lock Function	
Flag	**Meaning**
DDLOCK_NOSYSLOCK	Do not take the Win16Mutex. This flag is ignored when locking the primary surface.
DDLOCK_READONLY	The surface being locked will only be read.
DDLOCK_SURFACEMEMORYPTR	A valid memory pointer to the top-left corner of the specified rectangle should be returned. If no rectangle is specified, a pointer to the top of the surface is returned. This is the default and does not need to be entered explicitly.
DDLOCK_WAIT	Retries the Lock() function if it cannot be obtained because a blit operation is in progress.
DDLOCK_WRITEONLY	The surface being locked will be write-enabled.

The fourth parameter to the Lock() call was originally documented to be a handle to a system event that is triggered when the surface is ready to be locked. The newest version of the DirectDraw documentation states that it is not used and should always be set to NULL.

The DDLOCK_NOSYSLOCK flag relates to the fact that while a surface is locked DirectDraw usually holds the Win16Mutex (also known as the Win16Lock) so that gaining access to surface memory can occur safely. The Win16Mutex in effect shuts down Windows for the time that elapses between the Lock() and the Unlock() calls. If the DDLOCK_NOSYSLOCK flag is present, and the locked surface is not a primary surface, then the Win16Mutex does not take place. If a blit is in progress when Lock() is called, the function returns an error. You can prevent this by including the DDLOCK_WAIT flag, which causes the call to wait until a lock can be successfully obtained.

Lock() returns DD_OK if it succeeds or one of the following error codes if it fails:

DDERR_INVALIDOBJECT

DDERR_INVALIDPARAMS

DDERR_OUTOFMEMORY

DDERR_SURFACEBUSY

DDERR_SURFACELOST

DDERR_WASSTILLDRAWING

When Lock() succeeds, the application can retrieve a surface memory pointer and other necessary data and start accessing surface memory directly. Code can continue to access surface memory until a call to the Unlock() function is made. As soon as the surface is unlocked, the surface memory pointer becomes invalid. While the lock is in progress, applications cannot blit to or from surface memory. GDI functions fail when used on a locked surface.

Obtaining surface data

When the Lock() call returns DD_OK, the application can access the corresponding members of the DDSURFACEDESC2 structure variable passed in the call to obtain the data necessary for direct access. Assuming that application code knows the display mode and its corresponding pixel format, then the two data elements necessary for accessing the locked surface are its base address and the surface pitch. The base address is returned in a structure member of type LPVOID, and the surface pitch in a structure member of type LONG. Applications that plan to de-reference the surface pointer typically cast it into one that matches the surface's color format. For example, a program that has set a 24-bit True-color mode is likely to access surface memory in byte-size units. In this case the pointer can be cast into a variable of type LPBYTE. On the other hand, an application executing in a 16-bit real-color mode typecasts the pointer into a LPWORD type, and one that has set a 32-bit True-color mode may typecast into an LPLONG data type.

The following code fragment shows the use of the Lock() function in a routine that fills a 50×50 pixel box in a 24-bit True-color video mode. The box is arbitrarily located at screen row number 80 and pixel column number 300. The pixels are filled with the red attribute by setting each third surface byte to 0xff and the other three color bytes to 0x0.

```
LONG         localPitch;     // Local variable for surface pitch
LPBYTE       localStart;     // and for buffer start
LPBYTE       lastRow;        // Storage for row start
 . . .
// Attempt to lock the surface for direct access
if (lpDDSPrimary->Lock(NULL, &ddsd, DDLOCK_WAIT, NULL)\
   != DD_OK)
   DDInitFailed(hWnd, hRet, "Lock failed");
// Store video system data
   vidPitch = ddsd.lPitch;       // Pitch
   vidStart = ddsd.lpSurface;    // Buffer address

// Surface is locked. Global video data is as follows:
// vidPitch holds surface pitch
// vidStart holds video buffer start
// Copy to local variables typecasting void pointer
   localPitch = vidPitch;
   localStart = (LPBYTE) vidStart;

// Index to row 80
   localStart = localStart + (80 * localPitch);
// Move right 300 pixels
   localStart += (400 * 3);

// Display 50 rows, 50 times
   for(int i = 0; i < 50; i++){
      lastRow = localStart;        // Save start of row
   for(int j = 0; j < 50; j++) {
      *localStart = 0x0;           // blue attribute
      localStart++;
      *localStart = 0x0;           // green attribute
      localStart++;
      *localStart = 0xff;          // red attribute
      localStart++;
   }
 localStart = lastRow + localPitch;
}

lpDDSPrimary->Unlock(NULL);
```

Low-Level Programming

The maximum advantages of direct access to video memory are realized when the code is highly optimized: this means programming in 80x86 assembly language. Although an entire Windows application can be coded in assembly language, this approach usually entails more difficulties and complications than can be justified by the relatively few advantages. On the other hand, most C and C++ compilers provide in-line assemblers that allow embedding assembly language code in a C or C++ program. The result is an easy-to-produce multilanguage program with the advantages of both environments.

An added benefit of in-line assembly is that the low-level code can reference, by name, any C++ language variable or function that is in scope. This makes it easier to access data and processing routines than is the case when the assembly language source is in a module that must be assembled and linked separately. In-line assembly also avoids many of the complication and portability problems usually associated with parameter passing conventions in multilanguage programming. The resulting development environment has all the advantages of high-level programming, as well as the power and flexibility of low-level code. A graphics programmer cannot ignore the potential of this language combination. Visual C++ and Borland C Builder support in-line assembly.

DirectDraw has made assembly language coding in Windows applications an attractive option. Direct access to video memory, made possible by DirectX, opens the possibility of using assembly language to maximize performance and control. The result is a DOS-like development environment. However, in conventional GDI programming there is little justification for using low-level code.

_asm keyword

The _asm keyword is used in Visual C++ to produce assembly language instructions, one at a time, or in blocks. When the compiler encounters the _asm symbol it invokes the in-line assembler. The assembler, in turn, generates the necessary opcodes and inserts them into the object file. In this process the development system limits its action to that of an assembler program; no modification of the coding takes place and no interpretation or optimization effort is made. Thus, the programmer is certain that the resulting code is identical to the source. The fact that no separate assembly or linking is necessary considerably simplifies the development process.

Although the _asm keyword can precede a single instruction, it is more common to use it to generate a block of several assembly language lines. Braces are used to delimit the source block, as in the following example:

```
_asm
{
  ; Assembly language code follows:
    PUSH    EBX            ; EBX to stack
```

```
        MOV     EAX,vidPitch  ; vidPitch is a C variable
        MOV     EBX,80        ; Constant to register
        MUL     EBX           ; Integer multiply
        POP     EBX           ; Restore EBX
}
```

The second instruction of the preceding code fragment loads a variable defined in C++ code into a machine register. Accessing high-level language variables is one of the most convenient features of in-line assembly. Assembly language code can also store results in high-level variables.

Coding restrictions

There are a few rules and conventions that in-line assembly language code must follow. Perhaps the most important one is to preserve the registers that are used by C++. A source of problems is when the C++ program is compiled with the _fastcall switch or the /Gr compiler option. In these cases, arguments to functions are passed in the ECX and EDX machine registers; therefore, they must be preserved by the assembly language program section. The easiest way to avoid this concern is to make sure that programs that use in-line assembly are not compiled with either of these options. In Visual C++ the compiler options can be examined by selecting Settings in the Project Menu and then clicking the C/C++ tab. The Project Options window in this dialog box shows the compiler switches and options that are active. Make sure that you inspect the settings for both the Release and the Debug options, as shown in the Settings For: scroll box. Figure 9-3 is a screen snapshot of Developer Studio Project Settings dialog box.

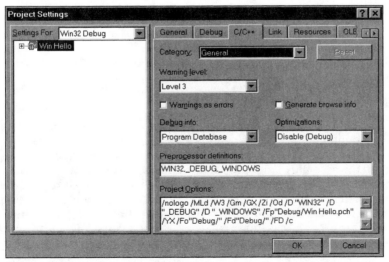

Figure 9-3: Inspecting compiler switches and options in the Project Settings dialog box

It has been consistently documented in the Microsoft literature that programs that do not use the _fastcall switch or the /Gr compiler options can assume that the four general- purpose registers do not need to be preserved. Consequently, EAX, EBX, ECX, and EDX are free and available to the assembly language code. In regards to the pointer registers and the direction flag, the Microsoft documentation is inconsistent. Some versions of the *Visual C++ Programmers Guide* state that ESI and EDI must be preserved, whereas other versions state the contrary. Regarding the direction flag, the original Microsoft C++ compilers required that the flag be cleared before returning, whereas the most recent manuals say that the state of the direction flag must be preserved. These newer documents also state that all other registers must be preserved.

Taking into account these discrepancies, and in fear of future variations, the safest approach is to use the general-purpose registers freely (EAX, EBX, ECX, and EDX) but to preserve all other machine registers and the direction flag. This means that on entry to the routine the in-line assembly code must push on the stack the registers that must be preserved, as well as the flags, and restore them before exiting the _asm block. This is the approach that we use in the book's sample code. The processing in a routine that uses the ESI and EDI registers can be as follows:

```
_asm
{
    PUSH      ESI              ; Save context
    PUSH      EDI
    PUSHF
    ; Processing operations go here
    ; .
    ; .
    ; .
    ; Exit code
    POPF                       ; Restore context
    POP       EDI
    POP       ESI
}
```

Assembly language functions

Often the low-level processing routines can be conveniently located in functions that can be called by the C++ code. When the assembly code is not created by means of the on-line feature of the compiler, that is, when it is written for a separate assembler, then the assembly language routine and the C++ must interface following the calling conventions adopted by the compiler. The usual procedure is that C++ places the parameters in the stack at the time the call is made, and the assembly language routine removes them from the stack making sure that the stack integrity is preserved. In this case the assembly and the C++ code usually reside in separate files that are referenced at link time.

For applications that use in-line assembly, the interlanguage protocol can be considerably simplified by creating a C++ function shell to hold the assembly code. In this case the use of the stack for parameter passing becomes almost unnecessary because the assembly code can reference the C++ variables directly. One possible drawback is that the in-line assembler does not allow the use of the data definition directives DB, DW, DD, DQ, and DT or the DUP operator. Therefore, the data elements used by the assembly language code must be defined as C++ variables. The following example is an assembly language routine to add three integers and return the sum to the calling code. The processing is contained in a C++ function shell, as follows:

```
int SumOf3(int x, int y, int z)
  {
   int total;          // C++ variable to hold sum

   _asm
   {
   MOV     EAX,x        ; move first parameter to accumulator
   ADD     EAX,y        ; add second parameter
   ADD     EAX,z        ; and third parameter
   MOV     total,EAX    ; store sum
   }
   return total;
}
The calling code could be as follows:
   int     aSum;            // local variable for sum
   . . .
   aSum = SumOf3(10, 20, 30);
```

This example shows that the assembly language code can access the parameters passed to the C++ function, as well as store data in a local variable that is also accessible to C++. This easy mechanism for sharing data is one of the major advantages of in-line assembly.

Direct Access Primitives

An application that uses direct access to the video buffer can usually benefit from a few primitive functions that perform the core processing operations. Depending on performance requirements these primitives can be coded in C++, or using in-line assembly. The primitive routines are mode-specific, and the code assumes that a particular display mode is available and has been selected. It is impossible to predict the specific functions and the number of primitives that are necessary for a particular graphics program. Among other factors, this depends on what portion of the processing is performed using direct access to video memory, and on the size and scope of the application. The resulting complexity can range from a few simple routines to a full-size, stand-alone graphics package. In this section we consider several direct access primitives that can be generally useful; they are:

✦ Function to lock a DirectDraw primary surface and store the video buffer's base address and pitch

✦ Function to release a DirectDraw primary surface

✦ Function to set an individual screen pixel at given coordinates and color attributes and to read the attributes of a screen pixel located at given coordinates

✦ Function to lock a DirectDraw primary surface, fill a pixel rectangle, at given coordinates, dimensions, and color attributes, and then release the surface

✦ Function to lock a DirectDraw primary surface, draw a single-line box, at given coordinates, dimensions, and color attributes, and then release the surface

Many of the routines that access video memory directly must perform calculations to determine the offset of a particular pixel in the display surface. For example, a call to fill a screen rectangle passes the address of its top-left corner as parameters. The processing must convert this address, often in column/row format, into a video memory offset. It is possible to develop a primitive function that calculates this pixel offset, but this approach introduces a call-return overhead that adversely affects performance. More often the address calculations are part of the processing routine. Therefore, before attempting to develop the direct access primitives, we take a closer look at the low-level operations necessary for calculating a pixel addresses.

Calculating a pixel address

A display mode's resolution, color depth, and pitch determine the location of each pixel on the surface. This makes pixel address calculations specific to a display mode. In the case of the hi-color modes, the variables that enter into the calculation of a pixel offset are the number of bytes per pixel and the surface pitch. In addition, the horizontal and vertical resolution of the display mode can be used to check for invalid input values because it is the responsibility of direct access routines not to read or write outside of the locked surface area. Figure 9-4 shows the parameters that define the location of a screen pixel and the formula used for calculating its offset.

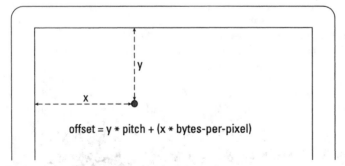

offset = y * pitch + (x * bytes-per-pixel)

Figure 9-4: Pixel offset calculation

Using the Lock() function

As discussed earlier, the DirectDraw Lock() function is used to lock the surface so that it can be accessed directly. The call also returns a pointer to the top-left corner of the rectangle that defines the surface, as well as its pitch. In the case of a primary surface, when the entire area is requested, Lock() returns the base address of the video buffer. The pitch, in this case, is the number of bytes in each screen buffer row.

Another effect of the Lock() call is that Windows relaxes its normal protection over video display memory. If a successful Lock() call has not been previously made, any instruction that attempts to access video memory immediately generates a protection violation exception and the application is terminated. This is important to keep in mind while designing direct access functions because it is this feature that makes the Lock() call necessary if a previous Lock() has been released. This is true even when the video buffer address and pitch have been previously obtained and stored. On the other hand, the surface lock can be retained during more than one access to video memory. This means that a routine that sequentially sets several screen pixels needs to call the Lock() function only once. After the pixel sequence is set, then the lock can be released. Also recall that the Lock() call requires a pointer to an IDirectDrawSurface4 object, which is usually obtained by means of the CreateSurface() function. The following is a simple locking function for the entire primary surface:

```
// Global variables for surface pitch and base address
LONG        vidPitch;
LPVOID      vidStart;
    . . . .
//****************************************************************
// Name: LockSurface
// Desc: Function to lock the entire DirectDraw primary surface
//       and store the direct access parameters
//
// PRE CONDITIONS:
// 1. First parameter is a pointer to DirectDraw surface
// 2. Video display globals have been declared as follows:
//     LONG    vidPitch; // Pitch
//     LPVOID  vidStart; // Buffer address
//
// POST CONDITIONS:
// Returns 1 if call succeeds and 0 if it fails
//****************************************************************
int LockSurface(LPDIRECTDRAWSURFACE4  lpSurface)
{
    // Attempt to lock the surface for direct access
    if (lpSurface->Lock(NULL, &ddsd, DDLOCK_WAIT, NULL)\
    != DD_OK)
    return 0;                        // Lock failed
    // Store video system data
```

```
        vidPitch = ddsd.lPitch;       // Pitch
        vidStart = ddsd.lpSurface;    // Buffer address
        return 1;                     // Surface locked
    }
```

Using the Unlock() function

A function call to release the locked surface is also necessary. In this case the processing is quite simple. In addition to the call to the Unlock() function, the code resets the access variables to zero. This makes it easier to determine if a lock is being held because a zero value is invalid for either variable. The routine itself tests one of these variables before attempting to release the lock.

```
//****************************************************************
// Name: ReleaseSurface
// Desc: Function to release locked surface
// PRE CONDITIONS:
// 1. Parameter is pointer to locked DirectDraw surface
// 2. Video display globals as follows:
//     LONG    vidPitch; // Pitch
//     LPVOID  vidStart; // Buffer address
//****************************************************************
void ReleaseSurface(LPDIRECTDRAWSURFACE4  lpSurface)
{
    if(vidStart != 0) {
        lpSurface->Unlock(NULL);
        // Clear global variables
        vidPitch = 0;
        vidStart = 0;
    }
    return;
}
```

This version of the ReleaseSurface() function assumes that the object of the lock was the entire surface.

Pixel-level primitives

Pixel-level operations are the lowest-level graphics routines available, to the point that they are often considered device driver components, rather than primitives. When you use pixel read and pixel write routines, it is possible to construct any graphics routine desired. The Windows GDI provides functions to set and read a single pixel. The disadvantage of using these functions is that they are extremely slow. A drawing operation that repeatedly calls GDI SetPixel() or ReadPixel() functions is likely to execute at an unacceptably slow speed. However, direct access pixel-level routines appear to execute several hundred times faster than the GDI counterparts. The code for the pixel-level read and write primitives is as follows:

```
// Global variables for surface pitch and base address
LONG        vidPitch;
LPVOID    vidStart;
  . . .
//*****************************************************************
// Name: DASetPixel
// Desc: Assembly language code to set a single screen pixel
//       using direct access to the video buffer
//
// PRE CONDITIONS:
// 1. Successful Lock() of surface
//    Video display globals are stored as follows:
//    LONG      vidPitch;    // Pitch
//    LPVOID    vidStart;     // Buffer address
// 2. First and second parameters are the pixel coordinates
// 3. Last three parameters are pixel RGB attributes
// 4. Assumes true color mode 640 x 480 x 28
//
// POST CONDITIONS:
// None
//*****************************************************************
void DASetPixel( int xCoord, int yCoord,
          BYTE redAtt, BYTE greenAtt, BYTE blueAtt)
{
    _asm
     {
    PUSH    ESI                 ; Save context
    PUSHF
    MOV     EAX,yCoord          ; Row number to EAX
    MUL     vidPitch;
    MOV     EBX,EAX             ; Store in EBX
    MOV     EAX,xCoord          ; x coordinate
    MOV     CX,3
    MUL     CX                  ; 3 bytes per pixel
    ADD     EAX,EBX             ; move right to x coordinate
    MOV     ESI,vidStart
    ADD     ESI,EAX
  ; Load color attributes into registers
    MOV     AL,blueAtt
    MOV     DH,greenAtt
    MOV     DL,redAtt
  ; Set the pixel
    MOV     [ESI],AL            ; Set blue attribute
    INC     ESI
    MOV     [ESI],DH            ; Set green
    INC     ESI
```

```
        MOV     [ESI],DL         ; Set red
        POPF                     ; Restore context
        POP     ESI
        }
    return;
}

//*****************************************************************
// Name: DAReadPixel
// Desc: Assembly language code to read a single screen pixel
//       using direct access to the video buffer
//
// PRE CONDITIONS:
// 1. Successful Lock() of surface
//    Video display globals are stored as follows:
//    LONG     vidPitch;    // Pitch
//    LPVOID   vidStart;    // Buffer address
// 2. First and second parameters are the pixel coordinates
//    values are returned in public variables named
//    pixelRed, pixelGreen, and pixelBlue
// 3. Assumes true color mode 640X480X28
//
// POST CONDITIONS:
// None
//*****************************************************************
void DAReadPixel( int xCoord, int yCoord)
{
    _asm
    {
    PUSH    ESI              ; Save context
    PUSHF
    MOV     EAX,yCoord       ; Row number to EAX
    MUL     vidPitch
    MOV     EBX,EAX          ; Store in EBX
    MOV     EAX,xCoord       ; x coordinate
    MOV     CX,3
    MUL     CX               ; 3 bytes per pixel
    ADD     EAX,EBX          ; move right to x coordinate
    MOV     ESI,vidStart
    ADD     ESI,EAX
    ; Read and store pixel attributes
    MOV     AL,[ESI]         ; Get blue attribute
    INC     ESI
    MOV     DH,[ESI]         ; green
    INC     ESI
    MOV     DL,[ESI]         ; and red
    MOV     pixelBlue,AL     ; Store blue
    MOV     pixelGreen,DH    ; green
    MOV     pixelRed,DL      ; and red
    POPF                     ; Restore context
    POP     ESI
    }
    return;
}
```

Rectangle filling

Filling rectangular areas with a particular color attribute is such a useful manipulation that most applications that access memory directly can profit from such a primitive. To define a screen rectangle you can use the coordinates of its diagonally opposite corners, or the coordinates of one corner and the rectangle's dimensions. The following listed function adopts the second approach. In addition, the routine needs to know the values for the RGB color attributes to use in the fill. The code is as follows:

```
//****************************************************************
// Name: DARectangle
// Desc: Assembly language code to draw a rectangle on the
screen
//       using direct access to the video buffer
//
// PRE CONDITIONS:
// 1. First parameter is pointer to surface
// 2. Second and third parameters are rectangle's x and y
//    coordinates
// 3. Fourth parameter is rectangle width, in pixels
// 4. Fifth parameter is rectangle height, in pixels
// 5. Last three parameters are RGB attributes
// 6. Assumes true color mode is 640 x 480 x 24

// POST CONDITIONS:
// Returns 1 if lock succeeded and 0 if it failed
//****************************************************************
int DARectangle(LPDIRECTDRAWSURFACE4 lpPrimary,
     int yCoord, int xCoord,
     int width, int height,
     BYTE redAtt, BYTE greenAtt, BYTE blueAtt)
{
 // Attempt to lock the surface for direct access
 if (!LockSurface(lpPrimary))
      return 0;                      // Lock failed

 _asm
 {
      PUSH      ESI              ; Save context
      PUSHF
      MOV       EAX,yCoord       ; Row number to EAX
      MUL       vidPitch;
      MOV       EBX,EAX          ; Store in EBX
      MOV       EAX,xCoord       ; x coordinate
      MOV       CX,3
      MUL       CX               ; 3 bytes per pixel
      ADD       EAX,EBX          ; move right to x coordinate
      MOV       ESI,vidStart
      ADD       ESI,EAX
      ; Load color attributes into registers
      MOV       AL,blueAtt
      MOV       DH,greenAtt
```

```
              MOV       DL,redAtt
              MOV       EBX,height      ; number of lines in rectangle
      NEXT_LINE:
              PUSH      ESI             ; Save start of line
              MOV       ECX,width       ; x dimension of rectangle
      SET_PIX:
              MOV       [ESI],AL        ; Set blue attribute
              INC       ESI             ; Next pixel
              MOV       [ESI],DH        ; Set green
              INC       ESI             ; Next pixel
              MOV       [ESI],DL        ; Set red
              INC       ESI             ; Next pixel
              LOOP      SET_PIX
          ; Pixel line is set
              POP       ESI
              ADD       ESI,vidPitch
              DEC       EBX
              JNZ       NEXT_LINE
              POPF                      ; Restore context
              POP       ESI
          }
      ReleaseSurface(lpPrimary);
      return 1;       // Exit
   }
```

Observe that the DARectangle() calls LockSurface() and ReleaseSurface()
functions previously developed. Alternatively, the function could be modified easily
to call Lock() and Unlock() directly.

Box-drawing

Drawing a box is a little more difficult than filling a rectangle. The actual processing
can be based on two simple routines: one to draw a horizontal line and another
one to draw a vertical line. The core routine sets up the machine registers with
the necessary data and then calls the horizontal and vertical line routines to do
the actual drawing. You would probably find other uses for the vertical and
horizontal line drawing functions. The parameters to the box drawing routine
are the same as those for the rectangle fill. They include the pointer to the
surface, the box coordinates, its dimensions, and the color attributes. The
code is as follows:

```
//*************************************************************
// Name: DABox
// Desc: Assembly language code to draw a screen box with
//       single-pixel wide lines, using direct access to the
//       video buffer
//
// PRE CONDITIONS:
// 1. First parameter is pointer to surface
// 2. Second and third parameters are the coordinates of the
//    top-left corner of the box
// 3. Fourth parameter is box width, in pixels
// 4. Fifth parameter is box height, in pixels
```

```
// 5. Last three parameters are RGB attributes
// 6. True color mode is 640X480X24
//
// POST CONDITIONS:
// Returns 1 if lock succeeds and 0 if it fails
//***************************************************************
int DABox(LPDIRECTDRAWSURFACE4 lpPrimary,
      int xCoord, int yCoord,
      int width, int height,
      BYTE redAtt, BYTE greenAtt, BYTE blueAtt)
{
  // Attempt to lock the surface for direct access
  if (!LockSurface(lpPrimary))
      return 0;                        // Lock failed

  _asm
  {
    PUSH     ESI            ; Save context
    PUSHF
    MOV      EAX,yCoord     ; Row number to EAX
    MUL      vidPitch;

    MOV      EBX,EAX        ; Store in EBX
    MOV      EAX,xCoord     ; x coordinate
    MOV      CX,3
    MUL      CX             ; 3 bytes per pixel
    ADD      EAX,EBX        ; move right to x coordinate
    MOV      ESI,vidStart
    ADD      ESI,EAX
    ; Load color attributes into registers
    MOV      AL,blueAtt
    MOV      DH,greenAtt
    MOV      DL,redAtt
    ; Draw top horizontal line
    MOV      ECX,width      ; x dimension of rectangle
    CALL     DAHorLine
    ; Draw bottom horizontal line
    PUSH     ESI            ; Save top left corner address
    PUSH     EAX            ; Save color
    PUSH     EDX
    MOV      EAX,height     ; Number of lines to EAX
    MUL      vidPitch;      ; Times the length of each line
    ADD      ESI,EAX        ; Add to start
    MOV      ECX,width      ; x dimension of rectangle
    POP      EDX            ; Restore color
    POP      EAX
    CALL     DAHorLine      ; Draw line
    POP      ESI            ; Restore start of rectangle
    ; Draw left vertical line
    MOV      EBX,vidPitch   ; Pitch to EBX
    MOV      ECX,height     ; Pixel height of vertical line
    CALL     DAVerLine
    ; Draw right vertical line
    ; ESI holds address of top-left corner
```

```
        PUSH    EAX             ; Save color
        PUSH    EDX
        MOV     EAX,width       ; Number of lines to EAX
        MOV     CX,3            ; Pixels per line
        MUL     CX
        ADD     ESI,EAX         ; Add to start
        MOV     ECX,height      ; Line y dimensions
        INC     ECX             ; One more pixel
        POP     EDX             ; Restore color
        POP     EAX
        CALL    DAVerLine       ; Draw line
        POPF                    ; Restore context
        POP     ESI
        }

    ReleaseSurface(lpPrimary);
    return 1;                   // Exit
}


//*************************************************************
// Name: DAHorLine
// Desc: Assembly language support function for DABox()
//                draws a horizontal pixel line
// PRE CONDITIONS:
//     ESI holds buffer address of start of line
//     ECX hold pixel length of line
//     AL = blue attribute
//     DH = green attribute
//     DL = red attribute
// POST CONDITIONS:
//     ECX is destroyed
//     All others are preserved
//*************************************************************
void DAHorLine()
{
    _asm
    {
    PUSH    ESI             ; Save start of line
DRAW_HLINE:
    MOV     [ESI],AL        ; Set blue attribute
    INC     ESI
    MOV     [ESI],DH        ; Set green
    INC     ESI
    MOV     [ESI],DL        ; Set red
    INC     ESI
    LOOP    DRAW_HLINE
    POP     ESI
    }
    return;
}
```

```
//*****************************************************************
// Name: DAVerLine
// Desc: Assembly language support function for DABox()
//       draws a vertical pixel line
// PRE CONDITIONS:
//     ESI holds buffer address of start of line
//     ECX hold pixel height of line
//     EBX holds surface pitch
//     AL = blue attribute
//     DH = green attribute
//     DL = red attribute
// POST CONDITIONS:
//     ECX is destroyed
//     All others are preserved
//*****************************************************************
void DAVerLine()
{
    _asm
    {
    PUSH      ESI               ; Save start of line
DRAW_VLINE:
    PUSH      ESI               ; Save start address
    MOV       [ESI],AL          ; Set blue attribute
    INC       ESI
    MOV       [ESI],DH          ; Set green
    INC       ESI
    MOV       [ESI],DL          ; Set red
    POP       ESI               ; Restore start
    ADD       ESI,EBX           ; Index to next line
    LOOP      DRAW_VLINE
    POP       ESI
    }
  return;
}
```

Raster Operations

Direct access to video memory, combined with low-level coding, provides
the programmer with a powerful, DOS-like, graphics toolkit. One of the many
possibilities consists of using logical operations to combine object and screen
data. These are sometimes called *raster operations*, raster ops, or mixes. A raster
operation determines how two or more source images are combined to produce a
destination image. Arithmetic and logical operators are used to produce the desired
effect. The simplest one is to replace the destination with the source. This is what
takes place when you write a pixel value to the video screen, as in the preceding
examples. When you use a MOV instruction to write a color value to the screen
we are actually replacing the destination with the source. The simplest way to
replace the destination with the source pixel is as follows:

```
    MOV     [ESI],AL
```

In many cases a raster operation requires a read-modify-write sequence. For example, you could increase the brightness of a pixel value by adding a constant to its value as follows:

```
MOV    AL,[ESI]       ; Read pixel
ADD    AL,20          ; Modify
MOV    [ESI],AL       ; Write
```

The problem with this type of processing is that the read-modify-write cycle takes considerable processing time. For this reason some graphics processors perform raster operations in hardware.

Nevertheless, the Pentium CPU has several logical operators that enable you to combine foreground and background data by means of a single instruction. For example, you can use a logical AND operation to combine foreground bits (object data) and background data. The result is that the background bits are preserved whenever the foreground bit is zero, and vice versa. The object data is sometimes referred to as a mask. For example, a graphics application can overlay a white grid over an existing image by ANDing a mask consisting of 1-bit in the solid portion of the grid and of 0-bits in the transparent portion. The Pentium contains opcodes for AND, OR, XOR, and NOT operations. For example, the following operation ANDs the value in the AL register with the screen data contained in the address pointed at by ESI:

```
AND    [ESI],AL
```

In C++ programming the bitwise operators perform a similar action. In the following sections we examine the XOR mix, which is one of the most popular raster operations in graphics programming.

XOR animation

Animating a screen object often requires that its image be erased from the current screen position before being redrawn at its new location. Graphics programmers sometimes call this sequence the save-draw-redraw cycle. If the object is not erased before it is redrawn, its apparent movement leaves an undesirable image track on the display surface. We can make an object appear to move laterally, left to right, by progressively redrawing and erasing its screen image at consecutively larger x coordinates. To do this in a conventional manner we have to perform a rather complex sequence of operations:

1. Preserve the screen image data in the area where the object is displayed.

2. Draw the object.

3. Erase the object by restoring the original screen image.

Step 1 requires reading all data in the screen area that is occupied by the animated object, while Step 3 requires redisplaying the saved image. Both operations are time-consuming, and in computer animation, time is always in short supply.

Several hardware and software techniques have been devised for performing the save-draw-redraw cycle. In later chapters we explore DirectDraw animation techniques that are powerful and versatile. These higher-level methods are based on flipping surfaces containing images and on taking advantage of the hardware blitters that are available in most video cards. Here we are concerned with the simplest possible approach to figure animation. This technique, which is made feasible by the high performance obtained with direct access to video memory, is based on the properties of the logical exclusive or XOR operation. Although it is theoretically possible to perform XOR animation using high-level code, the most efficient and powerful technique requires assembly language.

The action of the logical XOR can be described by saying that a bit in the result is set if both operands contain opposite values. It follows that XORing the same value twice restores the original contents, as in the following case:

```
                        10000001 <= original value  ----|
            XOR value => 10110011                        |
                        ---------                         |
                        00110010  <= first result        |
            XOR value => 10110011                        |
                        ---------                         |
                        10000001  <= final result ------|
```

XOR, like all bitwise operations, takes place on a bit-by-bit basis. In this example the final result (10000001) is the same as the original value.

Animation techniques can be based on this property of the bitwise XOR because it provides a convenient and fast way for consecutively drawing and erasing a screen object. The object is drawn on the screen by XORing it with the background data. XORing a second time erases the object and restores the original background. Therefore, the save-draw-redraw cycle now becomes an XOR-XOR cycle, which is considerably faster and simpler to implement. The XOR method is particularly useful when more than one animated object can coincide on the same screen position because it ensures that the original screen image is preserved automatically.

There are also disadvantages to using XOR in computer animation. The most important one is that the image changes according to the background. This is because each individual pixel in the object is determined both by the XORed value and by the destination pixel. For example, the following XOR operation produces a red object (in RGB format) on a bright white screen background:

```
                          R G B
            background => 1 1 1  ( white)
             XOR value => 0 1 1
                          -------
                result => 1 0 0  ( red )
```

However, if the same XOR operation is applied over a black background the results are as follows:

```
                              R G B
              background =>   0 0 0   ( black )
               XOR value =>   0 1 1
                            -------
                  result =>   0 1 1   ( cyan )
```

This property of the XOR operation, which makes the object's color change as it moves over different backgrounds, can be at times an advantage, or a disadvantage. For example, an object displayed by conventional methods can disappear as it moves over a background of its same color, while if this object is XORed onto the screen it remains visible over most backgrounds. On the other hand, it may happen that the color of a graphics object is an important characteristic. In this case the changes brought about by XOR display operations may not be acceptable. Figure 9-5 shows how the XOR operation changes the attributes of an object (circle) as it is displayed over different backgrounds.

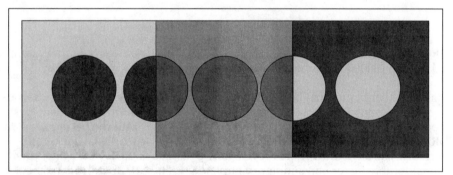

Figure 9-5: Effect of XOR operation on figure color

XORing a bitmap

One of the many possible uses of the XOR raster operation is to project a bitmap over an existing background. The graphics programmer can take advantage of the automatic draw-erase action of the XOR function to animate cursors and small sprites with minimal processing. The main drawback is that the object's color is partially determined by the background color, as already mentioned. The following function XORs a variable-size bitmap onto the video display, at any desired screen location. The function assumes a True-color display mode in $640 \times 480 \times 24$ format.

```
// Cross-shaped bitmap for demonstrating the DAXorBitmap()
// function
```

```
// 2 X 8 Bitmap      0   1   2   3   4   5   6   7
BYTE mapData[] ={ 0x00,0x00,0x00,0x7f,0x7f,0x00,0x00,0x00,// 0
                  0x00,0x00,0x00,0x7f,0x7f,0x00,0x00,0x00,// 1
                  0x00,0x00,0x00,0x7f,0x7f,0x00,0x00,0x00,// 2
                  0x7f,0x7f,0x7f,0x7f,0x7f,0x7f,0x7f,0x7f,// 3
                  0x7f,0x7f,0x7f,0x7f,0x7f,0x7f,0x7f,0x7f,// 4
                  0x00,0x00,0x00,0x7f,0x7f,0x00,0x00,0x00,// 5
                  0x00,0x00,0x00,0x7f,0x7f,0x00,0x00,0x00,// 6
                  0x00,0x00,0x00,0x7f,0x7f,0x00,0x00,0x00};// 7
    . . .


//****************************************************************
// Name: DAXorBitmap
// Desc: Assembly language code to XOR a bitmap onto the screen
//       using direct access to the video buffer
//
// PRE CONDITIONS:
// 1. First parameter is pointer to surface
// 2. Second and third parameters are x and y screen
//    coordinates
// 3. Fourth parameter is bitmap width, in pixels
// 4. Fifth parameter is bitmap height, in pixels
// 5. Sixth parameter is pointer to bitmap
// 6. Assumes true-color mode 640X480X28
//
// POST CONDITIONS:
// Returns 1 if call succeeds and 0 if it fails
//****************************************************************
int DAXorBitmap(LPDIRECTDRAWSURFACE4 lpPrimary,
                int xCoord, int yCoord,
                int bmWidth, int bmHeight,
                LPBYTE bitMapPtr)
{
    // Attempt to lock the surface for direct access
    if (!LockSurface(lpPrimary))
        return 0;                     // Lock failed

    _asm
    {
    PUSH    ESI               ; Save context
    PUSH    EDI
    PUSHF

    MOV     EAX,yCoord        ; Row number to EAX
    MUL     vidPitch;
    MOV     EBX,EAX           ; Store in EBX
    MOV     EAX,xCoord        ; x coordinate
    MOV     CX,3
    MUL     CX                ; 3 bytes per pixel
    ADD     EAX,EBX           ; move right to x-coordinate
    MOV     EDI,vidStart
```

```
        ADD     EDI,EAX
        MOV     ESI,bitMapPtr     ; Pointer to bitmap
        MOV     EBX,bmHeight      ; number of lines in bitmap
NEXT_BM_LINE:
        PUSH    EDI               ; Save start of line
        MOV     ECX,bmWidth       ; x-dimension of bitmap
XOR_PIX_LINE:
        MOV     AL,[ESI]          ; Bitmap data to AL
        XOR     [EDI],AL          ; Set blue attribute
        INC     EDI
        XOR     [EDI],AL          ; Set green
        INC     EDI
        XOR     [EDI],AL          ; Set red
        INC     EDI
        INC     ESI               ; Bitmap pointer to next byte
        LOOP    XOR_PIX_LINE
    ; End of line
        POP     EDI               ; Pointer to start of line
        ADD     EDI,vidPitch      ; Index to next line
        DEC     EBX               ; EBX is Lines counter
        JNZ     NEXT_BM_LINE
        ; Done!
        POPF                      ; Restore context
        POP     EDI
        POP         ESI
    }
    ReleaseSurface(lpPrimary);
    return 1;                     // Exit
}
```

In this function a single bitmap attribute is XORed with all three background colors. This keeps the bitmap small but limits the range of possible results. It would be quite easy to modify the routine so that the bitmap contains a byte value for each color attribute in a True-color mode.

DirectDraw Access Demo Project

The program named DD_Access.cpp, located in the DD Access Demo project folder of the book's CD-ROM, is a demonstration of the direct access techniques discussed in this chapter. The program contains all the functions listed in this chapter, plus some other ones not mentioned in the text. It executes in exclusive, full-screen display mode. The text messages are displayed using GDI graphics and the geometrical figures using the direct access functions developed in this chapter. Color plate 5 is a screen snapshot of the demo program. The labels list the program functions that perform the corresponding operations.

Summary

In this chapter you learned how to gain direct access to the video buffer using the facilities provided by DirectX. Direct access methods give the Windows programmer a level of control and the advantages of high performance coding that are characteristic of DOS graphics. At the same time, direct access techniques in Windows have greater coding facilities and operating system support. In Windows programming, the main disadvantages are that direct access is more difficult and that it introduces device-dependency concerns. Whether to use direct access, and if so, how much to use, are questions that must be answered in the context of each particular application. Fortunately, conventional Windows graphics and direct access techniques can be combined in DirectDraw applications that execute in exclusive mode.

In the following chapter we look at offscreen surfaces and bitBlt operations in DirectDraw. These are the fundamental mechanisms that support the fast manipulation of graphics images, one of the most important advantages of DirectDraw.

✦   ✦   ✦

Blitting and Blit-time Transformations

In this chapter we discuss the DirectDraw operations used in static rendering of bitmapped images. The fundamental mechanism for rendering bitmaps is called a *blit*, short for bit block transfer. The blit is one of the GDI functions but Direct-Draw provides its own versions, in the form of two functions named Blt() and BltFast(). A third variation, called BltBatch(), has been announced for future versions of the DirectX SDK. Another rendering operation is the *overlay*. As the name implies, overlays are like a drawing on transparent media, which can be placed over an image and then removed, restoring the original. The overlay technique simplifies many graphics rendering operations. At the present time overlays are supported by few video cards, and those that implement it do so inconsistently. For this reason we do not discuss overlays in this book.

Surfaces Revisited

Before discussing DirectDraw blits, we must expand some of the notions related to DirectDraw surfaces, first presented in Chapter 7. The following are the fundamental concepts introduced in this section:

 ◆ Surface operations
 ◆ Primary and off-screen surfaces
 ◆ Enumerating surfaces
 ◆ Losing and restoring surfaces
 ◆ Experimenting with surfaces

Surface operations

A DirectDraw surface is defined as a linear area of video memory, usually devoted to holding image data. Recall that a DirectDrawSurface is a COM object in itself, with its own interface, and that this interface is referenced in all surface-related operations. Applications create a DirectDraw surface by calling the CreateSurface() function. If the call is successful it returns a pointer to the surface. In DirectX 7 this pointer is of type LPDIRECTDRAWSURFACE4. It is this pointer that is used in calling the functions of the IDirectDrawSurface4 interface. Table 10-1 lists these functions.

Table 10-1
Surface-related Functions in DirectDraw

Type or topic	Function name
Allocating memory	Initialize() IsLost() Restore()
Attaching surfaces	AddAttachedSurface() DeleteAttachedSurface() EnumAttachedSurfaces() GetAttachedSurface()
Blitting	Blt() BltBatch() (not implemented in DirectX 6) BltFast() GetBltStatus()
Color keys	GetColorKey() SetColorKey()
Device contexts	GetDC() ReleaseDC()
Flipping	Flip() GetFlipStatus()
Locking surfaces	Lock() PageLock() PageUnlock() Unlock()

Type or topic	Function name
Overlays	AddOverlayDirtyRect() EnumOverlayZOrders() GetOverlayPosition() SetOverlayPosition() UpdateOverlay() UpdateOverlayDisplay() UpdateOverlayZOrder()
Private data	FreePrivateData() GetPrivateData() SetPrivateData()
Capabilities	GetCaps()
Clipper	GetClipper() SetClipper()
Characteristics	ChangeUniquenessValue() GetPixelFormat() GetSurfaceDesc() GetUniquenessValue() SetSurfaceDesc()
Miscellaneous	GetDDInterface()

Surface types

DirectDraw first attempts to create a surface in local video memory. If there is not enough video memory available to hold the surface, then DirectDraw tries to use nonlocal video memory, and finally, if no other option is available, it creates the surface in system memory. Code can also explicitly request that a surface be created in a certain type of memory by including the appropriate flags in the CreateSurface() call.

The primary surface is the one visible on the monitor, and it is identified by the DDSCAPS_PRIMARYSURFACE flag. There can be only one primary surface for each DirectDraw object. The size and pixel format of the primary surface matches the current display mode. For this reason, the surface dimensions, mode, and pixel depth are not specified in the CreateSurface() call for a primary surface. In fact, the call fails if these dimensions are entered, even if they match those of the display mode.

Off-screen surfaces are used often to store bitmaps, cursors, sprites, and other forms of digital imagery. Off-screen surfaces can reside in video memory or in system memory. For an off-screen surface to exist in video memory the total memory on the card must exceed the memory mapped to the video display. For example, a video card with 2MB of video memory (2,097,152 bytes), executing in mode with a resolution of 640×480 pixels, at a rate of 3 bytes per pixel, requires 921,600 bytes for storing the displayed image (assuming that there are no unused areas in the pixel mapping). This leaves 1,175,552 bytes of memory on the video card, which can be used as off-screen memory.

A common type of off-screen surface, called a *back buffer*, can be created if the amount of free video memory is sufficient to store a second displayable image. In the previous case, it is possible to create one back buffer because the display area requires 921,600 bytes, and there are 1,175,552 bytes of additional video memory available on the card. A back buffer would require the same space as the amount of free memory, that is, 921,600 bytes. Back buffers, which are frequently used in animation, are discussed in Chapter 11.

Off-screen surfaces are created with the CreateSurface() function. The call must specify the surface dimensions, which means that it must include the DDSD_WIDTH and DDSD_HEIGHT flags. The corresponding values must have been previously entered in the dwWidth and dwHeight members of the DDSURFACEDESC2 structure. The call must also include the DDSCAPS_OFFSCREENPLAIN flag in the DDSCAPS2 structure. If possible, DirectDraw creates a surface in display memory. If there is not enough video memory available, it creates the surface in system memory. Code can explicitly choose display or system memory by entering the DDSCAPS_SYSTEMMEMORY or DDSCAPS_VIDEOMEMORY flags in the dwCaps member of the DDSCAPS2 structure. The call fails and returns an error if DirectDraw cannot create the surface in the specified location. Figure 10-1 shows different types of DirectDraw surfaces.

A surface is lost when the display mode is changed or when another application receives exclusive mode. The Restore() function can be used to recreate lost surfaces and reconnect them to their DirectDrawSurface object. Applications using the IDirectDraw4 interface can restore all lost surfaces by calling Restore AllSurfaces(). Note that restoring a surface does not reload bitmaps that may have existed before the surface was lost. It is up to the application to reconstruct the graphics on each of the surfaces.

When a surface is no longer needed it should be released by calling the Release() function. Each surface must be explicitly released because there is no call to release all surfaces.

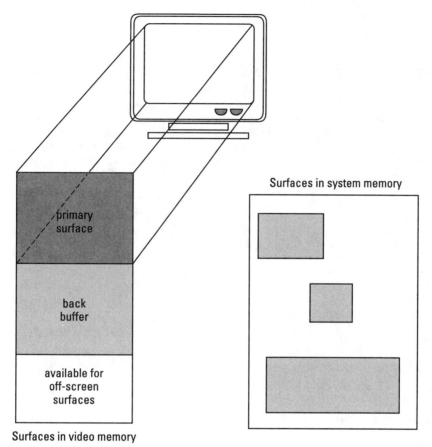

Surfaces in system memory

primary
surface

back
buffer

available for
off-screen
surfaces

Surfaces in video memory

Figure 10-1: Types of DirectDraw surfaces

Enumerating surfaces

A typical DirectDraw application operates on several surfaces during its execution.
In these manipulations an application often needs to know if a surface that matches
certain characteristics can be created. Or the application may need a list of the
existing surfaces and their properties. The `IDirectDraw4 EnumSurfaces()`
function is used to enumerate surfaces in a similar way as `EnumDisplayModes()`,
which is discussed in Chapter 8 in regards to display modes. The function's general
form is as follows:

```
HRESULT EnumSurfaces(
        DWORD dwFlags,                          // 1
        LPDDSURFACEDESC2 lpDDSD,                // 2
```

```
LPVOID lpContext,                          // 3
LPDDENUMSURFACESCALLBACK2 lpEnumCallback  // 4
);
```

The first parameter is a combination of a search-type flag and a matching flag. The search-type flag determines how the method searches for surfaces. Code can search for surfaces that can be created by using the description in the second parameter, or it can search for existing surfaces that already match that description. The matching flag determines whether the method enumerates all surfaces, those that match, or those that do not match the description specified in the second parameter. Table 10-2 lists the search and matching flags used in the EnumSurfaces() function.

Table 10-2 Flags Used in the EnumSurfaces() Function	
Flag	**Function name**
SEARCH-TYPE FLAGS	
DDENUMSURFACES_CANBECREATED	Enumerates the first surface that can be created and that meets the specifications in the second parameter. This flag can be used only with the DDENUMSURFACES_MATCH flag.
DDENUMSURFACES_DOESEXIST	Enumerates the already existing surfaces that meet the specification in the second parameter.
MATCHING-TYPE FLAGS	
DDENUMSURFACES_ALL	Enumerates all of the surfaces that meet the specification in the second parameter. This flag can be used only with the DDENUMSURFACES_DOESEXIST search type flag.
DDENUMSURFACES_MATCH	Searches for any surface that matches the specification in the second parameter.
DDENUMSURFACES_NOMATCH	Searches for any surface that does not match the specification in the second parameter.

The second parameter to EnumSurfaces() is the address of a structure variable of type DDSURFACEDESC2 that defines the characteristics of the surface. If the first parameter includes the DDENUMSURFACES_ALL flag, then this second parameter must be NULL. The third parameter is the address of an application-defined structure that is passed to each enumeration member. The fourth parameter is the address of a callback function, of type lpEnumSurfacesCallback, that is called every time the enumeration procedure finds a surface that matches the predefined characteristics.

If the call succeeds the return value is DD_OK. If it fails, the return value may be one of the following errors:

DDERR_INVALIDOBJECT

DDERR_INVALIDPARAMS

Implementing the callback function for EnumSurfaces() is very similar to the processing described in Chapter 8 for the EnumDisplayModes() callback function. The project DD Info Demo included in the book's CD-ROM contains sample code of the EdnumDisplayModes() callback.

An application often needs to know if a surface of certain characteristics is possible before it attempts to create it. In this case, code can combine the DDENUMSURFACES_CANBECREATED and DDENUMSURFACES_MATCH flags when it calls EnumSurfaces(). The DDSURFACEDESC2 structure variable is initialized to contain the desired surface characteristics. If the characteristics include a particular pixel format, then the DDSD_PIXELFORMAT flag also must be present in the dwFlags member of the DDSURFACEDESC2 structure. In addition, the DDPIXELFORMAT structure in the surface description must be initialized and the flags set to the desired pixel format flags. These can be DDPF_RGB, DDPF_YUV, or both. To specify surface dimensions, code must include the DDSD_HEIGHT and DDSD_WIDTH flags in DDSURFACEDESC2. The dimensions are then specified in the dwHeight and dwWidth structure members. If the dimension flags are not included, DirectDraw uses the dimensions of the primary surface.

The following code fragment shows a call to EnumSurfaces() to determine if a 640 × 480 × 24 bits RGB surface is available in the card's video memory space:

```
// Public variables
DDSURFACEDESC2      ddsd;
int                 surfCount = 0;
. . .
// Determine if a surface of 640 x 480 pixels, in 24-bits
// RGB color can be created in video memory
ZeroMemory(&ddsd, sizeof(ddsd));
ddsd.dwSize  = sizeof(ddsd);
ddsd.dwFlags = DDSD_CAPS |
               DDSD_PIXELFORMAT |
               DDSD_HEIGHT |
               DDSD_WIDTH;
ddsd.ddpfPixelFormat.dwFlags = DDPF_RGB;
ddsd.ddpfPixelFormat.dwRGBBitCount = 24;
ddsd.ddsCaps.dwCaps = DDSCAPS_VIDEOMEMORY |
                      DDSCAPS_LOCALVIDMEM;
ddsd.dwHeight = 480;
ddsd.dwWidth  = 640;
lpDD4->EnumSurfaces(
       DDENUMSURFACES_CANBECREATED | DDENUMSURFACES_MATCH,
       &ddsd, NULL,
       (LPDDENUMSURFACESCALLBACK2) SurfacesProc);
if (surfCount == 0)
```

```
            DDInitFailed(hWnd, hRet,
              "Surface not available");
        . . .
//************************************************
//    Callback function for EnumSurfaces()
//************************************************
static BOOL WINAPI SurfacesProc(LPDIRECTDRAWSURFACE4 aSurfPtr,
                LPDDSURFACEDESC2 aSurface, LPVOID Context)
{
    surfCount++;
    return DDENUMRET_OK;  // Continue
}
```

Because the DDENUMSURFACES_MATCH flag is present in the call, the callback function, in this case named SurfacesProc(), receives control only if a surface can be created. In the code, we made each iteration of the callback function increment the variable surfCount, which holds the number of similar surfaces that can be created, or zero if none can be created. The calling routine inspects this variable to determine the results of the EnumSurfaces() call. The previous code fragment uses the DDInitFailed() function, developed and listed in Chapter 9, to provide a terminal exit in case the surface cannot be created. In practice, an application may take another action, such as creating the surface in system memory instead of video memory. Note that the fourth parameter of EnumSurfaces() has to be typecast into a type LPDDENUMSURFACESCALL BACK2, otherwise a compiler error results.

Note that the call to EnumSurfaces() attempts to create a temporary surface with the desired characteristics. Code should be careful not to assume that a surface is not supported simply because it is not enumerated. DirectDraw attempts to create a temporary surface with the memory constraints that exist at the time of the call. This can result in a surface not being enumerated even when the driver actually supports it.

Restoring surfaces

It is possible to free surface memory associated with a DirectDrawSurface object, whereas the DirectDrawSurface objects representing these pieces of surface memory cannot be released. In this case several DirectDraw functions return DDERR_ SURFACELOST. Surfaces can be lost if the display mode was changed, or if another application requested and obtained exclusive mode and freed all of the currently allocated surface memory. The DirectDraw Restore() function recreates these lost surfaces and reconnects them to their DirectDrawSurface object. If the application uses more than one surface, code can call the RestoreAllSurfaces() function to restore all surfaces at once. However, restoring a surface does not reload any imagery that may have previously existed in the surface.

Surface manipulations

Most DirectDraw operations relate to surfaces; therefore, it is important for the programmer to gain familiarity with surface construction and characteristics. The DirectDraw application named ddtest that is furnished with DirectX allows you to experiment with DirectDraw options such as surfaces, blits, display modes, and capabilities, without actually writing code.

To create and examine a surface you first run ddtest and then click the Connect button to establish a DirectDraw interface. When the interface is recognized, you can click the Create button. On the Create DirectDraw Surface dialog box you can select the desired capabilities, dimensions, and pixel format for the surface, and then click OK. If the surface creation fails, a message is posted on the DirectDraw Test Application main screen and the Surface and Surface Info fields are blank. If the surface is created, then the surface box of the main screen contains the surface pointer and the Surface Info boxes have the pertinent surface information. Figure 10-2 shows two dialog boxes of the ddtest program.

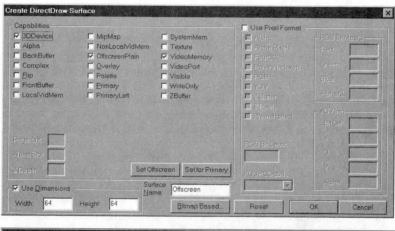

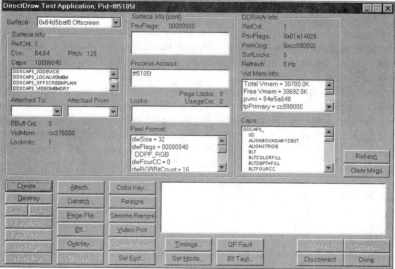

Figure 10-2: Surface operations using Microsoft's ddtest program

Transparency and color keys

Often you will need to display a new bitmap over an existing one. For example, you might want the bitmap of an airplane to be shown over a background of mountains, sky, and clouds, contained in another bitmap. Because bitmaps are rectangular areas, the airplane bitmap is actually a rectangle of some uniform color that contains the image of the airplane. If you display the airplane by simply projecting its rectangular bitmap over the background, the result is quite unnatural. The solution is to select the color of the framing rectangle of the airplane bitmap so that it is different from the colors used in drawing the airplane. The software can then be programmed to ignore the framing color while displaying the airplane bitmap. The processing logic is as follows:

> If bitmap pixel is equal to framing color, then leave the background pixel undisturbed. Else, replace background pixel with foreground image pixel.

The result is that the image of the airplane behaves as if it had been drawn on a sheet of transparent plastic. The selection of a framing color, called the *color key*, plays an important role in the result. If a color key can be found that is not present in the foreground image, then the transparency is perfectly achieved. If not, some pixels of the foreground image will not be shown. The greater the color range, the easier it is to find a satisfactory color key. It is difficult to imagine a 24-bit color bitmap (16.7 million colors) that will not have a single color value that is absent in the image.

An alternative option to achieve transparency is based on a color key located in the background image, also called the destination. In this case the color key determines if the foreground image pixel is used or not. The logic is as follows:

> If background pixel is color key, then use foreground pixel over background. Else, leave background undisturbed.

The result of using a destination color key is a window on which the foreground image is displayed. Here again, the programmer must find an attribute for the color key that is not used in the background.

DirectDraw supports both source and destination color keying for blits and overlay surfaces. Code supplies either a single color or a color range for source or destination color keying. Source and destination color keys can be combined on different surfaces. For example, a destination color key can be attached to a surface to create a window on which the mountains, sky, and clouds are visible. Then a source color key can be used in another surface to display the airplane bitmap transparently over this background. Figure 10-4 shows transparency based on the simultaneous use of source and destination color keys.

source bitmap

color key

destination bitmap

Figure 10-3: Transparency using a source color key

In Figure 10-4 we are manipulating three surfaces in implementing source and destination color key transparency. Surface 1 contains a window in which a destination color key is defined. Surface 2 is a bitmap image. Surface 3 is a sprite representing an airplane in which the background is a source color key. This sprite is transparently blitted onto the bitmap on surface 2, and then surface 2 is transparently blitted onto surface 1. The resulting image is shown at the bottom of the illustration.

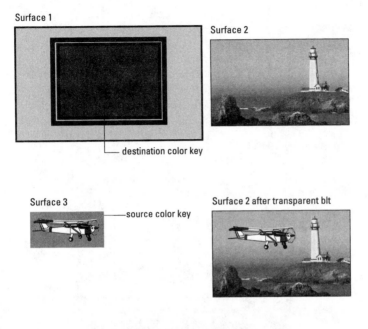

Surface 1

Surface 2

— destination color key

Surface 3

—source color key

Surface 2 after transparent blt

Surface 1 after transparent blt

Figure 10-4: Transparency using source and destination color keys

Setting the color key

In DirectDraw a color key is always associated with a surface. Code can set the color keys for a surface when it is created, or afterward. To set a color key or keys when creating a surface, you must first assign the desired color values to one or both of the ddckCKSrcBlt and ddckCKDestBlt members of the DDSURFACEDESC2 structure. When CreateSurface() is called, the color keys are assigned automatically. If the color key is used in blitting, one or both of DDSD_CKSRCBLT or DDSD_CKDESTBLT must be included in the dwFlags member.

The DirectDraw `SetColorKey()` function sets the color key for an existing DirectDrawSurface object. The function's general form is as follows:

```
HRESULT SetColorKey(
                DWORD dwFlags,              // 1
                LPDDCOLORKEY lpDDColorKey   // 2
                );
```

The first parameter is a flag that determines the type of color key to be used. Table 10-3 lists the predefined constants used in this parameter.

Table 10-3
Constants Used in SetColorKey() Function

Constant	Action
DDCKEY_COLORSPACE	The structure contains a color range. Bit not set if the structure contains a single color key.
DDCKEY_DESTBLT	The structure specifies a color key or color space to be used as a destination color key for blit operations.
DDCKEY_DESTOVERLAY	The structure specifies a color key or color space to be used as a destination color key for overlay operations.
DDCKEY_SRCBLT	The structure specifies a color key or color space to be used as a source color key for blit operations.
DDCKEY_SRCOVERLAY	The structure specifies a color key or color space to be used as a source color key for overlay operations.

The second parameter in the `SetColorKey()` function's general form is the address of a structure variable of type `DDCOLORKEY` structure that contains the new color key values for the `DirectDrawSurface` object. If this value is NULL, then the existing color key is removed from the surface.

If the call to `SetColorKey()` succeeds, the function returns `DD_OK`. If it fails, one of the following error codes is returned:

```
DDERR_GENERIC
DDERR_INVALIDOBJECT
DDERR_INVALIDPARAMS
DDERR_INVALIDSURFACETYPE
DDERR_NOOVERLAYHW
```

```
DDERR_NOTAOVERLAYSURFACE
DDERR_SURFACELOST
DDERR_UNSUPPORTED
DDERR_WASSTILLDRAWING
```

The color key is described in a DDCOLORKEY structure. The structure is used for a source color key, a destination color key, or a color range. A single color key is specified when both structure members have the same value. The structure is defined in the Windows header files as follows:

```
typedef struct _DDCOLORKEY{
    DWORD dwColorSpaceLowValue;
    DWORD dwColorSpaceHighValue;
} DDCOLORKEY,FAR* LPDDCOLORKEY;
```

The member dwColorSpaceLowValue contains the low value of the color range that is used as the color key. The member dwColorSpaceHighValue contains the high value (also inclusive). If both members have the same value, then the color key is a single color, not a range.

Color keys are specified using the pixel format of the surface. If a surface is palettized, then the color key is an index or a range of indexes. If the surface is in a 16-bit color space mode (high color), then the color key is a word-size value. If the surface's pixel format is RGB or YUV, then the color key is specified in an RGBQUAD or YUVQUAD structure, as in the following code fragments:

```
// High color mode is the single color key.
dwColorSpaceLowValue = 0xf011;
dwColorSpaceHighValue = 0xf011;

// RGB color 255,128,128 is the single color key.
dwColorSpaceLowValue = RGBQUAD(255,128,128);
dwColorSpaceHighValue = RGBQUAD(255,128,128);

// YUV color range used as a color key
dwColorSpaceLowValue = YUVQUAD(120,50,50);
dwColorSpaceHighValue = YUVQUAD(140,50,50);
```

Note that the YUV format was developed to more easily compress motion video data. It is based on the physics of human vision, which makes the eye more sensitive to brightness levels than to specific colors. The YUV acronym refers to a three-axis coordinate system. The Y-axis encodes the luminance component, while the U and V axes encode the chrominance, or color, element. Although several different implementations of the YUV format are available, no single format is directly supported by DirectDraw.

The previous example uses a YUV color range that extends from 120-50-50 to 150-50-50. In this case any pixel with a Y value between 120 and 150, and U and V values of 50, serves as a color key. Range values for color keys are used often when working with video data or photographic images; in this case there are often variations in the background color values. Artwork composed with draw or paint programs often use single-key colors.

Color key support

Transparency and color keys are supported by the HEL, so that these functions are always available; however, support for a color key range is hardware-dependent. Code should check the dwCKeyCaps member of the DDCAPS structure. The DDCAPS_COLORKEY constant of the dwCaps member identifies some form of color key support for either overlay or blit operations. The dwCKeyCaps member defines the options listed in Table 10-4.

<table>
<tr><td colspan="2" align="center">Table 10-4
Color Key Capabilities in DDCAPS Structure</td></tr>
<tr><td>*Constant*</td><td>*Meaning*</td></tr>
<tr><td>DDCKEYCAPS_DESTBLT</td><td>Supports transparent blitting. Color key identifies the replaceable bits of the destination surface for RGB colors.</td></tr>
<tr><td>DDCKEYCAPS_DESTBLTCLRSPACE</td><td>Supports transparent blitting. Color space identifies the replaceable bits of the destination surface for RGB colors.</td></tr>
<tr><td>DDCKEYCAPS_DESTBLTCLRSPACEYUV</td><td>Supports transparent blitting. Color space identifies the replaceable bits of the destination surface for YUV colors.</td></tr>
<tr><td>DDCKEYCAPS_DESTBLTYUV</td><td>Supports transparent blitting. Color key identifies the replaceable bits of the destination surface for YUV colors.</td></tr>
<tr><td>DDCKEYCAPS_DESTOVERLAY</td><td>Supports overlaying with color keying of the replaceable bits of the destination surface being overlaid for RGB colors.</td></tr>
</table>

Continued

Table 10-4 *(continued)*

Constant	Meaning
DDCKEYCAPS_DESTOVERLAYCLRSPACE	Supports a color space as the color key for the destination of RGB colors.
DDCKEYCAPS_DESTOVERLAYCLRSPACEYUV	Supports a color space as the color key for the destination of YUV colors.
DDCKEYCAPS_DESTOVERLAYONEACTIVE	Supports only one active destination color key value for visible overlay surfaces.
DDCKEYCAPS_DESTOVERLAYYUV	Supports overlaying using color keying of the replaceable bits of the destination surface being overlaid for YUV colors.
DDCKEYCAPS_NOCOSTOVERLAY	No bandwidth trade-offs for using the color key with an overlay.
DDCKEYCAPS_SRCBLT	Supports transparent blitting using the color key for the source with this surface for RGB colors.
DDCKEYCAPS_SRCBLTCLRSPACE	Supports transparent blitting using a color space for the source with this surface for RGB colors.
DDCKEYCAPS_SRCBLTCLRSPACEYUV	Supports transparent blitting using a color space for the source with this surface for YUV colors.
DDCKEYCAPS_SRCBLTYUV	Supports transparent blitting using the color key for the source with this surface for YUV colors.
DDCKEYCAPS_SRCOVERLAY	Supports overlaying using the color key for the source with this overlay surface for RGB colors.
DDCKEYCAPS_SRCOVERLAYCLRSPACE	Supports overlaying using a color space as the source color key for the overlay surface for RGB colors.
DDCKEYCAPS_SRCOVERLAYCLRSPACEYUV	Supports overlaying using a color space as the source color key for the overlay surface for YUV colors.
DDCKEYCAPS_SRCOVERLAYONEACTIVE	Supports only one active source color key value for visible overlay surfaces.
DDCKEYCAPS_SRCOVERLAYYUV	Supports overlaying using the color key for the source with this overlay surface for YUV colors.

Some hardware supports color ranges only for YUV pixel data, which is usually video. The transparent background in video footage (the blue screen against which the subject was photographed) might not be a pure color, so a range of colors in the color key is desirable in this case.

DirectDraw Blits

In the blit a rectangular block of memory bits, called the source, is transferred as a block into a rectangular memory area called the destination. If the destination of the transfer is screen memory, then the bitmapped image is immediately displayed. The source and destination bit blocks can be combined logically or arithmetically, or a unary operation can be performed on the source or the destination bit blocks.

GDI blits can be used in DirectDraw programming, although they rarely are used because of their low performance. DirectDraw contains its own blit functions that are usually more suitable to the programming environment and execute faster than the GDI counterparts. The DirectDraw blit functions, called `Blt()` and `BltFast()`, are both associated with DirectDraw surface objects. Microsoft announced a third method, called `BltBatch()`, which will be implemented in future versions of DirectDraw. In the context of Draw programming, blit operations usually take place from an off-screen surface onto the back buffer, or onto a primary surface. In fact, much of the processing time of a typical DirectDraw application is spent blitting imagery. Also, the performance capability (called the bandwidth) of a particular blitter determines the quality of the application's video output. Figure 10-5 shows the most common forms of the DirectDraw blit operation.

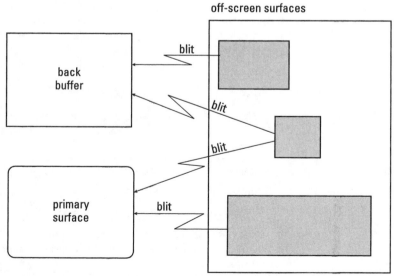

Figure 10-5: DirectDraw blit operations

Both Blt() and BltFast() operate on a destination surface, which is referenced in the call, and receive the source surface as a parameter. It is possible for both source and destination to be the same surface. In this case DirectDraw preserves all source pixels before overwriting them. Blt() is more flexible but BltFast() is faster, especially if there is no hardware blitter. Applications can determine the blitting capabilities of the hardware from the DDCAPS structure obtained by means of the GetCaps() function. If the dwCaps member contains DDCAPS_BLT, the hardware supports blitting.

BltFast()

BltFast requires a valid rectangle in the source surface from which the pixels are copied. If the entire surface is copied, then the source rectangle is NULL. It also requires x- and y-coordinates in the destination surface. If the source rectangle is larger than the destination, the call fails and BltFast() returns DDERR_INVALIDRECT. BltFast() cannot be used on surfaces that have an attached clipper. Neither does it support stretching, mirroring, or other effects that can be performed with Blt().

The function's general form is as follows:

```
HRESULT BltFast(
                DWORD dwX,                              // 1
                DWORD dwY,                              // 2
                LPDIRECTDRAWSURFACE4 lpDDSrcSurface,    // 3
                LPRECT lpSrcRect,                       // 4
                DWORD dwTrans                           // 5
                );
```

The first and second parameters are the x- and y-coordinates to blit on the destination surface. The third parameter is the address of an IDirectDrawSurface4 interface for the DirectDrawSurface object that is the source of the blit. The fourth parameter is a RECT structure that defines the upper-left and lower-right points of the rectangle on the source surface. The fifth parameter defines the type of blit, as listed in Table 10-5.

Table 10-5
Type of Transfer Constants in BltFast()

Constant	Action
DDBLTFAST_DESTCOLORKEY	Transparent blit that uses the destination's color key.
DDBLTFAST_NOCOLORKEY	Normal copy blit with no transparency.
DDBLTFAST_SRCCOLORKEY	Transparent blit that uses the source's color key.
DDBLTFAST_WAIT	Does not produce a message if the blitter is busy. Returns as soon as the blit can be set up or another error occurs.
DDERR_WASSTILLDRAWING	

If the call succeeds, BltFast() returns DD_OK. If it fails it returns one of the following self-explanatory values:

DDERR_EXCEPTION
DDERR_GENERIC
DDERR_INVALIDOBJECT
DDERR_INVALIDPARAMS
DDERR_INVALIDRECT
DDERR_NOBLTHW
DDERR_SURFACEBUSY
DDERR_SURFACELOST
DDERR_UNSUPPORTED
DDERR_WASSTILLDRAWING

BltFast() always attempts an asynchronous blit if it is supported by the hardware. The function works only on display memory surfaces and cannot clip when blitting. According to Microsoft, BltFast() is 10 percent faster than the Blt() method if there is no hardware support, but there is no speed difference if the display hardware is used. Figure 10-6 shows a diagram of the parameters and operation of the BltFast() function.

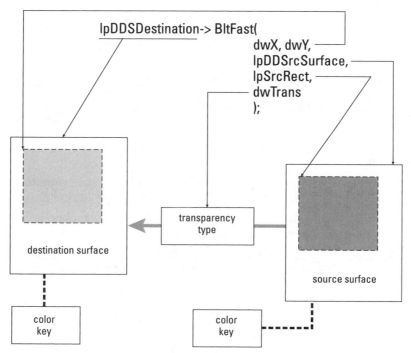

Figure 10-6: DirectDraw BltFast() function

Blt()

Blt() is the more flexible and powerful of the two DirectDraw blit functions. Like BltFast(), Blt() performs a bit block transfer from a source surface into a destination surface. Blt() allows a clipper to be attached to the destination surface, in which case clipping is performed if the surface falls outside of the destination rectangle. Blt() can also be used to automatically scale the source image to fit the destination rectangle. Scaling is disabled when both surfaces are the same size. The function's general form is as follows:

```
HRESULT Blt(
        LPRECT lpDestRect,                        // 1
        LPDIRECTDRAWSURFACE4 lpDDSrcSurface,      // 2
        LPRECT lpSrcRect,                         // 3
        DWORD dwFlags,                            // 4
        LPDDBLTFX lpDDBltFx                       // 5
        );
```

The first parameter is the address of a RECT structure that defines the upper-left and lower-right points of the source rectangle. If this parameter is NULL, the entire destination source surface is used. The second parameter is the address of the IDirectDrawSurface4 interface for the DirectDrawSurface object that is the source of the blit. The third parameter is the address of a RECT structure that defines the upper-left and lower-right points of the source rectangle from which the blit is to take place. If this parameter is NULL, then the entire source surface is used. The fourth parameter is one or more flags that determine the valid members of the associated DDBLTFX structure, which specifies color key information or requests a special behavior. Three types of flags are currently defined: validation flags, color key flags, and behavior flags. Table 10-6 lists the predefined constants for this parameter.

Table 10-6 Flags for the Blt() Function	
Flags	**Meaning**
Validation Flags:	
DDBLT_COLORFILL	The dwFillColor member of the DDBLTFX structure is the RGB color that fills the destination rectangle.
DDBLT_DDFX	The dwDDFX member of the DDBLTFX structure specifies the effects to use for the blit.
DDBLT_DDROPS	The dwDDROP member of the DDBLTFX structure specifies the raster operations (ROPS) that are not part of the Win32 API.

Flags	Meaning
DDBLT_DEPTHFILL	The dwFillDepth member of the DDBLTFX structure is the depth value with which to fill the destination rectangle.
DDBLT_KEYDESTOVERRIDE	The ddckDestColorkey member of the DDBLTFX structure is the color key for the destination surface.
DDBLT_KEYSRCOVERRIDE	The ddckSrcColorkey member of the DDBLTFX structure is the color key for the source surface.
DDBLT_ROP	The dwROP member of the DDBLTFX structure is the ROP for this blit. The ROPs are the same as those defined in the Win32 API.
DDBLT_ROTATIONANGLE	The dwRotationAngle member of the DDBLTFX structure is the rotation angle, in 1/100th of a degree unit, for the surface.
Color Key Flags:	
DDBLT_KEYDEST	The color key is associated with the destination surface.
DDBLT_KEYSRC	The color key is associated with the source surface.
Behavior Flags:	
DDBLT_ASYNC	Blit asynchronously in the FIFO order received. If no roomis available in the FIFO hardware, the call fails.
DDBLT_WAIT	Postpones the DDERR_WASSTILLDRAWING return value if the blitter is busy, and returns as soon as the blit can be set up or another error occurs.

The fifth parameter is the address of a structure variable of type DDBLTFX that defines special effects during the blit, including raster operations codes (ROP) and override information. Because of their complexity, special effects during blit operations are discussed in a separate section. Figure 10-7 shows the parameters and operation of the Blt() function.

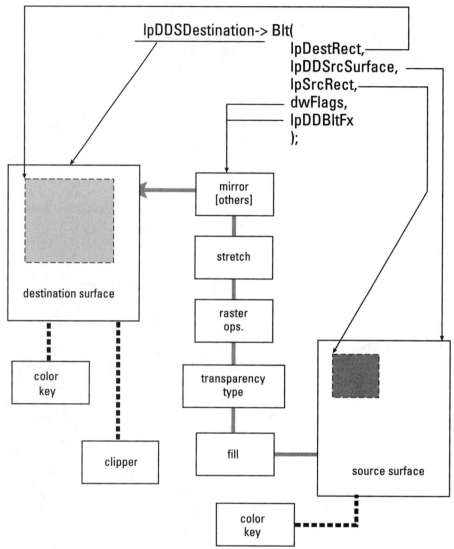

Figure 10-7: DirectDraw Blt() function

If the call succeeds, the return value is DD_OK. If it fails, the return value is one of the following error codes:

DDERR_GENERIC	DDERR_INVALIDRECT
DDERR_INVALIDCLIPLIST	DDERR_NOALPHAHW
DDERR_INVALIDOBJECT	DDERR_NOBLTHW
DDERR_INVALIDPARAMS	DDERR_NOCLIPLIST

DDERR_NODDROPSHW	DDERR_NOZBUFFERHW
DDERR_NOMIRRORHW	DDERR_SURFACEBUSY
DDERR_NORASTEROPHW	DDERR_SURFACELOST
DDERR_NOROTATIONHW	DDERR_UNSUPPORTED
DDERR_NOSTRETCHHW	DDERR_WASSTILLDRAWING

The Blt() function is capable of synchronous or asynchronous blits for display memory to display memory, display memory to system memory, system memory to display memory, or system memory to system memory. The default is asynchronous. The function supports both source and destination color keys. If the source and the destination rectangles are not the same size, Blt() performs the necessary stretching or shrinking. Blt() returns immediately with an error if the blitter is busy. If the code specifies the DDBLT_WAIT flag, then a synchronous blit takes place and the call waits until the blit can be set up or until another error occurs.

To use the Blt() function, code must supply a valid rectangle in the source surface (or NULL to specify the entire surface), and a rectangle in the destination surface to which the source image is copied. Here again, NULL means the destination rectangle is the entire surface. If a clipper is attached to the destination surface, then the bounds of the source rectangle can fall outside the surface and clipping is performed automatically. If there is no clipper, the source rectangle must fall entirely within the surface or else the method fails and returns DDERR_INVALIDRECT.

Blit Transformations

DirectDraw supports several transformations that take place at blit time. The most important ones are color fills, scaling, mirroring, and raster operations. Other effects, such as rotation, are not available in the HEL; therefore, they cannot be used if the hardware does not support them. Applications that do not require any special blit-time transformations other than scaling can pass NULL as in the fourth parameter of the Blt() function. Code can determine the hardware support for blit-time transformations by calling GetCaps().

Applications that require a particular blit-time transformation must pass the corresponding value in one of the members of the DDBLTFX structure. The appropriate flags must also be included in the fourth parameter of Blt(), which determines which members of the structure are valid. Some transformations require setting only a single flag, others require several of them.

You can use the dwFlags member of DDBLTFX named DDBLTFX_NOTEARING when blitting images directly to the front buffer. The action of this flag is to time the blit so that it coincides with the screen's vertical retrace cycle, thus minimizing the possibility of tearing. Tearing and screen update timing are discussed in the context of DirectDraw animation, in Chapter 11.

Applications that use surface color keys when calling BltFast() or Blt() must set one or both of the DDBLTFAST_SRCCOLORKEY or DDBLTFAST_DESTCOLORKEY flags in the corresponding function parameter. Alternatively, code can place the appropriate color values in the ddckDestColorkey and ddckSrcColorkey members of the DDBLTFX structure that is passed to the function in the lpDDBltFx parameter. In this case it is also necessary to set the DBLT_KEYSRCOVERRIDE or DDBLT_KEYDESTOVERRIDE flag, or both, in the dwFlags parameter. The resulting action is that the selected color keys are taken from the DDBLTFX structure rather than from the surface properties.

Color fills

Applications can use the blitter to fill the entire surface, or a part of it, with a single color. This operation is useful for creating backgrounds when using a destination color key, and for clearing large screen areas. When Blt() is used to perform a color fill, the call must reference the DDBLT_COLORFILL flag. The following code fragment fills an entire surface with the color blue. Code assumes that lpDDS is a valid pointer to an IDirectDrawSurface4 interface.

```
HRESULT          ddrval;
DDBLTFX          ddbltfx;
. . .
ZeroMemory(&ddbltfx, sizeof(ddbltfx));
ddbltfx.dwSize = sizeof(ddbltfx);

ddbltfx.dwFillColor = ddpf.dwBBitMask; // Pure blue
ddrval = lpDDS->Blt(
            NULL,          // Destination is entire
                           // surface
            NULL,          // No source surface
            NULL,          // No source rectangle
            DDBLT_COLORFILL, &ddbltfx);

if(ddrval != DD_OK)
// Error handler goes here
```

Scaling

The Blt() function automatically scales the source image to fit the destination rectangle. Scaling is implemented in the HEL, so it is always available. Some video cards have hardware support for scaling operations. Applications can inspect the dwCXCaps member of the DDCAPS structure to determine if hardware support is available and of which type. Table 10-7 lists the predefined constants used in the scaling capabilities flag.

Table 10-7
Scaling Flags for the Blt() Function

Flags	Meaning
DDFXCAPS_BLTALPHA	Supports alpha-blended blit operations.
DDFXCAPS_BLTARITHSTRETCHY	Arithmetic operations, rather than pixel-doubling techniques, are used to stretch and shrink surfaces along the *y*-axis.
DDFXCAPS_BLTARITHSTRETCHYN	Arithmetic operations, rather than pixel-doubling techniques, are used to stretch and shrink surfaces along the *y*-axis. Stretching must be integer-based.
DDFXCAPS_BLTSHRINKX	Arbitrary shrinking of a surface along the *x*-axis (horizontally).
DDFXCAPS_BLTSHRINKXN	Integer shrinking of a surface along the *x*-axis.
DDFXCAPS_BLTSHRINKY	Arbitrary shrinking of a surface along the *y*-axis.
DDFXCAPS_BLTSHRINKYN	Integer shrinking of a surface along the *y*-axis.
DDFXCAPS_BLTSTRETCHX	Arbitrary stretching of a surface along the *x*-axis.
DDFXCAPS_BLTSTRETCHXN	Integer stretching of a surface along the *x*-axis.
DDFXCAPS_BLTSTRETCHY	Arbitrary stretching of a surface along the *y*-axis (vertically).
DDFXCAPS_BLTSTRETCHYN	Supports integer stretching of a surface along the *y*-axis.

Scaling is disabled automatically when the source and destination rectangles are exactly the same size. An application can use the BltFast() function, instead of Blt(),to avoid accidental scaling because of differing sizes in the source and destination rectangles.

Some video cards support arithmetic scaling. In this case the scaling operation is performed by interpolation rather than by multiplication or deletion of pixels. For example, if an axis is being increased by one-third, the pixels are recolored to provide a closer approximation to the original image than would be produced by doubling every third pixel on that axis. Code has little control over the type of scaling performed by the driver. The only possibility is to set the DDBLTFX_ ARITHSTRETCHY flag in the dwDDFX member of the DDBLTFX structure passed to Blt(). This flag requests that arithmetic stretching be done on the *y*-axis. Arithmetic stretching on the *x*-axis and arithmetic shrinking are not currently supported in the DirectDraw API, but a driver may perform them on its own.

Mirroring

Mirroring is another transformation supported by the HEL. Applications can assume that it is available even if it is not supported in the hardware. Mirroring is defined in the x- and y-axes of the blit rectangle. Figure 10-8 shows mirroring along either axis.

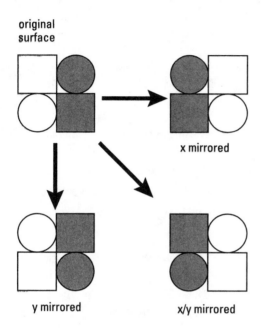

original
surface

x mirrored

y mirrored

x/y mirrored

Figure 10-8: Mirroring
transformations

Table 10-8 lists the predefined constants used in mirroring transformations during Blt().

Table 10-8	
Mirroring Flags for the Blt() Function	
Flags	*Meaning*
DDBLTFX_MIRRORLEFTRIGHT	Mirrors on the y-axis. The surface is mirrored from left to right.
DDBLTFX_MIRRORUPDOWN	Mirrors on the x-axis. The surface is mirrored from top to bottom.

Applications sometimes need several versions of a symmetrical sprite, in which the image faces in different directions. Rather than creating a bitmap for each image, it is possible to generate them by mirroring the original. Hardware support for mirroring can be determined by the presence of the DDFXCAPS_BLTMIRRORLEFTRIGHT and DDFCAPS_BLTMIRRORUPDOWN identifiers in the dwFXCaps member of the DDCAPS structure.

Raster operations

Blit-time transformations can include some of the standard raster operations (ROPs) used by the GDI BitBlt() functions. At present only SRCCOPY (the default), BLACKNESS, and WHITENESS are supported by the HEL. Hardware support for other raster operations can be determined by examining the DDCAPS structure. Code that uses any of the standard ROPs with the Blt() method must set the corresponding flag in the dwROP member of the DDBLTFX structure. The dwDDROP member of the DDBLTFX structure is for specifying ROPs specific to DirectDraw. No such ROPs have been defined at this time.

Summary

In this chapter we discussed the DirectDraw blit operation and the transformations that take place at blit time. We started by reviewing surfaces because DirectDraw bitmap rendering operations always take place at the surface level. We also looked at transparency and color keys as the fundamental tool for overlaying bitmaps. The basic rendering functions, Blt() and BltFast(), were analyzed in detail, as well as the blit-time transformations consisting of color fills, scaling, mirroring, and raster operations.

The next chapter is devoted to bitmap programming in DirectDraw.

✦   ✦   ✦

Rendering Bitmaps in DirectDraw

In This Chapter

Loading a bitmap

Obtaining bitmap data

Moving the bitmap onto a surface

Blitting the bitmap

Coding a DirectDraw window application

Bitmaps are one of the most powerful structures available to the graphics programmer. In today's technological world, with an abundance of real-color and True-color modes, bitmaps can be used to encode images with photo-realistic accuracy. The processing capabilities available in this generation of PCs make possible the effective manipulation of bitmapped images. DirectDraw implements a new dimension of functionality in bitmap processing and display operations. Many types of applications rely heavily on bitmaps; these include image processing, simulations, virtual reality, artificial life, and electronic games.

This chapter is devoted to bitmap rendering in the context of a DirectDraw windowed application. The use of bitmaps in animated programs that execute DirectDraw exclusive mode is the topic of Chapter 12.

Rendering a Bitmap

In DirectDraw programming bitmap manipulations consists of four basic steps:

+ Loading the bitmap into application memory
+ Obtaining bitmap data necessary for displaying it on the screen
+ Moving the bitmap onto a DirectDraw surface
+ Blitting the bitmap onto the video display

Loading the bitmap

Loading a bitmap onto the application's memory space is an operation of GDI graphics, not actually part of DirectDraw. In the demonstration program named Bitmap Demo, contained in the book's CD-ROM, we load several bitmaps during WM_CREATE message processing. In this case we used Developer Studio to define the bitmaps as program resources, and then used LoadBitmap() to load them into the application's memory space. Alternatively, instead of defining the bitmap as a program resource, you can use LoadImage() to load the bitmap directly from the disk file in which it is stored. At this time you can also perform certain preliminary checks to make sure that the DirectDraw surface is compatible with the bitmap to be displayed. Note that the sample code requires that the surface be nonpalettized. The GetSurfaceDesc() DirectDraw function is used to fill a DDSURFACEDESC2 structure, discussed in Chapter 9. The DDPIXELFORMAT structure, which is part of DDSURFACEDESC2, contains two relevant values: the flag DDPF_RGB indicates that the RGB data is valid, and the dwRGBBitCount member contains the number of RGB bits per pixel. If the DDPF_RGB flag is set and dwRGBBitCount is greater than 15, you can assume that the surface is nonpalettized, and therefore compatible.

Note that the LoadImage() function does not return palette information. Microsoft Knowledge Base Article Q158898 lists the function LoadBitmapFromBMPFile(), which uses the DIBSection's color table to create a palette. If no color table is present, then a half-tone palette is created. You can find the source for this function in the MSDN Library that is part of Visual C++.

When code has determined that a compatible surface is available, it can proceed to load the bitmap. The general form of the LoadImage() function is as follows:

```
HANDLE LoadImage(
            HINSTANCE hInst,          // 1
            LPCTSTR lpszName,         // 2
            UINT uType,               // 3
            int cxDesired,            // 4
            int cyDesired,            // 5
            UINT fuLoad               // 6
            );
```

The first parameter is a handle to an instance of the module that contains the image to be loaded. In the case of an image contained in a file, this parameter is set to zero. The second parameter is a pointer to the image to load. If it is nonNULL and the sixth parameter (described later) does not include LR_LOADFROMFILE, then it is a pointer to a null-terminated string that contains the filename of the image resource. The third parameter is the image type. It can be one of the following constants:

```
IMAGE_BITMAP

IMAGE_CURSOR

IMAGE_ICON
```

The fourth and fifth parameters specify the pixel width and height of the bitmap, cursor, or icon. If this parameter is zero and the sixth parameter is LR_DEFAULTSIZE, then the function uses the SM_CXICON or SM_CXCURSOR system metric value to set the width. If this parameter is zero, and if LR_DEFAULTSIZE is present in the sixth parameter, then the function uses the actual width and height of the bitmap.

The sixth, and last parameter, is one or more flags represented by the predefined constants listed in Table 11-1.

Table 11-1
Predefined Constants in LoadImage() Function

Constant	Meaning
LR_DEFAULTCOLOR	Default flag. Does nothing.
LR_CREATEDIBSECTION	When the third parameter is IMAGE_BITMAP, this flag causes the function to return a DIB section bitmap rather than a compatible bitmap. It is useful for loading a bitmap without mapping it to the colors of the display device.
LR_DEFAULTSIZE	For cursor and icons the width or height values are those specified by the system metric values, but only if the fourth and fifth parameters are set to zero. If this flag is not specified and the fourth and fifth parameters are set to zero, the function uses the actual resource size.
LR_LOADFROMFILE	Loads the image from the file specified by the second parameter. If this flag is not specified, lpszName is the name of the resource.
LR_LOADMAP3DCOLORS	Searches the color table for the image and replaces the following shades of gray with the corresponding 3D color:

	Color	RGB value	Replaced with
	Dk Gray	RGB(128,128,128)	COLOR_3DSHADOW
	Gray	RGB(192,192,192)	COLOR_3DFACE
	Lt Gray	RGB(223,223,223)	COLOR_3DLIGHT

Constant	Meaning
LR_LOADTRANSPARENT	Retrieves the color value of the top-left pixel in the image and replaces the corresponding entry in the color table with the default window color (COLOR_WINDOW). All pixels in the image that use that entry become the default window color. This value applies only to images that have corresponding color tables.
LR_MONOCHROME	Converts the image to black and white pixels.

Continued

Table 11-1 *(continued)*	
Constant	**Meaning**
LR_SHARED	Shares the image handle if the image is loaded multiple times. If LR_SHARED is not used, a second call to LoadImage() for the same resource loads the image again and returns a different handle. LR_SHARED should not be used for images that have nonstandard sizes, that may change after loading, or that are loaded from a file. In Windows 95 and Windows 98 LoadImage() finds the first image with the requested resource name in the cache, regardless of the size requested.
LR_VGACOLOR	Use true VGA colors.

LoadImage() returns the handle of the newly loaded image if the call succeeds. If the function fails, the return value is NULL. Although the system automatically deletes all resources when the process that created them terminates, applications can save memory by releasing resources that are no longer needed. DeleteObject() is used to release a bitmap, DestroyIcon() for icons, and DestroyCursor() for cursor resources.

The following function is used to load a bitmap into the application's memory space and obtain its handle. In this case the code checks for a compatible surface with a nonpalettized bitmap.

```
//****************************************************************
// Name: DDLoadBitmap
// Desc: Loads a bitmap file into memory and returns its handle
//
// PRE CONDITIONS:
// 1. Parameter 1 is pointer to a DirectDraw surface
//    Parameter 2 is pointer to bitmap filename string
//
// POST CONDITIONS:
// Returns handle to bitmap
//
// ERROR CONDITIONS:
// All errors exit through DDInitFailed() function
//****************************************************************

HBITMAP DDLoadBitmap( LPDIRECTDRAWSURFACE4 lpDDS, LPSTR
szImage)
{
```

```
HBITMAP          hbm;
DDSURFACEDESC2  ddsd;

ZeroMemory( &ddsd, sizeof( ddsd ) );
ddsd.dwSize = sizeof( ddsd );

if ( lpDDS->GetSurfaceDesc( &ddsd ) != DD_OK )
     DDInitFailed(hWnd, hRet,
       "GetSurfaceDesc() call failed in DDLoadBitmap()");

// Test for compatible pixel format
if ( ( ddsd.ddpfPixelFormat.dwFlags != DDPF_RGB ) ||
     ( ddsd.ddpfPixelFormat.dwRGBBitCount < 16 ) )
       DDInitFailed(hWnd, hRet,
        "Incompatible surface in DDLoadBitmap()");

// Load the bitmap image onto memory
hbm = ( HBITMAP )LoadImage( NULL, szImage,
        IMAGE_BITMAP, 0, 0, LR_LOADFROMFILE );

if ( hbm == NULL )
     DDInitFailed(hWnd, hRet,
       "Bitmap load failed in DDLoadBitmap()");

return hbm;
}
```

Note that in `DDLoadBitmap()` all errors are considered terminal and directed through the `DDInitFailed()` function, which was developed and listed in Chapter 9. This mode of operation can be changed if the code is to provide alternate processing in these cases.

Obtaining bitmap information

To display and manipulate a bitmap, the processing routines usually require information about its size and organization. The GDI `GetObject()` function is used for this purpose. This function fills a structure of type `BITMAP`, defined as follows:

```
typedef struct tagBITMAP {
    LONG    bmType;       // Must be zero
    LONG    bmWidth;      // bitmap width (in pixels)
    LONG    bmHeight;     // bitmap height (in pixels)
    LONG    bmWidthBytes; // bytes per scan line
    WORD    bmPlanes;     // number of color planes
    WORD    bmBitsPixel;  // bits per pixel color
    LPVOID  bmBits;       // points to bitmap values array
} BITMAP;
```

The bmWidth member specifies the width, in pixels, of the bitmap, whereas bmHeight specifies the height, also in pixels. Both values must be greater than zero. The bmWidthBytes member specifies the number of bytes in each scan line. Windows assumes that the bitmap is word-aligned; therefore, this value must be divisible by two. The member bmPlanes specifies the number of color planes. The member bmBitsPixel specifies the number of bits required to indicate the color of a pixel. The member bmBits points to the location of the bit values for the bitmap. It is a long pointer to an array of char-size (1 byte) values.

How much of the information in the BITMAP structure is used depends on the type of bitmap processing performed by the application. The direct access operations described in Chapter 9 enable code to manipulate bitmap data directly. In this case most of the BITMAP structure members are required in order to locate and access the bitmap data. On the other hand, applications can use high-level functions to display bitmap. Such is the case with the BitBlt() GDI function, and the DirectDraw Blt() and BltFast() functions. When high-level functions are used, only the bmWidth and bmHeight members are usually necessary.

Moving a bitmap onto a surface

Blit operations in DirectDraw take place between surfaces. Therefore, a useful function is one that loads a bitmap onto a surface. The function, named DDBmapToSurf(), copies a memory-resident bitmap, specified by its handle, into a DirectDraw surface.

```
//****************************************************************
// Name: DDBmapToSurf
// Desc: Moves a bitmap to a DirectDraw Surface
// PRE CONDITIONS:
// 1. Parameter 1 is pointer to a DirectDraw surface
//    Parameter 2 is handle to the bitmap
//
// POST CONDITIONS:
// Bitmap is moved to surface
// Returns 1 if successful
// /
// ERROR CONDITIONS:
// All errors exit through DDInitFailed() function
//****************************************************************
HRESULT DDBmapToSurf(LPDIRECTDRAWSURFACE4 pdds, HBITMAP hbm)
{
    HDC                     hdcImage;
    HDC                     hdc;
    DDSURFACEDESC2          ddsd;
    HRESULT                 hr = 1;
    BOOL                    retValue;
```

```
    if (hbm == NULL || pdds == NULL)
      DDInitFailed(hWnd, hRet,
            "Invalid surface or bitmap in DDBmapToSurf");

    // Create compatible DC and select bitmap into it
    hdcImage = CreateCompatibleDC(NULL);
      if (!hdcImage)
        DDInitFailed(hWnd, hRet,
            "CreateCompatibleDC() failed in DDBmapToSurf");
    SelectObject(hdcImage, hbm);

    // Get size of surface
    ddsd.dwSize = sizeof(ddsd);
    ddsd.dwFlags = DDSD_HEIGHT | DDSD_WIDTH;
    pdds->GetSurfaceDesc(&ddsd);

    if ((hr = pdds->GetDC(&hdc)) != DD_OK)
      DDInitFailed(hWnd, hRet,
            "GetDC() failed in DDBmapToSurf");

    retValue = BitBlt(hdc, 0, 0, ddsd.dwWidth, ddsd.dwHeight,
                      hdcImage, 0, 0, SRCCOPY);
    // Release surface immediately
    pdds->ReleaseDC(hdc);

    if(retValue == FALSE)
        DDInitFailed(hWnd, hRet,
            "BitBlt() failed in DDBmapToSurf");

        DeleteDC(hdcImage);
      return hr;
}
```

Displaying the bitmap

We mentioned that the BitBlt() GDI function provides a flexible, yet slow, mechanism for displaying bitmaps. In the case of a DirectDraw application, executing in exclusive mode, the device context must be obtained with the DirectDraw-specific version of the GetDC() function. IDirectDrawSurface4:GetDC **not only returns a** GDI-compatible device context, but also locks the surface for access. The following function displays a bitmap using a DirectDraw device context:

```
//***************************************************************
// Name: DDShowBitmap
// Desc: Displays a bitmap using a DirectDraw device context
//
// PRE CONDITIONS:
// 1. Parameter 1 is pointer to a DirectDraw surface
//     Parameter 2 is handle to the bitmap
```

```
//      Parameters 3 and 4 are the display location
//      Parameters 5 and 6 are the bitmap dimensions
//
// POST CONDITIONS:
// Returns TRUE if successful
//
// ERROR CONDITIONS:
// All errors exit through DDInitFailed() function
//****************************************************************

BOOL DDShowBitmap( LPDIRECTDRAWSURFACE4 lpDDS, HBITMAP hBitmap,
           int xLocation, int yLocation,
           int bWidth, int bHeight)
{

    HDC              hdcImage = NULL;
    HDC              hdcSurf  = NULL;
    HDC              thisDevice = NULL;

    // Create a DC and select the image into it.
    hdcImage = CreateCompatibleDC( NULL );
    SelectObject( hdcImage, hBitmap);

    // Get a DC for the surface.
    if(lpDDS->GetDC(&hdcSurf) != DD_OK) {
        DeleteDC( hdcImage );
        DDInitFailed(hWnd, hRet,
            "GetDC() call failed in DDShowBitmap()");
        }

    // BitBlt() is used to display bitmap
    if ( BitBlt( hdcSurf, xLocation, yLocation, bWidth,
        bHeight, hdcImage, 0, 0, SRCCOPY ) == FALSE ) {
            lpDDS->ReleaseDC( hdcSurf );
            DeleteDC( hdcImage );
        // Take terminal error exit
        DDInitFailed(hWnd, hRet,
            "BitBlt() call failed in DDShowBitmap()");
        }
    // Release device contexts
        lpDDS->ReleaseDC( hdcSurf );
        DeleteDC( hdcImage );
        return TRUE;
}
```

The following code fragment shows the processing required for loading and displaying
a bitmap onto the primary surface, as implemented in the project named DD Bmap
Demo contained in the book's CD-ROM.

```
// Load bitmap named hubble.bmp
aBitmap = DDLoadBitmap(lpDDSPrimary, "hubble.bmp");
```

```
// Get bitmap data for displaying
GetObject(aBitmap, sizeof (BITMAP), &bMap1);

// Display bitmap
DDShowBitmap(lpDDSPrimary, aBitmap, 130, 50,
             (int) bMap1.bmWidth,
             (int) bMap1.bmHeight);
```

DirectDraw Windowed Applications

The maximum power and functionality of DirectDraw are available only to applications that execute in exclusive mode. For this reason programmers usually associate DirectDraw applications with exclusive mode execution. However, this does not preclude conventional Windows programs from using many DirectDraw functions, usually with considerable gain in performance and also allowing some image manipulations that are not possible in GDI code. You should also consider the fact that DirectDraw programming in windowed mode restores most of the device-independence that is lost in exclusive mode. This means that program coding must return to the conventional multitasking, message-based paradigm that is characteristic of Windows.

Running in a window usually means that the program can be totally or partially obscured by another program, that it can lose focus, that surfaces may be unbound from their memory assignments, and that the application window can be minimized or resized by the user. Most of these circumstances, which are often ignored in exclusive mode, require careful attention in windowed DirectDraw. The following are the main differences between DirectDraw programs in exclusive and nonexclusive mode:

✦ Exclusive mode applications usually require window style `WS_POPUP`, whereas windowed applications use `WS_THICKFRAME` if they are resizable. The combination `WS_SYSMENU`, `WS_CAPTION`, and `WS_MINIMIZEBOX` is used if the window cannot be resized by the user. `WS_OVERLAPPEDWINDOW` style includes `WS_THICKFRAME`.

✦ Exclusive mode programs use `DDSCL_FULLSCREEN` and `DDSCL_EXCLUSIVE` cooperative level; windowed programs use `DDSCL_NORMAL`.

✦ Whereas exclusive mode programs can use page flipping in implementing animation (animation techniques are covered in Chapter 12), windowed programs have very limited flipping capabilities. This is one of the reasons why games and other animation-intensive applications are designed usually for DirectDraw exclusive mode.

✦ Full-screen programs can set their own display mode, whereas windowed programs must operate in the current desktop display mode. By the same token, exclusive mode programs can assume a particular display mode, whereas windowed programs must be designed with sufficient flexibility to execute in several display modes.

✦ Exclusive mode applications may use clipping to produce specific graphics effects. Nonexclusive mode programs often rely on clipping to facilitate interaction with other programs and with the Windows desktop.

✦ Although exclusive mode can be switched to the background, usually they cannot be minimized or resized by the user. Nonexclusive mode programs can be moved on the desktop, resized, minimized, or obscured by other applications.

✦ Exclusive mode programs have direct control over the palette and can be designed for a particular palette. Windowed programs must use the palette manager to make changes and must accommodate palette changes made by the user or by other programs.

✦ Exclusive mode programs can display or hide the system cursor but cannot use system-level mouse support, as is the case with the system menu or the buttons on the program's title bar. Furthermore, exclusive mode programs must furnish most of the cursor processing logic. On the other hand, DirectDraw windowed applications can make use of all the cursor and cursor-related support functions in the Windows API.

✦ Exclusive mode applications must implement their own menus. Windows applications can use the menu facilities in the API.

In summary, although windowed programs must address some specific issues in using DirectDraw services, they do have almost unrestricted access to the functionality of a conventional application. Thus, a DirectDraw program that executes in nonexclusive mode can have a title bar, resizable borders, menus, status bar, sizing grip, scroll bars, as well as most of the other GUI components discussed earlier in the book. As a result, there is no standard design for a DirectDraw windowed application. However, there are issues that are usually confronted by a typical DirectDraw application when executing in nonexclusive mode. In the following sections we discuss the most important ones.

Nonexclusive mode initialization

It is difficult to design a general-purpose template for a DirectDraw nonexclusive mode application. The same applies for the initialization operations required to set up such programs. At the same time, there are certain typical initialization steps that apply to many DirectDraw applications that execute in nonexclusive mode. The project named DD NonExc Mode, included in the book's CD-ROM, contains a template file with minimal initializations for a DirectDraw application in nonexclusive mode.

The first step in `WinMain()` processing is defining and filling the `WNDCLASSEX` structure variable and registering the window class. In the template file this is accomplished as follows:

```
// Defining a structure of type WNDCLASSEX
WNDCLASSEX  wndclass ;
```

```
wndclass.cbSize         = sizeof (wndclass) ;
wndclass.style          = CS_HREDRAW | CS_VREDRAW;
wndclass.lpfnWndProc    = WndProc ;
wndclass.cbClsExtra     = 0 ;
wndclass.cbWndExtra     = 0 ;
wndclass.hInstance      = hInstance ;
wndclass.hIcon          = LoadIcon (NULL, IDI_APPLICATION) ;
wndclass.hCursor        = LoadCursor (NULL, IDC_ARROW) ;
wndclass.hbrBackground  = (HBRUSH) GetStockObject
                          (WHITE_BRUSH) ;
wndclass.lpszMenuName   = szAppName;
wndclass.lpszClassName  = szAppName;
wndclass.hIconSm        = LoadIcon (NULL, IDI_APPLICATION) ;

// Register the class
RegisterClassEx(&wndclass);
```

Next, the code must create the window and define its show state. In the case of a resizable window with the three conventional buttons and the system menu box in the title bar you can use the WS_OVERLAPPEDWINDOW style. Because it is impossible to predict the window size and initial location in the template, we used CW_USEDEFAULT for these parameters.

```
hWnd = CreateWindowEx(0,          // Extended style
        szAppName,
        "DirectDraw Nonexclusive Mode Template",
        WS_OVERLAPPEDWINDOW,
        CW_USEDEFAULT,
        CW_USEDEFAULT,
        CW_USEDEFAULT,
        CW_USEDEFAULT,
        NULL,              // Handle of parent
        NULL,              // Handle to menu
        hInstance,         // Application instance
        NULL);             // Additional data
if (!hWnd)
    return FALSE;
ShowWindow(hWnd, nCmdShow);
```

The processing for creating a DirectDraw object and a primary surface is similar to that used in exclusive-mode programming. In the template we use the same support procedures previously developed. DD4Interface() attempts to find a DirectDraw4 object and returns 1 if found and 0 if not. If the call is successful, a global pointer variable named lpDD4, of type LPDIRECTDRAW4, is initialized. DDInitFailed() provides a terminal exit for failed initialization operations. The primary surface is created by means of a call to CreateSurface(). The surface pointer is stored in the public variable lpDDSPrimary. Code is as follows:

```
//*********************************
// Create DirectDraw object and
// create primary surface
//*********************************
// Fetch DirectDraw4 interface
hRet = DD4Interface();
if (hRet == 0)
  return DDInitFailed(hWnd, hRet,
        "QueryInterface() call failed");

// Set cooperative level to exclusive and full screen
  hRet = lpDD4->SetCooperativeLevel(hWnd, DDSCL_NORMAL);
  if (hRet != DD_OK)
      return DDInitFailed(hWnd, hRet,
          "SetCooperativeLevel() call failed");

//*********************************
//      Create the primary surface
//*********************************
// ddsd is a structure of type DDSRUFACEDESC2
  ZeroMemory(&ddsd, sizeof(ddsd));  // Clear structure
// Fill in other members
  ddsd.dwSize = sizeof(ddsd);
  ddsd.dwFlags = DDSD_CAPS ;
  ddsd.ddsCaps.dwCaps = DDSCAPS_PRIMARYSURFACE;

  hRet = lpDD4->CreateSurface(&ddsd, &lpDDSPrimary, NULL);
  if (hRet != DD_OK)
      return DDInitFailed(hWnd, hRet,
              "CreateSurface() call failed");
```

Clipping the primary surface

In Chapter 7 we discussed clipping as the DirectDraw operation by which output is limited to a rectangular area, usually defined in a surface. DirectDraw supports clipping in both exclusive and nonexclusive modes. Because exclusive mode applications have control over the entire client area, clipping is used mostly as a graphics output manipulation. Windowed applications, on the other hand, often share the display with the Windows desktop and with other applications. In this case clipping is often used to ensure that the application's output is limited to its own client area. Figure 11-1 shows the execution on the Windows desktop of three copies of a DirectDraw application that uses clipping. The program itself, whose source file DD_InWin.cpp is contained in the DD InWin Demo project in the book's CD-ROM, is discussed later in this session.

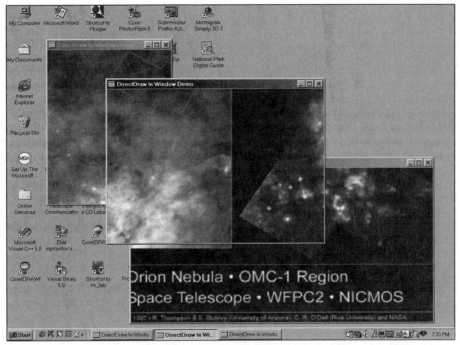

Figure 11-1: Clipping in a DirectDraw windowed application

In DirectDraw windowed applications a clipper is used to define the program's screen boundaries. The clipper ensures that a graphics object is not displayed outside the client area. Failure to define a clipper may cause the blit operation to fail because the destination drawing surface may be outside of the display limits. When the boundaries of the primary surface are defined in a clipper, then DirectDraw knows not to display outside of this area and the blit operation succeeds, as is the case in Figure 11-1. Recall that the `Blt()` function supports clipping but that `BltFast()` does not.

In a clip list, pixel coordinates are stored in one or more structures of type `RECT`. DirectDraw uses the clipper object to manage clip lists. Clip lists can be attached to any surface by using a DirectDrawClipper object. The simplest clip list consists of a single rectangle which defines the area within the surface to which a `Blt()` function outputs. Figure 11-2 shows a DirectDraw surface to which a clipper consisting of a single rectangle has been attached.

DirectDraw surface

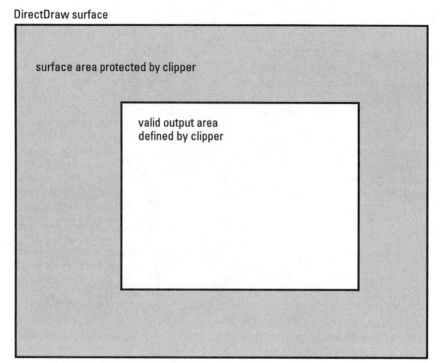

Figure 11-2: Establishing a surface's valid blit area by clipping

DirectDraw's Blt() function copies data only to the rectangles in the clip list. Clip lists consisting of several rectangles are often necessary to protect a specific surface area from output. For example, if an application requires a rectangular area in the top-center of the screen to be protected from output, it would need to define several clipping rectangles. Figure 11-3 shows such a case.

To manage a clip list, the application creates a series of rectangles and stores them in a data structure of type RGNDATA. One of the members of RGNDATA is the RGNDATAHEADER structure, which is used to define the number of rectangles that make up the region. The function SetClipList() is then called with the RGNDATA structure variable as a parameter. To delete a clip list from a surface, the SetClipList() call is made using NULL for the RGNDATA parameter.

DirectDraw surface

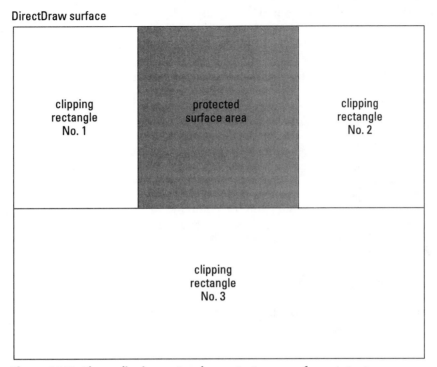

Figure 11-3: Three clipping rectangles protect an area from output

DirectDraw can manage the clip list for a primary surface automatically. Attaching a clipper to the primary surface requires several steps. In the first place, a clipper is a DirectDraw object in itself, which must be created using the DirectDraw4 interface object. The `CreateClipper()` function is used in this step. The function's general form is as follows:

```
HRESULT CreateClipper(
        DWORD dwFlags,                          // 1
        LPDIRECTDRAWCLIPPER FAR *lplpDDClipper, // 2
        IInknown FAR *pUnkOuter                 // 3
        );
```

The first and third parameters are not used in current implementations: the first one should be set to zero and the third one to NULL. The second parameter is the address of a variable of type `LPDIRECTDRAWCLIPPER`, which is set to the interface if the call succeeds; in this case the return value is DD_OK. If the call fails it returns one of the following constants:

```
DDERR_INVALIDOBJECT
DDERR_INVALIDPARAMS
DDERR_NOCOOPERATIVELEVELSET
DDERR_OUTOFMEMORY
```

After the clipper to the primary surface is created, it must be attached to the application's window. This requires a call to the SetHWnd() function. SetHWnd() takes two parameters: the first one must be set to zero in the current implementation and the second one is the handle to the window that uses the clipper object. This has the effect of setting the clipping region to the client area of the window and ensuring that the clip list is updated automatically as the window is resized, covered, or uncovered. After a clipper is set to a window, additional rectangles cannot be added.

Finally, the clipper must be associated with the primary surface. This is done by means of a call to the SetClipper() function that takes the surface pointer as its only parameter. The code in the template program is as follows:

```
//***********************************************
//  Create a clipper for the primary surface
//***********************************************
  hRet = lpDD4->CreateClipper(0, &lpDDClipper, NULL);
  if (hRet != DD_OK)
     return DDInitFailed(hWnd, hRet,
                       "Create clipper failed");
// Associate clipper with application window
hRet = lpDDClipper->SetHWnd(0, hWnd);
  if (hRet != DD_OK)
  return DDInitFailed(hWnd, hRet,
           "Clipper not linked to application window");
// Associate clipper with primary surface
hRet = lpDDSPrimary->SetClipper(lpDDClipper);
  if (hRet != DD_OK)
  return DDInitFailed(hWnd, hRet,
           "Clipper not linked to primary surface");
```

The remainder of the WinMain() function listed in the template program contains the regular message loop.

Rendering in Nonexclusive Mode

A simple rendering sequence in DirectDraw nonexclusive mode programming consists of storing a bitmap image in an offscreen surface and then blitting it to the primary surface. It is in the blitting stage that the windowed nature of the application introduces some constraints. The DirectDraw interface enables the program to access video memory directly, while the windowed nature of the application requires that video output be limited to the application's client area. A terminal error occurs if a windowed program attempts to display outside its own space. In GDI programming Windows takes care of clipping video output. In DirectDraw programming these restrictions must be observed and enforced by the application itself.

The most powerful rendering function for DirectDraw windowed applications is `Blt()`. DirectDraw windowed applications that use `Blt()` often create a destination surface clipper, and manipulate the size and position of the source and destination rectangles to achieve the desired effects. The `BltFast()` function can be used in cases that do not require clippers or the other output controls that are available in `Blt()`.

In this section we illustrate nonexclusive mode rendering with two sample programs, both contained in the DD InWin Demo project in the book's CD-ROM. Both programs display a bitmap of the Orion nebula images obtained by the Hubble Space Telescope.

Rendering by clipping

The first variation of the DD InWin Demo project is in the source file named DD_InWin.cpp. In this case the bitmap image is blitted to the entire primary surface and a clipper is used to restrict which portion of the image is displayed in the application's window. Figure 11-4 shows the original bitmap stretched to fill the primary surface. The clipper, which is the size of the application window, is attached to the primary surface. The lower part of the illustration shows three copies of the program on the Windows desktop. Each executing copy of the program shows the underlying portion of a virtual image according to the clipper, which is resized automatically by Windows to the application's client area. This ensures that video output is limited to the application's video space.

The DirectDraw windowed application is initialized as described earlier in this chapter. The wndclass.style member of the `WNDCLASSEX` structure is set to `CS_HREDRAW` and `CS_VREDRAW` so that the entire client area is redrawn if there is vertical or horizontal resizing.

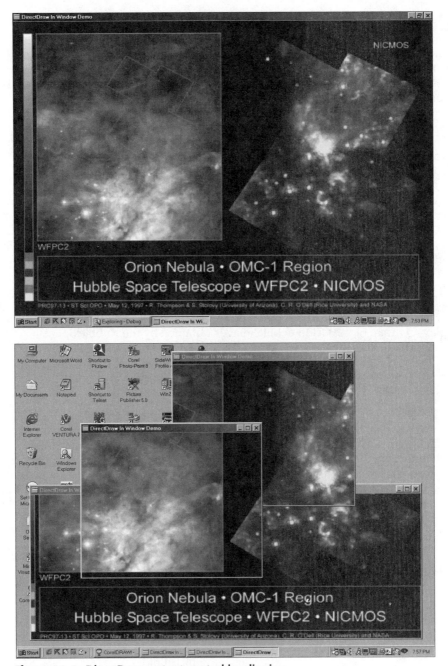

Figure 11-4: DirectDraw output control by clipping

The program design calls for creating an initial application window of the same size as the bitmap. Using the size of the original bitmap is an arbitrary decision because the program window is resizable. To obtain the bitmap dimensions, the code must load the bitmap into memory before creating the application window. The processing is as follows:

```
// Global handles and structures for bitmaps
HBITMAP     aBitmap;
BITMAP      bMap1;              // Structures for bitmap data
. . .
// Local data
RECT        progWin;           // Application window
                               // dimensions
//****************************************
//      Load bitmap into memory
//****************************************
// Load the bitmap image into memory
aBitmap = ( HBITMAP )LoadImage( NULL, "nebula.bmp",
           IMAGE_BITMAP, 0, 0, LR_LOADFROMFILE );
 if ( aBitmap == NULL )
     DDInitFailed(hWnd, hRet,
         "Bitmap load failed in DDLoadBitmap()");

// Get bitmap data
GetObject(aBitmap, sizeof (BITMAP), &bMap1);
// Store bitmap in RECT structure variable
progWin.left = 0;
progWin.top = 0;
progWin.right = bMap1.bmWidth;
progWin.bottom = bMap1.bmHeight;
```

At this point the bitmap dimensions have been stored in a structure variable named progWin, of type RECT. However, the application window is larger than the client area because it includes the title bar and the border. It is necessary to adjust the size by calling AdjustWindowRectEx(). This function corrects the data stored in a RECT structure variable according to the application's window style. The code is as follows:

```
//****************************************
//    Create a window with client area
//    the same size as the bitmap
//****************************************
// First adjust the size of the client area to the size
// of the bounding rectangle (this includes the border,
// caption bar, menu, etc.)

 AdjustWindowRectEx(&progWin,
                    WS_OVERLAPPEDWINDOW,
                    FALSE,
                    0);
```

```
hWnd = CreateWindowEx(0,          // Extended style
        szAppName,
        "DirectDraw In Window Demo",
        WS_OVERLAPPEDWINDOW,
        CW_USEDEFAULT,       // x of initial position
        CW_USEDEFAULT,       // y of initial position
        (progWin.right -- progWin.left),  // x size
        (progWin.bottom -- progWin.top),  // y size
        NULL,                // Handle of parent
        NULL,                // Handle to menu
        hInstance,           // Application instance
        NULL);               // Additional data

if (!hWnd)
    return FALSE;

ShowWindow(hWnd, nCmdShow);
```

In the call to `CreateWindowEx()` we used the default initial position and arbitrarily set the window's dimension to that of the bitmap, the size of which is stored in the `progWin` structure variables. The code now proceeds to create a DirectDraw object and a primary surface in the conventional manner. Note that the cooperative level in this case is `DDSCL_NORMAL`.

```
//**********************************
// Create DirectDraw object and
// create primary surface
//**********************************
 // Fetch DirectDraw4 interface
hRet = DD4Interface();
if (hRet == 0)
   return DDInitFailed(hWnd, hRet,
                   "QueryInterface() call failed");

 // Set cooperative level to exclusive and full screen
hRet = lpDD4->SetCooperativeLevel(hWnd, DDSCL_NORMAL);
if (hRet != DD_OK)
    return DDInitFailed(hWnd, hRet,
                   "SetCooperativeLevel() call failed");

// Create the primary surface
// ddsd is a structure of type DDSRUFACEDESC2
 ZeroMemory(&ddsd, sizeof(ddsd));  // Fill structure with
                                    // zeros
// Fill in other members
 ddsd.dwSize = sizeof(ddsd);
 ddsd.dwFlags = DDSD_CAPS ;
 ddsd.ddsCaps.dwCaps = DDSCAPS_PRIMARYSURFACE;

 hRet = lpDD4->CreateSurface(&ddsd, &lpDDSPrimary, NULL);
 if (hRet != DD_OK)
     return DDInitFailed(hWnd, hRet,
                   "CreateSurface() call failed");
```

Now the code must create a clipper associated with the application window and attached to the primary surface, as described previously in this chapter. The surface component tells DirectDraw which surface to clip. The window element defines the clipping rectangle to the size of the application's client area. The processing is as follows:

```
//*********************************
//     Create a clipper
//*********************************
 hRet = lpDD4->CreateClipper(0, &lpDDClipper, NULL);
 if (hRet != DD_OK)
      return DDInitFailed(hWnd, hRet,
                          "Create clipper failed");
// Associate clipper with application window
hRet = lpDDClipper->SetHWnd(0, hWnd);
 if (hRet != DD_OK)
    return DDInitFailed(hWnd, hRet,
             "Clipper not linked to application // window");
 // Associate clipper with primary surface
hRet = lpDDSPrimary->SetClipper(lpDDClipper);
 if (hRet != DD_OK)
    return DDInitFailed(hWnd, hRet,
             "Clipper not linked to primary surface");
```

Although the bitmap has been loaded, it has not yet been stored in an offscreen surface. Blt() requires that the bitmap is located on a surface; for this reason you have no other option in this case. Because speed is not a factor in this program, you can create the surface in system memory, which enables you to run several copies of the executable simultaneously. The code is as follows:

```
//***********************************
//    Store bitmap in offscreen surface
//***********************************
// First create an offscreen surface
// in system memory
ZeroMemory(&ddsd, sizeof(ddsd));   // Fill structure with
                                   // zeros
// Fill in other members
ddsd.dwSize = sizeof(ddsd);
ddsd.dwFlags = DDSD_CAPS | DDSD_HEIGHT | DDSD_WIDTH;
ddsd.ddsCaps.dwCaps = DDSCAPS_OFFSCREENPLAIN |
                      DDSCAPS_SYSTEMMEMORY;
ddsd.dwHeight = bMap1.bmHeight;
ddsd.dwWidth = bMap1.bmWidth;
hRet = lpDD4->CreateSurface(&ddsd, &lpDDSOffscreen, NULL);
if (hRet != DD_OK)
      return DDInitFailed(hWnd, hRet,
             "Offscreen surface creation failed");
  // Move bitmap to surface using DDBmapToSurf()function
hRet = DDBmapToSurf(lpDDSOffscreen, aBitmap);
```

```
        if(hRet != DD_OK)
            return DDInitFailed(hWnd, hRet,
                                "DDBMapToSurf() call failed");
    // ASSERT:
    //     Bitmap is in offscreen surface -> lpDDSOffscreen
```

Finally, the bitmap stored in the offscreen surface can be blitted to the primary surface using the clipper attached to the primary surface. The Blt() call is as follows:

```
    //**********************************
    //      Blit the bitmap
    //**********************************
    // Update the window with the new sprite frame. Note that the
    // destination rectangle is our client rectangle, not the
    // entire primary surface.
    hRet = lpDDSPrimary->Blt( NULL, lpDDSOffscreen, NULL,
                    DDBLT_WAIT, NULL );
        if(hRet != DD_OK)
            return DDInitFailed(hWnd, hRet,
                    "Blt() failed");
```

Because the window is resizable, we must also provide processing in the WM_PAINT message intercept. However, WM_PAINT is first called when the window is created; at this time the application has not yet performed the necessary initialization operations. To avoid a possible conflict, create a public switch variable, named DDOn, which is not set until the application is completely initialized. Another consideration is that the call to BeginPaint(), often included in WM_PAINT processing, automatically sets the clipping region to the application's update region. Because you are providing your own clipping, the call to BeginPaint() is undesirable. In the sample program, WM_PAINT message processing is as follows:

```
    case WM_PAINT:
        if(DDOn)
            hRet = lpDDSPrimary->Blt( NULL, lpDDSOffscreen, NULL,
                    DDBLT_WAIT, NULL );
        return 0;
```

Blit-time cropping

In the preceding section you saw the first variation of the DD InWin Demo sample program (source file is named DD_InWin.cpp) in which the bitmap image is stretch-blitted to the entire primary surface. A clipper that was previously attached to the primary surface automatically restricts which portion of the image is displayed in the application's window. An alternative rendering option, which produces entirely different results, is blitting to a destination rectangle in the primary surface that corresponds to the size of the application's client area. Because the destination of the blit is restricted to the client area there is no need for a clipper in this case; instead, the output is cropped by the Blt() function. Figure 11-5 graphically shows the basic operation of the two versions of the DD InWin Demo program.

Processing in DD_InWin.cpp sample program

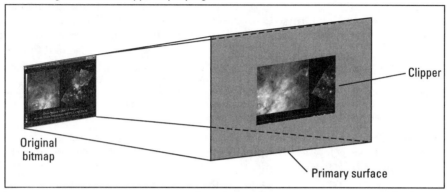

Processing in DD_InWinB.cpp sample program

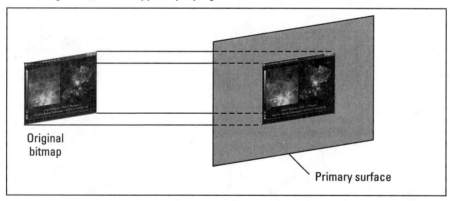

Figure 11-5: Comparing the two versions of the DD InWin Demo sample program

In the DD_InWinB.cpp version the WNDCLASSEX structure is defined similarly as in the first version of the sample program, except that the CS_HREDRAW and CS_VREDRAW window style constants are not necessary because the program window is not resizable. The fixed size of the program window also determines that the code uses WS_SYSMENU, WS_CAPTION, and WS_MINIMIZEBOX as the window style constants in both AdjustWindowRectEx() and CreateWindowEx() functions. Note that a resizable window requires the WS_THICKFRAME or WS_SIZEBOX styles. Also note that the WS_OVERLAPPEDWINDOW style, used in the first version of the sample program, includes WS_THICKFRAME and therefore also produces a resizable window. In the second version the program window is made the same size as the original bitmap, as is the case in the first version. In the first version the size of the display area is arbitrary because the program window is resizable anyway. In the second version we propose to display the bitmap identically, as it is stored; therefore, it is consequential that the display area correspond to the bitmap's size.

Much of the initialization and setup of the second version of the program is similar to the first version. The bitmap is loaded into memory and its size is stored in the corresponding members of a RECT structure variable. The DirectDraw4 object and the primary surface are created. In this case the clipper is not attached to the primary surface because it is not used. Then the offscreen surface is created and the bitmap is stored in it. It is now time to blit the bitmap from the offscreen surface to the primary surface, but before the blit can take place the code must determine the screen location and the size of the application's client area.

At blit time you need to define the destination rectangle as the first parameter of the Blt() function. One way to visualize the problem is to realize that at this point the program window is already displayed, with a blank rectangle on its client area, which is the same size as the bitmap. Also, the primary surface is the entire screen. Figure 11-6 shows the application at this stage and the dimensions necessary for locating the client area on the primary surface.

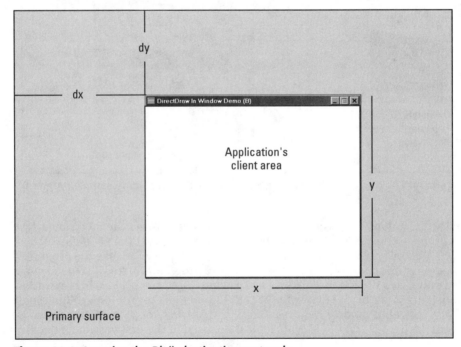

Figure 11-6: Locating the Blt() destination rectangle

The GetClientRect() API function returns the coordinates of the client area of a window. The function parameters are the handle of the target window and the address of a variable of type RECT, which holds the client area dimensions. The values returned by GetClientRect() correspond to the x and y dimensions shown in Figure 11-6. Because the coordinates are relative to the application's window, the value returned by the call for the upper-left corner of the rectangle is always (0,0). This makes the left and top members of the RECT structure variable passed to the call always zero. Because we need the location of application's window in the primary surface, the code must determine the values labeled *dx* and *dy* in Figure 11-6 and add them to the coordinates stored in the RECT structure.

The ClientToScreen() function performs this operation for you. Its parameters are the handle to the application's window and the address of a structure of type POINT containing two coordinate values that are updated to screen coordinates. ClientToScreen() actually performs an addition operation on the coordinate pair: it calculates the distances labeled *dx* and *dy* in Figure 11-6 and adds these values to those stored in the structure variable. If the POINT structure contains two members of type long, and the RECT structure contains four members, we can consider that the RECT structure member holds two structures of type POINT. The code in the sample program is as follows:

```
    RECT            clientArea;          // For Blt()
destination
    . . .
    // Obtain client rectangle and convert to screen coordinates
    GetClientRect(hWnd, &clientArea);
    ClientToScreen(hWnd, (LPPOINT) &clientArea.left);
    ClientToScreen(hWnd, (LPPOINT) &clientArea.right);

    // Blit to the destination rectangle
    hRet = lpDDSPrimary->Blt( &clientArea, lpDDSOffscreen, NULL,
                        DDBLT_WAIT, NULL );
      if(hRet != DD_OK)
        return DDInitFailed(hWnd, hRet,
                      "Blt() failed");
```

The ClientToScreen() function is called twice: First, for the coordinate pair that holds the top-left corner of the client area rectangle; these are the zero values returned by GetClientRect(). Then the ClientToScreen() function is called for the coordinate pair of the bottom-right corner of the client area rectangle, which correspond to the x and y dimensions in Figure 11-6. Similar processing must be performed in the WM_PAINT message intercept. Figure 11-7 shows the results of the DD_InWinB.cpp version of the demonstration program.

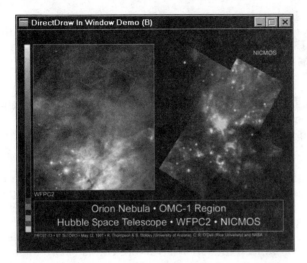

Figure 11-7: Screen snapshot of the DD_InWinB.cpp program version

The project folder DD InWin Demo in the book's CD-ROM contains both versions of the source program as well as the corresponding executable files.

Summary

In this chapter we discussed bitmap rendering operations in DirectDraw programming. The operations were illustrated in the context of two DirectDraw windowed applications. The emphasis has been on static rendering. In the next chapter we discuss dynamic rendering operations in the context of DirectDraw animation. Having learned bitmap operations in DirectDraw, we apply these techniques in producing animated applications in the next chapter.

✦   ✦   ✦

Animation Techniques

Animation is the most exacting and exciting task of graphics programming. This chapter is about computer animation using the facilities provided by DirectDraw. For many years animation in Windows was considered somewhat of an oxymoron. DirectDraw furnishes mechanisms and programming facilities that make possible graphics rendering at a high speed. It also provides the storage of image data in so-called back buffers, which can be flipped rapidly with the displayed surface to simulate screen movement. The results are often a smooth and natural simulation of movement that can be used in computer games, simulations, and in high-performance multimedia applications.

Palette animation techniques have been used effectively in DOS programming but we feel that today's video cards, even those in low-end systems, support such high resolutions and color depths that palette modes are no longer needed. On the other hand, overlays — although powerful and useful — are not supported by most video cards, and those that do support them do so inconsistently. Furthermore, overlay operations are not emulated in the HEL; therefore, if it is not available in the hardware, overlay operations cannot be used by code. We feel that overlays belong in the future of graphics programming, and palette manipulations in its past. Instead, we focus on animation techniques that are popular and practical.

Animation in Real-Time

Computer animation is the simulation of movement or lifelike actions by the manipulation of digital objects. It is a complex specialty field of graphics programming, on which many books have been written. The fundamentals of computer animation were discussed in Chapter 5. In this chapter we are concerned with real-time animation, rather than with computer-assisted techniques. Real-time animation is found in arcade machines, simulators, trainers, electronic games, multimedia applications, and in interactive programs of many kinds. In real-time animation the computing machine is often both the image generator and the display media, although most animations rely heavily on prestored images and on image sets.

Real-time animation is based on physiology of the human eye. In our vision system the image of an object persists in the brain for a brief period of time after it no longer exists. This phenomenon is called *visual retention*. Smooth animation is achieved by consecutively displaying images at a faster rate than the period of visual retention. It is the sequence of rapidly displayed images that creates in our minds the illusion a smoothly moving object.

Television and moving picture technologies use a critical image update rate for smooth animation between 22 and 30 images per second. In animation programming this is called the frame rate. Moving picture films are recorded and displayed at a rate of 24 images per second, while commercial television takes place slightly faster. The threshold rate, which is subject to variations in different individuals, is estimated at about 17 images per second. If the consecutive images are projected at a rate slower than this threshold, the average individual perceives jerkiness in the animation and feels uncomfortable watching it.

Surface tearing

Although the animator's principal concerns are usually speed and performance, too much speed can lead to image quality deterioration. A raster scan display system is based on scanning each horizontal row of screen pixels with an electron beam. The pixel rows are refreshed starting at the top-left screen corner of the screen and ending at the bottom-right corner. Each pixel row is called a *scan line*. The electron beam is turned off at the end of each scan line while the gun is re-aimed to the start of the next one. This period is called the *horizontal retrace*. When this process reaches the last scan line on the screen, the beam is turned off again while the gun is re-aimed to the top-left screen corner. The period of time required to re-aim the electron gun from the right-bottom of the screen to the top-left corner is known as the *vertical retrace* or *screen blanking* cycle. Figure 12-1 shows the scan and retrace cycles.

The problem arises when video data are changed by the CPU at the same time it is being displayed by the video controller. In the PC screen refresh rates are normally between 60 and 100 Hz. The fact that a CPU is capable of executing hundreds of thousands of instructions per second makes it possible that the image in video memory be modified before the video system has finished displaying it. The result is a breaking of the image, known as *tearing*. One way to avoid tearing is to limit video memory updates to the time that the electron guns are turned off. In practice, the vertical retrace cycle is used because it takes longer than the horizontal retrace.

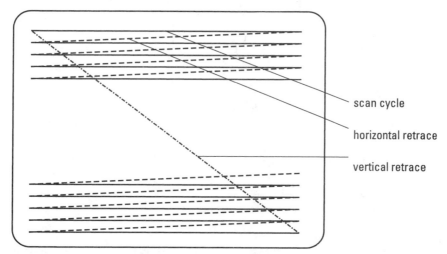

Figure 12-1: CRT scan and retrace cycles

DirectDraw programs that execute in exclusive mode can prevent or minimize tearing by using double-buffering and flipping techniques, discussed later in this chapter. Programs in windowed mode cannot use flipping and are limited to timing video updates with the vertical refresh cycle.

The animator's predicament

Several constraints make computer animation a battle against time. The animation programmer must resort to every possible trick in order to squeeze the maximum performance. Because execution speed is limited by the hardware, most of the work of the programmer-animator consists of making compromises and finding acceptable levels of undesirable effects. The animator often has to decide how small an image satisfactorily depicts the object, how much tearing is acceptable, how much bumpiness can be allowed in depicting movement, how little definition is sufficient for certain scenery, or with how few colors can an object be realistically represented.

Obtaining a Timed Pulse

Representing movement requires a display sequence, executed frame-by-frame, which creates the illusion of motion. Figure 12-2 shows several frames in the animation of a stick figure of a walking person.

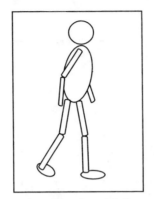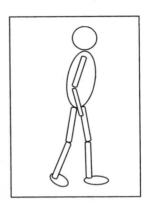

Figure 12-2: Frame-by-frame animation of a stick figure

The display of the frame-by-frame sequence in real-time requires a mechanism for measuring the time lapse between each frame; in other words, an update pulse. In DOS programming this can be accomplished by intercepting the system timer, which usually requires installing a dedicated interrupt vector. The result is that a routine in the application's code receives control every time that a preset timer counter expires. Because there is no multitasking in DOS, the resulting timing pulse is reasonably accurate. Windows, on the other hand, does not allow direct manipulation of the timer hardware.

A Windows application has several ways of generating a timed pulse. One is based on a program loop that reads the value in a ticker register and proceeds to update the frame whenever it matches or exceeds a predefined constant. A second approach is to enable a system timer pulse, which can be intercepted in a callback function or by a window message. In the following sections we discuss both methods. Other alternatives, sometimes called high-resolution timers, are discussed in the context of performance tuning, later in this chapter.

Tick counting method

Windows maintains a counter with the number of milliseconds elapsed since the system was started. This time period, sometimes called the Windows time, is stored in a `DWORD` variable that can be read by code. Two identical functions enable code to read this counter: `GetCurrentTime()` and `GetTickCount()`. However, Windows documentation states that `GetCurrentTime()` is now obsolete and should not be used.

`GetTickCount()`, which takes no parameters, returns the number of milliseconds elapsed since Windows was started. Application code can determine the number of milliseconds elapsed since the last call by storing the previous value in a static or public variable, as in the following function:

```
// Public variables for counter operation
DWORD          thisTickCount;    // New ticker value
DWORD          lastTickCount;    // Storage for old value
static DWORD   TIMER_VALUE = 25; // Constant for time lapse
    . . .
static void UpdateFrame()
{
   thisTickCount = GetTickCount();    // Read counter
   if(( thisTickCount - lastTickCount) < TIMER_VALUE)
     return;
   else
   {
     // Frame update operations go here
    lastTickCount = thisTickCount;    // Reset tick counts
   }
   return;
}
```

In order for the ticker counter reading method to produce a smooth animation, the value in the ticker counter must be polled frequently. One possible approach is to include the frame update function call as part of the application's message loop. The processing logic can be expressed in the following pseudocode:

If the application is active, and no other messages are waiting to be processed, then call the frame update routine.

The PeekMessage() function is used to check the thread's message queue without pausing for a message to be received. The function's general form is as follows:

```
BOOL PeekMessage(
             LPMSG lpMsg,         // 1
             HWND hWnd,           // 2
             UINT wMsgFilterMin,  // 3
             UINT wMsgFilterMax,  // 4
             UINT wRemoveMsg      // 5
             );
```

The first parameter points to an MSG structure variable that contains message information. The second parameter is the handle to the window whose messages are being checked. This parameter can be set to NULL to check messages for the current application. The third and the fourth parameters are used to specify the lowest and highest value of the messages to be checked. If both parameters are set to 0, then all messages are retrieved. The fifth parameter is one of two predefined constants: PM_REMOVE is used if the message is to be removed from the queue, and

PM_NOPREMOVE otherwise. The call returns TRUE if a message is available, and FALSE if not available.

Another API function often used in message polling routines is WaitMessage(). This function, which takes no parameters, suspends thread execution and does not return until a new message is placed in the queue. The result is to yield control to other threads when the current one has nothing to do with its CPU cycles. PeekMessage() and WaitMessage() can be combined with GetMessage() in the following message polling routine:

```
MSG         msg;            // Message structure variable
int         appActive = 0;  // Application active switch
                            // initialized to inactive
. . .
while(1) {
  if(PeekMessage(&msg, NULL, 0, 0, PM_NOREMOVE)) {
    if(!GetMessage(&msg, NULL, 0, 0)
      return msg.wParam;
    TranslateMessage(&msg);
    DispatchMessage(&msg);
  }
  else if (appActive)
  {
  // call to read ticker counter and/or update frame
  // go here
  }
  else
    WaitMessage();
}
```

In using this sample code the application must define when to set and reset the appActive switch. This switch determines if the frame update function is called, or if the thread just waits for another message.

The method just described, that is, reading the Windows tick count inside a program loop, is usually capable of generating a faster pulse than the system timer intercept, which is described in the next section. On the other hand, the system timer intercept is easier to implement and more consistent with the Windows multitasking environment. Therefore, it is preferred if the resulting pulse rate is satisfactory.

System timer intercept

An alternative way of obtaining a timed pulse is by means of the Windows system timer. The SetTimer() function is used to define a time-out value, in milliseconds. When this time-out value elapses, the application gets control either at the WM_TIMER message intercept or in an application-defined callback function that has the generic name TimerProc(). Either processing is satisfactory and which one is selected is a matter of coding convenience. SetTimer() has the following general form:

```
UINT SetTimer(
            HWND hWnd,              // 1
            UINT nIDEvent,          // 2
            UINT uElapse,           // 3
            TIMERPROC lpTimerFunc   // 4
            );
```

The first parameter is the handle to the window associated with the timer. The second parameter is the timer number. This allows more than one timer per application. The timer identifier is passed to the WM_TIMER intercept and to the TimerProc(). The third parameter is the number of milliseconds between timer intercepts. The fourth parameter is the address of the application's TimerProc(), if one is implemented, or NULL if processing is to be done in the WM_TIMER message intercept.

If the call succeeds, the return value is an integer identifying the new timer. Sixteen timers are available to applications, so it is a good idea for you to check if a timer is actually assigned to the thread. Applications must pass this timer identifier to the KillTimer() function to destroy a particular timer. If the function fails to create a timer, the return value is zero. After a system timer is initialized, processing usually consists of calling the application's frame update function directly because the timer tick need not be checked in this case.

Note that code cannot assume that system timer events are generated at the requested rate, only that the events are produced approximately at this rate and not more frequently. Windows documentation states that the minimum time between events is approximately 55 milliseconds.

Sprites

In graphics programming, particularly in game programming, a sprite is a rather small screen object, usually animated at display time. Sprite animation can be simple or complex. In simple animation an object represented in a single bitmap is animated by translating it to other screen positions, or the object itself performs an intrinsic action, for example, a rotating wheel. In complex animation both actions are performed simultaneously: a rocket moves on the screen until it reaches a point where it explodes. Sprites are typically encoded in one or more images that represent the object or its action sequence. The images can be stored in separate bitmaps, or in a single one. Figure 12-3 shows the image set of a dagger sprite that revolves around its own axis.

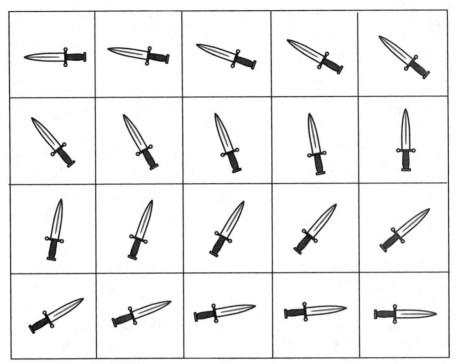

Figure 12-3: Image set for a dagger sprite

When the twenty images in the set of Figure 12-3 are rapidly displayed, the dagger appears to rotate 180 degrees. If the images are also translated from one screen position to another, the sprite simulates the movement of a thrown dagger. This last action would be a case of complex sprite animation.

Sprites often use a source color key to achieve transparency. To automate sprite color keying, some applications assume that the pixel at the top-left corner of the bitmap is the color key. Later in this chapter we discuss the use of dynamic color keys. It is possible to encode each image of the sprite image set in separate bitmaps, but this usually leads to many disk files and complicated file access operations. A better approach is to store the entire sprite image set in a single bitmap, and then use source rectangle selection capability of either the Blt() or BltFast() functions to pick the corresponding image.

Many factors determine how a sprite is actually rendered. One of the most important ones is if the application executes in exclusive mode or windowed. Exclusive-mode programs can use back buffers and flipping manipulations that considerably increase performance, whereas windowed programs are much more limited in the available rendering options. Other factors are the sprite's size, the number of images in the set, and the required rendering speed. Programmers often have to juggle these and other program elements to come up with a satisfactory animation.

Sprite art

Animated programs spend considerable resources in manipulating sprites and backgrounds. The better the image quality of these objects, the better graphics result you see. Because backgrounds are usually animated by simple panning and zooming transformations, the programmer's effort is often limited to scanning or drawing relatively few and relatively large images. But sprites can be a more complicated matter, especially if you want to create a sprite that has intrinsic movements or action. In this case the individual images in the sprite set must be tied to a common point. For example, if the various daggers in Figure 12-3 do not have a common center of rotation, the resulting animation is bumpy and unpleasant. The progression between each image in the set must also be proportional. In other words, the dagger must rotate by approximately the same angle to generate uniform screen movement.

Perhaps the most important factor in creating good sprites is the sprite itself. Until recently the creation of attractive sprites was considered some sort of black art. With the popularization of 3D graphics on the PC it is possible to easily create solid sprites that add a new dimension to the animation. Programs are now available which generate 3D graphics objects that can be animated. Some popular commercial drawing applications, such as CorelDRAW, now include 3D drawing capabilities. Figure 12-4 shows the rotation of a clipart 3D image using CorelDRAW. You can use the resulting image set to produce an intrinsic sprite animation.

Figure 12-4: Rotation of a 3D image using commercial software

The sprite image set

A computer animator often spends a large part of his or her time in designing, drawing, encoding, and testing sprites. This is particularly true in 3D graphics. The process of sprite design implies several apparently contradictory decisions, for instance:

✦ The larger the sprite is, the better its image quality, but it is more difficult to animate a larger sprite.

✦ The more images there are in the sprite image set, the smoother the animation, but it takes longer to display a large sprite image set.

✦ The higher the definition and color depth of the sprite bitmaps are, the better the quality of the image, but higher quality bitmaps take up more video memory and a longer time to blit.

Two hardware-dependent issues often must be taken into consideration as well: the processor speed of the host system and the capabilities of the video system. The second one of these issues comprises two other ones: the amount of video memory and the hardware support for DirectDraw operations. After the designers define the minimum system capabilities, and the acceptable performance levels, the next step usually is to experiment with several sprite image sets to determine the best possible image quality for the required levels of performance.

The details of how the sprite image sets are produced is more in the realm of graphics design than in programming. The higher the quality of the drawing or paint program used, and the more experienced and talented the sprite artist is, the better the resulting image set. The DD Animation Demo project, included in the book's CD-ROM, shows two rotating, meshed gears. The image set consists of 18 images. In each image the gears are rotated by an angle of 2.5 degrees. After 18 iterations the gears have rotated through an angle of 45 degrees. Because the gears have eight teeth each, the images are symmetrical after a rotation of 45 degrees. For this reason, this animation requires one-eighth the number of images that would be necessary to rotate a nonsymmetrical object by the same angle. Figure 12-5 shows the sequence of steps that we followed in creating the image set for the DD Animation Demo program.

In creating the image set of the DD Animation Demo program we started with a CorelDRAW clipart image of a gear, which was then edited and colored, as shown in Step 1 in Figure 12-5. In Step 2 we made a copy of the original gear. The copy was colored and rotated so that the two gears would mesh, as shown in Step 3. The meshed gear pair was then reproduced 18 times. In each reproduction the left-hand gear was rotated clockwise and the right-hand counterclockwise, by 2.5 degrees. The resulting image set is shown in Step 4 in Figure 12-5. This image set was then saved as a Windows bitmap for use by the code.

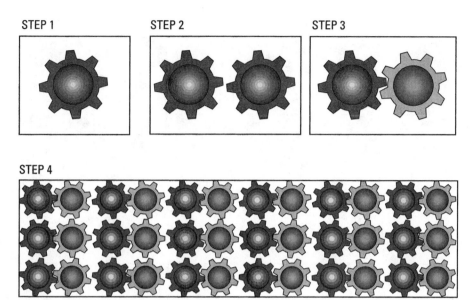

Figure 12-5: Image set for DD Animation Demo program

Sprite rendering

The actual display of the sprite consists of obtaining a timing pulse and blitting the image onto the screen. In each particular case you must decide whether the rendering is done using Blt() or BltFast(), with or without transparency, using source or destination color keys, or applying any blit-time transformations. The sprite image sequence is usually stored in a single bitmap, but it is also possible to store various bitmaps in different disk files and then read all of these files into a single surface. The final result, in either case, is a surface with multiple images. At blit time the program logic must select the corresponding image in the animation set.

The display of several images stored in a contiguous memory area or surface is made possible by the source area definition capabilities of both Blt() and BltFast(). In Chapter 10 we saw that a structure of type RECT is used to store the offset of the source rectangle in the surface. If an animation image set is stored in a rectangular bitmap, and the bitmap is then loaded onto a surface, then code can select which of the images in the set is displayed during each time-pulse iteration. You can do this by assigning values to the corresponding members of the RECT structure variable that defines the source surface. For example, the final bitmap image set in Figure 12-5 contains a sequence of 18 individual rotations of the gears. Each of these individual bitmaps is often called an animation frame, or simply, a frame. Figure 12-6 shows the image set partitioned into six columns and three rows. The dimensions labeled x and y refer to the size of each frame in the set.

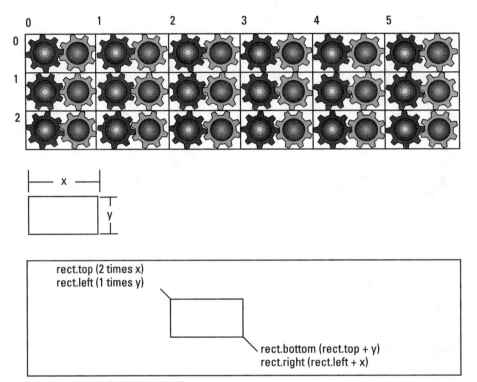

Figure 12-6: Rendering the sprite image set

Given the number of rows and columns in the image set, and the pixel size of each image, code can determine the coordinates of the RECT structure variable for each frame in the set. The dotted rectangle in Figure 12-6 binds each frame in the sequence. The members of a structure variable named rect, of type RECT, are calculated using the consecutive frame number and the number of columns in the bitmap. The case illustrated shows frame number 8, of a bitmap with six columns and three rows.

In the DD Animation Demo program the processing is generalized so that you can use the code to display any rectangular bitmap image set. This makes it useful for experimenting with various image sets before deciding which one is better suited for the purpose at hand. Code starts by creating global variables that define the characteristics of the image set. Code is as follows:

```
// Constants identifying the bitmap image set
static char bmapName[] = {"gearsy.bmp"};
static int        imageCols = 6;      // Number of image
columns
static int        imageRows = 3;      // Number of rows
```

```
// Variables, constants, handles, and structure for bitmaps
int        frameCount = (imageCols * imageRows) - 1;
int        bmapXSize;       // Calculated x size of bitmap
int        bmapYSize;       // Calculated y size of bitmap
HBITMAP    aBitmap;
BITMAP     bMap1;           // Structures for bitmap data
```

In this case the programmer defines the name of the bitmap and states the number of image columns and rows. Code uses these values to calculate the number of frames; this number is stored in the variable frameCount. The dimensions of the bitmap are obtained after it is loaded into memory. The *x* dimension is stored in the variable bmapXSize and the *y* dimension in bmapYSize. The bitmap dimensions are also used in the sample program to define the size of the application window, all of which is shown in the following code fragment:

```
//***************************************
//      Load bitmap into memory
//***************************************
// Load the bitmap image into memory
aBitmap = ( HBITMAP )LoadImage( NULL, bmapName,
        IMAGE_BITMAP, 0, 0, LR_LOADFROMFILE );
  if ( aBitmap == NULL )
        DDInitFailed(hWnd, hRet,
        "Bitmap load failed in DDLoadBitmap()");
// Get bitmap data
GetObject(aBitmap, sizeof (BITMAP), &bMap1);

// Calculate and store bitmap and image data
bmapXSize = bMap1.bmWidth / imageCols;
bmapYSize = bMap1.bmHeight / imageRows;

// Store bitmap in RECT structure variable
progWin.left = 0;
progWin.top = 0;
progWin.right = bmapXSize;
progWin.bottom = bmapYSize;

//***************************************
//    Create window with client area
//    the same size as the bitmap
//***************************************
// First adjust the size of the client area to the size
// of the bounding rectangle (this includes the border,
// caption bar, menu, etc.)

  AdjustWindowRectEx(&progWin,
        WS_SYSMENU | WS_CAPTION,
        FALSE,
        0);

  hWnd = CreateWindowEx(0,          // Extended style
        szAppName,
        "DirectDraw Animation Demo",
```

```
                    WS_SYSMENU | WS_CAPTION,
                    CW_USEDEFAULT,
                    CW_USEDEFAULT,
                    (progWin.right - progWin.left),
                    (progWin.bottom - progWin.top),
                    NULL,               // Handle of parent
                    NULL,               // Handle to menu
                    hInstance,          // Application instance
                    NULL);              // Additional data
        if (!hWnd)
            return FALSE;
```

The actual display of the bitmap is performed by a local function called Blit
Sprite(). The function begins by checking the tick counter. If the difference
between the old and the new tick counts is smaller than the predefined delay,
execution returns immediately. If it is equal to or larger than the delay, then the
offset of the next frame in the source surface is calculated and the bitmap is blitted
by means of the Blt() function. In this case the frame number counter is bumped;
if this is the last frame in the set, the counter is restarted. Execution concludes by
updating the tick counter variable. Coding is as follows:

```
//*************************************
//      update animation frame
//*************************************
static void BlitSprite()
{
    thisTickCount = GetTickCount();

    if((thisTickCount - lastTickCount) < TIMER_VALUE)
      return;
    else
    {
    // Update the sprite image with the current frame.
    bmapArea.top = ( ( frameNum / imageCols) * bmapYSize );
    bmapArea.left = ( ( frameNum % imageCols) * bmapXSize );
    bmapArea.bottom = bmapArea.top + bmapYSize;
    bmapArea.right = bmapArea.left + bmapXSize;

    hRet = lpDDSPrimary->Blt( &clientArea, lpDDSOffscreen,
            &bmapArea, DDBLT_WAIT, NULL );
        if(hRet != DD_OK)
            DDInitFailed(hWnd, hRet, "Blt() failed");
    // Update the frame counter
    frameNum++;
    if(frameNum > imageCount)
        frameNum = 0;
    lastTickCount = thisTickCount;
    return;
    }
}
```

Figure 12-7 is a screen snapshot of the DD Animation Demo program.

Figure 12-7: Screen snapshot of the DD Animation Demo program

Flipping

One of the most powerful animation tools provided by DirectDraw is page flipping. This technique finds common use in high-performance multimedia applications, in simulations, and in game software. The process is reminiscent of the schoolhouse method of drawing a series of images, each consecutive one containing a slight change. The figures are drawn on a paper pad. When you thumb through the package you perceive an illusion of movement. In the simplest version of computerized page flipping the programmer sets up two DirectDraw surfaces. The first one is the conventional primary surface and the other one is called a *back buffer*. Application code updates the image in the back buffer and then flips the back buffer and the primary surface. The result is usually a clean and efficient animation effect. Figure 12-8 shows the fade-out animation of a sphere.

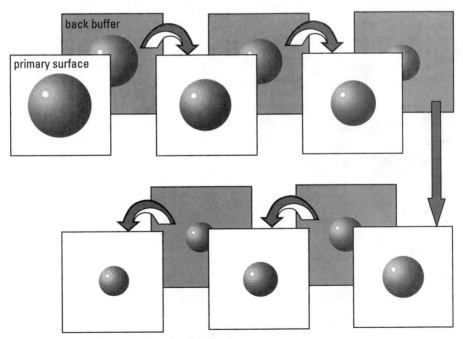

Figure 12-8: Fade-out animation by flipping

In Figure 12-8, you see that consecutively smaller images are drawn on the back buffer, which is then flipped with the primary surface. In this illustration the arrows represent the flip operations. The back buffers are shown in dark gray rectangles. The sequence of operations is draw to back buffer, flip, draw to back buffer, flip, and so on.

One limitation of multiple buffering and page flipping is that it can be used only in DirectDraw exclusive mode. This is because flipping requires manipulating video memory directly, which is not possible in a windowed environment. In the DirectDraw flip operation it is the pointers to surface memory for the primary surface and the back buffers that are swapped. In other words, flipping is actually a switching of pointers manipulation, not a data copying operation. Exceptions are when the back buffer cannot fit into display memory, or when the hardware does not support flipping, in which case DirectDraw performs the flip by copying the surfaces.

When programming a flip-based animation it is important to remember that code need only access the back buffer surface to perform the image updates. Every time the DirectDraw Flip() function is called the primary surface becomes the back buffer and vice versa. The surface pointer to the back buffer always points to the area of video memory not displayed, and the surface pointer to the primary surface or front buffer points to the video memory being displayed. If more than one back buffer is included in the flipping chain, then the surfaces are rotated in circular fashion. The case of a flipping chain with a primary surface and two back buffers is shown in Figure 12-9. In this case the flip operation rotates the surfaces as shown.

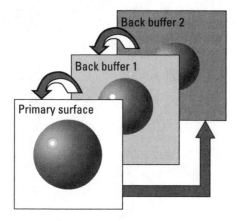

Figure 12-9: Flipping chain with two back buffers

Initializing and performing flip animation consists of several well-defined steps. In most cases the following operations are necessary:

✦ Creating a flipping chain
✦ Obtaining a back buffer pointer

✦ Drawing to the back buffer

✦ Flipping the primary surface and the back buffer

The first two steps of this sequence relate to initializing the flipping surfaces, and the second two steps refer to flip animation rendering operations. Table 12-1 lists the flipping-related functions in DirectDraw.

Table 12-1
Flipping-related DirectDraw Functions

Function	Object	Action
CreateSurface()	DIRECTDRAW4	Creates surface and attached back buffers
GetAttachedSurface()	DIRECTDRAWSURFACE4	Obtains back buffer pointer
Flip()	DIRECTDRAW4	Performs flipping
GetFlipStatus()	DIRECDRAWSURFACE4	Indicates whether a surface has concluded flipping

The function FlipToGDISurface() has very low performance since rendering takes place outside of DirectDraw. For this reason it is not discussed in this book.

Initializing the flipping surfaces

Any DirectDraw surface can be constructed as a flipping surface, although most commonly the flipping surfaces consist of a primary surface and at least one back buffer. The surfaces involved in the flipping are sometimes called the flipping chain. Creating the flipping chain requires two DirectDraw functions: CreateSurface() is used to create both the primary surface and the back buffer, and GetAttached Surface() to obtain the back buffer pointer. In the case of a flipping chain, the call to CreateSurface() must include the flag DDSD_BACKBUFFERCOUNT, which defines the member dwBackBufferCount, which in turn is used to set the number of back buffers in the chain. Other flags usually listed in the call are DDSCAPS_ PRIMARYSURFACE, DDSCAPS_FLIP, DDSCAPS_COMPLEX, and DDSCAPS_VIDEOMEMORY. The following code shows a call to CreateSurface() for a flipping chain consisting of a primary surface and a single back buffer:

```
DDSURFACEDESC2       ddsd;
. . .
// Create the primary surface with a back buffer
```

```
        ZeroMemory(&ddsd, sizeof(ddsd));  // Fill structure with
                                          // zeros
// Fill in other members
    ddsd.dwSize = sizeof(ddsd);
    ddsd.dwFlags = DDSD_CAPS | DDSD_BACKBUFFERCOUNT;
    ddsd.ddsCaps.dwCaps = DDSCAPS_PRIMARYSURFACE |
                          DDSCAPS_FLIP |
                          DDSCAPS_COMPLEX |
                          DDSCAPS_VIDEOMEMORY;
    ddsd.dwBackBufferCount = 1;
    hRet = lpDD4->CreateSurface(&ddsd, &lpDDSPrimary, NULL);
```

If the call to CreateSurface() returns DD_OK, then the flipping chain surfaces have been created. To use the flipping chain, code must first obtain the pointer to the back buffer because the call to CreateSurface() returns only the pointer to the primary surface (in its second parameter). The GetAttachedSurface() function has the following general form:

```
HRESULT GetAttachedSurface(
        LPDDSCAPS lpDDSCaps,                              // 1
        LPDIRECTDRAWSURFACE3 FAR *lplpDDAttachedSurface   // 2
        );
```

The first parameter is a pointer to a DDSCAPS2 structure that contains the hardware capabilities of the surface. The second parameter is the address of a variable that is to hold the pointer, of type IDIRECTDRAWSURFACE4, retrieved by the call. The retrieved surface matches the description in the first parameter. If the function succeeds, it returns DD_OK. If it fails it returns one of the following errors:

DDERR_INVALIDOBJECT

DDERR_INVALIDPARAMS

DDERR_NOTFOUND

DDERR_SURFACELOST

The following code fragment obtains the back buffer surface pointer for the primary surface previously described.

```
// Get back buffer pointer
    ddscaps.dwCaps = DDSCAPS_BACKBUFFER;
    hRet = lpDDSPrimary->GetAttachedSurface(&ddscaps,
                         &lpDDSBackBuf);
```

If the calls to CreateSurface() and GetAttachedSurface() are successful, DirectDraw creates two attached surfaces in display memory, and the application retrieves the pointers to each of these surfaces. The pointer to the back buffer surface is used at draw time, and the pointer to the primary surface at flip time. DirectDraw automatically switches the surface pointers, transparently to application code.

Flipping operations

After the application concludes drawing, and the frame timer count expires, the actual rendering is performed by calling DirectDraw Flip(). The Flip() function exchanges the surface memory of the primary surface and the back buffer. If more than one back buffer is specified when the flip chain is created, then each call to Flip() rotates the surfaces in a circular manner, as shown in Figure 12-9. When DirectDraw flipping is supported by the hardware, as is the case in most current video cards, flipping consists of changing pointers and no image data is physically moved. The function's general form is as follows:

```
HRESULT Flip(
        LPDIRECTDRAWSURFACE3 lpDDSurfaceTargetOverride,      // 1
        DWORD dwFlags                                        // 2
        );
```

The first parameter, sometimes called the *target override*, is the address of the IDirectDrawSurface4 interface for any surface in the flipping chain. The default value for this parameter is NULL, in which case DirectDraw cycles through the flip chain surfaces in the order they are attached to each other. If this parameter is not NULL, then DirectDraw flips to the specified surface instead of the next surface in the flipping chain, thus overriding the default order. The call fails if the specified surface is not a member of the flipping chain.

The second parameter specifies one of the predefined constants that control flip options. The constants are listed in Table 12-2.

<table>
<tr><td colspan="2" align="center">Table 12-2
DirectDraw Flip() Function Flags</td></tr>
<tr><td>*Flag*</td><td>*Action*</td></tr>
<tr><td>DDFLIP_EVEN</td><td>Used only when displaying video in an overlay surface. The new surface contains data from the even field of a video signal. Cannot be used with the DDFLIP_ODD flag.</td></tr>
<tr><td>DDFLIP_INTERVAL2</td><td></td></tr>
<tr><td>DDFLIP_INTERVAL3</td><td></td></tr>
</table>

Continued

	Table 12-2 *(continued)*
Flag	**Action**
DDFLIP_INTERVAL4	Indicate how many vertical retraces to wait between each flip. The default is 1. DirectDraw returns DERR_WASSTILLDRAWING until the specified number of vertical retraces has occurred. If DDFLIP_INTERVAL2 is set, DirectDraw flips on every second vertical retrace cycle. If DDFLIP_INTERVAL3 is set, DirectDraw flips on every third vertical retrace cycle, and so on. These flags are effective only if DDCAPS2_FLIPINTERVAL is set in the DDCAPS structure for the device.
DDFLIP_NOVSYNC	DirectDraw performs the physical flip as close as possible to the next scan line. Subsequent operations involving the two flipped surfaces do not check to see if the physical flip has finished, that is, they do not return DDERR_WASSTILLDRAWING. This flag enables an application to perform flips at a higher frequency than the monitor refresh rate. The usual consequence is the introduction of visible artifacts. If DDCAPS2_FLIPNOVSYNC is not set in the DDCAPS structure for the device, DDFLIP_NOVSYNC has no effect.
DDFLIP_ODD	Used only when displaying video in an overlay surface. The new surface contains data from the odd field of a video signal. This flag cannot be used with the DDFLIP_EVEN flag.
DDFLIP_WAIT	If the flip cannot be set up because the state of the display hardware is not appropriate, then the DDERR_WASSTILLDRAWING is immediately returned and no flip occurs. Setting this flag causes Flip() to continue trying if it receives the DDERR_WASSTILLDRAWING. In this case the call does not return until the flipping operation is successfully set up, or another error, such as DDERR_SURFACEBUSY, is returned.

If the Flip() call succeeds, the return value is DD_OK. If it fails, one of the following errors is returned:

DDERR_GENERIC	DDERR_SURFACEBUSY
DDERR_INVALIDOBJECT	DDERR_SURFACELOST
DDERR_INVALIDPARAMS	DDERR_UNSUPPORTED
DDERR_NOFLIPHW	DDERR_WASSTILLDRAWING
DDERR_NOTFLIPPABLE	

The Flip() function can be called only for surfaces that have the DDSCAPS_FLIP and DDSCAPS_FRONTBUFFER capabilities. The first parameter is used in rare cases when the back buffer is not the buffer that should become the front buffer. In most cases this parameter is NULL. In its default state, the Flip() function is always synchronized with the vertical retrace cycle of the video controller. When working with visible surfaces, such as a primary surface flipping chain, Flip() function is asynchronous, except if the DDFLIP_WAIT flag is included.

Many applications check if the Flip() returns with a DDERR_SURFACELOST. If so, code can make an attempt to restore the surface by means of the DirectDraw Restore() function, discussed in Chapter 10. If the restore is successful, the application loops back to the Flip() call and tries again. If the restore is unsuccessful, the application breaks from the while loop, and returns a terminal error.

Multiple buffering

The call to Flip() can return before the actual flip operation takes place, because the hardware waits until the next vertical retrace to actually flip the surfaces. While the Flip() operation is pending, the back buffer directly behind the currently visible surface cannot be locked or blitted to. If code attempts to call Lock(), Blt(), BltFast(), or GetDC() while a flip is pending, the call fails and the functions returns DDERR_WASSTILLDRAWING. The effect of the surface update time on the frame rate is shown in Figure 12-10.

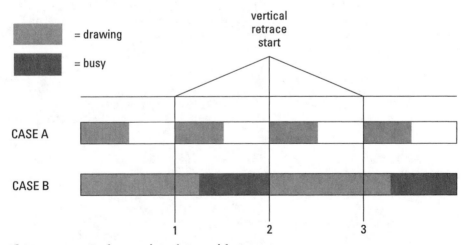

Figure 12-10: Surface update time and frame rate

Case A in Figure 12-10 shows an application with a relatively short surface update time. In this case the rendering is finished well before the next vertical retrace cycle starts. The result is that the image is updated at the monitor's refresh rate. In Case

B the rendering time is longer than the refresh cycle. In this case, the application's frame rate is reduced to one-half the monitor's refresh rate. In such situations, any attempt to access the back buffer during the period represented by the dark gray rectangles results in DDERR_WASSTRILLDRAWING error message.

A possible way to improve the frame rate in Case B, shown in Figure 12-10, is to use two back buffers instead of a single one. With two back buffers the application can draw to the back buffer that is not immediately behind the primary surface, thereby reducing the wasted time because the blits to this rear-most surface are not subject to the DDERR_WASSTILLDRAWING error condition.

In coding practice, creating a flipping chain with two or more back buffers requires no different processing than with a single one. DirectDraw takes care of flipping the surfaces, and the application code actually draws using the same back buffer pointer. In this case the middle buffer, or buffers, can be ignored by the code, which only sees the primary surface and a back buffer. The one drawback of multiple buffering is that each back buffer requires as much display memory as the primary surface. Also, the law of diminishing returns applies to back buffers: the more back buffers, the less increase in performance for each back buffer. At some point adding more back buffers degrades performance.

Exclusive-mode applications can select a lower resolution or color depth in the display mode to make possible multiple back buffers. For example, in a card with 2MB of video memory, executing in 640 by 480 pixels resolution in 24-bit color, you can create only one back buffer because the primary surface requires 921,600 bytes. By reducing the color depth to 16 bits, the sample application needs only 614,400 bytes for the primary surface, and you can now create two back buffers in display memory. The following code fragment shows the creation of a primary surface with two back buffers:

```
//Global variables
LPDIRECTDRAWSURFACE4        lpDDSPrimary = NULL;
LPDIRECTDRAWSURFACE4        lpDDSBackBuf = NULL;
DDSURFACEDESC2              ddsd;        // Surface description
HRESULT                     hRet;
. . .
// Create a primary surface with two back buffers
// ddsd is a structure of type DDSRUFACEDESC2
  ZeroMemory(&ddsd, sizeof(ddsd));   // Fill structure with
                                     // zeros
// Fill in other members
  ddsd.dwSize = sizeof(ddsd);
  ddsd.dwFlags = DDSD_CAPS | DDSD_BACKBUFFERCOUNT;
  ddsd.ddsCaps.dwCaps = DDSCAPS_PRIMARYSURFACE |
                        DDSCAPS_FLIP |
                        DDSCAPS_COMPLEX |
                        DDSCAPS_VIDEOMEMORY;
```

```
ddsd.dwBackBufferCount = 2;   // Two back buffers requested
hRet = lpDD4->CreateSurface(&ddsd, &lpDDSPrimary, NULL);
// At this point code can examine hRet for DD_OK and
// provide alternate processing if the surface creation
// call failed
// Get backbuffer pointer
ddscaps.dwCaps = DDSCAPS_BACKBUFFER;
hRet = lpDDSPrimary->GetAttachedSurface(&ddscaps,
                 &lpDDSBackBuf);
// At this point code can examine hRet for DD_OK and
// provide alternate processing if the back buffer pointer
// was not returned
```

Summary

Here we examined the fundamental techniques of computer animation using DirectDraw. Animation is one of the most exacting, as well as the most rewarding, tasks that can be undertaken in a graphics application. DirectDraw makes possible animation in Windows by furnishing direct access to the video hardware as well as specialized programming facilities, such as back buffers and flipping operations. In the following chapter we put this knowledge to work in animated applications.

✦   ✦   ✦

Animation Programming

Here we tackle some of the practical problems related to animation in DirectDraw programming. Animation programming is both exacting and rewarding. DirectDraw makes possible animation in Windows by furnishing direct access to the video hardware as well as specialized programming facilities, such as back buffers and flip operations, described in Chapter 12. We now put these techniques to work to create effects that simulate movement. The objective is to make these movements appear smooth and natural. Animation programming finds use in the development of computer games, simulations, in multimedia, and in many high-end graphics programs.

Flipping Techniques

Exclusive mode applications that use flipping animation start by initializing DirectDraw, setting a display mode, creating the flip chain, obtaining the corresponding pointers to the front and back buffers, and setting up a timer mechanism that produces the desired beat. After these housekeeping chores are finished, the real work can begin, which consists of rendering the imagery to the back buffer, usually by means of blits from other surfaces in video memory or offscreen. The design and coding challenge in creating an animated application using DirectDraw can be broken down into two parts: the first one requires the minimum resources that enable the program to perform satisfactorily. The second one makes the best use of these resources to produce the finest and smoothest animation possible.

Background animation

A typical computer game or real-time simulation often contains two different types of graphics objects: backgrounds and sprites. The backgrounds consist of larger bitmaps over which the action takes place. For example, in a flight simulator program there can be several background images representing views from the cockpit. These may include landscapes, seascapes, and views of airports and runways used during takeoff and landing. In a computer game that takes place in a medieval castle the backgrounds are the various castle rooms and corridors on which the action takes place. Sprites, on the other hand, are rather small, animated objects represented in two or three dimensions. In the flight simulator program the sprites are other aircraft visible from the cockpit as well as the cabin instruments and controls that are animated during the simulation. In the computer game the sprites are medieval knights that do battle in the castle, as well as the objects animated during the battle.

Panning animation

The design and display of background images is relatively straightforward and not complicated. In this sense the most difficult processing consists of creating backgrounds that are larger than the viewport and using clipping and blit-time rectangles to generate panning and zoom effects. Figure 13-1 shows a bitmapped galaxy, a portion of which is selected by a source rectangle.

background bitmap   source rectangle for blit

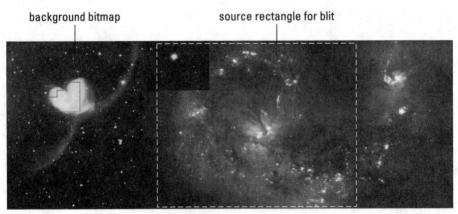

Figure 13-1: Source rectangle selection in panning animation

The project named DD Panning Demo in the book's CD-ROM demonstrates panning animation of a background bitmap. In the program the source rectangle has the same vertical dimension as the background bitmap, which is 480 pixels. The image bitmap is 1280 pixels wide and the source rectangle is one-half that size (640 pixels). This creates a source window that can be moved 639 pixels to the right from its original position. The white, dotted rectangle in Figure 13-1 represents the source rectangle within the background bitmap.

The program DD_Pan.cpp, which is located in the project DD Panning Demo, uses a simple processing logic to demonstrate panning animation. The program action is to pan to the right until the right border of the image is reached, and then reverse the panning direction until the left border is reached. The primary surface and a single back buffer are created and a clipper is installed in both surfaces. The background bitmap—in this case two colliding galaxies imaged by the Hubble Space Telescope— are stored in the panback.bmp file. This bitmap is twice as wide as the viewport; therefore, the source rectangle can be moved horizontally within the bitmap. The panning variables and the display routine are coded as follows:

```
// Global panning animation controls
RECT          thisPan;              // Storage for source
                                    // rectangle
LONG          panIteration = 0;  // panning iteration counter
LONG          panDirection = 0;  // 1 = left, 0 = right
// Constants
LONG          PAN_LIMIT_LEFT = 1;
LONG          PAN_LIMIT_RIGHT = 639;

. . .
//***************************************************
// Name: PanImage
// Desc: Update back with a source rectangle that
//       is a portion of the background bitmap
//       and flip to create a panning animation
//***************************************************
static void PanImage()
{

  thisTickCount = GetTickCount();
  if((thisTickCount - lastTickCount) < TIMER_VALUE)
     return;

  else
  {
    lastTickCount = thisTickCount;

  // Bump pan iteration according to direction
     if(panDirection == 1)
        panIteration--;
     else
        panIteration++;
```

```
                  // Reset panning iteration counter at limits
                     if(panIteration == PAN_LIMIT_RIGHT)
                        panDirection = 1;          // Pan left
                     if(panIteration == PAN_LIMIT_LEFT)
                        panDirection = 0;

                  // Set panning rectangle in source image
                  thisPan.left = panIteration;
                  thisPan.top = 0;
                  thisPan .right = 640 + panIteration;
                  thisPan.bottom = 480;

                  // Blit background bitmap to back buffer
                     hRet = lpDDSBackBuf->Blt(NULL,
                                 lpDDSBackGrnd,
                                 &thisPan,
                                 DDBLT_WAIT,
                                 NULL);
                     if(hRet != DD_OK){
                        DDInitFailed(hWnd, hRet,
                           "Blt() on background failed");
                        return;
                        }

                  // Flip surfaces
                     hRet = lpDDSPrimary->Flip(NULL, DDFLIP_WAIT);
                     if(hRet != DD_OK){
                        DDInitFailed(hWnd, hRet,
                             "Flip() call failed");
                        return;
                        }
                  return;
                     }
               }
```

The local function named PanImage() performs the panning animation. First it
bumps and checks the ticker counter. If the counter did not expire yet, execution
returns immediately. Code then checks the panDirection variable. If the direction
is 1, then panning is in the left-to-right cycle and the panIteration variable is
decremented. If not, then panning is right-to-left and the panIteration variable is
incremented. When either variable reaches the limit, as defined in the constants
PAN_LIMIT_LEFT and PAN_LIMIT_RIGHT, the panning direction is reversed. A
structure variable named thisPan, of type RECT, is used to define the source
rectangle for the blit. The panIteration variable is used to define the offset of the
source rectangle within the image bitmap. Because panning takes place on the
horizontal axis only, and the display mode is defined in the code, then the image
size can be hard-coded into the thisPan structure members. After the image is
blitted onto the back buffer, surfaces are flipped in the conventional manner.

Zoom animation

Zooming is another background animation that can be implemented by manipulating the source or destination rectangles, or both. This is possible because both Blt() and BltFast() perform automatic scaling when the source and destination areas are of a different size. The simplest approach to zooming animation consists of reducing the area covered by the source rectangle and letting Blt() or BltFast() perform the necessary adjustments. Figure 13-2 shows the initial and final source rectangles in zoom animation.

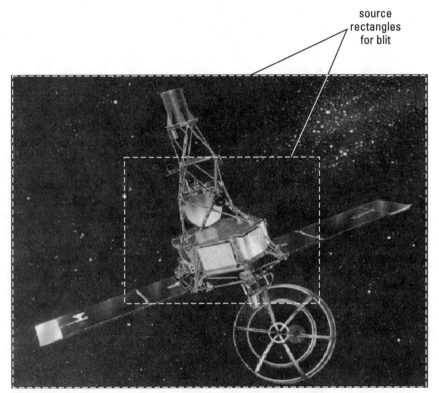

source
rectangles
for blit

Figure 13-2: Source rectangle selection in zoom animation

The program DD_Zoom.cpp, which is located in the project DD Zoom Demo, demonstrates zoom animation using an image of the Mariner spacecraft. The program action is to zoom into a bitmap by changing the position and progressively reducing the dimensions and the source rectangle. When an arbitrary maximum zoom value is reached, the process reverses and the source rectangle is made progressively larger until it is restored to the original size. As in the panning animation demo program, the primary surface and a single back buffer are created, and a clipper is installed in both surfaces. The background image, which in this case is stored in the zoomback.bmp bitmap, is then moved to an offscreen surface. This bitmap is the size of the viewport. In the following code fragment we show the zoom controls and display operations that are different from the panning animation, previously listed:

```
// Zoom animation controls
RECT      thisZoom;   // Storage for source rectangle
LONG      zoomIteration = 0;  // panning iteration counter
LONG      zoomDirection = 0;  // 1 = left, 0 = right
// Constants
LONG      ZOOM_LIMIT_OUT = 1;
LONG      ZOOM_LIMIT_IN = 200;
. . .
// Bump zoom iteration according to direction
if(zoomDirection == 1)
   zoomIteration--;
else
   zoomIteration++;

// Reset zoom iteration counter at limits
if(zoomIteration == ZOOM_LIMIT_IN)
   zoomDirection = 1;            // Pan left
if(zoomIteration == ZOOM_LIMIT_OUT)
   zoomDirection = 0;

// Set zoom rectangle in source image
   thisZoom.left = zoomIteration;
   thisZoom.top = zoomIteration;
   thisZoom.right = 640 - zoomIteration;
   thisZoom.bottom = 480 - ((zoomIteration * 3)/4);
```

Notice that in dimensioning the source rectangle for zoom animation we take into account the screen's aspect ratio, which is approximately 3:4. Therefore the *y* coordinate of the end point of the source rectangle is changed at a slower rate than the *x* coordinate. If both coordinates were reduced by the same amount, the resulting images would be stretched along this axis during the zoom.

Sprite operations

In the context of graphics programming a sprite is a rather small screen object, usually animated during program execution. It can be a fuel gauge on the dashboard of a race car simulation, a spaceship in a futuristic game, or a medieval warrior in another one. Designing, encoding, and manipulating sprites require all the talents and skills of the animator.

The project named DD Sprite Demo, in the book's CD-ROM, demonstrates sprite animation by simultaneously moving three screen objects at different speeds. Figure 13-3 is a screen snapshot of the demonstration program.

Sprite1   Sprite2   Sprite3

Figure 13-3: Screen snapshot of the sprite animation demo

The hot-air balloons and the blimp in Figure 13-3 are the sprites. During program execution the balloons and the blimp rise at different speeds. The blimp, which appears closer to the viewer, moves up one pixel during every iteration of the frame counter. The balloon on the left moves every second iteration and the one on the right every third iteration. The background is fixed in this sample.

Controlling several sprites, simultaneously displayed, can be a challenge in program design and data organization, but does not present any major programming problems in DirectDraw. The program named DD_Sprt.cpp, which performs the processing in the DD Sprite Demo project, starts by creating a primary surface and two back buffers. The use of a second back buffer improved program execution in most machines. A clipper is then installed on both surfaces. The clipper makes the animated objects appear to come into the display area, and disappear from it, softly and pleasantly. The background image, which is located in the bitmap named backgrnd.bmp, is stored in an offscreen surface. This bitmap is the size of the viewport. The code creates three additional surfaces, one for each of the sprites, and moves the sprite bitmaps into these surfaces. The sprite surfaces are assigned a source color key to make the bitmap backgrounds transparent at display time. To ensure a smooth animation, all the surfaces in the sample program are located in video memory.

Sprite control in the demo program is based on a structure of type SpriteCtrl defined globally, as follows:

```
// Sprite control structure
struct SpriteCtrl
{
    LONG     startY;        // Start x coordinate
    LONG     startX;        // Start y coordinate
    LONG     bmapX;         // Width of bitmap
    LONG     bmapY;         // Height of bitmap
    LONG     iterMax;       // Maximum iteration count
    LONG     skipFactor;    // Display delay
    LONG     iteration;     // Sprite iteration counter
} Sprite1, Sprite2, Sprite3;
```

Three structure variables, named Sprite1, Sprite2, and Sprite3, are allocated, one for each animated object. The sprites are numbered left-to-right as they are displayed, as shown in Figure 13-3. Each structure variable contains the members startX and startY that define the start coordinates for each sprite. The members bmapX and bmapY store the bitmap dimensions, which are obtained as the bitmaps are loaded from their files.

The sprite animation control is performed by the last three members of the SpriteCtrl structure. The iterMax member stores the value of the iteration counter at which the sprite is repositioned to the bottom of the screen. The skipFactor member determines how many iterations are skipped at display time. This value is used to slow down the smaller balloons. Sprite1 is assigned a skipFactor of 2. Sprite2, the largest one, has a skipFactor equal to 1. Sprite3, the smallest one, has a skipFactor of 3. The iteration member keeps track of the number of frame beats corresponding to each sprite. The counters are reset when the iterMax value is reached for each sprite. The iteration counters range from 0 to iterMax. The code initializes the structure members for each sprite, as follows:

```
//*******************************************************
//    Fill SpriteCtrl structure members for each sprite
//*******************************************************
// Sprite1 is balloon bitmap in bMap1
// Resolution is 640 by 480 pixels
Sprite1.startY = 479;     // Starts at screen bottom
Sprite1.startX = 70;      // x for start position
Sprite1.bmapX = bMap1.bmWidth;
```

```
Sprite1.bmapY = bMap1.bmHeight;
Sprite1.skipFactor = 2;
Sprite1.iterMax = (480+(bMap1.bmHeight)) * Sprite1.skipFactor;
Sprite1.iteration = 50;     // Init iteration counter
// Sprite2 is balloon bitmap in bMap2
Sprite2.startY = 479;       // Starts at screen bottom
Sprite2.startX = 240;       // x for start position
Sprite2.bmapX = bMap2.bmWidth;
Sprite2.bmapY = bMap2.bmHeight;
Sprite2.skipFactor = 1;
Sprite2.iterMax = 480+(bMap2.bmHeight);
Sprite2.iteration = 50;     // Init iteration counter
// Sprite3 is balloon bitmap in bMap3
Sprite3.startY = 479;       // Starts at screen bottom
Sprite3.startX = 500;       // x for start position
Sprite3.bmapX = bMap3.bmWidth;
Sprite3.bmapY = bMap3.bmHeight;
Sprite3.skipFactor = 3;
Sprite3.iterMax = (480+(bMap3.bmHeight)) * Sprite3.skipFactor;
Sprite3.iteration = 20;     // Init iteration counter
```

During initialization, the dimensions of each sprite are read from the corresponding bmWidth and bmHeight members of the BITMAP structure for each sprite. This ensures that the code continues to work even if the size of a sprite bitmap is changed. The maximum number of iterations for each sprite is calculated by adding the number of screen pixels in the selected mode (480), to the bitmap pixel height, and multiplying this sum by the sprite's skip factor. At display time the surface with the background bitmap is first blitted to the back buffer. Then the code calls a local function, named SpriteAction(), for each sprite. The FlipImages() function is coded as follows:

```
//**************************************************
// Name: FlipImages
// Desc: Update back buffer and flip
//**************************************************

static void FlipImages()
{
    thisTickCount = GetTickCount();
    if((thisTickCount - lastTickCount) < TIMER_VALUE)
       return;
    else
    {
        lastTickCount = thisTickCount;

       // Blit background bitmap to back buffer
       hRet = lpDDSBackBuf->Blt(NULL,
                                lpDDSBackGrnd,
                                NULL,
                                DDBLT_WAIT,
```

```
                                      NULL);
           if(hRet != DD_OK){
             DDInitFailed(hWnd, hRet,
                        "Blt() on background failed");
             return;
           }

     // Animate sprites. Farthest ones first
        SpriteAction(Sprite3, lpDDSBmap3);
        SpriteAction(Sprite2, lpDDSBmap2);
        SpriteAction(Sprite1, lpDDSBmap1);

    // Flip surfaces
       hRet = lpDDSPrimary->Flip(NULL, DDFLIP_WAIT);
        if(hRet != DD_OK){
          DDInitFailed(hWnd, hRet,
                     "Flip() call failed");
          return;
         }
        return;
      }
  }
```

The actual display of the sprites is performed by the local function named
SpriteAction(). This function receives the SpriteCtrl structure variable for
the sprite being animated, and the pointer to the surface that contains the sprite
image. The code checks the iteration number for the sprite against the maximum
count to determine if the iteration counter needs resetting. Then the position of the
sprite is calculated by dividing the current iteration number by the skip factor. This
information is stored in a RECT structure corresponding to the destination surface
rectangle, and the Blt() function is called. SpriteAction() code is as follows:

```
//*************************************************
// Name: SpriteAction
// Desc: Animate a sprite according
//       to its own parameters
// PRE CONDITIONS:
//    1. Pointer to structure containing
//       sprite data
//    2. Pointer to DirectDraw surface
//       containing sprite bitmap
//*************************************************
void SpriteAction(SpriteCtrl &thisSprite,
       LPDIRECTDRAWSURFACE4 lpDDSBmap)
{
    RECT       destSurf;
    LONG       vertUpdate;

    thisSprite.iteration++;
```

```
        if(thisSprite.iteration == thisSprite.iterMax)
            thisSprite.iteration = 0;

        vertUpdate = thisSprite.iteration / thisSprite.skipFactor;

        // Set coordinates for balloon1 display
        destSurf.left = thisSprite.startX;
        destSurf.top = thisSprite.startY - vertUpdate;
        destSurf.right = destSurf.left + thisSprite.bmapX;
        destSurf.bottom = destSurf.top + thisSprite.bmapY;

        // Use Blt() to blit bitmap from the off-screen surface
        // (->lpDDSBitamp), onto the back buffer (->lpDDSBackBuf)
        hRet = lpDDSBackBuf->Blt(&destSurf,
                            lpDDSBmap,
                            NULL,
                            DDBLT_WAIT | DDBLT_KEYSRC,
                            NULL);

    if(hRet != DD_OK){
        DDInitFailed(hWnd, hRet,
                "Blt() on sprite failed");
    return;
    }
  return;
}
```

After the background bitmap and all three sprites are blitted onto the back buffer, the code calls the `Flip()` function to render the results onto the primary surface.

Performance-Tuning the Animation

Computer animation is a performance-critical task. In the past, the programmer's greatest concern was to produce a smooth and uniform effect, with as little bumpiness, screen tearing, and interference as possible. Today's machines, with 400Mhz and faster CPUs, video cards with graphics coprocessors and 4 or 8MB of video memory, high-speed buses, and DirectX 6 software, can often produce impressive animations with straightforward code. For example, the executable in the DD Sprite Demo project, in the book's CD-ROM, smoothly animates three sprites, even when running in a 200Mhz Pentium machine equipped with a low-end display card with 2MB of video memory.

The basic paradigm of animation programming implies pushing graphics performance to its limits. If the animator finds that the code can manipulate three sprites successfully, then perhaps it can manipulate four, or even five. The rule seems to be: the more action, and the faster the action, the better the animation.

In this section we discuss several loosely linked topics that relate to improving program performance or to facilitating implementation.

Best-option processing

DirectDraw made it possible for Windows applications to achieve the graphics functionality and performance that, for a long time, was only possible in DOS. The price for the greater control and speed is a higher degree of device dependency. To accommodate this device dependency the applications developer can take several approaches. One of them is to require a minimum functionality in the host system. In this case the code can test the hardware for these requirements and abort execution if they are not available. This kind of program seems to say: "This is what I need to run. If you don't have it, I am out of here." Specialty and high-end programs, as well as dedicated applications, often do this. On the other hand, general-purpose programs, intended for a wide audience, must make the best possible use of whatever resources are available in the host machine. In this case the application seems to say: "This is what I would like to have. If it is not available, I'll make the best of what you have." The selection of the most suitable alternative among those available can be called "best-option" processing.

Programs that execute windowed applications have to accommodate the current desktop settings. If these are not adequate, there is little else that can be done except to notify the user and suggest changes. On the other hand, DirectDraw programs executing in exclusive mode can change display modes and hardware settings, thus controlling the execution environment to some degree. Most DirectDraw applications start by checking for a DirectDraw object and for the interface level. If DirectDraw is not installed, two actions are possible: one is to notify the user and to abort installation; the second one is to proceed to install the DirectX software, with varying levels of user participation. The DirectX setup facilities can be used to copy the required files to the host machine and to perform the necessary initialization. Because Microsoft furnishes these files at no cost, there is little justification for any major DirectDraw application not to provide this option.

Another possibility is that the version of DirectX installed in the host machine is not the current one. On encountering this problem you may be tempted to accommodate processing to whatever version of the SDK is already there. Although possible, the required processing presents some major complications. In the first place, the interface pointers are not generally interchangeable. That is, to use a function in the DirectDraw4 version of the SDK you need a pointer of type `LPDIRECTDRAW4`. The same applies to clippers, surfaces, palettes, and other objects of the interface. For this reason providing alternate processing for several interfaces amounts to furnishing separate code for each one. Here again, an easy way out is to notify the user of the problem and abort execution. A more reasonable one is to offer installing the updated drivers for the required SDK version.

Note that in very simple applications, as is the case in the DD Info Demo project in the book's CD-ROM, it is possible to typecast a pointer to an older interface to access methods in a newer one. However, this approach is dangerous and should be avoided because the functions in newer interfaces often have different parameter lists, processing options, and return types. If the call does not fail at compile time, it may fail at run time.

It is difficult to provide general guidelines on how to handle DirectDraw device dependencies. The project named DD Info Demo, in the book's CD-ROM, contains code showing how to read these capabilities in the host machine. In DirectDraw programming, the most critical device-dependency complication results from the fact that not all hardware functionalities are emulated in the HEL. For example, clipping and color fills can be implemented in hardware, but are also emulated. An application that uses these functions has better performance in a system with hardware support, but still executes in a system in which these operations are furnished by the HEL. On the other hand, overlays, alpha channels, and other DirectDraw operations are not emulated in the HEL. If an application attempts to use these functions in a machine that does not provide hardware support, execution fails with unpredictable results. In this book we avoid discussing DirectDraw operations that are not emulated by the software. Applications that require these nonemulated functions should make the necessary checks and adjustments.

DirectDraw programs that execute in exclusive mode virtually can tailor the system environment to suit their own requirements. Their first and most important decision is about the display mode. The project DD Info Demo contains code to list all available modes. The project DD Access Demo contains the function `HasDDMode()`, which can be used to test if a particular mode is available in the hardware. Applications can use this function in cascade fashion to determine the best available mode. Alternatively code can attempt to set the ideal mode; if an ideal mode is not available, it can then proceed to the next preferred one, and so forth.

Mode selection is complicated by the fact that different modes use various amounts of video memory. For example, an application that requires two back buffers needs to investigate not only if a particular mode is available, but if there is sufficient free memory in the mode so as to allocate the two back buffers. You can use the `GetCaps()` function and read the `dwVidMemTotal` or `dwVidMemFree` members to determine the video memory in a system. This is how it is done in the DD Info Demo project program. Alternatively, code can call the `GetAvailableVidMem()` function to obtain the total amount of memory available and the amount currently free. The results are identical with either function.

An application's video memory requirements are determined by the display mode and the number of surfaces necessary. For example, the demonstration program DD Sprites Demo, in the book's CD-ROM, executes in 640×480 pixels resolution, with a 16-bits- per-pixel color depth. In addition to the primary surface, it ideally requires two back buffers, and space for storing four bitmaps: one for the background and one for the three hot-air balloon sprites. The program's maximum memory requirements are as follows:

```
primary surface ...............    614,400 bytes
two back buffers ..............  1,228,800 bytes
background bitmap .............    614,400 bytes
Sprite 1 bitmap ..............      13,400 bytes
Sprite 2 bitmap ..............      30,600 bytes
Sprite 3 bitmap ..............       8,880 bytes
                                ===============
            Total .............  2,510,480 bytes
```

After the memory requirements are known, code can make sure that it is available by either calling GetCaps() or GetAvailableVidMem(). The following code fragment shows processing in the DD Sprite Demo project program:

```
// Variables for checking available memory
DDSCAPS2       ddCapsMem;
DWORD          memTotal;
DWORD          memFree;
static DWORD   MEM_REQUIRED = 2510480;
. . .
// Check for necessary free video memory
   ZeroMemory(&ddCapsMem, sizeof(ddCapsMem));
   lpDD4->GetAvailableVidMem(&ddCapsMem, &memTotal,
&memFree);
      if (memTotal < MEM_REQUIRED)
         return DDInitFailed(hWnd, hRet,
        "Insufficient video memory");
```

The code for performing display operations using one or more back buffers is identical in most cases. Applications can take advantage of this fact and start by requesting two or more back buffers. Then it reduces the number of back buffers if the call to CreateSurface() fails, and tries again. If you start by making sure that there is sufficient memory for at least one back buffer, the processing is ensured to succeed at some point. The following code shows this handling:

```
//****************************************************
// Create primary surface and one or more back buffers
//****************************************************
// ddsd is a structure of type DDSRUFACEDESC2
   ZeroMemory(&ddsd, sizeof(ddsd));  // Fill structure with
zeros
   // Fill in other members
   ddsd.dwSize = sizeof(ddsd);
   ddsd.dwFlags = DDSD_CAPS | DDSD_BACKBUFFERCOUNT;
   ddsd.ddsCaps.dwCaps = DDSCAPS_PRIMARYSURFACE |
                         DDSCAPS_FLIP |
                         DDSCAPS_COMPLEX |
                         DDSCAPS_VIDEOMEMORY;
```

```
// First request two back buffers
    ddsd.dwBackBufferCount = 2;
      hRet = lpDD4->CreateSurface(&ddsd, &lpDDSPrimary, NULL);
// If call failed, retry with one back buffer
      if (hRet == DDERR_OUTOFVIDEOMEMORY) {
          ddsd.dwBackBufferCount = 1;
          hRet = lpDD4->CreateSurface(&ddsd, &lpDDSPrimary, NULL);
      }
    if (hRet != DD_OK)
      return DDInitFailed(hWnd, hRet,
                          "CreateSurface() call failed");
```

High-resolution timers

In Chapter 12 we examined two methods of obtaining the timed beat that is necessary for the frame updates in an animation routine. One method is based on a milliseconds counter maintained by the system, which can be read by means of the GetTickCount() function. The other one sets an interval timer that operates as an alarm clock. When the timer lapse expires, the application receives control either in a message handler intercept or a dedicated callback function. Although both methods are used often, processing based on reading the windows tick counter has considerably better resolution than the alarm clock approach. Windows documentation states that the resolution of the timer intercepts is approximately 55 milliseconds. This produces a beat of 18.2 times per second, which is precisely the default speed of the PC internal clock. In many cases this beat is barely sufficient to produce smooth and lifelike animations.

There are several ways to improve the frequency and reliability of the timed pulse. The multimedia extensions to Windows include a high-resolution timer with a reported resolution of 1 millisecond. Furthermore, the multimedia timer produces more accurate results because it does not rely on WM_TIMER messages posted on the queue. Each multimedia timer has its own thread, and the callback function is invoked directly regardless of any pending messages. To use the multimedia library, code must include mmsystem.h and make sure that winmm.lib is available and referenced at link time. Several timer functions are found in the multimedia library. The most useful one in animation programming is timeSetEvent(). This function starts an event timer, which runs in its own thread. A callback function, defined in the call to timeSetEvent(), receives control every time the counter timer expires. The function's general form is as follows:

```
MMRESULT timeSetEvent(
                UINT uDelay,                    // 1
                UINT uResolution,               // 2
                LPTIMECALLBACK lpTimeProc,      // 3
                DWORD dwUser,                   // 4
                UINT fuEvent                    // 5
                );
```

The first parameter defines the event delay, in milliseconds. If this value is not in the timer's valid range, then the function returns an error. The second parameter is the resolution, in milliseconds, of the timer event. As the values get smaller, the resolution increases. A resolution of 0 indicates that timer events should occur with the greatest possible accuracy. Code can use the maximum appropriate value for the timer resolution to reduce system overhead. The third parameter is the address of the callback function that is called every time that the event delay counter expires. The fourth parameter is a double word value passed by Windows to the callback procedure. The fifth parameter encodes the timer event type. This parameter consists of one or more predefined constants listed in Table 13-1.

Table 13-1
Event-Type Constants in timeSetEvent() Function

Value	Meaning
TIME_ONESHOT	Event occurs once, after uDelay milliseconds.
TIME_PERIODIC	Event occurs every uDelay milliseconds.
TIME_CALLBACK_FUNCTION	Windows calls the function pointed to by the third parameter. This is the default.
TIME_CALLBACK_EVENT_SET	Windows calls the SetEvent() function to set the vent pointed to by the third parameter. The fourth parameter is ignored.
TIME_CALLBACK_EVENT_PULSE	Windows calls the PulseEvent() function to pulse the event pointed to by the third parameter. The fourth parameter is ignored.

Notice that the multimedia timers support two different modes of operation. In one mode (TIME_ONESHOT) the timer event occurs only once. In the other mode (TIME_PERIODIC) the timer event takes place every time that the timer counter expires. This mode is the one used in animation routines. If successful, the call returns an identifier for the timer event. This identifier is also passed to the callback function. When the timer is no longer needed, applications should call the timeKillEvent() function to terminate it.

Despite its high resolution, it has been documented that the multimedia timer can suffer considerable delays in Windows 95. One author states having recorded delays of up to 100 milliseconds. Applications requiring very high timer accuracy are recommended to implement the multimedia timer in a 16-bit DLL.

The WIN32 API first made available a high-resolution tick counter. These counters are sometimes called *performance monitors* because they were originally intended for precisely measuring the performance of coded routines. Using the high-performance monitors is similar to using the GetTickCount() function already described, but with a few special accommodations. Two Windows functions are associated with performance monitor counters: QueryPerformanceFrequency() returns the resolution of the counter, which varies according to hardware. QueryPerformanceCounter() returns the number of timer ticks since the system was started. QueryPerformanceFrequency() can also be used to determine if high-performance counters are available in the hardware, although the presence of the performance monitoring function can be assumed in any Windows 95, 98, or NT machine.

The function prototypes are identical for QueryPerformanceFrequency() and QueryPerformanceCount(): the return type is of type BOOL and the only parameter is a 64-bit integer of type LARGE_INTEGER. The general forms are as follows:

```
BOOL QueryPerformanceCounter(LARGE_INTEGER*);
BOOL QueryPerformanceFrequency(LARGE_INTEGER*);
```

Although it has been stated that the performance frequency on Intel-based PCs is 0.8 microseconds, it is safer for applications to call QueryPerformance Frequency() to obtain the correct scaling factor. The following code fragment shows this processing:

```
_int64          TIMER_DELAY = 15;  // Milliseconds
_int64          frequency;         // Timer frequency
. . .
QueryPerformanceFrequency((LARGE_INTEGER*) &frequency);
TIMER_DELAY = (TIMER_DELAY * frequency) / 1000;
```

After executing, the TIMER_DELAY value has been scaled to the frequency of the high-resolution timer. The QueryPerformanceCounter() can now be called in the same manner as GetTickCount(), for example:

```
_int64          lastTickCount;
_int64          thisTickCount;
. . .
QueryPerformanceCounter((LARGE_INTEGER*) &thisTickCount);
if((thisTickCount - lastTickCount) < TIMER_DELAY)
  return;
else {
  lastTickCount = thisTickCount;
  . . .
```

The DD Sprite Demo project program, in the book's CD-ROM, uses a high-performance timer to produce the animation beat.

Dirty rectangles

Looking at Figure 13-3 you notice that the background image is overlayed by three sprites. During every iteration of the animation pulse, code redraws the background to refresh those parts of the surface that have been overwritten by the sprites. The process is wasteful because most of the background remains unchanged. In fact, only the portion of the background that was covered by the sprite image actually needs to be redrawn. Figure 13-4 shows the rectangular areas that actually need refreshing in producing the next animation iteration of the image in Figure 13-3. These are called the "dirty rectangles."

Figure 13-4: Dirty rectangles in the animation of Figure 13-3

DirectDraw clipping operations can be used to identify the dirty rectangles. In this case a clip list defines the areas that require refreshing, and these are the only ones updated during the blit. The processing is simplified by the fact that the last position of the sprite, and its stored dimensions, can be used to define the dirty rectangles.

It is difficult to predict when a dirty rectangle scheme actually improves performance. The result depends on many factors: the total image area covered by the dirty rectangles, the number of rectangles, the processing overhead in calculating the rectangles and creating the clip list, and, above all, the efficiency of the DirectDraw clipping operations of the particular hardware. Unfortunately, in many cases, the screen update takes longer with dirty rectangle schemes than without them. The most rational approach is to develop the animation without dirty rectangles. If the results are not satisfactory, then try the dirty rectangles technique. The comparative results can be assessed by measuring the execution time in both cases. Methods for measuring performance of routines are discussed later in this section.

Dynamic color keys

Color keys are an integral part of sprite animation. It is difficult to image a sprite that can be transparently overlayed on a bitmapped background without the use of a source color key. When you create your own sprites using draw or paint programs, and these sprites are stored in 24- or 32-bit color depth bitmaps, the color key is usually known at coding time, or can be determined easily. If there is any doubt, the sprite can be loaded into a bitmap editor utility to inspect the RGB value of the background pixels. However, matters are not always that simple. One of the complicating factors with color keys occurs when the color depth of the application's video mode does not coincide with that of the sprite bitmap. This can be problematic in the palettized display modes, particularly when the palette changes during execution, or in applications that use best-option processing in regards to the video mode.

One possible solution is to determine the bitmap's color key dynamically, that is, at run time rather than at compile time. The method is usually based on the assumption that there is a fixed location in the bitmap, which is transparent at blit time. For example, the pixel at the bitmap's upper-left corner of the sprite image rectangle is typically part of the background. Figure 13-5 shows the fixed location of the color key for one of the balloon bitmaps used in the project DD Sprite Demo contained in the book's CD-ROM.

color key pixel
at bitmap (0,0)

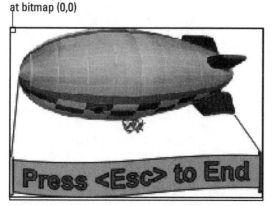

Figure 13-5: Color key in a fixed bitmap location

After the relative location of a color key pixel has been determined, code can load the bitmap onto a surface, and then read the surface data at the predefined location to obtain the color key. The manipulation is made possible by the direct access to memory areas that are available in DirectDraw, discussed in Chapter 10. Because the application knows the color depth of the target surface, it can read the color key directly from the surface. In this case you do not need to be concerned about how Windows converts a pixel value in one color depth into another one because the code is reading the resulting color key directly. The following code is used in the DD Sprite Demo program for dynamically loading the color key for Sprite1.

```
// Video display globals
LONG      vidPitch = 0;   // Pitch
LPVOID    vidStart = 0;   // Buffer address
// Color key data
DDCOLORKEY  bColorKey;
WORD        dynamicKey;

. . .
//*************************************************
// move first balloon bitmap to offscreen surface
//*************************************************
// Load the bitmap into memory
ball1Bitmap = ( HBITMAP )LoadImage( NULL, "balloon1.bmp",
              IMAGE_BITMAP, 0, 0, LR_LOADFROMFILE );
  if ( ball1Bitmap == NULL )
      DDInitFailed(hWnd, hRet,
        "Balloon1 bitmap load failed");
// Get bitmap dimensions to determine surface size
  GetObject(ball1Bitmap, sizeof (BITMAP), &bMap1);

// Create the offscreen surface for bitmap in system memory
  ZeroMemory(&ddsd, sizeof(ddsd));   // Fill structure with
                                     // zeros
// Fill in other members
  ddsd.dwSize = sizeof(ddsd);
  ddsd.dwFlags = DDSD_CAPS | DDSD_HEIGHT | DDSD_WIDTH;
  ddsd.ddsCaps.dwCaps = DDSCAPS_OFFSCREENPLAIN |
                        DDSCAPS_VIDEOMEMORY;
  ddsd.dwHeight = bMap1.bmHeight;
  ddsd.dwWidth = bMap1.bmWidth;
  hRet = lpDD4->CreateSurface(&ddsd, &lpDDSBmap1, NULL);
    if (hRet != DD_OK)
        return DDInitFailed(hWnd, hRet,
                "Offscreen surface1 creation failed ");

  // Move bitmap to surface using DDBmapToSurf()function
  hRet = DDBmapToSurf(lpDDSBmap1, ball1Bitmap);
    if(hRet != DD_OK)
        return DDInitFailed(hWnd, hRet,
                "DDMapToSurf() call failed");
```

```
//*******************************************
//   read color key from loaded sprite
//*******************************************
// Attempt to lock the surface for direct access
if (!LockSurface(lpDDSBmap1))
     return DDInitFailed(hWnd, hRet,
                     "Surface Lock failed ");
// Surface data is stored as follows:
//    LONG      vidPitch;  // Pitch (not used here)
//    LPVOID    vidStart;  // Buffer address
_asm
{
    PUSH    ESI             ; Save context
    PUSHF
    MOV     ESI,vidStart  ; Left-top pixel address
    ; Read and store pixel attributes
    MOV     AX,[ESI]        ; Get attribute
    MOV     dynamicKey,AX   ; Store value in variable
    POPF                    ; Restore context
    POP     ESI
}
ReleaseSurface(lpDDSBmap1);

// Set color key for balloon1 surface using values stored
// in variable dynamicKey
 bColorKey.dwColorSpaceLowValue = dynamicKey;
 bColorKey.dwColorSpaceHighValue = dynamicKey;
   hRet = lpDDSBmap1->SetColorKey(DDCKEY_SRCBLT, &bColorKey);
   if(hRet != DD_OK)
       return DDInitFailed(hWnd, hRet,
            "SetColorKey() for Balloon1 failed");
```

Measuring performance

The execution time of a coded routine or function is often the factor that determines its suitability for an animation application. Several software engineering techniques enable you to estimate the performance and efficiency of algorithms. These methods, which are based on mathematical analysis, are usually difficult and time-consuming. Instead of performing a complicated analysis of the algorithms that underlie a particular processing routine, a programmer can often obtain the necessary performance metrics by physically measuring its execution time.

In some cases time of execution ranges from several seconds to several minutes. In these situations it can sometimes be measured by observing the screen with a stopwatch in hand. More often the time of execution is in the milliseconds order, in which cases it may be possible to use the computer's timing mechanisms to determine the time lapsed between the start and the end of a processing routine or code segment. The QueryPerformanceCounter() function, described previously, has a resolution in the order of one-millionth of a second. To measure the execution time of a program segment, function, or routine you need to read the tick counter at the start and the end of the processing routine, and then subtract these values. The difference is the approximate execution time.

Unfortunately, there are many complicating factors that can affect the accuracy of this simple scheme. In the first place, the scheduler in a multitasking environment can interrupt a thread of execution at any time, thereby delaying it. Sometimes the unit-boundary at which a data item is located in memory affects the time required for a memory fetch operation. Another consideration relates to the occasional state of a memory cache, which can also change the fetch-time for data. This means that the measurements should be repeated as many times as practicable in order to obtain a more reliable value. Even with many repetitions the resulting numbers may not be accurate. However, for many practical programming situations the data obtained in this manner is sufficient for a decision regarding which of two or more routines is more suitable for the case at hand. The following code fragment shows measuring the execution time of two routines:

```
// Timer data
_int64          startCount;
_int64          endCount;
_int64          timeLapse1;    // First routine
_int64          timeLapse2;    // Second routine
. . .
// First routine starts here
QueryPerformanceCounter((LARGE_INTEGER*) &startCount);
//
// First routine code
//
QueryPerformanceCounter((LARGE_INTEGER*) &endCount);
timeLapse1 = endCount - startCount;
. . .
// Second routine starts here
QueryPerformanceCounter((LARGE_INTEGER*) &startCount);
//
// Second routine code
//
QueryPerformanceCounter((LARGE_INTEGER*) &endCount);
timeLapse2 = endCount - startCount;
```

The variables timeLapse1 and timeLapse2 now hold the number of timer ticks that elapsed during the execution of either routine. Code can display these values or a debugger can be used to inspect the variables.

Summary

In this chapter we tackled animation programming, one of the most difficult topics of 2D graphics. DirectDraw makes possible animation in Windows by furnishing direct access to the video hardware as well as specialized programming facilities, such as back buffers and flipping operations. We used these powers to create small demo programs that simulate movement. These techniques find use in many high-end or high-performance graphics programs.

With this we conclude Part II of the book. Having learned some general graphics theory as well as Windows API programming and DirectDraw, we are now ready to start with 3D. Our first approach is in the context of Microsoft's Direct3D package.

✦   ✦   ✦

3D Graphics with Direct3D

Introducing Direct3D

In this chapter we begin our discussion of Direct3D programming with the higher-level functions, called the retained mode. This chapter presents a smorgasbord of topics. The glue that holds them together is the fact that they are all necessary in order to understand and use Direct3D retained mode.

Before reading this chapter, make sure that you have grasped the material in Chapters 2, 3, and 4 that provide the necessary background in 3D graphics.

3D Graphics

There is some confusion regarding the scope and application of 3D graphics. One reason for this confusion is that 3D displays are not yet commercially available for the PC. Devices that render solid images, on a three-dimensional screen, are still experimental. Therefore, in a strict sense, 3D graphics do not yet exist commercially. However, systems capable of storing and manipulating images of solid objects and displaying these objects on two-dimensional media do exist. What we call 3D graphics in today's technology is actually a 2D rendering of a 3D object.

Direct3D is the component of Microsoft's DirectX software development kit that provides support for real-time, three-dimensional graphics, as available in today's machines. 3D programming is a topic at the cutting edge of PC technology. But cutting-edge infrastructures are rarely stable. Many of its features are undergoing revisions and redesigns, and there are still some basic weaknesses and defects. Furthermore, the performance of 3D applications depends on a combination of many factors, some of which are hidden in the software layers of the development environment. In today's world 3D applications developers spend much of their time working around the system's inherent weaknesses. Scores of video cards are on the market, each one supporting its own set of features and functionalities. Developing a 3D application that executes satisfactorily in most systems is no trivial task. The bright side of it is that the rewards can be enormous.

Historical origins of Direct3D

Direct3D can be described as a graphics operating system, although it would be less pretentious, and perhaps more accurate, to refer to it as a 3D graphics back end. Its core function is to provide an interface with the graphics hardware, thus insulating the programmer from the complications and perils of device-dependency. It also provides a set of services that enable you to implement 3D graphics on the PC. In this sense it is similar to other back ends, such as OpenGL and PHIGS. But Direct3D is also a provider of low-level 3D services for Windows. In Microsoft's plan the low-level components of Direct3D (immediate mode) serve and support its higher-level components (retained mode) and those of other 3D engines (OpenGL).

In the beginning 3D was exclusively in the realm of the graphics workstation and the mainframe computer. The standards were PHIGS (Programmer's Hierarchical Interactive Graphics Systems), and GKS (Graphical Kernel System). During the 1980s it was generally accepted that the processing power required to manipulate 3D images, with its associated textures, lighting, and shadows, was not available on the PC. However, some British game developers thought differently and created some very convincing 3D games that ran on a British Broadcasting Corporation (BBC) micro equipped with a 2MHz 6502 processor. This work eventually led Servan Keondjian, Doug Rabson, and Kate Seekings to the founding of a company named *RenderMorphics* and the development of the *Reality Lab* rendering engine for 3D graphics. Their first 3D products were presented at the SIGGRAPH '94 trade show.

In February 1995, Microsoft bought RenderMorphics and proceeded to integrate the Reality Lab engine into their DirectX product. The result was called Direct3D. Direct3D has been one of the components of DirectX since its first version, called DirectX 2. Other versions of the SDK, namely DirectX 3, DirectX 5, DirectX 6, and currently, DirectX 7, also include Direct3D. The functionality of Direct3D is available to applications running in Windows 95/98 and Windows NT 3.1 and later. The full functionality of DirectX SDK is part of Windows 98 and will also be found in Windows NT 5.0 and Windows 2000. This means that applications running under Windows 98 and later will be able to execute programs that use Direct3D without the loading of additional drivers or other support software.

Direct3D implementation

Direct3D is an application-programming interface for 3D graphics on the PC. The other major 3D API for the PC is OpenGL, which is discussed in Part IV. Figure 14-1 shows the structure of the graphics development systems under Windows.

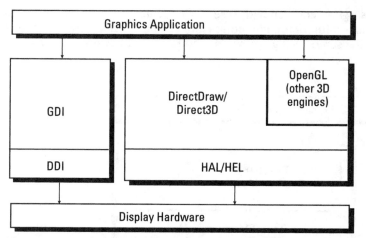

Figure 14-1: Windows graphics application development structure

Direct3D provides the API services and device independence required by developers, delivers a common driver model for hardware vendors, enables turnkey 3D solutions to be offered by personal-computer manufacturers, and makes it easy for end-users to add high-end 3D functions to their systems. Because the system requires little memory, it runs well on most of the installed base of computer systems.

The 3D graphics services in Direct3D execute in real time. The functions include rendering, transformations, lighting, shading, rasterization, z-buffering, textures, and transparent access to acceleration features available in the hardware. The Direct3D architecture consists of two well-defined modes: a low-level one called *immediate mode* and a high-level one called *retained mode*. The term retained mode originally referred to the images being preserved after rendering, but this notion is no longer literally true.

Retained mode overview

Retained mode was designed as a set of API for the high-level manipulation of 3D objects and managing 3D scenes. It is Microsoft's competition for OpenGL and other high-level 3D development environments. It is implemented as a set of interrelated COM objects that enable you to build and manipulate a 3D scene. Its intention was to make it easy to create 3D Windows applications or to add 3D capabilities to existing ones. The programmer working in retained mode can take advantage of its geometry engine, which contains advanced 3D capabilities, without having to create object databases or be concerned with internal data structures. The application uses a single call to load a predefined 3D object, usually stored in a file in .x format. The loaded object can then be manipulated within the scene and rendered in real-time. All of this is done without having to deal with the object's internals.

Retained mode is tightly coupled with DirectDraw, which serves as its rendering engine, and is built on top of the immediate mode. OpenGL and other high-level systems exist at the same level as retained mode. Figure 14-2 shows the elements of this interface.

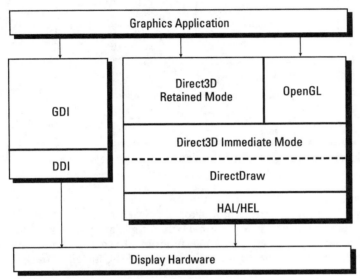

Figure 14-2: Architecture of the DirectX interface

Immediate mode overview

Direct3D immediate mode is a layer of low-level 3D API. Its original intention was to facilitate the porting of games and other high-precision and high-performance graphics applications to the Windows operating system. It allows access to hardware features in the 3D chip and offers software rendering when the function is not available in the hardware. The intention of immediate mode is to enable applications to communicate with the 3D hardware in a device-independent manner and to provide maximum performance.

In contrast with retained mode, immediate mode does not contain a graphics engine. Code that uses immediate mode must provide its own routines to implement object and scene management. This means that the effective use of immediate mode requires considerable knowledge and skills in 3D graphics.

Hardware abstraction layer

In Figure 14-2 you see that both the Immediate and the Retained Modes of Direct3D are built on top of the Hardware Abstraction Layer (HAL). It is this software layer that insulates the programmer from the device-specific dependencies. The

Hardware Emulation Layer (HEL) provides support for those features that are not present in the hardware. The combination of HEL and HAL ensure that the complete Direct3D functionality is always available.

DirectDraw

DirectDraw, the subject of Part II of this book, is the Windows rendering engine for 2D and 3D graphics. DirectDraw functions enable you to quickly compose images into front and back buffers, and to apply transformations, blitting, and flipping. The result is a capability of implementing smooth animation as required in computer games and other multimedia and high-performance graphics applications. DirectDraw functions can be used with images that originate in the Windows GDI, in Direct3D, or in OpenGL.

DirectDraw is implemented as an API layer that lies above the display hardware, as shown in Figure 14-2. It enables the graphics programmer to take advantage of the capabilities of graphics accelerators and coprocessors in a device-independent manner. DirectDraw is a COM-based interface.

The following are the most important connections between DirectDraw and Direct3D:

✦ IDirect3D, the interface to Direct3D, is obtained from a DirectDraw object by calling the QueryInterface() method.

✦ Direct3DDevice, the low-level interface to the 3D renderer, is similar to IDirectDrawSurface and is created by querying IDirectDrawSurface for a 3D device GUID. The 3D renderer will also render to a 2D surface and recognizes all DirectDraw 2D functions.

✦ IDirect3DTexture, the texture manager in Direct3D, is an extension of IDirectDrawSurface and is created by querying IDirectDrawSurface for an IID_IDirect3DTexture interface. Code can access all DirectDraw surface functions on a 2D surface.

✦ A Direct3D z-buffer is a DirectDraw surface created with the DDSCAPS_ZBUFFER flag. Code can use DirectDraw 2D functions in relation to z-buffers. Z-buffers are discussed later in this chapter.

OpenGL

OpenGL, the topic of Part IV, is an alternative 3D development environment that originated in graphics workstations. Its main area of application is in programs that require precise 3D image rendering, such as CAD/CAM, technical modeling and animation, simulations, scientific visualization, and others. OpenGL is part of Windows NT and is available for Windows 95 and 98. When installed, the system can execute programs that use the OpenGL APIs. Because of its high level, OpenGL appears to the programmer as an alternative to Direct3D retained mode.

Direct3D and COM

Like DirectDraw, Direct3D is based on Microsoft's Component Object Model (COM). COM is an object-oriented system that exists at the operating system level. In COM an interface is a group of related methods. COM's main purpose is to support and promote the reuse of interfaces. Direct3D is presented to the programmer using the Component Object Model. The COM object is a data structure that contains a pointer to the associated methods. Because it is not specific to C++, a program written in C, or even in a non-C development system, can use APIs based on the COM protocol.

There are several ways of accessing the COM interface. In C++ the COM object appears like an abstract class. In this case access is by means of the pointer to the DirectDraw COM object, which then allows code to obtain the Direct3D COM object. When programming in C the function must pass the pointer to the COM object as an additional parameter. In addition, the call must include a pointer to a property of the COM object called the *vtable*. In this book we use the simpler, C++ interface to the COM.

Direct3D Rendering Engine

Direct3D uses a 3D rendering engine composed of three separate modules:

✦ **Transformation Module.** This module consists of four modifiable state registers: viewport, viewing matrix, world matrix, and projection matrix. It supports arbitrary projection matrices, and allows perspective and orthographic views. As the name implies, the transformation module handles the geometrical transformations. It is also called the Geometry Module.

✦ **Lighting Module.** This module calculates lighting and color information. It uses a stack-like structure to maintain a record of the current lights. It supports ambient, directional, point, and spotlight light sources and two lighting models: monochromatic and RGB.

✦ **Rasterization Module.** This module uses the output of the transformation and lighting modules to render the scene. The rasterization module is the 3D renderer in Direct3D. The scene description is based on an extensible display-list that supports both 2D and 3D primitives. Raster options such as wireframe, solid fill, and texture map are defined in this module.

Figure 14-3 shows the modules of the Direct3D rendering engine and their interaction with the other modules and with the rest of the system.

Together, these three modules form the Direct3D rendering pipeline. Direct3D is furnished with one transformation module and a choice of two lighting and two rasterization modules. This ensures greater flexibility in lighting and rendering. For example, a scene can be rendered more realistically by switching the lighting module.

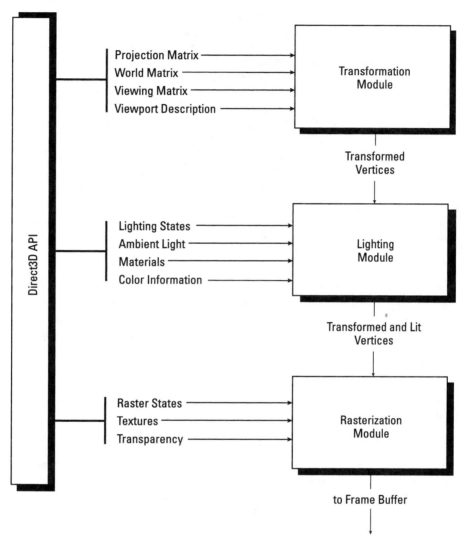

Figure 14-3: Action and interaction of the Direct3D rendering engine modules

Transformation module

The transformation module has four state registers: the viewport, the viewing matrix, the world matrix, and the projection matrix. All four are modifiable by code. Whenever one or more of the state registers are modified, they are recombined to form a new transformation matrix. The transformation matrix defines the rotation and projection of a set of 3D vertices.

In Direct3D a display list is the name given to a set of 3D commands. The transformation module supports a number of different vertex types in the display list. The

D3DTLVERTEX structure is a transformed and lit vertex that contains screen coordinates and colors. This structure contains the data and color information that is used by the lighting module. The D3DLVERTEX structure is used when the model contains data and color information only. Alternatively, the D3DHVERTEX structure is used when the application uses model-coordinate data with clipping. When this structure is used the transformations are performed in hardware. The D3DVERTEX structure is used if the hardware supports lighting. This type of vertex can be transformed and lit during rendering.

The transformation module contains two different types of methods: those that set the state and those that use the transformation module directly to act on a set of vertices. The second type of method is useful for testing bounding volumes or for acting on a set of vectors. These operations are based on the current transformation matrices. The structure used for all the direct transformation functions is D3DTRANSFORMDATA. Geometrical transformations were discussed in Chapter 3 and are revisited later in this chapter.

Lighting module

The lighting module maintains a stack-like structure representing the current lights, as well as the ambient light level, and a material. When the module is used directly, the input data includes a direction vector. If the light source is positional, as is the case with point- and spotlights, then the input also contains light source position information.

The monochromatic lighting model calculates the value for each light in a shade of gray. It is also called the ramp model. The RGB model uses the color component of light sources in order to produce more realistic and pleasant results. Internal color representations are always based on a palette-based color ramp.

In the ramp mode each color is represented by an index into a look-up table that can be located either in hardware or in software. Ramp modes use either 8- or 16-bit indices. In the ramp mode the lighting module has no knowledge of the particular color; it just works with a number of shades. Because color lights are treated as white lights, the ramp mode is sometimes called the *monochromatic mode*. The pre-calculated color ramps are divided into two sections. The first three-quarters of the ramp are the material's diffuse color. The values of this portion of the ramp range from the ambient color to the maximum diffuse color. The last quarter of the precalculated ramp encode the maximum diffuse color to the maximum specular color of the material. At rendering time the shade value is scaled by the size of the ramp and used as an index into the look-up table.

If the material does not have a specular component, the shade is calculated using the diffuse component of the light intensity. In this case the value ranges from 0 (ambient light) to 1 (full-intensity light). If the material has a specular component, then the shade calculation combines both the specular and diffuse components of the light according to the following equation

$$s = (\frac{3}{4}d \leftrightarrow (1 - s)) + sp$$

where *s* is the shade value, *d* is the diffusion, and *sp* is the specular value of the light. Notice that the first term of the equation takes into account the first three quarters of the ramp, which is equivalent to the material's diffuse color. The second term takes into account the last quarter of the ramp, which corresponds with the material's diffuse or specular color value.

Whether you use the RGB or the ramp color model depends mostly on the capabilities of the hardware. Ramp color is faster in software, but the RGB model supports color lights and is as fast, or even faster, than the ramp model if there is a hardware rasterizer.

Rasterization module

The rasterization module is the one that draws the triangles, lines, and points to the frame buffer. It responds only to execute calls. Instructions stored in the execute buffer determine the mode of operation of the rasterization module.

Execute buffers is just another name for display lists. They consist of self-contained, independent packets of information. The execute buffer contains a vertex list followed by an instruction stream. The instruction stream consists of individual instructions, each one containing an operation code (opcode), followed by the data. Figure 14-4 shows the format of the execute buffer.

The instructions determine how the vertex list is lit and rendered. One of the most common instructions is a triangle list, which consists of a list of triangle primitives that reference vertices in the vertex list.

The size of the execute buffer is determined by the hardware. Usually, 64K is considered satisfactory. How caching is implemented by the video card influences the best size for the buffer. The GetCaps() method can be used to retrieve the buffer size.

In processing execute buffers the transformation module runs through the vertex list, generating the transformed vertices. If clipping is enabled, the corresponding clipping information is attached. If there is no vertex in view at this point, the entire buffer can be rejected. Otherwise, vertices are processed by the lighting module, which adds color to them according to the lighting instructions in the execute buffer. Finally, the rasterization module parses the instruction stream. Primitives are rendered based on the generated vertex information.

The only geometry type that can be processed by the rasterization module are triangles. The screen coordinates range from (0, 0) for the top left of the screen or window device to width − 1, height − 1 for the bottom right of the device. The depth values range from zero at the front of the viewing frustum to one at the back. Rasterization is performed so that if two triangles that share two vertices are rendered, no pixel along the line joining the shared vertices is rendered twice. The rasterizer culls back facing triangles by determining the winding order of the three vertices of the triangle. Only those triangles whose vertices are traversed in a clockwise orientation are rendered.

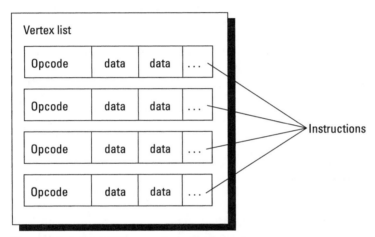

Figure 14-4: Direct3D execute buffer format

Retained Mode Elements

Retained mode programming consists of building 3D scenes out of components in Direct3D. The retained mode programmer does not need to be concerned with the development of geometrical primitives, or the structures of 3D objects and data-bases. You can load, rotate, scale, light, translate, and otherwise manipulate a 3D object, in real time, using high-level API functions. In this section we discuss the core elements of Direct3D retained mode. These are the building blocks that we use in the following chapter to construct a Direct3D program.

Frames

A *scene* in Direct3D, sometimes called a *scene graph*, is a collection or hierarchy of *frames*. The term frame relates to the notion of a *frame of reference*. It should not be confused with that of single animation image, also called a frame. In retained mode the role of a frame is to serve as a container for 3D objects, such as polygon meshes, lights, and cameras. These objects have no meaning by themselves. For example, a cube cannot be rendered until it is assigned a position within a frame, relative to a light and a camera, and possibly a material, color, and texture.

Each scene contains a root or master frame and any number of child frames, each of which can have other children of its own. It is a tree-like structure in which the root frame has no parent frame and the leaf frames have no children. The root frame is the highest level element of a 3D scene. Child frames inherit their characteristics from the parent frames and are physically attached to the parent. When a frame is moved, all the objects attached to it, including its child frames, move with it. For example, a helicopter in a 3D scene may consist of several frames. One frame could model the body, another one the lift rotor blades, and a third one the steering rotor blades. In this case the rotor blades would be child frames to the helicopter body. The helicopter is made to fly by rotating the blades in the main and tail rotors and by translating the helicopter body frame. Because the rotors are child frames of the helicopter body frame, the entire machine moves as a unit. Figure 14-5 shows the frame hierarchy in this case.

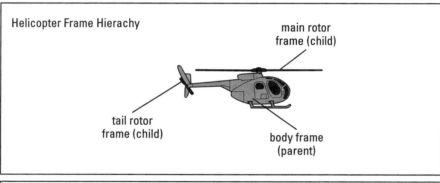

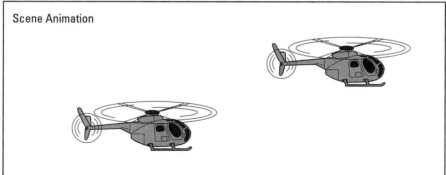

Figure 14-5: Frame hierarchy in a scene

Frame hierarchies in Direct3D are not rigid. Functions are available that enable you to change the reference frame, regardless of the parent-child relationships originally established. This flexibility adds considerable power to retained mode.

Meshes

The mesh is the principal visual object of a scene and the cornerstone of retained mode programming. Direct3D objects are made up of meshes. A mesh is described as a set of *faces*, each of which consists of a simple polygon. This makes a mesh equivalent to a set of polygons. Polygon meshes were discussed in Chapter 2.

The fundamental polygon type in Direct3D is the triangle. Retained mode applications can describe polygons with more than three vertices, but the system automatically translates them into triangles when rendering them. Immediate mode applications, on the other hand, are limited to triangles. Figure 14-6 shows two versions of the same mesh. The one at the top consists of 12 quadrilaterals. The one at the bottom is made up of 24 triangles.

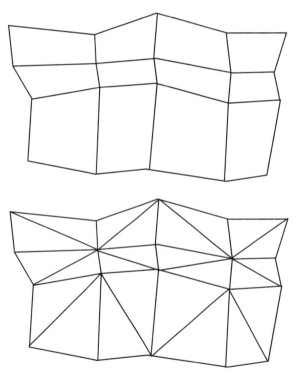

Figure 14-6: Quadrilateral and triangular meshes

The principal objection to modeling with nontriangular polygons is that in a polygon with more than three vertices it is possible for the vertices to lie on different planes (see Figure 2-1). In addition, polygons with more than three vertices can be concave. The triangle is not only the simplest of polygons, but all the points in the surface of a triangular polygon must lie on the same plane and any line drawn from two points in a triangle is inside it. In other words, a figure defined by three vertices is coplanar and convex. The renderer requires that polygons are convex and coplanar, so triangular modeling facilitates rendering.

Most graphics systems, including Direct3D, model objects by means of polygon meshes. Mesh information is stored in a database containing the vertices of each polygon and their attributes, such as color, texture, and shading. A state-of-the-art hardware-based renderer is capable of displaying hundreds of thousands to over one million of these polygons in one second, and at the same time applying texture, lighting, and other effects.

Mesh groups

The mesh group is an organizational concept used by Direct3D immediate mode. A mesh group consists of a collection of polygons. Each group can have its own material, color, texture, and rendering quality. Groups have no names and are not supported in retained mode.

Faces

If a face is a polygon, and a mesh is a collection of faces, then building a mesh consists of building the individual faces of which it is composed. Each face is a set of vertices. If the face is a triangle, then it is defined by three vertices. A front face is one in which vertices are defined in clockwise order. Figure 14-7 shows the front face of a triangular polygon in the Direct3D's left-handed coordinate plane.

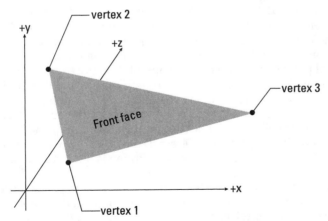

Figure 14-7: Front face of a triangular polygon

Each face has a normal vector, perpendicular to the face. If the normal vector of a face is oriented toward the viewer, that side of the face is its front. In Direct3D, only the front side of a face is visible. For this reason, if the vertices of the polygon in Figure 14-7 had been defined in counterclockwise order, the polygon's face would not be visible at rendering time. Face normals are used in Direct3D flat shading mode. Vertex normals are used in Phong and Gouraud shading. Figure 14-8 shows the face and vertex normals of a pyramidal object modeled with triangular polygons.

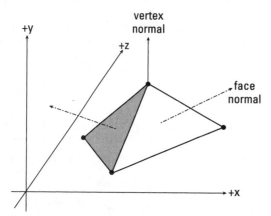

Figure 14-8: Vertex normals and face normals of a pyramid

Shading modes

Direct3D documents three shading modes: flat, Gouraud, and Phong shading, but Phong is not currently supported. These shading algorithms were described in Chapter 4. In the flat shading mode the color of the first vertex of the polygon is duplicated across all the pixels on the object's faces. The result is that each face is rendered in a single color. Often the only way of improving the rendering is by increasing the number of polygons, which can be computationally expensive. An improvement to flat shading is called interpolative or incremental shading. In this case each polygon is rendered in more than one shade by interpolating, for the polygon interior points, the values calculated for the vertices or the edges. This type of shading algorithm is capable of producing a more satisfactory shade rendering with a smaller number of polygons. Direct3D describes two incremental shading methods, called Gouraud and Phong shading. Phong is not yet supported.

In the Gouraud and Phong shade modes, vertex normals are used to give a more satisfactory appearance to a polygonal object. In Gouraud shading, the color and intensity of the polygon edges are interpolated across the polygon face (see

Figure 4-30). In Phong shading, the system calculates the appropriate shade value for each pixel. Because Gouraud shading is based on the intensity at the edges, it is possible to completely miss a highlight or a spotlight that is contained within a face. Figure 14-9 shows two possible cases in which Gouraud shading renders erroneously.

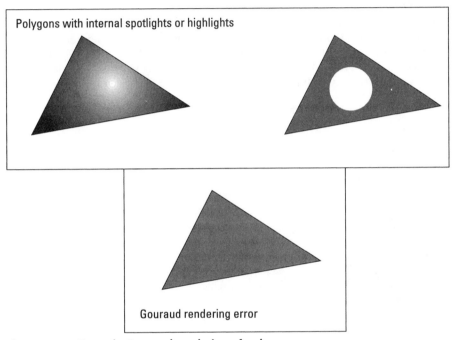

Figure 14-9: Errors in Gouraud rendering of polygons

Phong shading is the most effective shading algorithm in use today. This method, developed by Phong Bui-Toung is also called *normal-vector interpolation*. It is based on calculating pixel intensities by means of the approximated normal vector at each pixel point in the polygon. Phong shading improves the rendering of bright points and highlights that are misrendered in Gouraud shading. The one objection to Phong shading is that it takes considerably longer than Gouraud shading.

Interpolation of triangle attributes

At rendering time Direct3D interpolates the attributes of a triangle's vertices across the triangle face. Color, specular reflection, fog, and alpha blending attributes are interpolated. In interpolation the attributes are modified according to the current shade mode, as previously described. The interpolation of color and specular attributes depends on the color model. In the RGB model the red, green, and blue color components are used in the interpolation. In the monochromatic model only the blue component of the vertex color is taken into account. The alpha component of a color is treated as a separate interpolant. This is because device drivers can implement transparency in two different ways: by texture blending or by stippling.

Z-buffers

One of the problems encountered by the renderer refers to the display of over-lapping polygons. Figure 14-10 shows three triangles located between the viewer and the display buffer. In this case the question is whether the pixel should be rendered as dark gray, white, or light gray. The answer is obviously dark gray because the dark gray polygon is the one closest to the viewer.

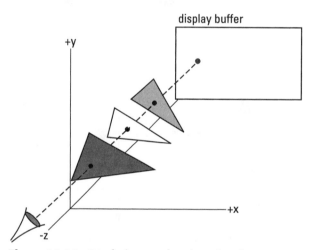

Figure 14-10: Rendering overlapping triangles

Several algorithms have been developed for eliminating hidden surfaces at render-ing time. One of the best known, attributed to Catmull, is called the *z-buffer* or *depth buffer* method. Because of its simplicity of implementation and relative efficiency it has become popular in 3D graphics. The z-buffer algorithm is described in Chapter 4.

Direct3D supports the z-buffer method for solving the so-called "polygon-on-top" problem. In Direct3D the z-buffer is a rather large block of memory where the depth value for each screen pixel is stored. Initially the depth value for a pixel is that of the background. As each polygon is rendered, its depth value is examined. This is the z-order. If its depth value is less than the one in the z-buffer, then the pixel is rendered with the polygon's attribute. Otherwise it is ignored.

In Direct3D z-buffering can be turned on and off. The general rule is that z-buffering improves performance when a screen pixel is set several times in succession. The average number of times a pixel is written to is called the scene overdraw. Although overdraw is difficult to calculate exactly, it is possible to estimate it. If the scene overdraw is less than 2, then best performance is achieved by turning z-buffering off.

Lights

Earlier in this chapter we discussed the lighting module in Direct3D as well as the RGB and ramp color models. In processing lights the lighting module uses information about the light source, and the normal vectors of the polygon vertices, to determine how to render the light source in each pixel.

The vertex normals are calculated from the face normals of the triangles adjacent to that vertex. Face normals are perpendicular to the polygon face, as shown in Figure 14-11. The angle between the vertex normals and the light source determines how much light intensity and color are applied to the vertex. The mathematical calculations are performed by the lighting module.

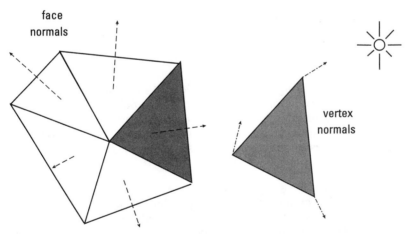

Figure 14-11: Calculating the vertex normals of a polygon

Lighting effects are used to improve the visual quality of a scene. Applications can attach lights to a frame to represent a light source in a scene. In this case the attached light illuminates the objects in the scene. The position and orientation for the light is defined in the frame. Code can move and redirect a light source simply by moving and reorienting the frame to which the light is attached.

Retained mode supports five types of light sources: ambient, directional, parallel point, point, and spotlight.

Ambient light

An ambient light source illuminates the entire scene, regardless of the orientation, position, and surface characteristics of the objects. All objects are illuminated with equal strength, therefore the position and orientation of the containing frame is inconsequential. Multiple ambient light sources can be combined within a scene.

Directional light

A directional light source has a specific orientation, but no position. The light appears to illuminate all objects with equal intensity, as if it were at an infinite distance from the objects. Directional lighting is often used to simulate distant light sources, such as the sun. It provides maximum rendering speed.

Parallel point light

The parallel point light can be considered a variation of direction light. In this case the orientation of the light is determined by the position of the light source. Whereas a directional light source has orientation, but no position, a parallel point light source has orientation and position. The parallel point light source has similar rendering-speed performance to the directional source.

Point light

A point light source radiates light equally in all directions. This makes it necessary to calculate a new lighting vector for every face it illuminates, which makes the method more computationally expensive than a parallel point light source. One advantage of the point light source is that it produces a more faithful lighting effect. When visual fidelity is a concern, a point light source is the best option.

Spotlight

A spotlight is a cone-shaped light source with the light at the cone's vertex. Objects within the cone are illuminated. The cone produces light of two degrees of intensity, with a central brightly lit section called the umbra, and a surrounding dimly lit section called the penumbra. In Direct3D the angles of the umbra and penumbra can be individually specified. Figure 14-12 shows the umbra and the penumbra in spotlight illumination.

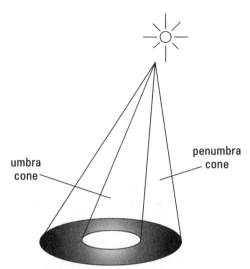

Figure 14-12: Umbra and penumbra in spotlight illumination

Textures

A texture is an image, usually encoded in a 2D bitmap that can be applied to the face of a polygon to improve its visual quality. Color plate 6 is a coffee cup to which a red marble texture has been applied.

Textures are usually stored in standard file formats, most commonly as a Windows bitmap, PCX, or GIF. Although any image can be used as a texture, not all images make good textures. Textures can be scaled at the time they are applied. Each element of a texture is called a *textel*, which is a composite of the words texture and pixel.

In its simplest implementation, sometimes called *point mapping*, the rendering software looks up each pixel in a texture map and applies it to the corresponding screen pixel. In most cases point sampling produces coarse effects that are unnatural and disturbing to the viewer. Satisfactory texturing requires that the distance between the object and the viewer be taken into account at the time of applying the texture, in other words, that the texture be rendered perspectively.

The *bilinear filtering* method of texture rendering uses the weighted average of four texture pixels. This results in more pleasant textures than those that result from point mapping.

Direct3D supports five texture-rendering styles:

✦ Decals

✦ Texture colors

✦ Mipmaps

✦ Texture filters and blends

✦ Texture transparency

Decals

A decal is a texture applied directly to a scene. Decals are not rendered on a polygon face, but as an independent object. They are rectangular in shape, the rectangle facing the viewport, and they grow and shrink according to their distance from the viewer. The fact that decals always appear facing the viewer considerably limits their usefulness.

The origin point of a decal is defined as an offset from the top-left corner of the containing rectangle. The default origin is (0,0). In Direct3D an application can set and retrieve the origin of a decal. When the decal is rendered, its origin is aligned with its frame's position.

Texture colors

Direct3D code in retained mode can set and retrieve the number of colors that are used to render a texture. Applications that use the RGB color model can encode textures in 8-, 24-, and 32-bit formats. In the ramp color model textures are represented in 8 bits. However, code that uses the ramp model should be careful regarding the number of texture colors. In this mode each color requires its own lookup table. If an application uses hundreds of colors, the system must allocate and manipulate as many lookup tables.

Mipmaps

The term mipmap originates in the Latin expression *multum in parvo,* which can be translated literally as *many in few* or *many objects in a small space.* This texture-rendering method, sometimes referred to as MIP maps, was described by L. Williams in 1983 and has since gained considerable favor.

In Direct3D a mipmap is a set of textures representing the same image at progressively lower resolutions. Each image in the set is one-quarter the size of the preceding one, which makes the entire mipmap take up 4/3 the memory of the original image. Mipmapping provides a computationally efficient way of improving the quality of rendered textures. Each scaled image in the mipmap is called a level. The image at level 0 is at the same resolution as the original. Figure 14-13 is a diagram of the mipmap structure.

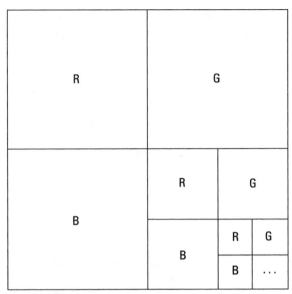

Figure 14-13: Mipmap structure

Mipmaps are created by the DirectDraw interface. Each mipmap level contains its own front and back surfaces, which can be flipped in the conventional manner. When the mipmap is created, code defines the number of levels, as well as the dimensions of the level 0 mipmap. Figure 14-14 shows the DirectDraw structure of a mipmap consisting of four levels. In the DirectDraw implementation of mipmaps, each level consists of a front and a back surface. As is the case with all mipmaps, successive levels have one half the resolution of the preceding one, and one-quarter the size.

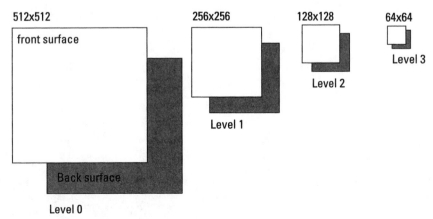

Figure 14-14: Example of a DirectDraw mipmap

Texture filters and blends

The elements of a texture (texels) rarely correspond to individual pixels in the original image. Texture filtering is used to specify how to interpolate texels to pixels.

Direct3D supports six texture-filtering modes. They are:

✦ Nearest

✦ Linear

✦ Mip-nearest

✦ Mip-linear

✦ Linear-mip-nearest

✦ Linear-mip-linear

The nearest mode uses the texel with coordinates nearest to the desired pixel value. The result is a point filter with no mipmapping. The linear mode uses a weighted average of an area of 2×2 texels surrounding the desired pixel. This is equivalent to bilinear filtering with no mipmapping. In the mip-nearest mode the closest mipmap level is chosen and a point filter is applied. In the mip-linear mode the closest mipmap level is chosen and a bilinear filter is applied. The linear-mip-nearest mode uses the two closest mipmap levels, and a linear blend is used between point filtered samples of each level. In the linear-mip-linear mode the two closest mipmap levels are chosen and then combined using a bilinear filter.

Texture blending consists of combining the colors of a texture with the colors of the surface to which the texture is applied. If done correctly, the result is a translucent surface. Because texture blending can result in unexpected colors, the color white is often used for the material texture. There are a total of seven texture blending modes:

✦ Decal

✦ Modulate

✦ Decal-alpha

✦ Modulate-alpha

✦ Decal-mask

✦ Copy

✦ Add

Texture blends are discussed in the context of retained mode texture programming, in Chapter 22.

Texture transparency

Direct3D contains methods to directly produce transparent textures. In addition, immediate mode programs can take advantage of DirectDraw support for color keys to achieve transparency. By selecting a color key that contains a color or color range in the texture, the material's color will show through the texture areas within the color key range. The result is a transparent texture. Color-key programming in DirectDraw was discussed in Chapter 12.

Wraps

In Direct3D a wrap is a way of applying a texture to a face or mesh. Four kinds of wraps are available:

✦ Flat

✦ Cylindrical

✦ Spherical

✦ Chrome

The flat wrap conforms to the faces of an object. The effect is sometimes compared to stretching a piece of rubber over the object. The cylindrical wrap treats the texture as if it were a sheet of paper wrapped around a cylinder. The left edge of the texture rectangle is joined to the right edge. The object is then placed in the middle of the cylinder and the texture is deformed inward onto the surface of the object. The spherical wrap is similar to the cylindrical wraps, but in this case the wrapping form is a sphere, instead of a cylinder. A chrome wrap allocates texture coordinates so that the texture appears to be reflected onto the objects. The chrome wrap takes the reference frame position and uses the vertex normals in the mesh to calculate reflected vectors, which are based on an imaginary sphere that surrounds the mesh. The resulting effect is that of the mesh reflecting whatever is wrapped on the sphere.

Texture wrapping is a complex procedure in which a two-dimensional surface is deformed to cover the surface of a three-dimensional object. The above analogies are coarse simplifications that do not take into account many of the complexities of wrapping. In practice, the results of wrapping operations are often different from what was expected. This has led some to believe that, in most cases, the complications do not justify the results. The reader interested in the more specific details on texture wrapping can refer to the article *Texture Wrapping Simplified* by Peter Donnelly that appears in Microsoft Developers Network documentation. The article includes a demonstration program for experimenting with texture wrapping operations.

Materials

Direct3D provides support for an object property called a material. A material determines how a surface reflects light. It has two components: an emissive property and a specular property. The emissive property determines whether the material emits light. This property is useful in modeling lamps, neon signs, or other light-emitting objects. The specular property determines if and how the material reflects light.

Code controls the emission property of a material by defining the red, green, and blue values for the emissive color. The specular property is also defined by the red, green, and blue values of the reflected light and by a power setting. The default specular color is white, but code can change it to any desired RGB value. The power setting determines the size, and consequently the sharpness, of the reflected highlights. A small highlight makes an object appear shiny or metallic. A large highlight gives a plastic appearance.

User-visuals

A user-visual object is an application-defined data structure that can be added to a scene and rendered, typically by means of a customized rendering module. For example, an application can add sound as a user-visual object in a scene, and then render the sound during playback. A user-visual object has no methods, but it does have a callback function that will be called by the renderer. The callback function is called twice: when the object is rendered and when the object is told to render itself. This property makes it possible for applications that execute in retained mode to use the user-visual mechanism to provide a hook into Direct3D immediate mode.

Viewports

The viewport contains a camera reference frame that determines which scene is to be rendered, as well as the viewing position and direction. Rendering takes place along the z-axis of the camera frame, assuming the conventional Direct3D Cartesian plane with the positive y-axis in the upward direction and the positive x-axis toward the right.

Viewing frustum

What the camera sees from the vantage point of a particular frame is called the viewing frustum. The viewport uses a frame object as a camera. In the perspective viewing mode, the viewing frustum is a truncated pyramid with its apex at the camera position. The camera's viewing axis runs from the pyramid's apex to the center of the base, as shown in Figure 14-15.

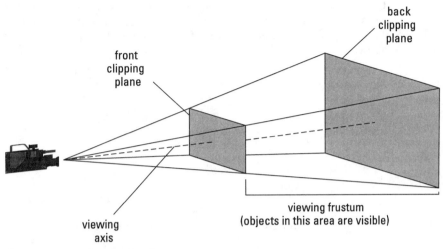

Figure 14-15: The viewing frustum

If we assume that the front clipping plane is at a distance D from the camera, and the back clipping plane is at a distance F from the front clipping plane, then the viewing angle A is determined by the formula

$$A = 2\,\mathrm{Tan}^{-1}\frac{h}{D}$$

where h is one half the height of the front clipping plane, if it is square. If the clipping plane is rectangular, then h is one half the height or the width of the front clipping plane, whichever is larger. The parameter h defines the field of view of the viewport. The above formula can be used to calculate the value of h for a specific camera angle. Figure 14-16 shows the viewport parameters.

Direct3D retained mode applications can set or retrieve the front and the back clipping planes, set the camera frame, as well as the viewport's field of view as defined by the parameter h in Figure 14-16. Direct3D supports two projection types: perspective and orthographic. Projections were discussed in Chapter 4.

Transformations

In the context of Direct3D viewports, transformations are used to convert between screen and world coordinates. Direct3D transformations are based on homogenous coordinates as described in Chapter 3. The projection matrix, which is a combination of a scaling and a translation transformation, produces a four-element homogenous coordinate $[x\ y\ z\ w]$. The three-element homogeneous coordinates are derived by performing x/w, y/w, z/w operations, where x/w and y/w are the coordinates to be used in the window and z/w is the depth. The depth ranges from 0 at the front clipping plane to 1 at the back clipping plane. The projection matrix is defined as follows:

$$
\begin{matrix}
\frac{D}{hF} & 0 & 0 & 0 \\
0 & \frac{D}{hF} & 0 & 0 \\
0 & 0 & \frac{F}{(F - D)} & 1 \\
0 & 0 & \frac{(-F \times D)}{(F - D)} & 0
\end{matrix}
$$

In the above matrix the parameters h and D are as in Figure 14-16.

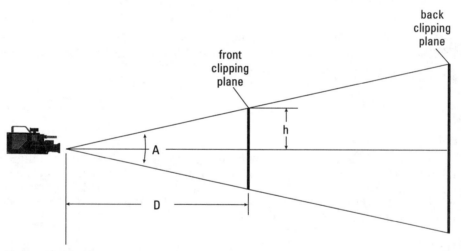

Figure 14-16: Viewport parameters

Picking

Direct3D supports the selection of an object by specifying its location in the viewport. This operation, called picking, is typically based on the position of the mouse cursor. Picking is accurate to the pixel; therefore it can be used in precise object selection by technical applications. The drawback of the picking operation is that it involves considerable processing, which may introduce a visible delay in the rendering.

To pick an object, code passes the *x* and *y* screen coordinates to the corresponding method. Usually these coordinates are those of the mouse cursor at the time of the pick action. The pick function returns either the closest object in the scene, or a depth-sorted list, called the *picked array*, of the objects found at that location.

Animations and animations sets

In retained mode an animation provides a mechanism for adding behavior to a 3D scene. An animation set consists of one or more animations and a time reference.

An animation is defined by a set of keys, which consist of a time value, an associated scaling operation, an orientation, or a position. A Direct3D animation object defines how a transformation is modified according to the time value. The animation can be set to animate the position, orientation, and scaling of visuals, lights, or viewport objects.

Applications can define position keys, rotation keys, and scale keys in the animation. Each key references a time value in zero-based arbitrary units. For example, if an application adds a position key with a time value of 99, a new position key with a time value of 49 would occur halfway between the beginning of the animation and the first position key. An animation is driven by calling a method that sets its time component. This call sets the visual object's transformation to the interpolated position, orientation, and scale of the nearby keys. As with the methods that add animation keys, the time value is arbitrary and based on the positions of keys that the application has already added. Rotation keys in an animation are based on quaternions. Quaternions, a mathematical structure that facilitates rotation transformations, are discussed later in this chapter.

A Direct3D animation set allows animation objects to be grouped together. The result is that all the animations in the set share the same time parameter, which simplifies the playback of complex sequences. Applications can add and remove animations to and from an animation set.

Direct3D Rendering Mathematics

The mathematical basis of 3D graphics was covered in Chapters 2, 3, and 4. At this time we lightly review some of the basic concepts as they relate to Direct3D programming in retained mode, and introduce some new ones that are specifically associated with this development environment. The material covered here refers to 3D programming at the API level, as takes place in Direct3D retained mode. System-level 3D graphics, which are necessary for immediate mode programming, requires a higher level of mathematical processing.

Direct3D coordinate system

The Cartesian coordinate system used in computer graphics was described in detail in Chapter 2. Recall now that the labeling of the axes in 3D space is arbitrary, although in computer graphics the most common labeling preserves the conventional representation of the x- and y-axes used in two-dimensional space, and adds the z-axis in the viewer's direction. The positive direction of the z-axis can point toward or away from the viewer. The case in which the positive values of the z-axis are in the direction of the viewer is called a right-handed coordinate system. The one in which the positive values of the z-axis are away from the viewer is called a left-handed system. Left- and right-handed systems are shown in Figure 14-17.

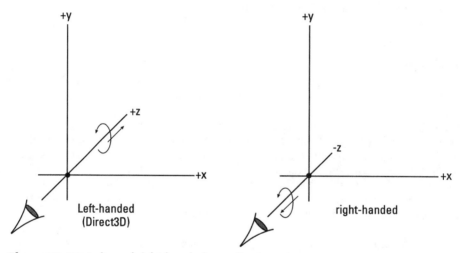

Figure 14-17: Left- and right-handed coordinate systems

It is easy to remember left- or right-handed systems by visualizing which hand needs to be curled over the z-axis so that the thumb points in the positive direction. In a left-handed system the left hand with the fingers curled on the z-axis has the thumb pointing away from the viewer. In a right-handed system the thumb points toward the viewer. Direct3D uses a left-handed coordinate system.

Points and vectors in Direct3D

Points and vectors are different entities. A point is a location in 3D space defined by its x, y, and z coordinates. A vector is a line segment defined by two points and a direction. Vectors do not have a location in 3D space. Vectors are usually represented by an arrow with its head pointing in the vector's direction and the length of the arrow shaft representing the vector's magnitude. Therefore, two line segments of equal length and the same direction represent the same vector quantity. In this case the vectors are said to be equivalent. Figure 14-18 represents a vector, labeled u, which extends from point A to point B in 3D space.

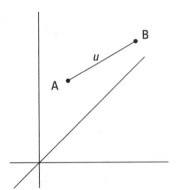

Figure 14-18: Vector representation in 3D space

Because a vector is defined by its end points, it can be described by subtracting the coordinates of the initial point from those of the terminal point. In the case of Figure 14-16 we can state

$u = B - A$

We can represent points A and B by their respective x-, y-, and z-coordinates. These coordinates can be placed in a column matrix, as follows:

$$A = \begin{matrix} A_x \\ A_y \\ A_z \end{matrix} \qquad B = \begin{matrix} B_x \\ B_y \\ B_z \end{matrix}$$

Subtracting the coordinates of points A from B ($B_x - A_x$, $B_y - A_y$, and $B_z - A_z$) yields the vector

$$u = \begin{matrix} u_x \\ u_y \\ u_z \end{matrix}$$

Notice that both vectors and points can be defined by their x, y, and z values.

Retained mode provides several functions for manipulating vectors, including

✦ Calculating the length of a vector

✦ Adding and subtracting vectors

✦ Calculating cross and dot product of two vectors

✦ Vector resizing

✦ Creating a unit vector

✦ Reflecting a vector about a given normal

✦ Rotating a matrix around a vector

✦ Scaling a vector

The length of a vector

Calculating the length of a vector is a simple matter of applying the Pythagorean theorem in 3D space. The length of a vector u, also called the modulus, is conventionally represented as

$$\|u\|$$

The length of vector u is calculated by means of the formula

$$\|u\| = \sqrt{u_x^2 + u_y^2 + u_z^2}$$

Figure 14-19 shows the vector u in 3D space.

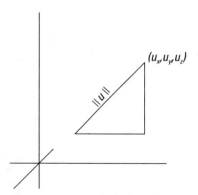

Figure 14-19: Calculating the length of a vector

Vector addition and subtraction

Vector addition and subtraction consists of performing either operation on the respective coordinate pairs. For example, the sum of vectors u and v is expressed as follows:

$$u + v = [(u_x - v_x)(u_y - v_y)(u_z - v_z)]$$

Dot product of two vectors

The dot product operation is a way of combining the angle between two vectors and their relative length into a single value. The dot product of vectors u and v is expressed as

$$u \, ?v = u_x v_x + u_y v_y + u_z v_z$$

The rule is, to obtain the dot product you multiply the x coordinates of both vectors and add to that the product of the y and the z coordinates. It is important to keep in mind that a dot product is a value, not a vector, and that this value is useful because it expresses the relationship between the vectors. The following are properties of the dot product of vectors v and u:

$$u \, ?0 = 0$$

$$u \, ?v = v \, ?u$$

$$\|v\| = \sqrt{v \, ?v}$$

$$u \, ?v = \|u\|\|v\| \cos a$$

Because the cosine of 90 degrees is zero, this last formula leads to the conclusion that the dot product of two perpendicular vectors is zero.

Calculating the unit vector

The unit vector is defined as a vector of one unit length. The unit vector notation is the caret (^) symbol. The unit vector is defined as follows:

$$u^\wedge = \frac{u}{\|u\|} = \frac{u}{\sqrt{u \, ?u}}$$

Cross product of two vectors

The cross product notation is named after the symbol used in conventional multiplication, which in the case of vectors is different from the period symbol used in the dot product notation, for example:

$$n = v \leftrightarrow u$$

In this case the vector n is called the cross product, or vector product. The result is a vector that is normal (perpendicular) to the plane that contains the two operand vectors. Figure 14-20 shows vector n, which is normal to the plane containing vectors u and v.

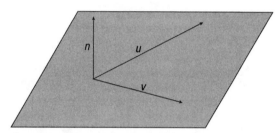

Figure 14-20: A normal vector

A normal vector is obtained by calculating the cross product of the two operand vectors. In this case the resulting vector is normal to the two operand vectors and also to the plane that contains them. It is also valid to say that a normal vector is perpendicular, orthogonal, or at right angles to the given vector pair.

Figure 14-21 graphically shows some interesting vector cross products.

3D plane

A plane, in 3D graphics, is a collection of points that have the same value for a common coordinate. A plane is named for the two axes that bind it, as shown in Figure 14-22.

In Figure 14-22 all the points in the x-z plane have the same y coordinate, the ones on the z-y plane have the same z coordinate, and those in the y-z plane have the same x coordinate. However, this fact is not sufficient to identify a plane because there could be a point that is simultaneously located in two intersecting planes. In fact, a point located at the origin in Figure 14-22 will be located in all three planes.

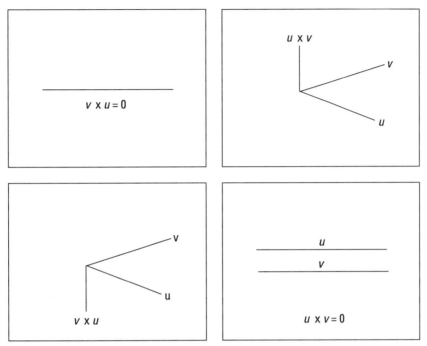

Figure 14-21: Some vector cross products

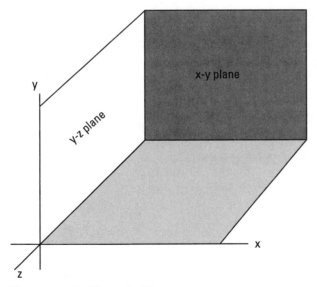

Figure 14-22: Planes in 3D space

Geometrically speaking, a plane can be defined uniquely in terms of its inclination and one of its points. Since a normal vector is perpendicular to a point, a vector can also serve to specify the plane. In this manner a plane can be defined as passing through a point $P0(x0, y0, z0)$ and having nonzero vector u as a normal vector. By the same token, another point P_1 is also on the plane if the vector from P_0 to P_1, designated as v, is perpendicular to the plane vector u. These relationships are shown in Figure 14-23.

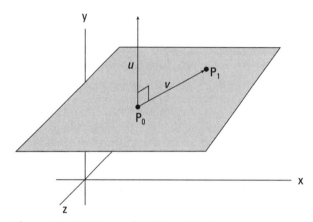

Figure 14-23: Vector definition of a plane

Because a vector has direction and magnitude, but no specific location in 3D space, then the vector definition of a plane is valid for any point that is perpendicular to the normal. Also, considering that the dot product of two perpendicular vectors is zero, then we can conclude that a point is in a plane if, and only if, the dot product of its vector to another point in the plane, and the plane vector, is zero. In reference to Figure 14-23 we can state that point *P1* is on the plane if

u ?v = 0

The general form of the equation for a plane is

ax + by + cz + d = 0

where a, b, c, and d are constants and x, y, and z are the coordinates of any point in the plane.

Quaternions

Direct3D retained mode supports a mathematical structure called a *quaternion* that has found use in 3D animation. The quaternion is described as an extension to complex numbers that describes both an orientation and a rotation in 3D space. In Direct3D the quaternion consists of a vector, that provides the orientation component, and a scalar, that defines the rotation component. This can be expressed as

q = (s , v)

where *s* is the rotation scalar of the quaternion and *v* is the orientation vector.

Quaternions provide a fast alternative to the matrix operations that are typically used for 3D rotations. The quaternion can be visualized as an axis in 3D space, represented by a vector, and a rotation around that axis, represented by a scalar, as shown in Figure 14-24.

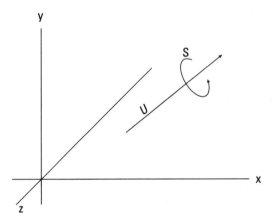

Figure 14-24: Vector/scalar interpretation of the quaternion

Two fundamental operations can be performed on quaternions: composition and interpolation. Composition consists of combining quaternions. For example, the composition of two quaternions, *q1* and *q2*, in reference to an object in 3D space, is interpreted to mean: rotate the object on the specified axis, by the rotation contained in quaternion *q1*, and then rotate the object on the specified axis by the rotation contained in quaternion *q2*. Quaternion interpolation is used to calculate a smooth path from one axis and orientation to another.

A common problem in computer animation is the generation of in-between frames that are necessary to simulate the smooth movement of an object from one position to another one. For example, Figure 14-25 shows images of an F-111 jet. The images at the top, called the key frames, represent the initial and final position of the aircraft in a planned animation. To simulate this movement, it is necessary to generate a set of in-between images that produce a smooth transition from the start frame to the end frame. Part of this image set, usually called the in-betweens, is shown in the lower part of Figure 14-25.

Rendering the in-between frames in the case of Figure 14-25 consists of performing several rotations on the image data for the F-111 aircraft. Aircraft dynamics use three angles: the yaw refers to the vertical axis, the pitch to a horizontal axis through the wings, and the roll through the fuselage axis. These angles are shown in Figure 14-26.

Generating the animation image set in Figure 14-25 requires rotating the aircraft along its yaw, pitch, and roll angles. Traditionally, rotations of 3D models have been by means of independent coordinates called Euler angles. This approach, although feasible, is computationally expensive because the composite rotation is based on three individual rotations along the axes shown in Figure 14-26.

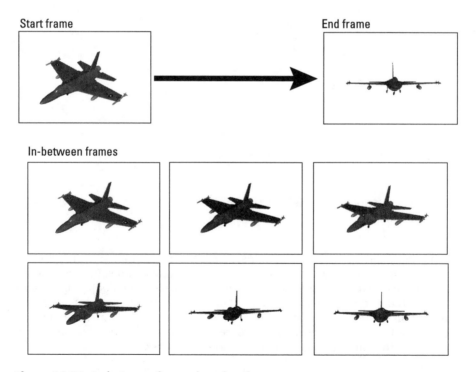

Figure 14-25: In-between frames in animation

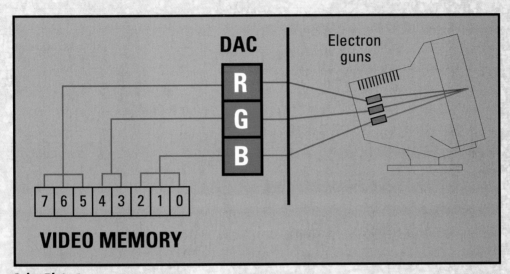

Color Plate 1
The illustration demonstrates bit-to-color mapping in a raster-scan system, which is discussed in Chapter 1. In this example, we have arbitrarily divided one memory byte into three separate bit fields, which encode the three-color values that determine each individual screen pixel.

Color Plate 2
The screen snapshot shows specular reflection on the surface of a teapot. Notice that the reflected highlights are the color of the incident light, not that of the surface material (see Chapter 4 for more information). The teapot in this example is a model for nonperfect reflectors as described by Phong Bui-Toung.

Rendered by incremental shading

Rendered by ray tracing

Color Plate 3
The screen snapshot in this example shows two renderings of a
coffee cup. The one on the top is obtained through incremental
shading, and the one on the bottom, through ray tracing, which is
discussed in Chapter 4.

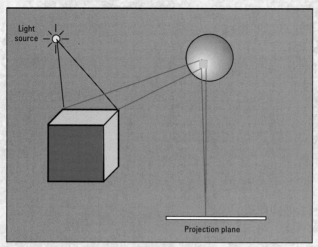

Color Plate 4
Reflected object imaged in ray tracing

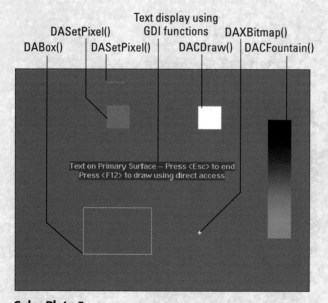

Color Plate 5
Screen snapshot of the DD Access Demo
project program

Color Plate 6
The screen snapshot shows a coffee cup to which a red marble texture has been
applied. The various methods used to apply textures are discussed in Chapter 14.

Ambient light intensity = 0.1

Ambient light intensity = 0.4

Ambient light intensity = 0.8

Color Plate 7
In this example, the screen snapshot shows three versions of a teapot image in which the intensity of the ambient light has been increased from 0.1 to 0.8 for all three primary colors. The effect of changing the ambient light intensity is discussed in Chapter 15.

Mesh color value not assigned

Mesh color value (0.0, 0.7, 0.0)

Color Plate 8
If you attempt to render a mesh without setting it to a color attribute
the result is an image in shades of gray, as shown in the top part of the
example above (see Chapter 15 for more information). The image in
the lower part of this example shows the object rendered after the
mesh is assigned the color value (0.0,0.7,0.0).

Color Plate 9
Building an object by loading individual meshes

Color Plate 10
Textured sphere

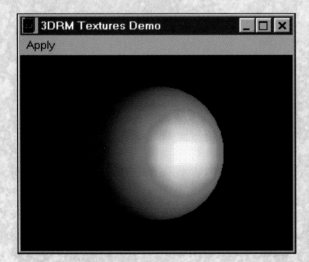

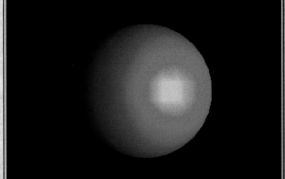

Color Plate 11
Metallic and plastic materials (D3DRM Textures Demo program)

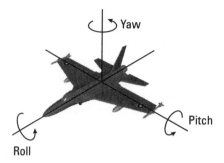

Figure 14-26: Yaw, pitch, and roll angles in aircraft dynamics

Quaternions provide a way of changing the orientation of the aircraft by performing a single rotation, that is a composite of the three primary ones along the yaw, pitch, and roll angles. This is achieved by using composition and interpolation together. A composition is first used to go from the original to the final frame. The smooth transition from the start frame to the end frame is then achieved through interpolation. In Direct3D programming code determines an angle, called the slerp value, that defines the position for the intermediate quaternion between two vectors. For example, a slerp value of 0.5 creates a quaternion that is midway between the two input quaternions. The quaternion method provides a much simpler and computationally faster approach to calculating in-between images for animation.

Direct3D File Formats

The information that defines a 3D object must be stored in a special file format. You cannot use the conventional BMP, GIF, or TIFF file types developed for 2D bitmaps for a 3D image, although a 3D application may be capable of rendering a particular view of a 3D object into one of the 2D file formats. Several 3D formats have been developed for the PC; in fact, it seems that every 3D drawing program supports its own proprietary format. What is worse, file conversion utilities that are relatively abundant for 2D imagery are difficult to develop for the 3D formats and, consequently, not always available.

Some of the 3D file formats have gained some level of prominence, usually proportional to the muscle of its corporate sponsors. One of the first PC programs that effectively used 3D was AutoCAD, a computer-assisted design application that enjoys a lion's share of this market. The .dxf file format was designed by AutoCAD primarily for the CAD environment. Its image handling capabilities are confined to 3D faces and polylines, which makes it quite crude for 3D modeling and authoring applications. However, these limitations also imply an inherent simplicity and ease of implementation, which have made the .dxf format quite popular. In many cases the only way of moving image data between two 3D applications is by means of a .dxf file, although the results usually leave much to be desired.

One of the leading 3D image editing programs is 3D Studio. The current version is named 3D Studio MAX. The native file format for 3D Studio, named .3ds, comes close to being the industry standard at the present time. Microsoft recognized this hegemony by providing a utility, named conv3ds, that converts 3ds files into the format supported by Direct3D.

Direct3D supports a single file format called .x. It is used to store objects, meshes, textures, and animation sets. It also supports animation sets, which allow playback in real-time. The .x format supports multiple references to a single object (such as a mesh) while storing the data for the object only once per file. Earlier versions of Direct3D used a file format named .xof, which is now considered obsolete. Direct3D retained mode uses the .x format for loading objects into an application and for writing mesh information, constructed by the application, in real time.

Description

The DirectX file format is a template-driven structure that allows the storage of user-defined objects, meshes, textures, animations, and animation sets. The format supports multiple references to an object, such as a mesh. Multiple references allow storing data only once per file. The format provides low-level data primitives as well as application-defined higher-level primitives via templates. The higher-level primitives include vectors, meshes, matrices, and colors.

File format architecture

The DirectX file format is context-free. Its template-driven architecture does not depend on any usage knowledge. The format is used in Direct3D retained mode to describe geometry data, frame hierarchies, and animations.

Reserved words

The following words are reserved for use by the DirectX format:

```
ARRAY
BYTE
CHAR
CSTRING
DOUBLE
DWORD
FLOAT
STRING
TEMPLATE
UCHAR
UNICODE
WORD
```

Header

The variable length header, which is compulsory, must be located at the beginning of the data stream. Table 14-1 lists the elements in the DirectX file header.

Table 14-1 **DirectX File Header**				
Type	*Sub Type*	*Size*	*Contents*	*Content Meaning*
Magic number (required)		4 bytes	xof	
Version number (required)	Major number Minor number	2 bytes 2 bytes	03 02	Major version 3 Minor version 2
Format Type (required)		4 bytes	txt bin com	Text File Binary File Compressed File Compression Type - required
if format is compressed		4 bytes	lzw zip etc...	
Float size (required)		4 bytes	0064 0032	64 bit floats 32 bit floats

For example, the header

```
xof 0302txt
```

corresponds to a file in text format. The code "xof" refers to the old extension for the .x format and, when found in the header, indicates an .x file. The digits 0302 correspond to the .x format version number, in this case 3.2. The digits 64 indicate that floating-point numbers are encoded in 64-bit. Because no compression code is listed, the file is not compressed.

The header

```
xof 0302bin 0032
```

corresponds to an .x file in binary format, version 3.2, in which floating-point numbers are encoded in 32-bits, uncompressed.

Comments

Comments, which are only applicable in text files, may occur anywhere in the data stream. A comment begins with either double slashes "//", or a hash character "#". The comment runs to the next new line.

```
# This is a comment.
// This is also a comment.
```

Templates

Templates are the basic element of the .x file format. A template contains no data but defines the type and order of the data objects in the file. A template is similar to a structure definition. The general template format is as follows:

```
template <template-name> {
<UUID>
<member 1>;
<member 2>;
...
<member n>;
[open/close/restricted]
[...]
}
```

The template name is a string that must not begin with a digit. The underscore character is allowed. UUID is the Windows universally unique identifier in OSF DCE format. The UUID is surrounded by angle brackets. The template members describe the data elements to which the template refers. The member format is as follows:

```
<data-type> <name>;
```

The primitive data types are listed in Table 14-2.

Table 14-2
Primitive Data Types for the .x file format

Type	Size
WORD	16 bits
DWORD	32 bits
FLOAT	IEEE float
DOUBLE	64 bits
CHAR	8 bits

Type	Size
UCHAR	8 bits
BYTE	8 bits
STRING	NULL terminated string
CSTRING	Formatted C-string (currently unsupported)
UNICODE	Unicode string (currently unsupported)

The template can contain any valid data type as an array. In this case the syntax is

```
array <data-type> <name>[<dimension-size>];
```

where `<dimension-size>` can be either an integer or a named reference to another template member whose value is then substituted. Arrays may be *n*-dimensional. In this case *n* is determined by the number of paired square brackets trailing the statement. For example:

```
array DWORD FixedArray[24];
array DWORD VariableArray[nElements];
array FLOAT Matrix8x8[8][8];
```

Templates may be open, closed, or restricted. These elements determine which data types may appear in the immediate hierarchy of a data object. An open template has no restrictions, a closed template rejects all data types, and a restricted template allows a named list of data types.

Data

The actual data of the .x file is contained in the data objects. Data objects are formatted as follows:

```
<Identifier> [name] {
<member 1>;
...
<member n>;
}
```

The `Identifier` element is compulsory and must match a previously defined data type or primitive. The `name` element is optional. The data members can be a data object, which can be nested, a data reference to a previous data object, an integer, float, or string list, in which the individual elements are separated by semicolons.

Retained mode templates

The following templates are used by Direct3D retained mode:

```
Template Name: Header
Template Name: Vector
Template Name: Coords2d
Template Name: Quaternion
Template Name: Matrix4x4
Template Name: ColorRGBA
Template Name: ColorRGB
Template Name: Indexed Color
Template Name: Boolean
Template Name: Boolean2d
Template Name: Material
Template Name: TextureFilename
Template Name: MeshFace
Template Name: MeshFaceWraps
Template Name: MeshTextureCoords
Template Name: MeshNormals
Template Name: MeshVertexColors
Template Name: MeshMaterialList
Template Name: Mesh
Template Name: FrameTransformMatrix
Template Name: Frame
Template Name: FloatKeys
Template Name: TimedFloatKeys
Template Name: AnimationKey
Template Name: AnimationOptions
Template Name: Animation
Template Name: AnimationSet
```

Summary

Although retained mode programming is the high-level interface to Direct3D, this does not mean that it is easy or intuitive. In this chapter you have encountered many of the core topics of Direct3D and of retained mode. Some of these elements are related only by the fact that they are necessary to understanding retained mode programming. At this point a reader could feel overwhelmed by the number of topics covered and by the complexity of some of them. Fortunately, not every direct mode program must use all the functionalities for modeling and rendering that are available. In the following chapter we begin programming in retained mode, at first using only a small subset of the system's functions.

✦   ✦   ✦

Fundamentals of Retained Mode Programming

We introduce retained mode by developing a very simple, windowed mode application. In order to make clear the fundamentals of retained mode programming we stripped off everything that is not essential. The result is that the processing described at this stage has minimal functionality: all we do in the code is render a static image from a file in DirectX format. The code executes by performing four clearly distinct steps:

1. Initializing the software interface. That is, creating the Direct3D and DirectDraw components that are necessary to the program.

2. Creating the objects. This implies creating the frames, meshes, lights, materials, and other objects that serve as parts of the scene.

3. Building the scene from the individual component objects.

4. Rendering the scene. In this step the viewport is cleared and the frame is rendered.

Each of these steps is explained in detail and packaged in its own function. All of the coding comes together in the sample project 3DRM InWin Demo1, which is furnished in the book's CD-ROM. We also include in this chapter a coding template for windowed retained mode programming.

Initializing the Software Interface

Direct3D, as does its parent DirectX, uses the Component Object Model (COM) interface specification defined by Microsoft. COM is a standard for a component-based architecture that aims at being language-independent, reusable, upgradable, and transparent to application code. Whether you like or dislike COM, in Direct3D programming you have no other option than to use it.

IUnknown

COM interfaces are derived from a general interface called IUnknown. All other COM interfaces inherit from IUnknown, therefore IUnknown methods are always polymorphically visible to COM client code. This means that any object instantiated as a COM object has access to the methods of IUnknown. There are three relevant methods in IUnknown:

✦ The QueryInterface() method interrogates the object about the features it supports. If the call is successful, it returns a pointer to the interface.

✦ AddRef() increments the object's reference count by 1 when an interface or another application binds itself to the object. Application code rarely uses this function.

✦ Release() decrements the object's reference count by 1. When the count reaches 0, the object is deallocated.

The reference count is a memory management technique that enables components to self-destroy. It is based on keeping a tally of the number of interfaces allocated to a COM object. Each time an interface is allocated, the reference count is incremented. When client code is finished using an interface it decrements the reference count by calling the Release() method. If at any time the reference count goes to zero, the interface object deletes itself. The AddRef() method is normally called by the function, whereas the Release() method is called by your code. When QueryInterface() successfully returns a pointer to an interface, it implicitly calls AddRef() to increment the reference count. This means that your application must call the Release() method before destroying the pointer to the interface.

Direct3DRMObject

We must first clarify that the use of the word *object* in the context of Direct3D is not related directly to object orientation. When you hear the word *object* in the context of Direct3D you should not interpret it as an instance of a class, but in its generic and more conventional sense. Textures, cameras, viewports, meshes, and many other elements of Direct3D are loosely referred to as objects. The common superclass of all these objects is the Direct3DRMObject. Direct3DRMObject is instantiated as a COM object and can, therefore, access the methods of the IUnknown interface.

Before an application can create the `Direct3DRMObject`, it must first instantiate a Direct3D retained mode object. This is achieved by calling `Direct3DRMCreate()`. The function's general form is as follows:

```
HRESULT Direct3DRMCreate(
        LPIRECT3DRM FAR * lplpD3DRM    // Address of interface
        );
```

The function returns `D3DRM_OK` if it succeeds. In this case the pointer is valid and can be used to access the interface. Any other return value indicates that the function failed and that the pointer is invalid.

QueryInterface()

The pointer returned by `Direct3DRMCreate()` is also a COM object and can therefore access the `IUnknown` methods. Of these methods, `QueryInterface()` is the one usually called first because it provides information on whether a particular COM interface is supported or not. The function's general form is as follows:

```
HRESULT QueryInterface(
                    REFIID riid,    // 1
                    LPVOID* obp      // 2
                    );
```

The first parameter is the reference to the unique identifier for the particular interface. It is sometimes called the *interface identifier*, or IID. In DirectX programming this parameter is passed to the call as a predefined constant. For example, in the DD Info Demo program developed in Chapter 8 we used cascaded calls to `QueryInterface()` using different IIDs in order to determine the most recent version of DirectDraw supported by the system. Code is as follows:

```
DDConnect = DirectDrawCreate ( NULL,
            &lpDD0,
            NULL);

// Store pointer and continue if call succeeded
if(DDConnect == DD_OK) {
    DDLevel = 1;        // Store level
    lpDD = lpDD0;       // copy pointer
// Query the interface to determine most recent version
    DDConnect = lpDD0->QueryInterface(
                                    IID_IDirectDraw2,
                                    LPVOID *) &lpDD2);
}
if(DDConnect == S_OK){
    DDLevel = 2;            // Update level
    lpDD0->Release();       // Release old pointer
    lpDD = lpDD2;
    DDConnect = lpDD->QueryInterface(
                                    IID_IDirectDraw4,
                                    (LPVOID *) &lpDD4);
```

```
    }
    if(DDConnect == S_OK){
        DDLevel = 4;                // Update level
        lpDD2->Release();           // Release old pointer
        lpDD = lpDD4;
    }
```

Notice that in the preceding code the call to QueryInterface() is first made with the identifier IID_IDirectDraw2, and then with IID_IDirectDraw4, to determine if either of these newer versions of DirectDraw is available. In this case the call returns S_OK if it succeeds. If it fails, QueryInterface() returns E_NOINTERFACE or one of the following interface-specific error values listed in Table 15-1.

Table 15-1	
Interface-Specific Error Values Returned by QueryInterface()	
DirectX Interface	*Returns (Comment)*
DirectDraw	DDERR_INVALIDOBJECT DDERR_INVALIDPARAMS DDERR_OUTOFMEMORY (IDirectDrawSurface2 only)
DirectSound	DSERR_GENERIC (IDirectSound and IDirectSoundBuffer only) DSERR_INVALIDPARAM
DirectPlay	DPERR_INVALIDOBJECT DPERR_INVALIDPARAMS
Direct3DRetainedMode	D3DRM_OK (No error) D3DRMERR_BADALLOC (Out of memory) D3DRMERR_BADDEVICE (Device not compatible) D3DRMERR_BADFILE D3DRMERR_BADMAJORVERSION D3DRMERR_BADMINORVERSION D3DRMERR_BADOBJECT D3DRMERR_BADTYPE D3DRMERR_BADVALUE D3DRMERR_FACEUSED (Face already used in a mesh) D3DRMERR_FILENOTFOUND D3DRMERR_NOTFOUND (Object not found) D3DRMERR_UNABLETOEXECUTE

When the application is finished using the interface retrieved by a call to this method, it must call the Release() method for that interface to free it.

The COM interface provides two macros, named SUCCEEDED and FAILED, which are defined as follows:

```
#define SUCCEEDED(Status) ((HRESULT)(Status) >= 0)
#define FAILED(Status) ((HRESULT)(Status)<0)
```

These macros are a convenient way to check for the success or failure of any COM function without having to deal with the specific error codes. We frequently use these macros in our code samples.

In Direct3D retained mode programs the call to QueryInterface() uses the IID_IDirect3DRM identifier. The call requires a Direct3DRM object. Code usually releases the object after the interface has been validated because there is no further use for it. The following code fragment is from a function listed later in this chapter.

```
// Create the Direct3DRM object.
LPDIRECT3DRM      pD3DRMTemp;
HRETURN            retval;
...
retval = Direct3DRMCreate(&pD3DRMTemp);
if (retval != D3DRM_OK)
{
    // Display error message here
    return FALSE;
}
retval = pD3DRMTemp->QueryInterface(IID_IDirect3DRM3,
                        (void **)&lpD3DRM)))
if(retval != D3DRM_OK)
{
    pD3DRMTemp->Release();
    // Display error message here
    return FALSE;
}
// Release the object
pD3DRMTemp->Release();
```

Creating the DirectDraw clipper

We mentioned that Direct3D is closely related to DirectDraw and uses much of its functionality. At this point we are interested in creating a DirectDraw clipper object that will determine which portion of the 3D scene is visible on the viewport. In a windowed mode application all you need to do is create a DirectDraw clipper object and then assign to it your application window as the clipping plane.

The DirectDraw clipper that you need for Direct3D must not be owned by a DirectDraw object. The DirectDraw API provides a function named Direct DrawCreateClipper() for this purpose. The resulting objects are known as *driver-independent* DirectDrawClipper objects. Notice that the function

`DirectDrawCreateClipper()` is not equivalent to `IDirectDraw::Create` `Clipper`, which creates a clipper owned by a specific DirectDraw object. The function's general form is as follows:

```
HRESULT DirectDrawCreateClipper(
            DWORD dwFlags,                          // 1
            LPDIRECTDRAWCLIPPER FAR *lplpDDClipper, // 2
            IUnknown FAR *pUnkOuter                 // 3
            );
```

The first parameter is currently not implemented and must be set to zero. The second parameter is the address of a pointer to be filled in with the address of the new `DirectDrawClipper` object. The third parameter is provided for future COM features but at the present time must be set to NULL. The function returns `DD_OK` if successful, or one of the following error codes if a failure results:

```
DDERR_INVALIDPARAMS
```

```
DDERR_OUTOFMEMORY
```

The object created by this function is not released automatically when an application's objects are released. They should be explicitly released by application code, although DirectDraw documentation states that they will be released automatically when the application terminates.

Defining the clip list

Clipping and clip lists were discussed in Chapter 7. In the context of Direct3D windowed applications a clip list is a series of rectangles that delimit the visible areas of the surface. You have seen that a `DirectDrawClipper` object can be attached to any surface and that a window handle can be attached to a `DirectDrawClipper` object. In this case DirectDraw updates the `DirectDrawClipper` clip list using the application window as a clipping plane. As the window changes, the clip list is updated.

The call to `DirectDrawCreateClipper()` creates the clipper but does not define the clip list. To do this, the application must use the pointer returned by `DirectDrawCreateClipper()` to call `SetHWnd()`. The function's general form is as follows:

```
HRESULT SetHWnd(
            DWORD dwFlags,            // 1
            HWND hWnd                 // 2
            );
```

The first parameter is currently not used and should be set to 0. The second parameter is the handle to the window that will be used as a clipping place. The call returns DD_OK if successful, or one of the following error codes:

```
DDERR_INVALIDCLIPLIST
DDERR_INVALIDOBJECT
DDERR_INVALIDPARAMS
DDERR_OUTOFMEMORY
```

The following code fragment creates a driver-independent DirectDrawClipper object and then attaches to it the current window as a clipping plane.

```
HRESULT          retval;
HWND             hwnd;
. . .
// Create a DirectDrawClipper object
    retval = DirectDrawCreateClipper(0, &lpDDClipper, NULL);
    if (retval != DD_OK)
    {
        // Display error message here
        return FALSE;
    }
    // Attach the program Window as a clipper
    retval = lpDDClipper->SetHWnd(0, hwnd);
    if (retval != DD_OK)
    {
        // Display error message here
        return FALSE;
    }
```

InitD3D() function

The function InitD3D() in the 3DRM InWin Demo1 project, included in the book's CD-ROM, performs the processing operations described in this section. A slightly modified version of this function is included in the retained mode windowed coding template described later in this chapter. Following is a listing of this function.

```
//*********************************************************
// Name: InitD3D()
// Description: Initialize Direct3D interface
//*********************************************************
BOOL InitD3D(HWND hwnd)
{
    HRESULT retval; // Return value
```

```
    // Initialize the entire global variable structure to zero.
    memset(&globVars, 0, sizeof(globVars));

    // Create the Direct3DRM object.
    LPDIRECT3DRM pD3DRMTemp;
    retval = Direct3DRMCreate(&pD3DRMTemp);
    if (FAILED(retval))
    {
        D3DError("Failed to create Direct3DRM.");
        return FALSE;
    }
    if( FAILED( pD3DRMTemp->QueryInterface(IID_IDirect3DRM3,
                        (void **)&lpD3DRM) ) )
    {
        pD3DRMTemp->Release();
        D3DError("Direct3DRM3 interface not found" );
        return FALSE;
    }
    pD3DRMTemp->Release();

    // Create DirectDrawClipper object
    retval = DirectDrawCreateClipper(0, &lpDDClipper, NULL);
    if (FAILED(retval))
    {
        D3DError("Failed to create DirectDrawClipper object");
        return FALSE;
    }
    // Attach the program Window as a clipper
    retval = lpDDClipper->SetHWnd(0, hwnd);
    if (FAILED(retval))
    {
        D3DError("Failed to set the window handle");
        return FALSE;
    }
    return TRUE;
}
```

Building the Objects

At this point in the code, the Direct3D retained mode windowed application performed the necessary initializations and is ready to start building the scene. To do this, code must first create the objects that are used in the scene. Before we tackle the details of object building, a few housekeeping chores need to be discussed.

Preliminary considerations

To create the objects, and later, the scene itself, you need the pointer to the Direct3D object, returned in the second parameter to the QueryInterface() call discussed previously. In the code used in this chapter the pointer is publicly defined as follows:

```
LPDIRECT3DRM3    lpD3DRM = NULL;
```

By giving the pointer public visibility you are able to use it from several functions without having to pass it as a parameter in each call.

In addition to the basic Direct3D retained mode pointer (lpD3DRM) just mentioned, you also need pointers to the specific objects and devices. For example, to load a file in DirectX format into the scene you need to create a meshbuilder object using the CreateMeshBuilder() function that is available in the IDirect3DRM interface. The pointer of type LPDIRECT3DRM (stored in the named variable lpD3DRM in these examples) provides access to the interface services in IDirect3DRM. The CreateMeshBuilder() function takes as a parameter a variable of the type LPDIRECT3DMESHBUILDER3. The returned pointer is then used to access the Load() method. Other Direct3D objects, such as devices, scenes, cameras, lights, frames, materials, and meshes also require pointers to their specific interfaces. In the code samples that follow we require the following subset of interface-specific pointers:

```
LPDIRECT3DRMDEVICE3

LPDIRECT3DRMFRAME3

LPDIRECT3DRMMESHBUILDER3

LPDIRECT3DRMLIGHT

LPDIRECT3DRMMATERIAL2
```

Sometimes the same pointer type is used for referencing different types of objects. For example, the type LPDIRECT3DRMFRAME3 is used to access a scene, a camera, a light, and a child frame.

Whether to make this pointer globally visible or not is mostly a matter of programming style. The most common guideline is that if the pointer is required in several functions then it should be public. The problem with this rule is that at the time you are developing code it is often difficult to predict if a pointer will be required in other functions. Our excuse for abusing public variables in the code samples presented in this book is that, today, wasting a few bytes of memory at run time is not as important an issue as it was in the memory-starved systems of a few years ago.

Direct3D retained mode applications frequently manipulate several objects, such as frames, scenes, cameras, lights, and textures. In this case it is useful to create one or more structures that define the individual pointers and variables and then instantiate structure variables as required for different objects used in the code. An additional benefit of using structures is that all the variables in the structure can be cleared simultaneously by means of the memset buffer manipulation routine. The following global structure and variables are used in the sample code listed in this chapter and in the 3DRM InWin Demo1 program included in the book's CD-ROM.

```
// Global variables
struct _globVars
{
    LPDIRECT3DRMDEVICE3   aDevice;     // Retained mode device
    LPDIRECT3DRMVIEWPORT2 aViewport;   // Direct3DRM viewport
    LPDIRECT3DRMFRAME3    aScene;      // Master frame
    LPDIRECT3DRMFRAME3    aCamera;     // Camera frame
    BOOL                  isInitialized; // All D3DRM objects
                                       // have been
                                       // been initialized.

} globVars;

LPDIRECT3DRM3 lpD3DRM = NULL;          // Direct3DRM object
manager
LPDIRECTDRAWCLIPPER lpDDClipper = NULL;
                                       // DirectDrawClipper
object
HWND                hWnd;
char                szXfile[] = "teapot.x" ;  // File to load
```

Notice that the template _globVars includes a Boolean variable that keeps track of the application's initialization state, named isInitialized.

In addition to global variables Direct3D applications often require local ones, typically located inside the functions that perform object creation and scene building. As you will see later in this chapter, the variables used in creating objects and building a scene can have local lifetime, as long as the resulting master frame and its component object are global. In our code the master frame is stored in the global structure variable globVars.aScene, listed previously.

Creating the objects

The following objects are needed to create a simple, Direct3D scene:

✦ A device

✦ A master scene frame

✦ A camera frame

✦ A viewport

The functions used in creating these objects commonly use the word "create" in their names; for example, CreateDeviceFromClipper(), CreateFrame(), and CreateViewport. After the objects are created they can be assembled into a master scene. A global variable, in this case the structure variable isInitialized, is used to record the fact that the master scene has been built.

The term *device* in the context of Direct3D retained mode is equivalent to a *display device*. It can be visualized as the video memory area to which the scene is rendered. In practice, a Direct3D device is always a DirectDraw surface. The viewport is a rectangular area within the device. You should also note that neither the device nor the viewport are equivalent to the video buffer, which is the area directly mapped to the display surface and shown on the screen.

In Direct3D the size of a device is defined when it is created and cannot be changed. To change the size of the device you must destroy the old device and create a new one with different dimensions. In Direct3D you can create a device from Direct3D objects, from a surface, or from a DirectDraw clipper. For the moment we will be concerned with this last method.

Because the size of the device must be defined at the time it is created, code needs to obtain the width and height of the client area. You can use the GetClientRect() function for this purpose. When the call returns, the *bottom* member of the RECT structure variable contains the height of the client area and the *right* member contains the width.

The CreateDeviceFromClipper() function of IDirect3DRM2 interface enables you to create a device from a DirectDraw clipper object. Previously in this chapter you called DirectDrawCreateClipper() and stored the resulting pointer in the variable lpDDClipper. This variable is now needed to create the device. CreateDeviceFromClipper() has the following general form:

```
HRESULT CreateDeviceFromClipper(
        LPDIRECTDRAWCLIPPER lpDDClipper,        // 1
        LPGUID lpGUID,                          // 2
        int width,                              // 3
        int height,                             // 4
        LPDIRECT3DRMDEVICE * lplpD3DRMDevice    // 5
        );
```

The first parameter is the address of the DirectDrawClipper object mentioned in the preceding paragraph. The second parameter is a globally unique identifier (GUID). Normally, this parameter is set to NULL. This forces the system to search for a device with a default set of capabilities. This is the recommended way to create a device in retained mode programming because the method always works, even if the user installs new hardware. Parameters 3 and 4 refer to the width and height of the device and usually correspond with the values obtained by the call to GetClientRect(). If the call succeeds, the fifth parameter will be filled with the address of a pointer to an IDirect3DRMDevice interface.

The call returns D3DRM_OK if successful, or an error otherwise.

The following code fragment shows creating a device using the
CreateDeviceFromClipper() function

```
HWND      hwnd;            // Handle to the window
HRESULT   retval;          // Return value
RECT      rc;              // Storage for viewport dimensions
. . .

// Obtain size of client area
GetClientRect(hwnd, &rc);

retval = lpD3DRM->CreateDeviceFromClipper(lpDDClipper,
                      NULL,            // Default device
                      rc.right,
                      rc.bottom,
                      &globVars.aDevice);
if (FAILED(retval))
{
    // Display error message here
    return FALSE;
}
```

CreateObjects() function

The function CreateObjects() in the 3DRM InWin Demo1 program in the book's
CD-ROM performs the processing operations discussed in this section. Following is
a code listing of this function.

```
//***********************************************************
// Name: CreateObjects()
// Description: Create the device and the scene objects
//***********************************************************
BOOL CreateObjects( HWND hwnd )
{
    // Local variables
    HRESULT retval;  // Return value
    RECT rc;         // Bounding rectangle for main window
    int width;       // Device's width
    int height;      // Device's height

    // Get client area dimensions
    GetClientRect(hwnd, &rc);
    // Create device from DirectDraw clipper
    retval = lpD3DRM->CreateDeviceFromClipper(lpDDClipper,
                      NULL, // Default aDevice
```

```
                            rc.right, rc.bottom,
                            &globVars.aDevice);
if (FAILED(retval))
{
    D3DError("Failed to create the D3DRM device");
    return FALSE;
}

// Create the master scene
retval = lpD3DRM->CreateFrame(NULL, &globVars.aScene);
if (FAILED(retval))
{
    D3DError("Failed to create the master scene frame");
    return FALSE;
}
// Create the camera frame
retval = lpD3DRM->CreateFrame(globVars.aScene,
                                &globVars.aCamera);
if (FAILED(retval))
{
    D3DError("Failed to create the camera frame");
    return FALSE;
}

// Create the Direct3DRM viewport using the device, the
// camera frame, and the device's width and height.
width = globVars.aDevice->GetWidth();
height = globVars.aDevice->GetHeight();

retval = lpD3DRM->CreateViewport(globVars.aDevice,
                                globVars.aCamera, 0, 0,
                                width, height,
                                &globVars.aViewport);
if (FAILED(retval))
{
    globVars.isInitialized = FALSE;
    globVars.aDevice->Release();
    return FALSE;
}
// Create the scene
if (!BuildScene(globVars.aDevice, globVars.aScene,
                globVars.aCamera))
    return FALSE;

// Record that global variables are initialized
globVars.isInitialized = TRUE;
return TRUE;
}
```

Creating the Master Scene

In Direct3D literature the notions of a scene and that of a frame sometimes overlap. A frame may have a parent frame from which it inherits all its attributes, even dynamic ones. For example, if a parent frame is rotating at a given rate, the resulting child frame rotates identically. A scene, on the other hand, is described as a frame with no parent. Some confusion results from the fact that you can create a scene (a frame with no parent) and later on associate it with a parent frame, at which time is ceases to be a scene and becomes a child frame. The CreateFrame() function of the IDirect3DRM2 interface is used for creating both frames and scenes. The function's general form is as follows:

```
HRESULT CreateFrame(
                  LPDIRECT3DRMFRAME lpD3DRMFrame,    // 1
                  LPDIRECT3DRMFRAME* lplpD3DRMFrame  // 2
                  );
```

The first parameter is the address of the frame that serves as a parent. If this parameter is NULL, then a scene is created. The second parameter is the variable that will be filled with a pointer to an IDirect3DRMFrame interface if the call succeeds.

The method returns D3DRM_OK if successful, or an error otherwise.

As previously discussed, we usually store the master scene in a global variable to make it visible throughout the code. The following code fragment shows the creation of a master scene.

```
// Create the master scene
retval = lpD3DRM->CreateFrame(NULL, &globVars.aScene);
if (FAILED(retval))
{
     // Display error message here
     return FALSE;
}
```

Notice that using NULL for the first parameter in the call to CreateFrame() ensures that the results are a scene; in other words, a frame with no parent.

Creating the scene's camera frame

In Direct3D retained mode the camera is implemented as a frame object. The camera frame determines the viewing position and direction because the viewport renders only what is visible along the positive z-axis of the camera frame. In addition, the camera frame determines which scene is rendered. Later in this chapter you will set the camera's position. For now, you need to create the camera frame, which you do by means of the same CreateFrame() function that was used in creating the master scene in the previous section. The one difference is that the camera frame is a child frame of the master scene. Therefore, in this case, the first parameter passed to CreateFrame() refers to the master scene, and the second one to the camera frame. The following code fragment shows the processing.

```
// Create the camera frame
retval = 1pD3DRM->CreateFrame(globVars.aScene,
                              &globVars.aCamera);
if (FAILED(retval))
{
    // Display error message here
    return FALSE;
}
```

Creating the scene's viewport

The viewport defines the rectangular area into which the scene is rendered. In this sense the viewport can be described as a 2D construct that is used in rendering 3D objects. Here again you should keep in mind that the viewport is not the video buffer, and that rendering to the viewport does not display the image.

We have seen that the viewport uses the camera frame object to define which scene is rendered as well as the viewing position and direction. A viewport is defined in terms of its viewing frustum, as explained in Chapter 14. The viewport is created by calling the CreateViewport() function of the IDirect3DRM interface. The function's general form is as follows.

```
HRESULT CreateViewport(
        LPDIRECT3DRMDEVICE 1pDev,                // 1
        LPDIRECT3DRMFRAME 1pCamera,              // 2
        DWORD dwXPos,                            // 3
        DWORD dwYPos,                            // 4
        DWORD dwWidth,                           // 5
        DWORD dwHeight,                          // 6
        LPDIRECT3DRMVIEWPORT* 1p1pD3DRMViewport  // 7
        );
```

The first parameter is the device on which the viewport will be created. The second parameter is the camera frame that defines the position and direction of the viewport. Parameters 3 and 4 refer to the position of the viewport and parameters 5 and 6 to its dimension. All of these are expressed in device coordinates.

If the call succeeds, parameter 7 is the variable that will be filled with a pointer to an IDirect3DRMViewport interface. The call returns D3DRM_OK if successful, or an error otherwise.

The position of the viewport relative to the device frame is specific to the application's design and the proposed rendering operations. However, the size of the viewport must not be greater than that of the physical device, otherwise the call to CreateViewport() fails. To make sure that the viewport is not larger than the physical device you can use the GetWidth() and GetHeight() functions, of IDirect3DRMDevice, to obtain the necessary dimensions. Note that the IDirect3DRMViewport interface also has GetWidth() and GetHeight() methods that retrieve the size of the viewport. At this time because the viewport has not yet been created you must use the functions of IDirect3DRMDevice. The following code fragment shows obtaining the device size and then creating the viewport.

```
int         width;          // Storage for device size
int         height;
. . .
// Obtain device size and store in local variables
width = globVars.aDevice->GetWidth();
height = globVars.aDevice->GetHeight();
// Create the viewport
retval = lpD3DRM->CreateViewport(globVars.aDevice,
                                 globVars.aCamera,
                                 0, 0,
                                 width, height,
                                 &globVars.aViewport);

if (FAILED(retval))
{
    // Display error message here
    globVars.isInitialized = FALSE;
    globVars.aDevice->Release();
    return FALSE;
}
```

Building the Master Scene

After all the global objects are built (in this case the device, the scene, the camera, and the viewport) you can proceed to build the master scene. In this example you assume that the mesh object is stored in a file in DirectX format, and that it is located in the same directory as the executable code. In the case that you are following, these steps are required:

1. Creating a meshbuilder object and using it to load the mesh file

2. Creating a child frame within the scene and adding the loaded mesh into the child frame

3. Setting the camera position

4. Creating the light frame

5. Creating the lights used in illuminating the scene and attaching them to frames

6. Creating a material and setting it in the mesh

7. Setting the mesh color

8. Releasing all local variables used in building the scene

In regards to this last step you must consider that in the process of building the master scene you create and use a host of Direct3D retained mode objects, such as meshes, cameras, lights, textures, and materials. After the scene is created, the individual objects that were used in building it are no longer needed because they have become part of the scene itself. For this reason, it is usually possible to limit the lifetime of these objects to the process of scene creation. This means that the pointers and variables required for creating the objects can have local scope and visibility. It also means that the individual objects can and should be released after they are incorporated into the scene.

Creating and using the meshbuilder object

As its name implies, the meshbuilder component is a tool for building meshes. The meshbuilder itself cannot be rendered. In this chapter we use the meshbuilder object to load a mesh previously stored in a file in DirectX format. You can use the meshbuilder functions to assemble 3D images manually. However, by far the most common way of creating images is by using a 3D image editor program, such as 3D Studio Max.

The first step is to create the meshbuilder object by means of the CreateMeshBuilder() function that is part of IDirect3DRM interface. The function has the following general form:

```
HRESULT CreateMeshBuilder(
        LPDIRECT3DRMMESHBUILDER* lplpD3DRMMeshBuilder  // 1
        );
```

The call's only parameter is the address of a pointer that is filled with the IDirect3DRMMeshBuilder interface if the call is successful. The function returns D3DRM_OK if it succeeds, or an error otherwise.

In the example that you are currently following you use the meshbuilder object's Load() function to load a file in DirectX format. The file is loaded into the meshbuilder itself and takes the form of a mesh. Later in the code this mesh is stored in a frame. The Load() function has the following general form:

```
HRESULT Load(
        LPVOID lpvObjSource,                              // 1
        LPVOID lpvObjID,                                  // 2
        D3DRMLOADOPTIONS d3drmLOFlags,                    // 3
        D3DRMLOADTEXTURECALLBACK d3drmLoadTextureProc,    // 4
        LPVOID lpvArg                                     // 5
        );
```

The first parameter is the source to be loaded. It can be a file, a resource, a memory block, or a stream, depending on the source flags specified in the third parameter.

The second parameter is the object name or position. This parameter depends on the identifier flags specified in the third parameter. If the D3DRMLOAD_BYPOSITION flag is specified, the second parameter is a pointer to a DWORD value that gives the object's order in the file. This parameter can be NULL. The third parameter is a flag of type D3DRMLOADOPTIONS describing the load options. Table 15-2 lists these flags.

Table 15-2
Flags in the D3DRMLOADOPTIONS Type

Flag	Description
Flags modifying the first parameter (lpvObjSource):	
D3DRMLOAD_FROMFILE	The lpvObjSource parameter is interpreted as a string representing a local filename.
D3DRMLOAD_FROMRESOURCE	The lpvObjSource parameter is interpreted as a pointer to a D3DRMLOADRESOURCE structure.
D3DRMLOAD_FROMMEMORY	The lpvObjSource parameter is interpreted as a pointer to a D3DRMLOADMEMORY structure.
D3DRMLOAD_FROMURL	The lpvObjSource parameter is interpreted as a URL.
Flags modifying the second parameter (lpvObjID):	
D3DRMLOAD_BYNAME	The lpvObjID parameter is interpreted as a string.
D3DRMLOAD_BYGUID	The lpvObjID parameter is interpreted as a GUID.
Other flags:	
D3DRMLOAD_FIRST	The first progressive mesh found is loaded. This is the default mode.

The fourth parameter to the Load() function is used when loading textures that require special formatting. In this case the specified callback function is called. This parameter can be NULL. The fifth parameter is the address of a data structure passed to the callback function in the fourth parameter. The function returns D3DRM_OK if successful, or an error otherwise.

The following code fragment shows the creation of a meshbuilder object and its use in loading a file in DirectX format.

```
char                   szXfile[] = "teapot.x" ; // DirectX
file
LPDIRECT3DRMMESHBUILDER3 meshbuilder = NULL;
HRESULT                retval;
. . .
```

```
// Create the meshbuilder object
retval = lpD3DRM->CreateMeshBuilder(&meshbuilder);
    if (FAILED(retval))
        // Meshbuilder creation error handler goes here
    . . .
// Use meshbuilder to load a mesh from a DirectX file
retval = meshbuilder->Load(szXfile,
                            NULL,
                            D3DRMLOAD_FROMFILE,
                            NULL,
                            NULL);
if (FAILED(retval))
{
    // Load error handler goes here
. . .
```

After this code executes, the file named teapot.x is converted into a mesh that becomes the meshbuilder object itself.

Add mesh to frame

Currently your mesh is stored in a meshbuilder object, which cannot be rendered. The next step consists of creating a frame and loading the mesh into this frame. You previously used CreateFrame(). Now you use this same method to create a child frame. The coding is as follows:

```
LPDIRECT3DRMFRAME3            childframe = NULL;
. . .
// Create a child frame within the scene
retval = lpD3DRM->CreateFrame(aScene, &childframe);
if(FAILED(retval))
        // Error in creating frame handler goes here
. . .
```

In Direct3D a visual object, or simply a visual, is one that is displayed when the frame is in view. Meshes, textures, and even frames can be visuals, although the most common visual is the mesh. When a texture object is labeled as a visual it becomes a decal. In this example we use the AddVisual() function, of the IDirect3DRMFrame interface, to add the mesh to the child frame as a visual. AddVisual() has the following general form:

```
HRESULT AddVisual(
            LPDIRECT3DRMVISUAL lpD3DRMVisual      // 1
            );
```

The function's only parameter is the address of a variable that represents the Direct3DRMVisual object to be added to the frame.

The call returns D3DRM_OK if successful, or an error otherwise. The following code fragment shows adding the mesh to the child frame.

```
// Add mesh into the child frame as a visual
retval = childframe->AddVisual(

(LPDIRECT3DRMVISUAL)meshbuilder);
if(FAILED(retval))
{
    // Failed AddVisual() error handler goes here
}
```

Notice that we used the pointer returned by the CreateFrame() call, which in this case is the variable childframe, of type LPDIRECT3DRMFRAME3, to access the AddVisual() function. The meshbuilder object is passed as a parameter and the result is that the mesh is added to the frame, and therefore to the scene.

Setting the camera position

Previously in this chapter you created the camera as a global object. The camera object was stored in the variable named aCamera, of type LPDIRECT3DRMFRAME3, which is a member of the globVars structure. The camera object was created with the following statement:

```
// Create the camera frame
retval = lpD3DRM->CreateFrame(globVars.aScene,
                              &globVars.aCamera);
```

You have seen that the camera frame determines which scene is rendered and the viewing position and direction. In Direct3D the viewport renders only what is visible along the positive z-axis of the camera frame, with the up direction being in the direction of the positive y-axis.

When a child frame is created, it is positioned at the origin of the parent frame, that is, at coordinates (0,0,0). Applications can call the SetPosition() function of the IDirect3DRMFrame interface to set the position of a frame relative to a reference point in the parent frame. To position the camera in its parent frame (the scene), you call SetPosition() using the variable aCamera as an interface reference. The general form of the SetPosition() function is as follows:

```
HRESULT SetPosition(
            LPDIRECT3DRMFRAME lpRef,      // 1
            D3DVALUE rvX,                 // 2
            D3DVALUE rvY,                 // 3
            D3DVALUE rvZ                  // 4
            );
```

The first parameter is the address of the parent frame that is used as a reference. The second, third, and fourth parameters are the x, y, and z coordinates of the new position for the child frame. The call returns D3DRM_OK if successful, or an error otherwise.

The camera position determines what, if anything, is visible when the scene is rendered. For example, changing the position of the camera along the z-axis makes the objects in the scene appear larger or smaller (see Figure 15-1). The default position of the camera frame at the scene origin may be so close to the viewing frustum that a small portion of the object is visible. The following code fragment shows positioning of the camera frame so that it is located -7 units along the z-axis.

```
retval = aCamera->SetPosition(aScene,
                              D3DVAL(0),        // x
                              D3DVAL(0),        // y
                              -D3DVAL(7)        // z
                              );
if (FAILED(retval))
{
      // Camera position error handler goes here
}
```

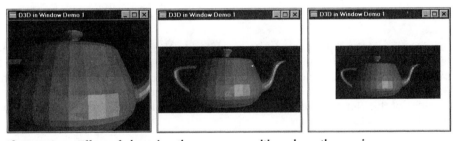

Figure 15-1: Effect of changing the camera position along the z-axis

Creating and positioning the light frame

There is no default lighting in Direct3D retained mode. The objects in a scene without lights are invisible. To illuminate the scene, code must create the light frame and position it in relation to the parent frame. After this is done, one or more lights can be added to the light frame and the scene illuminated. This means that you will be dealing with two different types of objects: the light frame object, which is of type LPDIRECT3DRMFRAME3, and one or more lights, which are of type LPDIRECT3DRMLIGHT.

You start by creating the light frame that is attached to the scene as a parent frame. Here again you use the `CreateFrame()` function, which is part of the `IDirect3DRM3` interface. The following code fragment shows the processing.

```
LPDIRECT3DRMFRAME3 lights = NULL;
. . .
// Create a light frame as a child of the scene frame
retval = lpD3DRM->CreateFrame(aScene, &lights);
if(FAILED(retval))
{
     // Light frame creation error handler goes here
}
```

To set the position of the light frame you use the `SetPosition()` function of `IDirect3DRMFrame` interface, as in the following code fragment.

```
// Position the light frame within the scene
retval = lights->SetPosition(aScene,
                        D3DVAL(5),          // x
                        D3DVAL(0),          // y
                        -D3DVAL(7));        // z
if(FAILED(retval))
{
     // Light frame positioning error handler goes here
}
```

The position of the light frame is often related to the position of the camera frame. Because our camera frame was located at coordinates (0,0,-7), we position the light frame at the same *y* and *z* coordinates as the camera, but at a greater *x* coordinate. The result is that the light or lights placed in this frame will appear to come from the right of the camera and at the same vertical level (*y* coordinate) and distance from the object (*z* coordinate).

Creating and setting the lights

Now that you have a light frame, you are able to create one or more lights. There are two methods in the IDirect3DRM interface that enable you to create lights: `CreateLight()` and `CreateLightRGB()`. `CreateLight()` requires that you specify the light color by referring to a structure of type `D3DCOLOR`, which is obtained by calling the macros `D3DRGB` or `D3DRGBA`. `CreateLightRGB()` allows defining the light color directly. Because it is easier to code, we will use `CreateLightRGB()` in the examples in this chapter. The function's general form is as follows:

```
HRESULT CreateLightRGB(
            D3DRMLIGHTTYPE ltLightType,        // 1
            D3DVALUE vRed,                     // 2
            D3DVALUE vGreen,                   // 3
            D3DVALUE vBlue,                    // 4
            LPDIRECT3DRMLIGHT* lplpD3DRMLight  // 5
            );
```

The first parameter is one of the lighting types defined in the D3DRMLIGHTYPE enumerated type. Table 15-3 lists the constants that enumerate the different light types.

<table>
<tr><td colspan="2" align="center">Table 15-3
Enumerator Constants in D3DRMLIGHTTYPE</td></tr>
<tr><td>**Constant**</td><td>**Description**</td></tr>
<tr><td>D3DRMLIGHT_AMBIENT</td><td>Light is an ambient source</td></tr>
<tr><td>D3DRMLIGHT_POINT</td><td>Light is a point source</td></tr>
<tr><td>D3DRMLIGHT_SPOT</td><td>Light is a spotlight source</td></tr>
<tr><td>D3DRMLIGHT_DIRECTIONAL</td><td>Light is a directional source</td></tr>
<tr><td>D3DRMLIGHT_PARALLELPOINT</td><td>Light is a parallel point source</td></tr>
</table>

The second, third, and fourth parameters are the RGB color values for the light. They are expressed in a D3DVALUE type, which is Direct3D's designation for a float data type. The valid range is 0.0 to 1.0. A value of 0.0 indicates the maximum dimness and a value of 1.0 the maximum brightness. The fifth parameter is the address that will be filled by a pointer to an IDirect3DRMLight interface. The call returns D3DRM_OK if successful, or an error otherwise.

The following code fragment creates a parallel point source light with a slight bluish tint.

```
LPDIRECT3DRMLIGHT light1 = NULL;
. . .
// Create a bright parallel point light
// Color values are as follows:
// 0.0 = totally dim and 1.0 = totally bright
retval = lpD3DRM->CreateLightRGB(D3DRMLIGHT_PARALLELPOINT,
                                 D3DVAL(0.8),    // Red intensity
                                 D3DVAL(0.8),    // Green
intensity
                                 D3DVAL(1.0),    // Blue
intensity
                                 &light1);
if(FAILED(retval))
{
     // Light creation error handler goes here
}
```

With the preceding call to CreateLightRGB() we have created a parallel point type light of a specific intensity and color composition. This light is stored in a variable of type LPDIRECT3DRMLIGHT, in this case named light1. However, it will not illuminate the scene until the light is attached to a frame. The light frame created in the preceding section can be used at this time. The code is as follows:

```
// Add light to light frame
retval = lights->AddLight(light1);
if(FAILED(retval))
{
     // Light-to-frame attachment error handler goes here
}
```

Often the visual quality of a scene improves considerably if a dim, ambient light is added. Nonambient lights (directional, parallel point, point, and spot lights) are usually attached to a frame so that the light source can be positioned within the scene. Ambient light sources have no position and, therefore, it is inconsequential to which frame they are attached. Most often we attach ambient lights to the master scene frame.

You create an ambient light using the same `CreateLightRGB()` or `CreateLight()` method used for a nonambient light. In this case the enumerator constant passed in the first parameter (see Table 15-3) is `D3DRMLIGHT_AMBIENT`. For ambient lights the values for the red, green, and blue component are usually in the lower part of the range. When created, the ambient light can be attached to any frame or to the master scene. Either option produces identical results because the light uniformly illuminates the scene independent of its position. The following code fragment shows creating a dim, ambient light and attaching it to the master scene.

```
LPDIRECT3DRMLIGHT light2 = NULL;
. . .
// Create a dim, ambient light and attach it to the scene
frame,
retval = lpD3DRM->CreateLightRGB(D3DRMLIGHT_AMBIENT,
                            D3DVAL(0.1),    // Red value
                            D3DVAL(0.1),    // Green value
                            D3DVAL(0.1),    // Blue value
                            &light2);
if(FAILED(retval))
{
     // Ambient light creation error handler goes here
}
// Attach ambient light to scene frame
retval = aScene->AddLight(light2);
    if(FAILED(retval))
{
     // Light attachment error handler goes here
}
```

Increasing the intensity of the ambient light often results in washed-out images. Color plate 7 shows three versions of a teapot image in which the intensity of the ambient light has been increased from 0.1 to 0.8 for all three primary colors.

Creating a material

The material property of an object determines how it reflects light. Two properties are associated with a material: emissive and specular. The emissive property of a material makes it appear to emit light and the specular property determines the sharpness of the reflected highlights thus making the surface appear hard and metallic or soft and plastic. The value of the specular property is defined by a power setting that determines the sharpness of the reflected highlights. A specular value of 5 gives a metallic appearance and higher values give a more plastic appearance.

Applications set the emissive property of a material using the SetEmissive() method of the IDirect3DRMMaterial interface. The function's general form is as follows:

```
HRESULT SetEmissive(
                D3DVALUE *lpr,            // 1
                D3DVALUE *lpg,            // 2
                D3DVALUE *lpb             // 3
                );
```

The function's three parameters are the intensity settings for the red, green, and blue components of the emitted light. The valid range for each color is 0.0 to 1.0. The function returns D3DRM_OK if it succeeds or an error otherwise.

The emissive property is useful in simulating self-luminous objects such as neon lights, radioactivity, or ghostly characters. The specular property of a material is more commonly used than the emissive property. The specular property has a power and a color component. The color component is set with the SetSpecular() function of the IDirect3DRMMaterial interface. The general form for this function is as follows:

```
HRESULT SetSpecular(
                D3DVALUE r,         // 1
                D3DVALUE g,         // 2
                D3DVALUE b          // 3
                );
```

The three parameters correspond to the value of the RGB color components for the specular highlights. The function returns D3DRM_OK if it succeeds, or an error otherwise.

The power setting for the specular property of a material can be defined when the material is created or afterwards. In the first case you use the CreateMaterial() method of the IDirect3DRM interface. To change the specular power of an existing material you can use the SetSpecular() method of IDirect3DRMMaterial interface. CreateMaterial() has the following general form:

```
HRESULT CreateMaterial(
                D3DVALUE vPower,                              // 1
                LPDIRECT3DRMMATERIAL * lplpD3DRMMaterial      // 2
                );
```

The first parameter is the sharpness of the reflected highlights, with a value of 5 corresponding to a metallic appearance. The second parameter is the address that will be filled with a pointer to an `IDirect3DRMMaterial` interface. The function returns `D3DRM_OK` if it succeeds, or an error otherwise.

After a material is created it must be attached to a mesh or to a specific face of a mesh. Retained mode provides two related functions, both of which are named `SetMaterial()`. The `SetMaterial()` function of the `IDirect3DRMFace` interface attaches the material to a specific face of a mesh. The `SetMaterial()` function of the `IDirect3DRMMeshBuilder` interface attaches the material to all the faces of a mesh. The latter function has the following general form:

```
HRESULT SetMaterial(
        LPDIRECT3DRMMATERIAL2 lpIDirect3DRMmaterial    // 1
        );
```

The function's only parameter is the address of `IDirect3DRMMaterial` interface for the `Direct3DRMMeshBuilder` object, which is of type `LPDIRECT3DMATERIAL2`. The function returns `D3DRM_OK` if it succeeds, or an error otherwise.

The following code fragment shows creating a material and assigning to it a specular power of 0.8. After the material is created, it is attached to an existing mesh.

```
LPDIRECT3DRMMATERIAL2 material1 = NULL;
. . .
// Create a material setting its specular property
retval = lpD3DRM->CreateMaterial(D3DVAL(8.0), &material1);
if(FAILED(retval))
{
    // Failed material creation error handler goes here
}
// Set the material on the mesh
retval = meshbuilder->SetMaterial(material1);
if(FAILED(retval))
{
    // Material attachment error handler goes here
}
```

Setting the mesh color

Meshes have no natural color. If you attempt to render a mesh without setting it to a color attribute the result is an image in shades of gray, as shown in the top part of color plate 8. Retained mode includes several methods to set the color of objects, all of which are named `SetColorRGB()`. One of these methods belongs to the `Direct3DRMFace` interface and is used to set the color of a mesh face. A second `SetColorRGB()` function is part of `IDirect3DRMFrame` interface and serves to set the color of a mesh contained in a mesh. In this case the material mode is set to

D3DRMMATERIAL_FROMFRAME. A third SetColorRGB() method is used to set the color of a light. The fourth one belongs to the IDirect3DRMMeshBuilder interface and is used to set all the faces of a mesh to a particular color attribute. This version of the SetColorRGB() function has the following general form:

```
HRESULT SetColorRGB(
                    D3DVALUE red,        // 1
                    D3DVALUE green,      // 2
                    D3DVALUE blue        // 3
                    );
```

The three parameters of this function determine the red, green, and blue color components of the mesh. The function returns D3DRM_OK if it succeeds, or an error otherwise.

The following code fragment shows using the SetColorRGB() function referenced by a meshbuilder object. In this case the color is set to bright green.

```
LPDIRECT3DRMMESHBUILDER3 meshbuilder = NULL;
. . .
// Set the mesh color (bright green in this case).
retval = meshbuilder->SetColorRGB(D3DVAL(0.0),   // red
                                  D3DVAL(0.7),   // green
                                  D3DVAL(0.0));  // blue

if(FAILED(retval))
{
    // Mesh color setting error handler goes here
}
```

The lower image in color plate 8 shows the object rendered after the mesh is assigned the color value (0.0,0.7,0.0).

Clean-up operations

After the master scene is built (usually by creating a meshbuilder and a mesh, loading the mesh into a child frame, setting the camera position, creating and positioning the lights, and creating the mesh material and color) you can proceed to release all the local objects used in the process. The individual objects are preserved in the scene and will be rendered on the screen. The Release() function of the IUnknown interface, mentioned earlier in this chapter, is used to deallocate the individual object and reduce the object count by one. The function's general form is as follows:

```
ULONG Release();
```

The function returns the new reference count in a variable of type ULONG. The COM object deallocates itself when its reference count reaches 0.

In reference to the code samples listed in this section, the clean-up operation is in the following code fragment:

```
// Local variables
LPDIRECT3DRMFRAME3 lights             = NULL;
LPDIRECT3DRMMESHBUILDER3 meshbuilder  = NULL;
LPDIRECT3DRMLIGHT light1              = NULL;
LPDIRECT3DRMLIGHT light2              = NULL;
LPDIRECT3DRMMATERIAL2 material1       = NULL;
. . .
// Release local objects
lights->Release();
meshbuilder->Release();
light1->Release();
light2->Release();
material1->Release();
```

The BuildScene() function

The BuildScene() function in the 3DRM InWin Demo1 program in the book's CD-ROM performs all of the processing operations discussed in this section. Following is a code listing of this function.

```
//**************************************************************
// Name: BuildScene()
// Description: Create the scene
//**************************************************************
BOOL BuildScene( LPDIRECT3DRMDEVICE3 aDevice,
                 LPDIRECT3DRMFRAME3  aScene,
                 LPDIRECT3DRMFRAME3  aCamera )
{
    // Local variables
    LPDIRECT3DRMFRAME3 lights             = NULL;
    LPDIRECT3DRMMESHBUILDER3 meshbuilder  = NULL;
    LPDIRECT3DRMFRAME3 childframe         = NULL;
    LPDIRECT3DRMLIGHT light1              = NULL;
    LPDIRECT3DRMLIGHT light2              = NULL;
    LPDIRECT3DRMMATERIAL2 material1       = NULL;
    HRESULT retval;

    // Create the meshbuilder object
    retval = lpD3DRM->CreateMeshBuilder(&meshbuilder);
      if (FAILED(retval))
          goto ERROR_EXIT;

    // Use meshbuilder to load a mesh from a DirectX file
    retval = meshbuilder->Load(szXfile,          // Source
                               NULL,
```

```
                                  D3DRMLOAD_FROMFILE, // Options
                                  NULL, NULL);
    if (FAILED(retval))
    {
        D3DError("Failed to load file.");
        goto DIRECT_EXIT;
    }

    // Create a child frame within the aScene.
    retval = lpD3DRM->CreateFrame(aScene, &childframe);
    if(FAILED(retval))
        goto ERROR_EXIT;

    // Add mesh into the child frame as a visual
    retval = childframe->AddVisual(

(LPDIRECT3DRMVISUAL)meshbuilder);
    if(FAILED(retval))
        goto ERROR_EXIT;
    // Set up the camera frame position
    retval = aCamera->SetPosition(aScene,
                                  D3DVAL(0),       // x
                                  D3DVAL(0),       // y
                                  -D3DVAL(7));     // z
    if (FAILED(retval))
    {
        D3DError("Failed to position the camera in the
                frame.");
        goto DIRECT_EXIT;
    }
    // Create a light frame as a child of the scene frame
    retval = lpD3DRM->CreateFrame(aScene, &lights);
      if(FAILED(retval))
        goto ERROR_EXIT;

    // Position the light frame within the scene
    retval = lights->SetPosition(aScene,
                                 D3DVAL(5),        // x
                                 D3DVAL(0),        // y
                                 -D3DVAL(7));      // z
    if(FAILED(retval))
        goto ERROR_EXIT;

    // Create a bright, parallel point light
    // Color values are as follows:
    // 0.0 = totally dim and 1.0 = totally bright
    retval = lpD3DRM->CreateLightRGB(D3DRMLIGHT_PARALLELPOINT,
                           D3DVAL(0.8),     // Red intensity
                           D3DVAL(0.8),     // Green intensity
                           D3DVAL(1.0),     // Blue intensity
                           &light1);
    if(FAILED(retval))
        goto ERROR_EXIT;
```

```
                    // Add light to light frame
                    retval = lights->AddLight(light1);
                    if(FAILED(retval))
                        goto ERROR_EXIT;

                    // Create a dim, ambient light and attach it to the scene
                    // frame,
                    retval = lpD3DRM->CreateLightRGB(D3DRMLIGHT_AMBIENT,
                                                     D3DVAL(0.2),      // red
                                                     D3DVAL(0.2),      // green
                                                     D3DVAL(0.2),      // blue
                                                     &light2);
                    if(FAILED(retval))
                        goto ERROR_EXIT;

                    retval = aScene->AddLight(light2);
                        if(FAILED(retval))
                            goto ERROR_EXIT;

                    // Create a material setting its specular property
                    retval = lpD3DRM->CreateMaterial(D3DVAL(8.0), &material1);
                    if(FAILED(retval))
                        goto ERROR_EXIT;

                    // Set the material on the mesh
                    retval = meshbuilder->SetMaterial(material1);
                    if(FAILED(retval))
                        goto ERROR_EXIT;

                    // Set the mesh color (bright green in this case).
                    retval = meshbuilder->SetColorRGB(D3DVAL(0.0),    // red
                                                      D3DVAL(0.7),    // green
                                                      D3DVAL(0.0));   // blue

                    if(FAILED(retval))
                        goto ERROR_EXIT;

                    //******************************
                    // Function succeeds. Clean up
                    //******************************
                    childframe->Release();
                    lights->Release();
                    meshbuilder->Release();
                    light1->Release();
                    light2->Release();
                    material1->Release();
                    return TRUE;

                    //******************************
                    //       Error exits
                    //******************************
```

```
        ERROR_EXIT:
        D3DError("Failure building the scene");
        DIRECT_EXIT:
        childframe->Release();
        lights->Release();
        meshbuilder->Release();
        light1->Release();
        light2->Release();
        material1->Release();
        return FALSE;
    }
```

Rendering the Scene

To render is to convert image data into an actual image. In all the processing operations performed so far in this chapter, all we have done is manipulate data. Nothing has been shown on the screen, or even formatted into a displayable construct.

In Chapter 14 you learned that Direct3D rendering takes place on three separate modules called the transformation, lighting, and rasterization modules. But when programming in retained mode, the individual modules are not visible. Instead, the rendering operation is conceptualized as consisting of four functions:

✦ The Move() function of the IDirect3DRMFrame interface applies the rotations and velocities to all the frames in the hierarchy.

✦ The Clear() function of the IDirect3DRMViewport interface clears the viewport to the current background color.

✦ The Render() function, that is part of the IDirect3DRNFrame, renders the scene into the viewport.

✦ The Update() function of the IDirect3DRMDevice interface copies the rendered image to the display surface.

The Move() function is discussed in the context of retained mode animation programming (see Chapter 25).

Clearing the viewport

In Direct3D retained mode the viewport is one of the objects of the IDirect3DRM interface. It is defined as a rectangular area in the device space. The viewport extent is always measured in device units, which are pixels for the screen device. The viewport origin is the offset of the viewport within the device space. Previously in this chapter we created a viewport using the CreateViewport() function of the lpD3DRM interface. At that time we assigned the viewport to a device frame and a camera frame. We also defined the viewport origin by means of its position in the device frame, as well as its extent.

Clearing the viewport is accomplished by calling the `Clear()` function of the `IDirect3DRMViewport` interface. The function's general form is as follows:

```
HRESULT Clear();
```

No parameters are necessary because the viewport to be cleared is the one calling the function, as in the following code fragment:

```
// Global Structure
struct _globVars
{
. . .
    LPDIRECT3DRMVIEWPORT2 aViewport;    // Direct3DRM viewport
. . .
} globVars;

// Clear the viewport.
retval = globVars.aViewport->Clear(D3DRMCLEAR_ALL);
if (FAILED(retval))
{
    // Viewport clearing error handler goes here
}
```

Rendering to the viewport

In Chapter 14 we showed you that a scene is organized in a tree-like structure that consists of a root, or master frame, and any number of child frames. Child frames inherit their characteristics from the parent frames to which they are physically attached. When a frame is moved, all the child frames move with it. The parent frame and its child frames are known as a frame hierarchy. In retained mode this frame hierarchy can be changed by code.

The `Render()` function of the `IDirect3DRMViewport` interface renders a frame hierarchy to a given viewport. The call renders the visual on a given frame and all of its child frames. Frames above it on the hierarchy are not rendered or affected. This mode of operation is sometimes described as being state based, which means that the state of the renderer is determined by the part of the frame tree currently being traversed. The general form of the `Frame()` function is as follows:

```
HRESULT Render(
            LPDIRECT3DRMFRAME lpD3DRMFrame      // 1
            );
```

The function's only parameter is the address of the variable that represents the Direct3DRMFrame object at the top of the frame hierarchy to be rendered. The function returns D3DRM_OK if it succeeds, or an error otherwise. The following code fragment shows a call to the Render() function.

```
// Global Structure
struct _globVars
{
.  .  .
    LPDIRECT3DRMVIEWPORT2 aViewport;     // Direct3DRM viewport
    LPDIRECT3DRMFRAME3    aScene;        // Master frame
.  .  .
} globVars;
.  .  .
// Render the scene
retval = globVars.aViewport->Render(globVars.aScene);
if (FAILED(retval))
{
     // Rendering failure error handler goes here
}
```

In this case, the argument of the Render() call is the master frame. This determines that all other frames attached to the master frame are rendered.

Updating the screen

We have now rendered the scene to the viewport, but nothing yet shows on the video display. For this to happen you must call the Update() function of the IDirect3DRMDevice interface. Update() copies the image in the viewport to the display surface. It also provides a system-level tick, called the *heartbeat*. This tick is discussed in the context of retained mode animation (see Chapter 25). The general form of the Update() function is as follows:

```
HRESULT Update();
```

No parameters are necessary because the device is referenced in the call. Each time Update() is called, the system optionally sends execution to an application-defined callback function. Applications define the callback function by means of the AddUpdateCallback() function of the IDirect3DRMDevice interface. The callback function is convenient when the application needs to update scene data during each beat of the renderer. AddUpdateCallback() is discussed in the context of retained mode animation (see Chapter 25). The Update() function returns D3DRM_OK if it succeeds, or an error otherwise.

RenderScene() function

The RenderScene() function that is part of the 3DRM InWin Demo1 program in the book's CD-ROM performs the processing operations discussed in this section. Following is a code listing of this function.

```
//*****************************************************************
// Name: RenderScene()
// Description: Clear the viewport, render the frame, and
//              update the window.
//*****************************************************************
static BOOL RenderScene()
{
    HRESULT retval;

    // Clear the viewport.
    retval = globVars.aViewport->Clear(D3DRMCLEAR_ALL);
    if (FAILED(retval))
    {
        D3DError("Clearing viewport failed.");
        return FALSE;
    }

    // Render the aScene to the viewport.
    retval = globVars.aViewport->Render(globVars.aScene);
    if (FAILED(retval))
    {
        D3DError("Rendering scene failed.");
        return FALSE;
    }
    // Update the window.
    retval = globVars.aDevice->Update();
    if (FAILED(retval))
    {
        D3DError("Updating device failed.");
        return FALSE;
    }
    return TRUE;
}
```

Sample Project 3DRM InWin Demo1

The project named 3DRM InWin Demo1 located in the Chapter 15 subfolder in the book's CD-ROM demonstrates the basic retained mode operations discussed in this chapter. The program displays a file in DirectX format. The filename is contained in a global string and can be edited by the user. The file furnished in the workspace directory is named teapot.x. This is one of the 3D files that comes with the DirectX SDK. Rendering is static because no animation is attempted at this point. Figure 15-2 is a screen snapshot of the 3DRM InWin Demo1 program.

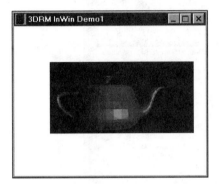

Figure 15-2: Screen snapshot of the 3DRM InWin Demo1 program

To facilitate reuse, we grouped the processing into four functions:

1. `InitD3D()` initializes the retained mode interface and creates a `DirectDraw Clipper` object based on the application window.

2. `CreateObjects()` creates the device and objects that form the 3D scene.

3. `BuildScene()` uses the objects created in the previous step to build the application's main frame.

4. `RenderScene()` renders the scene to the viewport and displays it.

The functions were discussed in detail and are listed in previous sections of this chapter.

Windowed Retained Mode Coding Template

The project directory 3DRM InWin Template, located in the Chapter 15 subfolder in the book's CD-ROM, contains a template program that could be useful in the initial stages of developing a Direct3D retained mode, windowed application. To use it you can copy the template file named 3DRM InWin Template.cpp to your own workspace. Then rename the file and edit it to suit your application. Alternatively you can copy or rename the entire directory. When using the template file make sure that you have referenced the libraries dxguid.lib, ddraw.lib, d3drm.lib, and winmm.lib. To include these libraries you must edit the Object/Libraries modules windows on the Link tab of Developer Studio Project Settings dialog box, as shown in Figure 15-3.

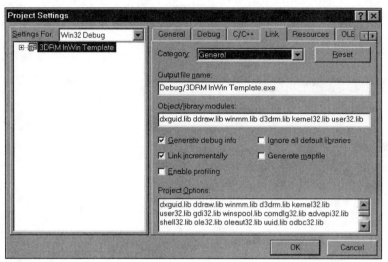

Figure 15-3: Direct3D Libraries referenced in the Project Settings dialog box

Summary

In this chapter we explained the coding that goes into a simple, windowed mode, Direct3D application that executes in retained mode. The program used as a model is contained in the 3DRM InWin Demo1 project folder in the book's CD-ROM. The sample program renders a 3D image stored in a file in Microsoft's DirectX format. We purposefully eliminated from the code everything that is not strictly necessary to accomplish this purpose. The fact that this extremely simple program requires approximately 450 lines of code indicates the complexity of 3D programming, even when it takes place in a high-level environment such as Direct3D retained mode. In the following chapter we use this same, basic code structure to introduce a finer level of object modeling and rendering.

✦   ✦   ✦

System-Level Operations

Having finished our overview of Direct3D retained
mode and having followed the coding of a simple
program, we are now ready to plunge into the details of the
application programming interface. We begin this chapter
with an introduction to the retained mode interface and its
organization. The remainder is devoted to discussing the
Direct3D retained mode highest-level controls. Lacking a
better term, we call these controls the *system-level interface*.
The functions at this level are used for creating the Direct3D
retained mode objects, accessing system-level variables, and
in performing top-level calculations and transformations. The
design and coding of a Direct3D application starts with the
system-level controls.

Direct3D Retained Mode API

The retained mode API is a set of interrelated, COM-based
interfaces. One of the difficulties in understanding Direct3D
is deciphering the organization of this interface. Figure 16-1
shows the retained mode interface hierarchy at the time of
this writing.

Some of the interfaces in Figure 16-1 are updates. The
digit following the interface name indicates its sequential
order. For example, `IDirect3DRMDEvice3` replaced
`IDirect3DRMDevice2`, which in turn replaced the original
`IDirect3DRMDevice` interface. In this case each successive
interface added methods to the preceding one. Figure 16-1
shows only the latest version of the interfaces.

Until the release of DirectX 6, each new interface inherited from its predecessor. For example, IDirect3DRMFrame2, introduced in DirectX 5.0, inherits from IDirect3DRMFrame. DirectX 6 changed this mode of operation; since its introduction the new interfaces do not inherit, but re-implement the functions in its predecessors. This means that the DirectX 6 IDirect3DRMFrame3 interface does not inherit from Direct3DRMFrame2 or IDirect3DRMFrame. However, Microsoft documentation states that all the methods in the previous interfaces remain unchanged and that existing code will not be broken by the new implementations.

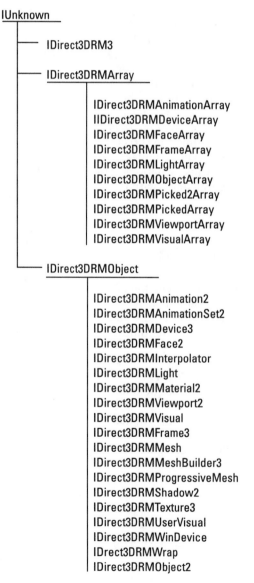

Figure 16-1: Retained mode interface hierarchy chart

Another change introduced in DirectX6refers to Microsoft's conventions for sequentially numbering functions. The interface inheritance mechanism that was in place up to DirectX 6 made it necessary for each new method to be identified by a sequential digit. This enabled code to conform to the new signatures. For example, `IDirect3DRMFrame::AddMoveCallback()` had two parameters. The new version of that method, which takes three parameters, was named `Direct3DRMFrame2::AddMoveCallback2()`. We already mentioned that, starting with DirectX 6.0, the new interfaces do not inherit from the old ones. Therefore this method numbering scheme became obsolete. For this reason, some retained mode method names that were appended with a digit in a previous interface have reverted to their original names in the post-DirectX 6 implementations. This is the case with the `AddModeCallback()` function of `IDirect3DRMFrame3`, which replaces `AddMoveCallback2()` of `IDirect3DRMFrame2`. Keep in mind that the practice of dropping the sequential digit applies to method names only, not to the interface designations. To avoid duplication and confusion, in this book we refer to the most recent version of the interface only.

In addition to the functions related to the specific interfaces listed in Figure 16-1, there are functions in the retained mode API that are not derived from any specific interface. These are sometimes called the nonmember or retained mode functions. In Chapter 14 you used one of the nonmember functions to create the Direct3D retained mode object. The code in the sample program 3DRM InWin Demo1 is as follows:

```
// Create the Direct3DRM object.
   LPDIRECT3DRM pD3DRMTemp;
   retval = Direct3DRMCreate(&pD3DRMTemp);
```

Notice that because `Direct3DRMCreate()` is a nonmember function, there is no interface pointer in the call statement. The remaining functions in this group perform auxiliary operations such as manipulating colors, matrices, vectors, and quaternions. Table 16-1 describes the Direct3D retained mode nonmember functions.

Table 16-1
Direct3D Nonmember Functions

Function	Description
Color manipulations	
D3DRMColorGetAlpha()	Retrieve alpha component
D3DRMColorGetBlue()	Retrieve blue component
D3DRMColorGetGreen()	Retrieve green component
D3DRMColorGetRed()	Retrieve red component
D3DRMCreateColorRGB()	Create color in RGB format

Continued

Table 16-1 *(continued)*

Function	Description
D3DRMCreateColorRGBA()	Create color in RGBA format
Matrix manipulations	
D3DRMMatrixFromQuaternion()	Calculate matrix from rotation of a unit quaternion
Vector manipulations	
D3DRMVectorAdd()	Sum of two vectors
D3DRMVectorCrossProduct()	Cross product of two vectors
D3DRMVectorDotProduct()	Dot product of two vectors
D3DRMVectorModulus()	Length of vector according to modulus formula
D3DRMVectorNormalize()	Scale vector to modulus 1
D3DRMVectorRandom()	Random unit of vector
D3DRMVectorReflect()	Reflect vector ray about a given normal
D3DRMVectorRotate()	Rotate vector around a given axis
D3DRMVectorScale()	Scale vector uniformly in all three axes
D3DRMVectorSubtract()	Subtract two vectors
Quaternion manipulations	
D3DRMQuaternionFromRotation()	Retrieves a unit quaternion from a rotation on a given axis
D3DRMQuaternionMultiply()	Product of two quaternion structures
D3DRMQuaternionSlerp()	Linear interpolation between two quaternion structures
Instance creation	
Direct3DRMCreate()	Create instance of Direct3DRM object

The System-Level Interface

Direct3D retained mode applications use the functions of the IDirect3DRM3 interface to create retained mode objects. The most important objects created by IDirect3DRM3 are the following:

✦ Viewports

✦ Devices

- ✦ Frames
- ✦ Meshbuilders and meshes
- ✦ Faces
- ✦ Lights
- ✦ Materials
- ✦ Shadows
- ✦ Textures
- ✦ Wraps
- ✦ ClippedVisuals
- ✦ Animations and animation sets
- ✦ UserVisuals
- ✦ Uninitialized objects

Table 16-2 lists the functions available in the `IDirect3DRM3` interface.

Table 16-2
Methods of IDirect3DRM Interface

Groups	Functions
Viewports	* CreateViewport()
Devices	CreateDevice() * CreateDeviceFromClipper() CreateDeviceFromD3D() CreateDeviceFromSurface() GetDevices()
Frames	* CreateFrame()
Meshes	CreateMesh() * CreateMeshBuilder() CreateProgressiveMesh()
Faces	CreateFace()
Lights	* CreateLight() * CreateLightRGB()
Materials	* CreateMaterial()
Shadows	CreateShadow()

Continued

Table 16-2 *(continued)*	
Groups	**Functions**

Textures	`CreateTexture()`
	`CreateTextureFromSurface()`
	`LoadTexture()`
	`LoadTextureFromResource()`
	`SetDefaultTextureColors()`
	`SetDefaultTextureShades()`

Wraps	`CreateWrap()`
Animations	`CreateAnimation()` `CreateAnimationSet()`

General support	`AddSearchPath()`
	`GetSearchPath()`
	`SetSearchPath()`
	`EnumerateObjects()`
	`CreateObject()`
	`CreateUserVisual()`
	`GetNamedObject()`
	`Load()`
	`Tick()`
	`SetOptions()`

We encountered some of these functions in Chapter 15, while developing the 3DRM InWin Demo1 program. Those that were discussed in detail in Chapter 15 are marked with asterisks in Table 16-2. These functions are not revisited in this chapter. The remaining topics are organized as follows:

✦ Creating devices

✦ Creating meshes and faces

✦ Creating materials, shadows, textures, and wraps

✦ Creating animations and animation sets

✦ General support functions

In this chapter we are mainly concerned with the processing operations that take place at the system level. Most of the topics discussed are revisited later in the book in the context of lower-level interfaces, or in chapters devoted to specific functionalities, as is the case with Direct3D animation.

Creating and Obtaining Devices

There are four documented methods in the IDirect3DRM interface for creating devices. One of them, CreateDevice(), is not implemented in Windows. The remaining methods are named CreateDeviceFromClipper(), CreateDeviceFromD3D(), and CreateDeviceFromSurface(). In Chapter 15 you used CreateDeviceFromClipper() passing NULL in the second parameter. Because this is the way that is recommended by Microsoft for creating a retained mode device, no further comment on this function is necessary at this time.

A common characteristic of all three device-creation methods is that they all return an IDirect3DRMDevice3 interface. This interface provides the functionality of an IDirect3DDevice3 immediate mode device, and it supports the DrawPrimitive interface and execute buffers. This interface is the one required for progressive meshes, alpha blending, and for sorting of transparent objects.

Creating a device from a Direct3D object

Program output is always associated with an output device. This output device represents the visual display destination for the renderer and determines the renderer's behavior. Applications can define multiple viewports on a device. This allows different aspects of the same scene to be viewed simultaneously. In addition, code can specify several output devices, allowing multiple destination devices for the same scene. Retained mode devices can render directly to the screen, to Windows, or into application memory.

In windowed applications the most useful and common way of creating a Direct3D display device is using CreateDeviceFromClipper() previously mentioned. This approach has the advantage that a DirectDraw clipper is attached to the window automatically. The CreateDeviceFromD3D() function creates a Windows device by using a specified Direct3D object. This function is used often in creating a device for full-screen mode programs. The function has the following general form:

```
HRESULT CreateDeviceFromD3D(
            LPDIRECT3D2 lpD3D,                     // 1
            LPDIRECT3DDEVICE2 lpD3DDev,            // 2
            LPDIRECT3DRMDEVICE3  *lplpD3DRMDevice  // 3
            );
```

The first parameter is a pointer to an instance of a Direct3D immediate mode object. The second parameter is a pointer to a Direct3D immediate mode Direct3DDevice2 object. If NULL is passed in the second parameter, the function searches for a hardware device with the minimum set of capabilities required for retained mode. The third parameter is the address that will be filled with a pointer to an IDirect3DRMDevice3 interface if the call succeeds. The call returns D3DRM_OK if it is successful, or an error otherwise.

Creating a device from a surface

The `CreateDeviceFromSurface()` function provides a mechanism for creating a Direct3D device based on a DirectDraw surface. `CreateDeviceFromSurface()` is used in full-screen Direct3D programs. The method's general form is as follows:

```
HRESULT CreateDeviceFromSurface(
                LPGUID lpGUID,                          // 1
                LPDIRECTDRAW lpDD,                      // 2
                LPDIRECTDRAWSURFACE lpDDSBack,          // 3
                LPDIRECT3DRMDEVICE2 * lplpD3DRMDevice   // 4
                );
```

The first parameter is the address of the globally unique identifier (GUID) used as the required device driver. As is the case in `CreateDeviceFromClipper()`, if this parameter is NULL, the default device driver is used. The second parameter is the address of the DirectDraw object that is used as a surface. The third parameter is the address of the `DirectDrawSurface` object that represents the back buffer. The fourth parameter is the address that is filled with a pointer to an `IDirect3DRMDevice2` interface. The function returns D3DRM_OK if it is successful, or an error otherwise.

Obtaining the device

The `GetDevice()` function of `IDirect3DRM3` returns all Direct3DRM devices that have been created in the system. The function has the following general form:

```
HRESULT GetDevices(
                LPDIRECT3DRMDEVICEARRAY *lplpDevArray    // 1
                );
```

The only parameter is the address of a pointer that is filled with the resulting array of Direct3DRM devices. The function returns D3DRM_OK if it succeeds, or an error otherwise.

If the call succeeds, an array of devices is filled with all the devices in the system. To obtain each particular device, code needs to call the functions in the `IDirect3DRMDeviceArray` interface. The `GetSize()` method returns the number of elements in the array. Its general form is as follows:

```
DWORD GetSize();
```

When the size of the array is known, code can proceed to examine each element by means of the `GetElement()` function of `IDirect3DRMDeviceArray`. The function's general form is as follows:

```
HRESULT GetElement(
                DWORD index,                             // 1
                LPDIRECT3DRMDEVICE *lplpD3DRMDevice      // 2
                );
```

The first parameter is the offset of the element in the array. The second parameter is filled with a pointer to the IDirect3DRMDevice interface. However, you cannot cast this parameter to a different version of the interface. For example, if the pointer you want is to IDirect3DRMDevice3, you must use QueryInterface() to obtain it. The function returns D3DRM_OK if it succeeds, or an error otherwise.

Creating Meshes and Faces

In Chapter 15 you created a mesh using the meshbuilder object. On that occasion the meshbuilder loaded a mesh file, in DirectX format. Then you created a child frame within the scene, and added the mesh into the child frame. Most retained mode applications use meshes developed in an image editing program. These meshes are stored in files and loaded into the scene as needed.

Alternatively, although rarely in retained mode, an application can create the individual faces of a polygon mesh using the methods in the IDirect3DRMFace2 interface. In this case the face is constructed using the AddVertex() and AddVertextAndNormalIndex() functions. Code can read the vertices using the GetVertex() and GetVertices() functions, or set the color, texture, and material of the face by using SetColor(), SetColorRGB(), SetTexture(), and SetMaterial(). Table 16-3 lists the methods in the IDirect3DRMFace2 interface.

Table 16-3 Functions in the IDirect3DRMFace2 Interface	
Function	Description
Color manipulations	
GetColor()	Retrieves the face color
SetColor()	Sets color and alpha component
SetColorRGB()	Sets color in RGB format
Materials	
GetMaterial()	Retrieves the material property
SetMaterial()	Sets the material property
Textures	
GetTexture()	Retrieves the applied texture
GetTextureCoordinateIndex()	Retrieves the index of the texture coordinate vertex

Continued

Table 16-3 *(continued)*

Function	Description
GetTextureCoordinates()	Retrieves the texture coordinates of a vertex
SetTexture()	Sets the face texture
SetTextureCoordinates()	Sets the texture coordinates of a vertex
SetTextureTopology()	Sets the texture topology of a face
Vertices and normals	
AddVertex()	Adds a vertex to a face
AddVertexAndNormalIndexed()	Uses the index for the vertex and the normal to add a vertex and a normal to a face
GetNormal()	Retrieves the normal vector of a face
GetVertex()	Retrieves the position and the normal of a vertex in a face
GetVertexCount()	Retrieves the number of vertices
GetVertexIndex()	Retrieves the index of the vertex in a face
GetVertices()	Retrieves the position and the normal vector of each vertex in a face

Because building meshes out of primitive components is not a common operation in retained mode programming, we do not discuss the mesh primitive functions at this point.

A progressive mesh is defined as a set of discrete steps that go from the coarsest to the most refined representation of the object. Progressive meshes were introduced to Direct3D in DirectX 5. In addition to rendering an image in a series of progressively refined steps, they also allow the progressive download of a mesh from a remote source.

One of the methods of IDirect3DRM is CreateProgressiveMesh(). This function creates a progressive mesh object. Its general form is as follows:

```
HRESULT CreateProgressiveMesh(
    LPDIRECT3DRMPROGRESSIVEMESH *lplpD3DRMProgressiveMesh  // 1
    );
```

The only parameter is the address that will be filled with a pointer to an IDirect3DRMProgressiveMesh interface if the call succeeds. The function returns D3DRM_OK if it succeeds, or an error otherwise.

After the progressive mesh object is created, it can be used to access any of the functions in `IDirect3DRMProgressiveMesh`. Table 16-4 lists the functions in this interface.

Table 16-4
Functions in the IDirect3DRMProgressiveMesh Interface

Function	Description
Creating and Copying Meshes	
Clone()	Creates a copy of the current mesh object.
CreateMesh()	Builds a mesh using the current level of detail.
Duplicate()	Creates a copy of the `Direct3DprogressiveMesh` object. The level of detail for the duplicate object can be set independently.
GetBox()	Retrieves the object's bounding box.
Loading	
Abort()	Terminates the current download.
GetLoadStatus()	Returns the current status of the load.
Load()	Loads a progressive mesh from a file, a resource, or a URL.
Mesh Quality	
SetQuality()	Sets the rendering quality of the progressive mesh.
GetQuality()	Retrieves the `D3DRMRENDERQUALITY` enumerated constant that specified the rendering quality of a progressive mesh.
Level of Detail	
GetDetail()	Returns the current level of detail (range is 0.0 to 1.0).
GetFaceDetail()	Retrieves the number of faces in a progressive mesh.
GetFaceDetailRange()	Retrieves the minimum and maximum face count.
GetVertexDetail()	Retrieves the number of vertices in a progressive mesh.
GetVertexDetailRange()	Retrieves the minimum and maximum vertex count.
SetDetail()	Sets the current level of detail (range is 0.0 to 1.0).

Continued

Table 16-4 *(continued)*	
Function	**Description**
SetFaceDetail()	Sets the level of detail for a face.
SetMinRenderDetail()	Sets the minimum level of detail, larger than the base mesh, that will be rendered during a load.
SetVertexDetail()	Sets the level of detail for a vertex.
Events Handling	
RegisterEvents()	Registers an event that will be signaled when a predefined condition is met.

Programming operations using progressive meshes is discussed in the context of Direct3D animation.

Creating Materials, Shadows, Textures, and Wraps

Materials, textures, shadows, and wraps are fundamental mesh attributes in Direct3D programming. An object's rendering quality depends largely on our abilities in manipulating these four attributes. In this chapter we consider the creation of these attributes and provide an overview of the interfaces that are used in their manipulation. The programming details are described beginning in Chapter 18.

Materials

In the 3DRM InWin Demo1 program presented in Chapter 15 you created a material using the CreateMaterial() function of IDirect3DRM. Notice that a material object can also be created in immediate mode using the CreateMaterial() function of IDirect3D3. Immediate mode provides a much finer degree of control over material properties than retained mode.

The call to CreateMaterial() of the IDirect3DRM3 interface returns a pointer to the IDirect3DRMMaterial2 interface if the call succeeds. This interface upgrade to IDirect3DRMMaterial became available in DirectX 6. The interface provides the methods listed in Table 16-5.

Table 16-5
Functions in the IDirect3DRMMaterial2 Interface

Function	Description
Ambient	
GetAmbient()	Retrieves the material's ambient value.
SetAmbient()	Sets the ambient value for the material. Default is the diffuse color.
Emissive property	
GetEmissive()	Retrieves the RGB components of the material's emissive property
SetEmissive()	Sets the RGB components of the material's emissive property.
Specular Power	
GetPower()	Retrieves the power value for the material's specular property.
SetPower()	Sets the power value for the material's specular property.
Specular property	
GetSpecular()	Retrieves the RGB components of the material's specular property.
SetSpecular()	Sets the RGB components of the material's specular property.

Manipulating materials properties is discussed in Chapter 18.

Shadows

In nature, illuminated objects produce shadows. In Direct3D, a shadow is a projection of a mesh, rendered as a visual and a light, onto a plane. The shadow is produced by calling the CreateShadow() method of the IDirect3DRM interface. The resulting shadow object is a visual. When this shadow object is attached to a frame it becomes visible at rendering time. The general form of CreateShadow() is as follows:

```
HRESULT CreateShadow(
              LPDIRECT3DRMVISUAL lpVisual,        // 1
              LPDIRECT3DRMLIGHT lpLight,          // 2
              D3DVALUE px,                        // 3
              D3DVALUE py,                        // 4
              D3DVALUE pz,                        // 5
              D3DVALUE nx,                        // 6
              D3DVALUE ny,                        // 7
              D3DVALUE nz,                        // 8
              LPDIRECT3DRMVISUAL * lplpShadow     // 9
              );
```

The first parameter is the address of the Direct3DRMVisual object that is casting the shadow. The second parameter is the address of the IDirect3DRMLight interface that is the light source. The third, fourth, and fifth parameters, represented by the variables px, py, and pz in the general form, are the coordinates of a point on the plane on which the shadow is projected. The sixth, seventh, and eight parameters, represented by the variables nx, ny, and nz in the general forms, define the normal to the plane on which the shadow is projected. In this manner the shadow's plane of projection is defined in terms of a point on this plane and its normal vector. The ninth parameter is an address that is initialized with a pointer to the shadow visual, if the call succeeds. The call returns D3DRM_OK if it succeeds, or an error otherwise.

Applications that use CreateObject() of the IDirect3DRM3 interface to create a shadow object then call the Init() function of IDirect3DRMShadow2 interface to initialize it. This function has the following general form:

```
HRESULT Init(
        LPDIRECT3DRMVISUAL lpVisual,      // 1
        LPDIRECT3DRMLIGHT lpLight,        // 2
        D3DVALUE px,                      // 3
        D3DVALUE py,                      // 4
        D3DVALUE pz,                      // 5
        D3DVALUE nx,                      // 6
        D3DVALUE ny,                      // 7
        D3DVALUE nz,                      // 8
        );
```

The meaning of the eight parameters to the Init() call are the same as those of the first eight parameters of the call to CreateShadow() described earlier.

In addition to the Init() function, the IDirect3DRMShadow2 interface contains functions that allow changing the visual, light, plane, and option shadow parameters. The interface provides the methods listed in Table 16-6.

Currently the only shadow option implemented is D3DRMSHADOW_TRUEALPHA. This option creates a shadow that does not have visual artifacts when true alpha is enabled.

Rendering shadows is discussed starting in Chapter 18.

Textures

In Chapter 14 you learned that a texture is a 2D image, usually encoded in bitmap form, that is used to enhance the rendering of a 3D mesh object. IDirec3DRM3 contains several texture-related functions, listed in Table 16-7.

Table 16-6
Functions in the IDirect3DRMShadow2 Interface

Function	Description
Initialization	
Init()	Initialized the shadow object
Parameter manipulations	
GetLight()	Retrieves the light source associated with the shadow
GetOptions()	Retrieves the shadow option flag (Currently D3DRMSHADOW_TRUEALPHA)
GetPlane()	Retrieves the shadow plane in point/normal form
GetVisual()	Retrieves the visual to be shadowed
SetLight()	Sets the light that produces the shadow
SetOptions()	Sets the shadow option (Currently D3DRMSHADOW_TRUEALPHA)
SetPlane()	Sets the plane onto which the shadow is projected (in point/normal form)
SetVisual()	Sets the visual to be shadowed

Table 16-7
Texture-related Functions in the IDirect3DRM3 Interface

Function	Description
CreateTexture()	Creates a texture from a memory image
CreateTextureFromSurface()	Creates a texture from a DirectDraw surface
LoadTexture()	Load a texture from a file in .bmp or .ppm format
LoadTextureFromResource()	Loads a texture from a program resource
SetDefaultTextureColors()	Sets the number of default colors to be used with a texture object
SetDefaultTextureShades()	Sets the number of default shades to be used with a texture object

The first four functions in Table 16-7 contain a parameter that is the address of a pointer to a IDirect3DRMTexture3 interface. This version of the interface, which was introduced in DirectX 6, provides a series of functions that perform texture management and control operations. IDirec3DRMTexture3 contains the functions listed in Table 16-8.

Table 16-8
Functions in the IDirect3DRMTexture3 Interface

Function	Description
Color	
GetColors()	Retrieves the maximum number of colors defined for a texture object
SetColors()	Sets the maximum number of colors for a texture object defined in the ramp color model
Decals	
GetDecalOrigin()	Retrieves the offset of the decal origin
GetDecalScale()	Retrieves the scale of a decal
GetDecalSize()	Retrieves the size of a decal
GetDecalTransparency()	Returns TRUE if decal is transparent
GetDecalTransparentColor()	Retrieves the transparent color of a decal
SetDecalOrigin()	Sets the offset of the decal origin
SetDecalScale()	Sets the decal scale
SetDecalSize()	Sets the decal size
SetDecalTransparency()	Sets the decal transparent attribute to TRUE or FALSE
SetDecalTransparentColor()	Sets the transparent color for a decal
Images	
GetImage()	Returns the address of the image used in creating the texture
Initialization	
InitFromFile()	Initializes a texture object using data contained in a file
InitFromImage()	Initializes a texture object from a memory image
InitFromResource2()	Initializes a texture object from a specified resource
InitFromSurface()	Initializes a texture object from a DirectDraw surface

Function	Description
Mipmap generation	
GenerateMIPMap()	Generates a mipmap from a single image source. The mipmap resolution is down to 1 × 1.
Miscellaneous	
GetCacheOptions()	Retrieves the relative importance of a texture and the flag that controls texture management priorities
GetSurface()	Retrieves the DirectDraw surface used in creating a texture
SetCacheOptions()	Sets the relative importance of a texture and the flag that controls texture management priorities
SetDownsampleCallback()	Specifies the callback function to be called when a texture is downsampled
SetValidationCallback()	Specifies the callback function that validates and updates the primary source texture
Renderer notification	
Changed()	Specifies the region of the texture that has changed
Shading	
GetShades()	Retrieves the number of shades per texture color
SetShades()	Sets the number of shades per texture color

Better performance is obtained if applications retain textures that are reused instead of creating them when they are needed. Square textures are handled better by the renderer. This is also the case with texture sizes that are powers of 2, such as 16, 32, 64, 128, 256, 512 pixels-per-side. Programming operations on textures are discussed in Chapter 22.

Wraps

A wrap is a specific way of deforming a 2D surface so that it covers a 3D object according to a particular scheme. Direct3D supports four types of wraps: flat, cylindrical, spherical, and chrome, which were discussed in Chapter 14. Applying wraps is a complex process. In most cases developers use the facilities of the 3D modeling tool, which allow wrapping textures on objects as they are created. However, we have seen that Direct3D provides primitives for creating meshes. Wraps may be of use when a mesh is created using these primitives.

The `CreateWrap()` function of the `IDirect3DRM3` interface creates a wrapping function that can be used to map texture coordinates to a face or mesh. The function's general form is as follows:

```
HRESULT CreateWrap(
            D3DRMWRAPTYPE type,              // 1
            LPDIRECT3DRMFRAME3 lpRef,        // 2
            D3DVALUE ox,                     // 3
            D3DVALUE oy,                     // 4
            D3DVALUE oz,                     // 5
            D3DVALUE dx,                     // 6
            D3DVALUE dy,                     // 7
            D3DVALUE dz,                     // 8
            D3DVALUE ux,                     // 9
            D3DVALUE uy,                     // 10
            D3DVALUE uz,                     // 11
            D3DVALUE ou,                     // 12
            D3DVALUE ov,                     // 13
            D3DVALUE su,                     // 14
            D3DVALUE sv,                     // 15
            LPDIRECT3DRMWRAP *lplpD3DRMWrap  // 16
            );
```

The first parameter is one of the constants defined in the `D3DRMWRAPTYPE` enumeration. They are listed in Table 16-9.

Table 16-9
Constants in the D3DRMWRAPTYPE Enumerated Type

Constant	Description
D3DRMWRAP_FLAT	Wrap is flat
D3DRMWRAP_CYLINDER	Wrap is cylindrical
D3DRMWRAP_SPHERE	Wrap is spherical
D3DRMWRAP_CHROME	Wrap allocates texture coordinates so that the texture appears to be reflected onto the objects

The second parameter is the frame that defines the object to which the wrap is applied. The parameters labeled `ox`, `oy`, and `oz` are the coordinates of the wrap origin. The parameters labeled `dx`, `dy`, and `dz` are the coordinates of the z-axis of the wrap. The parameters labeled `ux`, `uy`, and `uz` are the coordinates of the y-axis of the wrap. The parameters labeled `ou` and `ov` define the origin of the texture. The parameters `su` and `sv` are the scale factor of the texture. Finally, the sixteenth parameter is the address that is filled with a pointer to an `IDirect3DRMWrap` interface if the call succeeds. The function returns `D3DRM_OK` if it succeeds, or an error otherwise.

The IDirect3DRMWrap interface provides the two methods listed in Table 16-10.

<table>
<tr><td colspan="2" align="center">Table 16-10
Function in the IDirect3DRMWrap Interface</td></tr>
</table>

Function	Description
Apply()	Applies the wrap to the destination object, usually a face or mesh
ApplyRelative()	Applies the wrap to the vertices of the object

Because of the limited use of texture wraps we do not consider them any further.

Animations

Most 3D applications implement animation in one form or another. A 3D program whose execution is limited to displaying an object on a flat screen makes little use of the modeling and rendering powers of 3D graphics. But, in implementing animation, you encounter many difficulties and limitations, which make this field the most challenging one of 3D programming. Later in the book we devote several chapters to 3D animation. At this point the discussion is limited to those animation functions that are available at the highest rendering levels.

We must start by differentiating the generic term animation and the specific concept of a retained mode animation, as related to the CreateAnimation() or CreateAnimationSet() functions of the IDirect3DRM3 interface. In this latter sense an animation is a mechanism for adding behavior to a 3D scene. T he behavior is defined by a set of keys. The key contains a time value, as well as a scaling operation, an orientation, or a position. The Direct3DRMAnimation interface provides functions that define how a transformation is modified according to the key. Animations, in this sense, refer to the position, orientation, and scaling of Direct3DRMVisual, Direct3DRMLight, and Direct3DRMViewport objects.

Creating the animation

In creating retained mode animations, code usually starts by calling Create Animation() or CreateAnimationSet() functions of IDirect3DRM3. CreateAnimation() creates an empty IDirect3DRMAnimation2 object. When created, the animation object is usually attached to a frame. The function's general form is as follows:

```
HRESULT CreateAnimation(
        LPDIRECT3DRMANIMATION2  *lplpD3DRMAnimation     // 1
        );
```

The function's only parameter is the address of a pointer to the `IDirect3D RMAnimation2` interface, which is filled if the call succeeds. The function returns `D3DRM_OK` if it succeeds, or an error otherwise.

The pointer returned by the `CreateAnimation()` function provides access to the `IDirect3DRMAnimation2` interface. This interface provides functions to animate the position, orientation, and scale of a frame object. This frame object can be a visual, a light, or a viewport. Animation controls are based on keys, each one key containing a time and a value component. The functions allow adding and deleting keys, animating the frame, setting the animation time, and changing animation options. Table 16-11 lists the functions in `IDirect3DRMAnimation3`.

Table 16-11
Function in the IDirect3DRMAnimation3 Interface

Function	Description
Key operations	
AddKey()	Adds a new key to the animation
AddPositionKey()	Adds a position key based on a time key and the coordinates for each axis
AddRotateKey()	Adds a rotate key based on a time key and a rotation quaternion
AddScaleKey()	Adds a scale key based on a time key and a scale factor for each axis
DeleteKey()	Removes all keys at a particular time
DeleteKeyByID()	Removes a particular key
GetKeys()	Retrieves a key corresponding to a particular time range
ModifyKey()	Modifies the value of a key
Frame and time	
GetFrame()	Retrieves animation's frame
SetFrame()	Sets the animation frame
SetTime()	Sets the animation time
Animation options	
GetOptions()	Retrieves the animation options
SetOptions()	Sets the animation options

Several types of animation are supported in Direct3D. The variables representing these options are described in the D3DANIMATIONOPTIONS structure, as follows:

1. D3DRMANIMATION_CLOSED defines an animation that plays continually. When the end is reached, the animation loops back to the beginning. Code can ensure a smooth transition in the animation by making the last key in the animation a repeat of the first. In this case the IDirect3DRMAnimation2 and IDirect3DRMAnimationSet2 interfaces interpret the repeated key as the time difference between the last and first keys in the animation loop.

2. D3DRMANIMATION_LINEARPOSITION defines a linear animation position.

3. D3DRMANIMATION_OPEN defines an animation that plays once and stops.

4. D3DRMANIMATION_POSITION defines an animation's position matrix that should overwrite any transformation matrices set by other methods.

5. D3DRMANIMATION_SCALEANDROTATION defines an animation's scale and rotation matrix that should overwrite any transformation matrices set by other methods.

6. D3DRMANIMATION_SPLINEPOSITION defines an animation whose position is set using splines.

Animation keys, as used in the AddKey(), GetKeys(), and ModifyKey() functions listed in Table 16-11, are encoded in a structure of type D3DRMANIMATIONKEY. The structure is defined as follows:

```
typedef struct _D3DRMANIMATIONKEY
  {
    DWORD         dwSize;
    DWORD         dwKeyType;
    D3DVALUE      dvTime;
    DWORD         dwId ;
      union
       {
         D3DRMQUATERNION    dqRotateKey;
         D3DVECTOR          dvScaleKey;
         D3DVECTOR          dvPositionKey;
       };
  } D3DRMANIMATIONKEY;
```

The dwSize member defines the size of the animation. The dwKeyType member is the type of key, represented by one of the following values:

```
D3DRMANIMATION_ROTATEKEY   = 0x01
D3DRMANIMATION_SCALEKEY    = 0x02
D3DRMANIMATION_POSITIONKEY = 0x03
```

The `dvTime` member is the key's zero-based time value, in arbitrary units. For example, if an application adds a position key with a time value of 99, a new position key with a time value of 49 would occur exactly halfway between the beginning of the animation and the first position key. The time member is encoded in a `D3DVALUE` type. The `dwId` member is the key's identifier, encoded in a `DWORD` type. The `dqRotateKey` union member is the value of the `D3DRMQUATERNION` structure type that defines the rotation. The `dvScaleKey` union member is the value of the `D3DVECTOR` structure type that defines the scale.

The `dvPositionKey` union member is the value of the `D3DVECTOR` structure type that defines the position.

An animation is driven by calling the `SetTime()` function. This sets the visual object's transformation to the interpolated position, orientation, and scale of the nearby keys.

Creating the animation set

The `CreateAnimationSet()` function creates an object that contains several `Direct3DRMAnimation2` objects, which in turn can animate several frames. The `CreateAnimationSet()` function is used when you need to animate several frames at the same time. The fact that several frames are animated by the same time parameter provides a synchronization mechanism for implementing complex animations. The function's general form is as follows:

```
HRESULT CreateAnimationSet (
        LPDIRECT3DRMANIMATIONSET2  *lplpD3DRMAnimationSet  // 1
        );
```

The function's only parameter is the address that is filled with a pointer to an `IDirect3DRMAnimationSet2` interface if the call succeeds. The function returns `D3DRM_OK` if successful, or an error otherwise. The `IDirect3DRMAnimationSet2` interface contains functions for adding and deleting animations, loading animation sets, and for setting the time parameter. Table 16-12 lists the functions in `IDirec3DRMAnimationSet2`.

General Support Functions

Several functions available in the `IDirect3DRM3` interface perform auxiliary operations, or are difficult to classify. We have grouped them in this section and refer to them as general support functions. However, the grouping of these functions should not lead you to believe that they are of secondary significance. Some of the most useful functions of Direct3D are in this group.

Table 16-12
Function in the IDirect3DRMAnimationSet2 Interface

Function	Description
Animation manipulations	
AddAnimation( )	Adds an animation to an animation set
DeleteAnimation( )	Removes an animation from an animation set
GetAnimations( )	Retrieves an array containing the animations in an animation set
Load( )	Loads an animation set from a file, resource, memory, URL, or other sources
Time	
SetTime( )	Sets the time for a specific animation set

Search path functions

There is an environment variable in retained mode, named D3DPATH, that holds a list of directories, which are searched when the application needs to load a mesh, frame, animation, or texture, stored in a file. The path-related functions of IDirect3DRM3 enable you to obtain and set the search path and add directories to the current search path. Table 16-13 lists the path-related function in IDirect3DRM3.

Table 16-13
Path-related Functions in the IDirect3DRM3 Interface

Function	Description
AddSearchPath( )	Adds a directory list to the end of the current file search path
GetSearchPath( )	Returns a string containing the search path formatted as a series of directories separated by the ; symbols
SetSearchPath( )	Sets the current search path, which is passed as a string containing the various directories, separated by the ; symbols

Object-based functions

Three loosely-related functions in the IDirect3DRM3 interface are associated with Direct3D objects. These are CreateObject( ), GetNamedObject( ), and EnumerateObjects( ).

The CreateObject() function is used internally by the various creation methods in the IDirect3DRM interface, such as CreateAnimation(), CreateFace(), CreateLight(), and so on. The CreateObject() function creates a new object, but does not initialize it. The objects created by the other creation functions, on the other hand, are initialized automatically. The only documented use of this function is in implementing aggregation of Direct3DRM objects. The function's general form is as follows:

```
HRESULT CreateObject(
                REFCLSID rclsid,            // 1
                LPUNKNOWN pUnkOuter,        // 2
                REFIID riid,                // 3
                LPVOID FAR *ppv             // 4
                );
```

The first parameter is a class identifier for the object to be created. The second parameter is a pointer to the outer IUnknown object if COM aggregation is being used. The third parameter is the interface identifier GUID. The fourth parameter is the address of a pointer to the object created if the call succeeds. The function returns D3DRM_OK if successful, or an error otherwise.

The GetNamedObject() function of IDirect3DRM3 provides a way of finding a Direct3DRM object given its name. Objects loaded from files in DirectX format are named. The function's general form is as follows:

```
HRESULT GetNamedObject(
                const char  *lpName,            // 1
                LPDIRECT3DRMOBJECT *lplpD3DRMObject   // 2
                );
```

The first parameter is a pointer to a NULL terminated string containing the name of the object to be searched for. The second parameter is the address that is initialized with the Direct3DRMObject pointer if the call succeeds. The call returns D3DRM_OK if it succeeds, or an error code otherwise. If no object with the specified named is found, the function returns D3DRM_OK but, in this case, the lplpD3DRMObject parameter is NULL.

A Direct3D scene often contains several objects, which code may need to count or may have them to perform some specific task. The EnumerateObjects() function of IDirect3DRM3 calls a callback function for each object in the scene. The callback function, of type D3DRMOBJECTCALLBACK, can be used to count the objects or to perform object-specific operations. The function has the following general form:

```
HRESULT EnumerateObjects(
                    D3DRMOBJECTCALLBACK func,    // 1
                    LPVOID lpArg                 // 2
                    );
```

The first parameter is the address of the application-defined callback function that is called for each retained mode object in the scene. The second parameter is the address of the application-defined data passed to the callback function. The function returns D3DRM_OK if it succeeds, or an error otherwise.

The callback function is defined as follows:

```
void (*D3DRMOBJECTCALLBACK)(
                          LPDIRECT3DRMOBJECT lpD3DRMobj,   // 1
                          LPVOID lpArg);                   // 2
```

The first parameter passed to the callback function is a pointer to the IDirect3DRMObject interface for the object being enumerated. The application must use the Release() function for each enumerated object. The second parameter is the address of a pointer to application-defined data passed to the callback function. The function returns void.

Creating a UserVisual Object

Direct3D UserVisual objects provide a mechanism whereby a retained mode application can access immediate mode execute buffers or perform other low-level rendering operations. You can think of the UserVisual as a retained mode application's back door into immediate mode. In this manner applications can take advantage of the high-level convenience of retained mode, and still be capable of using immediate mode to improve rendering performance or to implement special effects.

The call to CreateUserVisual() defines the address of a callback function that is called during the rendering process. The function's general form is as follows:

```
HRESULT CreateUserVisual(
                 D3DRMUSERVISUALCALLBACK fn,           // 1
                 LPVOID lpArg,                         // 2
                 LPDIRECT3DRMUSERVISUAL *lplpD3DRMUV   // 3
                 );
```

The first parameter is the address of an application-defined callback function. The second parameter is the address of the application-defined data that is passed to the callback function. The third parameter is the address that is filled with a pointer to an IDirect3DRMUserVisual interface if the call succeeds. The function returns D3DRM_OK if it succeeds, or an error otherwise.

The third parameter to the CreateUserVisual() function returns a pointer to the IDirect3DRMUserVisual interface. The interface provides a single function, named Init(), which is used to initialize a user visual object created by calling the CreateObject() function of IDirect3DRM. Objects created with the CreateUserVisual() function are initialized automatically.

The callback function for the CreateUserVisual() call is of type D3DRMUSERVISUAL
CALLBACK and is defined as follows:

```
int (*D3DRMUSERVISUALCALLBACK)(
                LPDIRECT3DRMUSERVISUAL lpD3DRMUV,          // 1
                LPVOID lpArg,                              // 2
                D3DRMUSERVISUALREASON lpD3DRMUVreason,     // 3
                LPDIRECT3DRMDEVICE lpD3DRMDev,             // 4
                LPDIRECT3DRMVIEWPORT lpD3DRMview           // 5
                );
```

The first parameter to the callback function is the address of a pointer to the
Direct3DRMUserVisual object. The second parameter is the address of a pointer
to application-defined data passed to this callback function. The third parameter
is one of the members of the D3DRMUSERVISUALREASON enumerated type. The
following constants are defined in the enumeration:

1. D3DRMUSERVISUAL_CANSEE. The application should return TRUE if the
   user-visual object is visible in the viewport. The application uses the device
   specified in the lpD3DRMview parameter to determine if this is the case.

2. D3DRMUSERVISUAL_RENDER. The application should render the user-visual
   element. In this case, the application uses the device specified in the
   lpD3DRMDev parameter.

The fourth parameter is the address of a pointer to a Direct3DRMDevice
object used to render the Direct3DRMUserVisual object. The fifth parameter
is the address of a pointer to a Direct3DRMViewport object. This parameter is
used to determine whether the Direct3DRMUserVisual object is visible. The
callback function should return TRUE if the lpD3DRMUVreason parameter is
D3DRMUSERVISUAL_CANSEE, and the user-visual object is visible in the viewport.
It should return FALSE otherwise. If the lpD3DRMUVreason parameter is
D3DRMUSERVISUAL_RENDER, the return value is application-defined.
Microsoft documentation states that it is always safe to return TRUE.

The UserVisual callback function is called twice during the rendering process.
The first time it is called, the third parameter is set to D3DRMUSERVISUAL_CANSEE.
In this case the callback function is expected to determine if the UserVisual is
currently in view. If so, the callback should return TRUE. The application can use
the fifth parameter to determine this. Then the UserVisual callback is called
again with the third parameter set to D3DRMUSERVISUAL_RENDER. At this time
the callback function is expected to render the 3D image data.

Loading a retained mode object

The Load() function of IDirect3DRM3 provides a mechanism for loading an object stored in a file, resource, memory block, or a stream. These are objects typically stored in DirectX format files. The function's general form is as follows:

```
HRESULT Load(
        LPVOID lpvObjSource,                            // 1
        LPVOID lpvObjID,                                // 2
        LPIID *lplpGUIDs,                               // 3
        DWORD dwcGUIDs,                                 // 4
        D3DRMLOADOPTIONS d3drmLOFlags,                  // 5
        D3DRMLOADCALLBACK d3drmLoadProc,                // 6
        LPVOID lpArgLP,                                 // 7
        D3DRMLOADTEXTURE3CALLBACK d3drmLoadTextureProc, // 8
        LPVOID lpArgLTP,                                // 9
        LPDIRECT3DRMFRAME3 lpParentFrame                // 10
        );
```

The first parameter is the source for the object to be loaded. This can be a file, resource, memory block, or stream, depending on the source flags specified in the fifth parameter. The second parameter is the object name or position to be loaded. Which one it is depends on the identifier flags specified in the fifth parameter. If the D3DRMLOAD_BYPOSITION flag is specified, then the second parameter is a pointer to a DWORD value that gives the object's order in the file. The second parameter can be NULL. The third parameter is the address of an array of interface identifiers to be loaded. The following are possible GUIDs:

IID_IDirect3DRMProgressiveMesh

IID_IDirect3DRMMeshBuilder3

IID_IDirect3DRMAnimationSet2

IID_IDirect3DRMAnimation2

IID_IDirect3DRMFrame3

The fourth parameter is the number of elements specified in the third parameter. The fifth parameter is the value of the D3DRMLOADOPTIONS type describing the load options. Table 16-14 lists the constants that are defined in the D3DRMLOADOPTIONS data type.

Table 16-14 D3DRMLOADOPTIONS Constants	
Constant	**Value**
D3DRMLOAD_FROMFILE	0x00L
D3DRMLOAD_FROMRESOURCE	0x01L
D3DRMLOAD_FROMMEMORY	0x02L
D3DRMLOAD_FROMURL	0x08L
D3DRMLOAD_BYNAME	0x10L
D3DRMLOAD_BYPOSITION	0x20L
D3DRMLOAD_BYGUID	0x30L
D3DRMLOAD_FIRST	0x40L
D3DRMLOAD_INSTANCEBYREFERENCE	0x100L
D3DRMLOAD_INSTANCEBYCOPYING	0x200L
D3DRMLOAD_ASYNCHRONOUS	0x400L

The sixth parameter is the address of the callback function used when the system reads the specified object. This callback function is of type D3DRMLOADCALLBACK. The seventh parameter is the address of application-defined data passed to the D3DRMLOADCALLBACK callback function. The eighth parameter is the address of a D3DRMLOADTEXTURE3CALLBACK callback function used to load any textures that require special formatting. This parameter can be NULL. The ninth parameter is the address of application-defined data passed to the D3DRMLOADTEXTURE3CALLBACK callback function. The tenth parameter is the address of a parent of the Direct 3DRMFrame object. This argument only affects the loading of animation sets. The function returns D3DRM_OK if it succeeds, or an error otherwise.

Producing a heartbeat

Direct3D frames can contain moving positions and rotations that are used by the renderer in implementing animated effects. The Tick() function of the IDirect3DRM3 interface produces a heartbeat pulse that updates the positions of all moving frames according to their current motion attributes. At this time the scene is also rendered and the corresponding callback functions are called. Tick() is a synchronous method; control is not returned to the caller until rendering is complete. The function has the following general form:

```
HRESULT Tick(
        D3DVALUE d3dvalTick            // 1
        );
```

The function's only parameter is a value that defines the velocity and rotation step for the SetRotation() and SetVelocity() functions of the IDirect3DRMFrame3 interface. These functions are discussed in Chapter 17. Tick() returns D3DRM_OK if the call succeeds, or an error otherwise.

Microsoft documentation states that other retained mode methods enable implementing the heartbeat function with more rendering flexibility. The Move() method of IDirect3DRMFrame3 interface is one of them. Move() is discussed in Chapter 19.

Setting the retained mode geometry

Most applications use a left-handed coordinate system, which is the default in Direct3D. Nevertheless, DirectX 6 introduced a new function, named SetOption(), in the IDirect3DRM3 interface, which provides a way of changing to right-handed geometry. The function's general form is as follows:

```
HRESULT GetOptions(
                LPDWORD lpdwOptions             // 1
                );
```

The function's only parameter is a pointer to a flag value that indicates one of the following values:

> D3DRMOPTIONS_LEFTHANDED. Use left-handed geometry. This value is the default.
>
> D3DRMOPTIONS_RIGHTHANDED. Use right-handed geometry.

The function returns one of the following values:

> DDERR_INVALIDOBJECT
>
> DDERR_INVALIDPARAMS
>
> DD_OK

The selected retained mode geometry affects functions in the following interfaces:

> IDirect3DRMClippedVisual
>
> IDirect3DRMMesh
>
> IDirect3DRMMeshBuilder3
>
> IDirect3DRMProgressiveMesh
>
> IDirect3DRMShadow2
>
> IDirect3DRMTexture3
>
> IDirect3DRMViewport2

Summary

In this chapter we examined the retained mode interface and its organization. We also investigated the highest-level functions and controls that are available in Direct3D. The functions at this level are used for creating the Direct3D retained mode objects, accessing system-level variables, and performing calculations and transformations. In the following chapter we descend one notch in the retained mode hierarchy, and examine the functionality that is available at the device level. As we descend into this hierarchy, we progressively gain more knowledge of the modeling and rendering powers of Direct3D retained mode.

✦   ✦   ✦

Device-Level Operations

Direct3D retained mode device-level operations provide mechanisms for controlling the display device and the rendering output. Device-level functions enable applications to control the rendering quality; to set modes and retrieve information regarding shading, textures, transparency, and dithering; and to define the number of buffers used in rendering operations. In addition, device-level functions provide information regarding the device dimensions, the color model, the viewports associated with the device, and other useful data. Because operations at the device-level are independent of the scene or the scene components, device-level controls can be activated at the time the scene is being rendered.

It is important to realize that programming operations at the device level refer mostly to initialization, mode setting, performance control, and data retrieval. Although device-level controls influence the rendering, the actual rendering manipulations take place at lower levels and are discussed later in this book.

Retained Mode Device Interface

We have seen that Direct3D retained mode applications use the functions of the `IDirect3DRM` interface to create retained mode objects. One of the objects created is the Direct3D retained mode device. In program 3DRM InWin Demo1, listed in Chapter 15, the device was created with the following statement:

```
retval = lpD3DRM-
>CreateDeviceFromClipper(lpDDClipper,
                         NULL,
                         rc.right,
rc.bottom,
                         &globVars.aDevice);
```

The fact that the reference pointer is of type LPD3DRM ensures that the device is a retained mode device. After the device is created, applications can use the functions of the IDirect3DRMDevice3 interface. These methods provide interaction between the application and the output device, typically the video display.

Functions in IDirect3DRMDevice3

Applications use the methods of the IDirect3DRMDevice3 interface to interact with the output device. The interfaces support Draw Primitive methods and execute buffers. This interface is required for progressive meshes, alpha blending, and for sorting transparent objects. IDirect3DRMDevice3 includes all the functions in IDirect3DRMDevice2 and IDirect3DRMDevice interfaces, and adds FindPreferred TextureFormat() to select a specific texture format. It also adds four new functions that eliminate the possibility of setting a state to a value equal to its current value. These are GetStateChangeOptions(), LightStateChange(), RenderState Change(), and SetStateChangeOptions(). Table 17-1 lists the functions available in IDirect3DRMDevice3 interface.

Table 17-1
Functions of IDirect3DRMDevice3 Interface

Groups	Methods
Initialization	Init() InitFromClipper() InitFromD3D2() InitFromSurface()
State changes	GetStateChangeOptions() LightStateChange() RenderStateChange() SetStateChangeOptions()
Window updates and notifications	AddUpdateCallback() DeleteUpdateCallback() Update()
Rendering quality	GetQuality() SetQuality()
Rendering attributes	GetShades() SetShades() GetTextureQuality() SetTextureQuality() FindPreferredTextureFormat() GetRenderMode() **(transparency)** SetRenderMode() **(transparency)** GetDither() SetDither()

Groups	Methods
Device information	GetDirect3DDevice2() GetHeight() GetTrianglesDrawn() GetViewports() GetWidth() GetWireframeOptions() GetColorModel()
Buffer control	GetBufferCount() SetBufferCount()

Device initialization functions

The IDirect3DRMDevice3 interface contains four functions that perform initialization operations: Init(), InitFromClipper(), InitFromD3D2(), and InitFrom Surface(). Notice that the names of these initialization functions match those of the device creation functions described in Chapter 16 and listed in Table 16-2, namely CreateDevice(), CreateDeviceFromClipper(), CreateDeviceFromD3D(), and CreateDeviceFromSurface(). The Init() function, like its matching function CreateDevice(), is not implemented in Windows.

The device-creation functions, mentioned previously, automatically initialize the device at the time it is created. This is the way recommended by Microsoft for creating and initializing devices in Direct3D. Because the create device-type methods of IDirect3DRM3 encapsulate the functionality of device creation and initialization, most applications will not use the initialization function in the IDirect3DRMDevice3 interface. For this reason we do not discuss these function any further.

Render state changes

Device render states refer to controls in the Direct3D device rasterization module. Immediate mode applications can alter the render state by modifying attributes that relate to shading, fog, texture styles, texture filtering, and other rasterization options. Applications control the render state by using functions of the IDirect3DDevice3 interface, which is part of Direct3D immediate mode.

Earlier versions of retained mode could not assume that render and light states would remain the same from one call to the next. This resulted in retained mode often setting the state to a value equal to its current value. The IDirect3DRMDevice3 interface introduced several new functions that eliminated these redundant state changes. The functions are named GetStateChangeOptions(), LightStateChange(), Render StateChange(), and SetStateChangeOptions().

The only effect that results from avoiding redundant state changes is a minor increase in application performance. Furthermore, state changes are part of Direct3D immediate mode. For these reasons we do not discuss state change functions at this point.

Window Updates and Notifications

In the sample program presented in Chapter 15, named 3DRM InWin Demo1, and also in the one developed later in this chapter, we render a scene to a device by following three steps: first we clear the viewport, then we render the scene to the viewport, and finally we update the Window. The code is as follows:

```
// Clear the viewport.
   retval = globVars.aViewport->Clear(D3DRMCLEAR_ALL);
   if (FAILED(retval))
   {
       // Viewport clearing error handler goes here
   }

// Render the scene to the viewport.
   retval = globVars.aViewport->Render(globVars.aScene);
   if (FAILED(retval))
   {
       // Scene rendering error handler goes here
   }
   // Update the Window
   retval = globVars.aDevice->Update();
   if (FAILED(retval))
   {
       // Window update error handler goes here
   }
```

Notice that the third of these operations, updating the Window, is performed by means of the Update() function of the IDirect3DRMDevice3 interface. It is this call that copies the image in the viewport to the screen. The function's general form is as follows:

```
HRESULT Update( );
```

In addition to copying the image from the viewport to the display buffer, Update() provides an update pulse to the device driver. The function returns D3DRM_OK if it succeeds, or an error otherwise.

Each call to the Update() function causes the system to call an application-defined callback function of type D3DRMDEVICE3UPDATECALLBACK. The update callback mechanism is useful to code that needs to override the renderer's default behavior. Because this usually requires going into immediate mode programming, the mechanism is not frequently used by retained mode applications. The callback function's general form is as follows:

```
void (*D3DRMDEVICE3UPDATECALLBACK)(
                LPDIRECT3DRMDEVICE3 lpobj,           // 1
                LPVOID lpArg,                        // 2
                int iRectCount,                      // 3
                LPD3DRECT d3dRectUpdate              // 4
                );
```

The first parameter passed to the callback function is the address of a pointer to the Direct3DRMDevice3 object to which this callback function applies. The second parameter is the address of a pointer to application-defined data passed to the callback function. The third parameter is the number of rectangles specified in the fourth parameter. The fourth parameter is an array of one or more D3DRECT structures that describe the area to be updated. The coordinates are in device units. The function returns nothing.

Two other functions in IDirect3DRMDevice3 relate to update notifications: Add UpdateCallback() and DeleteUpdateCallback(). The first one is used to install an update notification callback and the second one to remove an installed update callback. AddUpdateCallback() has the following general form:

```
HRESULT AddUpdateCallback(
                D3DRMDEVICE3UPDATECALLBACK d3drmUpdateProc,    // 1
                LPVOID arg                                      // 2
                );
```

The first parameter is a pointer to an application-defined callback function, of type D3DRMDEVICE3UPDATECALLBACK, discussed previously. The second parameter is a pointer to the application-defined data to be passed to the update callback function. The function returns D3DRM_OK if it succeeds, or an error otherwise.

To remove an update callback function that was added by using the AddUpdate Callback() you use the DeleteUpdateCallback() function of IDirect3DRM Device3. The function has the following general form:

```
HRESULT DeleteUpdateCallback(
                D3DRMDEVICE3UPDATECALLBACK d3drmUpdateProc,    // 1
                LPVOID arg                                      // 2
                );
```

The arguments are the same as for the AddUpdateCallback() function. The function returns D3DRM_OK if it succeeds, or an error otherwise.

Rendering Quality

Retained mode code can manipulate the degree of realism with which an object is rendered. This is usually referred to as the *rendering quality*. The rendering quality consists of three individual elements:

✦ **The shading mode.** Currently flat and Gouraud shading modes are implemented. Direct3D retained mode assumes that the quality of the shading mode is lowest for the flat mode and highest for Gouraud. Phong mode has not yet been implemented.

✦ **The light mode.** This can be on or off. The on value is assumed to be of higher quality than the off value.

✦ **The fill mode.** Points, wireframe, and solid fill modes are currently available. Solid is assumed to be of the highest quality, followed by the wireframe and points modes.

Rendering quality rules

Rendering qualities can be applied to the devices as well as to mesh, progressive mesh, and meshbuilder objects. The resulting quality of rendering is determined by the quality values of the device and the objects according to predefined rules. These rules are as follows:

1. In regards to quality settings that affect the device, progressive mesh, and meshbuilder objects, retained mode uses the lowest quality at rendering time. For example, if the shading mode for a meshbuilder object is set to Gouraud and the rendering quality for the device is flat, then the rendering takes place using the flat quality setting.

2. In regards to mesh objects, the device quality setting is ignored and the quality setting for the mesh group is used.

Default quality settings

The default setting for the render quality changes for the device and the different objects. Table 17-2 shows the values.

The final rendered quality is determined by the installed settings for each of the object types, by the default setting of those not specifically changed by code, and by the rendering rules described previously. For example, if the application has created a mesh group, its quality settings will take precedence. If no mesh object exists, as is often the case in retained mode, then the lower settings of the meshbuilder, progressive mesh, and device objects will be used. For example, if code changes the device setting to Phong shading without modifying the default setting of the meshbuilder object, then the device Phong setting for the device is ignored and the meshbuilder setting (in this case Gouraud) is used by the renderer.

Table 17-2
Default Settings for Rendering Quality

Object	Shading	Light	Fill
Device	Flat	On	Solid
Mesh	Gouraud	On	Solid
Meshbuilder	Gouraud	On	Solid
ProgressiveMesh	Gouraud	On	Solid

After you destroy the objects used in creating the scene, the quality setting for these objects is no longer accessible to code. In this case changing the quality settings at the device level has no effect on the rendering. For example, if you created the scene by means of a meshbuilder object, using the default quality, as is the case in the sample program developed in Chapter 15, then changing the device quality to a higher value has no effect because the lowest one is used by the renderer. More concretely, because the default shading for a meshbuilder object is Gouraud, you cannot produce Phong shading by changing the device quality at rendering time. However, if you create the meshbuilder object with the highest possible settings (presently Phong shading, lights on, and solid fill) then you can change the rendering quality by manipulating the quality settings at the device level.

Changing the rendering quality

In the discussion that follows we assume that the mesh was created using a mesh-builder object, as is the case in the 3DRM InWin Demo1 program developed in Chapter 15 and the 3DRM InWin Demo2 program developed later in this chapter. For the moment we ignore objects created using the mesh or progressive mesh interfaces.

To set the rendering quality of a meshbuilder object, use the SetQuality() function of the IDirect3DRMMeshBuilder interface. To set the rendering quality of a device object, use the SetQuality() function of the IDirect3DRMDevice3 interface. Both functions have identical signatures. Their general form is as follows:

```
HRESULT SetQuality (
                    D3DRMRENDERQUALITY rqQuality          // 1
                    );
```

The only parameter is a value obtained from the D3DRMRENDERQUALITY enumeration, which is defined as follows:

```
typedef enum _D3DRMSHADEMODE {
    D3DRMSHADE_FLAT       = 0,
    D3DRMSHADE_GOURAUD    = 1,
```

```
        D3DRMSHADE_PHONG        = 2,
        D3DRMSHADE_MASK         = 7,
        D3DRMSHADE_MAX          = 8
    } D3DRMSHADEMODE;
    typedef enum _D3DRMLIGHTMODE {
        D3DRMLIGHT_OFF          = 0 * D3DRMSHADE_MAX,
        D3DRMLIGHT_ON           = 1 * D3DRMSHADE_MAX,
        D3DRMLIGHT_MASK         = 7 * D3DRMSHADE_MAX,
        D3DRMLIGHT_MAX          = 8 * D3DRMSHADE_MAX
    } D3DRMLIGHTMODE;
    typedef enum _D3DRMFILLMODE {
        D3DRMFILL_POINTS        = 0 * D3DRMLIGHT_MAX,
        D3DRMFILL_WIREFRAME     = 1 * D3DRMLIGHT_MAX,
        D3DRMFILL_SOLID         = 2 * D3DRMLIGHT_MAX,
        D3DRMFILL_MASK          = 7 * D3DRMLIGHT_MAX,
        D3DRMFILL_MAX           = 8 * D3DRMLIGHT_MAX
    } D3DRMFILLMODE;
```

D3DRMRENDERQUALITY contains three enumerations: one for the shade mode, one
for the light mode, and one for the fill mode. D3DRMRENDERQUALITY is defined in
terms of these enumerations, as follows:

```
    typedef DWORD D3DRMRENDERQUALITY;
        #define D3DRMRENDER_WIREFRAME
            (D3DRMSHADE_FLAT+D3DRMLIGHT_OFF+D3DRMFILL_WIREFRAME)
        #define D3DRMRENDER_UNLITFLAT
            (D3DRMSHADE_FLAT+D3DRMLIGHT_OFF+D3DRMFILL_SOLID)
        #define D3DRMRENDER_FLAT
            (D3DRMSHADE_FLAT+D3DRMLIGHT_ON+D3DRMFILL_SOLID)
        #define D3DRMRENDER_GOURAUD
            (D3DRMSHADE_GOURAUD+D3DRMLIGHT_ON+D3DRMFILL_SOLID)
        #define D3DRMRENDER_PHONG
            (D3DRMSHADE_PHONG+D3DRMLIGHT_ON+D3DRMFILL_SOLID)
```

Notice that each of the constants is defined as the sum of the three primitives
for shade mode, light mode, and fill mode listed previously. Table 17-3 lists the
descriptions and actions of these constants.

Table 17-3
Constants Defined for the SetQuality() Function

Constant	Action
D3DRMRENDER_WIREFRAME	Display only the edges
D3DRMRENDER_UNLITFLAT	Flat shading without lighting
D3DRMRENDER_FLAT	Flat shaded with lighting
D3DRMRENDER_GOURAUD	Gouraud shading
D3DRMRENDER_PHONG	Phong shading

Applications can use these predefined constants when setting the rendering quality, as in the following code fragment:

```
HERESULT         retval;
LPDIRECT3DRMMESHBUILDER3 meshbuilder = NULL;
. . .
// Set highest rendering quality for meshbuilder
retval = meshbuilder->SetQuality(D3DRMRENDER_PHONG);
   if(FAILED(retval))
   {
        // Failed quality setting error handler goes here
   }
```

Expressing quality numerically

The predefined constants listed in Table 17-3 are useful in cases in which you can determine the rendering quality at compile time and when it fits one of the preestablished settings. When you need to change the rendering quality at run time or select a combination of attributes that is not implemented in one of the five predefined constants, then the value of the quality attribute can be calculated numerically. The values for the enumerations are listed in Table 17-4.

Table 17-4 Numerical Values Used in Calculating the Render Quality	
Mode	**Value**
Shade mode	
Flat	0
Gouraud	1
Phong	2
Mask	7
Max	8
Light mode	
Off	$0 \ (0 \times 8)$
On	$8 \ (1 \times 8)$
Mask	$56 \ (7 \times 8)$
Max	$64 \ (8 \times 8)$
Fill Mode	
Points	$0 \ (0 \times 64)$
Wireframe	$64 \ (1 \times 64)$
Solid	$128 \ (2 \times 64)$

Continued

Table 17-4 *(continued)*	
Mode	**Value**
Mask	448 (7×64)
Max	512 (8×64)

Using Table 17-4, an application can calculate any quality setting combination by adding the values of the desired attributes. For example, the setting for wireframe fill, light on, and flat shading is 64 + 8 + 0 = 72. The following code fragment shows setting the rendering quality using numerical values.

```
// Variables for render quality setting
int        shadeValue = 0;      // Shade mode default is FLAT
int        lightValue = 8;      // Light mode default is ON
int        fillValue  = 128;    // Fill mode default is SOLID
. . .

HRESULT    retval;
int        qualityValue;
. . .
// Set device rendering quality
qualityValue = fillValue + lightValue + shadeValue;
retval = globVars.aDevice->SetQuality(qualityValue);
if(FAILED(retval))
    {
        // Device quality setting error handler goes here
    }
```

Interaction and visual effects

The rendering quality settings for shade, light, and fill attributes sometimes interact with each other. Of these, the most obvious one results from turning the light attribute off. In this case the rendering appears as a flat outline and the shade and fill attributes are ignored. The shade attributes, flat, Gouraud, and Phong, require a solid fill mode and the light mode should be turned on. On the other hand, the fill attributes wireframe and points are unaffected by the selected shade attribute.

The Set Quality command of the Rendering menu, in the 3DRM InWin Demo2 project in the book's CD-ROM, enables you to change the shade, light, and fill attributes to all the documented values. Figure 17-1 shows the dialog box used for setting the rendering qualities in the 3DRM InWin Demo2 program.

The fill mode settings of points, wireframe, and solid have different visual results. In the points mode only the vertex points are displayed. In the wireframe mode the vertex points are joined by straight lines. In both the points and the wireframe modes, the shade mode value is ignored. The solid fill mode renders the polygon faces using the flat, Gouraud, or Phong shade mode; whichever is currently selected. Figure 17-2 shows the effects of the various fill modes.

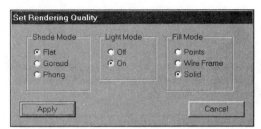

Figure 17-1: Set Rendering Quality dialog box in the 3DRM InWin Demo2 program

Figure 17-2: Points, wireframe, and solid fill mode

The shade modes, flat, Gouraud, and Phong, all required the solid fill mode value as well as the light attribute on. Figure 17-3 shows the same object rendered in each of the Direct3D shade modes.

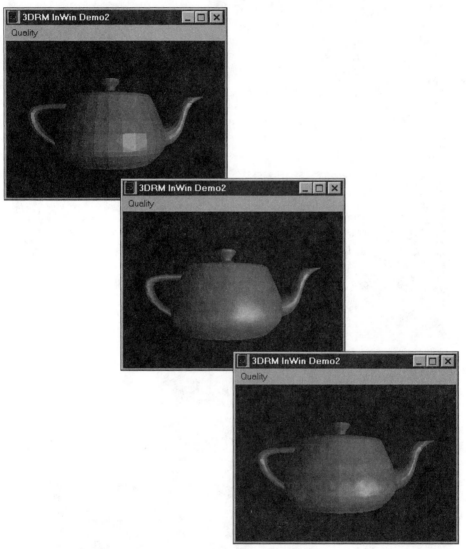

Figure 17-3: Flat, Gouraud, and Phong shade mode values

Obtaining the rendering quality

Applications can obtain the texture quality at the device level by calling the GetQuality() function of IDirect3DRMDevice3 interface. The function has the following general form:

```
D3DRMRENDERQUALITY GetQuality();
```

The returned value is the rendering quality encoded in one or more members of the enumerated type D3DRMRENDERQUALITY mentioned previously. Code can decipher which of the shading, light, and fill mode qualities are present by testing for the individual constants. Alternatively it is possible to mask out the individual bit fields that encode the shade, light, and fill mode attributes, as shown in Figure 17-4.

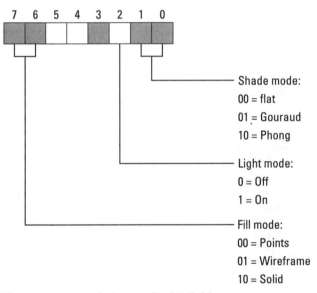

Figure 17-4: Rendering quality bit fields

Rendering Attributes

In this section we discuss four rendering attributes that are accessed at the device level: texture, shades, transparency, and dithering. IDirect3DRMDevice3 provides functions for setting and retrieving the values assigned to these attributes.

Texture

The notion of texture quality actually includes texture filters, blends, and transparency. However, the Direct3D `SetTextureQuality()` function, of the `IDirect 3DRMDevice3` interface, applies to texture filters only. Texture filtering is the texture rendering control that takes place at the device level. Therefore, we now focus our attention on this texture quality. Transparency is discussed later in this chapter and blends in other chapters.

Texture filters

Texture filters specify how to interpolate texels to pixels. The fundamentals of texture filtering were discussed in Chapter 14. We now recall that Direct3D supports the following texture filtering modes:

- ✦ nearest
- ✦ linear
- ✦ mip-nearest
- ✦ mip-linear
- ✦ linear-mip-nearest
- ✦ linear-mip-linear

In the nearest mode, the renderer uses the texel with coordinates nearest to the desired pixel value. The result is a point filter with no mipmapping. This is the default texture filter. In the linear mode the weighted average of an area of 2×2 texels surrounding the desired pixel is used. This mode does not support mipmapping. In the mip-nearest mode the closest mipmap level is chosen and a point filter is applied. In the mip-linear mode the closest mipmap level is chosen and a bilinear filter is applied. The linear-mip-nearest mode uses the two closest mipmap levels, and a linear blend is used between point filtered samples of each level. In the liner-mip-linear mode the two closest mipmap levels are chosen and then combined using a bilinear filter.

Setting the texture quality

Applications change the texture filter by means of the `SetTextureQuality()` function of the `IDirect3DRMDevice3` interface. The function's general form is as follows:

```
HRESULT SetTextureQuality(
                 D3DRMTEXTUREQUALITY tqTextureQuality   // 1
                 );
```

The function's only parameter is one of the members of the D3DRMTEXTUREQUALITY
enumerated type. The default is D3DRMTEXTURE_NEAREST. The enumerated type is
defined as follows:

```
typedef enum _D3DRMTEXTUREQUALITY{
    D3DRMTEXTURE_NEAREST,
    D3DRMTEXTURE_LINEAR,
    D3DRMTEXTURE_MIPNEAREST,
    D3DRMTEXTURE_MIPLINEAR,
    D3DRMTEXTURE_LINEARMIPNEAREST,
    D3DRMTEXTURE_LINEARMIPLINEAR
} D3DRMTEXTUREQUALITY;
```

The function returns D3DRM_OK if it succeeds, or an error otherwise.

The 3DRM InWin Demo2 project in the book's CD-ROM contains a menu entry
for setting the texture quality. Figure 17-5 shows the resulting dialog box.

Figure 17-5: Set Texture Quality dialog box
in the 3DRM InWin Demo2 program

In the 3DRM InWin Demo2 program changing the texture quality has no visible
effect on the displayed image because the coffeepot object contains no texture
wrap. In Chapter 22 we discuss creating and using textures and provide sample
code in which changing the texture filter affects the displayed image.

Obtaining the texture quality

Applications can obtain the texture quality presently associated with the device by
means of the GetTextureQuality() function of the IDirect3DRMDevice3 interface.
The texture quality is relevant only if the device is set in the RGB mode. The function
has the following general forms:

```
D3DRMTEXTUREQUALITY GetTextureQuality();
```

The returned value is the current texture quality constant for the device as defined in the D3DRMTEXTUREQUALITY enumerated type previously listed. Code can read the results numerically or by testing for one of the predefined constants.

The sample program 3DRM InWin Demo2 furnished in the book's CD-ROM contains a Get Quality command that obtains the device quality and displays the corresponding message box. The following code fragment shows the processing.

```
// Global variables
struct _globVars
{
    LPDIRECT3DRMDEVICE3 aDevice;      // Retained mode aDevice
. . .
} globVars;
D3DRMTEXTUREQUALITY  textQual;
. . .

// Get Texture quality menu command
case ID_TEXT_GETQUAL:
   textQual = globVars.aDevice->GetTextureQuality();
   if(textQual == D3DRMTEXTURE_NEAREST)
                       MessageBox(NULL, "Nearest",
                       "Texture Quality", MB_OK);
   if(textQual == D3DRMTEXTURE_LINEAR)
                       MessageBox(NULL, "Linear",
                       "Texture Quality", MB_OK);
   if(textQual == D3DRMTEXTURE_MIPNEAREST)
                       MessageBox(NULL, "Mip-Nearest",
                       "Texture Quality", MB_OK);
   if(textQual == D3DRMTEXTURE_MIPLINEAR)
                       MessageBox(NULL, "Mip-Linear",
                       "Texture Quality", MB_OK);
   if(textQual == D3DRMTEXTURE_LINEARMIPNEAREST)
                       MessageBox(NULL, "Linear-Mip-Nearest",
                       "Texture Quality", MB_OK);
   if(textQual == D3DRMTEXTURE_LINEARMIPLINEAR)
                       MessageBox(NULL, "Linear-Mip-Linear",
                       "Texture Quality", MB_OK);
  break;
```

Shading

In the present context the term shading is unrelated to the shade modes (flat, Gouraud, and Phong) that were discussed in previous sections. Instead, the term shades refers to shades-of-gray in Direct3D's monochromatic or ramp model. The SetShades() function of IDirect3DRMDevice3 sets the number of shades used in the monochromatic or ramp modes. The function has the following general form:

```
HRESULT SetShades(
              DWORD ulShades                    // 1
              );
```

The function's only parameter is the new number of shades. The default value is 32 and the value must be a power of 2. The function returns D3DRM_OK if it succeeds, or an error otherwise.

The function GetShades() of IDirect3DRMDevice3 retrieves the number of shades used in the ramp model. The function's general form is as follows:

```
DWORD GetShades();
```

The call returns the number of shades.

Transparency

Transparency controls were first implemented in the IDirect3DRMDevice2 interface of DirectX 5. The two transparency-related methods introduced at that time are named SetRenderMode() and GetRenderMode(). The IDirect3DRMDevice3 interface introduced in DirectX 6 added some new features to the transparency control functions.

Transparency determines how the color pixels of an object displayed, sometimes called the destination, interact with the color pixels of a previously displayed object, sometimes called the source. Notice that the Direct3D notion of source and destination is counter-intuitive.

Direct3D currently supports two major transparency modes (stippled and alpha blending) and several minor ones. The stippled transparency mode is the default setting. In this mode transparency is achieved by replacing some of the destination pixels with source pixels. The result is similar to viewing the scene through a screen that has been painted with the source image. For this reason it is also called screen door transparency.

Blended transparency refers to alpha blending of the source and the destination pixels. Alpha blending is discussed in detail later in this section.

In addition to the two major modes, stippled transparency and alpha blending, DirectX 6 introduced several submodes and transparency controls. In the sorted transparency mode transparent polygons in the scene are buffered, sorted, and rendered in a second pass. Sorted transparency is not compatible with alpha blending. Transparent polygons in external visuals or user visuals are not sorted. Only Direct3D retained mode visuals (such as D3DRMMesh objects and D3DRM MeshBuilder objects) are affected by this submode.

DirectX 6 also introduced a transparency control that takes into account the viewer's location and the light direction in providing a more realistic rendering of specular lights. Previous versions of DirectX supported flat specular light that did not take into account the viewer's location.

Setting and obtaining the render mode

The IDirect3DRMDevice3 interface contains a function to set the transparency mode and another one to obtain the currently installed transparency mode. SetRenderMode() determines how a transparent object is rendered. The function has the following general form:

```
HRESULT SetRenderMode(
                    DWORD dwFlags                    // 1
                );
```

The function's only parameter is one or more of the transparent mode flags. The default (dwFlags = 0) sets the transparency mode to stippled or screen door transparency. The other possible values for the transparency flag are as follows:

1. D3DRMRENDERMODE_BLENDEDTRANSPARENCY (dwFlags = 1) sets the transparency mode to alpha blending.

2. D3DRMRENDERMODE_DISABLESORTEDALPHAZWRITE (dwFlags = 32) specifies that no depth information will be written to the z-buffer when drawing sorted, transparent objects.

3. D3DRMRENDERMODE_LIGHTINMODELSPACE (dwFlags = 8) is defined in the documentation but not implemented.

4. D3DRMRENDERMODE_SORTEDTRANSPARENCY (dwFlags = 2) sets the transparency mode so that transparent polygons in the scene are buffered, sorted, and rendered in a second pass. This flag assumes alpha blending. Transparent polygons in external visuals or user visuals are not sorted. Only native Direct3D retained mode visuals (such as D3DRMMesh objects and D3DRMMeshBuilder objects) are sorted.

5. D3DRMRENDERMODE_VIEWDEPENDENTSPECULAR (dwFlags = 16) enables more realistic specular lights that depend both on the light direction and the viewer's location.

The function returns D3DRM_OK if it succeeds, or an error otherwise.

The function GetRenderMode() of IDirect3DRMDevice3 retrieves the current transparency flags. The function's general form is as follows:

```
DWORD GetRenderMode();
```

The return value is used to determine the state of one or more current transparency flags. These flags are bitmapped, as shown in Figure 17-6.

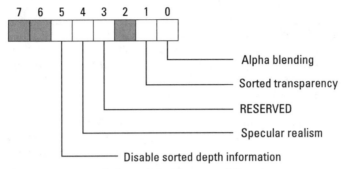

Figure 17-6: Rendering mode bitmapped flags

Code can test for the presence of the rendering mode flags by ANDing with the corresponding bit masks. The value of the individual constants are shown in Table 17-5.

Table 17-5 Numeric Value of Transparency Flags	
Flag	**Value**
D3DRMRENDERMODE_BLENDEDTRANSPARENCY	1
D3DRMRENDERMODE_DISABLESORTEDALPHAZWRITE	32
D3DRMRENDERMODE_LIGHTINMODELSPACE	8 (reserved)
D3DRMRENDERMODE_SORTEDTRANSPARENCY	2
D3DRMRENDERMODE_VIEWDEPENDENTSPECULAR	16

Alpha blending

Rendering transparent objects is computationally expensive and difficult to implement; transparent rendering in real time is even more painstaking. True-to-life, 3D rendering of transparent objects cannot be achieved with any method short of ray tracing. Alpha blending is a relatively simple technique for achieving a transparent quality that can be considered satisfactory in some applications. In alpha blending the pixels are given a transparent or semitransparent attribute in addition to their red, green, and blue values. This transparent attribute, called the alpha component, is stored separately from the RGB values. The resulting encoding is said to be in RGBA format, where the letter A represents the alpha channel or transparency value. Typically the alpha channel uses the same bit depth as the red, green, and blue components. For example, a 32-bit RGBA encoding uses 8 bits for each of the RGB color values and 8 bits for the alpha channel. In this case the bit field allows representing 256 transparency levels. A value of 0 indicates maximum transparency for that pixel, and a value of 255 maximum opacity.

Windows 98 and Windows 2000 support alpha blending in the GDI. DirectX, starting with version 6.0, also provides some alpha blending support, most of it in immediate mode. In this context the alpha channel value defines the pixel's transparency. When alpha blending is enabled, the colors, materials, and textures of a surface are blended with transparency onto another surface.

The SetRenderState() function of IDirect3DDevice3 (notice IDirect3DDevice3 is an immediate mode interface) enables you to set the render state. The function has the following general form:

```
HRESULT SetRenderState(
                  D3DRENDERSTATETYPE dwRenderStateType, // 1
                  DWORD dwRenderState                   // 2
                  );
```

The first parameter is the device state variable that is being modified. This parameter can be any of the members of the D3DRENDERSTATETYPE enumerated type. The following is a partial listing of the constants in this enumeration:

```
typedef enum _D3DRENDERSTATETYPE {
D3DRENDERSTATE_TEXTUREHANDLE      = 1,   // texture handle
D3DRENDERSTATE_ANTIALIAS          = 2,   // antialiasing mode
D3DRENDERSTATE_TEXTUREADDRESS     = 3,   // texture address
D3DRENDERSTATE_TEXTUREPERSPECTIVE = 4,   // perspective correction
D3DRENDERSTATE_WRAPU              = 5,   // wrap in u direction
D3DRENDERSTATE_WRAPV              = 6,   // wrap in v direction
D3DRENDERSTATE_ZENABLE            = 7,   // enable z test
D3DRENDERSTATE_FILLMODE           = 8,   // fill mode
D3DRENDERSTATE_SHADEMODE          = 9,   // shade mode
D3DRENDERSTATE_LINEPATTERN        = 10,  // line pattern
D3DRENDERSTATE_MONOENABLE         = 11,  // enable mono rendering
D3DRENDERSTATE_ROP2               = 12,  // raster operation
D3DRENDERSTATE_PLANEMASK          = 13,  // physical plane mask
D3DRENDERSTATE_ZWRITEENABLE       = 14,  // enable z writes
D3DRENDERSTATE_ALPHATESTENABLE    = 15,  // enable alpha tests
D3DRENDERSTATE_LASTPIXEL          = 16,  // draw last pixel in a line
```

```
D3DRENDERSTATE_TEXTUREMAG        = 17,   // how textures are magnified
D3DRENDERSTATE_TEXTUREMIN        = 18,   // how textures are reduced
D3DRENDERSTATE_SRCBLEND          = 19,   // blend factor is source
D3DRENDERSTATE_DESTBLEND         = 20,   // blend factor is destination
D3DRENDERSTATE_TEXTUREMAPBLEND   = 21,   // blend mode for map
D3DRENDERSTATE_CULLMODE          = 22,   // back-face culling mode
D3DRENDERSTATE_ZFUNC             = 23,   // z-comparison
D3DRENDERSTATE_ALPHAREF          = 24,   // reference alpha value
D3DRENDERSTATE_ALPHAFUNC         = 25,   // alpha-comparison function
D3DRENDERSTATE_DITHERENABLE      = 26,   // enable dithering
D3DRENDERSTATE_ALPHABLENDENABLE  = 27,   // enable alpha blending
D3DRENDERSTATE_FOGENABLE         = 28,   // enable fog
D3DRENDERSTATE_SPECULARENABLE    = 29,   // enable specular highlights
D3DRENDERSTATE_ZVISIBLE          = 30,   // enable z-checking
D3DRENDERSTATE_SUBPIXEL          = 31,   // enable subpixel correction
D3DRENDERSTATE_SUBPIXELX         = 32,   // x subpixel correction
D3DRENDERSTATE_STIPPLEDALPHA     = 33,   // enable stippled alpha
D3DRENDERSTATE_FOGCOLOR          = 34,   // fog color
D3DRENDERSTATE_FOGTABLEMODE      = 35,   // fog mode
D3DRENDERSTATE_FOGTABLESTART     = 36,   // fog table start
D3DRENDERSTATE_FOGTABLEEND       = 37,   // fog table end
D3DRENDERSTATE_FOGTABLEDENSITY   = 38,   // fog density
D3DRENDERSTATE_STIPPLEENABLE     = 39,   // enables stippling
D3DRENDERSTATE_EDGEANTIALIAS     = 40,   // antialias edges
D3DRENDERSTATE_COLORKEYENABLE    = 41,   // enable color-key
                                         // transparency
D3DRENDERSTATE_BORDERCOLOR       = 43,   // border color
D3DRENDERSTATE_TEXTUREADDRESSU   = 44,   // u texture address mode
D3DRENDERSTATE_TEXTUREADDRESSV   = 45,   // v texture address mode
D3DRENDERSTATE_MIPMAPLODBIAS     = 46,   // mipmap LOD bias
D3DRENDERSTATE_ZBIAS             = 47,   // z-bias
D3DRENDERSTATE_RANGEFOGENABLE    = 48,   // enables range-based fog
D3DRENDERSTATE_ANISOTROPY        = 49,   // maximum anisotropy
. . . ,
} D3DRENDERSTATETYPE;
```

The second parameter to the SetRenderState() function is the new value for the Direct3DDevice render state. The meaning of this parameter depends on the value of the first parameter. For example, if the first parameter is D3DRENDERSTATE_SRCBLEND or D3DRENDERSTATE_DESTBLEND, then the second parameter would be one of the members of the D3DBLEND enumerated type. The D3DBLEND enumeration constants, numeric values, and descriptions are shown in Table 17-6. In Table 17-6 RGBA values of the source and destination are indicated with the subscripts s and d.

Table 17-6
D3DBLEND Enumeration Constants

Constant	Value	Blend/Comment			
		R	G	B	A
D3DBLEND_ZERO	1	0	0	0	0
D3DBLEND_ONE	2	1	1	1	1
D3DBLEND_SRCCOLOR	3	s	s	s	s
D3DBLEND_INVSRCCOLOR	4	1-s	1-s	1-s	1-s
D3DBLEND_SRCALPHA	5	s	s	s	s
D3DBLEND_INVSRCALPHA	6	1-s	1-s	1-s	1-s
D3DBLEND_DESTALPHA	7	d	d	d	d
D3DBLEND_INVDESTALPHA	8	1-d	1-d	1-d	1-d
D3DBLEND_DESTCOLOR	9	d	d	d	d
D3DBLEND_INVDESTCOLOR	10	1-d	1-d	1-d	1-d
D3DBLEND_SRCALPHASAT	11	1-d	1-d	1-d	1
D3DBLEND_BOTHSRCALPHA	12	obsolete			
D3DBLEND_BOTHINVSRCALPHA	13	1-s 1-d	1-s 1-d	1-s 1-d	1-s/ 1-d

Applications use the D3DRENDERSTATE_ALPHABLENDENABLE enumerated constant (value = 27) to enable alpha transparency blending. Direct3D supports several types of alpha blending; however, keep in mind that they may not all be supported by the hardware.

The type of alpha blending depends on the D3DRENDERSTATE_SRCBLEND (value = 19) and D3DRENDERSTATE_DESTBLEND (value = 20) render states. Source and destination blend states are used in pairs. The following code fragment shows setting the source blend state set to D3DBLEND_SRCCOLOR and the destination blend state to D3DBLEND_INVSRCCOLOR.

```
// Code assumes that lpD3DDevice3 is a valid pointer to
// an IDirect3DDevice3 interface.
// Set the source blend state.
lpD3DDevice3->SetRenderState(D3DRENDERSTATE_SRCBLEND,
                    D3DBLEND_SRCCOLOR);
```

```
// Set the destination blend state.
lpD3DDevice3->SetRenderState(D3DRENDERSTATE_DESTBLEND,
                             D3DBLEND_INVSRCCOLOR);
```

After these calls to SetRenderState() Direct3D is configured to perform a linear blend between the source color (the color existing at the blend location) and the destination color (the color in the frame buffer). Recall that Direct3D's designation of source and destination is rather unconventional. In this case, the result simulates tinted glass, that is, some of the color of the destination object seems to be transmitted through the source object. The rest of the color appears to be absorbed. Code can create many interesting and intriguing effects by altering the source and destination blend states. For example, transparency can be used to simulate a light-emitting object in a foggy atmosphere.

Light mapping

Alpha blending is also used to control the lighting in a 3D scene. This is sometimes called light mapping. Setting the source blend state to D3DBLEND_ZERO and the destination blend state to D3DBLEND_SRCALPHA darkens a scene according to the value in the source's alpha channel. In this case the source is used as a light map that scales the contents of the frame buffer and darkens it when appropriate. The result is monochrome light mapping. Color light mapping can be achieved by setting the source alpha blending state to D3DBLEND_ZERO and the destination blend state to D3DBLEND_SRCCOLOR.

Alpha-testing

Code can use alpha testing to control when pixels are written to the target surface. By selecting the D3DRENDERSTATE_ALPHATESTENABLE enumerated value, the application sets the current Direct3D device so that it tests each pixel according to an alpha test function. If the test succeeds, the pixel is written to the surface. If not, Direct3D ignores it. Code selects the alpha test function with the D3DRENDERSTATE_ALPHAFUNC enumerated value. You can set a reference alpha value for all pixels to be compared against by using the D3DRENDERSTATE_ALPHAREF render state.

Alpha testing is most frequently used to improve performance when rendering objects that are nearly transparent. If the color data being rasterized is more opaque than the color already at a given pixel (D3DPCMPCAPS_GREATEREQUAL), then the pixel is written; otherwise the rasterizer ignores the pixel altogether, thus saving the processing required to blend the two colors.

Dithering

Dithering is a process whereby a color that is not available in a surface is simulated by displaying alternate pixels of approximate colors. In Direct3D, dithering is used to improve color resolution and reduce artifacts in display modes of less than 24 bits per pixel. Because dithering is on by default, and it has no undesirable effects in modes that do not require it, most applications can safely ignore this matter. The `IDirect3DDevice3` interface contains two functions related to dithering: one to set or reset the dither flag, named `SetDither()`, and another one to retrieve the dither flag, called `GetDither()`. The `SetDither()` function has the following general form:

```
HRESULT SetDither(
                  BOOL bDither                    // 1
                  );
```

The function's only parameter is the TRUE/FALSE state of the new dither flag. The default is TRUE. The function returns `DD3DRM_OK` if it succeeds, or an error otherwise.

The `GetDither()` function has the following general form:

```
BOOL GetDither();
```

The call returns TRUE if the dither flag is set, or FALSE otherwise.

Obtaining Device Information

Several functions in `IDirect3DRMDevice3` provide information regarding the device state or internal settings. These functions relate to each other by the fact that they provide information to the caller.

Gaining immediate mode access

The `GetDirect3DDevice2()` function of `IDirect3DRMDevice3` retrieves a pointer to the immediate mode device. It is used sometimes in conjunction with the `GetDirect3D()` function of `IDirect3DDevice` to obtain a pointer to the current Direct3D immediate mode object. This is necessary for retained mode applications that wish to access immediate mode functionality. The `GetDirect3DDevice2()` function has the following general form.

```
HRESULT GetDirect3DDevice2(
                           LPDIRECT3DDEVICE2 *lplpD3DDevice  // 1
                           );
```

The function's only parameter is the address that is initialized with a pointer to an `IDirect3DDevice2` immediate mode device object. The function returns `D3DRM_OK` if it succeeds, or an error otherwise.

Obtaining device specifications

Some auxiliary functions in IDirect3DRMDevice3 return information regarding the specifications of the display device. The information includes the selected color model, the wireframing option, the viewports, and the number of triangles drawn to a device since its creation.

Obtaining the color model

We have seen that Direct3D retained mode supports two color models: RGB and monochromatic or ramp. The RGB model treats color as a combination of red, green, and blue light. This model can have a depth of 8, 16, 24, and 32 bits. If the display depth is less than 24 bits, the display can show banding artifacts, which can be avoided by using optional dithering, as described earlier in this chapter.

In the monochromatic model each light source is set to a gray intensity. This model can be used with 8-, 16-, 24-, and 32-bit displays, although only 8-bit textures are supported in this mode. One consideration for using the monochromatic model over the RGB model is its better rendering speed.

Applications cannot change the color model of a Direct3D device. You can use the EnumDevices() or FindDevice() functions of IDirect3D to identify a driver that supports the desired color model. At the time of creating the device this driver can then be specified. The GetColorModel() function returns information regarding the color model used by the current device. The function has the following general form:

```
D3DCOLORMODEL GetColorModel( );
```

The return value is one of the constants in the D3DCOLORMODEL enumerated type. This enumeration is described as follows:

```
typedef enum _D3DCOLORMODEL
{
    D3DCOLOR_MONO = 1,
    D3DCOLOR_RGB  = 2,
} D3DCOLORMODEL;
```

Obtaining the wireframing option

Direct3DRM supports two wireframing options at the device level. The GetWireframe Options() function, of the IDirect3DRMDevice3 interface, can be used to retrieve which of these two options is enabled in the current display device. The function has the following general form:

```
DWORD GetWireframeOptions( );
```

The function returns one or more of the values listed in Table 17-7.

Table 17-7
Wireframing Flags in Direct3D Retained Mode

Constant	Bit	Description
D3DRMWIREFRAME_CULL	0	Backfacing faces are not drawn.
D3DRMWIREFRAME_HIDDENLINE	1	Wire-frame-rendered lines are obscured by nearer objects.

Application code can AND with the corresponding bit mask to determine if either or both of the wireframing options are available in the current display device.

Obtaining viewport information

In Chapter 16 you learned that applications can define multiple viewports on the same device in order to allow different aspects of the same scene to be viewed simultaneously. The GetViewports() function of IDirect3DRNDevice3 is used to obtain all the viewports associated with a display device. The function has the following general form:

```
HRESULT GetViewports(
            LPDIRECT3DRMVIEWPORTARRAY *lplpViewports  // 1
            );
```

The function's only parameter is the address of a pointer that is initialized with a valid Direct3DRMViewportArray object if the call succeeds. The call returns D3DRM_OK if it succeeds, or an error otherwise.

The pointer returned by the GetViewports() function can be used to access the functions in the IDirect3DRMViewportArray interface mentioned in Chapter 16. This interface contains two functions:

One named GetSize() returns the number of elements in the viewport object array. The other one, named GetElement(), retrieves a specified viewport object in the object array. The GetSize() function of IDirect3DRMViewport has the following general form:

```
DWORD GetSize( );
```

The returned value is the number of elements in the viewport array. After this value is known, code can loop through the array and inspect each of the contained viewports.

The GetElement() function of IDirect3DRMViewportArray can be used for this purpose. The function has the following general form:

```
HRESULT GetElement(
                DWORD index,                              // 1
                LPDIRECT3DRMVIEWPORT  *lplpD3DRMViewport  // 2
                );
```

The first parameter is the element's position in the array. The initial value for this parameter is usually based on the value returned by the call to the GetSize() function previously described. The second parameter is the address that will be filled with a pointer to the corresponding IDirect3DRMViewport interface. The function returns D3DRM_OK if it succeeds, or an error otherwise.

The pointer of type LPDIRECT3DRMVIEWPORT can be used to access any of the methods in IDirect3DRMViewport2 interface. Retained mode viewport programming is discussed in Chapter 20.

Obtaining the drawn triangles

A convenience function in IDirect3DRMDevice3, named GetTrianglesDrawn(), returns the number of triangles drawn to a device since its creation. This method, of little practical use to applications, includes the triangles actually drawn plus those that were passed to the renderer but were not drawn because they were facing away from the camera. The value returned by this function does not include triangles that were rejected for lying outside of the viewing frustum. The function has the following general form:

```
DWORD GetTrianglesDrawn();
```

Obtaining device dimensions

Two functions in the IDirect3DRMDevice3 interface allow retrieving the pixel size of the display device. The GetHeight() function returns the vertical dimensions and the GetWidth() function returns the horizontal dimension. The functions have the following general forms:

```
DWORD GetWidth();
DWORD GetHeight();
```

Both functions return a value in pixels.

Buffer Controls

In Chapter 12 we explored the possibility of creating a flipping chain consisting of multiple back buffers to improve rendering performance. Direct3D retained mode applications that use multiple buffering must inform the system of the number of buffers in use. This is required so that Direct3D knows how much of the window to clear and update on each frame.

Setting the number of buffers

The `SetBufferCount()` function of `IDirect3DRMDevice3` is used to set the number of buffers currently in use by an application. The function has the following general form:

```
HRESULT SetBufferCount(  DWORD dwCount  );
```

The function's only parameter is the number of buffers to be used. Applications pass the value one for a single buffer, two for double buffering, and so on. The default value is one. The function returns `D3DRM_OK` if it succeeds, or an error otherwise.

Obtaining the number of buffers

The `GetBufferCount()` function of the `IDirect3DRMDevice3` interface is used to retrieve the number of buffers currently in use by an application. The function has the following general form:

```
DWORD GetBufferCount();
```

The return value is the number of buffers. One indicates single-buffering, two for double-buffering, and so on.

Sample Program 3DRM InWin Demo2

The 3DRM InWin Demo2 program in the book's CD-ROM demonstrates the most useful functions discussed in this chapter. The Rendering menu contains a command that enables you to set the rendering quality. The resulting dialog is shown in Figure 17-1. The Texture menu contains commands to set and retrieve the texture quality. Figure 17-5 shows the program's dialog box for setting the texture quality. The program's Information menu contains a command to obtain device information. Figure 17-7 shows the resulting message box that displays the color model, wireframe mode, number of triangles drawn, device width and height, and the number of buffers.

Figure 17-7: Device information box in the
3DRM InWin Demo2 program

Summary

We have now explored the Direct3D functions that are available at the device level.
Device-level functions in Direct3D enable code to control the rendering quality, to
set modes and retrieve information regarding shading, textures, transparency, and
dithering, and to determine and retrieve the number of display buffers. Device-level
functions also provide information regarding the device dimensions, the color model,
the viewports associated with the device, and other data that may be useful to applications. Although the device-level functions refer to initialization, mode setting,
performance control, and information retrieval, they play an important role in defining
and controlling rendering.

In the next chapter we continue our tour of Direct3D retained mode at progressively
lower levels. Specifically, we explore programming at the viewport level.

✦   ✦   ✦

Viewport-Level Operations

T he viewport defines a rectangular area of the display device into which objects are rendered. Therefore, the viewport sets the vantage point for the scene and determines what is visible and what is not visible. This, in turn, determines how 3D objects are rendered into a 2D window. Viewport fundamentals were discussed in Chapter 14. In this chapter we are concerned with retained mode programming operations that relate to the viewport.

Retained Mode Viewport Interface

Viewport operations are part of Direct3D retained mode IDirect3DRMViewport2 interface. This version of IDirect3DRMViewport was introduced in DirectX 6. The new interface version added a flag parameter to the Clear() function and introduced two multi-element transformation functions.

Functions in IDirect3DRMViewport2

Applications use the methods of the IDirect3DRMViewport2 interface to determine how the objects of a 3D scene are mapped to a 2D surface. Through this interface application code can initialize the viewport, modify the clipping planes, and change the field of view, the viewport dimensions, projection type, scale, and offsets. In addition, the viewport interface provides functions for manipulating the camera, for performing transformations, and for rendering a scene. Table 18-1 lists the functions available in IDirect3DRMViewport2 interface.

Table 18-1
Methods of IDirect3DRMViewport2 Interface

Groups	Methods
Configuration	Init() Clear() Configure() ForceUpdate() GetDevice() GetDirect3DViewport()
Parameters	
Dimensions	GetHeight() GetWidth
Field of view	GetField() SetField()
Offsets	GetX() GetY()
Projection types	GetProjection() SetProjection()
Scaling	GetUniformScaling() SetUniformScaling()
Clipping planes	GetBack() GetFront() GetPlane() SetBack() SetFront() SetPlane()
Camera	GetCamera() SetCamera()
Picking	Pick()
Rendering	*Render()
Transformations	InverseTransform() InverseTransformVectors() Transform() TransformVectors()

The Render() function, marked with an asterisk in Table 18-1, was discussed in Chapter 15 and requires no further comment here.

Creating the viewport

In Chapter 15 you created a viewport using the `ViewportCreate()` function of the `IDirect3DRM3` interface. The call creates a viewport on a specific device, describing the position and direction of the camera frame, and determining the viewport's position and size within the display. The last function parameter is the address of a pointer that is filled with the `IDirect3DRMViewport2` interface if the call succeeds. This pointer is used by code to access the functions in `IDirect3DRMViewport2`. In the sample programs 3DRM InWin Demo1 and 3DRM InWin Demo2, the call for creating the viewport and retrieving the interface pointer is as follows:

```
// Global variables
struct _globVars
{
  LPDIRECT3DRMDEVICE3 aDevice;         // Retained mode aDevice
  LPDIRECT3DRMVIEWPORT2 aViewport;     // Direct3DRM viewport
  LPDIRECT3DRMFRAME3 aScene;           // Master frame
  LPDIRECT3DRMFRAME3 aCamera;          // Camera frame
  BOOL isInitialized;                  // D3DRM objects are
                                       // initialized.
} globVars;
. . .
// Local variables
    HRESULT retval;   // Return value
    int width;        // Device's width
    int height;       // Device's height
. . .
// Create the Direct3DRM viewport using the device, the
// camera frame, and the device's width and height.
    width = globVars.aDevice->GetWidth();
    height = globVars.aDevice->GetHeight();

    retval = lpD3DRM->CreateViewport(globVars.aDevice,
                                     globVars.aCamera,
                                     0,
                                     0,
                                     width,
                                     height,
                                     &globVars.aViewport);
    if (FAILED(retval))
    {
        // Viewport creation error handler goes here
    }
```

If the call to `CreateViewport()` is successful, code can then use the pointer returned in the variable `globVars.aViewport` to access any of the methods in `IDirect3DRMViewport2`.

Viewport Configuration

Several functions in IDirect3DRMViewport2 perform viewport initialization, configuration, and update operations and serve to retrieve the device or the immediate mode viewport object associated with the retained mode viewport.

Viewport initialization

The CreateViewport() function of the IDirect3DRM3 interface performs two simultaneous functions: it creates and initializes the viewport. In other words, CreateViewport() encapsulates the functionality of the CreateObject() function of IDirect3DRM3, and the Init() function of IDirect3DRMViewport2. Applications that use CreateViewport() need not call the Init() function. Init() is required when applications use CreateObject() of IDirect3DRM3. Init() has the following general form:

```
HRESULT Init(
        LPDIRECT3DRMDEVICE3 lpD3DRMDevice,         // 1
        LPDIRECT3DRMFRAME3 lpD3DRMFrameCamera,      // 2
        DWORD xpos,                                 // 3
        DWORD ypos,                                 // 4
        DWORD width,                                // 5
        DWORD height                                // 6
        );
```

The first parameter is the device on which the viewport is created. The second parameter is the camera frame that defines the position and direction of the viewport. Parameters 3 and 4 refer to the position of the viewport itself, and parameters 5 and 6 to its dimensions.

The position of the viewport relative to the device frame is determined by the application's design and the proposed rendering operations. However, the size of the viewport must not be greater than that of the physical device, otherwise the Init() call fails. To make sure that the viewport is not larger than the physical device you can use the GetWidth() and GetHeight() functions of IDirect3DRM Device to obtain the device dimensions. Note that the IDirect3DRMViewport2 interface also has GetWidth() and GetHeight() methods that retrieve the size of the viewport. However, at initialization time the viewport has not been created yet; therefore you must use the functions of IDirect3DRMDevice3. The function returns D3DRM_OK if it succeeds, or an error otherwise.

Clearing the viewport

Applications need to clear the viewport to the current background color before rendering. Before DirectX 6 the Clear() function of IDirect3DRMViewport simply set the viewport to the current background color. Clearing included the z-buffer and the target rendering surface. DirectX 6 introduced a flag parameter to the Clear() function which allows a finer degree of control on the viewport elements that are cleared by the call. The Clear() call has the following general form:

```
HRESULT Clear(
            DWORD dwFlags                    // 1
            );
```

The function's only parameter is one or more of the flags listed in Table 18-2.

Table 18-2
Viewport Clearing Flags

Name	Action
D3DRMCLEAR_TARGET	Clear the destination rendering surface.
D3DRMCLEAR_ZBUFFER	Clear the z-buffer surface.
D3DRMCLEAR_DIRTYRECTS	Clear the dirty rectangle list.
D3DRMCLEAR_ALL	Clear the destination, z-buffer, and dirty rectangle list. This flag is equivalent to using the previous version of the Clear() function.

You can enable more than one of the flags in Table 18-2 by performing a logical OR. The call returns DD_OK if it succeeds, or one of the following error values:

```
DDERR_INVALIDOBJECT

DDERR_INVALIDPARAMS
```

Re-configuring the viewport

When the viewport is initialized, either by the CreateViewport() function of IDirect3DRM3, or by the Init() function of IDirect3DRMViewport2, its position and dimensions are defined. Applications can reconfigure the viewport by changing its position and dimension. This is accomplished by calling the Configure() function of IDirect3DRMViewport2. The function has the following general form:

```
HRESULT Configure(
                LONG lX,                    // 1
                LONG lY,                    // 2
                DWORD dwWidth,              // 3
                DWORD dwHeight             // 4
                );
```

The first and second parameters define the new position of the viewport. The third and fourth parameters define the viewport's dimension, in terms of its width and height. Here again, the viewport dimensions cannot exceed those of the display device.

To make sure that this is not the case, code can call the GetWidth() and GetHeight() functions, of IDirect3DRMDevice, as previously described for the Init() function.

The call returns D3DRM_OK if it succeeds, or an error otherwise.

The value D3DRMERR_BADVALUE is returned if lX + dwWidth or lY + dwHeight are greater than the width or height of the device, or if any of lX, lY, dwWidth, or dwHeight is less than zero.

Forcing the image update

In Chapter 15 we discussed the image rendering mechanism in Direct3D which consists of three steps: clearing the viewport, rendering the scene to the viewport, and updating the screen. The third step, which is the one that actually displays the image, is performed by calling the Update() function of IDirect3DRMDevice3. The ForceUpdate() function, of IDirect3DRMViewport2, serves to redefine the area of the viewport that is displayed. The function's name is misleading because it does not force a screen update, as it seems to imply. Rather, it redefines an update area which is copied to the screen at the next call to the Update() function of IDirect 3DRMDevice3. In this manner it is possible to display an area larger than the one defined in the viewport. The ForceUpdate() function has the following general form:

```
HRESULT ForceUpdate(
                DWORD dwX1,                        // 1
                DWORD dwY1,                        // 2
                DWORD dwX2,                        // 3
                DWORD dwY2
                );
```

The function's four parameters define a new rectangular area to be updated. Parameters 1 and 2 defined the rectangle's upper-right corner and parameters 3 and 4 its lower-right corner. The function returns D3DRM_OK if it succeeds, or an error otherwise.

Retrieving the display device

On certain occasions code needs to obtain a pointer to the IDirect3DRMDevice3 interface to access its services. Because viewports are associated with a particular device at the time they are created, it is reasonable to expect that the viewport interface will provide information regarding its parent device. The `GetDevice()` function of `IDirect3DRMViewport2` returns the required pointer. Its general form is as follows:

```
HRESULT GetDevice(
               LPDIRECT3DRMDEVICE3 *lpD3DRMDevice      // 1
               );
```

The function's only parameter is the address of a variable that represents the device interface. The function returns `D3DRM_OK` if it succeeds, or an error otherwise.

Retrieving the immediate mode viewport

Direct3D supports mixed-mode programming via user visuals. The user visual mechanism allows a retained application to gain immediate mode functionality by having execute buffers rendered into an immediate mode viewport. To accomplish this, retained mode code needs to obtain access to the immediate mode viewport interface, `IDirect3DViewport`. This is accomplished by means of the `GetDirect 3DViewport()` function of `IDirect3DRMViewport2`. The function has the following general form:

```
HRESULT GetDirect3DViewport(
               LPDIRECT3DVIEWPORT  *lplpD3DViewport     // 1
                );
```

The function's only parameter is the address of a pointer that is initialized with the `IDirect3DViewport` interface. The function returns `D3DRM_OK` if it succeeds, or an error otherwise.

The following code fragment shows obtaining an immediate mode viewport from one in retained mode.

```
// Global variables
struct _globVars
{
  . . .
    LPDIRECT3DRMVIEWPORT2 aViewport;  // Retained mode viewport
  . . .
} globVars;

LPDIRECT3DVIEWPORT  iMViewport;     // Immediate mode viewport
. . .
// Obtaning the IDirect3DViewport interface using a retained
// mode viewport
retval = globVars.aViewport->GetDirect3DViewport(
```

```
                                                      &iMViewport);
if (FAILED(retval))
    {
        // Immediate mode viewport error handler goes here
    }
```

Setting and Acquiring Viewport Parameters

A viewport is defined in terms of its dimensions, its offset from the device origin, its field of view, the type of projection that it implements, its scaling mode, and the position and dimensions of its clipping plane. These elements can be called the viewport parameters. The Direct3D viewport interface contains several functions that enable you to set and acquire the viewport parameters. Application code often manipulates these parameters to change the rendered image.

Obtaining viewport size and position

The size of a viewport is defined by its width and height and its position by its x- and y-offsets. These four parameters are set at the time the viewport is created and can be changed only when the viewport is recreated or reconfigured, as discussed earlier in this chapter. Although there is no other way for changing the viewport size and position, code can retrieve these parameters by calling GetHeight(), GetWidth(), GetX(), and GetY() functions of IDirect3DRMViewport2. All four functions have a similar general form:

```
DWORD GetWidth();
DWORD GetHeight();
DWORD GetX();
DWORD GetY();
```

The returned value is the pixel width, height, x-offset, or y-offset of the viewport.

Viewport field of view

In Chapter 14 we introduced the notion of the viewing frustum as the 3D volume that determines which objects are visible in the viewport. Figure 14-15 is a diagram of the viewing frustum and Figure 14-16 relates the frustum to the viewport. At that time we described the device's viewing area as a pyramid intersected by front and back clipping planes. In perspective viewing (discussed later in this chapter) the frustum is the volume between these planes. Objects located between the camera and the front clipping plane are not rendered. Neither are objects located behind the back clipping plane or outside the lateral limits of the frustum. Therefore the viewing frustum determines which objects are visible in the viewport.

The viewing frustum is defined in terms of a field of view, sometimes called the fov, and the distance from the camera to the front and back clipping planes. Figure 18-1 shows the default values used in calculating the field of view.

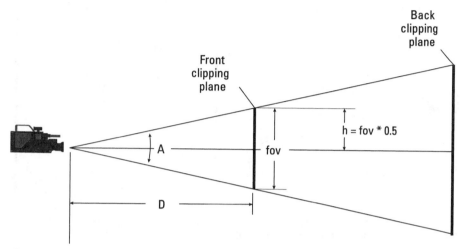

Figure 18-1: The default field of view

In Figure 18-1 the angle A is called the viewing angle. The value, in radians, of the viewing angle is calculated by the following formula:

$$A = 2\,\text{Tan}^{-1}\frac{h}{d}$$

The default value of *h* is half the *fov*, and *d* is the distance from the camera to the front clipping plane. Notice that the default value used by Direct3D retained mode in calculating the viewing angle is

$$h = fov \leftrightarrow 0.5$$

You can change the viewing angle by altering the value of *h* in the previous equation. For example, if you calculate *h* as 75 percent of the field of view, then the viewing angle changes, as shown in Figure 18-2.

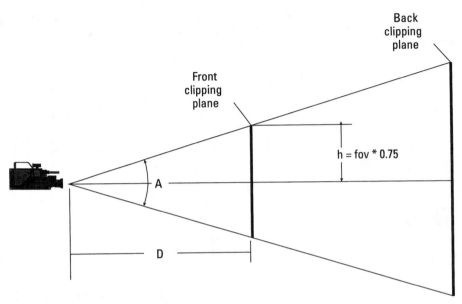

Figure 18-2: Changing the default field of view

The SetField() function of IDirect3DRMViewport2 enables you to set the field of view for a viewport, thus effectively changing the viewing angle. The function has the following general form:

```
HRESULT SetField(
              D3DVALUE rvField                          // 1
            );
```

The function's only parameter is the value for the new field of view. It is expressed as a fraction of the viewing angle. This corresponds to two times the arctangent of the angle of the front clipping plane. If the value for the SetField() parameter is less than or equal to zero, the method returns the D3DRMERR_BADVALUE error. If the call is successful it returns D3DRM_OK, or an error otherwise.

The parameter that determines the field of view can also be represented by the half-height of the front clipping plane. This value is labeled _h_ in Figures 18-1 and Figure 18-2, and in the formula for the viewing angle _A_ listed previously. A value larger than 0.5 enlarges the viewing angle, making objects appear smaller. A value smaller than 0.5 reduces the viewing angle, making objects appear larger. The visual result is similar to changing the magnification of a zoom lens, as shown in Figure 18-3.

fov = 0.5 (default) fov = 0.4

fov = 0.6 fov = 0.7

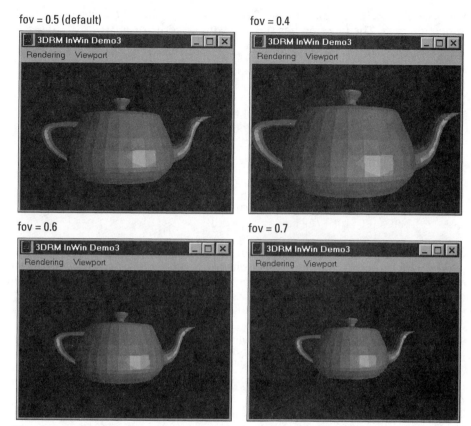

Figure 18-3: Effect of changing the field of view

The `SetField()` method is also used to add a field of view key to a `Direct3D RMViewportInterpolator` object. Interpolators are discussed in the context of retained mode animation.

Viewport projections

Projections were discussed in Chapter 4. Direct3D supports two projection types: perspective and orthographic. By far most applications use the perspective projection, which is the default. In perspective projection depth cues are used to enhance the relative position of objects, their distance to the camera, and their relative size. The orthographic projection, which is the simplest of the parallel projections, is used mostly in technical applications because of its scalability.

The `SetProjection()` function of `IDirect3DRMViewport2` enables you to set the projection type. The function has the following general form:

```
HRESULT SetProjection(
                      D3DRMPROJECTIONTYPE rptType        // 1
                      );
```

The function's only parameter is one of the members of the `D3DRMPROJECTIONTYPE` enumerated type, which is defined as follows:

```
typedef enum _D3DRMPROJECTIONTYPE{
    D3DRMPROJECT_PERSPECTIVE,
    D3DRMPROJECT_ORTHOGRAPHIC,
    D3DRMPROJECT_RIGHTHANDPERSPECTIVE,
    D3DRMPROJECT_RIGHTHANDORTHOGRAPHIC
} D3DRMPROJECTIONTYPE;.
```

The first two constants of the `D3DRMPROJECTIONTYPE` enumeration refer to the perspective and orthographic projections just mentioned. The last two relate to right-handed coordinate system first implemented in DirectX 6 and discussed in Chapter 16 in relation to the `SetOptions()` function of `IDirect3DRM3`. The `SetProjection()` function returns `D3DRM_OK` if it succeeds, or an error otherwise.

The `GetProjection()` function is used to retrieve the current projection type. The function has the following general form:

```
D3DRMPROJECTIONTYPE GetProjection();
```

The call returns one of the members of the `D3DRMPROJECTIONTYPE` enumerated type previously described.

Figure 18-4 shows the effect of changing the projection between perspective projection, which is the default, to orthographic.

Perspective projection (default)

Orthographic projection

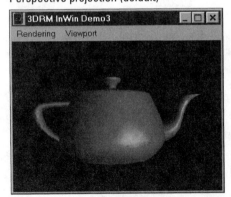

Figure 18-4: Effect of changing the projection type

Viewport scaling

Normally, the viewport is scaled into the window using the same scaling factor for the horizontal as for the vertical dimension. In this case uniform scaling ensures the correct image proportions. In nonsquare viewports it may be occasionally desirable to disable uniform scaling so that the vertical and horizontal components are rendered proportionally to the viewport dimensions. The SetUniform Scaling() function allows manipulating the uniform scaling property. The function's general form is as follows:

```
HRESULT SetUniformScaling(
                    BOOL bScale               // 1
                    );
```

The function's only parameter is a boolean value set to TRUE if you desire the same horizontal and vertical scaling factor in relation to the viewing volume. If the parameter is set to FALSE, then different scaling factors are used to scale the viewing volume exactly into the window. The default setting is TRUE. The function returns D3DRM_OK if it succeeds, or an error otherwise.

The SetUniformScaling() function is often used in relation to the SetPlane() function, described later in this chapter.

The GetUniformScaling() function retrieves the scaling property. The function has the following general form:

```
BOOL GetUniformScaling();
```

The call returns TRUE if the viewport is set to uniform scaling, or FALSE otherwise.

Clipping controls

Direct3D retained mode provides several functions that perform changes on the position and dimensions of the clipping planes, as well as other functions that retrieve the clipping plane's current position and dimensions.

Two functions allow positioning and retrieving the front clipping plane and two others perform similarly in relation to the back clipping plane. These functions are named GetFront(), SetFront, GetBack(), and SetBack(). The ones that retrieve the clipping plane positions have the following general form:

```
D3DVALUE GetFront();
D3DVALUE GetBack();
```

In both cases the returned value is the distance from the corresponding clipping place to the camera.

Two other functions allow setting the distance of the front and the back clipping planes to the camera. These have the following general form:

```
HRESULT SetFront(D3DVALUE rvFront);
HRESULT SetBack(D3DVALUE rvBack);
```

The distances to the clipping planes are based on the following default values: the front clipping plane is set at a distance of 1.0 units to the camera and the back clipping plane is set at a distance of 100 units. Here again, producing reasonable changes in the default settings of the clipping planes requires knowledge of the scene geometry and the resulting viewing frustum dimensions.

Direct3D retained mode applications normally define the viewing frustum by means of the SetField() function previously described. This method ensures that the front clipping plane (see Figure 18-1) is proportionally dimensioned to the viewing angle. Applications can produce unusual effects by modifying the normal proportions of the viewing frustum. The SetPlane() and GetPlane functions change and retrieve the dimensions of the front clipping plane in relation to the camera's z-axis.

The SetField() function has the following general form:

```
HRESULT SetPlane(
                D3DVALUE rvLeft,             // 1
                D3DVALUE rvRight,            // 2
                D3DVALUE rvBottom,           // 3
                D3DVALUE rvTop               // 4
                );
```

The function's first parameter determines the minimum x-coordinate of the left side of the front clipping plane rectangle, whereas the second parameter determines the maximum x-coordinate of the right side of the clipping plane. The third parameter determines the minimum y-coordinate of the bottom of the front clipping plane rectangle, and the fourth parameter the maximum y-coordinate of its top edge.

The GetPlane() function of IDirect3DRMViewport2 retrieves the current dimensions of the viewing plane. The function has the following general form:

```
HRESULT GetPlane(
                D3DVALUE rvLeft,             // 1
                D3DVALUE rvRight,            // 2
                D3DVALUE rvBottom,           // 3
                D3DVALUE rvTop               // 4
                );
```

The parameters have the same values as for the SetPlane() function previously described. Both functions return D3DRM_OK if they succeed, and an error otherwise.

The notion that the SetPlane() function changes the dimensions of the front clipping plane could lead us to think that these changes affect the objects that are visible in the viewport, and nothing more. In reality the SetPlane() function is capable of changing the proportion of the viewing frustum, which in turn can result in changes in the geometry of the image itself. For example, you can modify the *x*-coordinates of the front clipping plane to squeeze the image horizontally. The result of this manipulation is shown in Figure 18-5.

Proportional front clipping plane   Altered front clipping plane

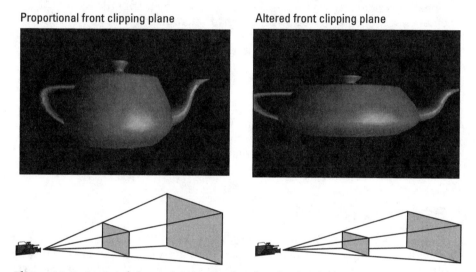

Figure 18-5: Image deformation by altering the viewing frustum

To produce the deformation in Figure 18-5 we first obtained the viewport dimensions using GetPlane() and then modified the frustum by calculating 75 percent of *x*-coordinates. The following code fragment shows the processing.

```
// Variables for viewport dimensions
D3DVALUE      left;
D3DVALUE      right;
D3DVALUE      top;
D3DVALUE      bottom;
. . .
// Obtain viewport dimensions
retval = globVars.aViewport->GetPlane(
                              &left, &right, &top, &bottom);
  if(FAILED(retval))
      }
        // Obtaining viewport dimensions error handler
        // goes here
      }
```

```
// Redimension front clipping plane x-coordinates to 75 percent
// of normal values
retval = globVars.aViewport->SetPlane(
                         left*0.75, right*0.75, top, bottom);
    if(FAILED(retval))
    {
         // Viewport dimensions setting error handler goes here
    }
```

Viewport dimensioning via the `SetPlane()` function and via the `SetField()` function cancel each other out. This means that code can change the viewing frustum by calling either the `SetPlane()` or `SetField()` functions, but not both. In fact, the `SetField()` function is but a compact way of setting all viewport dimensions to the same value. By the same token, if the `SetPlane()` function is called with the same value for all four parameters, the result is equivalent to a call to the `SetField()` function.

Although altering the dimensions of the viewing frustum can produce interesting and sometimes powerful effects, using these controls in a reasonable manner requires detailed knowledge of the geometry of the image being manipulated.

Camera Operations

In Chapter 15 you learned that the camera is a Direct3D retained mode object that defines the viewing position and direction. In that sense the camera defines the viewport because the renderer displays only what is visible along the positive z-axis of the camera frame. The actual sequence of operations in a typical retained mode application consists, first, of creating the camera frame by calling the `CreateFrame()` function of `IDirect3DRM3`, and then creating the viewport by calling the `CreateViewport()` function passing the frame that represents the camera as one of the parameters. In conclusion: the camera, represented by a frame that positions it, defines the viewing position and direction.

Two functions of `IDirect3DRMViewport2` relate to the camera: `SetCamera()` and `GetCamera()`. `SetCamera()` sets a viewport's position, direction, and orientation to that of the given camera frame. The view is oriented along the positive z-axis of the camera frame, with the up direction being in the direction of the positive y-axis. The `SetCamera()` function has the following general form:

```
HRESULT SetCamera(
                LPDIRECT3DRMFRAME3 lpCamera            // 1
                );
```

The function's only parameter is the address of a variable that contains a `Direct3DRMFrame` object that represents the camera. The function returns `D3DRM_OK` if it succeeds, or an error otherwise.

The GetCamera() function retrieves the frame object that represents the camera in the viewport. The function has the following general form:

```
HRESULT GetCamera(
             LPDIRECT3DRMFRAME3 *lpCamera          // 1
             );
```

The function's only parameter is the address of a variable that contains the Direct3DRMFrame object that represents the camera.

The call returns D3DRM_OK if it succeeds, or an error otherwise.

Camera manipulations are discussed in the context of frame programming, in Chapter 19.

Picking Viewport Objects

In Chapter 14 we discussed the fundamentals of Direct3D object selection by picking. Objects are picked using the viewport interface because picking consists of selecting objects in a 3D scene based on the their x- and y-coordinates of a 2D surface, in this case the viewport. Typically, picking is based on the position of the mouse cursor at the time of the pick.

The Pick() function of IDirect3DRMViewport2 finds a depth-sorted list of objects. This path includes the complete hierarchy, from the root, down to the frame that contains the object. Its general form is as follows:

```
HRESULT Pick(
             LONG lX,                               // 1
             LONG lY,                               // 2
             LPDIRECT3DRMPICKEDARRAY *lplpVisuals  // 3
             );
```

The first and second parameters are the screen coordinates of the object or objects to be picked. The third parameter is the address that is initialized with a pointer to the IDirect3DRMPickedArray interface if the call succeeds. The call returns D3DRM_OK if it succeeds, or an error otherwise.

The pointer returned by the Pick() function allows access to the IDirect3DRM PickedArray interface. This interface contains two functions: GetPick(), which retrieves the visuals and objects intersected in the pick, and GetSize() which returns the number of elements contained in the picked array. The elements in the array of frames are organized in a hierarchy in which the first element is the topmost element.

Viewport Transformations

3D applications deal with two different environments: the 3D environment of the modeled objects and the 2D environment of the rendering surface. Code often needs to convert from one coordinate system into the other one. Direct3D retained mode provides several methods that perform these coordinate system transformations. To understand these methods you must understand image transformations and coordinate systems, in particular homogeneous coordinates. Chapter 3, which is entirely devoted to these topics, serves as background for the present discussion.

Image transformations at the viewport level were introduced in Chapter 14. At that time we referred to the fact that, in the context of Direct3D viewports, transformations are used to convert between screen and world coordinates. Screen coordinates, which are defined in relation to the root frame, are represented as the four-element homogenous coordinate matrix [x y z w]. World coordinates refer to the two-dimensional viewport. Direct3D retained mode uses the D3DRMVECTOR4D structure for encoding screen coordinates and the D3DVECTOR structure for world coordinates. The structures are defined as follows:

```
typedef struct _D3DRMVECTOR4D {
    D3DVALUE x;
    D3DVALUE y;
    D3DVALUE z;
    D3DVALUE w;
}D3DRMVECTOR4D;
typedef D3DRMVECTOR4D, *LPD3DRMVECTOR4D;
```

The members x, y, z, and w are the homogenous coordinates. They are encoded in the D3DVALUE type.

```
typedef struct _D3DVECTOR
{
    union {
            D3DVALUE x;
            D3DVALUE dvX;
        };
    union {
            D3DVALUE y;
            D3DVALUE dvY;
        };
    union {
            D3DVALUE z;
            D3DVALUE dvZ;
        };
} D3DVECTOR, *LPD3DVECTOR;
```

World-to-screen transformation

The Transform() function of IDirect3DRMViewport2 converts world coordinates, encoded in a D3DRMVECTOR4D structure variable, into screen coordinates, encoded in a D3DVECTOR structure variable. The function has the following general form:

```
HRESULT Transform(
          D3DRMVECTOR4D  *lprvDest,        // 1
          D3DVECTOR  *lprvSrc              // 2
          );
```

The first parameter is the address of a D3DRMVECTOR4D structure variable that is the destination for the transformation. The second parameter is the address of a D3DVECTOR structure variable that is the source for the transformation. The function returns D3DRM_OK if it succeeds, or an error otherwise.

The result of the transformation is a four-element homogeneous matrix. The point represented by the resulting vector is visible if the following equations are true:

$$w \leftrightarrow x_{min} \leq x < w \leftrightarrow x_{max}$$

$$w \leftrightarrow y_{min} \leq y < w \leftrightarrow y_{max}$$

$$0 \leq z < w$$

where

$$x_{min} = viewport_x - (viewport_{width} / 2)$$

$$x_{max} = viewport_x + (viewport_{width} / 2)$$

$$y_{min} = viewport_y - (viewport_{height} / 2)$$

$$y_{max} = viewport_y - (viewport_{height} / 2)$$

Screen-to-world transformation

The InverseTransform() function of IDirect3DRMViewport2 converts screen coordinates into world coordinates. The function has the following general form:

```
HRESULT InverseTransform(
          D3DVECTOR  *lprvDest,           // 1
          D3DRMVECTOR4D  *lprvSrc         // 2
          );
```

The first parameter is the address of a D3DVECTOR structure variable that serves as the destination for the transformation. The second parameter is the address of a D3DRMVECTOR4D structure variable that represents the source of the operation. The function returns D3DRM_OK if it succeeds, or an error otherwise.

Vector array transformations

DirectX 6 introduced two new functions that allow screen-to-world and world-to-screen transformations on multiple elements. These functions, which have the word vectors in their names, perform the same transformations as their single-element counterparts discussed previously. The TransformVectors() function is the multiple-element version of the Transform() function. Its general form is as follows:

```
HRESULT TransformVectors(
                DWORD dwNumVectors,                   // 1
                LPD3DRMVECTOR4D lpDstVectors,         // 2
                LPD3DVECTOR lpSrcVectors             // 3
                );
```

The first parameter encodes the number of vectors to be transformed. The second parameter is an array of D3DRMVECTOR4D structures variables representing the vectors transformed to screen coordinates. The third parameter is the array of vectors to transform. The function returns DD_OK if it succeeds, or one of the following error codes:

> DDERR_INVALIDOBJECT
>
> DDERR_INVALIDPARAMS

The InverseTransformVectors() function is the multiple-element counterpart to TransformVectors(). Its general form is as follows:

```
HRESULT InverseTransformVectors(
                DWORD dwNumVectors,                   // 1
                LPD3DVECTOR lpDstVectors,             // 2
                LPD3DRMVECTOR4D lpSrcVectors         // 3
                );
```

The first parameter encodes the number of vectors for which coordinates are to be transformed. The second parameter is the array of vectors that serves as a destination of the transformation. The third parameter is the array of D3DRMVECTOR4D structure variables representing the vectors to transform. The function returns DD_OK if it succeeds, or one of the following error codes:

> DDERR_INVALIDOBJECT
>
> DDERR_INVALIDPARAMS

Sample Program 3DRM InWin Demo3

The 3DRM InWin Demo2 program in the book's CD-ROM demonstrates the most useful functions discussed in this chapter. The Rendering menu contains a command that enables you to set the rendering quality. In addition, there is a Viewport commands menu that enables you to experiment with the field-of-view, perspective and orthographic geometry, viewport proportions, and uniform and nonuniform scaling. The screen snapshots for the illustrations used in this chapter were obtained with this sample program.

Summary

We have now explored viewport-level programming in retained mode and learned how to configure the viewport, set and acquire viewport parameters, manipulate the camera, pick objects, and perform screen-to-world and world-to-screen coordinates transformations. The viewport defines the display device and sets the vantage point for the scene, thus determining what is visible and what is not visible in the scene. In the following chapter we continue our exploration of Direct3D retained mode at the frame level.

✦   ✦   ✦

Direct3D Programming

Local Frame Operations

In Chapter 14 we described a retained mode scene as a collection of frames, and indicated that, in this context, the term frame means a frame of reference. In retained mode the frame of reference serves as a container for the 3D objects that form the scene. Objects such as meshes, visuals, lights, and cameras cannot be rendered until they are given a frame of reference relative to the scene and to each other. In this chapter, we start discussing retained mode frame-level operations, as they are implemented in the IDirect3D RMFrame3 interface.

Frame-level operations are one of the richest and most powerful in the retained mode API. To better structure the material, we divided it into two chapters. In this one we concentrate on the basic rendering operations performed at the frame level. We call these the local frame operations. They include five categories: frame movements, frame transformations, vector-level manipulations, frame traversals, and frame move callback functions.

Retained Mode Frame Interface

The scene is a tree-like structure in which a root, or master frame, has any number of child frames, each of which can have other children in turn. In retained mode the scene object consists of a frame that has no parent. This root frame is the highest level component of a 3D scene. In this sense the terms scene, root frame, and master frame are usually considered synonyms. Child frames inherit their characteristics from the parent frames and are physically attached to it. When a frame is moved, all the child frames move with it. Figure 14-5 shows a frame hierarchy used to depict a helicopter.

Frame hierarchies are flexible. The IDirect3DFrame3 interface contains a rich set of functions for manipulating frames and frame elements. Some of the functions in the interface refer to the scene itself because the scene is defined as the root frame. Local operations on frames serve to position, move, load, and transform frames. In addition, the interface contains functions to manipulate child and parent frames, and to set and retrieve the frame sorting mode and the frame's visual attributes. Finally there are functions to add and remove frame attributes, to create visuals, and to perform ray picking. Figure 19-1 is a diagram of the retained mode frame interface.

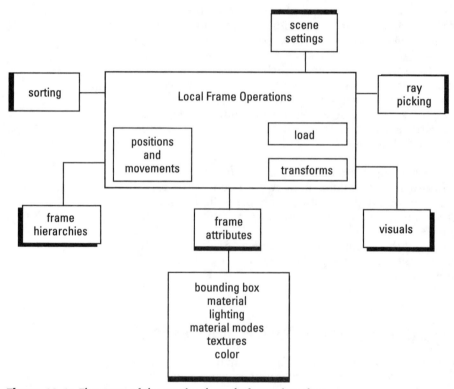

Figure 19-1: Elements of the retained mode frame interface

There are over seventy functions in IDirect3DFrame3. In Table 19-1 we classified these functions into the groups defined in Figure 19-1. This classification, although imperfect, provides us with a grouping on which to base the discussion of an extremely complex and lengthy topic.

Table 19-1
IDirect3DRMFrame3 Interface Functions

Local Frame Operations	Functions

Frame movements	`SetAxes()`
	`SetInheritAxes()`
	`AddRotation()`
	`AddScale()`
	`AddTranslation()`
	`GetOrientation()`
	`GetPosition()`
	`GetRotation()`
	`GetVelocity()`
	`LookAt()`
	`Move()`
	`SetOrientation()`
	`SetPosition()`
	`SetQuaternion()`
	`SetRotation()`
	`SetVelocity()`
	`Load()`

Matrix transformation	`AddTransform()` `GetTransform()`

Vector-level manipulations	`InverseTransform()`
	`InverseTransformVectors()`
	`Transform()`
	`TransformVectors()`

Traversal options	`GetTraversalOptions()` `SetTraversalOptions()`
Frame move callbacks	`AddMoveCallback()` `DeleteMoveCallback()`

Frame hierarchies	`AddChild()`
	`DeleteChild()`
	`GetChildren()`
	`GetParent()`
	`GetScene()`

Scene settings	`GetSceneBackground()`
	`GetSceneBackgroundDepth()`
	`SetSceneBackground()`
	`SetSceneBackgroundDepth()`

Continued

Table 19-1 *(continued)*	
Local Frame Operations	*Functions*

Scene settings *(continued)*	`SetSceneBackgroundImage()`(obsolete)
	`SetSceneBackgroundRGB()`
	`GetSceneFogColor()`
	`GetSceneFogEnable()`
	`SetSceneFogMethod()`
	`GetSceneFogMode()`
	`GetSceneFogParams()`
	`SetSceneFogColor()`
	`SetSceneFogEnable()`
	`SetSceneFogMethod()`
	`SetSceneFogMode()`
	`SetSceneFogParams()`

Ray picking	`RayPick()`

Sorting	`GetSortMode()`
	`GetZbufferMode()`
	`SetSortMode()`
	`SetZbufferMode()`

Frame Attributes	

Bounding box	`GetBox()`
	`GetBoxEnable()`
	`GetHierarchyBox()`
	`SetBox()`
	`SetBoxEnable()`

Color	`GetColor()`
	`SetColor()`
	`SetColorRGB()`

Lighting	`AddLight()`
	`DeleteLight()`
	`GetLights()`

Material	`GetMaterial()`
	`GetMaterialOverride()`
	`SetMaterial()`
	`SetMaterialOverride()`

Material modes	`GetMaterialMode()` `SetMaterialMode`
Textures	`GetTexture()` `SetTexture()`

Visuals	`AddVisual()`
	`DeleteVisual()`
	`GetVisuals()`

In the discussions that follow we describe the most useful functions in the local frame operations group. The remaining functions of the IDirect3DFrame3 interface are the topic of Chapter 20.

Frame Movement and Control Operations

One of the most extensive groups of frame-related functions are those that perform local operations and transformations. The functions in this group can be further classified as follows:

1. Operations that affect the position, axes, and orientation of the frame.

2. Operations that define and execute frame movements. These include functions to move, rotate, translate, and scale frames and to define the frame's velocity.

3. Operations that transform the frame coordinate systems.

4. Operation to load a frame from a file, resource, or memory area.

Orientation and position controls

The functions in this subgroup refer to the frame's orientation, axes, and position. We start with the frame's orientation controls.

The frame's orientation refers to two vectors that define its z-direction and y-direction respectively. The default orientation of a frame has a z-direction vector of [0, 0, 1] and a y-direction vector of [0, 1, 0]. The SetOrientation() function of IDirect3DRMFrame3 sets the orientation of a frame with respect to some other frame object. This reference frame can also be the scene itself. The function has the following general form:

```
HRESULT SetOrientation(
                LPDIRECT3DRMFRAME3 lpRef,        // 1
                D3DVALUE rvDx,                   // 2
                D3DVALUE rvDy,                   // 3
                D3DVALUE rvDz,                   // 4
                D3DVALUE rvUx,                   // 5
                D3DVALUE rvUy,                   // 6
                D3DVALUE rvUz                    // 7
                );
```

The first parameter is the address of a variable that represents the frame to be used as the reference. If this parameter is NULL the function uses the scene frame as a reference. The second, third, and fourth parameters specify the new z-axis for the frame. Each component vector must be in the range -1.0 to 1.0. The fifth, sixth, and seventh parameters specify the new y-axis for the frame. Here again, each component must be in the range -1.0 to 1.0. The function returns D3DRM_OK if it succeeds, or an error otherwise.

The following code fragment shows a call to set the default orientation of a camera frame within the scene.

```
LPDIRECT3DRMFRAME3 aCamera;
LPDIRECT3DRMFRAME3 aScene;

if (FAILED(aCamera->SetOrientation(aScene,      // reference
frame
                            D3DVAL(0),   //  ⎤
                            D3DVAL(0),   //  ⎥ z-axis values
                            D3DVAL(1),   //  ⎦
                            D3DVAL(0),   //  ⎤
                            D3DVAL(1),   //  ⎥ y-axis values
                            D3DVAL(0)))  //  ⎦
  {
      // Frame orientation error handler goes here
  }
```

The GetOrientation() function is used to retrieve the orientation of a frame in relation to another one. The function parameters include the reference frames and two vector structures that are filled with the z-axis and y-axis values that define the frame's orientation.

DirectX 6 added several axes-related functions to the frame-level API. The SetAxes() function is used to set the vectors that defined a coordinate space by which the SetOrientation() vectors are transformed. The method is used mainly to support left- and right-handed coordinate systems, and to specify that the front of an object is represented on the negative z-axis. A related method named GetAxes() retrieves the current frame axes. A pair of methods, named SetInheritAxes() and GetInheritAxes() respectively, allow setting and retrieving a boolean value that is TRUE if a frame inherits its axes from its parent frame, and FALSE otherwise.

A frame's position is the location of its origin in relation to the origin of another frame. When a child frame is created, its origin is placed at the origin of the parent frame. The SetPosition() function of IDirect3DRMFrame3 enables you to change the relative position of a frame. The function has the following general form:

```
HRESULT SetPosition(
                LPDIRECT3DRMFRAME3 lpRef,        // 1
                D3DVALUE rvX,                    // 2
                D3DVALUE rvY,                    // 3
                D3DVALUE rvZ                     // 4
                );
```

The function's first parameter is the address of a variable that represents the Direct3DRMFrame object to be used as the reference. If this parameter is NULL, the method uses the scene frame as a reference. The second, third, and fourth parameters define the new position for the frame within the coordinate system of the frame of reference specified in the first parameter. The function returns D3DRM_OK if it succeeds, or an error otherwise.

The following code fragment calls the SetPosition() function to move the position of the frame -5 units along the z-axis of the scene.

```
LPDIRECT3DRMFRAME3 aCamera;
LPDIRECT3DRMFRAME3 aScene;

if (FAILED(camera->SetPosition(scene,
                    D3DVAL(0),            // x
                    D3DVAL(0),            // y
                    -D3DVAL(5)))          // z
    {
        // Frame repositioning error handler goes here
    }
```

A related function called LookAt() is used to orient a frame so that its positive z-axis points in the direction of another frame. This function is often used to orient a light or viewport to point in the direction of another frame. The function's general form is as follows:

```
HRESULT LookAt(
            LPDIRECT3DRMFRAME3 lpTarget,          // 1
            LPDIRECT3DRMFRAME3 lpRef,             // 2
            D3DRMFRAMECONSTRAINT rfcConstraint    // 3
            );
```

The function's first parameter is the address of the variable that represents the Direct3DRMFrame object to be used as the target. This is the object that the function looks at. The second parameter is the address of the variable that represents the Direct3DRMFrame object to be used as the reference. If this object is NULL, then the scene is used. The third parameter specifies a member of the D3DRMFRAME CONSTRAINT enumerated type that defined one axis of rotation to constrain. The enumaration is defined as follows:

```
typedef enum _D3DRMFRAMECONSTRAINT {
    D3DRMCONSTRAIN_Z,    // Do not use z-rotations
    D3DRMCONSTRAIN_Y,    // Do not use y-rotations
    D3DRMCONSTRAIN_X     // Do not use x-rotations
} D3DRMFRAMECONSTRAINT;
```

The LookAt() function returns D3DRM_OK if it succeeds, or an error otherwise.

Frame movement controls

Retained mode provides a rather elaborate set of related functions that are used to scale, rotate, and translate frames.

The functions can be roughly classified into two groups: those that produce a single modification on the frame's matrix, and those that produce a continuous series of modifications. The functions in the second group are often used in producing simple animations at the frame level.

Frame-level animations are easy to set up and are often of sufficient quality to produce satisfactory results when implementing simple movements. You can use two functions of the IDirect3DRMFrame3 interface to provide simple rotation and translation of a frame: SetRotation() and SetVelocity(). In either case the movement is produced by a call to the Move() function, of IDirect3DRMFrame3, or the Tick() function, of IDirect3DRM3. Tick() was discussed in Chapter 16. The actions of the SetRotation() and SetVelocity() functions can be combined to produce interesting effects.

The AddRotation() function is used to set a frame rotating along one or more of its axes, by a given angle. The function has the following general form:

```
HRESULT SetRotation(
                LPDIRECT3DRMFRAME3 lpRef,          // 1
                D3DVALUE rvX,                       // 2
                D3DVALUE rvY,                       // 3
                D3DVALUE rvZ,                       // 4
                D3DVALUE rvTheta                    // 5
                );
```

The first parameter is the address of a variable that represents the Direct3DRM-Frame object to be rotated. If this parameter is NULL, then the function uses the scene's frame. The second, third, and fourth parameters define the axis or axes along which the rotation is to take place. Valid values are documented to be in the range -1.0 to 1.0. It appears that any nonzero value selects the corresponding axis, and a zero value deselects it. Positive values produce a clockwise rotation and negative values rotate the frame in a counterclockwise direction. Numeric variations appear to have no effect in this function because the angle and speed of rotation are determined elsewhere. The fifth parameter is the rotation angle, in radians, for each iteration of the Tick() or Move() function previously mentioned. Both Tick() and Move() scale the rotation angle according to a local parameter in these functions. SetRotation() returns D3DRM_OK if it is successful, or an error otherwise.

In our experiments with the SetRotate() function we detected some unexpected results. One of them is that if a zero value is entered for all three axes and a nonzero value for the angle of rotation, the frame is set to rotate along the *x*-axis anyway. The only way in which we have been able to call the SetRotate() function so that the frame remains stationary is by entering a zero value for the angle of rotation. In this case the value entered for the axes is meaningless.

The `SetVelocity()` function selects the axis to which a linear movement is applied, determines the velocity of the linear movement for each axis, and determines if the object's rotational velocity is taken into account when applying the linear movement.

Notice that `SetVelocity()` refers to a linear translation along the axes. Also notice that it allows defining the velocity independently for each axes, whereas the `SetRotation()` function, described previously, does not. In the case of the `SetVelocity()` function the linear movement refers to a given frame relative to a reference frame. The function has the following general form:

```
HRESULT SetVelocity(
            LPDIRECT3DRMFRAME3 lpRef,         // 1
            D3DVALUE rvX,                      // 2
            D3DVALUE rvY,                      // 3
            D3DVALUE rvZ,                      // 4
            BOOL fRotVel                       // 5
            );
```

The function's first parameter is the address of a variable that represents the Direct3DRMFrame object to be used as the reference. If this parameter is NULL, then the scene's frame is used. The second, third, and fourth parameters define the axis or axes along which the linear movement takes place. No range or units are defined for this function. Positive and negative values determine the direction of the movement along the axis. The numeric value determines the speed of the movement applied to each axis. Higher values make the frame move faster.

The `Move()` function of `IDirect3DRMFrame3` and the `Tick()` function of `Direct3DRM3` scale the value defined in these parameters. The fifth parameter is a flag that specifies whether the rotational velocity of the object is taken into account when setting the linear velocity. If TRUE, the object's rotational velocity is included in the calculation.

3DRM Move Demo project

The project named 3DRM Move Demo, in the book's CD-ROM, animates the frame containing a 3D image of a teapot by means of the `SetRotation()` and `SetVelocity()` functions. The program's Movement menu contains commands to control rotation and velocity values. Figure 19-2 is a screen snapshot of these dialog boxes.

The Rotation Setup dialog box provides three check boxes for selecting each of the rotation axes. The slider control enables the user to change the angular speed of rotation as defined by the fifth parameter of the `SetRotation()` function. The Velocity Setup dialog box also contains a check box for each axis. In this case there is a slider for controlling the speed of each axis independently, which is consistent with the `SetVelocity()` function. An additional check box enables the user to take into account the rotational component when performing the velocity calculations, as controlled by the fifth parameter of the `SetVelocity()` function.

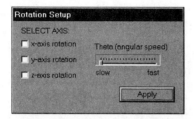

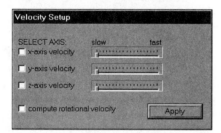

Figure 19-2: Rotation and velocity control dialog boxes in 3DRM Move Demo

The program makes successive calls to the `Move()` function of `IDirect3DRM Frame3` to produce the animation. This requires modifying the message loop so that calls to the `RenderScene()` function are made whenever the application is maximized and Direct3D has been correctly initialized. The code is as follows:

```
while (TRUE)
{
    // Process messages using PeekMessage()
    // Terminate execution when WM_QUIT is received
    if (PeekMessage(&msg, NULL, 0, 0, PM_REMOVE))
    {
        if (msg.message == WM_QUIT)
            break;
        TranslateMessage(&msg);
        DispatchMessage(&msg);
    }

    // Render object if the application is not minimized and
    // if Direct3D is initialized
    if (!globVars.isMinimized && globVars.isInitialized)
    {
        // Render one frame
```

```
                if (!RenderScene())
                {
                    D3DError("Rendering failed. Ending execution.");
                    PostMessage(NULL, WM_DESTROY, 0, 0);
                    break;
                }
            // Yield control to other threads
            } else
                WaitMessage();
```

Rendering is performed by the `RenderScene()` function. The function sets the rendering and the texture qualities, calls `Move()`, clears the viewport, renders the frame, and updates the window. Code is as follows:

```
//**********************************************************
// Name: RenderScene()
// Description: Set the rendering and texture qualities, move
//              the scene, clear the viewport, render the frame,
//              and update the window
//**********************************************************
static BOOL RenderScene()
{

    HRESULT retval;

    //**********************************
    //        Set Rendering Quality
    //**********************************
    retval = globVars.aDevice->SetQuality(D3DRMRENDER_GOURAUD);
    if(FAILED(retval))
    {
        D3DError("Device quality set failed.");
        return FALSE;
    }
    //**********************************
    //        Set Texture Quality
    //**********************************
    retval = globVars.aDevvce\
            ->SetTextureQuality(activeTexture);
      if(FAILED(retval))
      {
        D3DError("Texture quality set set failed.");
        return FALSE;
      }

    //**********************************
    //        Move the scene
    //**********************************
    retval = globVars.aScene->Move(D3DVAL(1.0));
```

```
        if (FAILED(retval))
        {
            D3DError("Moving scene failed");
            return FALSE;
        }

        //*****************************
        //      Clear the viewport
        //*****************************
        retval = globVars.aViewport->Clear(D3DRMCLEAR_ALL);
        if (FAILED(retval))
        {
            D3DError("Clearing viewport failed");
            return FALSE;
        }

        //*****************************
        //              render
        //*****************************
        retval = globVars.aViewport->Render(globVars.aScene);
        if (FAILED(retval))
        {
            D3DError("Rendering scene failed");
            return FALSE;
        }

        //*****************************
        //      update the window
        //*****************************
        retval = globVars.aDevice->Update();
        if (FAILED(retval))
        {
            D3DError("Updating device failed");
            return FALSE;
        }
        return TRUE;
}
```

The parameters that define the movements are entered during processing the BuildScene() function. The values, which are defined in global variables, are modified while the user interacts with the corresponding dialog boxes. The code is as follows:

```
// Rotation vectors
float    xRot  = 0.0;          // x axis rotation vector
float    yRot  = 0.0;          // y axis
float    zRot  = 0.0;          // z axis
float    theta = 0.02f;        // angular velocity of rotation

// Velocity vectors
float    xVel  = 0.0f;         // x axis velocity vector
float    yVel  = 0.0f;         // y-axis
float    zVel  = 0.0f;         // z-axis
```

```
BOOL     rotTF = FALSE;          // Include rotation flag
. . .

// Rotate the child frame
// If velocity controls are zero then use zero for rotational
// angle and set one axis. This makes it possible to use linear
// movements with no rotation
  if(xRot + yRot + zRot == 0)
  {
    theta = 0.0;
    xRot = 1;
  }
  if (FAILED(childframe->SetRotation(NULL,
                                     D3DVAL(xRot),
                                     D3DVAL(yRot),
                                     D3DVAL(zRot),
                                     D3DVAL(theta)))) // angle
    goto ERROR_EXIT;

// Set velocity
  if(xRot + yRot + zRot != 0)
  {
    if (FAILED(childframe->SetVelocity(NULL,
                              D3DVAL(xVel),
                              D3DVAL(yVel),
                              D3DVAL(zVel),
                              rotTF)))          // Include
rotational
                                                // velocity
    goto ERROR_EXIT;
  }
```

When the 3DRM Move Demo program first executes, the teapot object is static. The user can animate the object by manipulating the controls in the program's dialog boxes, shown in Figure 19-2. The result can be a simultaneous movement along one or more of the object's rotation or translation axes. Figure 19-3 shows three consecutive screen snapshots of the 3DRM Move Demo program. In this case three simultaneous rotations and translations have been enabled. As a result, the teapot appears to progressively fade into the background as it rotates on its axes.

Figure 19-3: Screen snapshots of the 3DRM Move Demo program

Changing the frame matrix

Another set of functions of IDirect3DRMFrame3 provides ways for making one-time changes on the frame's matrix. These functions differ from SetRotation() and SetVelocity(), described previously, in that they operate once on the frame's parameters, whereas the matrix changes produced by SetRotation() and SetVelocity() continue to take place at every iteration of the Move() or Tick() functions. The functions that perform one-time changes in the frame matrix discussed in this section are named AddRotation(), AddTranslation(), and AddScale(). A related function, named AddTransform(), is discussed in the context of frame-level transformations later in this chapter.

A common element in these three functions is that their first parameter is a constant of the D3DRMCOMBINETYPE enumeration, which determines how two matrices are combined. The enumeration is defined as follows:

```
typedef enum _D3DRMCOMBINETYPE{
    D3DRMCOMBINE_REPLACE,
    D3DRMCOMBINE_BEFORE,
    D3DRMCOMBINE_AFTER
} D3DRMCOMBINETYPE;
```

The constant D3DRMCOMBINE_REPLACE determines that the supplied matrix replaces the frame's current matrix. The constant D3DRMCOMBINE_BEFORE determines that the supplied matrix is multiplied with the frame's current matrix and precedes the current matrix in the calculation. On the other hand, the constant D3DRMCOMBINE_AFTER determines that the supplied matrix is multiplied with the frame's current matrix and follows the current matrix in the calculation. The order of the matrices is important because, as you know from Chapter 3, matrix multiplication is not commutative.

The AddRotation() function of IDirect3DRMFrame3 adds one or more rotation vectors to the matrix of the frame object making the call. The function has the following general form.

```
HRESULT AddRotation(
            D3DRMCOMBINETYPE rctCombine,     // 1
            D3DVALUE rvX,                    // 2
            D3DVALUE rvY,                    // 3
            D3DVALUE rvZ,                    // 4
            D3DVALUE rvTheta                 // 5
            );
```

The first parameter is one of the members of the D3DRMCOMBINETYPE enumerated type. This constant specifies the new rotation is combined with any current frame transformation. The second, third, and fourth parameters specify the axes about which the rotation is applied. Any nonzero value selects the axis and zero deselects it. The fifth parameter is the angle or rotation, in radians. The function returns D3DRM_OK if it succeeds, or an error otherwise.

Notice that the AddRotation() function, like its SetRotation() counterpart, allows selecting more than one axis of rotation but applies the same angular rotation to all the selected axes. However, in the case of AddRotation() it is possible to apply different rotations to two or more axes by selecting the D3DRMCOMBINE_AFTER mode. The AddRotation() function is then called independently for each axis, in each case with the desired value for the angle of rotation.

The AddTranslation() function of IDirect3DRMFrame3 adds one or more translation vectors to the matrix of the frame object making the call. The function has the following general form:

```
HRESULT AddTranslation(
                D3DRMCOMBINETYPE rctCombine,        // 1
                D3DVALUE rvX,                       // 2
                D3DVALUE rvY,                       // 3
                D3DVALUE rvZ                        // 4
                );
```

The first parameter is a member of the D3DRMCOMBINETYPE enumerated type. This constant specifies how to combine the new translation with any existing transformation. The second, third, and fourth parameters define the axis or axes along which the translation to takes place. Positive and negative values determine the direction of the movement along the axis. The numeric value determines the amount of translation applied to each axis. By entering different values for separate axes it is possible to generate a nonuniform translation in a single call. The function returns D3DRM_OK if it succeeds, or an error otherwise.

The AddScale() function of IDirect3DRMFrame3 adds one or more scaling vectors to the matrix of the frame object making the call. The function has the following general form:

```
HRESULT AddScale(
                D3DRMCOMBINETYPE rctCombine,        // 1
                D3DVALUE rvX,                       // 2
                D3DVALUE rvY,                       // 3
                D3DVALUE rvZ                        // 4
                );
```

The first parameter is a member of the D3DRMCOMBINETYPE enumerated type. This constant specifies how to combine the new translation with any existing transformation. The second, third, and fourth parameters define the axis or axes along which the scaling is to take place. Integer values determine a positive scaling and fractional values a negative scaling. A scaling value of 1 leaves the axis unchanged. The function returns D3DRM_OK if it succeeds, or an error otherwise.

Figure 19-4 shows the result of applying the AddScale() function.

x-axis scale = 0.5   x-axis scale = 1.0   x-axis scale = 1.5

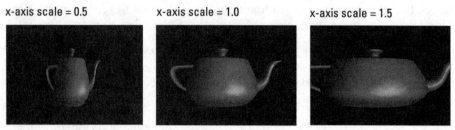

Figure 19-4: Scaling transformation using AddScale() function

Loading objects into frames

Retained mode provides a function named Load(), which is part of IDirect3DRM
Frame3, which allows loading an object into a frame. The function is sometimes
used to load textures and animation sets, although other, more suitable, functions
are also available for these purposes. The function's general form is as follows:

```
HRESULT Load(
        LPVOID lpvObjSource,                              // 1
        LPVOID lpvObjID,                                  // 2
        D3DRMLOADOPTIONS d3drmLOFlags,                    // 3
        D3DRMLOADTEXTURE3CALLBACK d3drmLoadTextureProc,   // 4
        LPVOID lpArgLTP                                   // 5
        );
```

The function's first parameter is a pointer to the source for the object to be loaded.
This can be a file, a resource, a memory block, or a stream, according to the setting
of the source flags specified in the third parameter. The second parameter is the
object's name or the position in which it is to be loaded. This parameter also
depends on the flag passed in the third parameter. The third parameter is a flag
that determines the load options. The load options are defined in a structure of
type D3DRMLOADOPTIONS, as follows:

```
typedef DWORD D3DRMLOADOPTIONS;
#define D3DRMLOAD_FROMFILE               0x00L
#define D3DRMLOAD_FROMRESOURCE           0x01L
#define D3DRMLOAD_FROMMEMORY             0x02L
#define D3DRMLOAD_FROMURL                0x08L
#define D3DRMLOAD_BYNAME                 0x10L
#define D3DRMLOAD_BYPOSITION             0x20L
#define D3DRMLOAD_BYGUID                 0x30L
#define D3DRMLOAD_FIRST                  0x40L
#define D3DRMLOAD_INSTANCEBYREFERENCE    0x100L
#define D3DRMLOAD_INSTANCEBYCOPYING      0x200L
#define D3DRMLOAD_ASYNCHRONOUS           0x400L
```

Table 19-2 describes the load option flags.

Table 19-2 Option Flags Used in the D3DRMLOADOPTIONS Structure	
Flag	**Description**
Source flags	
D3DRMLOAD_FROMFILE	Load from a file. This is the default setting.
D3DRMLOAD_FROMRESOURCE	Load from a resource. If this flag is specified, the lpvObjSource parameter of the calling Load function must point to a D3DRMLOADRESOURCE structure.
D3DRMLOAD_FROMMEMORY	Load from memory. If this flag is specified, the lpvObjSource parameter of the calling Load() function must point to a D3DRMLOADMEMORY structure.
D3DRMLOAD_FROMURL	Load from an URL.
Identifier flags	
D3DRMLOAD_BYNAME	Load any object by using a specified name.
D3DRMLOAD_BYPOSITION	Load a stand-alone object based on a given zero-based position within the file. Stand-alone objects can contain other objects, but are not contained by any other objects.
D3DRMLOAD_BYGUID	Load any object by using a specified globally unique identifier (GUID).
D3DRMLOAD_FIRST	The default setting. Load the first stand-alone object of the given type.
Instance flags	
D3DRMLOAD_INSTANCEBYREFERENCE	Check whether an object already exists with the same name as specified and, if so, use an instance of that object instead of creating a new one.
D3DRMLOAD_INSTANCEBYCOPYING	Check whether an object already exists with the same name as specified. If so, copy that object.
Source flags	
D3DRMLOAD_ASYNCHRONOUS	The Load call will return immediately. It is up to the application to use events to find out how the load is progressing. By default, loading is asynchronous.

The fourth parameter to the Load() function is a D3DRMLOADTEXTURE3CALLBACK callback function used to load any textures used by the object. This parameter can be NULL. The fifth parameter is a pointer to application-defined data passed to the D3DRMLOADTEXTURE3CALLBACK callback function. The function returns D3DRM_OK if it succeeds, or an error otherwise.

Frame Transformations

Chapter 3 is entirely devoted to matrix transformations as they are used in computer graphics. Here we discuss matrix transformations in the light of actual 3D retained mode programming practice. At this point in the text we assume that the reader has basic familiarity with the elements of matrix arithmetic, homogeneous coordinates, and matrix multiplication as presented in Chapter 3.

Most of the work of 3D graphics is based on translation, rotation, and scaling transformations. In addition, matrices and transformations are used to define the location of graphics objects and to change viewing positions, viewing direction, and in perspective rendering. Previously in this chapter you used functions to position and move frames. The AddTranslation(), AddRotation(), and AddScale() functions of the IDirect3DFrame3 interface are used to rotate, translate, and scale frames without accessing the frame's matrix directly. By means of these functions you can perform matrix transformations without dealing with the frame matrix itself. These frame-level local APIs provide a useful, elementary functionality. However, much greater power and control, as well as a simpler interface, is achieved by performing transformations by manipulating the frame matrices directly.

Review of basic notions

Briefly reviewing the fundamental concepts, we recall that we store the x-, y-, and z-coordinates of a point in 3D space as follows:

```
[x    y    z    1]
```

You can perform a translation, scaling, or rotation transformation on the coordinates of the point by multiplying the row vector by a corresponding homogeneous matrix. The matrices for the primitive transformations are as follows:

Translation:

Translation:

1	0	0	0
0	1	0	0
0	0	1	0
Tx	Ty	Tz	1

Scaling:

Scaling:

Sx	0	0	0
0	Sy	0	0
0	0	Sz	0
0	0	0	1

Rotation (x-axis):

Rotation (x-axis):

1	0	0	0
0	cos A	sin A	0
0	−sin A	cos A	0
0	0	0	1

Rotation (y-axis):

Rotation (y-axis):

cos A	0	−sin A	0
0	1	0	0
sin A	0	cos A	0
0	0	0	1

Rotation (z-axis):

Rotation (z-axis):

cos A	sin A	0	0
−sin A	cos A	0	0
0	0	1	0
0	0	0	1

In addition to the primitive transformations matrices, there is another matrix of interest. This matrix, called the *identity matrix*, has a similar property as the number 1 in scalar multiplication. That is, the product of multiplying any matrix by the identity matrix is the original matrix. The corresponding identity matrix for 3D operations is as follows:

Identity matrix:

$$
\begin{bmatrix}
1 & 0 & 0 & 0 \\
0 & 1 & 0 & 0 \\
0 & 0 & 1 & 0 \\
0 & 0 & 0 & 1
\end{bmatrix}
$$

The preceding matrices can be applied to the coordinates matrix of a point in 3D space to perform the transformation that it contains. The product of any arbitrary sequence of translation, scaling, and rotation transformations using these matrices have the property of preserving the parallelism, although not the line lengths or angles, of the original figure. For this reason they are described as affine transformations. Notice that the last column of all of the primitive transformations matrices listed previously have the following pattern:

$$
\begin{bmatrix}
0 \\
0 \\
0 \\
1
\end{bmatrix}
$$

It is this pattern in the matrices last column that ensures that the affine property is preserved.

The following matrix multiplication translates a point expressed in a row vector, with coordinates (x,y,z), according to the value contained in the translation matrix for each axis.

$$
\begin{bmatrix} x & y & z & 1 \end{bmatrix} \times
\begin{bmatrix}
1 & 0 & 0 & 0 \\
0 & 1 & 0 & 0 \\
0 & 0 & 1 & 0 \\
Tx & Ty & Tz & 1
\end{bmatrix}
$$

In this case Tx, Ty, and Tz represent the amount of translation performed in each axis.

Matrices in Direct3D

In C++ code, a matrix can be represented by an array of the corresponding dimensions. Conventionally, matrices are specified in row-major order. This means that a 2×4 matrix contains 2 rows and 4 columns. In this sense, a row vector that stores the coordinates of a point in 3D space can be represented in a one-dimensional array of four elements. For example:

```
D3DVALUE pointsArray[4];
```

The 4×4 matrix representing a 3D transformation can be stored in a two-dimensional array of 4 rows and 4 columns. In retained mode the D3DRMMATRIX4D data type is a 4×4, two-dimensional array that expresses a matrix-coded transformation. The array is defined as follows:

```
typedef D3DVALUE D3DRMMATRIX4D[4][4];
```

The first dimension corresponds to the matrix rows and the second one to the columns. The elements in the matrix array are of type D3DVALUE, which corresponds to a float data type. The D3DVAL macro is defined in the d3dtypes.h file as follows:

```
#define D3DVAL(val) ((float)(val))
```

The macro can be used, instead of typecasting, to create values of type D3DVALUE. The following code fragment shows a function that inserts values for an identity matrix in the matrix passed as a parameter by the caller.

```
//************************************************
// name: MakeIdentityMatrix()
// desc: Fills the values for an identity matrix,
//       that is, a matrix with 1's in the main
//       diagonal and 0's everywhere else
//************************************************
void MakeIdentityMatrix(D3DRMMATRIX4D aMatrix)
{

   aMatrix[0][0] = (D3DVALUE) 1.0;
   aMatrix[0][1] = (D3DVALUE) 0.0;
   aMatrix[0][2] = (D3DVALUE) 0.0;
   aMatrix[0][3] = (D3DVALUE) 0.0;

   aMatrix[1][0] = (D3DVALUE) 0.0;
   aMatrix[1][1] = (D3DVALUE) 1.0;
   aMatrix[1][2] = (D3DVALUE) 0.0;
   aMatrix[1][3] = (D3DVALUE) 0.0;

   aMatrix[2][0] = (D3DVALUE) 0.0;
```

```
        aMatrix[2][1] = (D3DVALUE) 0.0;
        aMatrix[2][2] = (D3DVALUE) 1.0;
        aMatrix[2][3] = (D3DVALUE) 0.0;

        aMatrix[3][0] = (D3DVALUE) 0.0;
        aMatrix[3][1] = (D3DVALUE) 0.0;
        aMatrix[3][2] = (D3DVALUE) 0.0;
        aMatrix[3][3] = (D3DVALUE) 1.0;

    return;
    }
```

The local transform

A retained mode frame is located and oriented by a 4×4 matrix located in the frame object itself. In this sense the terms *local* or *model* coordinates refer to the points in 3D space that define the modeled object. Consistently, the matrix associated with each frame is sometimes called the *local transform*. The default state of the local transform for a frame is the identity matrix. Applications can obtain the 4×4 affine matrix that is the local transform matrix for a frame by means of the GetTransform() function of IDirect3DRMFrame3. The function has the following general form:

```
HRESULT GetTransform(
                LPDIRECT3DRMFRAME lpRefFrame,        // 1
                D3DRMMATRIX4D rmMatrix               // 2
                );
```

The first parameter designates the frame that serves as the root of the scene. If this argument is NULL, the current root frame is used. The second parameter is an array of type D3DRMMATRIX4D that receives the frame's local transform. The function returns DD_OK if it succeeds.

Applying frame-level transformations

Several retained mode functions serve to simplify and implement matrix transformations. The most general one is named AddTransform(). The AddTransform() function applies the frame's local transform matrix to the coordinates of each point of the object contained in the frame. The result is a general transformation. The function's general form is as follows:

```
HRESULT AddTransform(
                D3DRMCOMBINETYPE rctCombine,         // 1
                D3DRMMATRIX4D rmMatrix               // 2
                );
```

The first parameter is one of the members of the D3DRMCOMBINETYPE enumeration described previously in this chapter. This determines how to combine the new transformation with any previously existing one. The second parameter is an array of type D3DRMMATRIX4D that defines the transformation matrix to be combined. The function returns D3DRM_OK if it succeeds, or an error otherwise.

Note that for the transformation to preserve its affine property the last column of the matrix passed in the call must contain the values:

0

0

0

1

Application code should carefully preserve this matrix column. Transformation can be applied to the frame at any point in the code, although the results are not visible until the frame is rendered. The following code fragment shows the processing operations required for performing an x- and y-axis translation using the AddTranslate() function.

```
// Translation matrix for x- and y-axis
D3DRMMATRIX4D transXY =
{    D3DVAL(1),      0,              0,            0,
     0,              D3DVAL(1),      0,            0,
     0,              0,              D3DVAL(1),    0,
     D3DVAL(0.5),    D3DVAL(0.5),    0,            D3DVAL(1)
};
. . .
FrameTransform(transXY);
. . .
//*************************************************
// name: FrameTransform()
// desc: Applies a transformation matrix to the
//       frame
//*************************************************
BOOL FrameTransform()
{
    // Add translation
        if(xTrans + yTrans + zTrans != 0)
        {
           retval = childframe->AddTranslation(CTTrans,
                                    D3DVAL(xTrans), // Axes
                                    D3DVAL(yTrans),
                                    D3DVAL(zTrans));

        if(FAILED(retval))
          {
```

```
                    RMError(retval);
                    return FALSE;
              }
        }
    return TRUE;
}
```

3DRM Matrix Ops Demo project

The project named 3DRM Matrix Ops Demo, in the book's CD-ROM, shows the action of the AddRotation(), AddTranslation(), and AddScale() functions and also illustrates matrix transformations. The program is intended as a minimal laboratory for experimenting with frame-level movements and matrix-based transformations. All transformations are applied to the scene frame. As the program executes it displays a modeless dialog box that contains the patterns for the matrices used in translation, scaling, and rotation transformations listed previously in this chapter. In addition, code reads and displays the current local transform. Figure 19-5 is a screen snapshot of the initial program display.

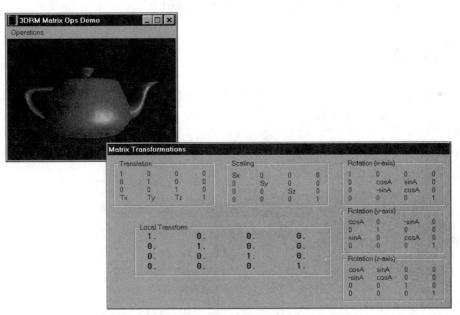

Figure 19-5: Initial screen of the 3DRM Matrix Ops Demo program

Notice in Figure 19-5 that the initial value for the local transform is the identity matrix. For this reason no change takes place in the frame object if the unmodified local transform is applied. Figure 19-5 also shows the program's main menu, which contains commands to execute some of the movements and transformation functions discussed in this chapter. The first three menu commands allow executing the `AddRotation()`, `AddTranslation()`, and `AddScaling()` functions of `IDirect3D RMFrame3`. Figure 19-6 shows the dialog boxes for each of these menu commands.

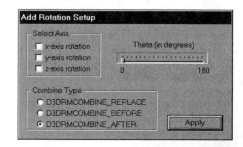

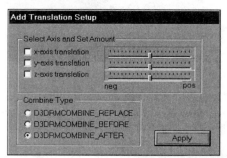

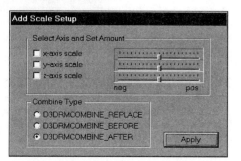

Figure 19-6: Dialog boxes for the first three commands in the 3DRM Matrix Ops Demo program

All three dialogs contain check boxes for selecting the axes on which the transformations are performed. They also contain radio buttons for selecting the combine type to be applied in the transformation. Consistently with the functions themselves, the Add Rotation Setup dialog box enables the user to enter a rotation angle (theta). The scale is encoded in degrees and the program performs the conversion into radians. The dialog boxes for setting up translation and scaling transformations enable the user to select a positive or negative value for each axis. This value determines the amount of transformations applied in each case. As the transformations are applied, the resulting local transform is shown in the program's Matrix Tranformations window.

The Add Transform command in the program's Operations menu allows applying an arbitrary transformation defined by the user. The command displays the dialog box shown in Figure 19-7.

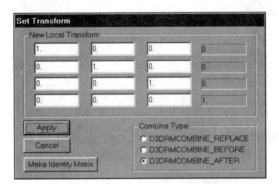

Figure 19-7: Add Transform dialog in the 3DRM Matrix Ops Demo program

When the Add Transform command executes the dialog box displays the values in the current local transform. The edit boxes allow entering new values in the matrix. The entries for the rightmost matrix columns are grayed to ensure that the resulting transformation preserves the affine characteristic. The button labeled Make Identity Matrix is used to change the matrix to the identity form, that is, with 1s in the main diagonal and 0s everywhere else. The button labled Apply closes the dialog box and produces the transformation. The one labeled Cancel closes the dialog box restoring the previous local transform. Here again, the user can select the combine type used in the call to the `AddTransform()` function.

The Apply All command in the Operations menu applies all transformations enabled with the Add Rotation, Add Translation, Add Scale, and Add Transform commands. The transformations are applied in the same order as they appear in the menu and according to the selected combine types.

Support Operations at the Frame Level

Three groups of frame-level operations serve mainly to support the major functions already discussed. These support operations consist of vector-level manipulations, frame traversal options, and the implementation of callback functions. Because of their simple nature they are discussed briefly in the following sections.

Vector-level manipulations

Four functions of IDirect3DRMFrame3 perform operations at the vector level. Although these functions are not as versatile or useful as those that perform matrix-level transformations, they do add a functionality that is occasionally necessary.

The functions and their operations are listed in Table 19-3.

Table 19-3 Vector-Level Functions in IDirect3DRMFrame3	
Function	**Action**
Transform()	Transforms a vector in model coordinates to world coordinates
TransformVectors()	Transforms an array of vectors in model coordinates to world coordinates
InverseTransform()	Transforms a vector in world coordinates to model coordinates
InverseTransformVectors()	Transforms an array of vectors in world coordinates to model coordinates

The functions in Table 19-3 perform transformations to and from model-space and world-space. In retained mode documentation, world coordinates are relative to the root frame and model coordinates relative to the child frame.

Frame traversal controls

Frame traversal options were first implemented in DirectX 6. The two new functions, named SetTraversalOptions() and GetTraversalOptions() enable you to control the render and the pick status of a frame. This status determines if a child frame is included in the frame hierarchy traversed during rendering and picking. The SetTraversalOptions() function has the following general form:

```
HRESULT SetTraversalOptions(
                    DWORD dwFlags              // 1
                    );
```

The function's only parameter consists of two flags that enable rendering and picking traversal for the frame. They are defined as follows:

✦ D3DRMFRAME_RENDERENABLE indicates to the function to render this frame or any children of this frame

✦ D3DRMFRAME_PICKENABLE indicates to the function to pick any visuals in this frame or any children of this frame

The default state of both flags is enabled. Code can disable one or another traversal option by setting the other one. Both traversal options are disabled by passing a value of zero for the function's parameter, as in the following statement:

```
childframe->SetTraversalOptions(0);
```

Thereafter, the child frame referenced in the call to SetTraversalOptions() is not visited during rendering or picking operations. The function returns DD_OK if it succeeds, or an error code otherwise.

The GetTraversalOptions() function returns the traversal option currently enabled.

Frame-level callback functions

Frames support a callback function that you can use to implement complex animations and other special manipulations at rendering time. After the callback function is registered, retained mode calls this function before the motion attributes are applied. When there is a hierarchy containing multiple frames, each frame can be associated with its own callback function. In this case the parent frames are called before the child frames. Callback functions are used to provide objects with new positions and orientations based on a preprogrammed animation sequence, or to implement dynamic motion in which the activities of visuals depend upon the positions of other objects in the scene.

DirectX retained mode currently provides nine different types of callback functions. One of them, named D3DRMFRAME3MOVECALLBACK, enables an application to receive control whenever a frame is moved or updated. The intercept can be used to produce powerful and sophisticated animation effects or other render-time operations. The use of the callback function in animation is discussed in Chapter 25. The callback function is defined as follows:

```
void (*D3DRMFRAME3MOVECALLBACK)(
                LPDIRECT3DRMFRAME3 lpD3DRMFrame,      // 1
                LPVOID lpArg,                         // 2
                D3DVALUE delta                        // 3
            );
```

The first parameter is the address of a pointer to the Direct3DRMFrame object that is being moved. The second parameter is the address of a pointer to application-defined data passed to this callback function. The third parameter encodes the amount of change that is to be applied to the frame movement. Two components are individually controllable: linear and rotational. The change in each component is equal to *velocity_of_component × delta*. Either or both of these velocities can be set relative to any frame; however, the system automatically converts them to velocities relative to the parent frame. The function has no return value.

The frame-level callback function enables code to control the acceleration of a frame relative to its parent frame. To accomplish this, you can reset the velocity of the child frame in relation to the parent frame during each tick. If *a* is the required acceleration, then each intercept code should set the velocity of the child frame relative to itself to (*a* units per tick) × 1 tick. This is equal to *a* × *delta* units per tick. Retained mode internally converts *a* × *delta* units per tick relative to the child frame to (*v* + (*a* × *delta*)) units per tick relative to the parent frame, where *v* is the current velocity of the child relative to the parent.

Two other functions of IDirect3DRMFrame3 are related to frame move callbacks: AddMoveCallback() and DeleteMoveCallback(). The first one is used to create a move callback intercept, as previously described. The function's general form is as follows:

```
HRESULT AddMoveCallback(
                    D3DRMFRAME3MOVECALLBACK d3drmFMC,    // 1
                    VOID *lpArg,                         // 2
                    DWORD dwFlags                        // 3
                    );
```

The first parameter is the application-defined D3DRMFRAME3MOVECALLBACK callback function previously discussed.

The second parameter is a pointer to an application-defined data structure passed to the callback function. The third parameter is one of the following flags:

✦ D3DRMCALLBACK_PREORDER. This is the default value. When the Move() function traverses the frame hierarchy, callbacks for a frame are used before any child frames are traversed.

✦ D3DRMCALLBACK_POSTORDER. When the Move() function traverses the hierarchy, callbacks for a frame are used after the child frames are traversed.

If multiple callbacks are implemented on the same frame, they are called in the order that they were created. The function returns D3DRM_OK if it succeeds, or an error otherwise.

The DeleteMoveCallback() function of IDirect3DRMFrame3 removes a callback function created with AddMoveCallback(). The function has the following general form:

```
HRESULT DeleteMoveCallback(
                        D3DRMFRAME3MOVECALLBACK d3drmFMC, // 1
                        VOID *lpArg                       // 2
                        );
```

The first parameter is the D3DRMFRAME3MOVECALLBACK callback function to be removed. The second parameter is a pointer to the application-defined data that was passed to the callback function. The function returns D3DRM_OK if it succeeds, or an error otherwise.

Summary

We have now concluded the first phase of our tour through frame-level programming in retained mode. In addition to an overview of the `IDirect3DRMFrame3` interface, we explored frame movements and controls, matrix-based transformations, vector manipulations, frame traversal options, and the use of application-defined callback functions. In this process we learned how to apply, in practical programming, the mathematical structures discussed in earlier chapters. This enabled us to perform frame-level transformations both indirectly and by manipulating primitive transformation matrices. In addition, we developed software that will enable us to experiment with these transformations.

In the next chapter we continue exploring frame-level programming in retained mode.

✦   ✦   ✦

Frame Attributes and Scene-Level Controls

In Chapter 19 we began our discussion of frame program-ming. At that time we mentioned that frame-level operations are one of the richest and most powerful in retained mode. Consequently, we divided the material into two chapters; this is the second one. The frame-related functions discussed here refer to the manipulation of frame attributes, scene-level opera-tions and programming, frame hierarchies, sorting modes, z-buffer controls, and visuals. Table 19-1, in the preceding chapter, lists all the functions of IDirect3DRMFrame3. There are close to fifty functions in this second part of the frame interface. We have only excluded a few functions that have very limited use, or that do not merit any explanation because of their simplicity or their similarity to other functions.

Manipulating Frame Components and Attributes

A rather broad group of frame-level functions refer to the manipulation of frame attributes or components. These include the following categories:

✦ Operations related to the frame's bounding box

✦ Operations that set and retrieve the frame's color

✦ Operations that add, delete, and retrieve lights

✦ Operations that set and retrieve materials, material modes, and material overrides

✦ Operations that set and retrieve textures

Bounding box operations

Bounding boxes for frames were first introduced in the IDirect3DRMFrame2 interface which is part of DirectX version 5. Bounding box–based testing is performed at render-time, as follows: the frame's bounding box is transformed into model space and checked for intersection with the viewing frustum. If the entire box is outside of the viewing frustum, none of the visuals in the frame, or in any child frame, are rendered. Otherwise, rendering takes place as normal. Bounding box operations at the frame level are useful in implementing hierarchical culling algorithms, but are not of much use in conventional application development.

The bounding box is delimited by a structure of type D3DRMBOX, which is defined as follows:

```
typedef struct _D3DRMBOX {
                        D3DVECTOR min, max;
                }D3DRMBOX;
typedef D3DRMBOX *LPD3DRMBOX;
```

The structure members min and max define the bounds of the box. These are D3DVECTOR structures.

Setting and retrieving the bounding box

Bounding box testing at the frame level must be explicitly enabled before it takes place. But, before bounding box testing is enabled, a valid bounding box must have been defined for the frame. The SetBox() function of IDirect3DRMFrame3 sets the bounding box for a frame. A valid bounding box must be equal to or smaller than the frame itself. The function has the following general form:

```
HRESULT SetBox(
            D3DRMBOX    *lpD3DRMBox                      // 1
            );
```

The function's only parameter is the address of a structure of type D3DRMBOX structure that contains the bounding box coordinates. The function returns D3DRM_OK if it succeeds, or an error otherwise.

The GetBox() function of IDirect3DRMFrame3 allows the retrieval of the bounding box for a frame object. The function has the following general form:

```
HRESULT GetBox(
            D3DRMBOX    *lpD3DRMBox                      // 1
            );
```

The function's only parameter is the address of a D3DRMBOX structure that is filled with the bounding box coordinates. The function returns D3DRM_OK if it succeeds, or an error otherwise. If a valid bounding box has not been previously defined for the frame, the call returns D3DRMERR_BOXNOTSET.

The GetHierarchyBox() function calculates and returns the bounding box required for holding all the objects in the hierarchy rooted in the calling frame. The function has the following general form:

```
HRESULT GetHierarchyBox(
                   D3DRMBOX    *lpD3DRMBox                    // 1
                   );
```

The function's only parameter is the address of a D3DRMBOX structure that is filled with the bounding box coordinates. The function returns D3DRM_OK if it succeeds, or an error otherwise.

Controlling bounding box testing

Bounding box testing at the frame level is off by default. Applications that intend to use this function must enable it by calling the SetBoxEnable() function of IDirect3DRMFrame3. This function can also be used to disable bounding box testing after it has been enabled. The function has the following general form:

```
HRESULT SetBoxEnable(
                   BOOL bEnableFlag                           // 1
                   );
```

The function's only parameter is a boolean that enables or disables bounding box checking for the frame making the call. The default value is FALSE, which corresponds to bounding box checking disabled. Enabling bounding box testing with a box of {0,0,0,0} completely prevents a frame from being rendered. The function returns D3DRM_OK if it succeeds, or an error otherwise.

The GetBoxEnable() function returns the state of the bounding box testing enabled flag. The function has the following general form:

```
BOOL GetBoxEnable();
```

The return value is TRUE if bounding box checking is enabled and FALSE otherwise.

Controlling frame color

Code can control the color of meshes in a frame by means of frame-level functions. This is possible only if the D3DRMMATERIALMODE enumerated type is D3DRMMATERIAL_FROMFRAME. Materials in frames are discussed later in this chapter. The color-related functions at the frame level are GetColor(),

SetColor(), and SetColorRGB(). The SetColor() function has the following general form:

```
HRESULT SetColor(
                D3DCOLOR rcColor                        // 1
              );
```

The function's only parameter is the address of a structure variable of type D3DCOLOR that contains the new color for the frame. The D3DCOLOR type is defined as a DWORD in the current implementation of DirectX. Because the alpha component of the color is not ignored, a typical application uses the RGBA_MAKE macro to specify the color value. The macro is defined as follows:

```
RGBA_MAKE(r, g, b, a)   \
    ((D3DCOLOR) (((a) << 24) | ((r) << 16) | ((g) << 8) | (b)))
```

The function returns D3DRM_OK if it succeeds, or an error otherwise.

A more direct way and easier way to set the frame color is by means of the SetColorRGB() function. The function has the following general form:

```
HRESULT SetColorRGB(
                D3DVALUE rvRed,             // 1
                D3DVALUE rvGreen,           // 2
                D3DVALUE rvBlue             // 3
              );
```

All three parameters define the red, green, and blue color components for the frame. Because each color is a D3DVALUE it must be in the range 0.0 to 1.0. The function returns D3DRM_OK if it succeeds, or an error otherwise. The following code fragment sets the material mode and the frame color.

```
retval = childframe->SetMaterialMode(D3DRMMATERIAL_FROMFRAME);
retval = childframe->SetColorRGB(D3DVAL(0.0),       // red
                                 D3DVAL(0.0),       // green
                                 D3DVAL(0.9));      // blue
```

The GetColor() function of IDirect3DRMFrame3 retrieves the color of a frame. The function's general form is as follows:

```
D3DCOLOR GetColor();
```

The returned value is a D3DCOLOR type, which is equivalent to a DWORD integer. Figure 20-1 shows the D3DCOLOR bitmap.

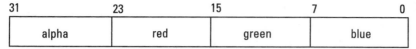

Figure 20-1: RGBA mapping in the D3DCOLOR data type

Application code can do some bitwise masking and shifting to isolate the individual color components into integer data types. Alternatively, code can use the nonmember functions discussed in Chapter 16 to obtain the individual color components in a D3DCOLOR variable. The functions are named D3DRMColorGetAlpha(), D3DRMColor GetBlue(), D3DRMColorGetGreen(), and D3DRMColorGetRed(). The return value for all four functions is of D3DVALUE type.

Controlling lights

In Chapter 14 we discussed lights in retained mode programming, and in Chapter 15 we developed code to create and position a light frame and to create and attach lights to this frame. At that time you learned that an unlighted scene is invisible and that lights can be used to increase the visual quality of a scene. You also learned that retained mode lights are attached to frames, which are used to position and orient the lights within the scene. The light is placed at the origin of the frame it is attached to. By moving and reorienting the frame code, you can redirect a light source.

Lights are discussed in detail in Chapter 24, in relation to the IDirect3DRMLight interface. Here we are concerned with the organization and management of lights at the frame level. Frame-level functions that relate to lights serve to add and remove lights from a frame and to obtain a list of the lights currently installed in the frame. Before you add a light to a frame you must create the light frame and position it within the scene. In the retained mode demo programs developed thus far in the book we have proceeded as shown in the following code fragment:

```
// Global variables
LPDIRECT3DRMFRAME3 lightsframe          = NULL;
LPDIRECT3DRMLIGHT light1                = NULL;
LPDIRECT3DRMLIGHT light2                = NULL;
. . .

// Create a light frame as a child of the scene frame
    retval = lpD3DRM->CreateFrame(aScene, &lightsframe);
        if(FAILED(retval))
            goto ERROR_EXIT;

// Position the light frame within the scene
    retval = lightsframe->SetPosition(aScene,
                                D3DVAL(5),        // x
```

```
                                              D3DVAL(0),        // y
                                             -D3DVAL(7));       // z
    if(FAILED(retval))
        goto ERROR_EXIT;

// Create a bright, parallel point light
// Color values are as follows:
// 0.0 = totally dim and 1.0 = totally bright
    retval = lpD3DRM->CreateLightRGB(D3DRMLIGHT_PARALLELPOINT,
                            D3DVAL(0.8),    // Red intensity
                            D3DVAL(0.8),    // Green intensity
                            D3DVAL(1.0),    // Blue intensity
                            &light1);
    if(FAILED(retval)){
        goto ERROR_EXIT;

// Attach first light to lights frame
    retval = lightsframe->AddLight(light1);
    if(FAILED(retval))
        goto ERROR_EXIT;

// Create a strong ambient light
    retval = lpD3DRM->CreateLightRGB(D3DRMLIGHT_AMBIENT,
                                D3DVAL(0.4),    // red
                                D3DVAL(0.4),    // green
                                D3DVAL(0.4),    // blue
                                &light2);
    if(FAILED(retval))
        goto ERROR_EXIT;
// Attach second light to lights frame
    retval = lightsframe->AddLight(light2);
        if(FAILED(retval))
            goto ERROR_EXIT;
. . .
```

The AddLight() function of IDirect3DRMFrame3 is used in the preceding code to attach each of the lights to the lights frame.

The function has the following general form:

```
HRESULT AddLight(
                LPDIRECT3DRMLIGHT lpD3DRMLight            // 1
            );
```

The function's only parameter is the address of a variable that represents the Direct3DRMLight object to be added to the frame.

The function returns D3DRM_OK if it succeeds, or an error otherwise.

As lights are added to the light frame, retained mode places each one at the end of an array of type `Direct3DRMLightArray`. Code accesses and manipulates the lights array through the functions in the `IDirect3DRMLightArray` interface. The first step in this process is to call the `GetLights()` function of `IDirect3DRMFrame3` to obtain the address of the lights array. `GetLights()` has the following general form:

```
HRESULT GetLights(
                LPDIRECT3DRMLIGHTARRAY *lplpLights          // 1
                );
```

The function's only parameter is the address of a pointer that is initialized with the address of a valid `Direct3DRMLightArray` variable. The function returns `D3DRM_OK` if it succeeds, or an error otherwise.

The pointer returned by the `GetLights()` function can be used to access the two functions of `IDirect3DRMLightArray`. The `GetSize()` function returns the number of elements in the lights array and the `GetElement()` function returns a pointer to the `IDirect3DRMLight` interface for the specific light. Through this pointer, application code can access the nineteen functions of `IDirect3DRMLight`, which enable you to control the light and retrieve its characteristics. The `GetSize()` function of `IDirect3DRMLightArray` has the following general form:

```
DWORD GetSize( );
```

The function returns the number of elements in the lights array.

The `GetElement()` function retrieves a pointer to the specific light element in the lights array. The function has the following general form:

```
HRESULT GetElement(
                DWORD index,                              // 1
                LPDIRECT3DRMLIGHT  *lplpD3DRMLight  // 2
                );
```

The first parameter is the element's position in the array. The second parameter is a pointer that is filled with the address of the `IDirect3DRMLight` interface. The function returns `D3DRM_OK` if it succeeds, or an error otherwise.

The `DeleteLight()` function of `IDirect3DRMFrame3` removes a light from a frame, effectively destroying the light. The light in question must have been previously created with the `AddLight()` function. `DeleteLight()` has the following general form:

```
HRESULT DeleteLight(
                LPDIRECT3DRMLIGHT lpD3DRMLight          // 1
                );
```

The function's only parameter is the address of a variable that represents the Direct3DRMLight object to be removed. The call returns D3DRM_OK if it succeeds, or an error otherwise.

When you use the functions described previously, it is possible to control lights at run time. Individual lights can be dimmed or augmented to change the scene's appearance, or they can be changed progressively to create very convincing fade-in and fade-out effects. Processing usually involves the following steps:

1. Retrieve the lights array and make sure that its size is as expected.

2. Obtain a pointer to the desired light using its offset in the array. This pointer, of type LPDIRECT3DRMLIGHT, provides access to the corresponding interface.

3. Use the pointer obtained in Step 2 to call the desired function in IDirect3D RMLight for the selected light. For example, code can call the SetColorRGB() function to reduce or augment the light or to change its color.

In the following example we assume that two lights were created in the scene. The first light is a strong parallel light and the second one is a softer, ambient light. The code fragment listed previously in this section creates these lights. Because lights are placed in the lights array in the order in which they were created, we know that the first one in the array (the one at offset zero) is the parallel light, and the second one is the ambient light. The following code fragment shows how you can retrieve the lights array and turn off the first light.

```
// Light-related variables
LPDIRECT3DRMLIGHTARRAY      lightsArray;
DWORD                       arraySize;
LPDIRECT3DRMLIGHT           aLight;
BOOL                        parallelIsOn = TRUE;
. . .
// Retrieve lights array
   retval = lightsframe->GetLights(&lightsArray);
// Check to see that there are two lights in the lights array
   arraySize = lightsArray->GetSize();
      if(arraySize < 2)
      {
      // Lights array size error handler here
      }

  // Check to see if parallel light is ON
  if(parallelIsOn)
   {
      retval = lightsArray->GetElement(0,     // Offset in array
                                  &aLight);
      if (FAILED(retval))
        {
         // Failed GetElement() call error handler here
        }
   // Turn off first light
```

```
retval = aLight->SetColorRGB(D3DVAL(0.0),        // red
                             D3DVAL(0.0),        // green
                             D3DVAL(0.0));       // blue
if (FAILED(retval))
{
    // Failed SetColorRGB() call error handler here
}
```

The sample program 3DRM Frame Ops Demo contained in the book's CD-ROM includes a menu command to turn on or off either one of the two lights used in the scene. Figure 20-2 shows the results.

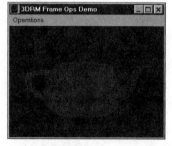

Figure 20-2: Manipulating scene lights in the 3DRM Frame Ops Demo program

Operating on materials

The material property of a retained mode object determines how its surface emits and reflects light. Material properties are normally applied to meshes and to faces, not as commonly to frames. Materials were mentioned in Chapter 14 and materials programming is discussed in Chapter 22.

In the context of frame-level programming there are six functions that relate to materials. Two of them, named `GetMaterialMode()` and `SetMaterialMode()`, are used to set and retrieve the source of material information for the object. These sources can be the mesh, the frame, or the object's parent frame. Two other functions, named `SetMaterial()` and `GetMaterial()`, set and retrieve the material for a frame object. These two functions were first implemented in `IDirect3DRMFrame2`, released with DirectX version 5. Finally, there are two functions introduced in DirectX version 6 named `SetMaterialOverride()` and `GetMaterialOverride()`, which enable applications to override the emissive properties of a material for the entire frame hierarchy.

Material modes

The material mode determines the source of material information for the visuals rendered with a frame. The `SetMaterialMode()` function has the following general form:

```
HRESULT SetMaterialMode(
                        D3DRMMATERIALMODE rmmMode           // 1
                        );
```

The function's only parameter is one of the members of the `D3DRMMATERIALMODE` enumerated type. The enumeration is defined as follows:

```
typedef enum _D3DRMMATERIALMODE{
    D3DRMMATERIAL_FROMMESH,
    D3DRMMATERIAL_FROMPARENT,
    D3DRMMATERIAL_FROMFRAME
} D3DRMMATERIALMODE;
```

Table 20-1 lists the retained mode material modes.

Table 20-1	
Material Mode Constants in D3DRMMATERIALMODE	
Constant	*Description*
D3DRMMATERIAL_FROMMESH	Material information is retrieved from the mesh. This is the default setting.
D3DRMMATERIAL_FROMPARENT	Material information is inherited from the parent frame.
D3DRMMATERIAL_FROMFRAME	Material information is retrieved from the frame, overriding any previous material information that the object may have possessed.

The `SetMaterialMode()` function returns `D3DRM_OK` if it succeeds, or an error otherwise.

The `GetMaterialMode()` function retrieves the material mode for a frame. The function has the following general form:

```
D3DRMMATERIALMODE GetMaterialMode();
```

The function returns one of the members of the `D3DRMMATERIALMODE` enumerated type listed in Table 20-1. The default mode is `D3DRMMATERIAL_FROMMESH`.

Frame-level materials control

Code interacts with materials by means of the `IDirect3DRMMaterial2` interface, discussed in Chapter 22. This interface contains functions to set and retrieve the ambient, emissive, and specular properties of materials and to set and retrieve the specular exponent. Two functions at the frame level allow access to this interface. The `SetMaterial()` function sets the material of a `Direct3DRMFrame3` object. The function has the following general form:

```
HRESULT SetMaterial(
                LPDIRECT3DRMMATERIAL2 *lplpMaterial     // 1
                );
```

The function's only parameter is the address of the `Direct3DRMMaterial` object that is applied to the frame. The function returns `D3DRM_OK` if it succeeds, or an error otherwise.

The `GetMaterial()` function of `IDirect3DRMFrame3` retrieves the material of a frame object. The function has the following general form:

```
HRESULT GetMaterial(
                LPDIRECT3DRMMATERIAL2 *lplpMaterial     // 1
                );
```

The function's only parameter is the address of a variable that is filled with a pointer to the `Direct3DRMMaterial` object that is applied to the frame. By default, the material is NULL. The function returns `D3DRM_OK` if it succeeds, or an error otherwise.

Material override functions

Two functions introduced in DirectX version 6, named `SetMaterialOverride()` and `GetMaterialOverride()`, enable you to override the emissive properties of a material for the entire frame hierarchy. The functions have the following general forms:

```
HRESULT GetMaterialOverride)
                LPD3DRMMATERIALOVERRIDE lpdmOverride    // 1
```

```
                            );

HRESULT SetMaterialOverride(
                    LPD3DRMMATERIALOVERRIDE lpdmOverride    // 1
                    );
```

In both functions the only parameter is a pointer to a D3DRMMATERIALOVERRIDE structure that describes the properties to be overridden. The structure is defined as follows:

```
typedef struct _D3DRMMATERIALOVERRIDE
{
    DWORD          dwSize;       // size in bytes
    DWORD          dwFlags;      // Flags
    D3DCOLORVALUE  dcDiffuse;    // Diffuse property setting
    D3DCOLORVALUE  dcAmbient;    // Ambient property setting
    D3DCOLORVALUE  dcEmissive;   // Emissive property setting
    D3DCOLORVALUE  dcSpecular;   // Specular property setting
    D3DVALUE       dvPower;      // Power setting
    LPUNKNOWN      lpD3DRMTex;
} D3DRMMATERIALOVERRIDE, *LPD3DRMMATERIALOVERRIDE;
```

The dwFlags structure member can be one or more flags indicating which fields in this structure are valid. The following values are possible:

```
D3DRMMATERIALOVERRIDE_DIFFUSE_ALPHAONLY
D3DRMMATERIALOVERRIDE_DIFFUSE_RGBONLY
D3DRMMATERIALOVERRIDE_DIFFUSE
D3DRMMATERIALOVERRIDE_AMBIENT
D3DRMMATERIALOVERRIDE_EMISSIVE
D3DRMMATERIALOVERRIDE_SPECULAR
D3DRMMATERIALOVERRIDE_POWER
D3DRMMATERIALOVERRIDE_TEXTURE
D3DRMMATERIALOVERRIDE_ALL
```

The dcDiffuse structure member defines the RGBA color setting for the diffuse property of the material. The value is of type D3DCOLORVALUE.

The dcAmbient structure member defines the RGB color for the ambient property of the material. The value is of type D3DCOLORVALUE.

The dcEmissive structure member defines the RGB color for the emissive color setting of the material. The value is of type D3DCOLORVALUE.

The dcSpecular structure member defines the RGB color of the specular property of the material. The value is of type D3DCOLORVALUE.

The dvPower structure member defines the power setting. The value is of type D3DVALUE.

The `lpD3DRMTex` structure member is a pointer to the texture interface.

The function returns `DD_OK` if it succeeds, or one of the following error codes:

```
DDERR_INVALIDOBJECT
DDERR_INVALIDPARAMS
```

Material property overrides always affect all elements lower in the hierarchy. When code overrides the emissive property in one frame, any attempts to override the same property farther down the hierarchy are ignored. This override also takes precedence over standard frame overrides, as well as material properties on specific meshes. Overrides that result from calls to `SetMaterial()` and `SetTexture()` functions have no effect on the action of the `SetMaterialOverride()` function.

Operating on textures

A texture, in retained mode programming, is a 2D bitmap image that is applied to the surface of an object to modify its visual qualities. Textures were mentioned in Chapter 14 and texture programming is discussed in Chapter 22.

In this section we are concerned with texture-related functions that are available at the frame level. It is interesting to note that, up to the `IDirectXFrame2` interface, there were two methods that related to texture topologies. They are named `GetTextureTopology()` and `SetTextureTopology()`. However, in the Microsoft documentation for `IDirect3DRMFrame3` (DirectX version 7) these methods are no longer described, with no explanation given for their disappearance. In any case, we do not discuss them in this section because these functions have limited usefulness at the frame level. Other texture topology functions at the mesh and face level are discussed later in this book.

Texture can be accessed at the frame level when the material mode is set to `D3DRMMATERIAL_FROMFRAME`. Setting material modes was discussed earlier in this chapter, and the material mode constants are listed in Table 20-1. The two texture-related functions described in `IDirect3DRMFrame3` are named `SetTexture()` and `GetTexture()`. The `GetTexture()` function has the following general form:

```
HRESULT GetTexture(
            LPDIRECT3DRMTEXTURE3 *lplpTexture        // 1
            );
```

The function's only parameter is a pointer variable that is filled with the address of the `Direct3DRMTexture` object representing the frame's texture. By default, the texture is NULL. The function returns `D3DRM_OK` if it succeeds, or an error otherwise.

After code obtains the pointer to IDirect3DRMTexture3 interface, it can use it to modify the frame's texture. The SetTexture() function has the following general form:

```
HRESULT SetTexture(
                    LPDIRECT3DRMTEXTURE3 lpD3DRMTexture    // 1
                   );
```

The function's only parameter is the address of a pointer that represents the Direct3DRMTexture object to be used. This object opens access to the IDirect3DRMTexture3 interface, which contains 20 texture manipulation functions. The function returns D3DRM_OK if it succeeds, or an error otherwise.

Scene-Level Attributes

In Chapter 14 we saw that a scene can be conceptually described as a hierarchy of individual frames that are organized in a tree-like structure. In actual programming the scene is defined by a root frame, also called the master frame, that anchors and serves as a reference for all the other visual objects. Two frame attributes are controlled at the scene-level: background and fog.

Scene background controls

Currently two background attributes are accessible at the frame level: color and depth. Up until DirectX 5 a function was available to use a texture to set the scene's background image. Current DirectX documentation states that the SetScene BackgroundImage() function is obsolete and should not be used. Now, it is recommended that applications that require a background image use a bit blit to display it on the screen.

Background color controls

Three functions in IDirect3DRMFrame3 relate to background color control. One function, named GetSceneBackground(), is used to obtain the current background color. The other functions, SetSceneBackground() and SetSceneBackgroundRGB(), are used to set a new background color. The GetSceneBackground() function has the following general form:

```
D3DCOLOR GetSceneBackground();
```

The function returns the scene's background color in a variable of type D3DCOLOR.

The SetSceneBackground() function is used to change the scene's background color. It has the following general form:

```
HRESULT SetSceneBackground(
                    D3DCOLOR rcColor          // 1
                    );
```

The function's only parameter is a variable of type D3DCOLOR that defines the new background color for the scene. The function returns D3DRM_OK if it succeeds, or an error otherwise.

Alternatively, the SetSceneBackgroundRGB() provides a way of setting the scene's background color by specifying each of the RGB components. The function has the following general form:

```
HRESULT SetSceneBackgroundRGB(
                    D3DVALUE rvRed,           // 1
                    D3DVALUE rvGreen,         // 2
                    D3DVALUE rvBlue           // 3
                    );
```

The function's three parameters are the red, green, and blue components for the new background color. Each color component must be in the range 0.0 to 1.0. The function returns D3DRM_OK if it succeeds, or an error otherwise.

The following code fragment shows setting the scene background color to red.

```
// Global variables
struct _globVars
{
. . .
    LPDIRECT3DRMFRAME3 aScene;        // Master frame
. . .
} globVars;
. . .
retval = globVars.aScene->SetSceneBackgroundRGB(
                                D3DVAL(0.8),      // red
                                D3DVAL(0.0),      // green
                                D3DVAL(0.0));     // blue
```

Background depth

Although immediate mode contains several functions for manipulating the background depth at the viewport level, the ones in retained mode appear in the IDirect3DRMFrame3 interface. The background depth is defined as a buffer that is used to initialize the z-buffer before rendering a scene. Two functions are provided at the scene level that relate to the background depth: GetSceneBackgroundDepth() and SetSceneBackgroundDepth(). We do not discuss these functions because direct z-buffer control is rarely used in retained mode programming.

Fog controls

Fog is a depth cueing technique that you can use to render a scene in order to enhance its realism, to provide a supernatural or mysterious mood, or to soften it. Fog control in retained mode is powerful, detailed, and effective. Fog effects are produced by blending the color of the objects in a scene with a chosen fog color. The blending is based on the depth of the object and on its distance from the viewpoint. More distant objects blend more into the chosen fog color, creating the illusion that the object is being increasingly obscured by tiny fog particles floating in the scene.

In retained mode, fog control relates to the following elements:

1. The fog enable state. Scene fog can be enabled or disabled.

2. The fog color.

3. The fogging method. Vertex- and table-based fog are available options. Another option is to base fogging effects in whatever capabilities are present in the device.

4. The fog mode. Retained mode documents three fogging formulas based on linear, exponential, and exponentially squared interpolations. Currently the linear mode is the only one supported.

5. The fog parameters refer to the distance to the point where the fog starts, where it ends, and its relative density in the exponential mode, for whenever it is implemented.

Functions in IDirect3DRMFrame3 enable you to set and retrieve all five fog control elements listed previously.

Fog enable state controls

Two functions in IDirect3DRMFrame3 enable you to set and retrieve the fog enabled state. The default state is that fog is disabled. The SetSceneFogEnable() function has the following general form:

```
HRESULT SetSceneFogEnable(
                    BOOL bEnable           // 1
                 );
```

The function's only parameter is a flag that sets the fog enable state. If TRUE, fog effects are produced. The function returns D3DRM_OK if it succeeds, or an error otherwise.

The GetSceneFogEnable() function retrieves that fog enable state. The function has the following general form:

```
BOOL GetSceneFogEnable();
```

The function returns TRUE if fog is enabled, and FALSE otherwise. The default state is FALSE.

Fog color controls

The fog color defines the color attribute used in producing the depth cueing. Sometimes the fog color is chosen to match the predominant color of the scene background. For other effects, white or shades of gray can be selected for the fog color. Two functions in IDirect3DRMFrame3 refer to the fog color, one to set it and another one to retrieve it. SetSceneFogColor() has the following general form:

```
HRESULT SetSceneFogColor(
                  D3DCOLOR rcColor                // 1
                  );
```

The function's only parameter is the new color for the fog contained in a variable of type D3DCOLOR. Applications can use the D3DRMCreateColorRGB() nonmember function of Direct3DRM to set an RGB triplet for the color value easily. The coding is shown later in this section. The call returns D3DRM_OK if it succeeds, or an error otherwise.

The GetSceneFogColor() function of IDirect3DRMFrame3 is used to retrieve the current fog color. The function has the following general form:

```
D3DCOLOR GetSceneFogColor();
```

The function returns the fog color, which is white by default. Code can use one of the following nonmember functions to get each of the RGB components of the fog color:

```
D3DRMColorGetBlue()
D3DRMColorGetGreen()
D3DRMColorGetRed()
```

Selecting the fogging method

Two methods, which were introduced in DirectX 6 for implementing fogging, are available in retained mode: vertex and table fog. Table fog is sometimes called pixel fog because it is calculated on a per-pixel base in the device driver. In vertex fog, Direct3D computes fog effects when it performs transformation and lighting, and interpolates the result to each vertex of the polygon during rendering. Some drivers implement table fog by means of a precalculated look-up table that is used to determine the fog factor for each pixel.

Two methods in IDirect3DRMFrame3 relate to the fogging method: GetSceneFog Method() and SetSceneFogMethod(). The SetSceneFogMethod() function has the following general form:

```
HRESULT SetSceneFogMethod(
                  DWORD dwFlags                // 1
                  );
```

The function's only parameter is one of the three flags described in Table 20-2.

Table 20-2 Fogging Method Flags in IDirect3DRMFrame3	
Flag	**Description**
D3DRMFOGMETHOD_ANY	Direct3D retained mode should choose one of the applicable methods
D3DRMFOGMETHOD_VERTEX	Use vertex fog
D3DRMFOGMETHOD_TABLE	Use table (pixel) fog

The default behavior is D3DRMFOGMETHOD_ANY. Fogging methods are chosen according to the capabilities of the device. If the device supports both vertex- and table-based fog, then vertex fogging will be used. If code requests table fog but it is not available in the hardware, then vertex fog is used. The function returns DD_OK if it succeeds, or one of the following errors:

D3DRMERR_BADVALUE

DDERR_INVALIDOBJECT

DDERR_INVALIDPARAMS

The GetSceneFogMethod() function retrieves the current fogging method. The function has the following general form:

```
HRESULT GetSceneFogMethod(
                LPDWORD lpdwFlags                // 1
                );
```

The function's only parameter and return values are the same as for the SetSceneFogMethod() function previously described.

Selecting the fogging mode

There are three fogging modes described in the retained mode documentation. They are named linear, exponential, and exponential-square. The SetSceneFogMode() and GetSceneFogMode() functions allow setting and retrieving the fogging mode. The SetSceneFogMode() function has the following general form:

```
HRESULT SetSceneFogMode(
                D3DRMFOGMODE rfMode               // 1
                );
```

The function's only parameter is one of the members of the D3DRMFOGMODE enumerated type. The enumeration is defined as follows:

```
typedef enum _D3DRMFOGMODE{
    D3DRMFOG_LINEAR,
    D3DRMFOG_EXPONENTIAL,
    D3DRMFOG_EXPONENTIALSQUARED
} D3DRMFOGMODE;
```

The linear fogging mode determines in what way the fog effect is calculated as the distance from the camera increases. Because the linear mode is the only one currently supported, code must always select the D3DRMFOG_LINEAR flag. The function returns D3DRM_OK if it succeeds, or an error otherwise.

The GetSceneFogMode() function returns the current scene mode, which currently must be D3DRMFOG_LINEAR for the reason explained in the previous paragraph.

Determining fog parameters

Fog parameters refer to the distance to the point where the fog starts and where it ends. There is a third parameter that determines the relative density in the exponential mode. Because this mode is not currently available, the value of this parameter is meaningless. Two functions are available in IDirect3DRMFrame3 that relate to fog parameters: one to set and one to retrieve the corresponding values. The SetSceneFogParams() function has the following general form:

```
HRESULT SetSceneFogParams(
                    D3DVALUE rvStart,        // 1
                    D3DVALUE rvEnd,          // 2
                    D3DVALUE rvDensity       // 3
                    );
```

The first parameter refers to the distance from the camera at which the fog effect first becomes visible. The second parameter sets the distance from the camera at which the fog reaches its maximum density. The third parameter sets the fog density in the exponential modes, and currently is ignored.

The GetSceneFogParams() function returns the current fog parameters for the scene. The function has the same parameters and returns type as the SetSceneFogParams() function.

Manipulating Frame Hierarchies

The frames in a scene are arranged in a tree-like structure. This structure is called the frame hierarchy. Frames can have parent and child frames. A frame with no parent is called the root frame and is referred to as the scene. Child frames have positions and orientations relative to their parent frames. This association between parent and child frames determines that if the parent frame moves, the child frames must also move.

Code can set the position and orientation of a frame relative to any other frame in the scene. Frame positions and orientations relative to the root frame are referred to as absolute. Frames can be detached from a parent and added as a child to another frame by means of the AddChild() function of IDirect3DRMFrame3. A frame can be deleted as a child frame by means of the DeleteChild() function. Other functions allow obtaining the parent of a frame, the children frames, and the root frame or scene.

In the context of frame hierarchies the term instance refers to the reuse of a frame hierarchy throughout the scene. When the parent frame is added as a visual to another frame all the child frames in the hierarchy are also added. This new hierarchy is an instance of the old one. However, retained mode documentation does not recommend instancing a parent frame into its children, thus creating a cyclic hierarchy. Cyclic hierarchies degrade performance and should be avoided.

Adding a child frame

Code can add a child to a parent frame by means of the AddChild() function of IDirect3DRMFrame3. If the frame being added as a child is attached to another parent, the existing connection is broken automatically before the frame is attached to the new parent. The new frame is added at the end of the frame array. The function has the following general form:

```
HRESULT AddChild(
              LPDIRECT3DRMFRAME3 lpD3DRMFrameChild    // 1
              );
```

The only parameter is the address of the Direct3DRMFrame object that is to be added as a child. The function returns D3DRM_OK if it succeeds, or an error otherwise.

At the time that the child frame is added to the parent frame its local transformation matrix is destroyed automatically. To preserve the child's local transform, code must call the GetTransform() function of IDirect3DRMFrame3 and store it in a variable. Then the transformation can be reapplied to the child frame by means of the AddTransform() function, after the AddChild() method has executed.

Deleting a child frame

A child frame can be removed from a frame hierarchy along with any of its children or attached lights and meshes. The DeleteChild() function has the following general form:

```
HRESULT DeleteChild(
                LPDIRECT3DRMFRAME3 lpChild          // 1
                );
```

The function's only parameter is the address of the frame object to be used as the child. The function returns D3DRM_OK if it succeeds, or an error otherwise.

As the function name implies, the child frame is deleted, not simply detached, from the parent. This means that the deleted frame will no longer be rendered. To break the frame's association with its parent, while preserving the child frame as a visual, code must call DeleteChild() followed by a call to reattach the frame to another frame or to the scene itself.

Retrieving frame hierarchies

Several functions in IDirect3DRMFrame3 are used for retrieving frame associations. The GetChildren() function is used to retrieve a frame array containing all the child frames in the hierarchy. The function has the following general form:

```
HRESULT GetChildren(
                LPDIRECT3DRMFRAMEARRAY *lplpChildren   // 1
                );
```

The function's only parameter is the address of a pointer that is initialized with the address of a valid Direct3DRMLightArray variable. The function returns D3DRM_OK if it succeeds, or an error otherwise.

The pointer returned by the GetChildren() function can be used to access the two functions of IDirect3DRMFrameArray. The GetSize() function returns the number of elements in the frame array, and the GetElement() function returns a pointer to the IDirect3DRMFrame interface for the specific light. Through this pointer application code can access all the functions of IDirect3DRMFrame3. The GetSize() function of IDirect3DRMFrameArray has the following general form:

```
DWORD GetSize( );
```

The function returns the number of elements in the frame array.

The GetElement() function retrieves a pointer to the specific element in the frame array. The function has the following general form:

```
HRESULT GetElement(
                DWORD index,                            // 1
                LPDIRECT3DRMFRAME3  *lplpD3DRMFrame  // 2
                );
```

The first parameter is the element's position in the array. The second parameter is a pointer that is filled with the address of the IDirect3DRMFrame3 interface. The function returns D3DRM_OK if it succeeds, or an error otherwise.

The GetParent() function of IDirect3DRMFrame3 returns the parent of the frame making the call. The function has the following general form:

```
HRESULT GetParent(
                LPDIRECT3DRMRAME3 *lplpParent            // 1
                );
```

The function's only parameter is the address of a pointer that is filled with the pointer to the Direct3DRMFrame object representing the frame's parent. The pointer is NULL if the current frame is the root. The call returns D3DRM_OK if it succeeds, or an error otherwise.

The GetScene() function returns the root frame of the hierarchy. The function has the following general form:

```
HRESULT GetScene(
                LPDIRECT3DRMFRAME3 lplpRoot              // 1
                );
```

The function's only parameter is the address of the pointer that will be filled with the pointer to the Direct3DRMFrame object representing the scene's root frame. The call returns D3DRM_OK if it succeeds, or an error otherwise.

3DRM Frame Hierarchy Demo program

The 3DRM Frame Hierarchy Demo program demonstrates some of the frame hierarchy functions described in the preceding sections. The program loads two meshes, one of them in the shape of a torus and the other one a sphere. The torus is green and the sphere is red. Figure 20-3 shows two screen snapshots of the 3DRM Frame Hierarchy Demo program.

In the initial state, the torus and the sphere frames are attached to the scene. In this case the rotation of the torus does not affect the sphere. By means of the dialog box the user can attach the sphere frame to the torus frame. In this case the sphere rotates with the torus.

initial program state
(sphere is child of scene frame)

sphere is child of torus frame

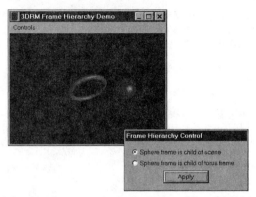
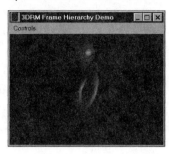

Figure 20-3: Manipulating frame hierarchies in the 3DRM Frame Hierarchy Demo program

The code for making and breaking the frame attachments is as follows:

```
// Global variables
LPDIRECT3DRMFRAME3 torusFrame             = NULL;
LPDIRECT3DRMFRAME3 sphereFrame            = NULL;
D3DRMMATRIX4D       sphereMatrix;
. . .
// Add sphere frame to torusFrame hierarchy
   retval = torusFrame->AddChild(sphereFrame);
     if(FAILED(retval))
        // Frame attachment error handler goes here
. . .
// Add sphere frame to scene
// First obtain and save the local transform
retval = sphereFrame->GetTransform(NULL, sphereMatrix);
    if(FAILED(retval))
       // Transform error handler goes here
// Remove sphereFrame from torusFrame hierarchy
retval = torusFrame->DeleteChild(sphereFrame);
    if(FAILED(retval))
       // Sphere frame removal error handler goes here
// Restore transform to sphere frame
retval = sphereFrame->AddTransform(D3DRMCOMBINE_REPLACE,
                                   sphereMatrix);
    if(FAILED(retval))
       // Transform operation error handler goes here
// Add sphere frame to scene frame
retval = globVars.aScene->AddChild(sphereFrame);
    if(FAILED(retval))
       // Sphere frame attachment error handler goes here
```

Sorting Modes and Z-buffer Control

Several functions of the IDirect3DRMFrame3 interface relate to the algorithms used by the rasterizer module. Although these controls are more applicable to immediate mode programming than to retained mode, we briefly mention them here.

Sort mode controls

Sorting modes determine the operation of hidden-surface removal algorithms by establishing the order in which child frames are processed. In immediate mode the sorting modes are defined in the D3DRMSORTMODE structure, as follows:

```
typedef enum _D3DRMSORTMODE {
    D3DRMSORT_FROMPARENT,
    D3DRMSORT_NONE,
    D3DRMSORT_FRONTTOBACK,
    D3DRMSORT_BACKTOFRONT
} D3DRMSORTMODE;
```

Table 20-3 describes the sorting mode constants in the enumeration.

Table 20-3 D3DRMSORTMODE Constants	
Constant	**Description**
D3DRMSORT_FROMPARENT	Child frames inherit the sorting order of their parents. This is the default setting.
D3DRMSORT_NONE	Child frames are not sorted.
D3DRMSORT_FRONTTOBACK	Child frames are sorted front-to-back.
D3DRMSORT_BACKTOFRONT	Child frames are sorted back-to-front.

The GetSortMode() function of IDirect3DRMFrame3 retrieves the current sorting mode used to process child frames. The function's general form is as follows:

```
D3DRMSORTMODE GetSortMode();
```

The function returns one of the constants defined in the D3DRMSORTMODE enumerated type. The default value is D3DRMSORT_FROMPARENT.

Sort modes are set with the SetSortMode() function. Its general form is as follows:

```
HRESULT SetSortMode(
                D3DRMSORTMODE d3drmSM              // 1
            );
```

The function's only parameter is one of the members of the D3DRMSORTMODE enumeration previously described. The function returns D3DRM_OK if it succeeds, or an error otherwise.

Z-buffer controls

The use of z-buffers is ubiquitous in modern-day video hardware, and they are the most common way of implementing depth buffer algorithms. However, z-buffer processing sometimes results in surface artifacts in distance objects, especially in applications that manage exterior scenes. Retained mode provides two functions that relate to z-buffer modes, one to set it and another one to retrieve it. Z-buffer states are defined in the D3DRMZBUFFERMODE enumeration, as follows:

```
typedef enum _D3DRMZBUFFERMODE {
    D3DRMZBUFFER_FROMPARENT,
    D3DRMZBUFFER_ENABLE,
    D3DRMZBUFFER_DISABLE
} D3DRMZBUFFERMODE;
```

Table 20-4 describes the constants in D3DRMZBUFFERMODE.

Table 20-4 Constants in **D3DRMZBUFFERMODE**	
Constant	**Description**
D3DRMZBUFFER_FROMPARENT	The frame inherits the z-buffer setting from its parent frame. This is the default mode.
D3DRMZBUFFER_ENABLE	Z-buffering is enabled.
D3DRMZBUFFER_DISABLE	Z-buffering is disabled.

The SetZbufferMode() function is used to set one of the z-buffer modes. The function's general form is as follows:

```
HRESULT SetZbufferMode(
                       D3DRMZBUFFERMODE d3drmZBM          // 1
                      );
```

The function's only parameter is one of the members of the D3DRMZBUFFERMODE enumerated type. The default value is D3DRMZBUFFER_FROMPARENT. The call returns D3DRM_OK if it succeeds, or an error otherwise.

The `GetZbufferMode()` function retrieves the z-buffer mode. The function has the following general form:

```
D3DRMZBUFFERMODE GetZbufferMode( );
```

The return value is one of the members of the `D3DRMZBUFFERMODE` enumerated type. The default value is `D3DRMZBUFFER_FROMPARENT`.

Operating on Visuals

The notion of a visual, or visual object, is one of the most difficult to grasp in retained mode architecture. The first difficulty is that visual objects are not components; instead, they are instances in the `IDirect3DRMVisual` interface. This interface has no methods per se, but from it the following retained mode interfaces are derived:

```
IDirect3DRMFrame3
IDirect3DRMMesh
IDirect3DRMMeshBuilder3
IDirect3DRMProgressiveMesh
IDirect3DRMShadow2
IDirect3DRMTexture3
IDirect3DRMUserVisual
```

Visuals are objects that can be rendered in a scene, but they only become visible when added to a frame in the scene by means of the `AddVisual()` function of `IDirect3DRMFrame3`. It is the frame that provides a position and orientation for rendering the visual object. In other words, it references the visual object. Visual objects include meshes, progressive meshes, meshbuilders, textures, shadows, and user visuals.

Adding and deleting visuals

A visual object is added to a frame by means of the `AddVisual()` function of `IDirect3DRMFrame3`. The function has the following general form:

```
HRESULT AddVisual(
                 LPUNKNOWN lpD3DRMVisual              // 1
                 );
```

The function's only parameter is a pointer to a variable that represents the visual object to be added to the frame. The function returns `D3DRM_OK` if it succeeds, or an error otherwise.

A visual object is deleted from a frame by means of the DeleteVisual() function. If the object has no other reference in the code it is effectively destroyed because the DeleteVisual() call cannot be reversed. The function has the following general form:

```
HRESULT DeleteVisual(
                LPUNKNOWN lpD3DRMVisual            // 1
                );
```

The function's only parameter is a pointer to a variable that represents the visual object to be deleted from the frame. The function returns D3DRM_OK if it succeeds, or an error otherwise.

Retrieving visuals

The GetVisual() function is used for retrieving visuals in IDirect3DRMFrame3. The function has the following general form:

```
HRESULT GetVisuals(
                LPDWORD pdwNumVisuals,            // 1
                LPUNKNOWN *ppUnk                  // 2
                );
```

The function's first parameter is a pointer to a DWORD type variable of which its contents depend on the second parameter. If the second parameter is NULL, then the first parameter returns the number of visuals contained by the frame. If the second parameter is not NULL, then the first parameter returns the number of visuals actually retrieved by the call.

The second parameter is a pointer to a Direct3DRMVisualArray object containing the array of visuals that is initialized by the call. Setting this second parameter to NULL causes GetVisuals() to return the number of visuals contained by the frame. If this second parameter is not NULL, then it represents a user-allocated array with sufficient space for the number of visuals in the first parameter.

This mode of operation determines that code often needs to make more than one call to the GetVisuals() function. For example, the first call to GetVisuals() can be made passing NULL as the second parameter in order to determine the number of visuals contained in the frame. When this value is known, code can allocate an array of visuals large enough to contain all the visuals in the frame and make a second call to GetVisuals() in order to retrieve the individual visual objects in the frame. In this second call to GetVisuals() we pass a pointer to an array of visuals in the second parameter and the total number of visuals in the first one. In this case the call returns an array of pointers to the IDirect3DRMVisualArray interface, one for each visual object in the frame.

IDirect3DRMVisualArray contains two functions: one named GetElement() and another one named GetSize(). The GetSize() function returns the number of elements in the visual array and the GetElement() function returns a pointer to the IDirect3DRMVisual interface for a specific visual element. IDirect3DRM Visual does not provide any retained mode functions but serves to derive other interfaces. The GetSize() function of IDirect3DRMVisualArray has the following general form:

```
DWORD GetSize();
```

The function returns the number of elements in the visual array.

The GetElement() function retrieves a pointer to the specific element in the visual array. The function has the following general form:

```
HRESULT GetElement(
                DWORD index,                        // 1
                LPDIRECT3DRMVISUAL  *lplpD3DRMVisual // 2
                );
```

The first parameter is the element's position in the array. The second parameter is a pointer that is filled with the address of the IDirect3DRMVisual interface. The function returns D3DRM_OK if it succeeds, or an error otherwise.

Summary

In this chapter we covered a smorgasbord of functions that are available at the frame level. We learned how to set and retrieve components and attributes of frame objects, manipulate backgrounds and fog, handle frame hierarchies, select sorting modes, enable and disable z-buffer rendering, and deal with visuals. The sample programs for this chapter contain code that show the implementation of the most used of these functions.

In the following chapters we continue our excursion into progressively lower levels of retained mode programming. The topic of Chapter 21 is meshes and meshbuilders. It is through mesh programming that we create the basic 3D objects for our programs.

✦　　✦　　✦

Mesh-Level Operations

Up to this point we discussed the higher-level interfaces of DirectX retained mode. In the preceding chapters of Part III we examined almost every function of these interfaces because most of them have been of interest to the graphics application programmer. For this reason the interfaces have been presented function-by-function. But as we descend into the lower-levels of retained mode programming, this ceases to be true because we begin to encounter functions that are less interesting to the application programmer.

This fact is particularly true in mesh-level programming, which is based on `IDirect3DRMMeshBuilder3` and `IDirect3DRMMesh` interfaces. Typically, the graphics application developer relies on imagery or on image data created with a 3D modeling program. However, many of the methods in the mesh-related interfaces are directed towards low-level mesh component manipulations and controls.

Consequently, we discuss the topic of mesh programming topically, bypassing the functions that are likely to be of limited interest in the context of typical retained mode programming. Although the chapter includes some discussion on the hard-coding of meshes by defining their elementary components, we do bypass most of the functions that relate to mesh components programming. In fact, it is difficult to imagine why these low- level functions are present in retained mode. Retained mode is intended as a high-level interface to Direct3D, while the control of the individual components of graphics objects, such as vertices, faces, and normals, is in the domain of immediate mode programming. Very few retained mode applications require these low-level controls.

Meshes in Retained Mode

The visual elements of our Direct3D retained mode programs are based on meshes. The mesh is the way Direct3D represents visual objects. A mesh consists of a group of polygonal faces, each one defined in terms of its vertices and normals. The mesh is a low-level construct, and each of its components, faces, vertices, and normals can be manipulated individually.

Building meshes by hard-coding their individual components is a time-consuming and laborious task. Most often the 3D applications use 3D modeling tools to create the meshes needed by their applications. However, Direct3D retained mode provides no way of manipulating proprietary graphics file formats directly. This means that before an application can load a mesh file into program code, it must convert it into Microsoft's DirectX (.x) format, described in Chapter 14.

Unfortunately, 3D file conversion utilities are presently in short supply. Microsoft's DirectX includes a DOS-mode application, named Conv3ds, that converts from the .3ds proprietary format, used by the 3D Studio program, into the DirectX format. Because DirectX cannot manipulate any format different than X, and because few other reliable conversion utilities are available, the application developer usually must create meshes using an application that saves into DirectX format directly, or into a file in .3ds format that can later be converted into X format by means of the Conv3ds program. The entire process often involves the following steps:

1. Create 3D objects using a modeling program that can save the objects into DirectX or .3ds formats.

2. If the mesh file is in .3ds format, convert it into X format by means of the Conv3ds program supplied with DirectX. The Conv3ds switches and options determine how the mesh or meshes must be loaded into the application.

3. Load the meshes, stored in one or more X files, into application code.

4. Manipulate the meshes and cast them into frames, where they can be changed further by code and visually rendered in the scene.

We discuss 3D image file manipulations at length later in this chapter.

Modeling the program imagery

This book is about programming; consequently the image creation phase is mentioned but incidentally. However, this does not mean that creating the program imagery is a trivial task. On the contrary, the quality of a 3D application depends on its design and the quality of its imagery. No amount of programming can fix a badly thought-out and poorly imaged application.

Designing and producing the digital imagery are art forms in themselves. When a programmer encroaches into the art of image creation the results usually leave much to be desired. It takes special talents and considerable skills to design and create the 3D imagery: it is much better to leave this part to the art professionals. However, often the programmer needs to create images to experiment with new techniques or implement algorithms in code. In this case it is useful to have at least minimal skills in using a 3D modeling program.

Many 3D modeling programs are available on the market, ranging in price from free to $50,000 or more. The CD-ROM furnished with this book contains examination copies of several 3D modeling applications. However, they are of little use to the programmer because file saving is disabled in most of these demos.

Hard-coding faces and meshes

In addition to using a 3D modeling program to generate imagery, Direct3D retained mode also supports building 3D objects, such as faces and meshes, directly in code. This means hard-coding the data that represents the faces, vertices, and normals to the mesh, and using the primitive function of IDirect3DRMMeshBuilder3 and IDirect3DRMMesh interfaces to construct the objects.

The usefulness of these hard-coding methods, in the context of this book, is limited to solving special processing and rendering problems and to the simplest of objects. For example, it is conceivable that an application developer could hard-code a flat, rectangular face to serve as a base or a background. Or, a developer can even create in code a simple, flat-faced, 3D object such as a cube or a pyramid. On the other hand, it is difficult to imagine a programmer spending time in hard-coding objects and imagery that is much more easily produced by using a 3D modeling tool.

There is one case in which manipulating hard-coded imagery may be a practical option. This is when you use a 3D modeling program to create one or more objects, export these objects into a text file, and then retrieve the object data from the text file so that it can be hard-coded into the application. In other words, you let the 3D modeler do the hard work of determining faces, vertices, and normals, and then move the data from the image file into your own code for faster rendering or for direct data manipulations.

Because there are cases, although not many, in which the programmer could conceivably find some use of hard-coding 3D imagery, in the following sections we briefly touch on this topic.

Creating Faces and Meshes

Several functions of IDirect3DRMMesh3 relate to the creation of faces and meshes directly in code. The functions can be classified into four groups:

1. Mesh and submesh operations

2. Face operations

3. Operations on normals

4. Vertex operations

Table 21-1 lists the functions of IDirect3DRMMeshBuilder3 that relate to the manipulation of meshes and mesh components.

Table 21-1
IDirect3DRMMeshBuilder3 Functions to Manipulate Meshes and Mesh Components

Group	Function
Meshes and Submeshes	AddMesh() CreateMesh() CreateSubMesh() DeleteSubMesh() GetParentMesh() GetSubMeshes()
Faces	AddFace() AddFaces() AddFacesIndexed() CreateFace() DeleteFace() GetFaceCount() GetFace() GetFaces()
Normals	AddNormal() DeleteNormals() GenerateNormals() GetNormal() GetNormals() GetNormalCount() SetNormal() SetNormals()

Group	Function
Vertices	AddVertex()
	DeleteVertices()
	GetGeometry()
	GetVertex()
	GetVertexColor()
	GetVertexCount()
	GetVertices()
	SetVertex()
	SetVertices()
	SetVertexColor()
	SetVertexColorRGB()

The retained mode programmer, typically working at developing applications, finds use but for a few of these functions.

Face and vertex normals

The rendering operation requires that each face contain a vector, perpendicular to its surface, which points outward from the face. This vector is called the face normal vector. In Direct3D, code does not have to specify face normals because they are calculated automatically as needed. Flat shading is implemented by means of these face normal vectors, which is to say, with no more information than the vertices that define the objects.

Gouraud shading (and Phong shading, whenever it becomes available) cannot be performed with face normals alone. In these cases figure data must include a vector that is normal to each vertex that defined the figure. These so-called vertex normals are used by the renderer in producing lighting and texturing effects. Because a vertex normal is anchored at the corresponding vertex point, its definition is made in terms of a single point in 3D space. Figure 21-1 shows flat shading of a plane using its face normal and Gouraud shading based on vertex normals.

Direct3D retained mode applications typically use the D3DVECTOR structure type to define vertices. Because a vertex normal requires but one additional point in 3D space, it is also defined by means of a structure member of type D3DVECTOR. The D3DVECTOR structure consists of three D3DVALUE types, as follows:

```
typedef struct _D3DVECTOR
{
    D3DVALUE x;
    D3DVALUE y;
    D3DVALUE z;
} D3DVECTOR;
```

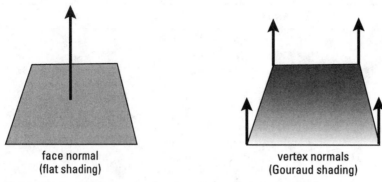

face normal
(flat shading)

vertex normals
(Gouraud shading)

Figure 21-1: Shading using face normal and vertex normals

In Gouraud shading Direct3D uses the vertex normals to calculate the angle between the light source and the surface. It calculates the color and intensity values for the vertices and interpolates them for every point across all of the surfaces. The light intensity is calculated based on the angle of each vector. The greater the angle, the less light that shines on the surface.

In a flat object the vertex normals should be perpendicular to the vertex points, as shown in Figure 21-1. If an object is not flat, as is often the case in 3D modeling, then the vertex normals are set at an angle with each of the vertices. If the vertex normal leans toward a surface, it causes the light intensity to increase or decrease for points on that surface, depending on the angle it makes with the light source.

Creating a face

The IDirect3DRMFace2 interface contains a host of functions for operating on faces. A face represents a single polygon in a mesh. An application can set the color, texture, and material of the face by using the functions in IDirect3DRMFace2. A face can be constructed from vertices or from vertices and their corresponding vertex normals.

Although there are several ways in which a face can be built using retained mode functions, the simplest and most direct one is by means of AddFaces() function of IDirect3DRMMeshBuilder3. The function adds one or more faces to a Direct3DRMMeshBuilder3 object. It has the following general form:

```
HRESULT AddFaces(
            DWORD dwVertexCount,                         // 1
            D3DVECTOR  *lpD3DVertices,                   // 2
            DWORD normalCount,                           // 3
            D3DVECTOR *lpNormals,                        // 4
            DWORD *lpFaceData,                           // 5
            LPDIRECT3DRMFACEARRAY *lplpD3DRMFaceArray    // 6
            );
```

The first parameter is a count of the number of vertices in the frame. The second parameter is the address of an array of D3DVECTOR structures that store the vertices. The third parameter is a count of the number of normals. This parameter is zero if no normals are defined for the face. The fourth parameter is the base address of an array of D3DVECTOR structures that store the normals. If the third parameter is zero, the fourth one is NULL. If the normals count is not zero, the fifth parameter contains a vertex count followed by pairs of indexes, with the first index of each pair indexing into the array of vertices, and the second indexing into the array of normals. If the third parameter (normals count) is zero, then the fifth parameter is a vertex count followed by the indexes into the array of vertices. In either case, the list of indexes terminates in zero. The sixth parameter is the address of a pointer to an IDirect3DRMFaceArray interface that is filled with a pointer to the newly created faces. This parameter can be NULL. The function returns D3DRM_OK if it succeeds, or an error otherwise.

Face with no vertex normals

We can use the AddFaces() function to define a face with no vertex normals. In this case the third parameter passed to the AddFaces() call is zero and the fourth one is NULL. In this case the array holding the face data consists of three elements: the number of vertices, the offset of each vertex, and the zero terminator. The resulting face can be shaded flat by the renderer only. For example, the following code fragment defines a set of vertices for a rectangular plane using the AddFaces() function of IDirect3DRMMeshBuilder3.

```
// Variables
LPDIRECT3DRMMESHBUILDER3   pMeshBuilder;
. . .
// Vertex definition for a plane. Direct3D uses by default
// a left-handed coordinate system in which the z axis
// points away from the viewer
//                          x       y       z
D3DVECTOR vertices[4] = { -1.0f,  -0.5f,  -1.0f,
                          -1.0f,   0.5f,   1.0f,
                           1.0f,   0.5f,   1.0f,
                           1.0f,  -0.5f,  -1.0f };

DWORD faceData[] = { 4, 0, 1, 2, 3, 0 };
//                   |  | | | | |
//                   |  | | | | |__ terminator
//                   |  |_|_|_|____ offset in arrays
//                   |_____ number of vertices

pMeshBuilder->AddFaces(4,         // Number of vertices
                       vertices,  // Vertex array
                       0,         // No normals
                       NULL,      // No normals array
                       faceData,  // Face data
                       NULL);
```

Face with vertex normals

If the face is to be rendered using Gouraud or Phong modes, then the face data must include the normal vectors to each vertex. In this case the third parameter to AddFaces() is nonzero and the fourth one is a pointer to an array of type D3DVECTOR containing the end coordinate of the normal for each vector. The following code fragments build the face in this case.

```
// Variables
LPDIRECT3DRMMESHBUILDER3   pMeshBuilder;
. . .
// Vertex definition for a plane
//                        x       y        z
D3DVECTOR vertices[4] = { -1.0f, -0.5f,  -1.0f,
                          -1.0f,  0.5f,   1.0f,
                           1.0f,  0.5f,   1.0f,
                           1.0f, -0.5f,  -1.0f };

// Array containing vertex normals.
//                       x        y        z
D3DVECTOR normals[4] =  { -1.0f, -0.25f,  -1.0f,
                          -1.0f,  0.25f,   1.0f,
                           1.0f,  0.25f,   1.0f,
                           1.0f, -0.25f,  -1.0f };

DWORD faceData[] = {4, 0, 0, 1, 1, 2, 2, 3, 3, 0};
//                  |  ---- ---- ---- ----  |
//                  |   |    |    |    |     |__ terminator
//                  |   |____|____|____|__ index pairs
//                  |_____ number of
vertices

pMeshBuilder->AddFaces( 4,            // Number of vertices
                        vertices,     // Vertex array
                        4,            // Number of normals
                        normals,      // Normals array
                        faceData,     // Face data
                        NULL );
```

In the preceding code fragment the vertex normals are defined for each vertex. The call to AddFaces() contains the number of normals and their corresponding indices into the data. The array holding the face data now contains ten elements: the number of vertices, two offsets for each vertex point, and the zero terminator. The resulting face can be rendered using the Gouraud mode. Because the vertex normals are perpendicular to the vertices, the shading depicts a surface with no curvature, as shown in Figure 21-1.

We can make the rendered surface appear curved by changing the angle of the vertex normals. If the vertex normals converge toward the center of the figure, then the rendered image appears convex. If the vertex normals converge away from the figure then the image appears concave. These effects are shown in Figure 21-2.

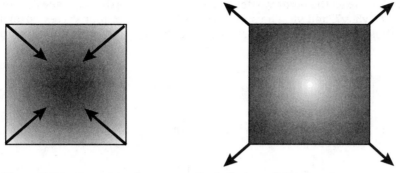

Figure 21-2: Convex and concave effects that result from vertex normal angles

Creating a cube

In hard-coding vertex and vertex normals for a cube you must deal with some additional complexity. A cube is defined by six faces, which share some of the same vertices. On the other hand, each face must be illuminated individually, so you must provide four vertex normals for each cube face. This means that data for a cube contains eight vertices and twenty-four vertex normals. It also means that the cube's face data must refer to each of the six faces. Figure 21-3 shows the faces, vertices, and vertex normals for a cube.

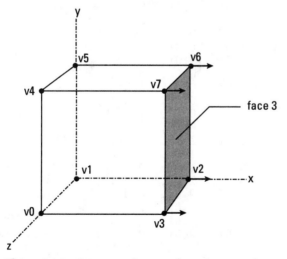

Figure 21-3: Faces, vertices, and vertex normals for a cube

In Figure 21-3 you see the eight vertices, labeled v0 to v7. Arbitrary face 3 is formed by vertices v2, v3, v7, and v6. The short arrows indicate the four vertex normals for face 3. The following code fragment shows the definition and creation of a hard-coded cube.

```
// Variables
LPDIRECT3DRMMESHBUILDER3   pMeshBuilder;
. . .

// A cube has six planar faces, defined by 8 vertices
D3DVECTOR vertices[]  = { -0.5f, -0.5f, -0.5f,   // first
vertex
                          -0.5f, -0.5f,  0.5f,
                          -0.5f,  0.5f, -0.5f,
                          -0.5f,  0.5f,  0.5f,
                           0.5f, -0.5f, -0.5f,
                           0.5f, -0.5f,  0.5f,
                           0.5f,  0.5f, -0.5f,
                           0.5f,  0.5f,  0.5f }; // last vertex

// Each of the cube's six faces has four vertex normals, for a
// total of 24
D3DVECTOR normals[]   = {  0.0f,  0.0f,  1.0f,   // First
normal
                           0.0f,  0.0f,  1.0f,
                           0.0f,  0.0f,  1.0f,
                           0.0f,  0.0f,  1.0f,
                           0.0f,  1.0f,  0.0f,
                           0.0f,  1.0f,  0.0f,
                           0.0f,  1.0f,  0.0f,
                           0.0f,  1.0f,  0.0f,
                           1.0f,  0.0f,  0.0f,
                           1.0f,  0.0f,  0.0f,
                           1.0f,  0.0f,  0.0f,
                           1.0f,  0.0f,  0.0f,
                           0.0f,  0.0f, -1.0f,
                           0.0f,  0.0f, -1.0f,
                           0.0f,  0.0f, -1.0f,
                           0.0f,  0.0f, -1.0f,
                           0.0f, -1.0f,  0.0f,
                           0.0f, -1.0f,  0.0f,
                           0.0f, -1.0f,  0.0f,
                           0.0f, -1.0f,  0.0f,
                          -1.0f,  0.0f,  0.0f,
                          -1.0f,  0.0f,  0.0f,
                          -1.0f,  0.0f,  0.0f,
                          -1.0f,  0.0f,  0.0f }; // Last normal
```

```
// Face data refers to each face of the cube
DWORD faceData[] = {   4,   1,   0,   5,   1,   7,   2,   3,   3,
                       4,   2,   4,   3,   5,   7,   6,   6,   7,
                       4,   5,   8,   4,   9,   6,  10,   7,  11,
                       4,   0,  12,   2,  13,   6,  14,   4,  15,
                       4,   0,  16,   4,  17,   5,  18,   1,  19,
                       4,   0,  20,   1,  21,   3,  22,   2,  23,  0 };

pMeshBuilder->AddFaces( 8,              // Number of vertices
                        vertices,       // Vertex array
                        24,             // Number of normals
                        normals,        // Normals array
                        faceData,       // Data for each face
                        NULL);
```

Sample program 3DRM Mesh Create Demo

The sample program 3DRM Mesh Create Demo in the book's CD-ROM illustrates the hard-coding of meshes and cubes, as discussed in the preceding sections. Figure 21-4 shows screen snapshots of the different commands in the program's menu.

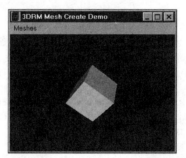

Mesh with no vertex normals

Mesh with perpendicular
vertex normals

Figure 21-4: Screen snapshots of the 3DRM Mesh Create Demo program

Loading Frames and Meshes from Files

We have mentioned that graphics applications that use, but do not manipulate 3D image data directly, often rely on imagery created by means of modeling programs. Retained mode requires that images are in Microsoft X format. Included in the DirectX SDK is a DOS-mode file conversion utility named Conv3ds that can be used to convert image data in 3D Studio's .3ds format into the X format. This determines that the imagery created in the 3D modeling program must be either in X or in .3ds formats. If in .3ds, the data can be converted into X format by means of Conv3ds.

Although there are several functions for loading images in retained mode, the ones most commonly used are in the IDirect3DRMFrame3 and IDirect3DRMMesh Builder3 interfaces. In the first case the image is loaded as a frame and in the second one it is loaded by a meshbuilder object. Which method is used depends on the internal structure of the X file. If the image data is contained in a frame, then the mesh is loaded using the Load() function of IDirect3DRMFrame3. If the image data is defined as a mesh, then we must use the Load() function of IDirect3DRMMesh Builder3. In the following sections we first discuss the Convs3ds utility and then examine loading image data as frames and as mesh objects.

The Conv3ds utility

The Conv3ds utility program furnished with the DirectX SDK converts three-dimensional models in Autodesk .3ds format into Microsoft's X file format. The Conv3ds utility is a DOS program and must be run from the command line. The program option switches, described in the next section, determine how the data is stored in the DirectX file and, therefore, how the contained meshes and frames must be loaded into the application. In the following discussion we use the name afile to indicate the filename of a file in .3ds format.

Default behavior

By default, Conv3ds produces binary X files with no templates. If the program is executed without specifying any of the optional switches, it produces an X file containing a frame hierarchy. For example, the command

```
conv3ds afile.3ds
```

produces the file afileX containing a hierarchy of frames. The frames can be loaded into an application by means of the Load() function of IDirect3DRMFrame3.

-A switch

The -A option produces an animation set. The command

```
conv3ds -A afile.3ds
```

produces a file in X format that can be loaded into the application using the `Load()` function of `Direct3DRMAnimationSet2`. Animating files in X format is discussed in Chapter 25.

-m switch

This option produces an X file that contains a single mesh made from all the objects in the .3ds source. The command

```
conv3ds -m afile.3ds
```

produces a file that can be loaded into the application using the `Load()` function of `IDirect3DRMMeshBuilder3`.

-T switch

This option is used to wrap all the objects and frame hierarchies in a single top-level frame. The first top-level frame hierarchy that results from using this option can be loaded with a single call to the `Load()` function of `IDirect3DRMFrame3`. The -T option has no effect if it is used with the -m option.

-s switch

This option allows entering a scale factor for all the objects in the .3ds file. The operand is an integer to make objects bigger and a decimal fraction to make them smaller. For example,

```
conv3ds -s5 afile.3ds
```

makes the objects in the file five times bigger. Whereas the command

```
conv3ds -s0.1 afile.3ds
```

makes the objects ten times smaller.

-r switch

The -r switch reverses the winding order of the faces when the .3ds file is converted. The switch should be used when the objects are inverted in the converted file.

-v switch

This switch turns on the verbose output mode. Table 21-2 lists the verbose modes supported by Conv3ds.

Table 21-2 Conv3ds Utility Verbose Switches	
Switch	*Action*
-v0	Default. Verbose mode off.
-v1	Prints warnings about bad objects and general information about what converter action.
-v2	Prints basic key frame information. Lists the objects being converted, and information about the objects being saved.
-v3	Very verbose. Mostly used for debugging.

-e switch

The -e option is used to change the extension of texture map files. For example, if the command

```
conv3ds -e"ppm" afile.3ds
```

is used for a .3ds file that references the texture map file Brick.gif, the X file references are changed to the texture map file Brick.ppm. The converter does not convert the texture map file. The texture map files must be in the D3DPATH when the resulting X file is loaded. D3DPATH D3DPath is a DOS-mode environment variable that sets the default search path.

-x switch

The default action of Conv3ds is to generate a binary file. The -x option forces the utility to produce a text X file. Text files are larger but they can be interpreted and modified.

-X switch

The -X option forces the inclusion of Direct3D retained mode X file templates in the output file. Templates are not included by default.

-t switch

This option specifies that the X file produced will not contain texture information.

-N switch

The -N option specifies that the X file produced will not contain vector normals. All Load() functions in Direct3D retained mode automatically generate vector normals for objects with no vector normals in the X file. Therefore, the action of this switch is to force the generation of vector normals at load time.

-c switch

The -c option specifies that the X file produced should not contain texture coordinates. By default, if you use the -m option, the mesh that is output will contain (0,0) uv texture coordinates if the .3ds object had no texture coordinates.

-f switch

The -f option specifies that the X file produced should not contain a frame transformation matrix. The frame transformation matrix encodes the position and scale of objects according to their appearance in the 3D modeling application.

- z and -Z switches

The -z and -Z options are used to adjust the alpha face color value of all the materials referenced by objects in the X file. The following command causes Conv3ds.exe to add 0.1 to all alpha values under 0.2

```
conv3ds -z0.1 -Z0.2 afile.3ds
```

The following command causes Conv3ds.exe to subtract 0.2 from the alpha values for all alphas:

```
conv3ds -z"-0.2" -z1 afile.3ds
```

-o switch

The -o option enables you to specify the filename for the X file produced. For example, to produce a file named newfile.x you can enter the command

```
conv3ds -o"newfile.x" afile.3ds
```

Notice that the X filename extension must be included in the quoted string.

-h switch

The -h option tells the converter not to try to resolve any hierarchy information in the .3ds file, which is produced by default. Instead, all the objects are output in top-level frames. The -h option is ignored if -m is used.

Loading images onto frames

Retained mode offers several possible ways of loading meshes onto a frame. To explore these possibilities we start by creating a 3D model using 3D Studio MAX. In this case the model is one of the built-in objects that is furnished with the modeling program. The 3D Studio MAX perspective window is shown in Figure 21-5.

Figure 21-5: Original model in 3D Studio MAX perspective window

Figure 21-5 shows the teapot model split into its four components. The image was exported into a file named tparts.3ds. This file can be found in the 3DRM Frame Load Demo folder in the book's CD-ROM. The four objects that form the teapot in Figure 21-5 were named Body, Handle, Spout, and Lid in 3D Studio MAX. The objects were created in that order. We can now use the Conv3ds utility furnished with DirectX to convert the file in .3ds format into a file in DirectX format which can be manipulated in retained mode. In the sections that follow we explore several of the most useful options.

Loading a frame hierarchy

When the .3ds file is converted into a DirectX format file without specifying the -m or -T switches discussed previously, the result is a file containing a frame hierarchy. For example, if we convert the file named tparts.3ds with the command

```
conv3ds -x -o"teapot0.x" tparts.3ds
```

the result is a text file named "teapot0.x". The file contains a frame hierarchy, as follows:

```
xof 0302txt 0064
Header {
 1;
 0;
 1;
```

```
}

Frame x3ds_Body {
 FrameTransformMatrix {
  1.000000, 0.000000, 0.000000, 0.000000,
  0.000000, 1.000000, 0.000000, 0.000000,
  0.000000, 0.000000, 1.000000, 0.000000,
  1.037232, -20.376945, -0.377255, 1.000000;;
 }
 Mesh Body {

   257;
   24.500000; 42.000000; 0.000000;,
   24.158203; 43.291992; 0.000000;

   . . . (additional data for Body mesh)

Frame x3ds_Handle {
 FrameTransformMatrix {
  1.000000, 0.000000, 0.000000, 0.000000,
  0.000000, 1.000000, 0.000000, 0.000000,
  0.000000, 0.000000, 1.000000, 0.000000,
  -13.010463, -24.609686, 0.665987, 1.000000;;
 }
 Mesh Handle {

   72;
   -28.000000; 35.437500; 0.000000;,
   -36.175781; 35.375977; 0.000000;,

   . . . (additional data for Handle mesh)

Frame x3ds_Spout {
 FrameTransformMatrix {
  1.000000, 0.000000, 0.000000, 0.000000,
  0.000000, 1.000000, 0.000000, 0.000000,
  0.000000, 0.000000, 1.000000, 0.000000,
  14.765121, -19.316219, -0.326592, 1.000000;;
 }
 Mesh Spout {

   72;
   29.750000; 24.937500; 0.000000;,
   38.144531; 26.865234; 0.000000;,

   . . . (additional data for Spout mesh)

Frame x3ds_Lid {
 FrameTransformMatrix {
```

```
  1.000000, 0.000000, 0.000000, 0.000000,
  0.000000, 1.000000, 0.000000, 0.000000,
  0.000000, 0.000000, 1.000000, 0.000000,
 -0.357211, -9.733930, -0.040901, 1.000000;;
 }
Mesh Lid {

  129;
  0.000000; 55.125000; 0.000000;,
  5.960938; 54.263672; 0.000000;,

  . . . (additional data for Lid mesh)
 }
 }
 }
```

Notice that the X format file that results from this conversion contains the four meshes that were defined in 3D Studio MAX. The names assigned to the individual meshes in the modeling program are preserved in the X file.

Because the file was created without the formatting switches (-T or -m) the objects contained in the X may be loaded into a frame, using the Load() function of IDirect3DRMFrame3. The following code fragment shows the processing.

```
// Program data
LPDIRECT3DRMFRAME3 teapartsFrame      = NULL;
char                szXfile0[]        = "teapot0.x";
  . . .
retval = lpD3DRM->CreateFrame(globVars.aScene,
                             &teapartsFrame);
    if(FAILED(retval))
        // Frame creation error handler goes here
// Load image into frame
retval = teapartsFrame->Load(szXfile1,              // Source
                             NULL,
                             D3DRMLOAD_FROMFILE, // Options
                             NULL, NULL);
    if(FAILED(retval))
        // Frame load error handler goes here
```

Because the file contains a frame hierarchy, an attempt to load the entire file into a frame results in loading the first frame in the hierarchy. In this case the first frame is the one named Body in the preceding listing of the resulting X file. Figure 21-6 shows the results in this case.

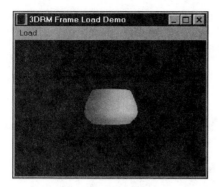

Figure 21-6: Screen snapshot of the 3DRM Frame Demo program after loading the first frame in a frame hierarchy

Loading a single frame

When the .3ds file is converted into a DirectX format by means of the -T switch, discussed previously, the result is a file in which all meshes are contained in a single frame. For example, if we convert the file named tparts.3ds with the command

```
conv3ds -x -o"teapot1.x" -T tparts.3ds
```

the result is a text file named "teapot1.x". The file contains a single frame, as follows:

```
xof 0302txt 0064
Header {
 1;
 0;
 1;
}

Frame x3ds_Teapot {

 Frame x3ds_Body {
  FrameTransformMatrix {
   1.000000, 0.000000, 0.000000, 0.000000,
   0.000000, 1.000000, 0.000000, 0.000000,
   0.000000, 0.000000, 1.000000, 0.000000,
   0.020745, -0.407539, -0.007545, 1.000000;;
  }
  Mesh Body {

    257;
    0.490000; 0.840000; 0.000000;,
    0.483164; 0.865840; 0.000000;,
    . . . (rest of file follows)
```

The principal difference between this file and the one created without the -T switch is the presence of a higher-level frame, in this case named x3ds_Teapot, which contains all others in the file. This first frame is the one accessed by the Load() function of IDirect3DRMFrame3. The result is that all meshes contained in the frame are loaded in a single call. The following code fragment shows the processing.

```
// Program data
LPDIRECT3DRMFRAME3 teapartsFrame        = NULL;
char               szXfile0[]           = "teapot0.x";
. . . .
retval = lpD3DRM->CreateFrame(globVars.aScene,
                              &teapartsFrame);
if(FAILED(retval))
   // Frame creation error handler goes here
// Load image into frame
retval = teapartsFrame->Load(szXfile1,              // Source
                             NULL,
                             D3DRMLOAD_FROMFILE, // Options
                             NULL, NULL);
if(FAILED(retval))
   // Frame load error handler goes here
```

Figure 21-7 shows the results in this case.

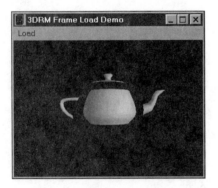

Figure 21-7: Screen snapshot of the 3DRM Frame Demo program after loading an X file created with the -T option

Loading frames by name

Notice that in an X file created with or without the -T switch each frame is assigned a unique name. The name consists of the x3ds prefix, the underscore symbol, and the name of the object as defined in the file. For example, the X file created by means of the -T switch, described in the previous section, contains the frames named

```
x3ds_Teapot
x3ds_Body
```

```
x3ds_Handle
x3ds_Spout
x3ds_Lid
```

The first of these named frames, `x3ds_Teapot`, does not appear in an X file created without the -T switch, but the other four frames are also present.

Applications can load any frame from an X file by using the `D3DRMLOAD_BYNAME` option and referencing the specific frame name.

The following code fragment shows loading the frame for the teapot handle.

```
// Program data
LPDIRECT3DRMFRAME3 teapartsFrame      = NULL;
char        szXfile1[] = "teapot1.x" ;  // Frame file to load
char        meshName[] = "x3ds_Handle"; // Frame name in file
. . .
retval = lpD3DRM->CreateFrame(globVars.aScene,
                              &teapartsFrame);
if(FAILED(retval))
   // Failed frame creation error handler goes here

// Load frame by name
retval = teapartsFrame->Load(szXfile2,               // Source
                             &meshName,
                             D3DRMLOAD_BYNAME,    // Options
                             NULL, NULL);
if(FAILED(retval))
   // Failed frame load error handler goes here
. . .
```

Figure 21-8 shows the results of loading a specific named frame.

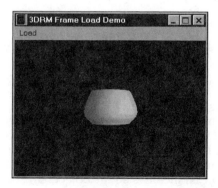

Figure 21-8: Screen snapshot of the 3DRM Frame Demo program after loading a named frame from an X file

Loading frames by position

Any one frame in an X format file created without the -T switch can be loaded by specifying its position in the file. In files created with the -T switch only the frame at offset zero can be loaded by position. An attempt to load any other frame results in an error.

The position of a frame can be obtained by examining its zero-based order in the file. For example, in the teapot0.x file, discussed in the section on loading a frame hierarchy, there are four individual frames. The frames appear in the file in the following order:

```
0 Body
1 Handle
2 Spout
3 Lid
```

The following code fragment shows loading the frame at offset 2, which is the one corresponding to the Spout object.

```
// Program data
LPDIRECT3DRMFRAME3 teapartsFrame      = NULL;
char         szXfile0[] = "teapot0.x" ;  // Frame file to load
DWORD        position = 2;               // Frame position
. . .
retval = lpD3DRM->CreateFrame(globVars.aScene,
                              &teapartsFrame);
if(FAILED(retval))
    // Frame creation error handler goes here

// Load image into frame by it offset in the file
retval = teapartsFrame->Load(szXfile0,            // Source
                     &position,
                     D3DRMLOAD_BYPOSITION,   // Options
                     NULL, NULL);
if(FAILED(retval))
    // Frame load error handler goes here
```

Loading meshes

Mesh data is present in X files. If the file was converted into X format by means of the Conv3ds utility, with no format switch entered in the command, then the mesh data is defined for each object in the file. In this case the individual meshes can be loaded by means of the Load() function of IDirect3DRMMeshBuilder3. On the other hand, if the mesh was created by means of the -m switch, described previously, then the X file contains a single mesh that includes all the objects present in the .3ds file. Note that the -m option performs a similar function in regards to meshes as the -T option in regards to frames.

Loading as a single mesh

If a .3ds file was converted in X format using the -m switch, then all the objects in the original file can be loaded using a single `Load()` call of `IDirect3DRMMesh Builder3`. In the sample program 3DRM Mesh Load Demo, furnished in the book's CD-ROM, the file named boxsph0.x was created from a .3ds format file with the command:

```
Conv3ds -m -o"boxsph0.x" -x boxsph.3ds
```

The result is a file named boxsph0.x, in text format, in which all objects are contained in a single mesh. The file listing is as follows:

```
xof 0303txt 0032

Header {
 1;
 0;
 1;
}

Mesh {
 122;
 -1.134496;0.272737;0.485547;,
 -0.254496;0.272737;0.485547;,
 -1.134496;1.152737;0.485547;,
 . . . (rest of file follows)
```

The following code fragment shows the loading of the file into a meshbuilder object.

```
// Data
char            szXfile[] = "boxsph0.x" ;  // Filename string
LPDIRECT3DRMMESHBUILDER3 multiMeshBuilder    = NULL;
. . .
retval = lpD3DRM->CreateMeshBuilder(&multiMeshBuilder);
if (FAILED(retval))
    // Meshbuilder creation failure error handler goes here
// Use meshbuilder to load a mesh from a DirectX file
retval = multiMeshBuilder->Load(szXfile,            // Source
                        NULL,
                        D3DRMLOAD_FROMFILE, // Options
                        NULL, NULL);
if (FAILED(retval))
    // File load error handler goes here
```

The resulting meshbuilder object can now be manipulated and rendered in the conventional manner.

Loading meshes by name

If the X file was not created with the -m switch, then the individual meshes can be referenced and loaded by name. For example, if the X file was created with the command

```
Conv3ds -o"boxsph1.x" -x boxsph.3ds
```

the result is a file named boxsph1.x, in text format, and in which objects are contained in separately named meshes. In this case the file boxsph.3ds contained two objects: a box and a sphere, which were named Box and Sphere in the original file. The resulting file after using Conv3ds is as follows:

```
xof 0302txt 0064
Header {
 1;
 0;
 1;
}

Frame x3ds_Box {
 FrameTransformMatrix {
  1.000000, 0.000000, 0.000000, 0.000000,
  0.000000, 0.000000, -1.000000, 0.000000,
  0.000000, 1.000000, 0.000000, 0.000000,
  -0.694496, 0.712737, 0.485547, 1.000000;;
 }
 Mesh Box {

   8;
   -0.440000; -0.000000; -0.440000;,
   0.440000; -0.000000; -0.440000;,
 . . . (additional data for Box mesh follows)

Frame x3ds_Sphere {
 FrameTransformMatrix {
  1.000000, 0.000000, 0.000000, 0.000000,
  0.000000, 0.000000, -1.000000, 0.000000,
  0.000000, 1.000000, 0.000000, 0.000000,
  0.674236, -0.636010, 0.000000, 1.000000;;
 }
 Mesh Sphere {

   114;
   0.000000; 0.551888; 0.000000;,
   0.000000; 0.509878; 0.211199;,
 . . . (additional data for Sphere mesh follows)
```

The following code fragment shows loading the Box mesh into a meshbuilder object.

```
// Data
char        szXfile1[] = "boxsph1.x" ;  // Second format
char        meshName[] = "Box";
. . .
retval = lpD3DRM->CreateMeshBuilder(&boxMeshBuilder);
if (FAILED(retval))
    // Meshbuilder creation failure error handler goes here
// Use meshbuilder to load a mesh from a DirectX file
retval = boxMeshBuilder->Load(szXfile1,          // Source
                    &meshName,
                    D3DRMLOAD_BYNAME, // Options
                    NULL, NULL);
if (FAILED(retval))
    // Mesh load error handler goes here
```

The program 3DRM Mesh Load Demo in the book's CD-ROM contains menu commands to load individual meshes. One of these commands loads all four individual meshes that are part of a teapot object. Each individual mesh is colored using the SetColorRGB() function of the IDirect3DRMMeshBuilder3 interface. The result is shown in color plate 9.

Although it is not explicitly stated in the documentation, it appears that the X file does not contain positional information regarding meshes. We make this deduction based on our failed attempts to load a mesh by position.

Interpreting X File Data

We have stated that the applications programmer is likely to rely on a modeling program for the construction of graphical objects. A typical scenario is to model 3D objects using 3D Studio MAX, TrueSpace4, or some other application. The resulting file can be already in X format or in .3ds format. In the latter case it can be converted into X format by means of the Conv3ds utility discussed previously in this chapter. The meshes in the X file are then loaded into program code either as frames, or as meshbuilder objects.

Considering the power and refinement of the available image editing tools, it is difficult to imagine a circumstance in which the programmer would hard-code a mesh by defining its faces, vertices, and normals. However, there are cases in which, for reasons of convenience or performance, it may be profitable to store mesh data directly in code. If the programmer is familiar with how mesh data is stored in the file, it is possible to use a 3D modeling program to create the mesh and then cut-and-paste the mesh data from the file into program code. In other words, let the modeling program do the hard work of finding the vertices, faces, and normals, and use this information to define the required data.

Decoding an X file cube

The DirectX file format templates can be of considerable assistance in interpreting the data contained in a DirectX text format file and in deciphering the encoding. Appendix C contains the templates for the DirectX file format. In the following example we use the data in the file boxsph1.x, which was obtained from the 3ds-format file named boxsph.3ds by means of the command:

```
Conv3ds -o"boxsph1.x" -x boxsph.3ds
```

Our purpose is to use the raw mesh data contained in the X file named boxsph1.x in order to hard-code a cube mesh. The data for the mesh object named "Box" appears in the file as follows:

```
Mesh Box {

    8;
    -0.440000; -0.000000; -0.440000;,
    0.440000; -0.000000; -0.440000;,
    -0.440000; -0.000000; 0.440000;,
    0.440000; -0.000000; 0.440000;,
    -0.440000; 0.880000; -0.440000;,
    0.440000; 0.880000; -0.440000;,
    -0.440000; 0.880000; 0.440000;,
    0.440000; 0.880000; 0.440000;;

    12;
    3;0,3,2;,
    3;3,0,1;,
    3;4,7,5;,
    3;7,4,6;,
    3;0,5,1;,
    3;5,0,4;,
    3;1,7,3;,
    3;7,1,5;,
    3;3,6,2;,
    3;6,3,7;,
    3;2,4,0;,
    3;4,2,6;;

    MeshNormals {
    24;
    -0.000000;-1.000000;-0.000000;,
    0.000000;0.000000;-1.000000;,
    -1.000000;0.000000;0.000000;,
    -0.000000;-1.000000;-0.000000;,
    0.000000;0.000000;-1.000000;,
    1.000000;0.000000;0.000000;,
    -0.000000;-1.000000;-0.000000;,
```

```
0.000000;0.000000;1.000000;,
-1.000000;0.000000;0.000000;,
-0.000000;-1.000000;-0.000000;,
1.000000;0.000000;0.000000;,
0.000000;0.000000;1.000000;,
0.000000;1.000000;-0.000000;,
0.000000;0.000000;-1.000000;,
-1.000000;0.000000;0.000000;,
0.000000;1.000000;-0.000000;,
0.000000;0.000000;-1.000000;,
1.000000;0.000000;0.000000;,
0.000000;1.000000;-0.000000;,
0.000000;0.000000;1.000000;,
-1.000000;0.000000;0.000000;,
0.000000;1.000000;-0.000000;,
1.000000;0.000000;0.000000;,
0.000000;0.000000;1.000000;;

12;
3;0,9,6;,
3;9,0,3;,
3;12,21,15;,
3;21,12,18;,
3;1,16,4;,
3;16,1,13;,
3;5,22,10;,
3;22,5,17;,
3;11,19,7;,
3;19,11,23;,
3;8,14,2;,
3;14,8,20;;
```

To decipher this data you can observe how it is formatted in the template for the Mesh component. The template appears in the Microsoft documentation (reproduced with minor editing in Appendix C) as follows:

```
Template: Mesh
UUID <3D82AB44-62DA-11cf-AB39-0020AF71E433>
```

Member Name	Type	Optional Array Size	Optional Data Objects (see list)
nVertices	DWORD		
vertices	array Vector	nVertices	
nFaces	DWORD		
faces	array MeshFace	nFaces	

Description

Defines a simple mesh. The first array is a list of vertices. The second array defines the faces of the mesh by indexing into the vertex array.

Optional data objects

The following optional data elements are used by Direct3D Retained Mode.

MeshFaceWraps	If not present, wrapping for both u and v defaults to false.
MeshTextureCoords	If not present, there are no texture coordinates.
MeshNormals	If not present, normals are generated using the GenerateNormals API.
MeshVertexColors	If not present, the colors default to white.
MeshMaterialList	If not present, the material defaults to white

If we now observe the X file data in light of the Mesh template we notice that the MeshNormals optional data object is the only one included with the mesh. This means that the mesh has no wraps, texture coordinates, vertex colors, or materials list. The first value (8) indicates the number of vertices and is followed by the coordinate triplets for each vertex, as follows:

```
8;
    -0.440000; -0.000000; -0.440000;,
    0.440000; -0.000000; -0.440000;,
    -0.440000; -0.000000; 0.440000;,
    0.440000; -0.000000; 0.440000;,
    -0.440000; 0.880000; -0.440000;,
    0.440000; 0.880000; -0.440000;,
    -0.440000; 0.880000; 0.440000;,
    0.440000; 0.880000; 0.440000;;
```

We can use this data to construct the array that encodes the coordinates for each vertex, as follows:

```
D3DVECTOR vertices[]  = {
    -0.440000, -0.000000, -0.440000,
    0.440000, -0.000000, -0.440000,
    -0.440000, -0.000000,  0.440000,
    0.440000, -0.000000,  0.440000,
    -0.440000,  0.880000, -0.440000,
    0.440000,  0.880000, -0.440000,
    -0.440000,  0.880000,  0.440000,
    0.440000,  0.880000,  0.440000 };
```

The mesh file also contains the optional MeshNormals data which you can use to obtain the array of normals for our hard-coded cube. The template for the MeshNormal (see Appendix C) is as follows:

```
Template: MeshNormals

UUID <F6F23F43-7686-11cf-8F52-0040333594A3>

Member Name          Type              Optional Array Size
nNormals             DWORD
normals              array Vector      nNormals
nFaceNormals         DWORD
faceNormals          array             nFaceNormals
                     MeshFace
```

Description

Defines normals for a mesh. The first array of vectors is the normal vectors themselves, and the second array is an array of indexes specifying which normals should be applied to a given face. The value of the nFaceNormals member should be equal to the number of faces in a mesh.

First we observe the array that contains the 24 mesh normal vectors:

```
MeshNormals {
    24;
    -0.000000;-1.000000;-0.000000;,
    0.000000;0.000000;-1.000000;,
    . . .
    1.000000;0.000000;0.000000;,
    0.000000;0.000000;1.000000;;
```

From this array we can obtain the data for the 24 vector normals as follows:

```
D3DVECTOR normals[]   = {
    -0.000000, -1.000000, -0.000000,    // Vector 1
     0.000000,  0.000000, -1.000000,    // Vector 2
    -1.000000,  0.000000,  0.000000,    // . . .
    -0.000000, -1.000000, -0.000000,
     0.000000,  0.000000, -1.000000,
     1.000000,  0.000000,  0.000000,
    -0.000000, -1.000000, -0.000000,
     0.000000,  0.000000,  1.000000,
    -1.000000,  0.000000,  0.000000,
    -0.000000, -1.000000, -0.000000,
     1.000000,  0.000000,  0.000000,
     0.000000,  0.000000,  1.000000,
     0.000000,  1.000000, -0.000000,
     0.000000,  0.000000, -1.000000,
```

```
-1.000000,  0.000000,  0.000000,
 0.000000,  1.000000, -0.000000,
 0.000000,  0.000000, -1.000000,
 1.000000,  0.000000,  0.000000,
 0.000000,  1.000000, -0.000000,
 0.000000,  0.000000,  1.000000,
-1.000000,  0.000000,  0.000000,
 0.000000,  1.000000, -0.000000,
 1.000000,  0.000000,  0.000000,
 0.000000,  0.000000,  1.000000 };  // Vector 24
```

To display the mesh using the AddFaces() function of IDirect3DRMMesh
Builder3, discussed earlier in this chapter, you need to construct the face data
array. This array encodes, for each face in the mesh, the number of vertices in the
face and the offset of the data in the arrays of vertices and the array of vertex
normals. The information is contained in the X file following the array of vertices
and the array of vertex normals, as follows:

```
12;
3;0,3,2;,
3;3,0,1;,
3;4,7,5;,
3;7,4,6;,
3;0,5,1;,
3;5,0,4;,
3;1,7,3;,
3;7,1,5;,
3;3,6,2;,
3;6,3,7;,
3;2,4,0;,
3;4,2,6;;
   . . .
12;
3;0,9,6;,
3;9,0,3;,
3;12,21,15;,
3;21,12,18;,
3;1,16,4;,
3;16,1,13;,
3;5,22,10;,
3;22,5,17;,
3;11,19,7;,
3;19,11,23;,
3;8,14,2;,
3;14,8,20;;
```

The first thing to notice is that there are 12 faces in the cube mesh. Earlier in this
chapter you hard-coded a cube consisting of six square faces. Meshes built by most
3D modeling programs are based on triangular surfaces. Therefore, the resulting
cube has 12 faces instead of 6. Figure 21-9 shows the faces, vertices, and vertex
normals of a 12-faced cube.

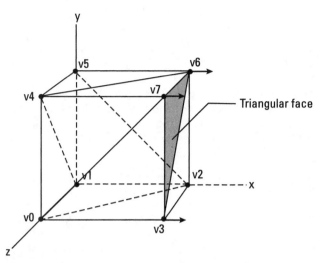

Figure 21-9: Faces, vertices, and vertex normals of a 12-faced cube

Comparing Figures 21-3 and 21-9 we notice that the total number of vertices and the number of vertex normals is the same for a six-faced cube based on rectangular surfaces, than for a twelve-faced cube based on triangles. However, each face of the cube in Figure 21-9 contains three vertices, instead of four vertices per face in the cube of Figure 21-3. Therefore the face data for the twelve-faced cube consists of 12 entries, each of which contains three offsets for the vertices and three offsets for the vertex normals.

With this knowledge you can now merge the face data for the vertices, and the face data for the vertex normals, contained in the X file to produce the face data array for the 12-faced cube. The resulting array is as follows:

```
// Face data for each of the 12 faces
//                              |-------|-------|----- vertex offsets
//                              |       |       |
DWORD faceData[] = { 3,  0,  0,  3,  9,  2,  6,        // Face 1
                     3,  3,  9,  0,  0,  1,  3,        // Face 2
                     3,  4, 12,  7, 21,  5, 15,        // . . .
                     3,  7, 21,  4, 12,  6, 18,
                     3,  0,  1,  5, 16,  1,  4,
                     3,  5, 16,  0,  1,  4, 13,
                     3,  1,  5,  7, 22,  3, 10,
                     3,  7, 22,  1,  5,  5, 17,
                     3,  3, 11,  6, 19,  2,  7,
                     3,  6, 19,  3, 11,  7, 23,
                     3,  2,  8,  4, 14,  0,  2,        // . . .
```

```
//                      3,  4, 14,  2,  8,  6, 20, 0 }; // Face 12
//                      |        |        |        |
//                      |        |--------|--------|-- vertex normals
//                      |                              offsets
//                      |_____ number of vertices
```

The comments fields in the previous code fragment indicate the origin of the offsets. Notice that the data is the same as the one in the X file. The following code fragment shows the call to the AddFaces() function of IDirect3DRMMeshBuilder3 to display the hard-coded cube listed previously.

```
pMeshBuilder->AddFaces( 8,          // Number of vertices
                vertices,           // Array of vertices
                      24,           // Number of vertex
normals
                 normals,           // Array of vertex normals
               faceData,            // Array of face data
                 NULL );
```

The sample program 3DRM Mesh Create Demo included in the book's CD-ROM demonstrates the encoding and display of a hard-coded cubes with six and twelve faces.

Summary

We visited in this chapter several mesh-related manipulations that are at the core of 3D application development. We started with the creation of simple faces and meshes by hard-coding the data into our programs. Due to the practical limitations of this technique, we then explored a more efficient mechanism for mesh creation based on the use of a 3D modeling program. Because such applications often output data in the .3ds proprietary format, we discussed the use of the Conv3ds utility. This program, which is furnished with the DirectX SDK, converts .3ds files into X format which can be handled in retained mode. We also examined how the frames and meshes contained in an X format file can be loaded and displayed by a retained mode application. The chapter concludes with the use of DirectX templates in the interpretation of mesh data contained in an X format file.

The following chapter is about how materials and textures are applied to retained mode objects to improve their visual quality.

✦   ✦   ✦

Textures and Materials

Our discussion of retained mode functions continues here with textures, materials, and other related topics such as wraps. More specialized uses of textures, such as decals, mipmaps, and transparency are discussed in Chapter 23. Some of the material in the present chapter was mentioned in Chapters 14 and 16. We now revisit these topics in an applied context. The programmer manipulates textures and materials to enhance the visual quality of 3D objects. A mesh is visually rendered with no other attribute than a surface color. By handling textures and materials, you can make 3D objects appear to have specific surface irregularities and color patterns. For example, you can make a wall appear to be constructed of red bricks, a teapot to be made of porcelain, or an airplane to shine as if it were built of metal.

Textures in Retained Mode

A texture is actually a 2D concept. Retained mode textures are encoded in 2D bitmaps, usually in .bmp or .ppm formats.

Any image can be used as a texture, but developing a good texture is a graphics art form. In the context of texture programming the term *textel*, a composite of texture and pixel, is used to represent each individual element of a texture.

The simplest texture rendering technique is called point mapping. In point mapping the rendering software looks up each pixel in a texture map and applies it to the corresponding screen pixel. Often point mapping produces an effect that is unnatural and disturbing. Satisfactory texturing requires that the distance between the object and the viewer be taken into account at the time of applying the texture. This means that the texture must be rendered perspectively. Bilinear filtering is a method of texture rendering that uses the weighted average of four texture pixels. This results in more pleasant textures than those that result from point mapping.

The Texture Bitmap

The texture is stored in a rectangular bitmap which can be in RGB or ramp color models. A texture bitmap in RGB format can be encoded in 8-, 24-, or 32-bit color. In the ramp model the texture color must be represented in 8 bits. Although texture bitmaps can be rectangular in shape, it is generally accepted that the renderer works better with square textures. In any case, a rectangular texture bitmap is scaled to a square shape at the time it is rendered. Textures are rendered more efficiently if the bitmap size is a power of 2, usually 32×32, 64×64, 128×128, 256×256, or 512×512 pixels. Here again, if the texture bitmap size is not a power of 2 it is scaled automatically to the nearest power of 2 size. For these reasons, in retained mode programming it is generally recommended that texture bitmaps are square and that their pixel size are a power of 2.

Creating a texture

Retained mode provides four ways of creating textures:

1. Create texture from a DirectDraw surface.
2. Create texture from a memory block.
3. Load texture from a bitmap file.
4. Load texture from a file in .xformat.

Most of the texture loading functions are in the IDirect3DRM3 interface, as listed in Table 22-1.

Table 22-1	
IDirect3DRM3 Texture-related Functions	
Function	**Description**
CreateTexture()	Creates a texture from a memory image.
CreateTextureFromSurface()	Creates a texture from a DirectDraw surface.
LoadTexture()	Loads a texture from a file. File must be in .bmp or .ppm format.
LoadTextureFromResource()	Loads a texture from a program resource.
SetDefaultTextureColors()	Sets the number of default colors to be used with a texture object.
SetDefaultTextureShades()	Sets the number of default shades to be used with a texture object.

In this section we discuss the texture-related functions that are auxiliary in nature, that is, the functions to create a texture from memory or from a DirectDraw surface and those to set the default texture colors and shades. The functions to load a texture from a bitmap, which are the most used, are discussed separately.

Texture from memory image

The `CreateTexture()` function of `IDirect3DRM3` is used to create a texture from an image resident in memory. The memory associated with the image is used each time the texture is rendered. This makes it possible to use the memory data both as a rendering target and as a texture. The function has the following general form:

```
HRESULT CreateTexture(
            LPD3DRMIMAGE lpImage,                      // 1
            LPDIRECT3DRMTEXTURE3 *lplpD3DRMTexture3    // 2
            );
```

The first parameter is the address of a structure describing the texture source. This structure, of type `D3DRMIMAGE`, is defined as follows:

```
typedef struct _D3DRMIMAGE {
    int                width, height;
    int                aspectx, aspecty;
    int                depth;
    int                rgb;
    int                bytes_per_line;
    void               *buffer1;
    void               *buffer2;
    unsigned long      red_mask;
    unsigned long      green_mask;
    unsigned long      blue_mask;
    unsigned long      alpha_mask;
    int                palette_size;
    D3DRMPALETTEENTRY  *palette;
}D3DRMIMAGE;
```

The members of the `D3DRMIMAGE` structure are described in Table 22-2.

Table 22-2 Members of D3DRMIMAGE	
Member	**Description**
`width` **and** `height`	Width and height of the image, in pixels.
`aspectx` **and** `aspecty`	Aspect ratio for nonsquare pixels.
`depth`	Number of bits per pixel.

Continued

	Table 22-2 *(continued)*	
Member	**Description**	
rgb	Flag that indicates whether pixels are RGB values or palette indices. If this member is FALSE, pixels are indices into a palette. Otherwise, pixels are RGB values.	
bytes_per_line	Number of bytes of memory for a scan line. This value must be a multiple of four.	
buffer1	Memory buffer to render into.	
buffer2	Buffer for double buffering. Set this member to NULL for single buffering.	
red_mask, green_mask, blue_mask, and alpha_mask	A mask for RGB pixels or pixel palette indices. If RGB is TRUE, these members are masks for the red, green, and blue parts of a pixel. Otherwise, they are masks for the significant bits of the red, green, and blue elements in the palette.	
palette_size	Number of entries in the palette.	
palette	Pointer to a D3DRMPALETTEENTRY structure describing the color palette to be used. Only if the D3DRMIMAGE RGB member is FALSE.	

If the call succeeds, the second parameter is the address of a pointer to an IDirect3DRMTexture3 interface. The function returns D3DRM_OK if it succeeds, or an error otherwise.

Texture from a DirectDraw surface

A DirectDraw surface can serve as the source for a retained mode surface. Retained mode documentation recommends that textures created from a DirectDraw surface are located in system memory. This optimizes performance and improves memory management. The CreateTextureFromSurface() function of IDirect3DRM3 serves to create the surface. The function has the following general form:

```
HRESULT CreateTextureFromSurface(
        LPDIRECTDRAWSURFACE lpDDS,                       // 1
        LPDIRECT3DRMTEXTURE3   *lplpD3DRMTexture3        // 2
        );
```

The first parameter is the address of the DirectDrawSurface object containing the texture. If the call succeeds, the second parameter is the address of the pointer to an IDirect3DRMTexture3 interface. The function returns D3DRM_OK if it succeeds, or an error otherwise.

Default texture parameters

Two functions of IDirect3DRM3 serve to set the default number of texture colors and shades respectively. The functions have similar general forms, as follows:

```
HRESULT SetDefaultTextureColors(
                          DWORD dwColors          // 1
                          );

HRESULT SetDefaultTextureShades(
                          DWORD dwShades          // 1
                          );
```

In both functions the only parameter is a double word value that defines in one case the number of default colors and in the other one the number of default texture shades. In either case the default parameters refer to textures that have not yet been created, and have no effect on existing textures. Both functions return D3DRM_OK if they succeed, or an error otherwise.

Retained mode texture programming

The IDirect3DRMTexture3 interface provides access to several texture-related functions. These are listed in Table 22-3.

Table 22-3	
Functions in IDirect3DRMTexture3	
Function	*Description*
Color	
GetColors()	Retrieves the number of colors used in rendering the texture
SetColors()	Sets the number of texture colors
Decals	
GetDecalOrigin()	Retrieves the origin of a decal
GetDecalScale()	Retrieves the scale of a decal
GetDecalSize()	Retrieves the size of a decal
GetDecalTransparency()	Retrieves the transparency attribute of a decal
GetDecalTransparentColor()	Retrieves the transparent color of a decal
SetDecalOrigin()	Sets the decal's offset from its top-left corner
SetDecalScale()	Sets the scaling property of a decal

Continued

Table 22-3 *(continued)*

Function	Description
SetDecalSize()	Sets the decal size if it is being scaled according to scene depth
SetDecalTransparency()	Sets the transparent property of a decal
SetDecalTransparentColor()	Sets the transparent color of a decal
Images	
GetImage()	Returns the address of the image used in creating a texture
Initialization	
InitFromFile()	Initializes a texture object from file data
InitFromImage()	Initializes a texture object from a memory image
InitFromResource2()	Initializes a texture object from a resource
InitFromSurface()	Initializes a texture object from a DirectDraw surface
Mipmaps	
GenerateMIPMap()	Creates a mipmap from a single image source
Shading	
GetShades()	Retrieves the number of shades used for each texture color
SetShades()	Sets the maximum number of shades for each texture color
Others	
GetCacheOptions()	Retrieves texture management information for the current texture
GetSurface()	Retrieves the DirectDraw surface used in creating a texture
SetCacheOptions()	Sets texture management parameters
SetDownsampleCallback()	Specifies a callback function to be used when texture is downsampled
SetValidationCallback()	Sets a callback function to be used to validate and update the primary texture source
Changed()	Notifies the renderer of the texture region that has changed

In the remainder of this chapter we discuss the most used of these functions. The ones related to decals and mipmaps are discussed in Chapter 23.

Wraps

In retained mode programming the notion of a wrap refers to how a texture is applied to a face or mesh. It is the wrap that determines how the texture conforms to the shape of the object. Four types of wraps are available in retained mode:

✦ Flat

✦ Cylindrical

✦ Spherical

✦ Chrome

In the flat wrap the texture behaves as if it were painted on a cloth that is wrapped over the object. The cylindrical wrap can be visualized as if the texture were located on a sheet of paper that is wrapped around a cylindrically shaped object. The spherical wrap is similar to the cylindrical wrap, except that in this case the wrapped object is spherical. A chrome wrap allocates texture coordinates so that the texture appears to be reflected onto the objects. The chrome wrap takes the reference frame position and uses the vertex normals in the mesh to calculate reflected vectors. These vectors are based on an imaginary sphere that surrounds the mesh. The resulting effect is the mesh reflecting whatever is wrapped on the sphere.

Texture wrapping is a complex task. Most retained mode applications apply materials and textures to objects as they are modeled in the art environment. 3D modeling programs, such as 3D Studio MAX and TrueSpace, have powerful texture functions, dozens of texture-related options, and include many texture bitmaps. In most cases the easiest way to visualize, create, and apply a texture is in the 3D modeling environment. Later in this chapter, we explore how to load textured objects into application code, either as meshes or as frames. Only on rare occasions will the applications programmer need to resort to manipulating wrapping modes directly. For this reason, our coverage of texture wraps is rather elementary. The article *Texture Wrapping Simplified* by Peter Donnelly that appears in Microsoft Developers Network documentation contains additional discussions of texture wraps. The article includes a demonstration program for experimenting with texture wrapping options. The program is included in the *Chapter 22/Texture Demo by Donnelly* directory in the book's CD-ROM.

Wrap arguments

The `CreateWrap()` function of `IDirect3DRM3` is used to create a wrapping function. The function has 16 parameters, which should be well understood. Its general form is as follows:

```
HRESULT CreateWrap(
           D3DRMWRAPTYPE type,              // 1
           LPDIRECT3DRMFRAME3 lpRef,        // 2
            D3DVALUE ox,                    // 3
            D3DVALUE oy,                    // 4
```

```
                D3DVALUE oz,                    // 5
                  D3DVALUE dx,                  // 6
                  D3DVALUE dy,                  // 7
                  D3DVALUE dz,                  // 8
                    D3DVALUE ux,                // 9
                    D3DVALUE uy,                // 10
                    D3DVALUE uz,                // 11
              D3DVALUE ou,                      // 12
              D3DVALUE ov,                      // 13
                D3DVALUE su,                    // 14
                D3DVALUE sv,                    // 15
              LPDIRECT3DRMWRAP *lplpD3DRMWrap   // 16
              );
```

The first parameter is one of the members of the D3DRMWRAPTYPE enumeration, which is defined as follows:

```
    typedef enum _D3DRMWRAPTYPE{
        D3DRMWRAP_FLAT,            // flat wrap
        D3DRMWRAP_CYLINDER,       // cylindrical wrap
        D3DRMWRAP_SPHERE,         // spherical wrap
        D3DRMWRAP_CHROME          // chrome wrap
    } D3DRMWRAPTYPE;
```

The four wrap types are discussed in detail later in this section. The second parameter is the reference frame for the wrap. If the call succeeds, the sixteenth parameter is the address of a pointer to an IDirect3DRMWrap interface. This interface contains three functions: Init(), Apply(), and ApplyRelative(). Init() uses a similar parameter list to CreateWrap() and is used to initialize a Direct3DRMWrap object. The Apply() function applies the wrap to a face or mesh. ApplyRelative() uses world transformation of the frame containing the wrap on the object vertices.

The remaining parameters (3 to 15), sometimes called the *wrap arguments*, determine how the texture is mapped to the object's surface. Figure 22-1 shows a texture seam that appears on the center of the object's surface and how this situation is corrected by remapping the texture bitmap to the object.

Parameters 3, 4, and 5 of the CreateWrap() function define the origin of the wrap. These arguments determine the location of the wrap's seam on the object. The default value is [0,0,0]. In the case of a rectangular object, the default position places the origin for the wrap at the center of the object. The resulting wrap is as shown in the top part of Figure 22-1. You can make the texture origin coincide with the edge of the object by resetting the x and y coordinates of the bitmap, represented by the ox and oy parameters in the general form of the CreateWrap() function listed previously. If you assume that w represents the width of the rectangular object and h its height, then, to set the origin of the bitmap to the bottom-left corner of the object you have to set the ox parameter to -0.5w and the oy parameter to -0.5h. Figure 22-2 shows recalculating the ox and oy parameters in the case of a square object that is exactly twice the size of a texture bitmap.

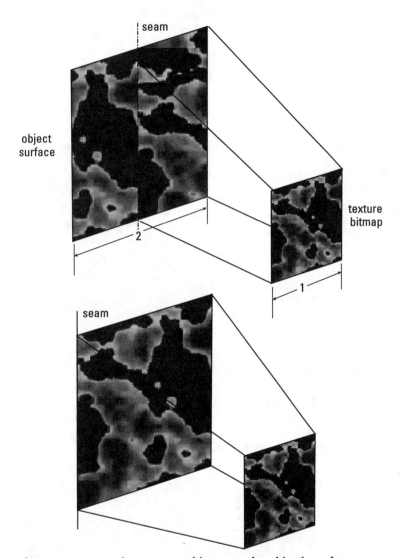

Figure 22-1: Mapping a texture bitmap to the object's surface

Parameters 6, 7, and 8 of the `CreateWrap()` function are called the *direction vectors*.
These parameters determine the *z*-axis of the wrap. Parameters 9, 10, and 11 are
called the *up vectors*. The action of the direction and the up vectors is to define a
coordinate system for the wrap, sometimes called the *wrap space*. The direction
vector defines the *z*-axis in the wrap space, and the up vector defines its *y*-axis.
The *x*-axis is always at right angles to both *y* and *z*, so usually it can be ignored.

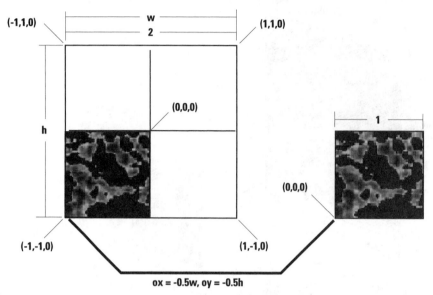

Figure 22-2: Resetting the wrap origin parameters

Parameters 12 and 13 define the texture origin, represented by the variables ou and ov in the function's general form. The values of these parameters determine which part of the texture coincides with the wrap origin. Normally they are set to zero. One possible use for these parameter is to extract portions of a large texture. For example, a 256×256 pixel texture may contain four individual images of 128×128 pixels. By setting the appropriate values for the ou and ov parameters, as well as the scaling parameters described in the next paragraph, only a portion of the texture is used in the wrap.

The orientation of the texture within the wrap depends on the sign of the scaling factors and on the bitmap format. When sv is positive, CreateWrap() places the bitmap's first scan line at the bottom of the wrap. This is satisfactory for bitmaps in .bmp format. However, .ppm bitmaps are inverted. In the case of .ppm bitmaps, you must set a negative value for sv to orient the top of the texture to the top of the wrap.

Parameters 14 and 15 define the texture scale, represented by the variables su and sv in the general form. These parameters determine how the texture is scaled to the object. In the calculations a square texture is considered to have dimensions of 1×1. In the case of a flat wrap su is the scale of the width of the texture to the width of the object, whereas sv is the scale of the height of the texture to the height of the object. For a cylindrical wrap, a value of 1 for su ensures that the texture wraps exactly once around the object so that the longitudinal edges will meet. In this case sv is used to scale the texture so that it covers the object from top to bottom. If the height of the object is represented by the variable h, then sv can be set to $1/h$. In the case of a spherical wrap su and sv are both set to 1 in order to stretch the texture to just cover the object.

Texture wrapping flags

Retained mode applications can create mesh groups that share common properties; among them are colors, materials, and textures. The functions for creating and manipulating mesh groups are located in the IDirect3DRMMesh interface and were discussed in Chapter 21. One of the shared characteristics of mesh groups determine how a texture is mapped to a surface. This is determined by a texture mapping flag that is set by the SetGroupMapping() function and retrieved by GetGroupMapping().

The texture mapping flags are defined in the D3DRMMAPPING type, as follows:

```
typedef DWORD D3DRMMAPPING, D3DRMMAPPINGFLAG;
   static const D3DRMMAPPINGFLAG D3DRMMAP_WRAPU       = 1;
   static const D3DRMMAPPINGFLAG D3DRMMAP_WRAPV       = 2;
   static const D3DRMMAPPINGFLAG D3DRMMAP_PERSPCORRECT = 4;
```

The wrapping flags determine how the rasterizer interprets texture coordinates. In flat wrapping mode no wrapping flag is set. In this case the plane specified by the u- and v-coordinates is an infinite tiling of the texture. Values greater than 1.0 are valid for both u and v. If neither D3DRMMAP_WRAPU or D3DRMMAP_WRAPV is set, the texture is a cylinder with an infinite length and a circumference of 1.0. Texture coordinates greater than 1.0 are valid only in the dimension that is not wrapped. If both D3DRMMAP_WRAPU and D3DRMMAP_WRAPV are set, the texture is a torus. In this case texture coordinates greater than 1.0 are invalid.

Applications usually set a wrap flag for cylindrical wraps when the intersection of the texture edges does not match the edges of the face. On the other hand, there is no need to set a wrap flag if more than half of a texture is applied to a single face. The D3DRMMAP_PERSPCORRECT flag ensures that the texture wrapping is corrected for perspective.

Flat wrap

The conventional description for a flat wrap is to say that it conforms to the faces of an object as if the texture were a piece of rubber stretched over the object. Peter Donnelly points out in the article, mentioned earlier in the chapter, that this description is inherently flawed. He proposes, instead, that we visualize the flat wrap as the projection of the texture image onto a flat, translucent plane, in which case the projector can be placed in any position relative to this plane.

In the case of a flat wrap the $[u,v]$ coordinates are derived from a vector $[x,y,z]$ by the following equations:

$u = sux - ou$

$v = svy - ov$

In the preceding formulas, s is the window-scaling factor and o is the window origin. Code should select the scaling factors and offsets so that the ranges of x and y are mapped to the range 0 to 1 for u and v.

Cylindrical wrap

In the cylindrical wrap the texture behaves as if it were a piece of paper wrapped around a cylindrical-shaped object that is placed so that its left and right edges are joined. The object is placed in the center of the cylinder and the texture is deformed inward onto its surface. Figure 22-3 shows the parameters used in cylindrical wrapping.

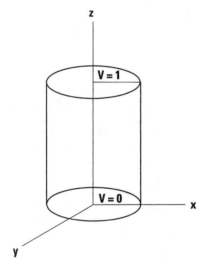

Figure 22-3: Cylindrical wrapping parameters

In cylindrical wrapping the direction vector specifies the axis of the cylinder, and the up vector the point on the outside of the cylinder where u equals 0. The following equations are used to calculate the texture coordinates $[u,v]$ for a vector $[x,y,z]$:

$$u = \frac{s_u}{2\pi}\tan^{-1}\frac{x}{y} - o_y$$
$$v = s_v z - o_v$$

The value u is typically not scaled, whereas v is scaled and translated so that the range of z maps to the range from 0 to 1 for v. Figure 22-4 shows the result of a cylindrical wrap.

Figure 22-4: Cylindrical wraps

Spherical wrap

The spherical wrap is similar to the cylindrical wraps, but in this case the wrapped form is a sphere, instead of a cylinder.

As in the cylindrical wrap, the u-coordinate is derived from the angle that the vector $[x,y,0]$ makes with the x-axis, whereas the v-coordinate is derived from the angle that the vector $[x,y,z]$ makes with the z-axis. Consequently, spherical mapping causes distortion of the texture at the z-axis. Figure 22-5 shows the location of the u and v parameters in spherical wrapping.

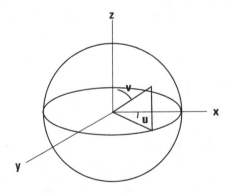

Figure 22-5: Spherical wrapping parameters

In the case of spherical wrapping, the $[u,v]$ coordinates are derived from a vector $[x,y,z]$ by using means of the following formulas:

$$u = \frac{s_u}{2\pi} \tan^{-1} \frac{x}{y} - o_u$$

$$v = \frac{s_v}{\pi} \tan^{-1} \frac{z}{\sqrt{x^2 + y^2 + z^2}} - o_v$$

Scaling factors and texture origin are often not needed in spherical wrapping because the unscaled range of u and v is already 0 through 1.

Chrome wrap

A chrome wrap makes the texture appear to be reflected onto the objects. The system uses the reference frame position and the vertex normals in the mesh to calculate the reflected vectors, which are based on an imaginary sphere that surrounds the mesh. The resulting effect is the mesh reflecting whatever is wrapped on this imaginary sphere.

The basic notion of the chrome wrap is that the texture is attached to the scene, not to the object itself. For example, if a conventional wrap is applied to a sphere, the wrap pattern rotates as the sphere rotates. However, if the same texture is applied to the sphere using a chrome wrap, then the texture does not rotate with the sphere, which produces the illusion of the texture being reflected by the object's surface. This implies, first, that chrome wraps are most effective in animated renderings. Second, this implies that the texture applied as a chrome wrap must be either part of the scene background, or part of another object, for the reflection to appear natural.

Implementing chrome wraps is computationally expensive because the wrap must be reapplied every time the object moves. This is because the orientation of the texture map is related to the scene, not to the object. The usual approach is to create a move callback function on the frame that contains the wrapped object. In this manner the application is notified of every movement of the object, at which time the wrap can be reapplied.

Materials in Retained Mode

A material property of a mesh, face, or frame determines how its surface reflects light. A material is not a texture but textures are effectively enhanced by selecting an adequate material to serve as its base. On the other hand, a miss-match between the material and the texture can produce disturbing and unnatural effects. For these reasons texture design usually starts with a material selection. Furthermore, many objects can be very effectively rendered by manipulating mesh color and materials alone. Textures are computationally expensive and should be used only when they play a crucial role in enhancing the image.

In retained mode the material component has an emissive property and a specular property. The first one determines whether the material emits light on its own. This is useful in modeling lamps, neon signs, or other self-luminous objects. Also, the emissive property is useful in producing unusual effects, such as ghostly or radioactive objects. The specular property determines if the material reflects light and, if so, how it reflects it. You can control the emissive property of a material by defining the red, green, and blue color values. The specular property is also defined by the red, green, and blue values of the reflected light and by a power setting. The default specular color is white. The power setting determines the size, and consequently the sharpness, of the reflected highlights. A small highlight makes an object appear shiny or metallic. A large highlight gives a plastic appearance.

Materials programming

The retained mode IDirect3DRMMaterial2 interface contains functions to interact with material objects. Table 22-4 lists the functions in IDirect3DRMMaterial2.

Table 22-4	
Functions in IDirect3DRMMaterial2	
Function	*Action*
Ambient controls	
GetAmbient()	Retrieve RGB ambient color value
SetAmbient()	Set RGB ambient color value
Emission controls	
GetEmissive()	Retrieve RGB intensity of emissive property
SetEmissive()	Set RGB intensity of emissive property
Power controls	
GetPower()	Retrieve power setting
SetPower()	Set power used in specular component
Specular controls	
GetSpecular()	Retrieve the RGB intensity of the specular component
SetSpecular()	Set RGB color value of specular highlights

DirectX version 6.0 introduced the GetAmbient() and SetAmbient() functions that allow a finer control over material properties. In previous versions of the interface the ambient color of a material was always equal to the face color and could not be modified. In IDirect3DRMMaterial2 an object uses the face color as the ambient color by default, but this value can be changed by calling the SetAmbient() function.

In addition to the functions in IDirect3DRMMaterial2, applications need to use other material-related functions to create and apply a material. Materials can be applied to a mesh, to a meshbuilder, to a face, or to a frame. To apply a material to a mesh object you must first create a group and then use the SetGroupMaterial() function of the IDirect3DRMMesh interface. To apply a material to a meshbuilder object you use the `SetMaterial()` function of `IDirect3DRMMeshBuilder3`. A material is applied to a face by means of the `SetMaterial()` function of `IDirect 3DRMFace2`. Finally, a material can be applied to a frame, thus overriding any material settings at the face, mesh, or meshbuilder levels. In this case you use the `SetMaterialMode()` function of `IDirect3DRMFrame3`.

Creating and applying a material

In applications programming materials are most often associated with meshes through the meshbuilder objects. Although occasionally, you may need to apply individual materials to the various faces of a mesh. Applying a material to a mesh is usually a two-step process: first you must create and specify the material, then the material must be set on the mesh.

To create a material you use the `CreateMaterial()` function of `IDirect3DRM3`. This function also defines the specular property of the material. Its general form is as follows:

```
HRESULT CreateMaterial(
        D3DVALUE vPower,                            // 1
        LPDIRECT3DRMMATERIAL2 *lplpD3DRMMaterial   // 2
        );
```

This first parameter defines the sharpness of the reflected highlights. A high value produces a metallic look and a lower one a more plastic appearance. This value can be changed in a material by means of the `SetPower()` function of `IDirect3DRMMaterial2`. The second parameter is filled with the address of a pointer to `IDirect3DRMMaterial2` interface if the call succeeds. This pointer can be used to access the functions listed in Table 22-4. The call returns `D3DRM_OK` if it succeeds, or an error otherwise.

The following function receives as parameters a meshbuilder object. It then creates a material according to the caller's specifications and applies it to the mesh. The function is part of the 3DRM Textures Demo program in the book's CD-ROM.

```
//*******************************************************
// name: MatToMesh()
// desc: Creates a material according to the caller's
//       parameters and applies it to the mesh
// Note: the function accumulates errors in a local
//       variable, which is inspected before the
//       function returns.
//*******************************************************
BOOL MatToMesh(LPDIRECT3DRMMESHBUILDER3 aMeshBuilder,
                   float meshRed,    // mesh/material color
                   float meshGreen,
                   float meshBlue,
                   float meshAlpha,
                   float ambientRed, // ambient color
                                     // values
                   float ambientGreen,
```

```
                              float ambientBlue,
                              float specRed,     // Specular
                              float specGreen,
                              float specBlue,
                              float emisRed,     // Emissive
                              float emisGreen,
                              float emisBlue,
                              float matPower)    // Power value
{

// Local variables
static HRESULT          rtnError = 0;
LPDIRECT3DRMMATERIAL2   aMaterial = NULL;

// Create material
// (power is set later)
retval = lpD3DRM->CreateMaterial(D3DVAL(0.0),
                                 &aMaterial);
rtnError = rtnError + retval;

// Set specular color and intensity
retval = aMaterial->SetSpecular(
                              D3DVAL(specRed),
                              D3DVAL(specGreen),
                              D3DVAL(specBlue));
rtnError = rtnError + retval;

// Set power
retval = aMaterial->SetPower(D3DVALUE(matPower));
rtnError = rtnError + retval;

// Set emissive property
retval = aMaterial->SetEmissive(
                              D3DVAL(emisRed),
                              D3DVAL(emisGreen),
                              D3DVAL(emisBlue));
rtnError = rtnError + retval;

retval = aMaterial->SetAmbient(
                              D3DVAL(ambientRed),
                              D3DVAL(ambientGreen),
                              D3DVAL(ambientBlue));
rtnError = rtnError + retval;

// Set the material on the mesh
retval = aMeshBuilder->SetMaterial(aMaterial);
rtnError = rtnError + retval;

// Set the mesh color according to caller's specs
retval = aMeshBuilder->SetColor(
                              RGBA_MAKE(int(255 * meshRed),
                              int(255 * meshGreen),
                              int(255 * meshBlue),
                              int(255 * meshAlpha)));
```

```
rtnError = rtnError + retval;

RELEASE(aMaterial);

if(rtnError)
   return FALSE;
else
   return TRUE;
}
```

Notice that, to simplify the coding, the function accumulates errors in a local variable which is inspected before it returns. Also notice that the material object is created and released locally.

Obtaining materials specifications

It is often difficult to empirically determine the specular, emissive, and ambient color of a specific material and its specular power. Experimenting in code with different settings for all four elements can be a fruitless task. A more reasonable approach is to use a 3D modeling program to simulate a desired material. Most 3D modeling applications include extensive libraries of materials from which the user can select. The material can then be applied to an object that is similar to the one in the application and the results rendered on the screen. When the desired material effect is achieved, the model can be saved to a file in X format, or to one that can later be converted into X format. In either case the resulting X file must be in text form. The material is stored in the file following the Material template specifications (see Appendix C). For example, a metallic surface appears as follows in the X file listing:

```
Material x3ds_mat_Metal {
  0.717647, 0.647059, 0.309804, 1.000000;;  // color
  30.000000;                                 // specular power
  1.000000, 1.000000, 1.000000;;            // specular color
  0.00, 0.00, 0.00;;                        // emissive color
```

The four values in the first row correspond to the material color, in RGBA format. These values can be used in coloring the mesh that contains the material and also in determining the ambient color for the material itself. The value in the second row is the specular power. The third row encodes the specular color and the fourth one the emissive color. These values can be used in the corresponding calls to SetAmbient(), SetEmissive(), SetSpecular(), and SetPower(). For example, the following code fragment shows a call to the MatToMesh() function previously listed to create a metallic material.

```
// Routine variables
BOOL             success;
LPDIRECT3DRMMESHBUILDER3 sphereMeshBuilder     = NULL;
. . .
```

```
    // Create gold material and attach to mesh
    success = MatToMesh(sphereMeshBuilder,
                        0.717647f,      // Mesh/ambient color red
                        0.647059f,      // green
                        0.309804f,      // blue
                        1.000000f,      // alpha
                        0.5f,           // ambient red
                        0.2f,           // green
                        0.2f,           // blue
                        1.0f,           // Specular red
                        1.0f,           // green
                        1.0f,           // blue
                        0.0f,           // Emissive red
                        0.0f,           // green
                        0.0f,           // blue
                        30.0f);         // Power
    if(!success)
        // Material creation error handler goes here
```

Color plate number 11 shows a metallic and a plastic material as they are rendered by the 3DRM Textures Demo program in the book's CD-ROM.

Applying Textures to Meshes

Retained mode applications can apply textures to mesh objects by performing a series of texture-related operations that originate in the `IDirect3DRM3`, `IDirect 3DRMTexture3`, and `IDirect3DRMMeshBuilder3` interfaces. In the following discussions we assume that a compatible texture file is located in the program's path. In many cases the safest location for the texture file is the same directory in which the application resides. At its simplest, the process of applying a texture to a mesh object in an already existing scene consists of the following steps:

1. The rendering quality is set using a light, fill, and shade mode that ensure adequate rendering of the texture.

2. A suitable wrap is created for applying the texture to the object.

3. The texture bitmap is loaded into the application.

4. The texture is associated with the object to which it is applied.

In some cases the above process can be one of the most complex in retained mode programming. On the other hand, when the texturing is not subject to many technical requirements, it can be applied in a straightforward manner with considerable improvement of the visual quality. It is this simpler case that we describe in the present section. Later in this chapter, we explore the use of 3D modeling software in creating and applying more complex textures.

Preliminary operations

An object of type LPDIRECT3DRMTEXTURE3 cannot be directly rendered by retained mode. To make the texture visible it must first be applied to a face, a mesh, a meshbuilder, or a frame. At higher levels of processing the meshbuilder approach is a reasonable one. In the example that follows we assume that a meshbuilder object has been previously created and that a spherically shaped mesh has been loaded, typically from a file in X format. Also, that a child frame is available in the scene.

Several preparatory operations are usually required before a texture can be applied to the mesh. These are as follows:

1. Create a material and set its properties.

2. Set the material on the mesh.

3. Set the quality for the meshbuilder.

4. Create a suitable wrap.

5. Apply the wrap to the meshbuilder object.

Much of the programming related to these preparatory operations was discussed previously in this chapter in the context of materials and wraps. In this case the coding can proceed as follows:

```
// General data for routine
HRESULT  retval;
LPDIRECT3DRMMATERIAL2 sphereMaterial            = NULL;
LPDIRECT3DRMMESHBUILDER3 sphereMeshBuilder      = NULL;
LPDIRECT3DRMWRAP aWrap                          = NULL;
// Variables for wrap and texture processing
D3DRMBOX        bBox;               // Bounding box
D3DVALUE        minY, maxY;         // y coordinates min and max
D3DVALUE        bHeight;            // Height
. . .
// Step 1:
//        Create a material and define its properties
    retval = lpD3DRM->CreateMaterial(D3DVAL(15.0),

&sphereMaterial);
    if(FAILED(retval))
    {
        // Material creation error handler goes here
    }
// Set ambient property color and intensity
    retval = sphereMaterial->SetAmbient(
                                    D3DVALUE(2.0),  // red
                                    D3DVALUE(2.0),  // green
                                    D3DVALUE(2.0)); // blue
    if(FAILED(retval))
```

```
    {
        // Ambient property error handler goes here
    }

// Step 2:
//          Set the material on the mesh
    retval = sphereMeshBuilder->SetMaterial(sphereMaterial);
    if(FAILED(retval))
    {
        // Material setting error handler goes here
    }
// Step 3:
//          Set quality for meshbuilder
// Use highest quality
    retval = sphereMeshBuilder->SetQuality(D3DRMRENDER_GOURAUD);
    if(FAILED(retval))
    {
        // Quality setting error handler goes here
    }
// Step 4:
//          Create a cylindrical wrap for the spherical mesh
// First obtain bounding box for sphere
    retval = sphereMeshBuilder->GetBox(&bBox);
    if(FAILED(retval))
    {
        // Bounding box error handler goes here
    }
// ASSERT:
//          D3DVECTOR types bBox.min and bBox.max now hold the
//          bounding box dimensions
// Store values in local variables
    maxY = bBox.max.y;
    minY = bBox.min.y;
    bHeight = maxY - minY;
// Using the bounding box data, create a cylindrical wrap
    retval = lpD3DRM->CreateWrap(
                    D3DRMWRAP_CYLINDR,     // Wrap type
                    NULL,                  // NULL reference
                    D3DVAL(0.0),           // x of Origin
                    D3DVAL(0.0),           // y
                    D3DVAL(0.0),           // z
                    D3DVAL(0.0),           // x of z-axis
                    D3DVAL(1.0),           // y
                    D3DVAL(0.0),           // z
                    D3DVAL(0.0),           // x of y-axis
                    D3DVAL(0.0),           // y
                    D3DVAL(1.0),           // z
                    D3DVAL(0.0),           // Texture origin
                    D3DDivide(minY, bHeight),
                    D3DVAL(1.0),           // Scale factor
                    D3DDivide(D3DVAL(1.0), bHeight),
                    &aWrap);               // Address of wrap
    if (FAILED(retval))
```

```
        {
             // Wrap creation error handler goes here
        }
    // Step 5:
    //        Apply wrap to meshbuilder
        retval = aWrap->Apply((LPDIRECT3DRMOBJECT)
    sphereMeshBuilder);
        if (FAILED(retval))
        {
             // Wrap application error handler goes here
        }
```

At this point you are ready to proceed with loading and applying the texture.

Loading the texture

A texture is a 2D bitmap. The source of a texture can be any image that is in a
compatible format (.bmp or .ppm) or that can be converted into these formats.
Scanned pictures, texture libraries from drawing and modeling programs, and
clip art provide easy access to many useful textures. In addition, applications often
create their own art for textures, usually by means of drawing or bitmap editing.
Whatever the origin, the retained mode texture file is a square bitmap whose
pixel size is a power of 2. Because the .ppm format exists mostly for compatibility
reasons, in the following examples we assume that texture files are in .bmp format.

The LoadTexture() function of IDirect3DRM3 provides a way for loading a
texture from a file. The call assumes that the texture file is in either .bmp of .ppm
formats and that it has a color depth of 8, 24, or 32 bits-per-pixel. The function's
general form is as follows:

```
HRESULT LoadTexture(
             const char  *lpFileName,                 // 1
             LPDIRECT3DRMTEXTURE3 *lplpD3DRMTexture   // 2
                 );
```

The first parameter is a pointer to the filename of the texture file. The filename can
be entered directly in the call by enclosing it in double quotation marks. If the call
succeeds, the second parameter is the address of a pointer that is initialized with
an object of IDirect3DRMTexture3 interface. This object provides access to all
the functions listed in Table 22-3. The function returns D3DRM_OK if it succeeds,
or an error otherwise.

The following code fragment shows loading a texture contained in a file named
limestn3.bmp and applying the texture to a mesh.

```
    // General data for routine
    LPDIRECT3DRMTEXTURE3 aTex                    = NULL;
    LPDIRECT3DRMFRAME3 childframe                = NULL;
    . . .
```

```
    // Load texture and set texture to mesh
    retval = lpD3DRM->LoadTexture("limestn3.bmp", &aTex);
    if (FAILED(retval))
    {
        // Load failure error handler goes here
    }
// Change the number of shades from default (16) to 32
    retval = aTex->SetShades(32);
    if (FAILED(retval))
    {
        // Texture shades change error handler goes here
    }
// Apply texture to meshbuilder object
    retval = sphereMeshBuilder->SetTexture(aTex);
    if (FAILED(retval))
    {
        // Set texture error handler goes here
    }

// Texture is made visible by adding the meshbuilder as a
// a visual to the child frame
    retval = childframe->AddVisual(
                (LPDIRECT3DRMVISUAL)sphereMeshBuilder);
    if (FAILED(retval))
    {
        // Adding visual error handler goes here
    }
```

If all has gone well, the application can now proceed to render the scene in the normal manner.

Textures from X Files

Retained mode provides an alternative approach to textures that does not require creating meshes, calculating wraps, and manipulating rendering properties. This option consists of the following steps:

1. The desired object and its texture are created in a modeling program.

2. The textured object is saved as an X format file, or converted into X format using the Conv3ds utility discussed in the previous chapter. The texture file itself, and the texture file reference in the X file, may require editing.

3. In the application, an object of type IDirect3DRMFrame3 is created and the Load() function of IDirect3DRMFrame3 is used to load the textured object, from the X file, into one or more frames. The material mode is set to D3DRMMATERIAL_FROMFRAME and the textured objects are rendered.

In many cases this easy approach to textures is a viable option.

Creating a textured object

The mechanics of applying textures to objects vary with different modeling programs. In most cases there are one or more texture-related services that enable you to load texture libraries, visualize them on objects of different shapes and colors, and apply the texture to one or more preexisting objects. The more powerful modeling applications, such as 3D Studio MAX and TrueSpace, contain several useful texture creation and editing facilities.

Although creating textures in a modeling program is often easy and convenient, there are many caveats regarding their use in application code. One of them is that the rendering engines in the modeling programs are sometimes more powerful and sophisticated than the one available in retained mode. This determines that a texture may not appear the same in the application as it did in the modeler. For example, a rendering program may have ray tracing or Phong rendering capabilities, whereas in retained mode programming you have to be content with Gouraud shading. Another source of possible differences between the modeled and the imported textures relates to lighting.

When creating a texture in the modeling program it is also important to make sure that the number, type, intensity, position, and color of the lights are the same as those used by the application. Small variations in lighting conditions often make textures appear quite different. In addition, you must be aware that the notions of textures and materials are often considered equivalent in the modeler. In this sense, a metallic surface luster may be labeled as a texture in the modeling program, whereas to the application this effect is achieved by means of a material.

Making a DirectX-compatible texture

One of the issues related to the use of software-created textures in retained mode applications is the texture file itself. Modeling programs are often capable of manipulating texture files in formats, sizes, and color ranges that are not compatible with retained mode. For example, 3D Studio MAX uses rectangular texture files in JPG format. DirectX texture files, on the other hand, must be in .bmp or .ppm formats; they must be square shaped; their size must be a power of 2; and the color range must be 8-, 24-, or 32-bits. This means that you must often convert the texture file from the format used by the modeling program into one that is compatible with DirectX retained mode.

The texture file format conversion is usually best performed by means of a bitmap editing application, such as Picture Publisher or Corel Photo Paint. To make the format conversion, you usually start by loading the original texture into the bitmap editor. If the texture is not square you must now crop it or stretch it as necessary. This is also a good time in which to edit the bitmap to improve it or make it more suitable for the purpose at hand. When edited, the bitmap is saved in a format, proportion, size, and color depth that is compatible with DirectX.

If the texture file used by the modeling program is in one of the formats supported by DirectX (.bmp or .ppm) the references in the X file will work correctly in retained mode code. However, it is more often the case that the modeling program uses file formats different from .bmp or .ppm. This means that you must manually edit the file reference before loading it into our application. For example, the following is a material template from a textured image created with 3D Studio MAX and then converted to X format using the Conv3ds utility.

```
Material x3ds_mat_Granite_Pink_Gra {
 0.854902, 0.552941, 0.533333, 1.000000;;
 29.000000;
 0.968627, 0.905882, 0.901961;;
 0.00, 0.00, 0.00;;
 TextureFilename {
  "GRANITPK.JPG";
 }
```

In this case the texture file, named GRANITPK.JPG, is one of the files that are found in 3D Studio MAX texture library. After you have edited the image in this file so that it conforms with DirectX requirements, and saved it in .bmp or .ppm format, you must then edit the material template to reflect this change. If the JPG file was changed to .bmp format, then the text reference will have to be edited as follows:

```
Material x3ds_mat_Granite_Pink_Gra {
 0.854902, 0.552941, 0.533333, 1.000000;;
 29.000000;
 0.968627, 0.905882, 0.901961;;
 0.00, 0.00, 0.00;;
 TextureFilename {
  "GRANITPK.BMP";
 }
```

Loading the textured frame

The process of loading the textured object into application code is identical to that used for loading into a frame, which was described in Chapter 21. The X file must contain a single, top-level frame or a frame hierarchy. This means that, if the file was converted from 3ds to X format by means of Conv3ds, it must have used the default option or the -T switch. The following code fragment shows the process of loading a textured object into a frame.

```
// Data for routine
struct _globVars
{
. . .
    LPDIRECT3DRMFRAME3 aScene;              // Master frame
. . .
} globVars;

LPDIRECT3DRMFRAME3 texturedFrame = NULL;
char               szXfile[] = "texcube.x" ;   // X format file
HRESULT            retval;
. . .
```

```
// Create the frame
retval = lpD3DRM->CreateFrame(globVars.aScene,
                              &texturedFrame);
if(FAILED(retval))
{
    // Frame creation error handler goes here
}
// Load image into frame
retval = texturedFrame->Load(szXfile,              // Source
                             NULL,
                             D3DRMLOAD_FROMFILE, // Options
                             NULL, NULL);
if(FAILED(retval))
{
    // Frame load error handler goes here
}
// Set material mode to frame
retval = globVars.aScene->SetMaterialMode(
                        D3DRMMATERIAL_FROMFRAME);
if(FAILED(retval))
{
    // Material mode creation error handler goes here
}
```

The project 3DRM Textures Demo in the book's CD-ROM contains examples of texture manipulations and display.

Summary

Here we have explored the fundamentals of using materials and textures in retained mode programming. We have seen how textures can be loaded into application code from memory, from DirectDraw surfaces, and from bitmaps. Several types of wraps are used to determine how the texture is applied to the object. One special wrap, called a chrome wrap, is used in implementing reflective textures.

Materials are fundamental to effective modeling because the material determines how the surface of the object reflects light. A well-selected material enhances the texture on which it is applied. In fact, many objects can be attractively rendered with a simple material. We also saw how textures are applied to meshes and frames and how textures created in a modeling program can be loaded into a retained mode application.

But we are not finished with textures and materials. In the following chapter we look at some special effects that relate to texture programming, such as decals, mipmaps, and transparency.

✦   ✦   ✦

Decals and Mipmaps

In this chapter we turn our attention to decals and mipmaps. These are two texture-related topics that, because of their specialized nature, were not covered in Chapter 22. Decals provide a useful mechanism for rendering a texture without having to attach it to a mesh or frame. Although they are a 2D object, you can use decals to solve many complex modeling problems in 3D programming. Mipmaps are a series of attached surfaces, of progressively lower resolution, which provide a computationally efficient way of simulating perspective effects for textures.

Decals in Retained Mode

In retained mode programming a decal is a texture rendered directly as a visual. That is, the texture bitmap is not wrapped to an object but displayed as a viewport-aligned rectangle. The IDirect3DRMTexture3 functions listed in Table 23-1 enable you to manipulate decals.

Decals and Pseudo 3D

Because the z-axis of the decal must be parallel to the z-axis of the viewport, the decal appears as a rectangular image floating in the scene. This limitation may lead us to think that decals are just postage-stamp-like objects that are used to decorate the scene. This would mean that the use of decals is limited to simulating pictures, windows, and other rectangular objects. In reality decals provide a powerful modeling tool. The fact that decals can be scaled and made transparent makes possible their use in creating sprites.

Table 23-1
Decal-related Functions in IDirect3DRMTexture3

Function	Description
GetDecalOrigin()	Retrieves the origin of a decal
GetDecalScale()	Retrieves the scale of a decal
GetDecalSize()	Retrieves the size of a decal
GetDecalTransparency()	Retrieves the transparency attribute of a decal
GetDecalTransparentColor()	Retrieves the transparent color of a decal
SetDecalOrigin()	Sets the decal's offset from its top-left corner
SetDecalScale()	Sets the scaling property of a decal
SetDecalSize()	Sets the decal size if it is being scaled according to scene depth
SetDecalTransparency()	Sets the transparent property of a decal
SetDecalTransparentColor()	Sets the transparent color of a decal

In Chapter 12, we discussed sprite animation techniques and developed software that uses animated sprites. The sample program DD Animation Demo, in the book's CD-ROM, uses a sprite image set to simulate the rotation of two gears. Figure 12-4 shows the fundamentals of this technique. In 3D graphics objects are modeled as solid, which can be scaled, rotated, translated, and even sheared. Therefore, a sprite for a 3D application can be modeled as a solid object and animated by applying the transformations that we have discussed in previous chapters. Quality-wise this is a much more effective solution than using an image set to implement animation or simulate 3D.

The main drawback to using 3D sprites is not a technical one, but a practical one. Animating 3D objects is computationally expensive. An application that requires several 3D sprites may find its performance degraded to a point in which its basic functionality is impaired. For this reason computer game designers and programmers often rely on simulating 3D by using a sequence of 2D images, usually in an image strip as the one shown in Figure 12-4. This technique is sometimes called pseudo 3D.

For example, consider a 3D simulation of air combat in which a fighter aircraft attacks a bomber from the rear. If the application simulates the view from the tail gunner turret, then the attacking fighter will appear to become large, and perhaps slightly change its pitch as it approaches the bomber. One way to depict this scene would be to use a 3D model of the fighter aircraft and manipulate the scale and rotation during the animation sequence. However, this technique is time-consuming and somewhat wasteful because the model of the fighter is always rendered from the same viewing angle. An alternative approach is to use a progressive sequence of 2D images of the fighter which are positioned in the viewport during the animation (see Figure 3-17). The result may not be as visually accurate as using a 3D model, but rendering the animation would consume less time.

Decals provide an alternative way of implementing pseudo 3D sprites. The decal-related functions listed in Table 23-1 allow scaling, resizing, positioning, and other–wise manipulating the sprite imagery in ways that are sometimes more convenient than the DirectDraw methods described in Chapter 12.

Decals in complex modeling

Some graphics effects are very difficult to model in 3D. For example, a game program may render a spaceship using a 3D model. But when the spaceship is impacted by an asteroid, the resulting explosion and disintegration would be very difficult to depict by manipulating the faces and meshes of the 3D object. In this case the application may use a 2D image set, rendered as decals, to represent the destruction of the spaceship. Many such cases arise in the design of an interactive 3D application and decals often offer a satisfactory, if not ideal, solution.

Decal Programming

From the previous discussion you may have gathered that decal programming can go from very simple to very complex. In one case an application may use a decal to decorate a scene by means of one or more square pictures. In the other case decals may serve to render sprites and other animated objects, often through callback functions, strip imagery, and using scaling and transparency effects.

Creating a decal

In creating a decal the first step is to load the decal bitmap into an object of type DIRECT3DRMTEXTURE3. This can be accomplished in any of the ways in which a texture can be loaded, described in Chapter 22. One approach already discussed is to load the texture from a bitmap file using the LoadTexture() function of IDirect 3DRM3. The result of this call is an object of type IDirect3DRMTexture3 which can be used to access the functions in the corresponding interface. At this point there is no difference between a conventional texture and a decal. For example, the following code fragment shows loading a bitmap named decal1.bmp into a texture object.

```
    // Routine data
    LPDIRECT3DRMTEXTURE3 aTex      = NULL;      // Texture object
    LPDIRECT3DRM3        lpD3DRM   = NULL;      // Direct3D RM
    object
```

```
. . .
// Load bitmap into texture object
   retval = lpD3DRM->LoadTexture( "decal1.bmp", &aTex );
   if(FAILED(retval))
   {
        // Texture loading error handler goes here
   }
```

After the texture object is satisfactorily created, you can proceed to set the decal attributes, which are origin, size, scale, and transparency.

Decal origin

The origin of a decal determines its position on the frame that contains it. The default position for a decal is its top-left corner aligned with the frame's center. The SetDecalOrigin() function of IDirect3DRMTexture3 enables you to reposition the origin in relation to the frame. The function's general form is as follows:

```
RESULT SetDecalOrigin(
                    LONG lX,              // 1
                    LONG lY              // 2
                    );
```

The first parameter is the new *x*-coordinate for the decal origin and the second one is the new *y*-coordinate. The default origin is at [0,0]. The function returns D3DRM_OK if it succeeds, or an error otherwise.

The values required for offsetting the decal origin are related to the size of the decal bitmap. Figure 23-1 shows a decal bitmap of 512 pixels per side. By offsetting the decal origin to [256,256] it is centered in the frame.

Decal Size

You can change the size of the decal by means of the SetDecalSize() function of IDirect3DRMTexture3. Resizing a decal is particularly useful when the decal is scaled according to its depth in the scene. The function has the following general form:

```
HRESULT SetDecalSize(
                    D3DVALUE rvWidth,        // 1
                    D3DVALUE rvHeight       // 2
                    );
```

The first parameter is the factor used in calculating the new width of the decal and the second one is used in calculating the height of a decal. Both are entered in model coordinates. A factor of 2 for the width and height parameters quadruples the displayed size of the decal. Because the data types are D3DVALUE fractional values are also allowed. The function returns D3DRM_OK if it succeeds, or an error otherwise.

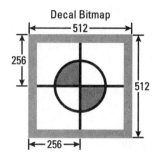

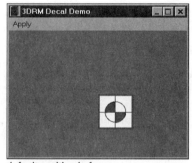

Figure 23-1: Centering a decal in the frame

Figure 23-2 shows a decal that has been scaled to twice its width and 1.5 times its height. The processing is shown in the 3DRM Decal Demo program in the book's CD-ROM.

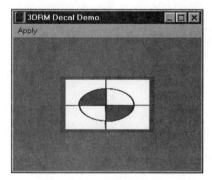

Figure 23-2: Changing the decal size

Decal scale

The decal's scaling attribute is set with the SetDecalScale() function of IDirect 3DRMTexture3. If this attribute is TRUE, then depth is taken into account at rendering time. If FALSE, then the depth of the frame holding the decal is ignored. In this case the decal is always displayed at the same size, independently of its position in relation to the camera. The default for the scaling property is TRUE. The function's general form is as follows:

```
HRESULT SetDecalScale(
                      DWORD dwScale                    // 1
                    );
```

The function's only parameter represents the new scaling property. A value of -1 or FALSE indicates that decal scaling is disabled. Otherwise, decal scaling is enabled. The function returns D3DRM_OK if it succeeds, or an error otherwise.

If the scale attribute is set to FALSE, then the decal is displayed at the original size of the bitmap that contains it. In this case any factor that could affect the size of the displayed image is ignored, such as camera or frame position within the scene, or the size of the decal set with the SetDecalSize() function. Figure 23-3 shows the same decal.

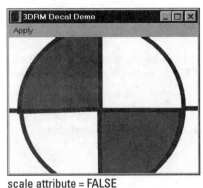

scale attribute = FALSE   scale attribute = TRUE

Figure 23-3: Effect of the decal scale attribute

On the left image the scale attribute is FALSE. In spite of the values passed by the SetDecalSize() function, the decal is displayed at the size of the bitmap. In the image to the right the scale attribute is set to TRUE.

It is interesting to note that the scaling parameter is a DWORD type, rather than a boolean. This seems to suggest that numeric scaling is possible with this function. In other words, that a higher value for the scaling parameter will determine that the decal is scaled differently than with a lower value. However, Microsoft documentation refers to the scaling attribute as being TRUE or FALSE and does not refer to any numeric property.

Decal transparency

In Chapter 10, we discussed DirectDraw transparency by means of color keys. In Chapter 13, we developed more effective dynamic color keying methods. A source color key is a single color or a color range that the artist selects so that pixels that match the color key are not written to the destination. Instead, the background pixel is shown through. The resulting effect of a color key is to make the object appear transparent for those pixels that match the color key.

Texture transparency can be achieved in decals by a method similar to the color keys used in DirectDraw. Two types of functions in IDirect3DRMTexture3 relate to decal transparency. One type enables you to set and retrieve the transparency property of a decal and another type enables you to set and retrieve the transparent color. For obvious reasons the transparent color setting is active only if the transparency attribute is enabled.

The SetDecalTransparency() function is used to set the decal transparency attribute. The function has the following general form:

```
HRESULT SetDecalTransparency(
                    BOOL bTransp            // 1
                    );
```

The function's only parameter is set to TRUE to enable decal transparency. If it is FALSE, then the decal is opaque. The default value is FALSE. The function returns D3DRM_OK if it succeeds, or an error otherwise. A companion function named GetDecalTransparency() allows retrieving the transparency attribute.

If the transparent attribute is enabled for a decal, we can set the single color that will be transparent by means of SetDecalTransparentColor() of IDirect3DRM Texture3. The function has the following general form:

```
HRESULT SetDecalTransparentColor(
                    D3DCOLOR rcTransp               // 1
                        );
```

The function's only parameter is a value of type D3DCOLOR that specifies the transparent color in RGB format. The default transparent color is black. The function returns D3DRM_OK if it succeeds, or an error otherwise. Figure 23-4 shows the results of an opaque and a transparent decal.

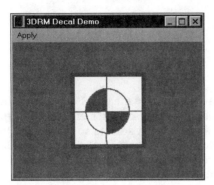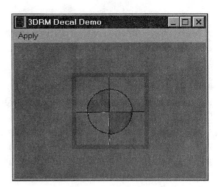

Figure 23-4: Opaque and transparent decals

Because there is no provision for setting a transparent color range in immediate mode, you must be careful in specifying the exact RGB values for the transparent color. For example, you may have created a True color bitmap in a paint program and assigned white as the transparent color. Therefore, we assume that the transparent color for this bitmap can be specified as RGB(0xff, 0xff, 0xff). However, it is possible that the actual RGB value for white used by the paint program could have been RGB(0xf0, 0xf0, 0xf0), which is almost pure white, but not the exact value specified for the transparent color. The difficulty in determining the exact value of the transparent color keys was addressed in Chapter 13 in the context of dynamic color keys. In regards to decals one way of simplifying this problem is by reducing the color range of the decal bitmap. This limits the values for the transparent color and makes it easier to find the exact RGB values.

Frames and decals

After a decal is created as a texture, and its properties defined by calling the functions of IDirect3DRMTexture3, it is usually attached to a child frame as a visual. This step ensures that the decal can be rendered. However, we must realize that, although a decal is attached to a frame, it is not a 3D object, such as a mesh or a face. Therefore, some of the frame-level transformations may not produce the same effect when applied to a decal as when applied to a 3D object. Because there is no vertex or vertex normal data in the case of a decal, it should not surprise us that some 3D transformations become inoperable in this case.

For example, if we attach a decal to a child frame as a visual and then use the AddRotation() or SetRotation() functions on the frame, the decal remains unchanged while other objects contained in the frame rotate as expected. The reason is that a decal is not a 3D object and contains no information so that immediate mode can apply a rotation transformation. However, if the decal's scale attribute is set to TRUE, then some of the frame-level transformations that relate to the decal's size are applied in the conventional manner. For example, if we call an AddTranslation() or SetVelocity() function on the frame, the results will affect the decal as well as the other objects in the frame.

This characteristic of decals can be used to produce many interesting effects in an uncomplicated manner. For instance, we could use transparency to create the image of a planet and attach it to the scene as a decal. Then several moons could be attached to the scene as mesh objects. The scene can then be animated by calling SetVelocity() and SetRotation(). Because the planet is a decal, it will respond to the scaling that results from the call to SetVelocity(), but remains unchanged by the call to SetRotation(). With little manipulation the scene can be made to simulate the moons rotating around a stationary planet.

In the 3DRM Decal Demo program in the book's CD-ROM we illustrate this processing. The program creates a decal and a 3D object, in the form of a teapot, which are both attached to the same frame. Then translation and rotation transformations are applied to the frame. The result is that the teapot appears to rotate and translate, while the decal is scaled but does not rotate. In the following listing we eliminated the error handlers to shorten the example:

```
// Routine variables
struct _globVars
{
. . .
    LPDIRECT3DRMFRAME3 aScene;        // Master frame
. . .
} globVars;

// Other global variables
LPDIRECT3DRMFRAME3 aChildFrame            = NULL;
LPDIRECT3DRMTEXTURE3 aTex                 = NULL;
LPDIRECT3DRMMESHBUILDER3 meshbuilder      = NULL;
. . .
//*************************
//   create mesh and decal
//*************************
// First create the child frame
    retval = lpD3DRM->CreateFrame(globVars.aScene,
                              &aChildFrame);
//*****************
//    create mesh
//*****************
// Create the meshbuilder object
    retval = lpD3DRM->CreateMeshBuilder(&meshbuilder);
// Use meshbuilder to load a mesh from a DirectX file
    retval = meshbuilder->Load(szXfile,            // Source
                         NULL,
```

```
                                    D3DRMLOAD_FROMFILE, // Options
                                    NULL, NULL);
    // Set the mesh color (bright green in this case).
        retval = meshbuilder->SetColorRGB(D3DVAL(0.0),    // red
                                          D3DVAL(0.7),    // green
                                          D3DVAL(0.0));   // blue
    // Set highest quality for meshbuilder
        retval = meshbuilder->SetQuality(D3DRMRENDER_PHONG);

    //******************
    //   create decal
    //******************
    // Load bitmap into texture object
        retval = lpD3DRM->LoadTexture( szTexFile0, &aTex );
    // Set decal attributes
        retval = aTex->SetDecalScale(TRUE);
        retval = aTex->SetDecalSize(4, 4);
        retval = aTex->SetDecalOrigin(256, 256);
        retval = aTex->SetDecalTransparency(FALSE);

    //******************
    // frame operations
    //******************
    // Set velocity to frame
        retval = aChildFrame->SetVelocity(NULL,
                                     D3DVAL(0.004f),
                                     D3DVAL(0.002f),
                                     D3DVAL(0.0125f),
                                     1);      // Rotational
                                              // velocity
    // Set rotation to frame
    // HAS NO VISIBLE EFFECT ON DECAL !!!
        retval = aChildFrame->SetRotation(NULL,
                                     D3DVAL(0.0f),
                                     D3DVAL(1.0f),
                                     D3DVAL(0.0f),
                                     D3DVAL(0.08f));// angle
    //***************
    //   add visuals
    //***************
    // Add decal frame as a visual
        retval = aChildFrame->AddVisual((LPDIRECT3DRMVISUAL) aTex);
    // Add mesh as a visual
        retval = aChildFrame->AddVisual(

(LPDIRECT3DRMVISUAL)meshbuilder);
    . . .
```

Figure 23-5 is a screen snapshot of the Decal movement command in the 3DRM Decal Demo program.

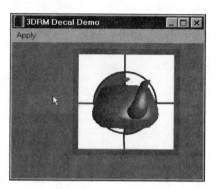

Figure 23-5: Decal movement within a frame in the 3DRM Decal Demo program

Mipmaps

Mipmaps were briefly mentioned in Chapter 14. Basically, a mipmap is a set of textures representing the same image at progressively lower resolutions. Each mipmap image is one-quarter the size of the preceding one, which determines that the entire mipmap take up 4/3 the memory of the original image. The technique provides a computationally inexpensive way of improving the quality of rendered textures by avoiding some of the artifacts that are produced during bitmap scaling operations. The DirectX SDK contains a sample program named mipmap that graphically shows the advantages of this method. However, this sample program is an immediate mode application. Neither the SDK nor MSDN contain sample programs that show mipmapping in retained mode. In fact, the information regarding retained mode mipmap programming is extremely scarce.

To implement mipmapping in retained mode, the following three steps are necessary:

1. The texture quality for the device must be set to one of the values that support mipmapping.

2. The mipmap must be generated.

3. The rendering loop must call the Changed() function so that the texture is rendered using the mipmap.

Setting the texture quality

In Chapter 17, we discussed the SetTextureQuality() in the context of device-level programming. When using retained mode mipmapping you must first set a compatible texture quality. The following listing of the D3DRMTEXTUREQUALITY structure lists the available texture qualities and marks those that support mipmapping.

```
typedef enum _D3DRMTEXTUREQUALITY{
    D3DRMTEXTURE_NEAREST,               // no mipmap support
    D3DRMTEXTURE_LINEAR,                // no mipmap support
    D3DRMTEXTURE_MIPNEAREST,            // supports mipmaps
    D3DRMTEXTURE_MIPLINEAR,             // supports mipmaps
    D3DRMTEXTURE_LINEARMIPNEAREST,      // supports mipmaps
    D3DRMTEXTURE_LINEARMIPLINEAR        // supports mipmaps
} D3DRMTEXTUREQUALITY;
```

Table 23-2 lists the individual texture qualities and their effect.

Table 23-2
Retained Mode Texture Qualities

Texture Quality	Description
D3DRMTEXTURE_NEAREST	Choose the nearest pixel in the texture. Does not support mipmapping.
D3DRMTEXTURE_LINEAR	Linear interpolation of the four nearest pixels. Does not support mipmapping.
D3DRMTEXTURE_MIPNEAREST	Similar to D3DRMTEXTURE_NEAREST. Uses the appropriate mipmap. Pixel sampling and mipmapping are both nearest.
D3D.RMTEXTURE_MIPLINEAR	Similar to D3DRMTEXTURE_LINEAR. Uses the appropriate mipmap. Pixel sampling is linear and mipmapping is nearest.
D3DRMTEXTURE_LINEARMIPNEAREST	Similar to D3DRMTEXTURE_MIPNEAREST. Interpolates between the two nearest mipmaps. Pixel sampling is nearest and mipmapping is linear.
D3DRMTEXTURE_LINEARMIPLINEAR	Similar to D3DRMTEXTURE_MIPLINEAR. Interpolates between the two nearest mipmaps. Pixel sampling and mipmapping are linear.

Generating the mipmap

Of all the mipmapping operations generating the mipmap is the easiest one. This is accomplished by calling the GenerateMIPMap() function of IDirect 3DRMTexture3. The function has the following general form:

```
HRESULT GenerateMIPMap(
                DWORD dwFlags                // 1
                );
```

The function's only parameter should be set to zero. The call returns D3DRM_OK if it succeeds, or an error otherwise.

The call to GenerateMIPMap() can be made at any time after a texture is created. The result is a mipmap of the source image down to a resolution of 1×1. Bilinear filtering is used between levels. After a mipmap has been generated, it will be updated whenever the Changed() function is called but only if the texture quality is set to one of the mipmap-compatible modes and the hardware supports it.

Changing the mipmap

After the texture quality has been set and the mipmap generated, all that is left is to call the Changed() function of IDirect3DRMTexture3 in the rendering loop. The Changed() function was modified in DirectX 6 in order to enable the application to specify the region where the texture has changed. The function has the following general form:

```
HRESULT Changed(
            DWORD dwFlags,                   // 1
            DWORD dwcRects,                  // 2
            LPRECT pRects                    // 3
            );
```

The first parameter is a flag that defines how the pixels have changed in the texture. Table 23-3 lists the flags associated with this parameter.

Table 23-3 Texture Change Flags	
Flag	**Interpretation**
D3DRMTEXTURE_CHANGEDPIXELS	The pixel values have changed
D3DRMTEXTURE_CHANGEDPALETTE	The palette has changed
D3DRMTEXTURE_INVALIDATEONLY	The texture regions are invalidated but do not need to be updated by the application

Applications can install a callback function, of type D3DRMVALIDATIONCALLBACK, that is called by retained mode whenever the primary source for the texture needs updating. The callback function is installed by means of the SetValidationCallback () function of IDirect3DRMTexture3. The D3DRMTEXTURE_INVALIDATEONLY flag is used to make the renderer call the validation callback function.

The second parameter to the Changed() call defines the number of RECT structures pointed to by the third parameter. If the second parameter is zero, and dwFlags contains D3DRMTEXTURE_CHANGEDPIXELS or D3DRMTEXTURE_INVALIDATEONLY, the whole texture is updated. The third parameter is an array of structures of type RECT that describes pixel regions that have changed. This parameter is valid only if the first parameter contains D3DRMTEXTURE_CHANGEDPIXELS or DRMTEXTURE_INVALIDATEONLY.

The function returns DD_OK if it succeeds or one of the following error codes:

```
DDERR_INVALIDOBJECT
DDERR_INVALIDPARAMS
```

Summary

Now we conclude our discussion of texture-related topics. In Chapter 22, we discussed the fundamentals of texture programming. In the present one we explored two specialized uses of textures, namely decals and mipmaps. Topics covered include the creation of decals, the definition of their origin and scale, and the use of decal transparency in rendering sprites. We also looked at creating and manipulating mipmaps.

In Chapter 24, we change our focus to lights and shadows in retained mode programming. The manipulation of lights and shadows greatly increases the visual fidelity of the scene and serves to enhance the texture and materials applied to 3D objects.

✦　　✦　　✦

Lights and Shadows

In retained mode light makes objects visible. There are
no default lights, therefore no objects are visible until we
create lights and attach them to the scene. In addition lighting
effects are used to enhance the visual quality of objects.
Retained mode has a rich set of light types and light controls.
It includes ambient lights and four types of directed lights:
parallel point, point, directional, and spot lights. The position,
color, and intensity of each light can be controlled by code. In
addition, lights can be attenuated over distance according to
two different formulae and three attenuation coefficients.
Because lights are placed in frames, all the manipulations and
movements that can be applied to frames are also applicable
to the contained lights.

In previous chapters we have looked at lights in general and
have created some basic lighting to make our scenes visible.
In this chapter we explore light programming in greater detail.
We also look at the creation of shadows in retained mode
programming.

Retained Mode Lights

In Chapter 14, we mentioned the retained mode lighting
module. At that time we said that retained mode uses two
different lighting models: monochromatic (or ramp) and RGB.
We also discussed how lighting is used to improve the visual
quality of a scene and looked at the five types of lights, which
can be summarized as follows:

1. An ambient light source illuminates the entire scene. It
   has no orientation or position and is unaffected by surface
   characteristics of the illuminated objects. Because all
   objects are illuminated with equal strength, the position
   and orientation of the frame is inconsequential.

2. A directional light has a specific orientation, but no position. It appears to illuminate all objects with equal intensity. This light source is often used to simulate the effect of distant sources, such as the sun. Rendering speed is maximum for directional lights.

3. The parallel point light is a variation of directional light. The orientation of a parallel point light is determined by the position of the source. Whereas a directional light source has orientation, but no position, a parallel point light source has orientation and position. The rendering performance is similar to the directional source.

4. A point light source radiates light equally in all directions. This light is computationally expensive to render because retained mode must calculate a new lighting vector for every face it illuminates. On the other hand, a point light source produces a more faithful lighting effect. When visual fidelity is a concern a point light source is the best option.

5. A spotlight is cone-shaped light with the source located at the cone's vertex. All objects within the cone are illuminated, but at two degrees of intensity. The central area of the cone is brightly lit. This section is called the umbra. The surrounding section, which is dimly lit, is called the penumbra. In retained mode the angles of the umbra and penumbra can be individually specified. Figure 14-12 shows the umbra and the penumbra in spotlight illumination.

Ambient and directed lights

The five light types listed in the preceding section can be further refined. Considering the variations in their fundamental characteristics you can classify them into ambient and directed groups. In this case the group of directed lights contains the directional, parallel point, point, and spotlight types. In this case you must be careful not to confuse the general group of directed lights with the more specific designation of directional light.

Ambient light is light that has been scattered so much that its direction and source have become indeterminate. It has a low level of intensity all over the scene. Ambient light has color and intensity, but no direction or source. It is independent of all objects in the scene and does not contribute to specular reflection.

Direct light, on the other hand, has color and intensity, and travels in a specified direction. Direct light interacts with material of a surface and creates specular highlights. Its direction is used in shading algorithms such as Gouraud and Phong shading. Reflected direct light does not contribute to the ambient light level in a scene. The objects in a scene that generate direct light are called lights or light objects. Each direct light illuminates the scene differently. Figure 24-1 graphically describes ambient and direct light sources.

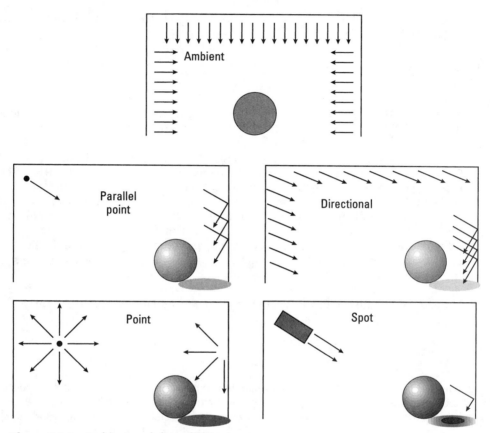

Figure 24-1: Ambient and direct light sources

Direct3D lighting model

Natural light is difficult to model in a computer environment. Every ray of light emitted by a source reflects hundreds, perhaps thousands, of times on the surface of every object in the scene. Each time the light encounters a surface, part of it is absorbed by it and parts of it are reflected in many directions. These reflections, in turn, then strike another object, with different properties, and the process continues until the attenuation makes the light invisible to the viewer.

The number and complexity of calculations required are such that it is currently impossible to simulate the natural effect of light. 3D systems rely on algorithmic simplifications based on mathematical formulas for determining attenuation, reflectance, and falloff. In the default mode Direct3D attenuation calculations are based on the following formula:

$$D_n = \frac{R - D}{R}$$

where *Dn* is the normalized distance, *R* is the light's range, and *D* is the distance from the light source to the vertex under consideration.

When the normalized distance has been determined, then Direct3D uses constant, linear, and quadratic attenuation factors to determine the attenuation effect. The resulting value for the attenuation ranges between 1.0 at the light source and 0.0 at the light's maximum range. Constant attenuation attenuates the light without taking into account the distance from the light to the vertex being lit. Linear and quadratic attenuation formulas are based on the distance from the light to the object. The attenuation is then applied to the red, green, and blue components of the light's color to make the light's intensity a factor of the distance that the light travels to the vertex.

In the default state Direct3D uses the following formula to calculate the total attenuation of light over distance:

$$A = dvAtt0 + D_n \times dvAtt1 + D_n^2 \times dvAtt2$$

where *A* is the total attenuation and *Dn* is the normalized distance from the light source to the vertex calculated using the formula listed previously in this section. The *dvAtt0*, *dvAtt1*, and *dvAtt2* values refer to the constant, linear, and quadratic attenuation factors for the light. In most cases, these attenuation factors are between 0.0 and 1.0, inclusive.

The formula applies to point lights and spotlights because directional and parallel point lights don't attenuate over distance. Applications can change the light attenuation formula by manipulating the flags passed to the SetRenderMode() function, as discussed later in this chapter.

The constant, linear and quadratic attenuation factors act as coefficients in the formula. It is possible to control the attenuation curves by making adjustments to these factors. Direct3D immediate mode provides a structure of type D3DLIGHT2, which enables you to control the three attenuation factors. Retained mode programmers rely on functions in the IDirect3DRMLight interface to accomplish this purpose. These functions are described later in this chapter. Microsoft documentation states that most applications should set the linear attenuation factor to 1.0 and the constant and quadratic attenuation factors to 0.0 to produce a light that steadily falls off over distance. Also, a constant attenuation factor of 1.0 makes a light that doesn't attenuate but is still limited by its range. Figure 24-2 shows the effect over distance of the three light attenuation factors.

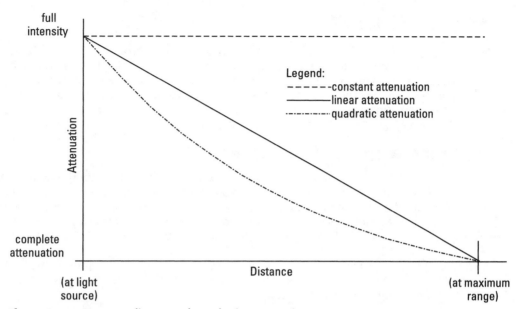

Figure 24-2: Constant, linear, and quadratic attenuation

With the light intensity attenuated, Direct3D calculates how much of the remaining light reflects from a vertex. The calculation is based on the angle of the vertex normal and the direction of the incident light. This step is not necessary for directional and parallel point lights because these sources do not attenuate over distance. In calculating reflection Direct3D uses two reflectance types: diffuse and specular. Each type is associated with a particular formula that determines how much light is reflected in each case. After the amount of reflection is determined according to type, then the reflectance properties of the material are taken into account for the vertex being lit. These are the color values of the diffuse and specular components that the rasterizer uses to produce specific shading effects, such as Gouraud and Phong, and specular highlighting.

Attenuation effect for spotlights require special considerations. We have seen that spotlights emit a cone of light that has a dark inner section, called the penumbra, and an outer, more brightly lit section, called the umbra. The varying intensity between the umbra and the penumbra requires a special form of attenuation calculations called the falloff. In this case the amount of light received by a vertex is a function of its location within the umbra or the penumbra. Direct3D uses the dot product of two vectors to calculate falloff. One vector is the spotlight's direction vector and the other one extends from the vertex being lit to the light source.

Scene Lighting

In Chapter 15, we discussed the fundamentals of lights programming in retained mode. This was necessary because there is no default lighting in retained mode; therefore, if the application does not create lights the objects in the scene are invisible. We now review some of these basic concepts and extend our view to other light controls.

Creating the lighting frame

The first step in illuminating a scene is creating a frame to contain the lights. This frame, usually called the lights frame, is a child frame of the scene. Light objects are then added to the lights frame so that the scene is illuminated. This means that in lights programming you deal with light frame and light objects. The light frame is of type LPDIRECT3DRMFRAME3, and the light objects are type LPDIRECT3DRMLIGHT.

The light frame is created from the scene in the conventional manner. This is done by means of the CreateFrame() function of IDirect3DRM3. The following code fragment shows the processing.

```
// Routine data
struct _globVars
{
.  .  .
    LPDIRECT3DRMFRAME3 aScene;        // Master frame
.  .  .
} globVars;
LPDIRECT3DRMFRAME3 lights = NULL;
.  .  .
// Create a light frame as a child of the scene
retval = lpD3DRM->CreateFrame(aScene, &lights);
if(FAILED(retval))
{
    // Light frame creation error handler goes here
}
```

After the lights frame is created, it can be positioned in the scene. This position is often related to that of the camera frame. For example, if the camera frame is located at coordinates (0,0,-7), you can position the light frame at the same y- and z-coordinates as the camera, but at a greater x-coordinate. The result is that the light or lights placed in this frame will appear to come from the right of the camera and at the same vertical level and distance. The SetPosition() function of IDirect3DRMFrame3 is called, as in the following code fragment.

```
// Position the light frame within the scene
retval = lights->SetPosition(aScene,
                    D3DVAL(5),           // x
                    D3DVAL(0),           // y
```

```
                             -D3DVAL(7));          // z
    if(FAILED(retval))
    {
        // Light frame positioning error handler goes here
    }
```

Positioning the lights close to the camera produces relatively flat lighting with simple shadows. Interesting lighting effects can be achieved by more aggressive positioning of the lights.

Creating the lights

When the light frame exists you can proceed to create the lights that it will contain. Two methods of IDirect3DRM allow creating lights: CreateLight() and Create LightRGB(). CreateLight() uses a structure of type D3DCOLOR to define the light color. In current implementations of DirectX D3DCOLOR is a word-size variable type whose bit mapping is shown in Figure 20-1. The function's general form is as follows:

```
HRESULT CreateLight(
                D3DRMLIGHTTYPE d3drmltLightType,   // 1
                D3DCOLOR cColor,                   // 2
                LPDIRECT3DRMLIGHT *lplpD3DRMLight  // 3
                );
```

The first parameter is one of the lighting types defined in the D3DRMLIGHTTYPE enumerated type. Table 24-1 lists the constants that enumerate the different light types.

Table 24-1	
Enumerator Constants in D3DRMLIGHTTYPE	
Constant	**Description**
D3DRMLIGHT_AMBIENT	Light is an ambient source
D3DRMLIGHT_POINT	Light is a point source
D3DRMLIGHT_SPOT	Light is a spotlight source
D3DRMLIGHT_DIRECTIONAL	Light is a directional source
D3DRMLIGHT_PARALLELPOINT	Light is a parallel point source

The second parameter is the light color specified in a variable of type D3DCOLOR. The third parameter is the address that will be filled by a pointer to an IDirect3DRMLight interface. The call returns D3DRM_OK if successful, or an error otherwise. The following code fragment shows the creation of a white, parallel point light using the CreateLight() function.

```
// Create a bright, parallel point light
    retval = lpD3DRM->CreateLight(D3DRMLIGHT_PARALLELPOINT,
                                  (D3DCOLOR) 0x00ffffff,
                                  &light1);
    if(FAILED(retval))
    {
        // Light creation error handler goes here
    }
```

The CreateLightRGB() function can also be used to create a light. This function was discussed in Chapter 15.

Attaching the light to the light frame

After the type and color of a light is defined, the light must be attached to the lights frame (or any other frame for that matter) in order for it to illuminate the scene. The AddLight() function of IDirect3DRMFrame3 is used for this purpose. The function was discussed in Chapter 20. The code proceeds as follows:

```
// Add light to light frame
retval = lights->AddLight(light1);
if(FAILED(retval))
{
    // Light-to-frame attachment error handler goes here
}
```

Creating an ambient light

Often you can improve the visual quality of a scene by adding an ambient light. Ambient light sources have no position and, therefore, it is inconsequential to which frame they are attached. Often ambient lights are attached to the master scene frame. The ambient light is created using the same CreateLightRGB() or CreateLight() function used for a directed lights. In this case the constant passed in the first parameter (see Table 24-1) is D3DRMLIGHT_AMBIENT. To make a dim, ambient light, the values for the red, green, and blue component can be placed in the lower part of the range. The following code fragment shows creating a dim, ambient light and attaching it to the master scene.

```
LPDIRECT3DRMLIGHT light2 = NULL;
. . .
// Create a dim, ambient light and attach it to the scene frame,
retval = lpD3DRM->CreateLightRGB(D3DRMLIGHT_AMBIENT,
                                 D3DVAL(0.1),    // Red value
```

```
                                        D3DVAL(0.1),    // Green value
                                        D3DVAL(0.1),    // Blue value
                                        &light2);
   if(FAILED(retval))
   {
        // Ambient light creation error handler goes here
   }
   // Attach ambient light to scene frame
   retval = aScene->AddLight(light2);
        if(FAILED(retval))
   {
        // Light attachment error handler goes here
   }
```

Lighting Control

Retained mode applications may not need to perform any additional manipulation of the scene lighting after it has been created. On the other hand, the IDirect3DRMLight interface provides a rich set of functions for controlling lights whenever it is necessary. Table 24-2 lists the functions in this interface.

Table 24-2
Functions in IDirect3DRMLight

Function	Description
Attenuation controls	
GetConstantAttenuation()	Retrieves the constant attenuation factor
GetLinearAttenuation()	Retrieves the linear attenuation factor
GetQuadraticAttenuation()	Retrieves the quadratic attenuation factor
SetConstantAttenuation()	Sets the constant attenuation factor
SetLinearAttenuation()	Sets the linear attenuation factor
SetQuadraticAttenuation()	Sets the quadratic attenuation factor
Color controls	
GetColor()	Retrieves the light's color
SetColor()	Sets the light's color using a DD3DCOLOR value
SetColorRGB()	Sets the light's color using RGB values

Continued

Table 24-2 *(continued)*	
Function	*Description*
Frame enable	
GetEnableFrame()	Retrieves frame illuminated by the light
SetEnableFrame()	Sets frame illuminated by the light
Light types	
GetType()	Retrieves the light type
SetType()	Sets the light type
Spotlight controls	
GetRange()	Retrieves the spotlight's range
SetRange()	Sets the spotlight's range
GetPenumbra()	Retrieves the penumbra angle of a spotlight
GetUmbra()	Retrieves the umbra angle of a spotlight
SetPenumbra()	Sets the penumbra angle of a spotlight
SetUmbra()	Sets the umbra angle of a spotlight

Light attenuation controls

Earlier in this chapter we saw that Direct3D attenuates lights over distance using a formula that takes into account three factors called constant, linear, and quadratic attenuation. The effect of these factors is shown graphically in Figure 24-2. The retained mode IDirect3DRMLight interface contains methods to set and retrieve each of the three attenuation factors for a light. In addition, retained mode applications can set a render mode flag that makes retained mode use an immediate mode D3DLIGHT2 structure to define the light type.

Enabling realistic highlights

The SetRenderMode() function was introduced in DirectX 6. This function provides a way of producing more realistic specular highlights in retained mode. The new style of highlights depends both on the light direction and the viewer's location. Previously highlights were rendered without taking into account the viewer's location. Realistic highlights, also called view-dependent highlights, are enabled by calling the SetRenderMode() function of IDirect3DRMDevice3 and passing the D3DRMRENDERMODE_VIEWDEPENDENTSPECULAR flag as a parameter. If this flag is set, Direct3D retained mode uses the D3DLIGHT2 structure to define the light type. If it is not set, then lighting behavior reverts to the flat specular highlights of previous DirectX versions.

Direct3D changes the rendering of highlights by using different formulas for calculating the total attenuation factor. The default formula applies when the D3DRMRENDERMODE_VIEWDEPENDENTSPECULAR is not set. In this case the total attenuation is calculated as follows:

$$A = dvAtt0 + D_n \times dvAtt1 + D_n^2 \times dvAtt2$$

where A is the total attenuation and Dn is the normalized distance from the light source to the vertex calculated using the formula listed previously in this section. The $dvAtt0$, $dvAtt1$, and $dvAtt2$ values refer to the constant, linear, and quadratic attenuation factors for the light. If the D3DRMRENDERMODE_VIEWDEPENDENTSPECULAR is set, then the following formula is used to determine the total attenuation.

$$A = \frac{1}{dvAtt0 + D_n \times dvAtt1 + D_n^2 \times dvAtt2}$$

Observing these formulas you can see that when the view-dependent specular highlights flag is clear the attenuation factor is greater than in the default state.

The default attenuation factors are shown in Table 24-3.

Table 24-3		
Default Attenuation Factors for Lights		
Attenuation Type	*Constant*	*Value*
Constant attenuation	dvAtt0	1.0
Linear attenuation	dvAtt1	0.0
Quadratic attenuation	dvAtt2	0.0

Applying these values to the preceding formulas results in the following calculations for total attenuation:

```
default         1.0 + 0.0 + 0.0    = 1.0
enhanced        1/1.0 + 0.0 + 0.0  = 1.0
```

This means that the default mode is constant attenuation and that the state of the D3DRMRENDERMODE_VIEWDEPENDENTSPECULAR flag is inconsequential in this default state. This can be confirmed by observing the constant attenuation curve in Figure 24-2.

You have seen that setting or clearing the D3DRMRENDERMODE_VIEWDEPENDENTSPECULAR is done by calling the SetRenderMode() function of IDirect3DRMDevice3. Retained mode documentation states that this flag is associated with bit number 4. Therefore, you can use the mask 0x10 to manipulate this bit without affecting the other render mode flags. The following code fragment shows the manipulation to set and clear the view-dependent specular flag.

```
// Routine data
static DWORD    renderMode;    // Storage for render mode flags
. . .
// Set render mode to view-dependent specular highlights
// flag = 0001 0000 binary = 0x10
renderMode = globVars.aDevice->GetRenderMode();
renderMode = renderMode | 0x10;
retval = globVars.aDevice->SetRenderMode(renderMode);
if(FAILED(retval))
    // Failed setting render mode set handler goes here
. . .
// Clear render mode view-dependent specular highlights flag
renderMode = globVars.aDevice->GetRenderMode();
renderMode = renderMode & 0xffffffef;
retval = globVars.aDevice->SetRenderMode(renderMode);
if(FAILED(retval)) RMError(retval);
    // Failed render mode set error handler goes here
```

Changing light attenuation

Retained mode applications can change the light attenuation from the default state of constant attenuation to linear or quadratic attenuation, or use a combination of these factors. Recall that constant attenuation is actually no attenuation. In most cases an application that requires light attenuation effects over distance will set the linear attenuation factor to 1.0 and the constant and quadratic attenuation factors to 0.0. However, because the attenuation factors are the coefficients of the formulas listed in the preceding section, all three factors can be assigned values independently, usually with unpredictable and unexpected results.

The IDirect3DRMLight interface contains functions to set and retrieve the three attenuation factors. The functions are quite similar for each of the factors. The general form for the functions to set the attenuation factors are as follows:

```
HRESULT SetLinearAttenuation(. . .
HRESULT SetConstantAttenuation(. . .
HRESULT SetQuadraticAttenuation(
                        D3DVALUE rvAtt        // 1
                        );
```

The only parameter is a value of type D3DVALUE that represents the new attenuation factor in each case. The functions return D3DRM_OK if they succeed, or an error otherwise.

The functions to retrieve the attenuation factors have the following general forms:

```
D3DVALUE GetLinearAttenuation()
D3DVALUE GetConstantAttenuation();
D3DVALUE GetQuadraticAttenuation();
```

The return value is the attenuation factor for the light object referenced in the call. The following code fragment shows setting the light attenuation factor.

```
// Routine data
LPDIRECT3DRMLIGHT light1                    = NULL;
LPDIRECT3DRM3 lpD3DRM                       = NULL;

// Light attenuation coefficients
float constAtt  =  1.0f;
float linearAtt =  0.0f;
float quadAtt   =  0.0f;
. . .
// Create a bright, parallel point light
   retval = lpD3DRM->CreateLight(D3DRMLIGHT_PARALLELPOINT,
                                (D3DCOLOR) 0x00ffffff,
                                &light1);
   if(FAILED(retval))
   {
       // Light creation error handler goes here
   }
   // Set attenuation coefficients
   retval = light1->SetConstantAttenuation((D3DVALUE)
constAtt);
   if(FAILED(retval))
       // Error handler goes here
   retval = light1->SetLinearAttenuation((D3DVALUE) linearAtt);
   if(FAILED(retval))
       // Error handler goes here
   retval = light1->SetQuadraticAttenuation((D3DVALUE)
quadAtt);
   if(FAILED(retval))
       // Error handler goes here
```

Light attenuation is active in relation to directed lights only. Ambient light is not attenuated over distance. In regards to the four types of directed lights, attenuation effects are also different. Directional light types have no position and therefore are not attenuated. Neither are parallel point lights. Point lights and spotlights are the only directed lights attenuated over distance. In addition, retained attenuation is more evident if view-dependent specular highlights are disabled.

Spotlight controls

In the listing of the functions of the IDirect3DRMLight interface (see Table 24-2) you will notice a group of functions that relate specifically to spotlights. This is because spotlights have three attributes that are not present in the other types. These are the spotlight range and the angles of the umbra and penumbra cones.

The spotlight range limits the effects of the light to objects located within these values. The default range for a spotlight is 256 units of model space. The SetRange() function can be used to shorten or lengthen the default range. The GetRange() function returns the current range of a spotlight.

The angle of the centrally lit cone of light of a spotlight, called the umbra, can also be set and retrieved by means of the SetUmbra() and GetUmbra() functions of IDirect3DRMLight. The default value for the umbra is 0.4 radians, or approximately 23 degrees. The angle of the outer, dimly light area of a spotlight, called the penumbra, can also be set and retrieved by means of the GetPenumbra() and SetPenumbra() functions of IDirect3DRMLight. The default angle for the penumbra is 0.5 radians, or approximately 28.5 degrees.

3DRM Light Demo program

The 3DRM Light Demo program in the book's CD-ROM enables you to experiment with ambient and directed lights. The program executes by displaying the image of a teapot and a modeless dialog box, as shown in Figure 24-3.

With this program you can enable and disable an ambient light and control its intensity, as well as select any one of the four types of directed lights and the attenuation mode. The rendering of view-dependant specular highlights can be enabled or disabled and the directed light can be moved along the x-axis and along the z-axis.

Shadows

In retained mode a shadow is the result of the projection of a mesh onto a plane by a single light. Consequently, the elements of a shadow are the mesh that casts it, the light that generates it, and the plane onto which it is rendered. The shadow is a visual object that is attached to the same frame that contains the mesh that casts the shadow.

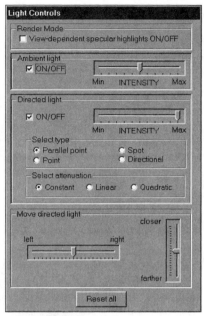

Figure 24-3: Screen snapshot of the 3DRM Light Demo program

The elements of a retained mode shadow make evident some of its limitations. The fact that each shadow is associated with a mesh and a single light source indicate that adding shadow functionality onto an elaborate scene is not a simple task. In this case each shadow requires a particular mesh and a particular light source. Furthermore, because retained mode shadows are only projected onto a plane, it is not possible to generate shadows on the surface of objects that are not flat. But perhaps the most important limitations of retained mode shadows are their computational cost. 3D applications that perform animation must often do without shadows because of the processing time that they require.

There are two ways for creating a shadow. The simplest one is by calling the `Create Shadow()` function of `IDirect3DRM3`. Alternatively, you can create a shadow using the `CreateObject()` function of this same interface and then call the `Init()` function of `IDirect3DRMShadow2`. Both approaches were discussed in detail in Chapter 16, as well as the functions in `IDirect3DRMShadow2` interface. At this point we are interested in the programming required to generate shadows in retained mode.

Creating a shadow

In creating a shadow you must define the three elements mentioned previously; that is, the object that casts the shadow, the light that produces the shadow, and the plane onto which the shadow is projected. These elements can be seen in Figure 24-4.

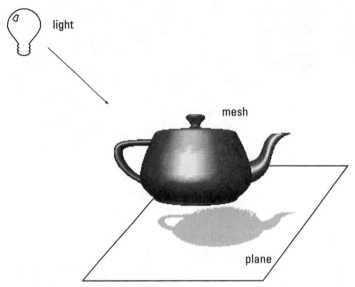

Figure 24-4: Elements of a shadow

The only retained mode object that can cast a shadow is a mesh. In practical programming we sometimes use the meshbuilder object to add a visual onto a frame, this saving having to create a mesh. However, when programming shadows we must have available the mesh object that casts the shadow, therefore we must specifically create the mesh.

The light that produces the shadow must be a directed light. Ambient lights are multidirectional and produce no shadows. In addition, the position of the camera, the light, the mesh, and the plane must be such that the shadow is visible at rendering time. It is quite possible to position one or more of these elements so that the generated shadow lies outside of the viewing frustum. Assuming that the mesh object that generates the shadow has already been created, and also that there is a directed light conveniently positioned, then producing a shadow consists of three steps: creating the shadow, defining the shadow option, and attaching the shadow as a visual to the frame. The following code fragment shows the processing.

```
// Routine variables
LPDIRECT3DRMFRAME3 aChildFrame            = NULL;
LPDIRECT3DRMLIGHT dirLt                   = NULL;
LPDIRECT3DRMSHADOW2 aShadow               = NULL;
LPDIRECT3DRMMESH teapotMesh               = NULL;
. . .
// Code assumes that a teapotMesh and a directed light object
// already exist in the scene
retval = lpD3DRM->CreateShadow( teapotMesh, // Mesh object
                                dirLt,      // Light
                                D3DVAL(0),  // |
                                D3DVAL(-2), // | Plane for
                                            // | shadow
                                D3DVAL(0),  // |
                                D3DVAL(0),  // |
                                D3DVAL(1),  // | Shadow plane
                                D3DVAL(0),  // | normal
                                &aShadow);  // Shadow object
if(FAILED(retval))
{
    // Shadow creation error handler goes here
}
// Set shadow options
retval = aShadow->SetOptions(D3DRMSHADOW_TRUEALPHA);
if(FAILED(retval))
{
    // Shadow option error handler goes here
}
// Attach shadow to frame as visual
retval = aChildFrame->AddVisual(aShadow);
if(FAILED(retval))
{
    // Add visual error handler goes here
}
```

3DRM Shadow Demo program

The 3DRM Shadow Demo program in the book's CD-ROM shows a rotating teapot that generates a shadow onto the x-plane. The code used in the sample program is similar to the one listed previously.

Summary

We have now concluded our tour of retained mode light and shadow programming. In it we explored the lighting models and formulas, the creation and control of ambient and directed lights, the positioning of lights within a scene, and the generation of shadows. It is through light programming that the objects of our scenes become visible at rendering time. What is more, by the adequate selection and placement of lights and shadows we can significantly enhance the visual quality of 3D objects.

With the discussion of lights and shadows we conclude our discussion of static rendering in DirectX retained mode, which includes the simple movements that can be directly applied to frames. In the following chapter we explore retained mode animation. It is animation that makes 3D applications unique and powerful. The static rendering of a 3D object is visually identical to the display of a 2D image.

✦   ✦   ✦

3D Animation

Animation is often the central feature of a 3D application. We have already encountered Direct3D animation in the context of frame movements. In Chapter 19, we covered topics related to the continuous scaling, rotation, and translation of frames which make possible a rudimentary level of animation. The SetRotation() and SetVelocity() functions implement this functionality at the frame level, whereas the Move() and Tick() functions of IDirect3DRM provide a timing mechanism that drives the animation. The 3DRM Move Demo program in the book's CD-ROM shows the basic processing.

Simple, frame-level manipulations by means of SetVelocity() and SetRotation() provide an easy way of producing interesting effects. In some cases, these methods are all that is required for an animated application. However, in programs that require more powerful animations the controls that are available with SetRotation() and SetVelocity() are too limited. For these cases retained mode provides other more powerful and flexible animation mechanisms.

In addition to the animation facilities provided by retained mode functions there is a simple, often overlooked, approach to animation. The technique is based on creating an intercept routine that receives control at every beat of the animation pulse, then executing step-by-step image changes within this intercept. This approach usually requires implementing a move callback function that is called by the rendering loop. Code can use this intercept to produce any desired changes in the visuals. We start our discussion of animation techniques by examining this approach. An alternative animation method is based on a technique called key-framing. Retained mode contains extensive support for several flavors of key frame animation. Key frame animation by tranformation keys and by interpolators are also discussed in this chapter.

Direct Intercept Animation

A simple approach to animation consists of creating a callback function that is called at every animation beat, and providing the necessary processing in the intercept routine. This technique, which could be called the direct intercept method, is both powerful and laborious. It is powerful because you can use the intercept routine to produce any scene change that is available in retained mode. There is no limit to the number or types of movements, or to the number of changes that can be applied to a single scene. For example, you can use the callback function to transform objects, to morph meshes, to change the color, intensity, or position of lights, to modify the color tint of objects, to change materials and textures, to manipulate fog intensity, or to perform any other valid action on the scene's objects. The only limits to what can be accomplished are those imposed by bandwidth and by rendering performance.

The major limitation of this method is that it requires that you calculate and execute all the individual steps of the animation. In direct intercept animation there is no assistance from the system in calculating in-betweens or in producing the intermediate calls. Later in this chapter you will see that retained mode provides other animation methods that take advantage of considerable help from the system.

Implementing direct intercept animation consists of two steps:

1. Creating the direct intercept routine, sometimes called the move callback function

2. Calculating and implementing the step-by-step changes in the intercept routine

Creating the move callback function

The AddMoveCallback() function of IDirect3DRMFrame3 provides a way of creating a callback function that is called every time frame motion attributes are applied. The AddMoveCallback() function was discussed in Chapter 19. Creating a move callback function for direct intercept animation consists of calling the AddMoveCallback() function and passing as a parameter the name of the intercept routine.

```
// Create a frame intercept callback function
 retval = aChildFrame->AddMoveCallback(FrameInterceptCallback,
                                       NULL,
                                       D3DRMCALLBACK_PREORDER );
if(FAILED(retval))
{
    // Move callback creation failure error handler goes here
}
```

Implementing the step changes

The actual animation is performed in the intercept routine. It is up to the programmer to decide what actions are to be executed and to provide some form of iteration control for these actions.

Suppose that you want to implement an animation consisting of a z-axis translation combined with a simultaneous color tint change of the object. This means that the object is to move away from the viewer as its color progressively fades to black.

The first design decision in implementing direct intercept animation for this case is determining the number of discrete steps in the image update sequence. The more steps, the slower the changes. Let's assume that the object is to be translated from a z-axis coordinate of 0 to a z-axis coordinate of 40. Also assume that the animation consists of 40 discrete steps. This means that you must translate the object one unit along the z-axis at every beat of the animation pulse. At the same time you need to fade the object's color from its maximum intensity to black. Because the retained mode RGB color attributes are defined in the range 1.0 to 0.0, you can produce the desired tint fade by subtracting 1/40th (0.025) to the color intensity during each iteration. This means that you start with a color attribute of 1.0 and subtract 0.025 at every iteration of the animation pulse. At the 40th iteration the color will fade to black and the object will move 40 units along the z-axis. The intercept routine can be coded as follows:

```
//********************************************************
// Name: FrameInterceptCallback()
// Desc: Intercept routine for performing a simultanous
//       translation and color tint change animation.
// Note: Code assumes that delta = 1.0. No error handling
//       is provided.
//********************************************************
void FrameInterceptCallback( LPDIRECT3DRMFRAME3 aFrame,
                             void *arg,
                             D3DVALUE delta )
{

   static D3DVALUE   colorTint    = D3DVAL(1.0);   // Initial
                                                   // color
   static D3DVALUE   changeRate   = D3DVAL(0.025); // 1/40 units
   static D3DVALUE   frameAction  = D3DVAL(0.0);   // Initial z

   // Set the color
   aFrame->SetColorRGB(D3DVAL(0.0),
                   D3DVAL(colorTint),  // Green tint
                   D3DVAL(0.0));
   // Move the frame
   aFrame->SetPosition(NULL,             // Use local transform
               D3DVAL(0.0),              // x
```

```
                        D3DVAL(0.0),             // y
                        D3DVAL(frameAction));  // z

    // Update tint
    colorTint = colorTint - changeRate;
    if(colorTint < 0)
        colorTint = 1.0f;

    // Update frame position
    frameAction = frameAction + delta;
    if(frameAction > 40)
        frameAction = 0.0f;
}
```

The program 3DRM Mode Intercept Demo in the book's CD-ROM implements the preceding animation.

Key Frame Animation

In Chapter 5, we discussed several low-level controls used in animation. At that time we discussed the in-between, or tweening, techniques used in cartoon animation. This method is based on defining two key positions, which serve to mark the beginning and the end of an action sequence, and then creating the in-between images. At that time we mentioned that computers can be used to generate the in-betweens by performing geometrical transformations on the key frames. The process is illustrated in Figure 25-1.

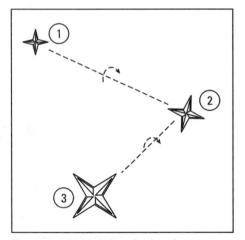

Figure 25-1: Defining the key frames

The animation shown in Figure 25-1 consists of moving the four-pointed star from its initial position on the top-left corner of the viewing area to its final position in the bottom-left corner. At the same time the star is rotated by approximately 30 degrees. To accomplish this animation we define three key frames, labeled with the numbers 1, 2, and 3 in the illustration. The movement of the star from key frame number 1 to key frame number 2 is accomplished by performing a translation, a scaling, and a rotation transformation. The same is true to move from key frame number 2 to key frame number 3. Once the key frames are defined, the system calculates and generates the intermediate images between key frames.

Computer-Generated In-Betweens

In computer-based animation it is the computer that can generate the in-betweens. The fundamental algorithm for transformation-based animations consists of establishing a *range of motion* for the action that is to take place between two key frames. The calculations require defining the number of images that are used for each second of animation. In the United States, television technology uses a rate of 30 images per second, whereas professional motion pictures use 24 images per second. Next, you define the time lapse between the key frames. When the image rate and the time lapse are known, the system can calculate the number of in-betweens that are required. Usually the calculations are based on a linear interpolation.

Suppose you decide that the animation shown in Figure 25-1 is to take place in two-thirds of a second, and that the frame rate is of 30 images per second. In this example the area of motion between key frame number 1 and key frame number 2 requires one-third of a second, or 10 frames at 30 fps. Given this information, the system can proceed to determine the total translation, rotation, and scaling required between key frame number 1 and key frame number 2. These totals for each transformation are divided by the number of frames, in this case 10, and the resulting transformation applied to each set of image coordinates.

One of the problems that occasionally arises in key frame animation is that there can be more than one path-of-motion between key frames. This ambiguity can be seen in Figure 25-2.

In the case in Figure 25-2 you can see that the animation between key frames requires a translation and a rotation transformation. Also the rotation can take place either in a clockwise or a counter-clockwise direction, creating two possible image sets between key frames. The resolution of ambiguities such as this one usually requires the definition of additional key frames. For example, to make sure that sequence option A is the one generated, you can define a new key frame in which the dagger appears in a vertical position, with the tip facing up, as shown in the illustration.

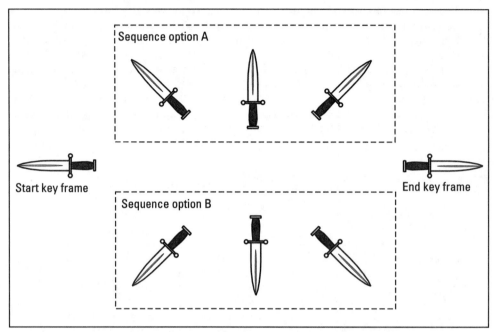

Figure 25-2: Ambiguity in key frame animation

Key Frame Animation in Retained Mode

Retained mode supports basic key frame animation. The key frame animation functionality is found in the `IDirect3DRM3`, `IDirect3DRMAnimation2`, `IDirect 3DRMAnimationSet2`, `IDirect3DRMAnimationArray`, and `IDirect3DRM Interpolator` interfaces.

In the key frame method of retained mode animation the application code starts by creating an animation object. To the animation object code you can add position, rotation, and scaling keys. Each key contains an arbitrary time value. The animation is driven by calling the `SetTime()` function of `IDirect3DRMAnimation2`.

A higher level of animation programming is by means of animation sets. In this case a complex animation is created by combining several animation objects. Animation sets can be built by adding individual animations, or by loading the animation set from a file, resource, memory block, or stream. This last option opens up the possibility of using a modeling program to create the animation sets, which can then be loaded from a file in X format into the application. Modeling and animation programs simplify the process of creating complex animations by providing visual tools and technical controls. Many application developers use this approach to creating animations, rather than constructing the key frames in code.

Retained mode animation programming

The `Direct3DRMAnimation2` interface contains functions to animate the position, orientation, and scale of a frame object. This frame object can be a visual, a light, or a viewport. Animation controls are based on keys, each one key containing a time and a value component. The functions allow adding and deleting keys, animating the frame, setting the animation time, and changing animation options. Table 25-1 lists the functions in `IDirec3DRMAnimation3`.

Table 25-1
Functions in the IDirect3DRMAnimation3 Interface

Function	Description
Key operations	
AddKey()	Adds a new key to the animation
AddPositionKey()	Adds a position key based on a time key and the coordinates for each axis
AddRotateKey()	Adds a rotate key based on a time key and a rotation quaternion
AddScaleKey()	Adds a scale key based on a time key and a scale factor for each axis
DeleteKey()	Removes all keys at a particular time
DeleteKeyByID()	Removes a particular key
GetKeys()	Retrieves a key corresponding to a particular time range
ModifyKey()	Modifies the value of a key
Frame and time	
GetFrame()	Retrieves animation frame
SetFrame()	Sets the animation frame
SetTime()	Sets the animation time
Animation options	
GetOptions()	Retrieves the animation options
SetOptions()	Sets the animation options

Creating an Animation

The creation of animations and animation sets was discussed in Chapter 16 in the context of the `IDirect3DRM3` interface. Here we present a brief revisiting of the fundamental concepts, starting with a single animation and continuing with animation sets.

The first step in creating a retained mode animation consists of calling `Create Animation()` function of `IDirect3DRM3`. This call creates an empty `IDirect3DRM Animation2` object. The object can be used to access the methods of `IDirect3DRM Animation2`. The function's general form is as follows:

```
HRESULT CreateAnimation(
        LPDIRECT3DRMANIMATION2   *lplpD3DRMAnimation     // 1
        );
```

Its only parameter is the address of a pointer to the `IDirect3DRMAnimation2` interface, which is filled if the call succeeds. The function returns `D3DRM_OK` if it succeeds, or an error otherwise.

After the animation object is successfully created, code can implement the animation by using the methods of `IDirect3DRMAnimation2` and other retained mode interfaces. In the following discussion we assume that the application contains a time-driven pulse that calls the rendering routine. The 3DRM Move Demo program developed in Chapter 19 can serve as a template for the message loop and the basic implementation of the `RenderScene()` function. We also assume that the master scene has been created, and that there is a child frame available that contains the visual object to be animated. Given this basic program skeleton, the process of creating the animation consists of the following steps:

1. Some suitable animation options are selected.

2. The animation parameters are defined for the animation object created in Step 1. These include the frame to be animated, the key frames, and the animation's time element.

3. A frame move callback is attached to the child frame that contains the animation object.

The actual animation is performed by means of time pulse that drives the rendering loop. The easiest way of implementing a time pulse for the animation is to use the program thread itself. This is what you do when you call the rendering function inside the program's message loop. Alternatively you can use other timing mechanisms to drive the animation. Two of these were discussed in Chapter 12 in the context of DirectDraw animation. Typically, the rendering loop calls the `Move()` or the `Tick()` functions which, in turn, call the animation callback function. The image updating is performed in the animation callback.

Selecting the animation options

Several types of animation are supported in Direct3D. The SetOptions() function of IDirect3DRMAnimation2 is used to select the animation options that are adequate for the case at hand. The function has the following general form:

```
HRESULT SetOptions(
                D3DRMANIMATIONOPTIONS d3drmanimFlags      // 1
                );
```

The function's only parameter is a structure variable of type D3DRMANIMATIONOPTIONS. It is defined as follows:

```
typedef DWORD D3DRMANIMATIONOPTIONS;
#define D3DRMANIMATION_CLOSED               0x02L
#define D3DRMANIMATION_LINEARPOSITION       0x04L
#define D3DRMANIMATION_OPEN                 0x01L
#define D3DRMANIMATION_POSITION             0x20L
#define D3DRMANIMATION_SCALEANDROTATION     0x10L
#define D3DRMANIMATION_SPLINEPOSITION       0x08L
```

Table 25-2 lists the various animation options.

Table 25-2
Animation Options in D3DRMANIMATIONOPTIONS Structure

Constant	Action
3DRMANIMATION_CLOSED	Animation plays continually. When the G end is reached, the animation loops back to the beginning.
D3DRMANIMATION_LINEARPOSITION	Defines a linear animation position.
3DRMANIMATION_OPEN	Animation plays once and stops.
3DRMANIMATION_POSITION	Animation position matrix overwrites any transformation matrices set by other functions.
D3DRMANIMATION_SCALEANDROTATION	Animation's scale and rotation matrix overwrites any transformation matrices set by other functions.
3DRMANIMATION_SPLINEPOSITION	Animation position is set using splines.

When selecting the 3DRMANIMATION_CLOSED flag you can ensure a smooth transition by making the last key in the animation a repeat of the first one. In this case the IDirect3DRMAnimation2 and IDirect3DRMAnimationSet2 interfaces interpret the repeated key as the time difference between the last and first keys in the loop. Selecting the incorrect animation option could make our animation effects invisible at rendering time. For example, an application that is to use rotation keys must select the D3DRMANIMATION_SCALEANDROTATION option. The call to SetOptions() returns D3DRM_OK if it succeeds, or an error otherwise.

The GetOptions() function of IDirect3DRMAnimation2 provides a way for code to retrieve the current animation options flags. The function has the following general form:

```
D3DRMANIMATIONOPTIONS GetOptions( );
```

The call returns a D3DRMANIMATIONOPTIONS type describing the animation options. Because these flags are bitmapped, they can be examined by performing a bitwise AND operation with the corresponding mask.

Defining the key frames

Retained mode animation requires that code defines a minimum of two key frames. The system uses the key frames to calculate the in-betweens. The animation is rendered according to the timing parameters specified by the code.

Animation keys are used by the AddKey(), AddPositionKey(), AddRotateKey(), AddScaleKey(), DeleteKey(), DeleteKeyByID(), GetKey(), and ModifyKey() functions listed in Table 25-1. Animation keys are encoded in a structure of type D3DRMANIMATIONKEY, which is defined as follows:

```
typedef struct _D3DRMANIMATIONKEY
  {
    DWORD         dwSize;
    DWORD         dwKeyType;
    D3DVALUE      dvTime;
    DWORD         dwId ;
      union
       {
        D3DRMQUATERNION    dqRotateKey;
        D3DVECTOR          dvScaleKey;
        D3DVECTOR          dvPositionKey;
       };
  } D3DRMANIMATIONKEY;
```

The dwSize member defines the size of the animation. The dwKeyType member is the type of key, represented by one of the following values:

```
D3DRMANIMATION_ROTATEKEY    = 0x01
D3DRMANIMATION_SCALEKEY     = 0x02
D3DRMANIMATION_POSITIONKEY  = 0x03
```

The dvTime member is the key's zero-based time value, in arbitrary units. If an application adds a position key with a time value of 99, a new position key with a time value of 49 occurs exactly halfway between the beginning of the animation and the first position key. The time member is encoded in a D3DVALUE type. The dwId member is the key's identifier, encoded in a DWORD type. The dqRotateKey union member is the value of the D3DRMQUATERNION structure type that defines the rotation. The dvScaleKey union member is the value of the D3DVECTOR structure type that defines the scale. The dvPositionKey union member is the value of the D3DVECTOR structure type that defines the position.

Adding an animation key

IDirect3DRMAnimation2 contains four functions for adding animation keys. The first one, named AddKey(), is generic. It enables you to add either a position, a rotation, or a scaling key to the animation. The other three functions, AddPosition Key(), AddRotateKey(), and AddScaleKey() are specific for the individual key types.

All four key adding functions contain a time element defined in a D3DVALUE type. This time element actually defines the zero-based sequential position for the key. For example, in an animation consisting of four keys the time element can be assigned values 0, 1, 2, and 3 for each of the keys. However, if you define an animation consisting of 20 keys, then the value assigned to the time element would be 0 to 19.

The time element can also be used to modify the rate of change of the animation. For example, consider an animation consisting of five key frames has the values 0, 7, 11, 13, and 14 assigned to its sequential positions. In this case the total time for the animation is of 15 arbitrary units. Seven of these time units elapse between the first and the second key frames, four time units elapse between the second and the third key frames, two units between the third and the fourth key frames, and so on. When the animation is rendered the object will appear to accelerate. Figure 25-3 shows the manipulating of the key frame sequence to simulate acceleration of an object in a gravitational field.

In Figure 25-3 we assume that the change in image data is the same between the key frames. If the animation consists of a translation along the y-axis, this means that the difference between y-axis values is the same for any key frame pair. In the example in Figure 25-3 acceleration is produced by manipulating the sequence number assigned to each key frame. Alternatively, it is possible to simulate acceleration by changing the animation parameters themselves. For example, you could simulate acceleration of a falling object by assigning progressively large y-axis movement to each key frame. A combination of both elements is also possible.

Simulating acceleration by varying the key frame sequence numbers usually requires careful calculations. For example, to realistically simulate the fall of an object in a gravitational field you could use the formulas for gravitational attraction to calculate the rate of change in the object's speed. The number of key frame points, sometimes called motion points, determine the accuracy of the simulation. The more motion points, the more natural the animation. If the animation contains few motion points the acceleration effect may appear bumpy.

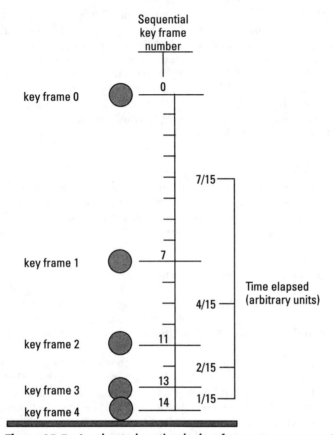

Figure 25-3: Accelerated motion by key frame sequence control

In the following sections we refer to the so-called time element of a key frame as its sequential number. We reserve the notion of *animation time* as the element that determines the rendering speed, which is determined by the Move() and the SetTime() functions, discussed later in this chapter.

Creating a translation animation

The AddPositionKey() function of IDirect3DRMAnimation2 enables you to create a new position key by performing a translation transformation. The function has the following general form:

```
HRESULT AddPositionKey(
                D3DVALUE rvTime,        // 1
                D3DVALUE rvX,           // 2
                D3DVALUE rvY,           // 3
                D3DVALUE rvZ            // 4
                );
```

The first parameter represents the animation sequence number for the key frame. The second, third, and fourth parameters are the new *x*-, *y*-, and *z*-axis coordinates for the key frame. The function returns D3DRM_OK if it succeeds, or an error otherwise.

In actual programming, position keys and sequential key frame numbers are often stored in arrays. The values for the various key frame elements are then set in a loop. Figure 25-4 shows the two key frames for an animation consisting of a translation transformation.

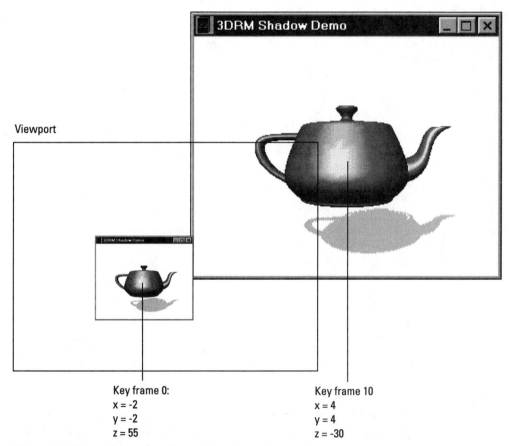

Key frame 0:
x = -2
y = -2
z = 55

Key frame 10
x = 4
y = 4
z = -30

Figure 25-4: Key frames for a translation-based animation

To produce the animation that translates the image of the teapot from the position in key frame number 0 to that in key frame number 1 you must add the two position keys to an animation object. The coordinates for the two position keys, as well as the count of the number of keys in the animation, can be stored in corresponding arrays. The following code fragment shows the necessary processing in this case.

```
// Routine data
LPDIRECT3DRMANIMATION2 anim                    = NULL;
HRESULT                retval;
int motionPoints    = 2;              // Number of key frames
D3DVECTOR pointCoords[2] =
{
   { -2.0f, -2.0f,  55.0f },  // Coordinates for key frame 0
   {  4.0f,  4.0f, -30.0f }   // Coordinates for key frame 1
};
. . .
// Create the animation
retval = lpD3DRM->CreateAnimation( &anim);
if(FAILED(retval))
{
    // Animation creation error handler goes here
}
// Set the animation options
retval = anim->SetOptions( D3DRMANIMATION_CLOSED |
                           D3DRMANIMATION_LINEARPOSITION |
                           D3DRMANIMATION_POSITION);
if(FAILED(retval))
{
    // Option selection error handler goes here
}

// Loop to add position keys to animation object
for (int i = 0; i < motionPoints; i++)
{    retval = anim->AddPositionKey( D3DVAL(i),   // Key frame
                                                 // sequence
                                                 // number
                                    pointCoords[i].x,
                                    pointCoords[i].y,
                                    pointCoords[i].z);
if(FAILED(retval))
{
    // Add position key error handler goes here
}
```

Creating a scaling animation

Producing an animation based on a scaling transformation is very much like producing one based on a translation transformation. In the case of a scaling transformation you use the AddScaleKey() function of IDirect3DRMAnimation2. The function has the following general form:

```
HRESULT AddScaleKey(
                D3DVALUE rvTime,         // 1
                D3DVALUE rvX,            // 2
```

```
                    D3DVALUE rvY,              // 3
                    D3DVALUE rvZ              // 4
                    );
```

The first parameter represents the animation sequence number for the key frame. The second, third, and fourth parameters are the new x-, y-, and z-axis coordinates for the key frame. The function returns D3DRM_OK if it succeeds, or an error otherwise.

Creating a rotation animation

To create an animation based on a rotation transformation, use the SetRotateKey() function of IDirect3DRMAnimation2. The function has the following general form:

```
HRESULT AddRotateKey(
                    D3DVALUE rvTime,          // 1
                    D3DRMQUATERNION *rqQuat    // 2
                    );
```

The first parameter represents the animation sequence number for the key frame. The second parameter is a quaternion representing the rotation. The function returns D3DRM_OK if it succeeds, or an error otherwise.

A quaternion, discussed in Chapter 14, is a structure that represents an axis in 3D space and a rotation along that axis. The power of quaternions relates mostly to the possibility of performing the operations of composition and interpolation. Here we are concerned with defining a rotation by means of a quaternion. The D3DRMQuaternionFromRotation() nonmember function comes to our assistance in this case. We call the function passing to it a scalar and a vector that define the transformation, and the call returns the corresponding quaternion. The following code fragment shows the processing for performing two 180-degree rotations along the x-axis.

```
// Routine data
D3DRMQUATERNION   quat;
int   motionPoints = 3;
D3DVECTOR axis[]=
{
    { D3DVALUE(1), D3DVALUE(0), D3DVALUE(0) },
    { D3DVALUE(1), D3DVALUE(0), D3DVALUE(0) },
    { D3DVALUE(1), D3DVALUE(0), D3DVALUE(0) }
};
const D3DVALUE angle[]=
{
    (float)PI,        // + 180 degrees
    (float)0,
    (float)-PI        // - 180 degrees
};
```

```
// Create the rotation animation
for (i = 0; i < motionPoints; i++)
{
// Calculate the quaternion
D3DRMQuaternionFromRotation(&quat,
                            &axis[i],
                            angle[i]);
// Add rotate key using quaternion
retval = anim->AddRotateKey( D3DVAL(i),   // Sequential key
                             &quat);       // Quaternion
if(FAILED(retval))
{
    // Rotation key error handler goes here
}
```

Note that in the preceding code fragment the array named axis[], of type D3DVECTOR, serves as the axis selector for the rotation.

The angle of rotation is defined in the array named angle[]. The function D3DRMQuaterionFromRotation() is called with the values obtained from these arrays. The quaterion returned by the call is then passed as a parameter to the AddRotateKey() function. The resulting rotation can be seen in the program 3DRM Animation Demo in the book's CD-ROM.

Driving the animation

The sequential display of the animation is usually performed by means of a frame-level callback function. The creation and setup of a frame callback function was discussed in detail in Chapter 19. The following code fragment shows the creation and definition of a callback function to be used in driving an animation. The code assumes the existence of a child frame that contains the animation object.

```
// Routine data
LPDIRECT3DRMFRAME3 aChildFrame                    = NULL;
LPDIRECT3DRMANIMATION2 anim                       = NULL;
D3DVALUE        t = D3DVAL(0.0);        // Time lapse control
D3DVALUE        speed = D3DVAL(0.02);   // Speed control
. . .
retval = aChildFrame->AddMoveCallback( FrameAnimCallback,
                (void *) aChildFrame,
                D3DRMCALLBACK_PREORDER );
. . .
//*****************************************************
// name: FrameAnimCallback()
// desc: Implements a callback for frame animation
//*****************************************************
```

```
void FrameAnimCallback(
                    LPDIRECT3DRMFRAME3 aFrame, // Calling frame
                    void *arg,
                    D3DVALUE delta)          // Speed factor
{
// Local variable
LPDIRECT3DRMFRAME3 scene;

aFrame->GetScene(&scene);    // Obtain scene
t += D3DVAL(speed);          // Add speed constant
anim->SetFrame(aFrame);      // Select frame
anim->SetTime(t);            // Drive the animation

RELEASE(scene);              // Safe release function
}
```

The animation callback function is called by means of the Move() or the Tick() functions. The Move() function is generally preferred because it produces a smoother animation, in most cases. The call to Move() is usually part of the rendering routine which is, in turn, called by the timer- or message-driven animation pulse.

An animation is driven by calling the SetTime() function. This sets the visual object's transformation to the interpolated position, orientation, and scale of the nearby keys. The speed of the animation can be based on the value passed as a parameter to the callback function, on the setting of a global variable, or on both factors.

Animation Sets

An animation set is a group of animation objects. It was designed to facilitate the playback of animations that share the same time parameter and to make possible the creation of complex animation sequences. The CreateAnimationSet() function creates an empty Direct3DRMAnimationSet object that can be used to gain access to the functions of IDirect3DRMAnimationSet2. The function's general form is as follows:

```
HRESULT CreateAnimationSet (
        LPDIRECT3DRMANIMATIONSET2  *lplpD3DRMAnimationSet  // 1
        );
```

Its only parameter is the address that is filled with a pointer to an IDirect3DRM AnimationSet2 interface if the call succeeds. The function returns D3DRM_OK if it succeeds, or an error otherwise.

The IDirect3DRMAnimationSet2 interface, discussed in Chapter 16, provides functions for manipulating animation sets. Table 25-3 lists the functions in this interface.

<table>
<tr><td colspan="2" align="center">Table 25-3
Function in IDirect3DRMAnimationSet2</td></tr>
<tr><td>*Function*</td><td>*Description*</td></tr>
<tr><td colspan="2">**Animation manipulations**</td></tr>
<tr><td>AddAnimation()</td><td>Adds an animation to an animation set</td></tr>
<tr><td>DeleteAnimation()</td><td>Removes an animation from an animation set</td></tr>
<tr><td>GetAnimations()</td><td>Retrieves an array containing the animations in an animation set</td></tr>
<tr><td>Load()</td><td>Loads an animation set from a file, resource, memory, URL, or other sources</td></tr>
<tr><td colspan="2">**Time**</td></tr>
<tr><td>SetTime()</td><td>Sets the time for a specific animation set</td></tr>
</table>

Animations in X Files

Although it is possible to create animation sets by adding individual animation objects, the most frequent use of the IDirect3DRMAnimationSet2 interface is in loading and manipulating animations contained in X files. The typical scenario in 3D animation programming is to use a specialized tool, such as 3D modeling application, to create the meshes and the animations. These tools simplify an otherwise difficult and laborious task. In addition, these tools contain controls that make possible the creation of more complex and precise animations.

3D Studio MAX and TrueSpace4 contain functions for generating animations. In 3D Studio MAX the animation is saved in a file in 3ds format and the -A switch of the Conv3ds utility is then used to convert the file into X format. The creation of animations using modeling and specialty software is beyond the scope of this book.

An animation set in the X file format appears as one of the following templates:

✦ AnimationKey
✦ AnimationOptions
✦ Animation
✦ AnimationSet

The `AnimationSet` template describes an object equivalent to the retained mode concept. It usually contains one or more `Animation` templates that define the animated frame and set the keys. The `AnimationOptions` template is used to determine if the animation is open or closed, as well as to determine the interpolation mode as linear or spline. The most important information for rendering the animation is contained in the `AnimationKey` template. This element defines a set of key frames and determines whether the keys represent a rotation, a scaling, or a translation transformation.

Figure 25-5 is a screen snapshot of one of the animation sets contained in the program 3DRM Animation Set Demo in the book's CD-ROM.

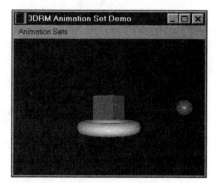

Figure 25-5: Screen snapshot of animation set in 3DRM Animation Set Demo

The animation was created using 3D Studio MAX and saved in a file in 3ds format. The file was then converted to the X format by means of the Conv3ds utility funished with the DirectX SDK. The command switches were as follows:

```
conv3ds -A -s0.02 -x box_sph0.3ds
```

The resulting file in X format contains the animation set for a cube, a torus, and a sphere. The following is a partial listing of this file. We have added comments to clarify the contents.

```
AnimationSet x3ds_animset_0 {      // Animation set
 Animation x3ds_anim_0 {           // First animation in set
  {x3ds_Cube}                      // Cube object
  AnimationKey {                   // First animation key set
   0;                              // 0 = rotation
   5;                              // 5 keys follow
   0; 4; 1.000000, 0.000000, 0.000000, 0.000000;;,
   25; 4; 0.922201, 0.000000, -0.386711, 0.000000;;,
   50; 4; 0.707107, 0.000000, -0.707107, 0.000000;;,
   75; 4; 0.378649, 0.000000, -0.925540, 0.000000;;,
   100; 4; 0.000000, 0.000000, -1.000000, 0.000000;;;
  }
  AnimationKey {                   // Second key set for cube
```

```
 2;                                // 2 = translation
 1;                                // 1 key follows
 0; 3; 0.000107, -0.300209, -0.010889;;;
 }
}
Animation x3ds_anim_1 {            // Second animation in set
 {x3ds_Sphere}                     // Sphere object
 AnimationKey {                    // First animation key set
 0;                                // 0 = rotation
 1;                                // 1 key follows
 0; 4; 1.000000, 0.000000, 0.000000, 0.000000;;;
 }
 AnimationKey {                    // Second key set for sphere
 2;                                // 2 = translation
 101;                              // 101 keys follow
 0; 3; -1.375861, 0.000000, -1.362754;;,
 1; 3; -1.432249, 0.000000, -1.200597;;,
 2; 3; -1.484094, 0.000000, -1.042808;;,
 3; 3; -1.531396, 0.000000, -0.889388;;,

 99; 3; -1.255123, 0.000000, -1.464121;;,
 100; 3; -1.424272, 0.000000, -1.411225;;;
 }
}
Animation x3ds_anim_2 {            // Third animation in set
 {x3ds_Torus}                      // Torus object
 AnimationKey {                    // First animation key set
 0;                                // 0 = rotation
 1;                                // 1 key follows
 0; 4; 1.000000, 0.000000, 0.000000, 0.000000;;;
 }
 AnimationKey {                    // Second animation key set
 1;                                // 1 = scaling
 1;                                // 1 animation key follows
 0; 3; 1.098252, 1.098252, 1.098252;;;
 }
 AnimationKey {                    // Third animation key set
 2;                                // 2 = translation
 101;                              // 101 keys follow
 0; 3; -0.001230, 0.000646, -0.004002;;,
 1; 3; -0.001140, 0.046207, -0.004002;;,
 2; 3; -0.001052, 0.089906, -0.004002;;,
. . .
 98; 3; -0.000385, -0.092070, -0.004002;;,
 99; 3; -0.000346, -0.046086, -0.004002;;,
 100; 3; -0.000304, 0.001852, -0.004002;;;
 }
 }
}                                  // End of X file
```

X file templates are listed in Appendix C.

Loading an animation set

As discussed in Chapter 21, a file in 3ds format containing an animation can be converted into the X format by means of the Conv3ds utility. The -A switch creates an X file that contains an animation set. This animation set can be loaded into an object of type DIRECT3DRMANIMATIONSET2 by means of the Load() function of IDirect3DRMAnimationSet2. The function has the following general form:

```
HRESULT Load(
        LPVOID lpvObjSource,                            // 1
        LPVOID lpvObjID,                                // 2
        D3DRMLOADOPTIONS d3drmLOFlags,                  // 3
        D3DRMLOADTEXTURE3CALLBACK d3drmLoadTextureProc, // 4
        LPVOID lpArgLTP,                                // 5
        LPDIRECT3DRMFRAME3 lpParentFrame                // 6
        );
```

The first parameter represents the source for the object to be loaded. This can be a file, resource, memory block, or stream, depending on the source flags specified in the third parameter. The second parameter is the name or position of the object to be loaded. The use of this parameter depends on the identifier flags specified in the third parameter. If the D3DRMLOAD_BYPOSITION flag is specified, this parameter is a pointer to a DWORD value that gives the object's order in the file. This parameter can be NULL. The third parameter is the value Value of the D3DRMLOADOPTIONS type describing the load options. These options were discussed in Chapter 19 and are listed in Table 19-2. The fourth parameter is the address of a D3DRMLOADTEXTURE3 CALLBACK callback function used to load any textures used by the object. This parameter can be NULL if no textures are to be loaded at this time. The fifth parameter is the address of application-defined data passed to the D3DRMLOAD TEXTURE3CALLBACK callback function.

The sixth parameter is the address of a parent object of type Direct3DRMFrame3. This argument only affects the loading of animation sets. If an animation that is loaded from an X file references a frame with no parent, then the frame's parent is set automatically to this argument. However, if the Load() function is used to load any frames in the X file, the parent frame argument is not used. In other words, the parent frame argument is used only when you load animation sets. The value of this argument can be NULL. The function returns D3DRM_OK if it succeeds, or an error otherwise.

By default, the Load() function loads the first animation set in the file specified by the first parameter. Perspective correction is on by default. The following code fragment shows loading an animation set. Code assumes that the child frame already exists.

```
// Routine data
LPDIRECT3DRMFRAME3 aChildFrame              = NULL;
LPDIRECT3DRMANIMATIONSET2 animSet           = NULL;
```

```
char     szXFile1[] = "box_sph0.x" ;     // x file with animation
. . .
retval = lpD3DRM->CreateAnimationSet( &animSet);
if(FAILED(retval))
{
     // Animation set creation error handler goes here
}

// Load the X file into the animation set
retval = animSet->Load(szXFile1,              // Source
                       NULL,
                       D3DRMLOAD_FROMFILE, // Options
                       NULL, NULL,
                       aChildFrame);
if (FAILED(retval))
{
   // Animation set loading error handler goes here
}
```

Driving the animation set

The real-time rendering of an animation set is performed by methods quite similar to those already described for driving an individual animation. The application usually sets up a frame-level callback function, as discussed earlier. The following code fragment shows the creation and definition of a callback function to be used in driving an animation set. The code assumes the existence of a child frame that contains the animation object.

```
// Routine data
LPDIRECT3DRMFRAME3 aChildFrame                = NULL;
LPDIRECT3DRMANIMATIONSET2 animSet             = NULL;
D3DVALUE        t = D3DVAL(0.0);         // Time lapse control
D3DVALUE        speed = D3DVAL(0.02);    // Speed control
. . .
retval = aChildFrame->AddMoveCallback( SetAnimCallback,
                (void *) aChildFrame,
                D3DRMCALLBACK_PREORDER );
. . .
//***************************************************
// name: SetAnimCallback()
// desc: Implements a callback for frame animation
//       of an animation set
//***************************************************
void SetAnimCallback(LPDIRECT3DRMFRAME3 aFrame,
                     void *arg,
                     D3DVALUE delta)
{
     LPDIRECT3DRMFRAME3 scene;     // Scene frame
```

```
        aFrame->GetScene( &scene);     // Get scene
        t = t + D3DVAL(speed);         // Iteration timer
        animSet->SetTime(t);           // Set time

        RELEASE(scene);
    }
```

As is the case with the animation callback function, the animation set callback function is usually called by the Move() function. The call to Move() is typically located in the rendering routine, which is, in turn, called by the timer- or message-driven animation pulse. The animation set is driven by calling the SetTime() function. SetTime() sets the visual object's transformation to the interpolated position, orientation, and scale of the nearby keys. The speed of the animation can be based on the value passed as a parameter to the callback function, on the setting of a static or global variable, or on both factors.

Interpolators

We have seen that retained mode animation techniques are based on generating the in-between images by interpolating between the key frames. Starting with version 5, Direct X supports an object type called an interpolator. Interpolators provide a more general approach to in-between techniques by extending their use into color tint manipulations, mesh morphing, as well as materials and textures. In this manner interpolators extend the functionality of the Direct3DRMAnimation2 interface. The interpolator functions are located in the IDirect3DRMInterpolator interface. Table 25-4 lists the methods in this interface.

<table>
<tr><th colspan="2">Table 25-4
Methods in IDirect3DRMInterpolator</th></tr>
<tr><th>Method</th><th>Description</th></tr>
<tr><td>AttachObject()</td><td>Connects an object to the interpolator</td></tr>
<tr><td>DetachObject()</td><td>Detaches an object from the interpolator</td></tr>
<tr><td>GetAttachedObjects()</td><td>Retrieves the array of objects currently attached to the interpolator</td></tr>
<tr><td>GetIndex()</td><td>Retrieves the current interpolator index</td></tr>
<tr><td>Interpolate()</td><td>Calculates and generates the actions previously defined for the interpolator.</td></tr>
<tr><td>SetIndex()</td><td>Sets the current interpolator index.</td></tr>
</table>

Like animations and animation sets, interpolators are associated with key frames. When you define an interpolator you set a range of keys, sometimes called the *index span* of the interpolator, and assign values to the key frames. The interpolator logic calculates the in-between values from the key frames. When the `Interpolate()` function is called, the system applies the calculated values to the corresponding object automatically.

Suppose you create an interpolator to perform a translation animation on a frame. In this case you establish the index span for the interpolator as a value in the range 0 to 40. Next, you define the object's position for index number 0. To do this you use the frame interpolator object to call the `SetPosition()` function. Next you define the object's position for the last index in the span. In the move callback function you simply call the `Interpolate()` function passing as arguments the current index number and the object to which the interpolation is to be applied. The system automatically calculates the in-betweens and calls `SetPosition()` for the target object. The result is a translation animation of the frame.

Types of interpolators

Retained mode recognizes the following types of interpolator objects:

✦ `FrameInterpolator`

✦ `LightInterpolator`

✦ `MaterialInterpolator`

✦ `MeshInterpolator`

✦ `TextureInterpolator`

✦ `ViewportInterpolator`

The object attached to an interpolator must be of the same type as the interpolator itself. This means that a frame object can be attached to a `FrameInterpolator`, a mesh object to a `MeshInterpolator`, and so on. It is also possible to attach another interpolator to an interpolator, thus creating a hierarchical chain. Changing the index of an interpolator changes the indices of all attached interpolators to the same value. Table 25-5 lists the methods supported by the `IDirect3DRM` `Interpolator` interface.

Interpolator index and keys

The notion of an interpolator key is related to that of an animation key frame. An interpolator key defines the values for a procedure call. Each key is associated with an index. The interpolator automatically calculates between the key values.

An interpolator key is stored by calling one of the supported interface methods listed in Table 25-5. The key contains two components: the key index and the parameter values to be applied. Once set, the index value for a key never changes.

Table 25-5
Functions Supported by IDirect3DRMInterpolator

Function Category	Function Name
Viewport	SetFront() SetBack() SetField() SetPlane()
Frame	SetPosition() SetRotation() SetVelocity() SetOrientation() SetColor() SetColorRGB() SetSceneBackground() SetSceneBackgroundRGB() SetSceneFogColor() SetSceneFogParams() SetQuaternion()
Mesh	Translate() SetVertices() SetGroupColor() SetGroupColorRGB()
Light	SetColor() SetColorRGB() SetRange() SetUmbra() SetPenumbra() SetConstantAttenuation() SetLinearAttenuation() SetQuadraticAttenuation()
Texture	SetDecalSize() SetDecalOrigin() SetDecalTransparentColor()
Material	SetPower() SetSpecular() SetEmissive()

Interpolation modes

Retained mode interpolators recognize several operation modes, sometimes called options in the DirectX literature. These modes are defined in D3DRMINTERPOLATION OPTIONS, as follows:

```
typedef DWORD D3DRMINTERPOLATIONOPTIONS;
#define D3DRMINTERPOLATION_OPEN 0x01L
#define D3DRMINTERPOLATION_CLOSED 0x02L
#define D3DRMINTERPOLATION_NEAREST 0x0100L
#define D3DRMINTERPOLATION_LINEAR 0x04L
#define D3DRMINTERPOLATION_SPLINE 0x08L
#define D3DRMINTERPOLATION_VERTEXCOLOR 0x40L
#define D3DRMINTERPOLATION_SLERPNORMALS 0x80L
```

Table 25-6 lists the action of each of the constants.

Table 25-6 Retained Mode Interpolation Options	
Constant	**Effect on Interpolation**
D3DRMINTERPOLATION_OPEN	First and last keys of each key chain fix the interpolated values outside of the index span.
D3DRMINTERPOLATION_CLOSED	Cyclic interpolation. The keys repeat infinitely with a period equal to the index span. A key with an index equal to the end of the span is ignored.
D3DRMINTERPOLATION_NEAREST	Nearest key value is used for determining in-between values.
D3DRMINTERPOLATION_LINEAR	Linear interpolation between the two nearest keys is used for determining in-between values.
D3DRMINTERPOLATION_SPLINE	B-spline blending function on the four nearest keys is used for determining in-between values.
D3DRMINTERPOLATION_VERTEXCOLOR	Specifies that vertex colors should be interpolated.
D3DRMINTERPOLATION_SLERPNORMALS	Specifies that vertex normals should be spherically interpolated (not currently implemented).

The interpolation mode is set by the call to the Interpolate() function.

Programming interpolators

The convenience of interpolators is that they facilitate obtaining the in-betweens. For this reason interpolators are particularly useful in animations that are not based on conventional transformations. We have seen that animations and animation sets based on rotation, translation, or scaling transformations can be readily coded as animations or animation sets. In these cases interpolators are not too useful. However, there is no built-in mechanism for animating meshes, colors, textures, or materials. In these cases the use of interpolators facilitates the programming.

On the other hand, you should remember that interpolators are a convenience that makes it easier to calculate and apply the in-betweens required for some types of animation, but that these effects can also be achieved by performing the actual calculations in code. For example, an application that needs to produce a color change to simulate a fade-in or fade-out effect can do so by means of a color interpolator, or by creating a move callback function and then calculating and applying the changes in object color during callback processing. In this case the main advantage of using an interpolator is that it makes the programming easier. At the same time, interpolators are black boxes that sometimes produce unexpected results.

Interpolator programming usually consists of the following steps:

1. Creating the interpolator object and defining its type.

2. Setting the interpolator index span and establishing the individual keys. Attaching the interpolator to an object in the application.

3. Creating an interpolator callback function that receives control with every animation tick. It is this function that typically performs the actual interpolation.

Creating the interpolator object

Most retained mode objects can be defined in a data declaration. To keep the coding as simple as possible, we have followed this method almost exclusively in this book. In regards to interpolators you can define a generic pointer to an interpolator as follows:

```
LPDIRECT3DRMINTERPOLATOR interp1              = NULL;
```

However, retained mode does not define data types for the specific interpolator types FrameInterpolator, LightInterpolator, MaterialInterpolator, MeshInterpolator, TextureInterpolator, and ViewportInterpolator. This means that in order to obtain access to the corresponding interfaces you must obtain the corresponding object from the COM. In the case of a frame interpolator the coding is as follows:

```
// Routine data
LPDIRECT3DRMINTERPOLATOR interp1              = NULL;
LPDIRECT3DRMFRAME3 frameInterp                = NULL;
```

```
HRESULT retval;
. . .
retval = lpD3DRM->CreateObject(

CLSID_CDirect3DRMFrameInterpolator,
                            NULL,
                            IID_IDirect3DRMInterpolator,
                            (VOID**) &interp1);
if(FAILED(retval))
{
    // Interpolator object creation error handler goes here
}
retval = interp1->QueryInterface(IID_IDirect3DRMFrame3,
                            (VOID**) &frameInterp);
if(FAILED(retval))
{
    // Failed interface query error handler goes here
}
```

Defining the index span and keys

After you have obtained the interpolator object, you make calls to any of the functions listed in Table 25-5 to define the interpolator keys. Because each key is associated with an index value, code usually calls the SetIndex() function of IDirect3DRMInterpolator prior to setting the key parameters. For example, to add a position key to a frame interpolator you start by calling SetIndex() with a parameter that corresponds to the current interpolator index. Then you record the position by calling SetPosition() of IDirect3DRMFrame3. Notice that the values passed in the call to SetPosition() are applied to the interpolator, rather than to a real frame. The function call and its parameters are stored in the interpolator as a new index and key. These values are used in calculating the in-betweens during the call to the Interpolate() function.

The SetIndex() function of IDirect3DRMInterpolator sets the interpolator's index to the specified value. If other interpolators are attached to the interpolator, this method recursively synchronizes their indices to the one passed in the call. The function has the following general form:

```
HRESULT SetIndex(
            D3DVALUE d3dVal                         // 1
            );
```

The only parameter is the value of the interpolator's index.

The function returns D3DRM_OK if it succeeds, or an error otherwise.

There is an interesting characteristic to interpolators that execute in the D3DRMINTER POLATION_CLOSED mode. In this case the value assigned to a key at the end of the index span is ignored (see Table 25-6). This means that when assigning key values in the closed mode you must usually include a dummy key, with no associated value, at the end of the span.

After all the indices and keys have been defined for the interpolator, the application must connect the interpolator to a real object. In the case of a frame, the interpolator must be attached to a real frame. The following code fragment shows the creation of three interpolator keys for a translation animation and the attachment of the interpolator to a frame object.

```
// Routine data
LPDIRECT3DRMINTERPOLATOR interp1              = NULL;
LPDIRECT3DRMFRAME3 frameInterp                = NULL;
LPDIRECT3DRMFRAME3 aChildFrame                = NULL;
HRESULT retval;
. . .
// Create first interpolator key
retval = interp1->SetIndex(D3DVAL(0));
if(FAILED(retval))
{
    // Index creation error handler goes here
}

retval = frameInterp->SetPosition(NULL,
                                  D3DVAL(0.0),     // x
                                  D3DVAL(0.0),     // y
                                  D3DVAL(40.0));   // z
if(FAILED(retval))
{
    // Setting interpolator attribute error handler goes here
}
// Create second interpolator key
retval = interp1->SetIndex(D3DVAL(39));
if(FAILED(retval))
{
    // Index creation error handler goes here
}
retval = frameInterp->SetPosition(NULL,
                                  D3DVAL(0.0),
                                  D3DVAL(0.0),
                                  D3DVAL(0.0));
if(FAILED(retval))
{
    // Setting interpolator attribute error handler goes here
}
// Set extra index
retval = interp1->SetIndex(D3DVAL(40));
if(FAILED(retval))
{
    // Index creation error handler goes here
}
// Attach frame object to interpolator
retval = interp1->AttachObject(aChildFrame);
if(FAILED(retval))
{
    // Frame attachment error handler goes here
}
```

The interpolator callback

Actual interpolation usually takes place within a callback function. The creation of the callback function for interpolation is similar to that described earlier in this chapter for other forms of animation. Optionally, the application can also create a destroy callback function. For example, in the case of a frame interpolator the callback function and the destroy callback function are created as follows:

```
// Routine data
LPDIRECT3DRMINTERPOLATOR interp1                      = NULL;
LPDIRECT3DRMFRAME3 aChildFrame                        = NULL;
HRESULT retval;
. . .
// Create an interpolator callback function
retval = aChildFrame->AddMoveCallback(InterpolateCallback,
                                      (void *) interp1,
                                      D3DRMCALLBACK_PREORDER );
if(FAILED(retval))
{
    // Callback function creation error handler goes here
}
// Create destroy callback
retval = aChildFrame->AddDestroyCallback(
DestroyInterpCallback,
                                        interp1);
if(FAILED(retval))
{
    // Destroy callback creation error handler goes here
}
```

The actual processing performed in the callback function is application dependent. Usually, the intercept routine contains a call to the `Interpolate()` function of `IDirect3DRMInterpolator`. The following code fragment shows a simple interpolation callback function.

```
//****************************************************************
// Name: InterpolateCallback()
// Desc: Frame interpolator callback function
// Note: The parameter delta is passed by the Move() function
//       call
//****************************************************************
void InterpolateCallback( LPDIRECT3DRMFRAME3 aFrame,
                          void *arg,
                          D3DVALUE delta )
{
    LPDIRECT3DRMINTERPOLATOR frameInt;

    // Retrieve target frame
    frameInt = (LPDIRECT3DRMINTERPOLATOR) arg;

    frameInt->Interpolate(pulse += delta,
                          NULL,
                          D3DRMINTERPOLATION_CLOSED |
```

```
                        D3DRMINTERPOLATION_LINEAR);
}
```

If the interpolation refers to a translation animation, the call to `Interpolate()` calls the `SetPosition()` function for the frame attached to the interpolator. The interpolator mode constants passed in the third parameter have the action described in Table 25-6. The actual parameters for the call, the so-called in-betweens, are calculated automatically by the interpolator.

Alternatively, the call to `Interpolate()` can reference a specific object in the second parameter. In this case the interpolation is applied directly to the specified object bypassing any previous attachments. The same interpolator can be used to store more than one key. For example, if the defined keys refer to other object attributes, such as color, orientation, or scale, these are all simultaneously applied to the attached frames.

You can use the same interpolator to store other keys such as orientation, scale, velocity, and color keys. Each property exists on a parallel timeline, and calling `Interpolate()` assigns the interpolated value for each property to the attached frames. The program 3DRM Interpolator Demo in the book's CD-ROM contains an example of a simultaneous translation and color tint change interpolation.

Summary

In this chapter we have examined animation techniques in retained mode programming. Most 3D applications require some form of animation, so the topic is a crucial one. We discussed several animation techniques, starting with the simplest approach which consists of creating a callback function for object movements and then hand-coding the necessary transformations and manipulations in the intercept handler. We also discussed retained mode animation techniques that take advantage of facilities provided by the system. These include animations, animation sets, and interpolators. We also explored the advantages of using animations contained in X files.

♦   ♦   ♦

Windows and DirectX Structures

This appendix contains the structures mentioned in the text. Structures are listed in alphabetical order.

```
BITMAP
   typedef struct tagBITMAP {  /* bm */
        int     bmType;
        int     bmWidth;
        int     bmHeight;
        int     bmWidthBytes;
        BYTE    bmPlanes;
        BYTE    bmBitsPixel;
        LPVOID  bmBits;
   };

BITMAPCOREHEADER
   typedef struct tagBITMAPCOREHEADER { // bmch
        DWORD   bcSize;
        WORD    bcWidth;
        WORD    bcHeight;
        WORD    bcPlanes;
        WORD    bcBitCount;
   } BITMAPCOREHEADER;

BITMAPCOREINFO
   typedef struct _BITMAPCOREINFO {      // bmci
        BITMAPCOREHEADER  bmciHeader;
        RGBTRIPLE         bmciColors[1];
   } BITMAPCOREINFO;

BITMAPFILEHEADER
   typedef struct tagBITMAPFILEHEADER { // bmfh
        WORD    bfType;
        DWORD   bfSize;
        WORD    bfReserved1;
        WORD    bfReserved2;
        DWORD   bfOffBits;
   } BITMAPFILEHEADER;
```

```
BITMAPINFO
    typedef struct tagBITMAPINFO { // bmi
        BITMAPINFOHEADER bmiHeader;
        RGBQUAD          bmiColors[1];
    } BITMAPINFO;

BITMAPINFOHEADER
    typedef struct tagBITMAPINFOHEADER{ // bmih
        DWORD  biSize;
        LONG   biWidth;
        LONG   biHeight;
        WORD   biPlanes;
        WORD   biBitCount
        DWORD  biCompression;
        DWORD  biSizeImage;
        LONG   biXPelsPerMeter;
        LONG   biYPelsPerMeter;
        DWORD  biClrUsed;
        DWORD  biClrImportant;
    } BITMAPINFOHEADER;

CHOOSECOLOR
    typedef struct {     // cc
        DWORD          lStructSize;
        HWND           hwndOwner;
        HWND           hInstance;
        COLORREF       rgbResult;
        COLORREF*      lpCustColors;
        DWORD          Flags;
        LPARAM         lCustData;
        LPCCHOOKPROC   lpfnHook;
        LPCTSTR        lpTemplateName;
    } CHOOSECOLOR;

COLORADJUSTMENT
    typedef struct  tagCOLORADJUSTMENT {     /* ca */
        WORD   caSize;
        WORD   caFlags;
        WORD   caIlluminantIndex;
        WORD   caRedGamma;
        WORD   caGreenGamma;
        WORD   caBlueGamma;
        WORD   caReferenceBlack;
        WORD   caReferenceWhite;
        SHORT  caContrast;
        SHORT  caBrightness;
        SHORT  caColorfulness;
        SHORT  caRedGreenTint;
    } COLORADJUSTMENT;

CREATESTRUCT
```

```
typedef struct tagCREATESTRUCT { // cs
    LPVOID    lpCreateParams;
    HINSTANCE hInstance;
    HMENU     hMenu;
    HWND      hwndParent;
    int       cy;
    int       cx;
    int       y;
    int       x;
    LONG      style;
    LPCTSTR   lpszName;
    LPCTSTR   lpszClass;
    DWORD     dwExStyle;
} CREATESTRUCT;

DDBLTFX
    typedef struct _DDBLTFX{
        DWORD   dwSize;
        DWORD   dwDDFX;
        DWORD   dwROP;
        DWORD   dwDDROP;
        DWORD   dwRotationAngle;
        DWORD   dwZBufferOpCode;
        DWORD   dwZBufferLow;
        DWORD   dwZBufferHigh;
        DWORD   dwZBufferBaseDest;
        DWORD   dwZDestConstBitDepth;
    union
    {
            DWORD                dwZDestConst;
            LPDIRECTDRAWSURFACE  lpDDSZBufferDest;
    };
        DWORD   dwZSrcConstBitDepth;
    union
    {
            DWORD                dwZSrcConst;
            LPDIRECTDRAWSURFACE  lpDDSZBufferSrc;

    };
        DWORD   dwAlphaEdgeBlendBitDepth;
        DWORD   dwAlphaEdgeBlend;
        DWORD   dwReserved;
        DWORD   dwAlphaDestConstBitDepth;
    union
    {
            DWORD                dwAlphaDestConst;
            LPDIRECTDRAWSURFACE  lpDDSAlphaDest;
    };
        DWORD   dwAlphaSrcConstBitDepth;
    union
    {
```

```
                    DWORD                  dwAlphaSrcConst;
                    LPDIRECTDRAWSURFACE    lpDDSAlphaSrc;
            };
            union
            {
                    DWORD                  dwFillColor;
                    DWORD                  dwFillDepth;

                    LPDIRECTDRAWSURFACE    lpDDSPattern;
            };
            DDCOLORKEY  ddckDestColorkey;
            DDCOLORKEY  ddckSrcColorkey;
            } DDBLTFX,FAR* LPDDBLTFX;

DDCAPS
    typedef struct _DDCAPS{
            DWORD     dwSize;
            DWORD     dwCaps;
            DWORD     dwCaps2;
            DWORD     dwCKeyCaps;
            DWORD     dwFXCaps;
            DWORD     dwFXAlphaCaps;
            DWORD     dwPalCaps;
            DWORD     dwSVCaps;
            DWORD     dwAlphaBltConstBitDepths;
            DWORD     dwAlphaBltPixelBitDepths;
            DWORD     dwAlphaBltSurfaceBitDepths;
            DWORD     dwAlphaOverlayConstBitDepths;
            DWORD     dwAlphaOverlayPixelBitDepths;
            DWORD     dwAlphaOverlaySurfaceBitDepths;
            DWORD     dwZBufferBitDepths;

            DWORD     dwVidMemTotal;
            DWORD     dwVidMemFree;
            DWORD     dwMaxVisibleOverlays;
            DWORD     dwCurrVisibleOverlays;
            DWORD     dwNumFourCCCodes;
            DWORD     dwAlignBoundarySrc;
            DWORD     dwAlignSizeSrc;
            DWORD     dwAlignBoundaryDest;
            DWORD     dwAlignSizeDest;
            DWORD     dwAlignStrideAlign;
            DWORD     dwRops[DD_ROP_SPACE];
            DDSCAPS   ddsCaps;
            DWORD     dwMinOverlayStretch;
            DWORD     dwMaxOverlayStretch;
            DWORD     dwMinLiveVideoStretch;

            DWORD     dwMaxLiveVideoStretch;
            DWORD     dwMinHwCodecStretch;
            DWORD     dwMaxHwCodecStretch;
```

```
        DWORD     dwReserved1;
        DWORD     dwReserved2;
        DWORD     dwReserved3;
        DWORD     dwSVBCaps;
        DWORD     dwSVBCKeyCaps;
        DWORD     dwSVBFXCaps;
        DWORD     dwSVBRops[DD_ROP_SPACE];
        DWORD     dwVSBCaps;
        DWORD     dwVSBCKeyCaps;
        DWORD     dwVSBFXCaps;
        DWORD     dwVSBRops[DD_ROP_SPACE];
        DWORD     dwSSBCaps;
        DWORD     dwSSBCKeyCaps;

        DWORD     dwSSBCFXCaps;
        DWORD     dwSSBRops[DD_ROP_SPACE];
        DWORD     dwReserved4;
        DWORD     dwReserved5;
        DWORD     dwReserved6;
    } DDCAPS,FAR* LPDDCAPS;

DDCOLORKEY
    typedef struct _DDCOLORKEY{
        DWORD   dwColorSpaceLowValue;
        DWORD   dwColorSpaceHighValue;
    } DDCOLORKEY,FAR* LPDDCOLORKEY;

DDPIXELFORMAT
    typedef struct _DDPIXELFORMAT{
        DWORD   dwSize;
        DWORD   dwFlags;
        DWORD   dwFourCC;
    union
    {
            DWORD   dwRGBBitCount;
            DWORD   dwYUVBitCount;
            DWORD   dwZBufferBitDepth;
            DWORD   dwAlphaBitDepth;
    };
    union
    {
            DWORD   dwRBitMask;
            DWORD   dwYBitMask;
    };
    union
    {
            DWORD   dwGBitMask;
            DWORD   dwUBitMask;
    };
    union
    {
```

```
          DWORD   dwBBitMask;
          DWORD   dwVBitMask;
    };
    union
    {
          DWORD   dwRGBAlphaBitMask;

          DWORD   dwYUVAlphaBitMask;
    };
  } DDPIXELFORMAT, FAR* LPDDPIXELFORMAT;
```

DDSCAPS2
```
  typedef struct _DDSCAPS2 {
      DWORD   dwCaps;   // Surface capabilities
      DWORD   dwCaps2;  // More surface capabilities
      DWORD   dwCaps3;  // Not currently used
      DWORD   dwCaps4;  // .
  } DDSCAPS2, FAR* LPDDSCAPS2;
```

DDSURFACEDESC2
```
  typedef struct _DDSURFACEDESC2 {
      DWORD          dwSize;
      DWORD          dwFlags;
      DWORD          dwHeight;
      DWORD          dwWidth;
      union
      {
          LONG       lPitch;
          DWORD      dwLinearSize;
      } DUMMYUNIONNAMEN(1);
      DWORD          dwBackBufferCount;
      union
      {
          DWORD      dwMipMapCount;
          DWORD      dwRefreshRate;
      } DUMMYUNIONNAMEN(2);
      DWORD          dwAlphaBitDepth;
      DWORD          dwReserved;
      LPVOID         lpSurface;
      DDCOLORKEY     ddckCKDestOverlay;
      DDCOLORKEY     ddckCKDestBlt;
      DDCOLORKEY     ddckCKSrcOverlay;
      DDCOLORKEY     ddckCKSrcBlt;
      DDPIXELFORMAT  ddpfPixelFormat;
      DDSCAPS2       ddsCaps;
      DWORD          dwTextureStage;
  } DDSURFACEDESC2, FAR* LPDDSURFACEDESC2;
```

DIBSECTION

```
typedef struct tagDIBSECTION {
    BITMAP             dsBm;
    BITMAPINFOHEADER   dsBmih;
    DWORD              dsBitfields[3];
    HANDLE             dshSection;
    DWORD              dsOffset;
} DIBSECTION;
```

DIDATAFORMAT
```
typedef struct {
    DWORD dwSize;
    DWORD dwObjSize;
    DWORD dwFlags;
    DWORD dwDataSize;
    DWORD dwNumObjs;
    LPDIOBJECTDATAFORMAT rgodf;
} DIDATAFORMAT;
```

DIDEVCAPS
```
typedef struct {
    DWORD dwSize;
    DWORD dwDevType;
    DWORD dwFlags;
    DWORD dwAxes;
    DWORD dwButtons;
    DWORD dwPOVs;
} DIDEVCAPS;
```

DIDEVICEINSTANCE
```
typedef struct {
    DWORD dwSize;
    GUID  guidInstance;
    GUID  guidProduct;
    DWORD dwDevType;
    TCHAR tszInstanceName[MAX_PATH];
    TCHAR tszProductName[MAX_PATH];
} DIDEVICEINSTANCE;
```

DIDEVICEOBJECTDATA
```
typedef struct {
    DWORD dwOfs;
    DWORD dwData;
    DWORD dwTimeStamp;
    DWORD dwSequence;
} DIDEVICEOBJECTDATA;
```

DIJOYSTATE
```
typedef struct DIJOYSTATE {
    LONG    lX;
    LONG    lY;
    LONG    lZ;
```

```
        LONG    lRx;
        LONG    lRy;
        LONG    lRz;
        LONG    rglSlider[2];
        DWORD   rgdwPOV[4];
        BYTE    rgbButtons[32];
    } DIJOYSTATE, *LPDIJOYSTATE;

DIJOYSTATE2
    typedef struct DIJOYSTATE2 {
        LONG    lX;
        LONG    lY;
        LONG    lZ;
        LONG    lRx;
        LONG    lRy;
        LONG    lRz;
        LONG    rglSlider[2];
        DWORD   rgdwPOV[4];
        BYTE    rgbButtons[128];
        LONG    lVX;
        LONG    lVY;
        LONG    lVZ;
        LONG    lVRx;
        LONG    lVRy;
        LONG    lVRz;
        LONG    rglVSlider[2];
        LONG    lAX;
        LONG    lAY;
        LONG    lAZ;
        LONG    lARx;
        LONG    lARy;
        LONG    lARz;
        LONG    rglASlider[2];
        LONG    lFX;
        LONG    lFY;
        LONG    lFZ;
        LONG    lFRx;
        LONG    lFRy;
        LONG    lFRz;
        LONG    rglFSlider[2];
    } DIJOYSTATE2, *LPDIJOYSTATE2;

DIMOUSESTATE
    typedef struct {
        LONG lX;
        LONG lY;
        LONG lZ;
        BYTE rgbButtons[4];
    } DIMOUSESTATE;

DIPROPDWORD
```

```
typedef struct {
    DIPROPHEADER      diph;
    DWORD             dwData;
} DIPROPDWORD;
```

DIPROPHEADER
```
typedef struct {
    DWORD   dwSize;
    DWORD   dwHeaderSize;
    DWORD   dwObj;
    DWORD   dwHow;
} DIPROPHEADER;
```

DIPROPRANGE
```
typedef struct {
    DIPROPHEADER diph;
    LONG         lMin;
    LONG         lMax;
} DIPROPRANGE;
```

```
DISPLAY_DEVICE
typedef struct _DISPLAY_DEVICE {
    DWORD   cb;
    WCHAR   DeviceName[32];
    WCHAR   DeviceString[128];
    DWORD   StateFlags;
} DISPLAY_DEVICE, *PDISPLAY_DEVICE, *LPDISPLAY_DEVICE;
```

DSETUP_CB_UPGRADEINFO
```
typedef struct _DSETUP_CB_UPGRADEINFO
{
    DWORD UpgradeFlags;
} DSETUP_CB_UPGRADEINFO;
```

LOGBRUSH
```
typedef struct tag LOGBRUSH { /* lb */
    UINT     lbStyle;
    COLORREF lbColor;
    LONG     lbHatch;
} LOGBRUSH;
```

LOGPEN
```
typedef struct tagLOGPEN {   /* lgpn */
    UINT     lopnStyle;
    POINT    lopnWidth;
    COLORREF lopnColor;
} LOGPEN;
```

LV_KEYDOWN
```
typedef struct tagLV_KEYDOWN {
    NMHDR hdr;
```

```
        WORD wVKey;
        UINT flags;
    } LV_KEYDOWN;

MONITORINFO
    typedef struct tagMONITORINFO {
        DWORD   cbSize;
        RECT    rcMonitor;
        RECT    rcWork;
        DWORD   dwFlags;
    } MONITORINFO, *LPMONITORINFO;

MONITORINFOEX
    typedef struct tagMONITORINFOEX {
        DWORD   cbSize;
        RECT    rcMonitor;
        RECT    rcWork;
        DWORD   dwFlags;
        TCHAR   szDevice[CCHDEVICENAME]
    } MONITORINFOEX, *LPMONITORINFOEX;

MSG
    typedef struct tagMSG {        // msg
        HWND    hwnd;
        UINT    message;
        WPARAM  wParam;
        LPARAM  lParam;
        DWORD   time;
        POINT   pt;
    } MSG;

NMHDR
    typedef struct tagNMHDR {
        HWND hwndFrom;
        UINT idFrom;
        UINT code;
    } NMHDR;

PAINTSTRUCT
    typedef struct tagPAINTSTRUCT { // ps
        HDC  hdc;
        BOOL fErase;
        RECT rcPaint;
        BOOL fRestore;
        BOOL fIncUpdate;
        BYTE rgbReserved[32];
    } PAINTSTRUCT;

POINT
    typedef struct tagPOINT {
        LONG x;
```

```
        LONG y;
    } POINT;

    RECT
    typedef struct tagRECT {
        LONG left;
        LONG top;
        LONG right;
        LONG bottom;
    } RECT;

RGBQUAD
    typedef struct tagRGBQUAD { // rgbq
        BYTE      rgbBlue;
        BYTE      rgbGreen;
        BYTE      rgbRed;
        BYTE      rgbReserved;
    } RGBQUAD;

RGBTRIPLE
    typedef struct tagRGBTRIPLE { // rgbt
        BYTE rgbtBlue;
        BYTE rgbtGreen;
        BYTE rgbtRed;
    } RGBTRIPLE;


RGNDATA
    typedef struct _RGNDATA { /* rgnd */
        RGNDATAHEADER rdh;
        char          Buffer[1];
    } RGNDATA;

RGNDATAHEADER
    typedef struct _RGNDATAHEADER { // rgndh
        DWORD dwSize;
        DWORD iType;
        DWORD nCount;
        DWORD nRgnSize;
        RECT  rcBound;
    } RGNDATAHEADER;

SCROLLINFO
    typedef struct tagSCROLLINFO {  // si
        UINT cbSize;
        UINT fMask;
        int  nMin;
        int  nMax;
        UINT nPage;
        int  nPos;
        int  nTrackPos;
```

```
        }   SCROLLINFO;
    typedef SCROLLINFO FAR *LPSCROLLINFO;

SIZE
    typedef struct tagSIZE {
        int cx;
        int cy;
    } SIZE;

TBBUTTON
    typedef struct _TBBUTTON { \\ tbb
        int iBitmap;
        int idCommand;
        BYTE fsState;
        BYTE fsStyle;
        DWORD dwData;
        int iString;
    } TBBUTTON, NEAR* PTBBUTTON, FAR* LPTBBUTTON;
    typedef const TBBUTTON FAR* LPCTBBUTTON;

TEXTMETRICS
    typedef struct tagTEXTMETRIC {   /* tm */
        int   tmHeight;
        int   tmAscent;
        int   tmDescent;
        int   tmInternalLeading;
        int   tmExternalLeading;
        int   tmAveCharWidth;
        int   tmMaxCharWidth;
        int   tmWeight;
        BYTE  tmItalic;
        BYTE  tmUnderlined;
        BYTE  tmStruckOut;
        BYTE  tmFirstChar;
        BYTE  tmLastChar;
        BYTE  tmDefaultChar;
        BYTE  tmBreakChar;
        BYTE  tmPitchAndFamily;
        BYTE  tmCharSet;
        int   tmOverhang;
        int   tmDigitizedAspectX;
        int   tmDigitizedAspectY;
    } TEXTMETRIC;

TOOLINFO
    typedef struct {   // ti
        UINT     cbSize;
        UINT     uFlags;
        HWND     hwnd;
        UINT     uId;
        RECT     rect;
```

```
        HINSTANCE hinst;
        LPTSTR    lpszText;
    } TOOLINFO, NEAR *PTOOLINFO, FAR *LPTOOLINFO;

WNDCLASSEX
    typedef struct _WNDCLASSEX {      // wc
        UINT    cbSize;
        UINT    style;
        WNDPROC lpfnWndProc;
        int     cbClsExtra;
        int     cbWndExtra;
        HANDLE  hInstance;
        HICON   hIcon;
        HCURSOR hCursor;
        HBRUSH  hbrBackground;
        LPCTSTR lpszMenuName;
        LPCTSTR lpszClassName;
        HICON   hIconSm;
    } WNDCLASSEX;
```

✦   ✦   ✦

Ternary Raster Operation Codes

This appendix describes the ternary raster operation codes used by the Windows GDI and DirectX. These codes determine how the bits in a source are combined with those of a destination, taking into account a particular pattern.

The following abbreviations are used for the ternary operands and the Boolean functions:

D = destination bitmap

P = pattern (determined by current brush)

S = Source bitmap

& = bitwise AND

~ = bitwise NOT (inverse)

| = bitwise OR

^ = bitwise exclusive OR (XOR)

The most commonly used raster operations have been given special names in the Windows include file, windows.h. The following table, taken from Developer Studio help files, lists all 256 ternary raster operations.

Raster Operation	ROP code	Boolean operation	Common name
00	00000042	0	BLACKNESS
01	00010289	~(P|S|D)	–
02	00020C89	~(P|S)&D	–
03	000300AA	~(P|S)	–
04	00040C88	~(P|D)&S	–
05	000500A9	~(P|D)	–
06	00060865	~(|P~(S^D))	–
07	000702C5	~(P|(S&D))	–
08	00080F08	~P&S&D	–
09	00090245	~(P|(S^D))	–
0A	000A0329	~P&D	–
0B	000B0B2A	~P(|(S&~D))	–
0C	000C0324	~P&S	–
0D	000D0B25	~P|(~S&D))	–
0E	000E08A5	~P|~(S|D)	–
0F	000F0001	~P	–
10	00100C85	P&~(S|D)	–
11	001100A6	~(S|D)	NOTSRCERASE
12	00120868	~(S|~(P^D))	–
13	001302C8	~(S|(P&D))	–
14	00140869	~(D|~(P^S))	–
15	001502C9	~(D|(P&S))	–
16	00165CCA	P^(S^(D&~(P&S)))	–
17	00171D54	~(S^((S^P)&(S^D)))	–
18	00180D59	(P^S)&(P^D)	–
19	00191CC8	~(S^D&~(P&S)))	–
1A	001A06C5	P^(D|(S&P))	–
1B	001B0768	~(S^(D&(P^S)))	–
1C	001C06CA	P^(S|(P&D))	–

Raster Operation	ROP code	Boolean operation	Common name
1D	001D0766	~(D^(S&(P^D)))	–
1E	001E01A5	P^(S|D)	–
1F	001F0385	~(P&(S|D))	–
20	00200F09	P&~S&D	–
21	00210248	~(S|(P^D))	–
22	00220326	~S&D	–
23	00230B24	~(S|(P&~D))	–
24	00240D55	(S^P)&(S^D)	–
25	00251CC5	~(P^(D&~(S&P)))	–
26	002606C8	S^(D|((P&S))	–
27	00271868	S^(D|~(P^S))	–
28	00280369	D&(P^S)	–
29	002916CA	~(P^(S^(D|(P&S))))	–
2A	002A0CC9	D&~(P&S)	–
2B	002B1D58	~(S^((S^P)&(P&D)))	–
2C	002C0784	S^(P&(S|D))	–
2D	002D060A	P^(S|~D)	–
2E	002E064A	P^(S|(P^D))	–
2F	002F0E2A	~(P&(S|~D))	–
30	0030032A	P&~S	–
31	00310B28	~(S|(~P&D))	–
32	00320688	S^(P|S|D)	–
33	00330008	~S	NOTSRCCOPY
34	003406C4	S^(P|(S&D))	–
35	00351864	S^(P|~(S^D))	–
36	003601A8	S^(P|D)	–
37	00370388	~(S&(P|D))	–
38	0038078A	P^(S&(P|D))	–
39	00390604	S^(P|~D)	–

Continued

Raster Operation	ROP code	Boolean operation	Common name
3A	003A0644	S^(P^(S^D))	-
3B	003B0E24	~(S&(P|~D))	-
3C	003C004A	P^S	-
3D	003D18A4	S^(P|~(S|D))	-
3E	003E1B24	S^(P|(~S&D))	-
3F	003F00EA	~(P&S)	-
40	00400F0A	P&S&~D	-
41	00410249	~(D|(P^S))	-
42	00420D5D	(S^D)&(P^D)	-
43	00431CC4	~(S^(P&~(S&D)))	-
44	00440328	S&~D	SRCERASE
45	00450B29	~(D|(P&~S))	-
46	004606C6	D^(S|(P&D))	-
47	0047076A	~(P^(S&((P^D)))	-
48	00480368	S&(P^D)	-
49	004916C5	~(P^(D^(S|(P&D))))	-
4A	004A0789	D^(P&(S|D))	-
4B	004B0605	P^(~S|D)	-
4C	004C0CC8	S&~(P&D)	-
4D	004D1954	~(S^((P^S)|(S^D)))	-
4E	004E0645	P^(D|(P^S))	-
4F	004F0E25	~(P&(~S|D))	-
50	00500325	P&~D	-
51	00510B26	~(D|(~P&S))	-
52	005206C9	D^(P|(S&D))	-
53	00530764	~(S^(P&(S^D)))	-
54	005408A9	~(D|~(P|S))	-
55	00550009	~D	DSTINVERT
56	005601A9	D^(P|S)	-

Raster Operation	ROP code	Boolean operation	Common name
57	00570389	~(D&(P|S))	–
58	00580785	P^(D&(P|S))	–
59	00590609	D^(P|~S)	–
5A	005A0049	P^D	PATINVERT
5B	005B18A9	D^(P|~(S|D))	–
5C	005C0649	D^(P|(S^D))	–
5D	005D0E29	~(D&(P|~S))	–
5E	005E1B29	D^(P|(S&~D))	–
5F	005F00E9	~(P&D)	–
60	00600365	P&(S^D)	–
61	006116C6	~(D^(S^(P|(S&D))))	–
62	00620786	D^(S&(P|D))	–
63	00630608	S^(~P|D)	–
64	00640788	S^(D&(P|S))	–
65	00650606	D^(~P|S)	–
66	00660046	S^D	SRCINVERT
67	006718A8	S^(D|~(P|S))	–
68	006858A6	~(D^(S^(P|~(S|D))))	–
69	00690145	~(P^(S^D))	–
6A	006A01E9	D^(P&S)	–
6B	006B178A	~(P^(S^(D&(S|P))))	–
6C	006C01E8	S^(P&D)	–
6D	006D1785	~(P^(D^(S&(P|D))))	–
6E	006E1E28	S^(D&(P|~S))	–
6F	006F0C65	~(P&~(S^D))	–
70	00700CC5	P&~(S&D)	–
71	00711D5C	~(S^((S^D)&(P^D)))	–
72	00720648	S^(D|(P^S))	–
73	00730E28	~(S&(~P|D))	–

Continued

Raster Operation	ROP code	Boolean operation	Common name
74	00740646	D^(S|(P^D))	–
75	00750E26	~(D&(~P|S))	–
76	00761B28	S^(D|(P&~S))	–
77	007700E6	~(S&D)	–
78	007801E5	P^(S&D)	–
79	00791786	~(D^(S^(P&(S|D))))	–
7A	007A1E29	D^(P&(S|~D))	–
7B	007B0C68	~(S&~(P^D))	–
7C	007C1E24	S^(P&(~S|D))	–
7D	007D0C69	~(D&~(S^P))	–
7E	007E0955	(P^S)|(S^D)	–
7F	007F03C9	~(P&S&D)	–
80	008003E9	P&S&D	–
81	00810975	~((P^S)|(S^D))	–
82	00820C49	~(P^S)&D	–
83	00831E04	~(S^(P&(~S|D)))	–
84	00840C48	S&~(P^D)	–
85	00851E05	~(P^(D&(~P|S)))	–
86	008617A6	D^(S^(P&(S|D)))	–
87	008701C5	~(P^(S&D))	–
88	008800C6	S&D	SRCAND
89	00891B08	~(S^(D|(P&~S)))	–
8A	008A0E06	(~P|S)&D	–
8B	008B0666	~(D^(S|(P^D)))	–
8C	008C0E08	S&(~P|D)	–
8D	008D0668	~S(^(D|(P^S)))	–
8E	008E1D7C	S^((S^D)&(P^D))	–
8F	008F0CE5	~(P&~(S&D))	–
90	00900C45	P&~(S^D)	–

Raster Operation	ROP code	Boolean operation	Common name
91	00911E08	~(S^(D&(P|~S)))	-
92	009217A9	D^(P^(S&(P|D)))	-
93	009301C4	~(S^(P&D))	-
94	009417AA	P^(S^(D&(P|S)))	-
95	009501C9	~(D^(P&S))	-
96	00960169	P^S^D	-
97	0097588A	P^(S^(D|~P|S))	-
98	00981888	~(S^(D|~(P|S)))	-
99	00990066	~(S^D)	-
9A	009A0709	(P&~S)^D	-
9B	009B07A8	~(S^(D&(P|S)))	-
9C	009C0704	S^(P&~D)	-
9D	009D07A6	~(D^(S&(P|D)))	-
9E	009E16E6	(S^(P|(S&D)))^D	-
9F	009F0345	~(P&(S^D))	-
A0	00A000C9	P&D	-
A1	00A11B05	~(P^(D|(~P&S)))	-
A2	00A20E09	(P|~S)&D	-
A3	00A30669	~(D^(P|(S^D)))	-
A4	00A41885	~(P^(D|~(P|S)))	-
A5	00A50065	~(P^D)	-
A6	00A60706	(~P&S)^D	-
A7	00A707A5	~(P^(D&(P|S)))	-
A8	00A803A9	(P|S)&D	-
A9	00A90189	~((P|S)^D)	-
AA	00AA0029	D	-
AB	00AB0889	~(P|S)|D	-
AC	00AC0744	S^(P&(S^D))	-
AD	00AD06E9	~(D^(P|(S&D)))	-

Continued

Raster Operation	ROP code	Boolean operation	Common name
AE	00AE0B06	(~P&S)|D	-
AF	00AF0229	~P|D	-
B0	00B00E05	P&(~S|D)	-
B1	00B10665	~(P^(D|(P^S)))	-
B2	00B21974	S^((P^S)|(S^D))	-
B3	00B30CE8	~(S&~(P&D))	-
B4	00B4070A	P^(S&~D)	-
B5	00B507A9	~(D^(P&(S|D)))	-
B6	00B616E9	D^(P^(D|(P&D)))	-
B7	00B70348	~(S&(P^D))	-
B8	00B8074A	P^(S&(P^D))	-
B9	00B906E6	~(D^(S|(P&D)))	-
BA	00BA0B09	(P&~S)|D	-
BB	00BB0226	~S|D	MERGEPAINT
BC	00BC1CE4	S^(P&~(S&D))	-
BD	00BD0D7D	~((P^D)&(S^D))	-
BE	00BE0269	(P^S)|D	-
BF	00BF08C9	~(P&S)|D	-
C0	00C000CA	P&S	MERGECOPY
C1	00C11B04	~(S^(P|(~S&D)))	-
C2	00C21884	~(S^(P|~(S|D)))	-
C3	00C3006A	~(P^S)	-
C4	00C40E04	S&(P|~D)	-
C5	00C50664	~(S^(P|(S^D)))	-
C6	00C60708	S^(~P&D)	-
C7	00C707AA	~(P^(S&(P|D)))	-
C8	00C803A8	S&(P|D)	-
C9	00C90184	~(S^(P|D))	-
CA	00CA0749	D^(P&(S^D))	-

Raster Operation	ROP code	Boolean operation	Common name
CB	00CB06E4	~(S^(P|(S&D)))	–
CC	00CC0020	S	SRCCOPY
CD	00CD0888	S|~(P|D)	–
CE	00CE0B08	S|(~P&D)	–
CF	00CF0224	S|~P	–
D0	00D00E0A	~(^(S|(P^D)))	–
D1	00D1066A	P^(~S&D)	–
D2	00D20705	~(S^(P&(S|D)))	–
D3	00D307A4	S^((P^S)&(P^D))	–
D4	00D41D78	(~(D&~(P&S))	–
D5	00D50CE9	P^(S^(D|(P&S)))	–
D6	00D616EA	~(D&(P^S))	–
D7	00D70349	~(D&(P&S))	–
D8	00D80745	P^(D&(P^S))	–
D9	00D906E8	~(S^(D|(P&S)))	–
DA	00DA1CE9	D^(P&~(S&D))	–
DB	00DB0D75	~((P^S)&(S^D))	–
DC	00DC0B04	S|(P&~D)	–
DD	00DD0228	S|~D	–
DE	00DE0268	S|(P^D)	–
DF	00DF08C8	S|~(P&D)	–
E0	00E003A5	P&(D|S)	–
E1	00E10185	~(P^(S|D))	–
E2	00E20746	D^(S&(P^D))	–
E3	00E306EA	~(P^(S|(P&D)))	–
E4	00E40748	S^(D&(P^S))	–
E5	00E506E5	~(P^(D|(P&S)))	–
E6	00E61CE8	S^(D&~(P&S))	–
E7	00E70D79	~((P^S)&(P^D))	–

Continued

Raster Operation	ROP code	Boolean operation	Common name
E8	00E81D74	S^((P^S)&*S^D))	–
E9	00E95CE6	~(D^(S^(P&~(S&D))))	–
EA	00EA02E9	(P&S)|D	–
EB	00EB0849	~(P^S)|D	–
EC	00EC02E8	S|(P&D)	–
ED	00ED0848	S|(~(P^D)	–
EE	00EE0086	S|D	SRCPAINT
EF	00EF0A08	~P|S|D	–
F0	00F00021	P	PATCOPY
F1	00F10885	P|(~(S|D)	–
F2	00F20B05	P|(~S&D)	–
F3	00F3022A	P|~S	–
F4	00F40B0A	P|(S&~D)	–
F5	00F50225	P|~D	–
F6	00F60265	P|(S^D)	–
F7	00F708C5	P|(~(S&D)	–
F8	00F802E5	P|(S&D)	–
F9	00F90845	P|~(S^D)	–
FA	00FA0089	P|D	–
FB	00FB0A09	P|~S|D	PATPAINT
FC	00FC008A	P|S	–
FD	00FD0A0A	P|S|~D	–
FE	00FE02A9	P|S|D	–
FF	00FF0062	1	WHITENESS

✦   ✦   ✦

DirectX Templates

Templates used in the Microsoft's DirectX file format and retained mode programming, are described in the DirectX version 7 documentation. The following templates are listed in this appendix:

Header	MeshTextureCoords
Vector	MeshNormals
Coords2d	MeshVertexColors
Quaternion	MeshMaterialList
Matrix4 × 4	Mesh
ColorRGBA	FrameTransformMatrix
ColorRGB	Frame
Indexed Color	FloatKeys
Boolean	TimedFloatKeys
Boolean2d	AnimationKey
Material	AnimationOptions
TextureFilename	Animation
MeshFace	AnimationSet
MeshFaceWraps	

Template: Header

UUID: <3D82AB43-62DA-11cf-AB39-0020AF71E433>

```
Member Name Type
major        WORD
minor        WORD
flags        DWORD
```

Description
Defines the application-specific header for the Direct3D retained mode usage of the DirectX file format. The retained mode uses the major and minor flags to specify the current major and minor versions for the retained mode file format.

Template: Vector

UUID: <3D82AB5E-62DA-11cf-AB39-0020AF71E433>

```
Member Name Type
x           FLOAT
y           FLOAT
z           FLOAT
```

Description
Defines a vector.

Template: Coords2d

UUID <F6F23F44-7686-11cf-8F52-0040333594A3>

```
Member Name Type
u           FLOAT
v           FLOAT
```

Description
A two-dimensional vector used to define a mesh's texture coordinates.

Template: Quaternion

UUID <10DD46A3-775B-11cf-8F52-0040333594A3>

```
Member Name Type
s           FLOAT
v           Vector
```

Description
Currently unused.

Template: Matrix4 × 4

UUID <F6F23F45-7686-11cf-8F52-0040333594A3>

```
Member Name    Type
matrix         array FLOAT 16
```

Description

Defines a 4 × 4 matrix used as a frame transformation matrix.

Template: ColorRGBA

```
UUID <35FF44E0-6C7C-11cf-8F52-0040333594A3>

Member Name Type
red          FLOAT
green        FLOAT
blue         FLOAT
alpha        FLOAT
```

Description

Defines a color object with an alpha component. Used for the face color in the material template definition.

Template: ColorRGB

```
UUID <D3E16E81-7835-11cf-8F52-0040333594A3>

Member Name Type
red          FLOAT
green        FLOAT
blue         FLOAT
```

Description

Defines the basic RGB color object.

Template: Indexed Color

```
UUID <1630B820-7842-11cf-8F52-0040333594A3>

Member Name  Type
index        DWORD
indexColor   ColorRGBA
```

Description

Consists of an index parameter and an RGBA color and is used for defining mesh vertex colors. The index defines the vertex to which the color is applied.

Template: Boolean

UUID <4885AE61-78E8-11cf-8F52-0040333594A3>

```
Member Name    Type
DWORD          true/false
```

Description

Defines a simple Boolean type. This template should be set to 0 or 1.

Template: Boolean2d

UUID <4885AE63-78E8-11cf-8F52-0040333594A3>

```
Member Name  Type
u            Boolean
v            Boolean
```

Description

Defines a set of two Boolean values used in the MeshFaceWraps template to define the texture topology of an individual face.

Template: Material

UUID <3D82AB4D-62DA-11cf-AB39-0020AF71E433>

```
Member Name     Type
faceColor       ColorRGBA
power           FLOAT
specularColor   ColorRGB
emissiveColor   ColorRGB
```

Description

Defines a basic material color that can be applied to either a complete mesh or a mesh's individual faces. The power is the specular exponent of the material. Note that the ambient color requires an alpha component.

TextureFilename is an optional data object used by Direct3D Retained Mode. If this object is not present, the face is untextured.

Template: TextureFilename

UUID <A42790E1-7810-11cf-8F52-0040333594A3>

Member Name	Type
filename	STRING

Description

Specifies the file name of a texture to apply to a mesh or a face. This template should appear within a material object.

Template: MeshFace

UUID <3D82AB5F-62DA-11cf-AB39-0020AF71E433>

Member Name	Type	Optional Array Size	Optional Data Objects
nFaceVertexIndices	DWORD		None
faceVertexIndices	array		
	DWORD	nFaceVertexIndicies	

Description

Used by the Mesh template to define a mesh's faces. Each element of the nFaceVertexIndices array references a mesh vertex used to build the face.

Template: MeshFaceWraps

UUID <4885AE62-78E8-11cf-8F52-0040333594A3>

Member Name	Type
nFaceWrapValues	DWORD
faceWrapValues	Boolean2d

Description

Used to define the texture topology of each face in a wrap. The value of the nFaceWrapValues member should be equal to the number of faces in a mesh.

Template: MeshTextureCoords

UUID `<F6F23F40-7686-11cf-8F52-0040333594A3>`

Member Name	Type	Optional Array Size
nTextureCoords	DWORD	
textureCoords	array Coords2d	nTextureCoords

Description

Defines a mesh's texture coordinates.

Template: MeshNormals

UUID `<F6F23F43-7686-11cf-8F52-0040333594A3>`

Member Name	Type	Optional Array Size
nNormals	DWORD	
normals	array Vector	nNormals
nFaceNormals	DWORD	
faceNormals	array MeshFace	nFaceNormals

Description

Defines normals for a mesh. The first array of vectors is the normal vectors, and the second array is an array of indexes specifying which normals should be applied to a given face. The value of the nFaceNormals member should be equal to the number of faces in a mesh.

Template: MeshVertexColors

UUID `<1630B821-7842-11cf-8F52-0040333594A3>`

Member Name	Type	Optional Array Size
nVertexColors	DWORD	
vertexColors	array IndexedColor	nVertexColors

Description

Specifies vertex colors for a mesh, instead of applying a material per face or per mesh.

Template: MeshMaterialList

UUID <F6F23F42-7686-11cf-8F52-0040333594A3>

Member Name	Type	Optional Data Objects
nMaterials	DWORD	Material
nFaceIndexes	DWORD	
FaceIndexes	array DWORD nFaceIndexes	

Description

Used in a mesh object to specify which material applies to which faces. The nMaterials member specifies how many materials are present, and materials specify which material to apply.

Template: Mesh

UUID <3D82AB44-62DA-11cf-AB39-0020AF71E433>

Member Name	Type	Optional Array	Optional Data
Size	Objects		
nVertices	DWORD		(see list)
vertices	array Vector	nVertices	
nFaces	DWORD		
faces	array MeshFace	nFaces	

Description

Defines a simple mesh. The first array is a list of vertices, and the second array defines the faces of the mesh by indexing into the vertex array.

Optional Data Objects

The following optional data elements are used by Direct3D Retained Mode.

MeshFaceWraps	If not present, wrapping for both u and v defaults to false.
MeshTextureCoords	If not present, there are no texture coordinates.
MeshNormals	If not present, normals are generated using the GenerateNormals API.
MeshVertexColors	If not present, the colors default to white.
MeshMaterialList	If not present, the material defaults to white.

Template: FrameTransformMatrix

UUID <F6F23F41-7686-11cf-8F52-0040333594A3>

```
Member Name      Type
frameMatrix      Matrix4x4
```

Description

Defines a local transform for a frame (and all its child objects).

Template: Frame

UUID <3D82AB46-62DA-11cf-AB39-0020AF71E433>

```
Member Name                      Optional Data Objects
None                             (see list)
```

Description

Defines a frame. Currently, the frame can contain objects of the type Mesh and a
FrameTransformMatrix.

Optional Data Objects

The following optional data elements are used by Direct3D retained mode.

```
FrameTransformMatrix        If this element is not present, no
                            local transform is applied to the
                            frame.
Mesh                        Any number of mesh objects that
                            become children of the frame.
                            These objects can be specified
                            inline or by reference.
```


Template: FloatKeys

UUID <10DD46A9-775B-11cf-8F52-0040333594A3>

```
Member Name      Type
nValues          DWORD
values array     FLOAT nValues
```

Description

Defines an array of floating-point numbers and the number of floats in that array.
This is used for defining sets of animation keys.

Template: TimedFloatKeys

UUID <F406B180-7B3B-11cf-8F52-0040333594A3>

```
Member Name     Type
time            DWORD
tfkeys          FloatKeys
```

Description

Defines a set of floats and a positive time used in animations.

Template: AnimationKey

UUID <10DD46A8-775B-11cf-8F52-0040333594A3>

```
Member Name     Type         Optional Array Size
keyType         DWORD
nKeys           DWORD
keys            array        nKeys
                TimedFloatKeys
```

Description

Defines a set of animation keys. The keyType member uses the integers 0, 1, and 2 to specify whether the keys are rotation, scale, or position keys, respectively.

Template: AnimationOptions

UUID <E2BF56C0-840F-11cf-8F52-0040333594A3>

```
Member Name      Type
openclosed       DWORD
positionquality  DWORD
```

Description

Enables setting the Direct3D retained mode animation options. The openclosed member can be either 0 for a closed or 1 for an open animation. The positionquality member is used to set the position quality for any position keys specified and can either be 0 for spline positions or 1 for linear positions. By default, an animation is closed.

Template: Animation

UUID <3D82AB4F-62DA-11cf-AB39-0020AF71E433>

Member Name   Optional Data Objects
None   (see list)

Description

Contains animations referencing a previous frame. It should contain one reference to a frame and at least one set of AnimationKeys. It also can contain an AnimationOptions data object.

Optional Data Objects

The following optional data elements are used by Direct3D retained mode.

AnimationKey   An animation is meaningless
                                without AnimationKeys.
AnimationOptions   If this element is not present,
                                an animation is closed.

Template: AnimationSet

UUID <3D82AB50-62DA-11cf-AB39-0020AF71E433>

Member Name   Optional Data Objects
none   Animation

Description

Contains one or more Animation objects and is the equivalent to the Direct3D retained mode concept of animation sets. This means each animation within an animation set has the same time at any given point. Increasing the animation set's time will increase the time for all the animations it contains.

✦   ✦   ✦

What's On the CD-ROM

The CD-ROM that accompanies this book contains all the programs and projects discussed in the text. The project files were developed with Microsoft Visual C++ version 5 and have been tested in version 6. The directories containing the project files are named for the book chapters in which the programs are first mentioned.

We have not provided an installation program with the CD-ROM because most users are likely to prefer using the files directly from the CD or to load them into their systems as needed.

Please note that CD-ROM files are sometimes tagged by Windows with the read-only attribute and that this attribute is retained when the files are copied to a hard disk drive. When this happens, a development environment, such a Visual C++, is unable to make the required changes in sources or executables. One solution to this problem is to highlight the file or files in Windows Explorer, right-click, and then select the Properties option in the drop-down menu. The Properties dialog screen contains a check box for the read-only attribute. Make sure that this box is unchecked and click on the Apply button.

Unfortunately, the DirectX SDK must still be considered as work in progress. Professional developers of 3D applications are often advised to test their programs in no less than one hundred different hardware systems before commercially releasing their product. This means that it would not surprise us if one or more of the sample programs fail in a particular system. In some cases the authors may be able to explain the malfunction or provide a solution. You can contact us by e-mail at the following addresses:

julio.sanchez@mankato.msus.edu

cantom@mail.mankato.msus.edu

Bibliography

Bargen, Bradley and Peter Donnelly. *Inside DirectX.* Microsoft Press, 1998.

Box, Don. *Essential COM.* Addison-Wesley, 1998.

Bronson, Gary. *A First Book of C++.* West Publishing Company, 1995.

Cluts, Nancy Winnick. *Programming the Windows 95 User Interface.* Microsoft Press, 1995.

Coelho, Rohan, and Maher Hawash. *DirectX, RDX, RSX, and MMX Technology.* Addison-Wesley, 1998.

Conger, James L. *Windows API Bible: the Definite Programmer's Reference.* Waite Group, 1992.

Cooper, Alan. *About Face: Essentials of User Interface Design.* IDG Books, 1995.

Egerton, P. A., and W. S. Hall. *Computer Graphics: Mathematical First Steps.* Prentice Hall, 1999.

Ezzell, Ben, and Jim Blaney. *Windows 98 Developer's Handbook.* Sybex, 1998.

Foley, James D., Andries van Damm, Steven K. Feiner, and John F. Hughes. *Computer Graphics: Principles and Practice.* Addison-Wesley, 1997.

Glidden, Rob. *Graphics Programming with Direct3D.* Addison-Wesley, 1997.

Giambruno, Mark. *3D Graphics & Animation.* New Riders, 1997.

Giesecke, Frederick E, et al. *Engineering Graphics. Fourth Edition.* Macmillan, 1987.

Hearn, Donald, and M. Pauline Baker. *Computer Graphics.* Prentice-Hall, 1986.

Hearn, Donald, and M. Pauline Baker. *Computer Graphics: C Version. Second Edition.* Prentice-Hall, 1997.

Hoggar, S.G. *Mathematics for Computer Graphics.* Cambridge, 1992.

Kawick, Mickey. *Real-Time Strategy Game Programming using DirectX 6.0.* Wordware, 1999.

Kernigham, Brian W., and Dennis M. Ritchie. *The C Programming Language.* Prentice-Hall, 1978.

Kold, Jason. *Win32 Game Developer's Guide with DirectX 3.* Waite GRoup Press, 1997.

Kovach, Peter J. *The Awesome Power of Direct3D/DirectX.* Manning. 1998.

Mandelbrot, Benoit B. *The Fractal Geometry of Nature.* W.T. Freeman and Co., 1982.

Microsoft Corporation. *Programmer's Guide to Microsoft Windows 95.* Microsoft Press, 1995.

Micosoft Corporation. *The Windows Interface Guidelines for Software Design.* Microsoft Press, 1995.

Microsoft Corporation. *DirectX 5 SDK documentation.* 1998.

Microsoft Corporation. *DirectX 6 SDK documentation.* 1999.

Microsoft Corporation. *DirectX 7 SDK documentation.* 1999.

Minasi, Mark. *Secrets of Effective GUI Design.* Sybex, 1994.

Moller, Thomas, and Eric Haines. *Real-Time Rendering.* A. K. Peters Ltd., 1999.

Morris, Charles W. *Signs, Language and Behaviors.* George Braziller, 1955.

O'Rourke, Michael. *Principles of Three-Dimensional Computer Animation.* Norton, 1998.

Petzold, Charles. *Programming Windows. Fifth Edition.* Microsoft Press, 1999.

Ratner, Peter. *3-D Human Modeling and Animation.* Wiley, 1998.

Rector, Brent E. and Joseph M. Newcomer. *Win32 Programming.* Addison-Wesley, 1997.

Redmond, Frank E. III. *DCOM: Microsoft Distributed Component Object Model.* IDG Books, 1997.

Rimmer, Steve. *Windows Bitmapped Graphics.* McGraw-Hill, 1993.

Ritcher, Jeffrey. *Advanced Windows. Third Edition.* Microsoft Press, 1997.

Rogerson, Dale. *Inside COM.* Microsoft Press, 1997.

Root, Michael, and James Boer. *DirectX Complete.* McGraw-Hill, 1999.

Salmon, Rod, and Mel Slater. *Computer Graphics: Systems and Concepts.* Addison-Wesley, 1987.

Sanchez, Julio, and Maria P. Canton. *Space Image Processing.* CRC Press, 1999.

Sanchez, Julio, and Maria P. Canton. *Windows Graphics Programming.* M & T Books, 1999.

Schildt, Herbert. *C++ The Complete Reference. Second Edition.* McGraw-Hill, 1995.

Schildt, Herbert. *Windows 98 Programming from the Ground Up.* Osborne, 1998.

Simon, Richard. *Win32 Programming API Bible.* Waite Group Press, 1996.

Stein, Michael L, Eric Bowman, and Gregory Pierce. *Direct3D Professional Reference.* New Riders, 1997.

Thompson, Nigel. *3D Graphics Programming for Windows 95.* Microsoft Press, 1996.

Timmins, Bret. *DirectDraw Programmming.* M & T Books, 1996.

Trujillo, Stan. *High Performance Windows Graphics Programming.* Coriolis Group Books, 1998.

Trujillo, Stan. *Cutting-Edge Direct3D Programming.* Coriolis Group Books, 1996.

Walmsley, Mark. *Graphics Programming in C++.* Springer, 1998.

Watt, Alan, and Mark Watt. *Advanced Animation and Rendering Techniques: Theory and Practice.* Addison-Wesley, 1992.

Watt, Alan, and Fabio Policarpo. *The Computer Image.* Addison-Wesley, 1998.

Walnum, Clayton. *Windows 95 Game SDK Strategy Guide.* Que, 1995.

Young, Michael J. *Introduction to Graphics Programming for Windows 95: Vector Graphics Using C++.* AP Professional, 1996.

Zaratian, Beck. *Microsoft Visual C++ Owner's Manual.* Version 5.0. Microsoft Press, 1997.

Index

Continued

Continued

Notes

Notes

Notes

IDG Books Worldwide, Inc.
End-User License Agreement

READ THIS. You should carefully read these terms and conditions before opening the software packet(s) included with this book ("Book"). This is a license agreement ("Agreement") between you and IDG Books Worldwide, Inc. ("IDGB"). By opening the accompanying software packet(s), you acknowledge that you have read and accept the following terms and conditions. If you do not agree and do not want to be bound by such terms and conditions, promptly return the Book and the unopened software packet(s) to the place you obtained them for a full refund.

1. **License Grant.** IDGB grants to you (either an individual or entity) a nonexclusive license to use one copy of the enclosed software program(s) (collectively, the "Software") solely for your own personal or business purposes on a single computer (whether a standard computer or a work-station component of a multiuser network). The Software is in use on a computer when it is loaded into temporary memory (RAM) or installed into permanent memory (hard disk, CD-ROM, or other storage device). IDGB reserves all rights not expressly granted herein.

2. **Ownership.** IDGB is the owner of all right, title, and interest, including copyright, in and to the compilation of the Software recorded on the disk(s) or CD-ROM ("Software Media"). Copyright to the individual programs recorded on the Software Media is owned by the author or other authorized copyright owner of each program. Ownership of the Software and all proprietary rights relating thereto remain with IDGB and its licensers.

3. **Restrictions On Use and Transfer.**

   (a) You may only (i) make one copy of the Software for backup or archival purposes, or (ii) transfer the Software to a single hard disk, provided that you keep the original for backup or archival purposes. You may not (i) rent or lease the Software, (ii) copy or reproduce the Software through a LAN or other network system or through any computer subscriber system or bulletin-board system, or (iii) modify, adapt, or create derivative works based on the Software.

   (b) You may not reverse engineer, decompile, or disassemble the Software. You may transfer the Software and user documentation on a permanent basis, provided that the transferee agrees to accept the terms and conditions of this Agreement and you retain no copies. If the Software is an update or has been updated, any transfer must include the most recent update and all prior versions.

4. **Restrictions on Use of Individual Programs.** You must follow the individual requirements and restrictions detailed for each individual program in Appendix D of this Book. These limitations are also contained in the individual

license agreements recorded on the Software Media. These limitations may include a requirement that after using the program for a specified period of time, the user must pay a registration fee or discontinue use. By opening the Software packet(s), you will be agreeing to abide by the licenses and restrictions for these individual programs that are detailed in Appendix D and on the Software Media. None of the material on this Software Media or listed in this Book may ever be redistributed, in original or modified form, for commercial purposes.

5. **Limited Warranty.**

   (a) IDGB warrants that the Software and Software Media are free from defects in materials and workmanship under normal use for a period of sixty (60) days from the date of purchase of this Book. If IDGB receives notification within the warranty period of defects in materials or workmanship, IDGB will replace the defective Software Media.

   (b) **IDGB AND THE AUTHOR OF THE BOOK DISCLAIM ALL OTHER WARRANTIES, EXPRESS OR IMPLIED, INCLUDING WITHOUT LIMITATION IMPLIED WARRANTIES OF MERCHANTABILITY AND FITNESS FOR A PARTICULAR PURPOSE, WITH RESPECT TO THE SOFTWARE, THE PROGRAMS, THE SOURCE CODE CONTAINED THEREIN, AND/OR THE TECHNIQUES DESCRIBED IN THIS BOOK. IDGB DOES NOT WARRANT THAT THE FUNCTIONS CONTAINED IN THE SOFTWARE WILL MEET YOUR REQUIREMENTS OR THAT THE OPERATION OF THE SOFTWARE WILL BE ERROR FREE.**

   (c) This limited warranty gives you specific legal rights, and you may have other rights that vary from jurisdiction to jurisdiction.

6. **Remedies.**

   (a) IDGB's entire liability and your exclusive remedy for defects in materials and workmanship shall be limited to replacement of the Software Media, which may be returned to IDGB with a copy of your receipt at the following address: Software Media Fulfillment Department, Attn.: *DirectX 3D Graphics Programming Bible*, IDG Books Worldwide, Inc., 7260 Shadeland Station, Ste. 100, Indianapolis, IN 46256, or call 1-800-762-2974. Please allow three to four weeks for delivery. This Limited Warranty is void if failure of the Software Media has resulted from accident, abuse, or misapplication. Any replacement Software Media will be warranted for the remainder of the original warranty period or thirty (30) days, whichever is longer.

   (b) In no event shall IDGB or the author be liable for any damages whatsoever (including without limitation damages for loss of business profits, business interruption, loss of business information, or any other pecuniary loss) arising from the use of or inability to use the Book or the Software, even if IDGB has been advised of the possibility of such damages.

(c) Because some jurisdictions do not allow the exclusion or limitation of liability for consequential or incidental damages, the above limitation or exclusion may not apply to you.

7. **U.S. Government Restricted Rights.** Use, duplication, or disclosure of the Software by the U.S. Government is subject to restrictions stated in paragraph (c)(1)(ii) of the Rights in Technical Data and Computer Software clause of DFARS 252.227-7013, and in subparagraphs (a) through (d) of the Commercial Computer — Restricted Rights clause at FAR 52.227-19, and in similar clauses in the NASA FAR supplement, when applicable.

8. **General.** This Agreement constitutes the entire understanding of the parties and revokes and supersedes all prior agreements, oral or written, between them and may not be modified or amended except in a writing signed by both parties hereto that specifically refers to this Agreement. This Agreement shall take precedence over any other documents that may be in conflict herewith. If any one or more provisions contained in this Agreement are held by any court or tribunal to be invalid, illegal, or otherwise unenforceable, each and every other provision shall remain in full force and effect.

my2cents.idgbooks.com

Register This Book — And Win!

Visit **http://my2cents.idgbooks.com** to register this book and we'll automatically enter you in our fantastic monthly prize giveaway. It's also your opportunity to give us feedback: let us know what you thought of this book and how you would like to see other topics covered.

Discover IDG Books Online!

The IDG Books Online Web site is your online resource for tackling technology — at home and at the office. Frequently updated, the IDG Books Online Web site features exclusive software, insider information, online books, and live events!

10 Productive & Career-Enhancing Things You Can Do at www.idgbooks.com

- Nab source code for your own programming projects.

- Download software.

- Read Web exclusives: special articles and book excerpts by IDG Books Worldwide authors.

- Take advantage of resources to help you advance your career as a Novell or Microsoft professional.

- Buy IDG Books Worldwide titles or find a convenient bookstore that carries them.

- Register your book and win a prize.

- Chat live online with authors.

- Sign up for regular e-mail updates about our latest books.

- Suggest a book you'd like to read or write.

- Give us your 2¢ about our books and about our Web site.

You say you're not on the Web yet? It's easy to get started with IDG Books' *Discover the Internet,* available at local retailers everywhere.

CD-ROM Installation Instructions

The CD-ROM that accompanies this book contains the complete code examples from the text as well as the DirectX 7 SDK. These are stored on the CD in their own subfolders. See Appendix D for further information.

Microsoft Product Warranty and Support Disclaimer

The Microsoft program on the CD-ROM was reproduced by IDG Books Worldwide, Inc. under a special arrangement with Microsoft Corporation. For this reason, IDG Books Worldwide, Inc. is responsible for the product warranty and for support. If your CD-ROM is defective, please return it to IDG Books Worldwide, Inc. which will arrange for its replacement. PLEASE DO NOT RETURN IT TO MICROSOFT CORPORATION. Any product support will be provided, if at all, by IDG Books Worldwide, Inc. PLEASE DO NOT CONTACT MICROSOFT CORPORATION FOR PRODUCT SUPPORT. End users of this Microsoft program shall not be considered "registered owners" of a Microsoft product and therefore shall not be eligible for upgrades, promotions or other benefits available to "registered owners" of Microsoft products.